Christendom and its discontents

From the eleventh century onward, Latin Christendom was torn by discontent and controversy. As the Church and secular rulers defined more clearly than ever before the laws and institutions on which they based their power, they demanded greater uniformity and obedience to their authority. Under increasing pressure to conform to the prevailing orthodoxy, minorities and dissenters struggled to define themselves and to survive. The resulting tensions led to outright challenges to the Church and to the repression of any group that could be branded as heretic or deviant.

The essays in this book cast new light on the dynamics of repression, highlighting the controversies and discontent that troubled medieval society. Looking especially at the mechanisms underlying the dissemination of heterodoxy and its repression, the religious aspirations of women, the fate of non-Christian minorities in Europe, and changing boundaries between orthodoxy and heterodoxy, the authors provide a new understanding of the Church's response to the diversity of belief and practice with which it was confronted.

Christendom and its discontents

Exclusion, persecution, and rebellion, 1000–1500

Edited by

Scott L. Waugh

University of California, Los Angeles

and

Peter D. Diehl

Western Washington University, Bellingham

CAMBRIDGE
UNIVERSITY PRESS

Published by the Press Syndicate of the University of Cambridge
The Pitt Building, Trumpington Street, Cambridge CB2 1RP
30 West 20th Street, New York, NY 10011–4211, USA
10 Stamford Road, Oakleigh, Melbourne 3166, Australia

First published 1996

Printed in Great Britain at the University Press, Cambridge

A catalogue record for this book is available from the British Library

Library of Congress cataloguing in publication data

Christendom and its discontents: exclusion, persecution, and
rebellion, 1000–1500 / edited by Scott L. Waugh and Peter D. Diehl.
     p.   cm.
Includes index.
ISBN 0 521 47183 4
1. Dissenters, Religious – Europe. 2. Persecution – History – Middle
Ages, 600–1500. 3. Heresies, Christian – History – Middle Ages,
600–1500. I. Waugh, Scott L., 1948– . II. Diehl, Peter D.
BR1609.5.C47 1995
273'.6–dc20   94–40753 CIP

ISBN 0 521 47183 4 hardback

WD

Contents

Preface

This volume grew out of a conference held at the University of California, Los Angeles, on 5–7 January 1991. The conference was conceived and organized by Clifford Backman and Peter Diehl with the able assistance of the Center for Medieval and Renaissance Studies at UCLA. Like many volumes of conference papers, this one has been too long in the making, the victim of budgetary crisis in California and the many demands on the time of the authors and editors. Everyone who attended the conference had a hand in shaping the essays in this volume, for the conference was characterized by lively and stimulating discussion over each paper. In particular, however, we would like to thank the National Endowment for the Humanities, the Ahmanson Foundation, and the Del Amo Foundation, the Center for Medieval and Renaissance Studies, Robert L. Benson, Jeffrey Burton Russell, Alexander Patchovsky, Benjamin Kedar, Elizabeth A. R. Brown, Richard Landes, John Edwards, Lothar Kolmer, Barbara Newman, Michael McVaugh, Robert Lerner, Jill Webster, Thomas Head, Kurt-Viktor Selge, Peter Reill, and John Van Engen for their support of the conference and the production of this volume. The conference would never have materialized if not for the expert assistance of Suzanne Kahle, Pegeen Connelly, and Abigail Bok, and the encouragement given by the Director of the Center, Michael Allen. We are also indebted to William Davies for taking on this project at Cambridge University Press.

Abbreviations

The following abbreviations are used for source collections cited by more than one author. Other abbreviations used by individual authors are explained in the bibliographies of their articles.

MGH	*Monumenta Germaniae Historica*
Const.	*Constitutiones et acta publica imperatorum et regum*
Ep. saec. XIII	*Epistolae saeculi XIII e regestis Vaticanis selectae*
Ep. sel.	*Epistolae selectae*
LdL	*Libelli de lite imperatorum et pontificum*
Leges	*Leges*
Schriften	*Schriften der Monumenta Germaniae Historica*
SS	*Scriptores* (in folio)
SS rer. Germ.	*Scriptores rerum Germanicarum in usum scholaru*
PG	J. P. Migne, ed., *Patrologia graeca*
PL	J. P. Migne, ed., *Patrologia latina*

Introduction

In April 1198, Innocent III likened the diverse heretical sects of the Languedoc to "little foxes having differing faces but tied together at the tail because they stem from the same source of vanity."[1] The image of foxes destroying the vineyard of the Lord (taken from the Song of Songs 2.15) was widely used to denounce the potential destruction of Christendom threatened by heretics. This fear of the dissolution of social and religious order mounted in the second half of the Middle Ages, when not only heretics, but political rebels, Jews, Muslims, lepers, homosexuals, and women came under suspicion as threats to the authority of the Church and state. The conception of an alliance or conspiracy among these variously complexioned "foxes" remained quite strong through the later Middle Ages. The persistent accusation of an unholy plot by Jews and lepers to poison the wells of France in the early fourteenth century or the rumor that the Templars had allied themselves with the Saracens provide good examples of this phenomenon.[2] Our purpose in this volume is to examine the commonalties among seemingly disparate expressions of discontent that so troubled Innocent and other medieval authorities, even if conspiratorial linkages existed more in their collective minds than among the suspected groups.

Latin Christendom had always encompassed great variety within its nominal unity of religious faith. The vision of a uniform Christendom under the leadership of a single Church barely concealed the heterogeneity of the peoples it embraced or the diversity of beliefs they held. The process of conversion by which Christianity spread through Europe left numerous cultural minorities incompletely assimilated to the faith and many others who found themselves in disagreement with the Church's view of what was orthodox. The clergy's early reaction to these minorities displayed a shifting range of emotions – curiosity, distrust, fear, and indulgence. It was typified by Gregory the Great's response to St. Augustine's questions about how Augustine should treat the pagan

---

[1] Innocent, Reg. 1/94. For a fuller discussion of this image, used for heretics at least since Bernard of Clairvaux's time, see Oliver 1957: 180–3.
[2] For the nature of these conspiratorial rumors, see Ginzburg 1991: 33–62.

1

customs he found among the Anglo-Saxons: "For in these days the Church corrects some things strictly, and allows others out of leniency; others again she deliberately glosses over and tolerates and by so doing often succeeds in checking an evil of which she disapproves."[3] Despite the delicacy and pragmatism of Gregory's approach, the ecclesiastical hierarchy required the subordination, if not eradication, of dissident groups. Numerical minorities were not the only ones affected. Churchmen found what they considered good biological, biblical, as well as legal/historical reasons to distrust women and to deny them an authoritative place or voice in the institution. Nonetheless, early enforcement of this clerical hegemony varied considerably, from Charlemagne's forced baptism of the Saxons to the frequent disregard for anti-Jewish legislation in his and other kingdoms.[4] Only after the millennium would churchmen seek consistent application of norms previously honored often in the breach.

The eleventh century thus proved to be a crucial turning point in the fortunes of various groups within Christendom. The tensions, apprehensions, and opportunities that accompanied the development of a new Christendom created the framework for persecution. In his essay "Heresy, repression, and social change in the age of Gregorian reform," R. I. Moore highlights three features of that development to explain the rise of heresy and its suppression: the consolidation of seigneurial authority, the articulation of a literate, clerical culture, and the formation of new communities in response to the accelerating growth of population and economic activity.[5] It was a Europe in which the material and institutional landscape was undergoing massive restructuring. It was also a Europe that was adjusting its religious values, emphasizing Christ as a mediator with profoundly human characteristics especially manifested in his suffering.

Anxiety arising from the displacement of customary relationships in new social and economic circumstances could lead to suspicion of outsiders, leaving those who failed to conform, who refused to obey, or who broke their oaths extremely vulnerable. Authorities were more than ever willing to wield their newly refined institutions against the disobedient or those banished from the community. The process was perhaps clearest in the realm of faith, where the treatment of heretics, Jews, or Muslims offers sensational, recurring

---

[3] Gregory the Great, *Libellus responsionum*, quoted by Bede, *Ecclesiastical History of the English People*, 1.27 as translated in Sherley-Price 1968: 74–5.

[4] On the Saxons, see McKitterick 1983: 62; Bacharach 1977: 136–40 and *passim* argues forcefully that early medieval rulers rarely enforced the harsh anti-Jewish statutes they and the Church promulgated but often instead fostered Jewish communities in their realms. Wemple 1981: 160, notes that some abbesses in Merovingian Gaul heard confession and granted absolution to members of their monasteries, a practice imported from the Irish Church. (See p. 191 for a summary of her arguments.)

[5] For a recent account of these changes, see Bournazel and Poly 1991.

examples of repression. It occurred in the secular realm as well with the identification and banishment of outlaws, felons, and traitors. The expansion of the crusading ideal to embrace warfare against heretics or political opponents is symptomatic of this willingness to resort to force and to use claims of deviance to justify it. Similar motivations led to the sharpening of ethnic differences all around the geographic fringes of Europe where expansion took place at the expense of native inhabitants, now brought under the domination of Christian Europeans and classified as inferior – at first on religious rather than ethnic or racial grounds – if only to justify conquest.[6] The anxiety produced on the intellectual and geographic frontiers thus manifested itself in the widespread tendency to lump outsiders, aliens, or opponents together through common identifying characteristics and then eradicate them.

Yet the changes sometimes produced contradictory effects. For example, the renewed emphasis on Christ's humanity, as both Robert Chazan and Gavin I. Langmuir remind us in their essays in this volume, highlighted his suffering and death, making Christians more receptive to the stereotyping of Jews as his murderers and making the crime all the more horrible in their eyes. For Jews, popular enthusiasm roused by Christ's suffering, particularly as manifested in the Eucharist, could have deadly consequences. In contrast, Caroline Bynum has argued that Christ's accessibility and role as mediator empowered women excluded from the male clerical culture to find religious voice and authority through mysticism.[7] In the face of an exclusionist culture, women and heretics formulated alternative approaches to religious sensibility, even if their formulations sometimes drew them into conflict with religious authority.

The consolidation of ecclesiastical authority from the eleventh century onward demanded a more rigorous examination of all that was suspect. As the Church asserted its view of orthodox religious belief, a gulf necessarily opened up between what Gavin Langmuir has termed "religion" and "religiosity," that is, between institutional demands for uniformity and personal conviction.[8] One may draw a broad analogy to Freud's essay, *Civilization and its Discontents*, to which the title of this volume alludes. Freud argued that the constraints on individual behavior required for the functioning of a civilized society inevitably produced neuroses and unresolved conflicts among individuals in that society.[9] While not advocating a Freudian approach to interpreting medieval history, we would say that the increasingly powerful claims of the Church and secular authority to universality and uniformity in Christendom provoked inevitable conflicts between individuals' religious practices and aspirations and the Church's claims to obedience. Peter Damiani underscored the goal when he stated that "the sacred canons brand as heretics those who do

6 Bartlett 1993; Davies 1990.   7 Bynum 1982.
8 Langmuir 1990: 135–7.   9 Freud 1961.

not agree with the Roman Church."[10] If obedience becomes a litmus test of orthodoxy, then disobedience places one outside the Church, in league with Satan and subject to "righteous persecution" by the Church. The stakes have suddenly increased. No longer do glaring heterodoxies alone raise suspicions capable of bringing the full weight of the institution to bear on a group or individual. Innocent III showed that a skeptical institution was prone to see the seemingly innocuous opinions of marginalized groups as manifestations of a single conspiracy of vulpine guile. Any deviation, however slight or ostensibly benign, became all the more hazardous.

These are the tensions and contradictions that the essays in this volume seek to understand. The "discontent" in our title threaded its way throughout religious encounters from the eleventh through the fourteenth centuries: doctrinal discontent manifested itself in challenges, sometimes subtle, some-times overt, to the prevailing orthodoxy; religious discontent drove women and men to find different forms of pious expression than those routinely offered by the Church; while social and economic discontent could impel the Church to violent repression of those who tested its authority.

These confrontations have generated two overlapping trends in medieval scholarship. One has been to reassess the motives and methods that underlay the pursuit of obedience. R. I. Moore, for example, has recast the problem of heresy into a deeper analysis of Christendom's reaction to outsiders and the violence of its reaction to diversity. He has argued that the systematic condemnation of heretics, lepers, Jews, male homosexuals, and female prostitutes after 1100 is best ascribed not to any realistic threat that they posed to Christendom, particularly since authorities attributed to them common characteristics, but rather to the anxieties and fears of the dominant culture.[11] In a landmark study of that reaction, John Boswell has shown that the Church's treatment of homosexuality changed from tolerance to aggressive hostility during this period.[12] The policies of ecclesiastical and secular authorities toward the Jews similarly worsened after 1100, a transformation that has been the subject of several studies.[13] Like many of these writers, Brian Stock, in his exploration of the spread of literacy after 1000, has tried to understand medieval discontent from the standpoint of both authorities and dissidents. What he has termed "textual communities" developed among preachers, heretics, and reformers alike. In each case, written texts provided a means of communication and group cohesion, but more importantly shaped the group's

---

[10] Peter Damiani, *Epistolae* 1.20, as quoted by Robinson 1988: 275.
[11] Moore 1987. The literature on heresy and related topics has become quite vast, as can be seen in the notes to the essays in this volume. For a summary and brief bibliography of the current literature, see Russell 1992.
[12] Boswell 1980.
[13] Bachrach 1977; Cohen 1982; Chazan 1988, 1989; Jordan 1989; Langmuir 1990.

internal identity and its identity in the minds of others.[14] It is this problem of understanding the nature of dissident or minority groups themselves, as well as their motives and beliefs, that forms a second scholarly path, which has as its source the recent upsurge of interest in popular culture and popular religion.[15] *Montaillou* provides one model of the microscopic imaging of a heretic community in the Middle Ages and the problems that confront such a study.[16] Other scholars, directing their gaze toward Christian beliefs and practices, have discovered many different streams of piety, especially among women, which at once enriched the Christian religion and aroused suspicion, if not hostility, within the Church hierarchy.[17] Studies of magic and witchcraft have similarly demonstrated the existence of myriad beliefs and practices at all levels of medieval society, and religious authorities did not react consistently when confronted with evidence of behavior which seemed to challenge their own dogma.[18] Analysis of these intellectual and spiritual strata as well as the struggle between tolerance and repression in the Middle Ages has led to a renewed appreciation of the diversity of medieval society, thought, and religious sensibility. As Carlo Ginzburg and others have noted, until recently, European historical traditions largely dismissed evidence of the heterogeneity of cultural practices as interesting epiphenomena or reflections of elite neuroses.[19] Yet the study of heretics, Jews, Muslims, homosexuals, prostitutes, witches, and other minorities in medieval Europe has revealed a highly variegated social and intellectual landscape. Simple models of conspiracy or opposition between well-defined and organized opponents have to be replaced with a more nuanced interpretation of the interchange between different cultures.

The essays presented here thus explore how religious faith shaped cultural and personal identity within Christendom by including or excluding certain individuals and groups. Moore sets the stage in "Heresy, repression, and social change in the age of Gregorian reform" by seeking to account for the rise of heresy after the eleventh century. Material explanations, whether Marxist or Weberian, he argues, have been as unsuccessful as either conspiratorial theories of a unified heretical movement or cultural explanations based on changes in spirituality in explaining why heresy arose and why authorities reacted to it as strongly as they did. For Moore, the explanation lies in the changing relationship between dissenters and seigneurial and ecclesiastical authorities, who were refining their techniques of power to demand stricter obedience to their rule. Focusing on the Peace of God movement in trying to

---

[14] Stock 1983.   [15] Ginzburg 1980, 1974; Sabean 1984.
[16] Le Roy Ladurie 1979.
[17] Schmitt 1984, 1994; Christian 1981; Head 1990; Newman 1987; Bynum 1987.
[18] Ginzburg 1991.
[19] Ginzburg 1991.

disentangle the fear of heresy and the actual practice of heresy, Moore shows how secular and clerical authorities were eager to demarcate their zones of power, leaving dissidents vulnerable to accusation and attack: "The identification of heresy is by definition a political act, requiring both that obedience be demanded and that it be refused."

In this context, if medieval Christendom was, to use Benedict Anderson's term, an "imagined community," mediated through the images and rituals of the Church, it is crucial to understand how authorities as well as those on whose allegiance they depended conceived the boundaries of their community and how the give and take between them could redraw those borders where obedience became the prime test of membership. The effective power to set and enforce limits depended ultimately not just on the fiat of popes and emperors but on the willingness or unwillingness of those under them to accept and enforce the boundaries set by authorities. It was along the margins that the question of religious or cultural identity became most acute and troublesome; where confrontations between alternative interpretations of the "true" faith or with another faith altogether created anxiety and uneasiness. Since the Christian community was defined by faith and its borders were mental as well as geographic, the drama of interchange was played out all across Europe, subject to the exigencies and interests of each local society.

Ecclesiastical authority thus had to operate within the mechanisms of local power. James Given and Peter Diehl provide case studies of how the Church's drive for conformity, if it was to be successful, had to accommodate itself to these local power structures and patterns of social conflict. Studying the work of inquisitors in later thirteenth- and early fourteenth-century Languedoc, Given offers the salutary warning that the vision from the top, where the drive for uniformity and the appearance of administrative competence were strongest, is not necessarily accurate at all times. His concern is to demonstrate the actual mechanisms by which authorities could secure compliance, and he concludes that the inquisitors were successful because they exploited fractures in local society to isolate and punish individuals. Similarly, Diehl's essay "Overcoming reluctance to prosecute heresy in thirteenth-century Italy" shows how ambivalence about the prosecution of heresy, arising out of doubts about the validity of condemnation as well as about the relationship between secular and ecclesiastical authorities, created a reluctance within thirteenth-century Italian cities to enforce the laws against heresy urged on them by the emperor and papacy. Both studies show that through astute maneuvering, the Church could successfully induce local collaboration with its policies, especially by enlisting the help of preachers, and that such collaboration was necessary for the exercise of central authority.

Moore, Diehl, and Given work toward a sociology of heresy and repression, seeking to understand how the local dynamics of authority and conflict reconfigured the broader dispute between Church and dissidents. Decisions to segregate, condemn, and repress had to be made over and over again in the centuries after 1000 in many different contexts. That the impulse to simplify the problem and eliminate any deviancy increased dramatically in those centuries there can be little doubt. How that impulse worked itself out in particular instances is not always so clear. Local circumstances could impinge upon the process in various ways and sometimes produce different results. Compliance by local powers was not axiomatic; and repression did not proceed directly, channeled instead through the fault lines of local antagonisms.

Another practical problem for authorities was the identification of heretical ideas; intellectual exclusion and condemnation were not necessarily predictable. As Clifford Backman traces the idiosyncratic intellectual career of Arnau de Vilanova in "The reception of Arnau de Vilanova's religious ideas," it becomes clear that the determination of orthodoxy could be influenced by many forces. Indeed, a sub-theme running throughout all of the essays, and brought to light in Arnau's case, is the way in which pragmatic considerations impinged on ecclesiastical or theological judgments. Arnau trod a fine line on the borders of intellectual propriety but escaped censure because in other respects, whether social, medical, or ideological, he found support in the papal curia. The identification of dissent, like its repression, functioned through, rather than in place of, the traditional avenues of power and politics.

The identification and repression of heresy were the most dramatic aspects of the relationship between religious authority and its potential challengers. Both sides also wanted to disseminate their opinions, and the prime tool for publicizing doctrine, for orthodox and heterodox alike, was preaching. Indeed, the rise of heresy is intimately connected with the spread of preaching as a medium of instruction and propaganda. The sermon, to paraphrase Anne Hudson, was at the core of the heretics' efforts to win converts as well as the Church's efforts to combat heresy. In its battle with forces seeking to seduce Christians away from the true faith, the Church needed arguments and inducements to convince them to stay within the fold. The tension between the offensive and defensive stance of the Church is evident, as Moore has pointed out, in the decrees of the Fourth Lateran Council.[20] If, on the one hand, the council sought explicitly to define, identify, and condemn heretics, it also tried to clarify the tenets of the true faith, improve the quality of the priesthood charged with overseeing the faith, and urge mechanisms such as synods and confession which would strengthen the faith.

How preaching, the instrument of public debate, developed is therefore of the greatest concern in conceiving how the boundaries between what was proper and improper were set and defended. Mary A. Rouse and Richard A.

[20] Moore 1987: 6–11.

Rouse provide important insight by exploring a hitherto unknown work of Durand of Huesca in "The schools and the Waldensians." They show how sermon models were disseminated from the intellectual centers of northern Europe through the channels of personal acquaintance, in this case through relations among Durand of Huesca, Peter of Capua, and Bernard of Pavia. That Durand had experience in the worlds both of heresy and of orthodoxy makes the connections even more compelling. Durand worked at the dawn of the great age of preaching, but at the other end, in the era of the Lollards, sermons remained the prime medium for gaining adherents. Anne Hudson's paper on Lollard sermons not only demonstrates the centrality of preaching to the Lollard movement but brings to life the experience of sermons, providing an understanding of content, audience, and impact that is usually lacking for earlier heretical groups. Little wonder, then, that the control of preaching, the licensing of teaching by Church authorities, remained contentious throughout the Middle Ages.

Another area of contention, filled with ambiguities and ambivalence, was the role of women in the Church. Ecclesiastical authority had been built, in part, on a powerful misogyny which not only denied women a public role in ecclesiastical institutions as well as in the state and local community but also cast doubt on the validity of their religious ideas. Despite that inhospitable environment, women had laid the foundations of a vigorous religious and intellectual tradition, beginning with their work in convents and double monasteries. The flowering of a new religious sensibility after 1000 brought with it new expressions of women's spirituality, often based on the incorporation of routine elements of their daily lives into religious symbolism. The presence of women becomes a notable feature of religious life after the twelfth century, whether as mystics, pilgrims, nuns, or heretics. The yearning for spiritual expression within the context of secular life, especially among the growing urban population, led to the proliferation of new forms of communal organization, such as the beguine and tertiary movements. The increasing number of female saints in the later Middle Ages testifies to the strength of this religious activity and spiritual engagement. Yet the increased visibility of religious women also rekindled clerical misgivings about the propriety of women's role in spiritual matters.

Anne Clark takes as her theme this dialectic between the ideology of the ecclesiastical hierarchy and women's religious aspirations, arguing that the relationship itself helped to contour medieval Christendom. In exploring the association between Elisabeth and Ekbert of Schönau, Clark wants to move away from a view of repression as a static, unchanging fact, toward an appreciation of the shifting nature of domination and subordination in which men and women could both exercise a kind of intellectual opportunism, enlarging, to some extent, their range of religious expression. E. Ann Matter raises similar issues in the realm of religious patronage through her exploration of the relationship between a female mystic, Lucia Brocadelli da Narni, and her patron Ercole d'Este, the duke of Ferrara. Like Clark, she finds that an asymmetrical relationship in terms of power could produce a profound spiritual interdependence. Moving from the context of individual religious women to organized groups, Katherine Gill comes to a similar conclusion. Her study of women's religious communities in late medieval Italy shows that the relationship between Church authorities and communities was quite variable through the fourteenth and fifteenth centuries and that the expression of women's religious aspirations flourished through many different institutional forms. Nor did male authorities always respond to this diversity with strict conformity to the regulations. Through petitioning and appeals, women managed to fashion environments that were most nearly conducive to their spiritual needs, and, until the late sixteenth century, they were often successful.

In contrast to the ambiguities of the relationship between the Church and religious women, the boundary between Christendom and non-Christians would seem to be more concrete, though even there, Christian reaction to Jews and Muslims was sometimes ambivalent and certainly changed over time. The Mediterranean region and Spain in particular provide an important laboratory for testing these ideas, for it was here that three great monotheistic religions – Judaism, Christianity, and Islam – overlapped, forcing some form of accommodation. Military cooperation between peoples of a different faith or the assimilation of conquered Muslims as well as Jews challenged the Christian hierarchy to find pragmatic solutions to problems of intolerance and mutual exclusivity. The religious frontier had to be defended at the level of personal relations, where daily contact might lead to a blurring of differences.

These problems, however, were rooted in the origins of Christianity and its expansion as an international institution. In "The conversion of Minorcan Jews (417–418): an experiment in history of historiography," Carlo Ginzburg uses an episode in the discovery of the relics of St. Stephen in the early fifth century and their translation to Africa, Spain, and Minorca on the one hand to explore the ambivalence towards Jews which accompanied the development of the cult of the saints, and on the other to caution how modern historians' choice of language can diminish or repress the anti-Jewish attitudes of early Christians. The violence that marked relations between the Jewish and Christian communities in the early fifth century presaged (and should eliminate any misplaced surprise about) the systematic use of force against the Jews that would become the norm later in the Middle Ages. Nevertheless, Jews through the early Middle Ages in Europe enjoyed a stable though precarious existence under the protection of kings and lords. Their position, however, deteriorated rapidly from the twelfth century onward. Accused of murdering Christ, of ritual murders, and of defaming the Eucharist, Jews became the focus of hatred and violence. Efforts at conversion, which had been aired before but never systematically pursued, were stepped up, and those Jews who refused became subject to slavery, expulsion, or execution. Robert Chazan's goal is to explain the complex set of changes within Christendom that led to the unreasonable perception of the Jewish community as a threat to the predominant culture, at a time when Jews hardly constituted any threat at all. He finds in twelfth-century Christendom a combination of positive changes – a new emphasis on reason and the humanity of Christ – and rising anxieties – brought on by external threats and rapid internal change in Europe – which worked to the particular disadvantage of the Jews and made their vulnerability to changes in the Christian psyche all the more frightening.

The destructive confluence of religious attitudes and political power is brought to light in David Abulafia's study of the policies of the kings of Majorca and Naples towards Muslims and Jews within their realms at the end of the thirteenth century. Like Chazan, he rejects simplistic explanations of the oppression of these communities based on purely material considerations, whether they be the financial needs of kings, the moneylending of the Jews, or the wealth of the Muslims. These studies thus reinforce Moore's argument that the reasons for persecution cannot be found in the practices of the oppressed communities; they can only be located in changes within the policies and psyche of the oppressors. Abulafia considers not only the religious fervor which undoubtedly underlay the royal acts against minorities, though it is seen to be uneven, but also the development of state power itself, which used the persecution of minorities to display its authority and assert a religious uniformity to strengthen governmental centralization. Hostility between the Muslim and Christian faiths was played out in a slightly different, and less tense, fashion along the frontier in Spain. By tracing the changing currents of the trade in Christian and Muslim slaves, Olivia Remie Constable adds an instructive commercial dimension to the picture. Christians, Jews, and Muslims collaborated in this exchange of human merchandise during the thirteenth century, providing an unfortunate platform for cooperation, even though each religion forbade the enslavement of their own people. The ethnic mix of the slave trade fluctuated according to the changing military fortunes along the Spanish frontier, providing a means of gauging interfaith conflict.

In all of these studies of Christendom's confrontation with other faiths, the issue of the nature of Christian belief itself is brought to the forefront of analysis, focusing attention on the obscure dynamic between religious belief and psychological motivation. What they lay bare is the degree of uncertainty, whether emotional, religious, or rational, which haunted Christians. These uncertainties in turn produced anxieties which struck at the heart of Christendom and help explain the aggressiveness with which Christians attacked minorities.

The central mystery of the Christian religion, the real presence in the bread and wine of the Eucharist, was one such source of anxiety. Gavin Langmuir explores the role of this fundamental Christian doubt in producing the massacres of Jews from 1298 to 1338. Like Chazan, he is interested not only in the derogatory image of Jews but in the ambiguities and discontents within the Christian faith itself which can help explain its violent reaction to Jewish believers. Accusations against Jews for torturing the body of Christ can only be understood in the context of a long theological development in Christendom concerning the real presence and the change in religious sensibilities which dramatically highlighted Christ's humanity and suffering. Those changes left believers uncomfortable about their relationship with the Eucharist, a discomfort which had to be repressed and which finally erupted in terrible violence against those who were imagined to mock their doubts.

In developing his argument about the real presence, Langmuir shows that conceptions of permissible ecclesiastical criticism, intellectual exploration, or religious expression were the subject of continual debate at various levels of the ecclesiastical hierarchy. From its inception, Christianity had been characterized by a fruitful exploration of the meaning of the central tenets of the faith. The magnitude of commentary quickly outstripped the amount of scripture, setting in motion a tension within the community over the definition of "true" faith and proper interpretation. Religious diversity sprang from many different causes and motives, presenting religious authorities with a daunting task of detection as well as discrimination.

The papers by Richard Kieckhefer and Edward Peters examine the issue of permissible exploration from two different angles. The problem in distinguishing the holy and unholy was that they manifested themselves in strikingly similar ways, leaving the interpretation of visions or ecstasies to outsiders, to those who could not partake and could only view the crude manifestations in the saint's/heretic's/witch's behavior. Interpretation was likewise at stake in the expression of ideas and reading of texts. In each case, authority was put to the test of whether to acknowledge as genuine modes of expression which lay outside traditional experience.

Kieckhefer examines the complexities involved in distinguishing boundaries of sainthood, witchcraft, and magic in the later Middle Ages. The period is important because the spread of lay literacy opened the doors to new expressions of piety which did not always follow traditional, and permissible, paths. Kieckhefer finds that saints, witches, and necromancers crudely mirrored one another's activities but were at base fundamentally different. Their similarities created problems for their interpreters. At the opposite end of the intellectual spectrum, there was the problem of scriptural exegesis. How far did human reason and curiosity dare to go in explicating scripture and what place did tradition and authority have in declaring limits to intellectual exploration? Edward Peters shows how the frontier between these forces moved backward and forward over the long sweep of Christendom from the later Empire to the eve of the Reformation, igniting controversy yet changing the notion of acceptable interpretation. There might be broad agreement about the extremes, when understanding or practice pushed into clearly forbidden realms, yet at the center there was ample room for debate. Categorizing the issue too neatly can present a deceptive impression of the complete segregation of heterodoxy and orthodoxy, as though those categories were equally clear to all parties. Interpretation and dissent repeatedly raised anew the issue of where the boundary between proper and improper, between orthodox and heterodox should be drawn.

This uncertainty and a corresponding hesitancy to apply repressive measures in some cases appear to have been as important attributes of medieval Christian culture as outright repression. They raise the underlying question of what determined medieval Christendom's response to minorities and outsiders, an issue touched upon in one form or another by all of the essays in this volume. Most accounts rely on the notion of "anxiety" to help explain Christian violence against outsiders or deviants, whether arising from a fear of pollution, from theological doubt, or the strain of abrupt social change. Anxiety has been cited, for example, as a product of economic expansion in the twelfth and thirteenth centuries as well as economic contraction in the fourteenth. Assuredly, the use of the concept in two such radically different contexts does not invalidate either explanation. It does, however, suggest that the nature of anxiety and the psychic mechanisms by which it led to hate and oppression need further refinement. The hope is that the essays presented here will point out lines of inquiry, hypotheses for further investigation.

Explanations based on anxiety, moreover, raise the question of whether other cultures shared the same degree of apprehension, or whether Christendom was unique in the way it assuaged its internal doubts through outward aggression. In the discussion of the papers during the conference, it became apparent that a comparison of Latin Christendom, Byzantium, Judaism, and Islam would be necessary to round out the exploration of Christendom's discontents. How these different cultures handled diversity and criticism and how they determined uniformity and conformity are crucial for understanding their peculiarities and commonalties. As these religions were forced to share the increasingly cramped quarters of the Mediterranean, they not only had to stake out their own religious and intellectual territories but they also borrowed from one another. A comparative analysis would help clarify the dynamics of faith, reason, and emotion which produced intolerance and repression. With the exception of women's religious outlook, what is largely represented in this volume is the view of the dominant group in Latin Christendom: its tensions and contradictions which rebounded to the detriment of dissenters, minorities, or nonconformists. We need to know more about how different groups viewed their troubled oppressor.[21]

If the contours of Christian and non-Christian faith and practice are coming to be better understood than in the past, there nevertheless remain many corners and whole territories needing further exploration. This volume is part of an endeavor to illuminate the diversity of religious experience and the controversies it caused in Europe during the Middle Ages. The discontents of medieval Christendom were many and varied; the essays here expose the mechanics underlying that turmoil.

REFERENCES

Bacharach, Bernard S. 1977 *Early Medieval Jewish Policy in Western Europe*. Minneapolis: University of Minnesota Press.

Bartlett, Robert 1993 *The Making of Europe: Conquest, Colonization, and Cultural Change*. London: Allen Lane.

Boswell, John 1980 *Christianity, Social Tolerance, and Homosexuality: Gay People in Western Europe from the Beginning of the Christian Era to the Fourteenth Century*. Chicago: University of Chicago Press.

Bournazel, Eric, and Poly, Jean-Pierre 1991 *The Feudal Transformation 900–1200*. Trans. Caroline Higgitt. New York and London: Homes and Meier.

Bynum, Caroline Walker 1982 *Jesus as Mother: Studies in the Spirituality of the High Middle Ages*. Berkeley and Los Angeles: University of California Press.

1987 *Holy Feast and Holy Fast: The Religious Significance of Food to Medieval Women*. Berkeley and Los Angeles: University of California Press.

Chazan, Robert 1973 *Medieval Jewry in Northern France: A Political and Social History*. Baltimore: Johns Hopkins University Press.

1988 *New Christian Missionizing of the Thirteenth Century*. Cambridge, Mass.: Harvard University Press.

1989 *Daggers of Faith: Thirteenth-Century Christian Missionizing and Jewish Response*. Berkeley and Los Angeles: University of California Press.

Christian, William A. 1981 *Apparitions in Late Medieval and Renaissance Spain*. Princeton: Princeton University Press.

Cohen, Jeremy 1982 *The Friars and the Jews: The Evolution of Medieval Anti-Judaism*. Ithaca: Cornell University Press.

Davies, R. R. 1990 *Domination and Conquest: The Experience of Ireland, Scotland and Wales 1100–1300*. Cambridge: Cambridge University Press.

Flint, Valerie 1991 *The Rise of Magic in Early Medieval Europe*. Princeton: Princeton University Press.

Freud, Sigmund 1961 *Civilization and its Discontents*. Trans. James Strachey. New York: W. W. Norton.

Ginzburg, Carlo 1980 *The Cheese and the Worms: The Cosmos of a Sixteenth-Century Miller*. Trans. John and Anne Tedeschi. Baltimore: Johns Hopkins University Press.

[21] Powell 1990; Chazan 1973.

1984 *The Night Battles: Witchcraft and Agrarian Cults in the Sixteenth and Seventeenth Centuries*. Trans. John and Anne Tedeschi. Baltimore: Johns Hopkins University Press.

1991 *Ecstasies: Deciphering the Witches' Sabbath*. Trans. Raymond Rosenthal. New York: Pantheon.

Head, Thomas 1990 *Hagiography and the Cult of the Saints: The Diocese of Orléans 800–1200*. Cambridge: Cambridge University Press.

Jordan, William Chester 1989 *The French Monarchy and the Jews from Philip Augustus to the Last Capetians*. Philadelphia: University of Pennsylvania Press.

Kieckhefer, Richard 1976 *European Witch Trials: Their Foundations in Popular and Learned Culture, 1300–1500*. Berkeley and Los Angeles: University of California Press.

1989 *Magic in the Middle Ages*. Cambridge: Cambridge University Press.

1994 The Specific Rationality of Medieval Magic. *American Historical Review* 99: 813–36.

Le Roy Ladurie, Emmanuel 1979 *Montaillou: The Promised Land of Error*. Trans. Barbara Bray. New York: Vintage Books.

Langmuir, Gavin I. 1990 *History, Religion, and Anti-Semitism*. Berkeley and Los Angeles: University of California Press.

McKitterick, Rosamond 1983 *The Frankish Kingdoms under the Carolingians*. London: Longman.

Moore, R. I. 1987 *The Formation of a Persecuting Society: Power and Deviance in Western Europe 950–1250*. Oxford: Basil Blackwell.

Murray, Alexander 1992 Missionaries and Magic in Dark-Age Europe. *Past and Present* 136: 186–205.

Newman, Barbara 1987 *Sister of Wisdom: St. Hildegard's Theology of the Feminine*. Berkeley and Los Angeles: University of California Press.

Oliver, Antonio 1957 *Táctica de propaganda y motivos literarios en las cartas anti-heréticas de Innocentio III*. Rome: Regnum Dei.

Powell, James M., ed. 1990 *Muslims under Latin Rule, 1100–1300*. Princeton: Princeton University Press.

Robinson, I. S. 1988 Church and Papacy. In J. H. Burns, ed., *The Cambridge History of Medieval Political Thought c. 350–c. 1450*, 252–305. Cambridge: Cambridge University Press.

Russell, Jeffrey Burton 1992 *Dissent and Order in the Middle Ages: The Search for Legitimate Authority*. New York: Twayne.

Sabean, David Warren 1984 *Power in the Blood: Popular Culture and Village Discourse in Early Modern Germany*. Cambridge: Cambridge University Press.

Schmitt, Jean-Claude 1983 *The Holy Greyhound: Guinefort, Healer of Children since the Thirteenth Century*. Trans. Martin Thom. Cambridge: Cambridge University Press.

1994 *Les Revenants: les vivants et les morts dans la société médiévale*. Paris: Gallimard.

Sherley-Price, Leo 1968 Bede, *Ecclesiastical History of the English People*. Ed. and trans. Leo Sherley-Price. Harmondsworth: Penguin.

Stock, Brian 1983 *The Implications of Literacy: Written Language and Models of Interpretation in the Eleventh and Twelfth Centuries*. Princeton: Princeton University Press.

Wemple, Suzanne Fonay 1981 *Women in Frankish Society: Marriage and the Cloister 500 to 900*. Philadelphia: University of Pennsylvania Press.

Part I

Heterodoxy, dissemination, and repression

1   Heresy, repression, and social change in the age of Gregorian reform

R. I. Moore

Almost the only proposition about medieval popular heresy which has always commanded general assent (despite Jeffrey Russell's gallant attempt to subvert it)[1] is that it began in the eleventh century – which is not to say that nothing before that time could be so described, but that this is when we can begin to trace a history which was more or less continuous, though extremely various, for the rest of the Middle Ages.

What it is the history of is another question. At this time two things happened in western Europe which were logically and sociologically quite distinct from one another: (i) the conviction grew among the *literati* and holders of authority that the Catholic Church and faith were threatened by heresy, especially among the people; and (ii) a number of new religious movements appeared, mainly among the *rustici*, which doubted, or even disputed, the authority of the Church, and substituted certain other convictions for its teachings. The ancient debate about "the origins of medieval heresy" is, in effect, a discussion of the relationship between these two facts. Unfortunately, much confusion has arisen from failure to distinguish them clearly. Upon doing so we see immediately that there is no necessary or fixed relationship between them.

For many centuries the simplest possible view prevailed, that the first of these developments was the direct result of the second. Inquisitors, antiquarians, and scholars accepted at face value the perception of the Church of Innocent III, that it was confronted by a similarly organized and motivated counterpart of diabolic origin, which over the previous 200 years had infiltrated the Latin west from the heresy-ridden Byzantine lands, and now lurked hidden in every corner of Christendom (except where the rulers were depraved or feeble enough to allow it to flaunt itself openly), seducing numberless Christian souls and undermining the authority and integrity of the Church itself.[2] Hence eleventh- and twelfth-century bishops believed that they were

---

[1] Russell 1965: 10–17, 247–9.
[2] A tradition widely accepted even by anti-Catholic historians, including e.g. H. C. Lea. Its most complete modern exemplar is Runciman 1947, still maintained in the reprint of 1982. Russell

threatened by a great heretical movement because they encountered its emissaries and converts. They characterized it as Manichaean because the emissaries whom they questioned professed dualistic convictions and behaved in accordance with them. This characterization was vindicated in the thirteenth century when direct and irrefutable evidence began to accumulate that western Europe was indeed being successfully infiltrated by a Bulgarian or Byzantine dualist Church (or Churches) which was itself by a long but plain descent the heir of Mani. The secrecy which it must have preserved in its operations for so long was seen not only as essential to its success, but as one of the plainest indications of its sinister and disreputable nature: as Guibert of Nogent had remarked, it was the habit of these heretics to assent to Catholic propositions while mentally attaching a different meaning to them, so that "with them a good saying covers much wickedness."[3] Accordingly, even historians not otherwise notorious for their credulity interpreted every hint to be found in the scanty surviving records that people who were accused of heresy might have questioned Catholic teaching in respect of sexuality, diet, the sacraments, and the priesthood as expressions of their dualist theology; every intimation that they might hold meetings or have leaders or rituals of their own as confirmation of their elaborate ecclesiastical organization; every reminder that they were not always natives of the places in which they were arraigned as confirmation of its universal ramifications and oriental origin.[4] In a happy phrase of Christopher Brooke's (describing the historiography, not his own position) the evidence of popular heresy in the eleventh- and twelfth-century west could be, and for long was read as confirming, that "we are shown by the sources a variety of aspects of a Bogomil iceberg."[5]

From about the end of the second world war increasing skepticism of this simple equation began to be expressed by scholars approaching the question (it is important to remember) from the study both of western and of eastern dualistic heresy.[6] It was easily established that there was, as there still is, no unequivocal evidence of any direct connection or relations between heretics in east and west before 1141 at the earliest. Although many, even most, of the

---

1963 remains a valuable survey and evaluation to *c.* 1960 of a very large literature; for bibliography see also Grundmann 1967 (also in Le Goff 1968, a collection which gives a useful conspectus of the state of the field in the early 1960s, at pp. 407–67); Russell and Berkhout 1981. The following paragraphs are based on a paper entitled "Dualisme mitigé ou dualisme absolu? Les origines de l'hérésie médiévale," presented to the 24th International Congress on Medieval Studies, Kalamazoo 1989; I am grateful to the organizers and participants for the stimulus they provided to clarify my views on the subject.

[3] Guibert of Nogent, *De vita sua* III.22, ed. Labande 1981: 428–35, at pp. 432–3.

[4] A method comprehensively exemplified by Dondaine 1952.

[5] Brooke 1968: 120.

[6] Notably by Ilarino da Milano 1947 and Morghen 1953: 212–86, and in many subsequent papers up to Morghen 1966; for references and discussion see Moore 1970; Musy 1975.

essential propositions of Balkan dualism appeared in the accounts of eleventh-century heretics, no individual or single group was shown to maintain them all as a coherent body of doctrine.[7] Nor did any trace appear in the west before the end of the twelfth century of the myths and legends which embodied the gnostic tradition in the east.[8] More rigorous study of the heresies of the Byzantine world showed that the chain of dualist belief and organization which had once been believed to stretch from Mani to Bogomil was itself something of a myth, owing its continuity to the theological consistency and precon-ceptions of orthodox observers rather than to any set of historical identities or affiliations.[9] The Bogomil heresy itself, taken to be by far the most important progenitor of western dualism, was less extreme, theologically speaking, in its initial propositions, slower in its evolution, and milder in its demeanor and organization than either Byzantine or still less Latin contemporaries had been inclined to suppose. A flood of new light on the Cathars and their problems – deriving, ironically enough, from the skillful editing of inquisitorial sources – showed that they were as fragmented, disorganized, and quarrelsome as radical fundamentalist sects usually are, and everywhere (with only a partial exception even in the Languedoc) weaker by far in numbers, wealth, and intellectual coherence than the ravening monster of Antichrist which terrified the imagination of their age.[10] More careful scrutiny of the earlier western sources and increasingly sophisticated understanding of Catholic spirituality under the influence of late Carolingian Neoplatonism,[11] of the various and vigorous currents of reform in the early eleventh-century Church,[12] and of the sociology of religious enthusiasm and nascent literacy,[13] permitted the evolution of a cogent and coherent account of the growth of heretical movements in the eleventh-century west which required no recourse to the *diabolus ex machina* of Bogomil missionaries to render them comprehensible. By the 1970s it was accepted by most scholars active in the field that Catharism was not only a much weaker and less united force in the west than had usually been supposed, but a newer one, making its first inroads no earlier

[7] Puech 1957: 80–2.

[8] Bozoky 1980: 186–217; Culianu 1989: 259–92.

[9] Led by Puech and Vaillant 1945 and Obolensky 1948, whose insights have been confirmed and extended by much subsequent work, including notably Garsoian 1971, Lemerle 1973, and Sanjek 1976. For a survey and discussion see Moore 1977a: 139–67.

[10] This, despite his continuing belief in an element of Bogomil influence at the origin of western heresy, was the consistent tenor of Dondaine's masterly editions of fundamental texts, above all Dondaine 1949, 1950, reprinted in Dondaine 1990, which may be regarded as inaugurating the modern history of Catharism.

[11] Cracco 1971; Taviani 1974.

[12] Originally by Grundmann 1935; for a good recent discussion and bibliography of some of these aspects of the reform movement see Leyser 1984.

[13] Nelson 1972; Stock 1983: 88–151. Among many influences from outside the field of medieval heresy those of Cohn 1957 and Brown 1971 and 1981 have been especially fruitful.

than the 1140s into a world already widely, though perhaps not deeply, infected by a variety of anti-clerical and enthusiastic heresies which had their own histories and their own causes, demanding study and understanding in their own right. Although the ancient temptation to account for deviance by contamination from outside will always be with us,[14] it is now very generally agreed that the appearance of popular heresy in the eleventh-century west must be explained by what was happening in the west in the eleventh century, and not by attributing it to sinister machinations from the orient.

The heretics have been no easier to embrace in a single framework of social than of doctrinal explanation. Most attempts of the cold war period to account for them in such terms suffered from excessive generality and a doctrinaire inflexibility which left them open to somewhat perfunctory rebuttals, themselves for similarly ideological reasons accepted more easily than they ought to have been. It should not need saying that neither in Marx's terms nor in anybody else's is the proposition that popular heresy was inspired by class interest and conflict refuted by the mere though undoubted fact that both heretical preachers and their followers came from all social classes. Nevertheless, although it introduced valuable insights into the discussion even the best Marxist work relied on an oversimplified account of social change as well as of the heresies themselves.[15] Among the religious movements of the eleventh century there is no consistent or objectively definable frontier between those which were characterized as heretical and those which were not. Once we set aside the presumption of some (but by no means all) of the authors of our sources that they were confronted by various manifestations of a single heretical movement it is quickly seen that the episodes in which heresy was involved differed widely in content, inspiration, and membership, even though they also shared a good deal in the social and spiritual climate which gave rise to them.[16]

Equally, although heresy was much more widely disseminated among the population of western Europe after the middle of the twelfth century than before, and although the rulers of Church and state were firmly convinced that it was a revolutionary force which would overthrow Christian society, there is very little to suggest that they were right. However radical the logical

---

[14] The acknowledged excellence of Poly and Bournazel 1980 on so many other matters makes it the more necessary to point out that their discussion of the heretical movements (pp. 382–427), to the best of my knowledge the most sweeping and detailed assertion of the Bogomil conspiracy theory in modern times, rests not only on much misplaced ingenuity, but on readings of eleventh- and early twelfth-century texts long since exploded in a body of scholarship of which a small sample is mentioned in nn. 5–10 above, from which further directions may easily be obtained.

[15] E.g. Werner 1957; Koch 1962; Anguélov 1972. Cf. Russell 1965: 230–8; Moore 1977a: 265–70.

[16] Moore 1977a: 23–45.

implications of the pacifism and contempt for worldly institutions and authority which the Cathars and Waldensians preached in their heyday, there is no
serious justification for suggesting that it was translated into an immediate or
direct challenge to the structure or institutions of lay society. Nor was heresy
in thirteenth-century southern France or Italy associated particularly, let alone
exclusively, with the poor, either in town or country. Indications of the involvement of nobles – whatever exactly that may mean – are much more evident.
Indeed, where there are clear signs of substantial popular support, as perhaps
in the Languedoc at the time of the Albigensian crusade, it seems to be in
association with noble leadership and patronage rather than in opposition to
it.[17] Where there was persistent conflict between different sections or factions,
especially in thirteenth-century Italy, one side or the other was often more or
less regularly associated with an heretical sect. A good example which has
recently been elegantly demonstrated by Valerie Ramseyer[18] comes from
Orvieto, where in the early years of the thirteenth century the cult of S. Pietro
Parenzo, the papal *podestà* who had been murdered by the Cathars, was
promoted by one group of families which rose to power in the city at that time,
while it was resisted and the Cathars were supported by their rivals. This by no
means suggests that heresy in any sense caused either the social division or the
violence associated with it: as some Brescian nobles complained when they
were accused of persecuting Catholics (in 1233), their families had been
enemies for generations and they defended their towers not because they were
heretics but as members of their party.[19]

The cult of S. Pietro Parenzo also illustrates why crude Weberianism has
fared no better. Heresy was not especially characteristic of merchants. As
Giacchino Volpe argued for the Italian cities and John Mundy from the studies
of Toulouse which he has conducted over so many years, far from being
associated with new social forces it was often the resort of those who felt
themselves the victims of social and economic change – for example, members
of old families whose income came predominantly from rents, at a time when
there was a great deal more to be made in trade by those who were vulgar
enough to engage in it.[20] Conversely, then as now the vigorous championship
of Catholic orthodoxy through membership of Leagues for the glory of
the Holy Virgin and the suppression of heresy and sodomy, like generous

---

[17] Wakefield 1974: 68–88 offers a helpful summary on this and related points.
[18] Valerie Ramseyer, "The Political Cult of Saint Peter Parenzo," 25th International Congress on
Medieval Studies, Kalamazoo, 1990. I am grateful to Valerie Ramseyer for a copy of her paper,
and for permission to cite it here.
[19] Volpe 1992: 106.
[20] Volpe 1992; Mundy 1954: 76–80, 1966, 1974, 1985: 54–64, noting the caution in the last
(p. 56) that the difficulties of the families in question "seem to have been caused by the war
rather than an economic crisis." An early caution against glib equations was provided by Evans
1931, still a useful discussion.

contributions to the church building fund, could serve as a path to social acceptability and respectability for those whose money was new and perhaps not delicately come by.

In the absence of a convincing interpretation of the earliest popular heresies in their social context the present tendency to account for them essentially in terms of spiritual and intellectual influences is not altogether surprising. There is a good deal to support it. They drew much of their language and their interpretation of the scriptures from the current of piety which originated in the Neoplatonism that was Eriugena's legacy to the schools of the late Carolingian world, and which in many forms and through many channels was becoming increasingly influential in the thoughts and concerns of the Church and churchmen by the middle of the tenth century, spreading from Italy and the Low Countries. It was characterized by an inner-directed contemplative and personal, as opposed to a ritual-oriented, mediatory, and collective spirituality, emphasizing the New Testament rather than the Old, personal austerity in respect of diet, sexuality, property, and demeanor, and individual responsibility for the condition and destiny of the soul; it was profoundly mistrustful of power and its exercise, and hence if not of established institutions and authority *per se*, at least of their human representatives.[21] To mention this new spirituality is to evoke at once its pervasiveness in the Europe of the eleventh and early twelfth centuries, the immense variety of new impulses and institutions to which it gave rise, and the force of its impact on so many old ones, including its contribution to what was nevertheless (at least to my mind) the quite distinct movement for the reform and aggrandizement of the Roman papacy. The universality and evident power of this message, and especially perhaps the attraction which it was capable of exercising among all social classes, have constituted a persuasive case for adding the emergence of popular heresy to the long list of its achievements, an overspill, at it were, of enthusiasm, doubtless excessive or ill-judged, but at bottom an expression of Christian piety nonetheless.[22]

Although the debt of the eleventh-century heresies to the new spirituality is proclaimed in almost everything we know of them, which is not a great deal, this can hardly be accepted as a sufficient explanation of their appearance. The very ubiquity and regularity of the spirit of reform contrasts too greatly with the fitful and irregular appearance of heresy. That fitfulness was not simply a product of imperfect definition, or of the scantiness of the surviving evidence, but a direct reflection of the fact that heresy is, by canonical definition, a social and a political matter. To establish its existence two things were necessary: that a bishop should require a formal affirmation of orthodoxy in respect of a particular doctrine or doctrines, from a particular person or

[21] Cracco 1971; Tavani 1974, 1977.   [22] Grundmann 1935; Brooke 1968.

persons, in particular circumstances; and that the person or persons in question should consciously, deliberately, and publicly refuse it.[23]

It is hardly necessary to insist that both the exigency of bishops and the intransigence of their flocks were subject to considerable fluctuation, beyond what can be accounted for by personal whim. It is not always easy to assess the proportionate contributions of the variables on any particular occasion. The first two trials of which descriptions survive present in this respect an instructive contrast. The trial at Orléans of 1022, which resulted in the burning of fourteen (or sixteen) people who refused to renounce their beliefs, was the climax of an elaborate preparation and complex maneuvers, including the infiltration of the alleged sect by an *agent provocateur*.[24] At Arras, less than two years later, a group who readily, indeed proudly, acknowledged that they had been openly preaching the denial of infant baptism and impugning the authority of the clergy were allowed to go their way, having provided the bishop with the opportunity of denouncing a variety of more exotic errors and signed a confession of faith which he dictated and which, on their insistence, had first been translated into the vernacular so that they could satisfy themselves of its acceptability to them.[25]

No doubt there were many reasons for the differences in the treatment accorded to the two groups. Among them, and with some significance for the argument that lies ahead as well as for the present point, is that the affair at Orléans was but a single chapter in a long, complex, and highly-charged series of political stratagems around the Capetian court, involving the weightiest considerations of royal succession, diplomacy, and patronage.[26] It may

---

[23] Gratian, II cxxiv, Q. iii, cc. 27–31 (ed. Friedberg 1879–91: I.997–8). During our period ecclesiastical, though not always secular, authorities were scrupulous to act accordingly: cf. Moore 1977a: 250–5.

[24] Bautier 1975. Another and baffling dimension has recently been added to the complexity by Eleanor Searle, who shows that Herfast – Aréfast, as he has been known in the context of his part in the Orléans affair – was not just related to the Norman counts, as the Orléans sources had told us, but the brother of Richard I's wife Gunnor, and that his conversion to the monastic life was a critical episode in the dynastic policy of the ruling house. Searle 1988: 115–16, 291 n. 11.

[25] *Acta synodi Atrebatensis*, PL CXLII.1271–312. Cf. Moore 1977a: 8–18; Duby 1980: 29–36.

[26] Without contesting Bautier's 1975 analysis of the political context of the Orléans trials upon which my comments are chiefly based the important discussions of Stock 1983: 106–20 and Head 1990: 266–9 adduce substantial indications that its victims were members of a coterie characteristic of the circles of lay piety increasingly evident at this time. Head's discussion, significantly developed by "Ascetic Circles in the Orléanais: Aristocratic Ambition and Religious Dissent," presented to the "Medieval Christendom and its Discontents" conference, but regrettably unavailable for publication in this volume, is particularly valuable for its demonstration that such groups were linked to both of the factions whose bitter political rivalries Bautier uncovered: once again "reform" turns out to be no monolithic concept, the prerogative of no single party. However, the natural emphasis of both Stock and Head on the lay character of these groups tends to blur the fact that on all the evidence presented they remain firmly aristocratic and privileged, not popular, in their composition and ambience: *pace* Head

also represent – though this is speculative – the broader tendency to the politicization of heresy charges in western France at this time which is discussed below with particular reference to events in Aquitaine. The heretics who were confronted by Gerard of Cambrai were in humble circumstances, and the relaxed view which he took of the danger they presented, though in striking contrast with the attitudes of so many of his successors, was quite in harmony with its time and place. The century's first three bishops of Châlons-sur-Marne all found heretics spreading similar doctrines among their people. The first was content to denounce the heresy without, apparently, confining or otherwise punishing the heretic; the second, in the case we have just mentioned, was rebuked by his neighbor Gerard of Arras (who had just done exactly the same thing) for letting them go after questioning; and the third solicited and received the famous advice of Wazo of Liège against recourse to violence or physical coercion, even through the agency of the secular power.[27]

If their language is correctly reported the clerks of Orléans may have been influenced by Neoplatonic spirituality, but even if it led them into heresy it was no more than a pretext for a prosecution of which, though the victims, they were neither the cause nor the object. The same appears to be true of the victims of the other great conflagration of the century, which took place at Milan about six years later, except that the Neoplatonism of the aristocratic coterie which had gathered at Monforte d'Asti is very plainly revealed by Landulf Senior's account of their interrogation, whereas Archbishop Aribert's political motive for tracking them down is a matter of inference.[28] There is nothing to suggest so sophisticated a foundation for the convictions of any of those who were interrogated in the Châlons region, who were undoubtedly illiterate, though that does not exclude the possibility, even probability, that the stream of evangelism upon which they were borne had sprung from a school or monastery which was inspired by it. Their beliefs amounted to a simple and direct assertion, as it was put by a leader of the group questioned by Gerard of

---

(1990: 267 n. 141) the new material vindicates my judgment that "the origin of the affair lies in the world of the court and political power, and not even in that of learned, let alone popular heresy" (Moore 1987: 16). This is not, of course, to deny the authenticity or religious quality of the private motivations of the victims.

[27] R. Glaber, *Historiarum libri* v, ii. xi, ed. France 1989: 88–91; Anselm of Liège, *Gesta episcoporum . . . Leodiensis, MGH SS* VII.226–8; Moore 1977a: 35–8. The heretics mentioned by Egbert of Liège in the 1020s and by Theoduin of Liège in the 1040s (Lambert 1977: 360) should be included with these, though the references are too fragmentary to be usefully discussed.

[28] For the possibility of Neoplatonism at Orléans Beryl Smalley, reviewing Moore 1977a in *English Historical Review* 93 (1978), 855; at Monforte, Landulf Senior, *Historia mediolanensis* II, ed. D. L. C. Bethmann and W. Wattenbach, *MGH SS* VIII.65–6, with excellent discussion by Stock 1983: 139–45 and Violante 1968.

Cambrai in 1024, that "they had learned the precepts of the Gospels and the apostles and would accept no other scripture but them."[29] "This," he went on, "is its tenor: to abandon the world, to restrain the appetites of the flesh, to live by the labor of our own hands, to do no injury to anyone, to extend charity to everyone of our own faith."

That remarkable series of equations would be particularly striking if, as may be the case, these were townsmen, in the decades which have supplied the first evidence of legal differentiation of status among the people of Arras, and which might even have seen in that city the introduction of the standing loom, fixed capital equipment which must be operated by workers on the employer's premises.[30] But though my interpretation would be spectacularly supported by spokesmen of Europe's first industrial proletariat, as these may have been, it sits equally well with the greater probability that the exploitation of which their disapproval was so clearly articulated took place in the countryside. It is unnecessary to labor the point that every heretic who came from or appealed to the people now and in the next hundred years can be seen in one way or another to invoke resentment of the consolidation of the seigneurie in both its secular and its ecclesiastical aspects, or that heretics were very far from being alone in doing so. Leutard of Vertus, the first of this series of Champenois heretics, preached against tithes only a few years after Rodulf of Caen had the hands and feet cut off the emissaries of the Norman peasants who came to him for justice.[31] In the monastic movement in Tuscany and Lombardy during these decades disavowal of seigneurial power itself, as well as of revenues associated with it, was a firm and explicit condition of acceptance among the holy.[32] The enforcement of servile obligations was the theme of many a famous miracle story and many a clerical nervousness in the rest of the century.[33] There is nothing new in that. What is new, however, is recent work on the movement for the Peace of God and its connection with Cluny. Exciting for many reasons, it has thrown a flood of light on the relationship between religious and social change in the crucial decades on either side of the millennium. One of the

[29] *PL* CXLII.1272.

[30] Lestocquoy 1952: 20–1. The origin of the fixed loom in early eleventh-century Flanders was proposed by Pirenne on the basis of references to broad cloth (*pannus*) in the poem *Conflictus ovis et lini*; see Verlinden 1972. Nicholas 1991: 17–41 gives further references to discussion, but shows that the innovation was more probably associated with Champagne than with Flanders. This would not preclude a connection with the accused at Arras, since it seems probable that they or their teachings had come there from the diocese of Châlons-sur-Marne: cf. Noiroux 1954.

[31] Guillaume de Jumièges, *Gesta Normannorum Ducum*, ed. J. Marx (Rouen, 1914), quoted by Searle 1988: 111.

[32] Moore 1980:53–5.

[33] This is a subject which would bear more systematic exploration than I am aware of its having received, but for examples from Andrew of Fleury see Rollason 1985: 87–8, and for the uneasiness of Guibert of Nogent on the subject, Moore 1985: 110.

shapes which that light reveals, or at the very least one of the shadows which it throws, is that of the birth of popular heresy.

Everyone is familiar with the great alliance between Church and people which was the movement for the Peace of God,[34] classically described in this account of the first Council of Charroux, probably in 990 or thereabouts:

> When evildoers had sprung up like weeds, and wicked men ravaged the vineyard of the lord like thorn bushes and briars choking the harvest, the abbots and bishops and other holy men decided to call a council at which *praeda* would be forbidden, what had been taken unjustly restored to the church, and other blemishes on the face of the holy church of God scraped away with the sharp blade of anathema. The council was summoned to the monastery of Charroux, and great crowds of people went from Poitou, the Limousin and neighboring regions. The bodies of many saints were brought along to reinforce the pious by their presence and dull the threats of the wicked. The divine will, moved as we believe by the presence of the saints, illuminated that council by frequent miracles.[35]

As a result the archbishop of Bordeaux and five of his suffragans declared excommunicate those who robbed churches or the poor, or offered violence to unarmed clerics. The council was followed by several more, where crowds rallied around the relics brought out from the monasteries, and swore to protect each other and the Church against the depredations of the *milites*, the knights and castellans who were taking advantage of the collapse of royal power to assert their own control over the countryside.

Quantitatively speaking it is difficult to assess Cluny's role in the peace movement with any exactness. The vast prestige of the abbey in the tenth and eleventh centuries has always tended to breed exaggeration of its part in the movements both for ecclesiastical reform and secular regeneration. However, Cluny's most imperial figure, Abbot Odilo, appeared at the Council of Anse, in Burgundy, in 994, shortly after his election. Several of the bishops and abbots who led the councils in Aquitaine had Cluniac connections, and it is not immaterial that Duke William was himself an important patron of Cluny and the descendant of its effective founder, since the peace movement in his duchy considerably enhanced his authority. In a number of other regions, such as Provence, the Peace was introduced by Cluniac prelates, and if, as some believe, the ideology of the Peace contributed to that of the crusade, the latter was unquestionably promulgated by a Cluniac pope. There are also some *prima facie* grounds for seeing Cluniac influence at work in the techniques of the movement. If it is not easy to be sure that the Cluniacs exploited any more than everybody else the cult of relics which played so prominent a part in the

---

[34] For a comprehensive and judicious review of scholarship see Paxton 1987. I am extremely grateful to Thomas Head and Richard Landes for allowing me to use and to cite unpublished materials prepared for the expanded version of Head and Landes 1987, Head and Landes 1992, and for stimulating my interest in the peace movement.

[35] *Delatio corporis sancti Juniani in synodum Karrofensis, PL* CXVII.824–5.

manipulation of popular enthusiasm it is certainly the case, as manifested by their preaching and miracle working, that the abbots of Cluny were pioneering experts in that field.[36] It has been nicely demonstrated by Geoffrey Koziol that some of the histrionic techniques used by Flemish monks later in the eleventh century to bring public opinion to bear upon the recalcitrant pursuers of a particularly disruptive feud were directly derived from the Cluniac liturgy.[37]

Closer inspection of the inspiring picture of Church and people united for faith and freedom against a licentious and (in the traditional account) *arriviste* soldiery reveals some intriguing inconsistencies. The writings of these years are full of lamentations about the wickedness with which the goods of the poor were seized, their animals stolen, their persons held to ransom. Behind the rhetoric, however, was something more subtle than mere anarchy. The words which are used to describe the deprecated practices – *praedae, rapinae, redemptiones*, and others – turn out to refer not to mere brigandage, but to the powers conferred by the Carolingian monarchs on their counts, vicomtes, provosts, and other officers, including ecclesiastical officers, to collect royal revenues and services, raise and provision armies, see to the construction of public works, and so forth.[38] These rights and powers constituted by far the most lucrative access to the profits of the land, and by definition, being owed to the king by all free men, represented a source of wealth which was as yet untapped by the lords. They were also precisely the royal powers and rights whose diffusion from count to castellans in the last decades of the tenth and the early ones of the eleventh century defined the final collapse of the Carolingian state and the consolidation of the seigneurie.[39]

If the practices denounced by the Peace councils were not entirely illegal, neither were they entirely forbidden. The Council of Charroux prohibited a comprehensive list of them, except in one circumstance – *nisi per propriam culpam*.[40] Who was to decide what constituted *propria culpa*? This was saying that rights of justice were to be reserved to those who already possessed them. Similarly, at a council held at Le Puy, probably in 993, anathema was pronounced upon those who committed a vast repertory of abuses, including seizing hostages and building castles, the very practice from which all these evils have commonly been held to flow – unless they did it on their own

---

[36] Töpfer 1956, translation by Janos Bak in Head and Landes 1992.
[37] Koziol 1987.
[38] Magnou-Nortier 1992.
[39] The classic analyses of the process are still those of Lemarignier 1951 and Duby, e.g. in several of the papers reprinted in Duby 1977; there are now many fine surveys, including those of Poly and Bournazel 1980; Fossier 1982. Outstanding even among these, and bearing particularly on the regions under consideration here, is Bonnassie 1991, especially at pp. 104–31, 288–313.
[40] J. D. Mansi, ed., *Sacrorum conciliorum nova et emplissima collectio* (Venice, 1774, repr. Paris and Leipzig, 1902), XIX, vol. 90.

lands.[41] The councils, in short, did not resist the consolidation of the seigneurie in the hands of the lords. They endorsed it, on the condition that each should respect the boundaries of the others. Certainly this did mean offering protection, at least in principle, to the small alodial holders who were prominent among both the victims of seigneurial aggrandizement and the supporters of the Peace.[42] That is not an insignificant exception, but it remains the case that in reality the councils were a very long way from spreading their mantle over the mass of the *pauperes*, in the Carolingian sense of those who lacked power.

The reason is not far to seek: the next clause from Le Puy says that nobody shall dare to take various levies from "ecclesiastical, episcopal, canonical or monastic land" – unless it has been acquired from the bishop or the brethren as a voluntary gift.[43] The protection of anathema, in other words, is not extended to those who work the land, from whose surplus the exaction in question must come, but to the Church which claimed its lordship. In the following year Abbot Odilo of Cluny appeared at the Council at Anse in Burgundy, to secure from the assembled prelates protection for a long list of properties which had been given to his abbey, against *invasores aut raptores* – which is to say, against indignant or unconsenting relations of the donors. Barbara Rosenwein has recently demonstrated in detail that Cluny at this time was consolidating its hold over many properties by interpreting the terms of donations much more inflexibly than had previously been customary or intended by the donors, in respect both of boundaries and of exclusive long-term control over the land in question. The properties listed by the Council of Anse constituted the strategic core of Cluny's future domain, which was enormously expanded during Odilo's long abbacy to provide the foundation of perhaps the greatest monastic estate of the *ancien régime* in France.[44]

It is in no way surprising that in promulgating the Peace of God the Cluniacs and other great magnates who led the peace movement were not endorsing or promoting a radical or egalitarian program. It would be truly astonishing if they had been. Nevertheless, the movement derived an indispensable impetus from popular fervor which was clearly millenarian in character, and which had been quite consciously and deliberately orchestrated by its monastic leaders. There can be no doubt, whatever was actually said in the sermons preached at the rallies and other occasions of the Peace, that the emotions engendered were those associated with the longing for social unity, the dissolution of barriers and differences of power and status, which Victor Turner called the sense of *communitas*, and for which we have learned to look

---

[41] *Ibid.*, cols. 271–2.
[42] Lauranson-Rosaz 1992; Bachrach 1987: 416–17. Cf. Cowdrey 1970: 47–8.
[43] Mansi, ed., *Sacrorum conciliorum*, XIX, cols. 99–102.
[44] Rosenwein 1989: 85–92, 165–72.

out on all such occasions.[45] Its ultimate source was the tension and grievance created by the collapse of Carolingian institutions and the danger and deprivation to which the weak were exposed in consequence. Yet what emerged from the collapse, in what Georges Duby has called the feudal revolution,[46] was a society in which power and wealth were concentrated far more completely than formerly in the hands of the lords at the expense of the princes and the peasants – but not of the churches, which were conspicuous among the beneficiaries. The first indications that this would be the case coincided in time and space with the first indications of popular hostility to ecclesiastical power and wealth, and with the first accusations that those who articulated and expressed such hostility were heretics.

The character of the Peace of God as an alliance between Church and people was clearly announced by the Council of Charroux and reiterated by Duke William V a few years later, when he presided over the next great rally, at Poitiers. It was fostered quite deliberately, and with great skill. Beyond the familiar rallies and relics Daniel Callahan has shown how the tropes and sequences which were being added to the mass in Aquitaine at exactly this time (and soon widely imitated) emphasized both the idea of peace and the involvement of the people as active participants in the liturgy – this latter point in direct contrast to the sharp distinction now being drawn in other parts of France between the *oratores* who performed the liturgy and the *laboratores*, who stood apart and listened.[47] One of the abbeys especially associated with that innovation was St. Martial at Limoges, and one of St. Martial's most skilled liturgists was Ademar of Chabannes. Yet Ademar ended his life and completed his writings bitterly suspicious of popular religious enthusiasm, and in a famous paragraph of his chronicle, concluding his account of certain events of the year 1018, became the first western authority to allege that it had been infected by Manichaeism:

Shortly thereafter Manichaeans arose throughout Aquitaine, seducing the promiscuous populace, negating holy baptism and the power of the cross, the Church and the Redeemer of the world, marriage and the eating of meat, whatever was sound doctrine. Abstaining from food they seemed like monks and faked chastity. But in fact among themselves they practiced every depravity and were the messengers of Antichrist, and they turned away simple people from faith.[48]

This is one of the earliest descriptions of popular heresy in medieval Europe. Earlier appearances are recorded, but the sources for them are not

---

[45] Turner 1969: 96–7, 111–12, and for a striking and pertinent illustration Turner and Turner 1978: 95–7.
[46] Duby 1980: 147–65.
[47] Callahan 1987; Landes 1987: 488–91.
[48] Ademar of Chabannes, *Historiarum Libri* III, ed. G. Waitz, *MGH SS* IV.138.

contemporaneous. Radulfus Glaber, who gives us the stories of the school-master Vilgard of Ravenna, apparently located in the 970s, and of Liutard the shepherd of Champagne, just after 1000, apparently wrote what became the second book of his *Histories* at St. Bénigne, Dijon, at just about the same time, in the 1020s.[49] Ademar composed his chronicle around 1025, but Richard Landes has shown that within three or four years he revised his paragraph in such a way as to uncouple it from his description of the trampling of some fifty-two people in the basilica of St. Martial, also in 1018, removing his previous implication of a causal connection between the two.[50] The revision appears to be connected with what Ademar describes as a sequel to the appearance of the "Manichees" in 1028 when: "Duke William summoned a council of bishops and abbots to Charroux, to wipe out the heresies which the Manichaeans had been spreading among the people."

In other words, the alliance between prelates and people over which William had presided so enthusiastically only a few years earlier had turned sour. As Landes argues, Ademar's revision of his text strongly implies that the souring was in some way connected with the trampling in the basilica. Ademar gives no clue as to the nature of the connection, but we will recall that criticism of the cost and ostentation of ecclesiastical buildings became one of the regular charges against those accused of heresy.

Other episodes in the tale of disillusionment are suggested by Landes's account of two more incidents. In 1019 Geoffrey, Abbot of St. Martial of Limoges and brother of the vicomte, died. Bishop Gerard was his nephew, and to keep the abbatial revenues in the family refused for two years to consecrate the duly elected successor, until he was forced to do so by popular pressure. And in August 1029 Ademar himself suffered a devastating public humiliation when a Lombard monk named Benedict of Chiusa confronted him with the accusation that the campaign to establish the apostolicity of St. Martial to which Ademar had devoted his life and writings was nothing but a fraud to increase the revenues of the monastery. What is particularly significant from our point of view, as well as particularly painful for Ademar, is that Benedict was vociferously supported by a crowd of local onlookers.[51]

Cluny represented itself in the rhetoric of the Peace of God as the champion of an old social order, while in fact the Peace councils were providing ecclesi-astical sanction for a new one, of which Cluny was itself a pioneer and a

---

[49] It appears that Book II, which contains the story of Leutard, was written before 1030: France 1989: xxxiv–xlv, at xl.

[50] Landes 1987: 499–502, and for the suggestion that the entry was composed in the years 1025–8, followed by revisions in 1027–32 and 1029–32, p. 470n, anticipating Landes's forth-coming study of Ademar and his writings.

[51] Landes 1987: 470–1, 495–8, and for the confrontation between Ademar and Benedict of Chiusa, Wolff 1978.

conspicuous beneficiary. This did not escape the notice of prelates like Adalbero of Laon and Gerard of Cambrai, who did not share the fashionable admiration for Cluniac ways,[52] of monks who resisted the incorporation of their houses into Cluny's rapidly growing and now increasingly formalized and hierarchical order,[53] or (it seems likely) of popular preachers who observed a contrast between the wealth and power which the abbot exercised and the precepts of the gospels which some of his monks were helping to disseminate. It looks very much as though what we have seen in Aquitaine is a series of incidents during which popular enthusiasm for alliance with the Church against the *milites* gave way to the suspicion, and then to the conviction, on the part of the people that the Church had been manipulating them for its own purposes, and on the part of the Church and the duke that popular enthusiasm was a dangerous and fickle force, as easily manipulated by their enemies as by themselves. There may be some danger in drawing out these speculations of extending the implications of Landes's heavily documented and technically sophisticated argument from the realm of the sublime to that of the ridiculous. Nevertheless, even if these connections are deemed too tenuous to amount to a hypothesis plausible in itself, they have at least the merit of providing a model or form of explanation, otherwise lacking, for what seems to be both plain and important: between the Council of Poitiers (sometimes dated *c.* 1000, sometimes *c.* 1011), and the second Council of Charroux in 1028 relations between Church and people degenerated from the ecstatic harmony of the early peace rallies to bitter accusations and counter-accusations of heresy and avarice.

Even if this is correct, it does not answer the traditionally crucial question – was the heresy real, in the sense that heretical doctrines were in fact being propounded, or were the accusations of heresy simply invented as a means of discrediting popular opposition to the policy of ecclesiastical leaders? The latter is exactly what is implied by yet another powerful revision, this time Guy Lobrichon's discussion of the curious letter purportedly written by a monk named Heribert to warn Christians against "false prophets who are trying to pervert Christianity" in the region of Périgueux.[54] Heribert offers a number of disquieting observations about his "heretics," including their refusal to eat meat, drink wine, or accept money, their contempt for the mass and hostility to the cross, and the difficulty of imprisoning them, since "even if they are bound in iron chains and shackles and put in a winebutt turned upside down and watched by the strongest guards they will not be found the next day unless they choose to be, and the empty butt will be turned up again full of the wine which had been emptied from it." Until recently this text had always been thought to

---

[52] Duby 1980: 139–40.
[53] Lobrichon 1987: 439–40.
[54] *Ibid.*, with a reedition of the text; for earlier interpretations Moore 1977a: 197–9.

come from the second half of the twelfth century. However, Lobrichon has found a new version of it, which dates not only from the early eleventh century, but from the monastery of St. Germanus at Auxerre. St. Germanus belonged to Cluny, and was the centre at which a number of texts were produced which in various ways contributed to the ideology and propagation of the peace movement and of the "imperial" policies, the aggressive expansion of the order and of the liturgy, associated with Abbot Odilo. Lobrichon makes a strong case for regarding the Heribert letter not as a genuine report of popular heresy – even in this brief summary an element of the burlesque will be apparent – but a polemic designed to discredit critics within the circles of the monastery who were opposed to the elaboration of its liturgy and the extension of its power over other monastic houses, by satirizing them, and at the same time suggesting that their arguments in favour of simplicity, austerity, and poverty tended in the direction of Manichaeism.

Among Heribert's accusations is that "nobody is so stupid that if he joins [the heretics] he will not become literate in eight days, so that he can be reconverted neither by argument nor example." In this he anticipates the complaint of Bishop Roger of Châlons *c.* 1043 that "if *idiotae et infacundi* become members of their sect they immediately become more eloquent than the most learned Catholics, so that even the pure argument of the truly wise seems to be conquered by their fluency."[55] This is the most direct expression of the regularly voiced concern that those suspected or accused of heresy had been led into it by means of unauthorized access to the scriptures which is also represented by the shadowy figures sometimes said to be responsible for spreading heresy – the Italian Gundolfo who (according to Gerard of Cambrai) was quoted as their leader by the men examined at Arras in 1024, and the woman, also Italian, whom Radulphus Glaber credited with the seduction of the clerks of Orléans. The absurdity of invoking such a phantom to account for the deviation of the sophisticated protagonists of the last case, however, alerts us to the real significance of these anxieties, which has been exposed by Brian Stock. They are tide-marks of the slow diffusion of literacy, among whose consequences a new demarcation of social boundaries is particularly germane to our present inquiry. They illustrate the determination that both literacy itself and the power and status associated with it should be reserved to its proper guardians. In describing heresy as an infection or pollution emanating from the people Ademar of Chabannes and Radulphus Glaber betray their nervousness of the permeability of the boundary that separated – and protected – them from the unprivileged.[56]

It had not always been so. From the perspective of late antiquity the

---

[55] Anselm of Liège, *Gesta episcoporum*, p. 226; Moore 1986: 49–51.
[56] Stock 1983: 115–18.

Carolingian world had experienced a considerable deepening of the gulf between the cleric and the layman, and between the literate and the illiterate. Nevertheless, by the standards of the twelfth century and afterwards the evolution was far from complete, especially perhaps in the conception of literacy as a marker of social position. Nobody would expect to find extensive diffusion of literacy outside the ranks of the nobility in the ninth century, but it does not appear that there was a sharply delineated conceptual boundary between the literate and the illiterate, or any sense that literacy was inappropriate or undesirable in the *miserabiles*. Indeed, the *admonitio generalis* is specifically to the contrary,[57] and though examples of the spread of literacy beyond the higher nobility are not numerous the public ideal, expressed by Theodulf of Orléans's insistence that priests should hold schools *per villas et vicos*, was a universal one.[58] It is noteworthy that an analogous discrimination in respect of women was also lacking in the ninth century. By contrast the work of Clanchy, Murray, Stock, and others has not only reminded us forcefully that the fact of literacy was the great instrument of the power and position of the *clerici* of the high Middle Ages, but shown how they claimed literacy itself as a possession and prerogative of their class. Their equation of illiteracy with the notions of paganism, rusticity, and heresy not only served particular purposes, such as discrediting popular acclaim (as opposed to clerical approbation) as a basis for the veneration of relics, but helped much more broadly to establish a sense of solidarity and community among the clerks themselves and to associate them firmly with the ranks of privilege, in contradistinction from the ever more despised and terrifying world of the ignorant and brutish peasantry.[59]

The social revolution of the eleventh century, in short, rested upon the redefinition and universalization not of one great social division, but of two. By means of the usurpation of the ban and its vigorous extension in terms both of the variety of impositions it sanctioned and of the range and number of people from whom they were exacted the seigneurie united the powers of the crown over free men with those of landlords over tenants and serfs. An infinitely diverse patchwork of status and obligation became a well-nigh universal subjection to the "customs" which in the early eleventh century began to embody all the profits and prerogatives of lordship over land and men. The

---

[57] McKitterick 1989: 220 n. 35.

[58] *Ibid.*, 220–3; Riché 1978: 199–200. Nelson 1990, a beautifully differentiated discussion which, like the important volume in which it appears, came to hand too late to be taken into account in this essay, seems to be broadly consistent with this view, in that the distinction which it demonstrates between the "active literacy" of the ruling elite and the "passive or pragmatic literacy" to be found widely among the *mediocres* and even some *pauperes* (see especially pp. 269–76) is functionally quite different from the twelfth-century distinction between the literate and the illiterate, separates and unites quite different social categories, and is much less sharply drawn and conceptualized.

[59] Clanchy 1979: 175–201; Murray 1978 especially at pp. 234–44; Stock 1983: 244–51.

establishment and diffusion of the seigneurie therefore made the division between free and unfree very much starker and more general than it had been in the Carolingian world, as well as placing a very large number of people on the wrong side of it. Similarly, the separation of the clergy from the laity which was the main underlying and uniting objective of the religious reform movements of the eleventh century was sharpened and clarified by renewed emphasis on the distinction between the literate and the illiterate, and in particular by the insistence on literacy as a prerequisite of religious leadership at every level. Nothing illustrates the identification between the burgeoning power and authority of the clerks and their all-purpose, universally potent cause of reform more vividly than the swiftness with which accusations of heresy were leveled against those who resisted "reform" at every level, from the wretched architects of every evil of the age, the proponents of the *simoniaca heresis*, to the peasants who resented the expense of the new basilica at St. Martial, or the citizens of Le Mans who followed the advice of Henry of Lausanne not to take too seriously the impediment to their marital aspirations represented by a vastly extended definition of incest.[60]

In the light of all this there is an obvious temptation to dismiss popular heresy as a mere artefact of class formation, a device to enable the emerging clerical elite to proclaim its identity, suppress its critics, and develop its bureaucratic muscle by exercising and extending its authority. Certainly, like other forms of persecution which developed in this period, the repression of heresy possessed that aspect, but to leave it there would do a great deal less than justice not only to the clerks but to the heretics themselves. The most elementary objection, in both senses of the word, is that so many of them chose death in preference to renunciation. From the followers of Gerard of Monforte, of whom "many leapt into the flames, holding their hands in front of their faces, and dying wretchedly were reduced to ashes" to the first Cathars (or proto-Cathars) found in the west, at Cologne in 1141, who "entered and endured the torment of the flames not merely courageously but joyfully", showing to Eberwin of Steinfeld "such fortitude as is seldom found among the truly religious in the faith of Christ,"[61] to the *perfecti* who hurled themselves by the score onto the fires of Béziers, Minerve, and the rest, they present a poignant contrast to the helpless, miserable, and protesting victims of so many other purges and massacres. The inquisitors did not rejoice alone in the certainty that they possessed the right.

The great achievement of Brian Stock's study of *The Implications of Literacy* is precisely that it did not rest content with describing the process of

---

60 Below, n. 71.
61 Landulf Senior, *Historia mediolanensis* II, ed. Bethmann and Wattenbach, *MGH SS* VIII.65–6; Eberwin, letter to Bernard of Clairvaux, *PL* CLXXXII.676–80.

labeling which it illustrated in so original a manner, but discovered in mediated literacy a new principle of association.[62] The power of the sect (or potential sect, for by no means all such groupings were excluded from the Church, especially in this period) to focus and command the identity of its members was derived very largely from its capacity to replace all other principles of allegiance – lordship, kinship, even place of habitation – by its own. That was what made it the nursery of martyrs.[63] Nevertheless, just as the band of enthusiasts transformed by the news of the Gospels as their leader told it is only one example of Stock's textual community, so we should think of the textual community itself as occupying one position – in certain respects no doubt an extreme position – on a spectrum of community formation which is manifested in almost every activity and development of an inordinately active period. Its exuberance and variety, as the merciless erudition of Susan Reynolds demonstrates so cogently,[64] defies even the most persuasive attempts at characterization or generalization in any of its multitudinous aspects. The closing pages of this essay are no place to rush in where the footprints of so many angels bear mute witness to their obliteration, and need not venture beyond Reynolds's contents page to make the simple point that the proliferation of fraternities and gilds, of parishes, villages, and communes and all the rest, as well as of religious associations of every conceivable variety, advertises a world undergoing rapid differentiation in every dimension of social existence. Nor is it necessary to labor the equally obvious point that the growth in productivity and population upon which it all rested was achieved not so much by the expansion of existing communities as by the creation of new ones. But it must be said, if only to remind ourselves that for perhaps the only time in European history we are dealing with a world which constructed far more of itself than it inherited.[65]

At the level of the material world this notoriously involved conceding, even advertising, greater autonomy to individuals and groups, both negatively in breaking down or moving away from customary exactions and controls, and positively by way of incentive to attract settlers and investment. That meant the construction of communities – physically in the collection of people into

---

[62] Stock 1983: 88–151. The textual community as Stock describes it was not confined to the illiterate, but might be formed by any group founded on allegiance to a common interpretation of a particular text, or set of texts – such as, for example, the highly literate clerks of Orléans. However, the only significant qualification I would propose to this important discussion of eleventh-century heresy is that it attaches insufficient weight to the distinction between groups like that one, all or most of whose members had direct access to their scriptures, and those like the one interrogated by Gerard of Cambrai whose members, being illiterate, depended entirely on the mediation of their master or leader. Cf. above n. 26.

[63] Moore 1986.

[64] Reynolds 1984: especially pp. 67–154. Now see also Génicot 1990.

[65] I am greatly indebted to Constantin Fasolt for insisting on this point in many conversations.

localities, socially in organization for common tasks, and juridically in the conferment of collective privileges and status.[66] Religiously the spirit of community formation found many modes of expression, including acclaiming saints without waiting for them to win episcopal endorsement, and even if necessary fighting to secure possession of their bodies.[67] Among the most general and durable of these expressions of community was the parish, whose resemblance to the African land shrines described by Max Gluckman is very striking.[68] It was organized around the sanctuary which provided shelter for all the activities that required the witness and approval of the community – markets, marriages, settlements of disputes, and the rest.[69] The history of marriage provides an increasingly familiar reminder that it did not remain so for long, but during the exuberant decades on either side of 1100 when the creative springs of the people of western Europe outran the capacity to control them, the churchyard was firmly identified with the community and not with its masters: as Robert Fossier has observed, it was often the first collective possession of these new communities.[70] When in 1116 Henry of Lausanne called the people of Le Mans to the sacrilegious meeting so shocking to the chronicler, in which he denounced the clergy of the city and proclaimed his own utopia by marrying repentant prostitutes to the young men and collecting money for their dowries, it was not by accident that he summoned them to the churchyard of St. Germain and St. Vincent.

The confrontation between Henry of Lausanne and Hildebert of Lavardin, bishop of Le Mans, may present a moment not dissimilar, in spiritual terms, from that which we have postulated a hundred years earlier in Aquitaine, when Church and people realized that despite their shared enthusiasm for suppressing the activities of the *milites* their real interests were opposed. When Henry sent his messengers, barefoot and clad as penitents, bearing an iron cross before them on a pole, for permission to preach in the town during Lent, Hildebert had no reason to regard him as an antagonist.[71] The bishop was himself a committed reformer, and the friend and patron of Robert of Arbrissel, who had denounced the sins of the clergy across western France with

---

66 Fossier 1974: 42–7.
67 Murray 1978: 400; Dalarun 1985: 154–75.
68 Gluckman 1965: 104–7. The salient characteristics of the land shrines which Gluckman describes are that they tended to be maintained by the people responsible for the clearance and cultivation of a particular area, and to be associated with ritual declarations that peace is to be observed at particular times and places, and often with the name of the first settler on the land in question, or of a prophet from outside the community.
69 Fossier 1982: 345–58; Duparc 1969: 483–504. I hope to consider this subject more fully on another occasion.
70 Fossier 1974: 35.
71 *Gesta Pontificum Cenomannensium*, ed. M. Bouquet, *Recueil des historiens de Gaule et de la France* (Paris: Aux depens des librairies, 1877), XII.547–51; Moore 1977b: 82–90.

unexampled eloquence for the quarter century before his recent death. It may even be that Henry, still young, was naive enough to think that his message would be welcome in the see of such a man; certainly to seek the bishop's license, a delicacy not always indulged by his spiritually distinguished forerunners in these parts, was not the action of a determined heretic.[72] At any rate Hildebert gave his permission, and set out on his planned journey to Rome for the Easter synod. He returned to find that the canons had fled, leaving the city in the hands of Henry, whom he eventually contrived to expel, denounced, exposed as a fraud and excommunicate.

If it is fanciful to suspect in these events the disillusionment of each man with what the other had seemed to stand for, it is reasonable at least to suppose that neither had foreseen that this was how it would turn out. Just as in Aquitaine the *milites* had provided a convenient target for universal opprobrium, rightly to be blamed for what all good men must agree to be wrong, so did lascivious clerks in Maine and Anjou. Nor is it always easy to identify the right: when Henry began to denounce the clergy of Le Mans some of them helped to prepare the platform, and sat weeping at his feet while he preached, and two of the younger among them, Cyprian and Peter, followed him from the city even after Hildebert's denunciation, later to repent and return to the fold.[73] It was possible to work a long way down the agenda of reform, and it was not quick or easy work, before reaching the point of decision. But sooner or later, as Peter Damiani had insisted to his erstwhile allies among the Patarenes of Milan in 1059, and as that dreadful old reactionary Gerard of Cambrai had known all along,[74] the choice between the light of conscience and the voice of authority would have to be made – and made on both sides, not only by the heretics, for it is a fine thing to march with the people and we are not entitled to presume that Hildebert, or Damiani for that matter, turned his back on them without a sigh.

The choice they faced is familiar enough in theological terms. It also had profound social implications. If, as we have argued – and it is scarcely a contentious point – the creation of a new and cosmopolitan clerical elite, formally defined by ordination but distinguished and united above all by its common Latin culture, was a central goal and consequence of the eleventh-century revolution, then Hildebert of Lavardin was the very model of its success, a veritable twelfth-century renaissance man. The account of this whole episode in the *Gesta Pontificum Cenomannensium* is a literary artefact so

72 Compare Bernard of Tiron, who made no bones about telling the archdeacon of Coutances that his holiness of life was his license (*Vita B. Bernardi, PL* CLXXII.172, 1399), and Henry's own brusque reply when challenged for his license to preach some twenty years later, "I was sent by him who said, Go ye, preach to all nations" (Manselli 1953: 44).
73 Hildebert, *Epistolae*, II. 24, *PL* CLXXI.242.
74 Moore 1977a: 42–3, 60–1; Cracco 1971: 452–6.

skillfully wrought and highly polished as to place in question how literally it should be accepted as a historical narrative. It tells the story of how the good and enlightened bishop traveled to Rome, returning in the nick of time to save his flock from the wolf which had been ravaging it in his absence. The journey to Rome emphasizes not only the ultimate source of Hildebert's authority – the apostolic authority by which, in the dénouement, he expelled Henry from the city – but his membership of the wider world by which the reforms he was introducing to the diocese were inspired, including those relating to incest and marriage which Henry had attacked with such effect. The canons of the cathedral, whose reputation the chronicler is little enough concerned to defend against Henry's assault (he mentions that one of them was nicknamed Guillelmus Qui-non-bibit-aquam), stand for the old world, for which Hildebert had little more regard than Henry himself. As for Henry, what Hildebert set out to establish in order to discredit him was that he did not possess knowledge of the daily offices consistent with the rank of deacon which he claimed, and was therefore a fraud. Whether or not this was true – on the whole it seems unlikely – the relevance of the test to the present argument is obvious.

If Hildebert was a model spokesman for the high culture, or the large community, Henry was equally so for the small, at least *in posse*. Some time in the next twenty years or so he was engaged in debate by a monk named William, whose record, hostile though it is, reveals Henry as the possessor of a formidably articulate and consistent theology.[75] Central to it was his repudiation of infant baptism, probably the single heresy most commonly avowed in these generations, but here worked out with rare vigor and originality. Baptism was the ceremony of acceptance into the community: considered as a rite of passage the crucial question which it raised, therefore, was whether on the one hand the new-born infant must bear the burden of others' sins – a contention which Henry denounced with eloquent passion – and on the other whether the transition to membership of the community should not be equated with that from infancy to maturity. To deny that someone who has not reached the age of reason could bear the responsibilities of citizenship is to deny that his godparents can be trusted to represent him in the spiritual world or his kin in the material one.[76] In this light doubt of infant baptism clearly reflects the instability of an age of geographical and social mobility, and of changing family structures. The stark individualism which lay behind all Henry's teachings, on confession, marriage, and priesthood as well as baptism, his absolute rejection of large and abstract structures of authority in favor of those firmly rooted in the community itself, represent a plain affirmation of a world in which small groups of men and women stand together as equals, dependent

[75] Ed. Manselli 1953: 36–62, trans. Moore 1975: 46–60; Moore 1977a: 92–101.
[76] Moore 1977b.

on each other, suspicious of outsiders, and hostile to every external claim upon their obedience, allegiance, or wealth.

We began with the assertion that there is no simple or direct connection between the growth of the fear of popular heresy among the *literati* and the powerful on the one hand, and on the other the appearance among the people of leaders and movements prepared to defy the authority of the Church. The logic of the distinction is incontestable in the sense in which it was then stated, that the former cannot be accepted as a mere product of the latter. No account of popular heresy in this or any period can be founded on a ready or uncritical acceptance of the assertions of those who believed on *a priori* grounds that heresy would appear in certain circumstances, and therefore persecuted what they believed to be its manifestations. At another level, however, the question is more complex. Heresy and the accusation of heresy are not to be seen discretely as the product of accused and accusers respectively, but rather as the expression of a changing relationship between the two. That is why it is not enough to trace influences, whether in the form of Greek or Italian persons diffused by the currents of international trade, or of Greek or Italian ideas diffused by the disciples of John Scotus Eriugena. One or the other – in fact, unequivocally the latter – is certainly a necessary part of the explanation, but by no means a sufficient one. The identification of heresy is by definition a political act, requiring both that obedience be demanded and that it be refused. The "appearance" of popular heresy in the eleventh-century west for the first time since antiquity therefore registers the disruption of the existing social and political order, and dispute over what should replace it.

There can be no doubt that this was a direct result of the transformation of social relations brought about by the upheavals commonly if inadequately referred to as the feudal revolution and the Gregorian reform, and the attendant reconceptualization of society as comprising "the three orders" which has been the object of so much attention in recent years. Those who were condemned as heretics consistently disputed both the morality of the surplus extraction associated with a new mode of production, the seigneurie, and the legitimacy of the power relations founded upon it. The undoubted fact that the critics originated among the privileged as well as the underprivileged cannot obscure the unfailing regularity with which they not only complained of every source of clerical income, spiritual and temporal alike, but denounced the uses to which it was put as destroying the spiritual authority of those who enjoyed it. They were denounced in their turn, and their claims dismissed as lacking the legitimacy conferred by membership of the reinvigorated and redefined clerical elite, which, magnifying the danger, took full advantage of the attack to discredit its enemies, entrench its privilege, and enhance its solidarity with the powerful. Both heresy and repression resulted from the realization that, contrary to the heady expectations of its millennial dawn, the new world placed the interests of the powerful (among whom the monks were now included, as they had not been in Carolingian times) inescapably in conflict with those of the poor, and of the literate (whose designation now carried implications of power and privilege, which it had not done in Carolingian times) with those of the illiterate.

Yet elite formation is not everything. The creation of that new world – the urban revolution which made northwestern Europe for the first time the seat of an indigenous complex civilization – depended equally on the proliferation of communities, and especially of peasant communities. The subordination of the countryside to the city in economic function, ecclesiastical and secular administration, and cultural prestige is another radical social division, not touched on in this essay, which is notoriously reflected in the vocabulary of heresy and persecution. The leadership of enthusiastic movements of every kind was a communal leadership, conferred by popular acclamation and exercising upwardly directed authority. The representatives of the larger structures pitted their own authority against it, across a whole range of issues from the payment of tithes to the canonization of saints. Popular heresy was not a simple manifestation either of popular sentiment or of clerical repression, but a paradigmatic expression of the relationship between them. It was always a complicated relationship, but always at the bottom of it was the simple fact that community's meat was often culture's poison.

REFERENCES

Anguélov D. 1972 *Le bogomilisme en Bulgarie*. Trad. Fr., Toulouse: Privat.

Bachrach, Bernard 1987 The Northern Origins of the Peace Movement at Le Puy in 975. In Head and Landes 1987: 405–21.

Bautier, R. H. 1975 L'Hérésie d'Orléans et le mouvement intellectuel au début du xie. siècle. In *Enseignement et vie intellectuelle IXe–XVIe siècle: Actes du 95e. Congrès national des sociétés savantes (Reims, 1970), Section philologique et historique*, I.63–88. Paris: Bibliothèque Nationale.

Bonnassie, Pierre 1991 *From Slavery to Feudalism in South-Western Europe*, trans. Jean Birrell. Cambridge: Cambridge University Press.

Bozoky, Edina 1980 *Le Livre secret des cathares: Interrogatio Iohannis*. Paris: Beauchesne.

Brooke, C. N. L. 1968 Heresy and Religious Sentiment, 1000–1250. *Bulletin of the Institute of Historical Research* 41.

Brown, Peter 1971 The Rise and Function of the Holy Man in Late Antiquity. *Journal of Roman Studies* 61: 80–101.

1981 *The Cult of the Saints*. Chicago: University of Chicago Press.

Callahan, Daniel F. 1987 The Peace of God and the Cult of the Saints in Aquitaine in the Tenth and Eleventh Centuries. In Head and Landes 1987: 443–61.

Clanchy, Michael T. 1979 *From Memory to Written Record*. London: Edward Arnold.

Cohn, Norman 1957 *The Pursuit of the Millennium*. London: Secker and Warburg.

Cowdrey, H. E. J. 1970. The Peace and Truce of God. *Past & Present* 46: 42–67.

Cracco, Giorgio 1971 Riforma ed eresia in momenti della cultura Europea tra x e xi secolo. *Rivista di storia e letteratura religiosa* 7: 411–77.

Culianu, Ioan 1989 *I miti dei dualismi occidentali*. Milan.

Dalarun, Jacques 1985 *L'impossible sainteté: la vie retrouvée de Robert d'Arbrissel*. Paris: Cerf.

Dondaine, Antoine 1949, 1950 L'Hiérarchie cathare en Italie. *Archivum Fratrum Praedicatorum* 19: 280–312 and 20: 234–324.

1952 Aux origines de l'hérésie médiévale. *Rivista di Storia della Chiesa in Italia* 6: 43–78.

1990 *Les Hérésies et l'inquisition*. Aldershot: Variorum.

Duby, Georges 1977 *The Chivalrous Society*. Berkeley and Los Angeles: University of California Press.

1980 *The Three Orders: Feudal Society Imagined*. Chicago and London: University of Chicago Press.

Duparc, Pierre 1969 Les Cimetières, séjours des vivants (xie–xiie siècles). *Bulletin philologique et historique 1964*. Paris: Bibliothèque Nationale.

Eberwin of Steinfeld, letter to Bernard of Clairvaux, Migne, PL. 182 cols. 676–80.

Evans, Austin P. 1931 Social Aspects of Medieval Heresy. In *Persecution and Liberty: Essays in Honor of George Lincoln Burr*, 93–116. New York: The Century Company.

Fossier, Robert 1974 *Chartes de coutume en Picardie (xie–xiiie siècles)*. Paris: Biblothèque Nationale.

1982 *Enfance de l'Europe, xe–xiie siècles*. Paris: Presses Universitaires de France.

France, John 1989 *Rodulfus Glaber Opera*. Oxford: Oxford University Press.

Friedberg, A., ed. 1879–81 *Corpus Iuris Canonici*. 2 vols. Leipzig: Bernhard Tauchnitz.

Garsoian, Nina 1971 Byzantine Heresy: A Reinterpretation. *Dumbarton Oaks Papers* 25: 87–113.

Génicot, Leopold 1990 *Rural Communities in the Medieval West*. Baltimore: Johns Hopkins University Press.

Gluckman, Max 1965 *Politics, Law and Ritual in Tribal Society*. Oxford: Blackwell.

Grundmann, Herbert 1935 *Religiöse bewegungen im mittelalter*. Berlin: E. Ebering. 2nd edn. Darmstadt, 1970.

1967 *Bibliographie zur Ketzergeschichte des Mittelalters*. Rome: Edizioni di Storia e Letteratura.

Head, Thomas 1990 *Hagiography and the Cult of Saints: The Diocese of Orléans 800–1200*. Cambridge: Cambridge University Press.

Head, Thomas, and Landes, Richard, eds., 1987 Essays on the Peace of God: The Church and the People in Eleventh-Century France. *Historical Reflections/ Réflexions historiques*, 14/3.

1992 *The Peace of God: Violence and Religion in France around the Year 1000*. Ithaca, N.Y.: Cornell University Press.

Ilarino da Milano 1946 L'eresia popolare del secolo xii nell' Europa occidentale. *Studi Gregoriani* (ed. G. B. Borino) 2: 43–89.

Iogna-Prat, Dominic 1988 Agni Immaculati, *Recherches sur les sources hagiographiques relatives à St. Maieul de Cluny (854–994)*. Paris: Les Editions du Cerf.

Koch, Gottfried 1962 *Frauenfrage und Ketzertum in Mittelalter*. Berlin: Akademie-Verlag.

Koziol, Geoffrey 1987 Monks, Feuds and the Making of Peace in Eleventh Century Flanders. In Head and Landes 1987: 531–49.

Labande, Edmond René 1981 *Guibert de Nogent, Autobiographie*. Paris: Société d'édition "Les Belles Lettres."

Lambert, Malcolm D. 1977 *Medieval Heresy from Bogomil to Hus*. London: Holmes & Meier Publishers.

Landes, Richard 1987 The Dynamics of Heresy and Reform in Limoges. In Head and Landes 1987: 467–512.

Lauranson-Rosaz, Guy 1992 Peace from the Mountains: The Auvergnat Origins of the Peace of God. In Head and Landes 1992: 104–34.

Le Goff, Jacques, ed., 1968 *Hérésies et sociétés dans l'Europe pré-industrielle*. Paris and The Hague: Le Haye Mouton.

Lemarignier, J. F. 1951 La Dislocation du *pagus* et le problème des *consuetudines*. In *Mélanges dédiées à la mémoire de Louis Halphen*, 401–10. Paris: Presses Universitaires de France.

Lemerle, Paul 1973 L'Histoire des Pauliciens de'Asie mineure d'après les sources grecques. *Travaux et Mémoires* 5: 1–135.

Lestocquoy, Jean 1952 *Aux origines de la Bourgeoisie: les Villes de Flandre et de l'Italie sous le gouvernement des patriciens*. Paris: Presses Universitaires de France.

Leyser, Henrietta 1984 *Hermits and the New Monasticism*. London: Macmillan.

Lobrichon, Guy 1987 Le Clair-obscur de l'hérésie au début du xie siècle en Aquitaine. Une lettre d'Auxerre. In Head and Landes 1987: 423–44.

McKitterick, Rosamond 1989 *The Carolingians and the Written Word*. Cambridge: Cambridge University Press.

Magnou-Nortier, Elisabeth 1992 The Enemies of the Peace: Reflections on a Vocabulary, 500–1100. In Head and Landes 1992: 58–79.

Manselli, Raoul 1953 Il monaco enrico e la sua eresia. *Bulletino dell' Istituto storico italiano per il medio evo* 65: 36–63.

Moore, R. I. 1970 The Origins of Medieval Heresy. *History* 55: 21–36.

    1975 *The Birth of Popular Heresy*. London: Edward Arnold.

    1977a *The Origins of European Dissent*. London: Allen Lane; Oxford: Blackwell, 1985.

    1977b Some Heretical Attitudes to the Renewal of the Church. In Derek Baker, ed., *Renaissance and Renewal in Christian History*, 87–93. Studies in Church History 14. Oxford: Blackwell.

    1980 Family, Community and Cult on the Eve of the Gregorian Reform. *Transactions of the Royal Historical Society* 5/30: 49–69.

    1985 Guibert of Nogent and his World. In Henry Mayr-Harting and R. I. Moore, eds., *Studies in Medieval History Presented to R. H. C. Davis*, 107–17. London and Ronceverte WVA: Hambledon Press.

    1986 New Sects and Secret Meetings: Association and Authority in the Eleventh and Twelfth Centuries. In J. Sheils and Diana Wood, eds., *Voluntary Religion*, 47–68. Studies in Church History 25. Oxford: Blackwell.

    1987 *The Formation of a Persecuting Society: Power and Deviance in Western Europe, 950–1250*. Oxford: Blackwell.

Morghen, Raffaello 1953 *Medioevo Cristiano*. Bari: Laterza.
1966 Problèmes sur l'origine de l'hérésie au moyen-âge. *Revue historique* 336: 1–16.
Mundy, John 1954 *Liberty and Political Power in Toulouse, 1050–1230*. New York: Columbia University Press.
1966. Charity and Social Work in Toulouse, 1100–1250. *Traditio* 22: 203–88.
1974 Une famille cathare: les Maurand. *Annales: Economies, Sociétés Civilisations* 29: 1211–23.
1985 *The Repression of Catharism at Toulouse: The Royal Diploma of 1279*. Toronto: Pontifical Institute of Mediaeval Studies.
Murray, Alexander 1978 *Reason and Society in the Middle Ages*. Oxford: Oxford University Press.
Musy, J. 1975 Mouvements populaires et hérésies au xie siècle en France. *Revue historique* 352: 33–76.
Nelson, Janet L. 1972 Society, Theodicy and the Origins of Heresy. In Derek Baker, ed., *Schism, Heresy and Religious Protest*, 65–77. Studies in Church History 9. Cambridge: Cambridge University Press.
1990 Literacy in Carolingian Government. In Rosamond McKitterick, ed., *The Uses of Literacy in Medieval Europe*, 258–96. Cambridge: Cambridge University Press.
Nicholas, David M. 1991 Of Poverty and Primacy: Demand, Liquidity and the Flemish Economic Miracle, 1050–1200. *American Historical Review* 1: 17–41.
Noiroux, J. M. 1954 Les Deux Premiers Documents concernants l'hérésie aux Pays Bas. *Revue d'histoire écclésiastique* 49: 842–55.
Obolensky, D. 1948 *The Bogomils*. Cambridge: Cambridge University Press.
Paxton, Frederick S. 1987 The Peace of God in Modern Historiography: Perspectives and Trends. In Head and Landes 1987: 385–404.
Poly, J. P., and Bournazel, E. 1980 *La Mutation féodale*. Paris: Presses Universitaires de France.
Puech, H. C. Catharisme médiévale et bogomilisme. In Accademia dei Lincei, Fondazione Volta Convegno 12, *Oriente ed Occidente nel Medio Evo*, 56–84. Rome.
Puech, H. C., and Vaillant, A. 1945 *Le Traité contre les bogomiles de Cosmas le prêtre*. Paris: Imprimerie Nationale.
Reynolds, Susan 1984 *Kingdoms and Communities in Western Europe 900–1300*. Oxford: Oxford University Press.
Riché, Pierre 1978 *Daily Life in the World of Charlemagne*. Philadelphia: University of Pennsylvania Press.
Rollason, D. W. 1985 The Miracles of St. Benedict: a Window on Early Medieval France. In Henry Mayr-Harting and R. I. Moore, eds., *Studies in Medieval History Presented to R. H. C. Davis*, 73–90. London and Ronceverte WVA: Hambledon Press.
Rosenwein, Barbara 1989 *To Be the Neighbor of St. Peter: The Social Meaning of Cluny's Property, 909–1046*. Ithaca and London: Cornell University Press.
Runciman, Steven 1947, 1982 *The Medieval Manichee*. Cambridge: Cambridge University Press.
Russell, Jeffrey Burton 1963 Some Interpretations of the Origins of Medieval Heresy. *Medieval Studies* 25: 26–53.

46   *R. I. Moore*

1965 *Dissent and Reform in the Early Middle Ages*. Berkeley and Los Angeles: University of California Press.

Russell, Jeffrey Burton, and Berkhout, Carl 1981 *Medieval Heresies: A Bibliography*. Toronto: Pontifical Institute of Mediaeval Studies.

Sanjek, Franjo 1976 *Les Chrétiens bosniaques et le mouvement cathare, xii–xv siècles*. Paris: Diffusion, Vander-Oyez; Brussels: Nauwelaerts.

Searle, Eleanor 1988 *Predatory Kinship and the Creation of Norman Power 840–1066*. Berkeley and Los Angeles: University of California Press.

Stock, Brian 1983 *The Implications of Literacy*. Princeton: Princeton University Press.

Taviani, Huguette 1974 Naissance d'une hérésie en Italie du nord au xie. siècle. *Annales: Economies, Sociétés Civilisations* 29: 1224–52.

1977 Le Mariage dans l'hérésie de l'an mil'. *Annales: Economies, Sociétés Civilisations* 32: 1074–89.

Töpfer, Bernhard 1956 Reliquienkult und Pilgerbewegung zur Zeit der Kolsterreform in burgundisch-aquitanischen Gebeit. In H. Kretzschmar, ed., *Von Mittelalter zur Neuzeit. Zum 65 Geburtstag von Heinrich Spromberg*, 420–39. Berlin: Ruetten & Loening.

Turner, Victor 1969 *The Ritual Process*. London: Routledge & Kegan Paul.

Turner, Victor, and Turner, Edith 1978 *Image and Pilgrimage in Christian Culture*. New York and London: Columbia University Press.

Verlinden, Charles 1972 Marchands ou tisserands: à propos des origines urbaines. *Annales: Economies, Sociétés Civilisations* 27: 396–406.

Violante, Cinzio 1968 Hérésies rurales et hérésies urbaines en Italie du 11e au 13e siècle. In Le Goff 1968: 171–201. Volpe, Giacchino 1922 *Movimenti religiosi e sette ereticali nella società medievale italiana*. Florence: Vallecchi. Repr. Florence: Sansoni, 1961.

Wakefield, Walter L. 1974 *Heresy, Crusade and Inquisition in Southern France, 1100–1250*. London: Allen & Unwin.

Werner, Ernst 1957 *Pauperes Christi. Studien zu sozial-religiösen Bewegungen im Zeitalter des Reformpapsttums*. Leipzig: Kochler & Amelang.

Wolff, Robert Lee 1978 How the News was Brought from Byzantium to Angoulême; or, The Pursuit of a Hare in an Oxcart. *Byzantine and Modern Greek Studies* 4: 162–209.

2   Overcoming reluctance to prosecute heresy in thirteenth-century Italy

Peter D. Diehl

The first series of mass executions for heresy in Italy began in the early 1230s, when large groups of heretics were burned at the stake in Rome, Milan, and Verona. Executions for heresy occurred frequently for the rest of the thirteenth century.[1] Yet many people in northern and central Italy doubted the legitimacy of criminal prosecution for heresy. In the *Liber supra stella*, a massive antiheretical treatise written in 1235, the nobleman Salvo Burci of Piacenza devoted a lengthy chapter to justifying criminal prosecution and penalties for heresy.[2] At one point in an imaginary dialogue with a heretic, an orthodox speaker provided a lengthy justification of temporal punishments for crimes including heresy, and his opponent congratulated him thus: "you have shown that punishment should be imposed not only for criminals but also for heretics, and this is a great proof. Why? Because many men believe that the punishment of criminals [is ordained] by almighty God the Father, who do not believe the punishment of heretics can be done."[3] These doubters included both heretics and orthodox persons; Salvo Burci implies this by identifying them simply as

References to canon law and papal letters follow the conventions established by the *Bulletin of Medieval Canon Law*.

[1] Earlier instances of capital punishment for heresy in Italy occurred in isolation. Two centuries earlier, in 1028, a group of dissenters from Monforte in Piedmont was executed in Milan. Arnold of Brescia was hanged by the prefect of Rome in 1155, perhaps for heresy (contemporary sources say little about Arnold's trial and do not give the exact charges). On these instances, see Moore 1977: 35, and Frugoni 1954: 131–4.

[2] The *Liber supra stella* survives in one manuscript, Florence, Biblioteca Mediceo-Laurenziana, Mugellanus (De nemore) 12. The text occupies the entire manuscript of 224 folios. The chapter "De gladio temporali" runs from fol. 140ra to 158vb. No complete edition of the text exists, but selections have been published by Döllinger 1890: II, 52–84, and by Ilarino da Milano 1945: 307–41. Döllinger gives poorly transcribed excerpts drawn from the entire work but presented as if all of a piece. Ilarino's excerpts are more completely edited, with indications of folios, chapter headings, and biblical citations. I am preparing an edition of the *Liber supra stella*.

[3] Ilarino da Milano 1945: 325 (MS fol. 151ra): "ostendisti quod uindicta non tantum debet esse facta de malefactoribus, immo etiam de errecticis [*sic* MS]; et hec est magna probatio. Quare? Quia multi homines credunt uindictam malefactorum a Deo Patre omnipotente, qui non credunt fieri posse de errecticis." The spelling *errecticus* occurs consistently throughout the manuscript and probably implies a derivation of *hereticus* from *error*.

homines and not as *heretici*. The Dominican Moneta of Cremona confirms this interpretation in his anti-heretical *summa* written *c.* 1241. In the midst of a lengthy argument directed at Cathars and Waldensians, Moneta pauses to address a few words justifying the use of criminal prosecution against heretics "for the instruction of the unlearned in the Church."[4] Reluctance to prosecute heresy thus constituted a major obstacle to anti-heretical campaigns in Italy and persisted throughout the thirteenth century.[5] But this resistance began to crumble under the weight of ecclesiastical, particularly papal, pressure to put anti-heresy laws into the statute books of the Italian communes.

I

In recent years historians have greatly revised our picture of medieval responses to religious dissent. Close study of the social and political context of individual cases has revealed a considerable ambiguity in attitudes towards persecution of dissenters not only in Italy but throughout Latin Christendom in the period from 1000 to 1350. Doubts about the use of force to impose orthodoxy waned in the latter half of the period but never entirely disappeared.[6] This ambiguity had deep roots. Churchmen of the high Middle Ages confronted by organized religious dissent found conflicting precedents in patristic writings on heresy. Some of the Fathers had opposed the coercion of heretics to orthodoxy, while others, most notably Augustine, had come to accept it. In the eleventh century, ecclesiastics were divided over the legitimacy of invoking secular authorities to help suppress dissent.[7] This division persisted into the twelfth century, but the tide of clerical opinion generally turned to favor forcible repression. About 1140, Gratian's *Decretum* came down squarely in favor of requiring secular authorities to assist in the suppression of heresy, effectively turning heresy into a secular crime.[8] Some

---

[4] Moneta of Cremona 1743: 530: "Ista ad haereticos sufficiunt, tamen ad instructionem rudium in Ecclesia hoc dico." The passage appears in Book V, chapter 13, "De isto mandato: *non occides*" (pp. 508–46).

[5] For examples of resistance to heresy prosecution in the later thirteenth and early fourteenth centuries, see Webb 1984. To some extent, the growth in heresy prosecutions in thirteenth-century Italy was part of a larger shift in criminal law, as the prosecution of crimes went from a private matter between individuals to a chief concern of governments acting in the public interest. On this see Fraher 1984: 577–81 and *passim*, who attributes much of the transformation to leading theorists and practitioners of papal monarchy, including Innocent III and Hostiensis. I wish to thank Professor Edward Peters of the University of Pennsylvania for this reference and discussion on this point during the conference.

[6] Webb 1984: 110-13.

[7] Manselli 1971: 176–7 discusses the opposition of Wazo of Liège and other leading eleventh-century churchmen to the use of force against heretics.

[8] *Decretum Gratiani*, c. 23, q. 4, 5, and 6. Later Roman imperial law had prescribed criminal penalties for heresy and legal disabilities for heretics; see in particular the *Codex Justinianus*,

churchmen still preferred peaceable persuasion to the use of force; their ranks included such notable figures as Bernard of Clairvaux (d. 1153) and later Peter the Chanter (d. 1198).[9] On the whole, however, ecclesiastical opinion shifted strongly towards favoring coercion of heretics by 1200.[10]

A similar shift in lay opinion occurred, though it is harder to define precisely, particularly outside of elite circles. Emperors, kings, and other rulers accepted the responsibility of protecting the faith by forcibly suppressing dissent, arguably already in the eleventh century.[11] Certainly by the later twelfth century, secular authorities agreed with leading churchmen that heresy posed a threat which required forcible suppression, an agreement symbolized by the Emperor Frederick Barbarossa's issuance of an anti-heretical edict in conjunction with Lucius III's decretal *Ad abolendam* in 1184. It is not clear, however, that lay people below the ruling circles agreed with the legitimacy of prosecuting heretics. Recent scholarship has greatly modified the older view that spontaneous popular revulsion towards heresy led to many of the lynchings, executions, and other judicial punishments of heretics in the eleventh and twelfth centuries.[12] In Italy at least, serious doubts about the righteousness of prosecuting dissenters persisted well into the thirteenth century, as the polemics quoted above show. Even later resistance to prosecution occurred occasionally; executions of heretics provoked riots at Parma in 1279 and Bologna in 1299.[13] Such incidents were, however, rare by the later thirteenth century. Inquisitors generally received the necessary support for their work from the powerful in lay society and encountered little opposition from others.[14] Partly as a result of inquisitorial efforts, the major sects of the earlier thirteenth century, the Cathars, Waldensians, and Poor Lombards, declined numerically and were forced into hiding. Improved

book 1, title 5. This legal background underlay the patristic citations (particularly from Augustine's works against the Donatists) used in the *Decretum*'s treatment of heresy, but Gratian did not cite Roman law directly here. On the development of the medieval canon law of heresy through the twelfth century, see Maisonneuve 1960: 29–91.

[9] On Bernard, see Manselli 1971: 181; on Peter the Chanter, see Baldwin 1970: I, 320–3.

[10] Baldwin 1970: I, 322–3 notes that Peter the Chanter's position on the issue was a minority view in his time, and that many of his students, including Robert of Courson, disagreed with him.

[11] Moore 1987: 14–16, notes the political undercurrents of eleventh-century heresy trials, particularly the famous case at Orléans in 1022. Heresy here appears to have served as a pretext for an attack by one court faction on another. Some other cases (the burning of the heretics of Monforte at Milan in 1028, the hanging of heretics by Emperor Henry III at Goslar in 1052) may also have had underlying political motivations. See also Professor Moore's essay in this volume.

[12] A hotly debated point. For the view that persecution of heretics (and other marginal groups) did not arise from popular horror of deviance, see Moore 1984, and Moore 1987 *passim*. For an opposing view, see Manselli 1983.

[13] Webb 1984: 104.

[14] On lay confraternities established to assist inquisitors and bolster the orthodoxy of the laity, see Meersseman 1951.

preaching, especially by the mendicants, also diminished the appeal of heresy. Religious dissent became less acceptable to lay society during the course of the thirteenth century. In what follows, I will discuss the insertion of anti-heretical measures in the statute books of Italian cities between about 1180 and 1260 as a measure of increasing recognition of heresy as a crime by lay persons.

II

The most straightforward attempt to criminalize heresy came directly from the papacy. From 1184 onward, the popes attempted to get the communes of northern and central Italy to adopt anti-heretical statutes. These laws were usually but not always derived from imperial sources, either indirectly from Justinian or directly from medieval emperors. Up to the 1230s, these efforts met with limited success; most cities, loathe to compromise their legislative autonomy, ignored papal entreaties.[15] Furthermore, many cities spent much of the early thirteenth century at odds with the papacy over the liberty of the Church, and especially over the cities' attempts to tax local churches and monasteries. Popes wrote frequently to the rulers of cities, ordering them to strike from their statute books laws which infringed on the privileges of the Church and threatening excommunication and interdict to those who refused. These weapons had already lost much of their effectiveness, as many cities called a pope's bluff and endured lengthy interdicts.[16] In this climate of conflict and confrontation, complicated further by papal–imperial struggles, few communes at first accepted papal dictation of anti-heretical legislation.

The first significant action against heresy in Italy came in November 1184 at the Council of Verona, a meeting between Pope Lucius III and Emperor Frederick Barbarossa. This conference failed in its primary objective of settling several issues left hanging at the end of the schism between Frederick and Lucius's predecessor Alexander III, but it ended with a joint papal–imperial

---

[15] The cities of the first Lombard League obtained the right to legislate for themselves in the Treaty of Constance, which took the form of an imperial privilege granted by Frederick Barbarossa to the cities in 1183 as part of his peace settlement with them (*MGH Const.* I.408–18 no. 293). Many pro-imperial cities received similar privileges around the same time. For an overview of legal developments in thirteenth-century Italian cities, see Blanshei 1983, who surveys the scholarship on communal legislation and legal practices. I wish to thank Professor Edward Peters for this reference.

[16] A few examples: (1) On 18 May 1222, Honorius III ordered the *podestà* and people of Pavia to cease taxing the churches of the city or else face interdict and excommunication (Pressutti 3962; Po. —). (2) On 1 June 1222, Honorius ordered the excommunication of the people of Milan, who had exiled the archbishop-elect and a significant portion of the clergy of Milan. This excommunication lasted for three years until the Milanese relented (Pressutti 4015; Po. —). (3) On 7 March 1237, Gregory IX ordered the *podestà* and Council of Vercelli to remove laws infringing the *Libertas ecclesiae* from the communal statute book (Auvray II.577–9 no. 3539; Po. —).

pronouncement against heresy.[17] Frederick issued an edict subjecting heretics to the ban of the Empire.[18] Frederick's edict did not survive and left few traces in later secular and canonical jurisprudence. Frederick himself undertook no campaigns against heresy before or after the meeting at Verona.[19] Lucius's contribution had greater impact. He issued the decretal *Ad abolendam*, a wide-ranging measure calling for bishops to comb their dioceses for heresy using a proto-inquisitorial procedure. Lucius required lay rulers to support this effort, ordering

that counts, barons, rectors, and consuls of cities and other places . . . should promise, having sworn an oath in person, that . . . they will aid the Church against heretics and their accomplices, and that they will strive . . . to see to the execution of both ecclesiastical and imperial statutes concerning the matters of which we have spoken.[20]

By "ecclesiastical statutes" Lucius meant the anti-heretical provisions of Gratian's *Decretum*, causae 23 and 24, augmented by recent legislation including canon 27 of the Third Lateran Council (1179).[21] The "imperial statutes" probably included both the provisions against heresy in the *Codex* of Justinian and Frederick's ban.[22]

Like Frederick's edict, Lucius's decretal had a limited impact at first, but its lasting influence was far greater, since it was diffused in several decretal collections, most notably *Compilatio prima* and *Liber extra*.[23] Furthermore, some cities adopted anti-heretical measures after the meeting at Verona. Few, however, enforced them regularly. On 2 October 1185, Lucius complained to the bishop and clergy of Rimini

that although a certain edict had recently been established by common consent concerning the expulsion of heretics and . . . that rectors succeeding each year in the government of the city must swear that they will observe it, the *podestà* who was recently installed omitted this oath at the behest of the people, whence it is said that the

---

[17] Robinson 1990: 501–3.

[18] This is confirmed by three contemporary or near-contemporary sources: a letter written from Verona by Archbishop Adalbert III of Salzburg, Mansi XXII.489–91; the *Continuatio Zwetlensis altera* to the *Annales Mellicenses*, *MGH SS* XVIII.452; and the *Chronicon universale anonymi Laudunensis, MGH SS* XXVI.450. These and other sources on the meeting at Verona are discussed more fully in Diehl 1989.

[19] On Frederick's attitude to heresy, see Diehl 1989: 7–8.

[20] JL 15109: "Statuimus [*scil.* Lucius] insuper, ut comites, barones, rectores et consules civitatum et aliorum locorum . . . praestito corporaliter iuramento promittant quod . . . ecclesiam contra haereticos et eorum complices adiuvabunt et studebunt . . . ecclesiastica simul et imperialia statuta circa ea, quae diximus, exsecutioni mandare."

[21] Alberigo 1973: 225. This canon, like canon 4 of the Council of Tours (1163) was directed against heretics in southern France. On the Council of Tours, see Somerville 1977: 50–3.

[22] On another occasion, Lucius approved the use of Roman law as a supplement for canon law (JL 15189, 1181–5); on this ruling, see Kuttner 1952: 92–5. Frederick appropriated Roman law on occasion; see Benson 1982: 360–9, and Appelt 1961–2.

[23] 1 Comp. 5.6.10; X 5.7.9.

leaders of the Patarines, who had earlier been expelled for the most part, have returned.[24]

The outcome of Lucius's complaint is not known; his death on 25 November 1185 may have caused the matter to drop.

Lucius's immediate successors, by and large a frail and elderly lot, took no significant actions against heresy. Urban III (1185–7) was preoccupied with a vendetta against Frederick Barbarossa stemming from his family's losses during Barbarossa's sack of Milan two decades earlier. His hostility to the emperor led to a virtual siege of the papal court in Verona by imperial forces during much of 1186, with no chance for the cooperation of *regnum* and *sacerdotum* against heresy envisaged by Lucius.[25] Gregory VIII, his successor (November–December 1187), attempted to mend papal–imperial relations but died after only two months in office.[26] Clement III (1187–91) focused on reaching an accord with the Senate of Rome and regaining control of parts of the papal patrimony in central Italy. During his pontificate, Frederick Barbarossa left Europe for the Third Crusade and died on his way there.[27] His successor Celestine III (1191–8) struggled to thwart the aspirations of Frederick's son Henry VI to the crown of Sicily while avoiding an open breach with the emperor. Celestine aimed to preserve the balance of power in the Italian peninsula and to prevent the encirclement of Rome and the papal state by territories controlled by the emperor.[28] None of these popes seems to have done anything about heresy in Italy. Interestingly, Henry VI used the suppression of heresy as the rationale for military campaigns in Rimini and parts of Tuscany in 1194–6, although one may suspect political expediency lay behind such claims since these campaigns strengthened the imperial position in central Italy.[29]

---

[24] JL 15621; text in Pflugk-Harttung 1880–6: III.317 no. 353: "quod nuper de fugandis hereticis edictum quoddam communi fuerit deliberatione statutum et . . . quod succedentes sibi rectores in regimine civitatis se iurare debent annis singulis servaturos, nuper potestas, que ad civitatis regimen est assumpta, iuramentum illud, faciente populo, pretermisit, unde iam Paterinorum principes qui prius eiecti fuerant ex magna parte, ut dicitur, redierunt." Pflugk-Harttung dated the letter as 2 October 1184 or 1185 (dating clauses of papal letters did not use regnal years regularly until the pontificate of Innocent III). Since Lucius refers later in the letter to the "decreta, que nuper edidimus, in universos patarinos, receptatores et fautores eorum," probably meaning *Ad abolendam* (4 November 1184), the later date is more likely.

[25] Robinson 1990: 503–5.

[26] *Ibid.* 506.

[27] *Ibid.* 507–9.

[28] *Ibid.* 510–18. Henry succeeded after several years in obtaining Sicily, but his early death in 1197 staved off the envelopment feared by the pope.

[29] Theloe 1913: 104, 141–2 discusses Henry's use of heresy as a pretext for intervention in Rimini and Fucecchio, a village near Lucca. Lami 1766: II.523–4 prints a document in which an imperial legate describes his actions at Prato during one of these campaigns: "Venientes Pratum . . . bona Paterinorum et Paterinarum ibi morantium fecimus publicari, et domos eorum fecimus subverti et destrui." The political nature of this campaign is made clear later in the

Innocent III (1198–1216) sought new ways to combat heresy. He welcomed movements of pious lay persons such as the Humiliati and the Poor Catholics which his predecessors had anathematized, and by accepting the Franciscans and the Dominicans, he explored new forms of peaceable opposition to heresy.[30] At the same time, he opposed Catharism and other radical heresies far more vigorously than his predecessors had. In southern France, he eventually opted for force in the form of the Albigensian Crusade. In Italy, however, nothing like a crusade was possible, since the pope could not afford to lose potential allies in the Italian cities while the imperial throne was in dispute. Additionally, he may have felt that the situation in northern and central Italy was not as desperate for the Church as in Languedoc. Persuasion, not force, was needed here.

Innocent's famous decretal *Vergentis*, sent to Viterbo in 1199, used law as a weapon against heresy. The decretal ordered the authorities of Viterbo to banish all heretics from the city, and by equating heresy with *lèse majesté*, it applied to heretics the penalties for treason in Roman law: confiscation of property and disinheritance of the convicted person's heirs.[31] *Vergentis* imposed these measures as law in territories like Viterbo subject to the pope's temporal authority, but Innocent added that "we prescribe that the same be done in other lands by secular powers and princes, and we order that if they should be negligent, they be compelled by ecclesiastical censure to carry it out."[32] *Vergentis* circulated widely and quickly found its way into decretal collections, but it does not seem to have been adopted by many Italian cities.[33] *Vergentis* prescribed radical punishments which struck at the standing of heretics and their sympathizers in their communities by proclaiming them infamous, incapable of holding office, and unable to have recourse to the law courts. The provision of disinheritance and hereditary infamy for even orthodox heirs threatened the status of entire families and would have produced severe dislocations in the politics of many cities.[34] Few cities if any found

---

document: "Addicimus etiam ipsi Communi sub eadem poena [*scil.* ducentarum marcarum] ut Praepositum Pratensem, qui nunc est, vel ad tempus ibi fuerit, Cappellanum videlicet D. Imperatoris, et suos fratres in nullo offendere debeat; sed potius honoret et custodiat velut fidelis D. Imperatoris."

[30] Grundmann 1961: 70–157 remains fundamental on this aspect of Innocent's policies.

[31] On *Vergentis* and this unusual use of Roman law, see Ullmann 1965; Maisonneuve 1965; and Hageneder 1963.

[32] Po. 643; X 5.7.10: "in aliis [terris] idem praecipimus fieri per potestates et principes saeculares, quos ad id exsequendum, si forte negligentes exstiterint, per censuram ecclesiasticam . . . compelli volumus et mandamus."

[33] *Vergentis* appears in numerous decretal collections of the early thirteenth century including the official collections *Compilatio tertia* and *Liber extra* (3 Comp. 5.4.1; X 5.7.10). See Hageneder *et al.* 1964–83: II.3 no. 1 for a complete listing.

[34] Families formed the basic political units in Italian urban politics; on this see Heers 1977: 101–16 and *passim*.

the rigor of this measure acceptable, and canonists remarked that it exceeded Roman laws against heresy in its severity.[35] One leading commentator, Tancred of Bologna, reported that *Vergentis* was not applied outside of the Patrimony of St. Peter, and he justified the non-observance of the decretal on the grounds that equity was preferable to the severity of strict law.[36]

Innocent failed to follow up on *Vergentis* within the Patrimony of St. Peter since he faced a strong challenge to his authority in Rome from the Orsini faction.[37] Only in 1205 did he renew the attack on heresy with a letter to the people of Viterbo demanding that they cease sheltering heretics and dismiss the consuls and other officials who favored heresy.[38] This letter marked the opening of a new campaign to reduce the cities of the Patrimony to obedience, for which the repression of heresy provided a convenient pretext.[39] By the middle of 1207, Innocent succeeded in subduing Viterbo, Orvieto, and the surrounding cities. On 24 September 1207 he convened an assembly of consuls and other rulers of cities at Viterbo and promulgated a statute against heresy which he required all the cities to adopt.[40] Significantly, it reduced the punishment of supporters of heresy (*fautores et credentes*) from the total confiscation, disenfranchisement, and hereditary infamy prescribed by *Vergentis* to the mere confiscation of one quarter of their goods.

Innocent also pressured cities outside of the Patrimony to take measures against dissent. In 1206, Innocent wrote to three cities about statutes against heresy and the expulsion of heretics. In the first case, on 4 March, he praised the consuls and people of Prato "because you have expelled these violent and impious people from your boundaries, decreeing laudably that nobody in your

---

[35] Pennington 1978: 139 cites the commentaries of Laurentius (*c.* 1212) and Johannes Teutonicus (*c.* 1218), both of whom noted the discrepancy with Roman law. Johannes attempted the explanation that Innocent was correcting and superseding the relevant Roman laws (*Cod.* 1.5.4, 1.5.19; *Nov.* 115.3.14).

[36] Tancred to 3 Comp. 5.4.1 (*Vergentis*) v. exheredatio filiorum: "In aliis autem terris preualent leges predicte [*scil.* Romane] qui maiori equitate nituntur. Hec decretalis de seueritate loquitur, ut ex littera patet. Equitas enim iuri stricto preferenda est" (Vat. lat. 1377, fol. 264v, quoted by Pennington 1978: 141 n. 17).

[37] Waley 1961: 45–7. Innocent abandoned Rome and stayed away for nearly a year from May of 1203 to Easter 1204 and did not reach a lasting accord with his Roman opponents until 1205.

[38] *PL* CCXV.654–7; Po. 2532. The letter later appeared in official decretal collections as 3 Comp. 5.4.2 and X 5.7.11.

[39] Some Cathars did reside in the cities of the Patrimony, but many of the persons accused by name of heresy were actually opponents of papal power. After they came to terms with Innocent, their orthodoxy no longer was questioned. More extensive discussion of this in Diehl 1991: 240–3.

[40] *PL* CCXV.1226–7; Po. 3187. On this assembly, the so-called Parliament of Viterbo, see Waley 1961: 52–3. This measure repeated almost verbatim a statute he had imposed on Viterbo on 26 June 1207 (*PL* CCXV.1200; Po. 3158).

land henceforth shall hold the consulate who is suspect in faith."[41] The next day, 5 March, he wrote to the Florentines to urge them to greater zeal against heretics, particularly by "observing the statute which you laudably decreed against the said impious ones."[42] This letter apparently had some effect: on 6 December, Innocent wrote to the *podestà*, consuls, and people of Faenza and called on them to follow the example of the Florentines, who had made "a certain statute by which they intend to eliminate the filth of heretical wickedness from their city."[43] This letter represents a significant development; it was the first occasion in which a pope urged another commune's statute on a city government rather than Roman laws or general provisions such as banishment or confiscation.

Innocent's initiatives against heresy in Italy were necessarily sporadic, and the attention given to communal statutes in 1206 and 1207 seems to have been unusual. For the most part, he sought the reconciliation of borderline groups such as the Humiliati and relied on local ecclesiastical authorities to combat more intractable dissenters. Few Italian cities appear to have adopted anti-heretical statutes as a result of his efforts. His successors would raise the issue of communal statutes to a central position in their campaigns against heresy in Italy. In so doing, they encountered considerable resistance from the communes, resistance which required decades to overcome.

Honorius III (1216–27) used the imperial coronation of Frederick II in December 1220 as the occasion for a new legal assault on heresy. Frederick had recently returned to Italy after spending eight years in Germany establishing his authority there. The presence of a strong emperor in the peninsula would significantly change the balance of power, and Honorius sought guarantees of benevolence towards the Church from Frederick. He also wanted imperial help against heresy. For several months before the coronation, negotiations took place between the would-be emperor and the pope's representatives concerning the terms under which Honorius would consent to perform the coronation. These negotiations covered a wide array of topics including Honorius's attempt to prevent Frederick from uniting the kingdom of Sicily to the Empire.[44] In September 1219, Frederick repeated an oath he had first taken at Innocent III's behest on 13 July 1213. He promised to abandon the throne of Sicily to his son on attaining the imperial crown, to protect the liberties of the

---

[41] Po. 2702; *PL* CCXV.815: "quod huiusmodi violentes et impios a vestris finibus expulistis, . . . laudabiliter statuentes, ut nullus in terra vestra de caetero habeat consulatum, qui fuerit de fide suspectus."

[42] Po. 2704; *PL* CCXV.814: "institutionem, quam contra impios predictos fecistis laudabiliter, observantes."

[43] Po. 2932; *PL* CCXV.1043: "quoddam . . . statutum, per quod intendunt a civitate sua haereticae pravitatis eliminare spurcitiam."

[44] Frederick had tried to allay the pope's fears of imperial encirclement in a number of letters in 1219 and 1220 (Huillard-Bréholles 1859–66: I.2.628–9, 673–4, 740, 741).

Church, and to help eradicate heresies.[45] This did not satisfy Honorius, who wanted further evidence of Frederick's goodwill. Soon after his arrival from Germany in September 1220, Frederick met with papal legates in Verona. On 16 September, he sent out a letter to all the cities of Italy in which he rescinded all local statutes infringing on ecclesiastical liberty: "By the authority of the present letter, we annul them as deriving from a root of heretical wickedness."[46]

But the pope wanted more. In a letter of late September, Honorius stipulated: "since the vice of heresy is reported to have grown greatly in Lombardy, . . . you must decree something worthy of the royal dignity against heretics and their supporters."[47] In another letter, the pope obligingly supplied Frederick with the text of this "something worthy of the royal dignity" that he wanted from him, as well as other laws protecting the liberty of the Church.[48] Frederick raised no objection, and preparations for the coronation proceeded.[49] Frederick issued these laws during the coronation.[50] Honorius then ordered that they be promulgated in the cities of northern and central Italy and accepted as binding by these cities. He also required his legate Ugolino, cardinal-bishop of Ostia, to see that these laws were added to the corpus of Roman law studied at the schools of Bologna.[51]

When Honorius's legates attempted to impose the coronation laws on the communes, they met with a very mixed response. Mantua adopted less severe measures. Cardinal Ugolino of Ostia persuaded the *podestà* there to order the expulsion of all heretics and their supporters on 21 July 1221 and to fine those who sheltered them or provided them with any assistance.[52] The measure was renewed and the fines increased on 13 September.[53] On 28 July 1221, Ugolino brokered a settlement between the *milites* and *populus* of Piacenza, where

---

[45] *Ibid.* I.2.676–7.

[46] *Ibid.* I.2.855: 'Nos ea tanquam de radice pravitatis provenientia auctoritate cassamus."

[47] Po. 6358; *MGH Ep. saec.* XIII 1.101 no. 141: "quatinus cum vitium heresis dicatur in Lombardia plurimum excrevisse, . . . contra haereticos et fautores ac receptatores eorum statuas et servari facias aliquid dignum regia maiestate."

[48] Po. 6395; *MGH Ep. saec.* XIII 1.103 no. 144.

[49] Frederick had every reason to placate Honorius; he had repeatedly deferred his departure on crusade after taking the crusader's vow on 25 July 1215 (Abulafia 1988: 120–1). This tardiness had displeased the pope, and Frederick may have anticipated further delays while settling affairs in the kingdom of Sicily, from which he had been absent for eight years. The promulgation of these laws was a small price to pay to gain the coronation and the continued goodwill of the pope.

[50] *MGH Const.* II.106–9 no. 85.

[51] Po. 6598; *MGH Ep. saec.* XIII 1.118 no. 169. The latter measure would promote the diffusion of the new anti-heretical statute among the future *podestà* and other practitioners of the nascent *ius commune* of the Italian cities who received their legal training at Bologna.

[52] Levi 1890: 86–7 no. 63. The fines were £10 for *pedites* and £20 for *milites*, and after a second offense, a house in which heretics had taken refuge would be destroyed.

[53] *Ibid.* 87–8 no. 64. The fine for sheltering heretics rose to £100, regardless of social class.

factional strife had been endemic. Measures imposed on the city included the expulsion of all heretics, whether citizens or foreigners. Ugolino further commanded

that you cause to be put word for word in the statute of the commune of Piacenza, on which future rectors of your city will swear, the statute of the last Lateran Council and the laws of the lord Emperor Frederick promulgated on the day of his coronation in the basilica of St. Peter concerning the expulsion of heretics and the preservation of ecclesiastical liberty.[54]

Ugolino also succeeded at Bergamo, where the *podestà* and council agreed on 24 September to erase all laws in the city's statute book which infringed on ecclesiastical liberty and to adopt the emperor's coronation laws concerning heresy and the liberty of the Church.[55]

Few other cities appear to have adopted the coronation laws. In some cases, resistance to their introduction occurred. At Genoa a confrontation flared up when the *podestà* Lotaringo Martinengo refused to show the statute book of the commune to the bishop of Tortona, who wanted to insert Frederick's coronation laws. The Genoese resisted all attempts to add anti-heresy laws to their statutes until 1256 at least.[56] Even when communal authorities did accept Frederick's statute, as at Rimini, they met with great resistance within the commune. In February 1227, Honorius complained to the *podestà* and people of this city about the harsh treatment received by a former *podestà* who had turned over some heretical women to the emperor for punishment and had added the imperial law against heresy to the city's statute book.[57] Honorius did not prosecute his campaign for reform of communal statutes vigorously after 1221, for the crusade at Damietta and the frustrations of trying to get Frederick II to live up to his crusading vow and the promises made before his coronation nearly monopolized his energies. His successors would renew the effort.

Honorius's immediate successor, Ugolino, cardinal-bishop of Ostia, who took the name of Gregory IX, had experienced firsthand the limited success of Honorius's program. Early in his pontificate, on 29 April 1227, Gregory wrote to the cities of Lombardy. He complained that many cities had failed entirely to prosecute heresy and that others made only token efforts: "you make your statutes about expelling heretics and punishing their supporters, . . . and

---

[54] *Ibid.* 54 no. 48: "quatinus in statuto communis Placentini, super quo iurabunt futuri rectores civitatis vestre, poni faciatis de verbo ad verbum statutum ultimi Lateranensis concilii et leges domini imperatoris Frederici super ereticis expellendis et conservanda ecclesiastica libertate." The canon referred to was c. 3 of the Fourth Lateran Council (1215).

[55] *Ibid.* 94–6 no. 72.

[56] Vitale 1951: 32.

[57] Po. 7672; *MGH Ep. saec.* XIII 1.259 no. 341. The law in question here was probably Frederick's second anti-heretical statute, issued in 1224 (*MGH Const.* II.126 no. 100).

carrying out these statutes superficially, you banish these heretics, and they return after a brief time, and you allow this under a pretence, as if God could be fooled by your cleverness."[58] Gregory prescribed that the cities adopt the canons of the Fourth Lateran Council and the Emperor Frederick's laws against heresy.[59] The response to this command was not impressive. Milan adopted a statute ordering the punishment of heretics according to imperial law in 1228 at the urging of a papal legate.[60] Guala, bishop of Brescia, procured the insertion of Frederick's laws in his city's statute book in late 1230 or early 1231.[61] Apparently few other cities followed suit, since Gregory eventually turned to a new strategy.

In February 1231, Gregory issued a blanket condemnation of heretics. At the same time, Annibaldo, the senator of Rome, issued an edict against heretics, doubtless at Gregory's behest.[62] In May the pope wrote to the archbishop of Milan and his suffragans and also to the bishops of Tuscany. He ordered these prelates to publicize the excommunication and Annibaldo's statute and to press the officials of their cities to add them to their statute books. Presumably Gregory felt that the cities would find Annibaldo's statute more palatable than imperial laws against heresy, given their growing suspicions of Frederick II. If so, he was disappointed; to the best of my knowledge, no cities adopted it. Some were content with existing legislation. Others were even less satisfactory to the pope. The Florentines obstinately refused Annibaldo's statute, as Gregory complained in April 1233.[63] Up to this point, Gregory's efforts had found little more success than his predecessors'. Several cities had statutes on the books, but few enforced them regularly. Fewer still were eager to change their statutes to conform to every new formulation from the papal curia.

III

Another force than the papacy influenced a number of cities which had previously sheltered heretics to begin energetic prosecutions for heresy in the

---

[58] Po. —; Auvray I.28 no. 54: "facitis statuta vestra de expellendis hereticis et eorum fautoribus puniendis . . . ipsaque statuta superficialiter exequentes, hereticos ipsos a finibus vestris expellitis, qui post tempus modicum revertuntur, vosque, quasi Deus vestra possit astutia irrideri, id sub dissimulatione transitis."

[59] *Ibid.* pp. 29–30.

[60] Baroni 1976–88: I.327–8 no. 220, dated 22 January 1229, ratifying an act of the previous year's *podestà*.

[61] Havet 1880: 602, citing *Historiae patriae monumenta* 16, col. 1584[125], which I have been unable to see.

[62] Auvray I.351–2 no. 539 (Gregory's excommunication) and I.352–3 no. 540 (Annibaldo's edict). It is no doubt significant that Annibaldo's edict was recorded in Gregory's register, as the coronation statutes of Frederick II had been in Honorius's register in 1220. It was extremely rare for any letter or proclamation of a secular ruler to be included in the papal registers.

[63] Po. 9170 (28 April 1233); Ughelli 1717–22: III.112.

mid-1230s. Preaching by the mendicant orders powerfully swayed public opinion, most notably during the Alleluia of 1233. A vast movement of religious revival in the lower Po valley, the Alleluia pursued orthodox goals, but it began as a local initiative of mendicant preachers in the Veneto rather than a centrally planned campaign from Rome. Among other objectives, the friars persuaded the citizens to enforce existing anti-heretical laws or to add new ones to their cities' statutes.[64] The Dominican John of Vicenza, the leading preacher of the Alleluia, had sixty Cathars burned at Verona in the summer of 1233, though he seems not to have added any statutes there.[65] Another preacher, Gerard of Modena, overhauled the statutes of Parma, adding new provisions to an existing law against heresy.[66] Mendicant preaching also had considerable impact west of the main area of the Alleluia proper, where three cities received new anti-heretical statutes in 1233 or 1234. In September 1233, the Dominican Peter of Verona induced the Milanese to add a stringent new statute on the punishment of heretics and their supporters. He then carried out an inquisition in which several heretics were convicted and burned at the stake.[67] Two nearby cities, Monza and Vercelli, invited Franciscan preachers to revise their statute books in 1234 to conform to the teachings of the Church. The friars included lengthy statutes against heretics and their various degrees of supporters.[68] Significantly, only the legislative activity at Milan had prior papal approval, although Gregory IX moved quickly to regain control as the early zeal of the Alleluia faded.

The excitement of the Alleluia proved momentary, but the mendicant orders' permanent presence in the cities radically altered the terms of religious discourse. By the mid-1230s, the friars had established houses in most of the major cities of Italy.[69] Both the Franciscan and Dominican orders had begun in part as orthodox responses to heresy, the Dominicans explicitly and the Franciscans implicitly at least.[70] They began this mission by preaching against heresy and providing an example of apostolic austerity and rigor to counter

---

[64] The primary goal of the Alleluia movement was to secure peace in northeastern Italy. On the movement, see Sutter 1891; Vauchez 1966; and Thompson 1988.

[65] Thompson 1988: 190–1.

[66] *Statuta communis Parmae digesta anno 1255*, Monumenta historica ad provincias Parmensem at Placentinam pertinentia 1 (Parma, 1856), 269–71; Thompson 1988: 188. The old law had provided for the expulsion of heretics along the lines of the imperial legislation of 1220; Gerard's new provisions added fines of 100s. imp. for knights and 50s. imp. for commoners who conducted public or private disputations on the Catholic faith; the reformed law also required that the statute be read thrice yearly in public.

[67] Baroni 1976–88: I.452–4 no. 308; *Memoriae Mediolanenses* s.a. 1233, *MGH SS* XVIII.402.

[68] Vauchez 1966: 525–6.

[69] Moorman 1968: 155–60; Hinnebusch 1966–73: I.251–78. Moorman 1983 *passim*.

[70] On the Dominicans, see Hinnebusch 1966–73: I.39–67 and *passim*; on the attitudes of St. Francis and the first two generations of Franciscans to heresy, see among others, Mariano d'Alatri 1979.

heretical critiques of ecclesiastical wealth and claims to a monopoly on the *vita apostolica*.[71] As loyal servants of the papacy, the mendicants agitated for anti-heretical legislation. Given the ineffectiveness of most bishops in countering heresy, the friars also became the logical choice for papal commissions as heresy inquisitors in the 1230s and beyond. Required thus to advocate forcible repression of heresy both as preachers and inquisitors, they sometimes encountered violent opposition, as for example in the riot provoked by the preaching of the Dominican Roland of Cremona at Piacenza in 1234 or the assassination of Peter of Verona in 1252.[72]

Notwithstanding considerable opposition from heretics and from cities anxious to keep their legislative autonomy, the persistence of the popes' efforts to impose anti-heretical legislation on the communes and the ability of the mendicant orders to sway public opinion produced results. Whereas in 1216 the famous preacher James of Vitry complained that nobody in Milan or other cities of northern Italy except the Humiliati opposed the growth of heresy, two decades later the situation had changed significantly.[73] In a remarkable passage of the *Liber supra Stella*, a heretic complains:

> The prelates of this church give their strength and work as hard as they can, so that it may be ordained in the writings of cities that those whom they call heretics should be tortured with various torments. And if the commune of the cities does not want to do this, they attack them [*sic*], saying "We will excommunicate you, and it is right that this be done." And if they do not do it, they do not say their office nor their other frauds, and in this, the commune is foolish and follows their follies.[74]

This passage was written in 1235, just after the Alleluia, when the communes began to give in to papal and mendicant pressure for repression of dissent. Debate on religious matters was forced underground. At least one of the laws imposed by the mendicants during the Alleluia forbade public and private disputation on questions of faith.[75] Early procedural manuals written by mendicant inquisitors mandated examination of suspects' beliefs but prohibited attempts to convert them through disputation.[76] These measures did

---

[71] Little 1978: 146–69.

[72] On Piacenza, see Racine 1979: 857–60; on Peter of Verona, see Merlo 1984: 473–88, with survey of earlier works.

[73] James of Vitry 1960: 71–2 no. 1.

[74] Ilarino da Milano 1945: 326–7 (= fol. 153ra–rb): "Prelati huius ecclesie dant uim et laborant in quantum possunt, ut ponatur in scriptis ciuitatum quod uariis tormentis crucientur hii quos ipsi erreticos appellant; et si commune ciuitatum non uult hoc facere, pugnant eos [*sic*] dicentes: 'Excommunicabimus uos, et oportet quod fiat.' Et si non faciunt, neque dicunt officium neque quasdam suas truphas; et in hoc commune est stultum et sequitur stulticias suas." (I have altered the punctuation at one point and have rendered consonantal u as u rather than v as Ilarino did.) On this passage, see also Merlo 1984: 484–5.

[75] At Parma; see n. 49 above.

[76] Dondaine 1947: 88–96.

not entirely succeed in suppressing religious dissent, but they pushed it outside of the bounds of acceptable public discourse.

Heresy did not dwindle obviously in the latter years of Gregory IX's pontificate nor in that of Innocent IV, largely because the struggle waged by these popes with Frederick II outweighed all other concerns. Lombardy still served as a refuge for Cathars fleeing increasingly effective repression in Languedoc.[77] The renewed papal–imperial conflict did, however, produce one event significant for later campaigns against heresy. In 1239 Frederick augmented his laws against heresy and reissued them to forestall papal propaganda which impugned his own orthodoxy.[78] Somewhat ironically, Innocent IV adopted these laws of 1239 as the definitive norm for secular laws against heresy, but he did so only in May 1252, after Frederick had been safely dead for a year and a half.[79] Innocent ordered the cities to insert these laws into their statute books. Innocent renewed this command in October 1252, and again in May and July 1254, assigning mendicant inquisitors to execute the task and granting them the authority to excommunicate all civic officials who resisted.[80]

Innocent IV's use of the imperial laws set a precedent for his successors. Alexander IV repeated his command to the cities in September and November 1258.[81] Clement IV did likewise in October and November 1265, and Nicholas IV in 1288.[82] The repetition of this command may indicate continuing resistance to forcible repression of heresy or perhaps continuing resistance by independent-minded communes to papally imposed legislation. A decretal of Urban IV prohibited local laws which interfered with the work of inquisitors, an indication of continuing resistance to forcible repression of dissent.[83] But many cities complied with papal orders, adding anti-heretical statutes when inquisitors appeared bearing papal decretals. Como added Frederick's laws and five of Innocent IV's decretals against heresy into the communal statute book on 10 September 1255 at the behest of the Dominican Rainerio Sacconi, head inquisitor of Lombardy.[84] Padua likewise adopted Frederick's laws in 1258 at

---

[77] Guiraud 1935–8: II.245–65.

[78] MGH Const. II.280–5 nos. 209–11.

[79] Po. 14607, 28 May 1252. On Frederick II's attitude to heresy and the nature of papal propaganda against him, see Abulafia 1988: 155, 293–6.

[80] Po. 14672, 31 October 1252; Po. 15378, 22 May 1254; Po. 15448, 7 July 1254.

[81] Po. 17383, 27 September 1258; Po. 17405, 7 November 1258.

[82] Po. 19423, 21 October 1265; Po. 19428, 1 November 1265; Po. 22839, 23 December 1288 (addressed to rulers in southern France but apparently universally applicable).

[83] VI 5.2.9. Such laws may also indicate local opposition to the political program of the papacy with which inquisitors were associated.

[84] Milan, Biblioteca Trivulziana, cod. 404, fol. 54r. The council unanimously adopted Innocent's decretals Ad extirpanda (20 May 1254, Po. 15375), Cum in constitutionibus (20 July 1254, Po. 15474), Nouerit uniuersitas (15 June 1254, Po. 15425), Cum aduersus hereticam (22 May 1254, Po. 15378), and Malitia huius temporis (15 July 1254, Po. 15429).

the behest of Pope Alexander IV.[85] On 15 July 1259, the council of San Gimignano received into the city's statutes a group of papal decretals against heresy which had been presented by the Franciscan inquisitor Giovanni da Oliva.[86] Instances such as these and the presence of anti-heresy laws in the statute books of many cities in the late thirteenth and fourteenth centuries indicate that reluctance to prosecute heresy waned significantly by the third quarter of the thirteenth century.

To conclude: this essay has suggested that little enthusiasm for the prosecution of heresy existed in medieval Italy before the thirteenth century. During the first half of this century, this situation changed considerably, with heresy increasingly being treated as a criminal offense. This change resulted in part from papal pressures on the communes to adopt anti-heretical measures into their statute books and to enforce these laws. The diffusion of preachers from the mendicant orders in the cities during the first half of the thirteenth century also contributed to the increasing marginalization and criminalization of heresy, most notably in the great mass movement of the Alleluia in 1233. As a result of these influences, by the third quarter of the century, heresy prosecutions became common and large heretical groups such as the Cathars, the Waldensians, and the Poor Lombards began to dwindle in numbers and visibility. While religious dissent did not disappear completely as a result of the papal campaigns for anti-heretical statutes and mendicant preaching, toleration of dissent decreased significantly, and official tolerance disappeared entirely.

BIBLIOGRAPHY

PRIMARY SOURCES

Florence, Biblioteca Mediceo-Laurenziana, Mugellanus (De nemore) 12. Salvo Burci, *Liber supra stella.*
Milan, Biblioteca Trivulziana, cod. 404. A collection of inquisitorial texts.

Printed sources

Sources cited in short form or according to guidelines of the *Bulletin of Medieval Canon Law*
Auvray, Lucien ed. *Les Registres de Grégoire IX.* Bibliothèque des Ecoles françaises d'Athènes et de Rome. 4 vols. Paris: A. Fontemoing, 1892–1955. Cited as Auvray and item no.

---

[85] Gloria 1873: 423 no. 1364.
[86] *Carte di San Gimignano* 90, fol. 5v, Archivio di Stato, Florence, cited by Davidsohn 1896–1904: II.104. On 25 October 1258, the *podestà* of San Gimignano had sentenced a heretic to death by burning at the behest of the same inquisitor (*Carte* 88, fol. 10r, cited by Davidsohn 1896–1904: II; 103). Presumably these decretals were a package of anti-heresy measures similar to the one accepted by Como in 1255.

Corpus iuris canonici. Ed. Emil Friedberg. 2 vols. Leipzig: Bernhard Tauschnitz, 1879–90. Contains *Decretals of Gregory IX* in vol. II. Cited as X.

Jaffé, Philipp. *Regesta pontificum Romanorum.* Ed. P. Ewald (to AD 604), E. Kaltenbrunner (604–881), and S. Loewenfeld (881–1198). 2nd edn. 2 vols. Berlin, 1885–8. Reprint Graz: Akademische Druck und Verlaganstalt, 1956. Cited as JE, JK, or JL and item no.

Mansi, J. D. *Sacrorum conciliorum nova et amplissima collectio.* 53 vols. Florence, 1759–67; Venice, 1769–98. Repr. Paris: Welter, 1901–27. Cited as Mansi.

Potthast, August. *Regesta pontificum Romanorum 1198–1304.* 2 vols. Berlin: Rudolf von Deckel, 1871. Cited as Po. and item number.

Pressutti, Paulus. Regesta Honorii tertii. 2 vols. Rome: Typographia Vaticana, 1890. Cited as Pressutti and item number.

Quinque compilationes antiquae. Ed. Emil Friedberg. Leipzig: Bernhard Tauschnitz, 1882. Cited as Comp.

Other source collections

Alberigo, Giuseppe *et al.*, eds. 1973 *Conciliorum oecumenicorum decreta.* 3rd edn. Bologna: Istituto per le scienze religiose.

Baroni, Maria Franca, ed. 1976–88 *Gli atti del comune di Milano nel secolo XIII.* 2 vols. (to date). Milan: O. Capriolo.

Gloria, Andrea, ed. 1873 *Statuti del Comune di Padova dal secolo XII all'anno 1285.* Padua: F. Sacchetto.

Hageneder, Othmar, *et al.* 1964–83 *Die Register Innocenz' III.* Publikationen des Österreichischen Kulturinstituts in Rom, 2. Abteilung, Quellen 1. Reihe. 2 vols. (to date). Graz: H. Boehlaus Nachfolger.

Huillard-Bréholles, J. L. A. 1859–66 *Historia diplomatica Friderici secundi.* 7 vols. in 11. Paris: Plon.

James of Vitry 1960 *Lettres de Jacques di Vitry.* Ed. R. B. C. Huygens. Leiden: Brill.

Lami, G. B. 1766 *Lezioni di antichità toscane e spezialmente di Firenze.* 2 vols. Florence: A. Bonducci.

Levi, Guido, ed. 1890 *Registri dei cardinali Ugolino d'Ostia e Ottaviano degli Ubaldini.* Rome: Istituto storico italiano per il Medio Evo.

Moneta of Cremona 1743 *Adversus Catharos et Valdenses libri quinque.* Ed. Thomas Augustinus Ricchinius. Rome: Ex Typographia Palladis. Repr. Ridgewood, N.J.: Gregg, 1964.

Pflugk-Harttung, J. von 1880–6 *Acta pontificum romanorum inedita.* 3 vols. Stuttgart. Repr. Graz: Akademische Druck und Verlaganstalt, 1958.

Statuta communis Parmae digesta anno 1255. Monumenta historica ad provincias Parmensem et Placentinam pertinentia 1. Parma: P. Fraccodori, 1856.

Ughelli, Ferdinando 1717–22 *Italia sacra.* 9 vols. Venice: Apud Sebastianum Coleti. Repr. 1970.

SECONDARY REFERENCES

Abulafia, David 1988 *Frederick II: A Medieval Emperor.* London: Allen Lane.

Appelt, Heinrich 1961–2 Friedrich Barbarossa und das römisches Recht. *Römische historischen Mitteilungen* 5: 18–34.

Baldwin, John W. 1970 *Masters, Princes, and Merchants: The Social Views of Peter the Chanter and His Circle*. 2 vols. Princeton: Princeton University Press.

Benson, Robert L. 1982 Political *Renovatio*: Two Models from Roman Antiquity. In Robert L. Benson and Giles Constable, eds., with Carol D. Lanham, *Renaissance and Renewal in the Twelfth Century*, 339–86. Cambridge, Mass.: Harvard University Press.

Blanshei, Sarah R. 1983 Criminal Justice in Medieval Perugia and Bologna. *Law and History Review* 1: 251–75.

Davidsohn, Robert 1896–1904 *Forschungen zur älteren Geschichte von Florenz*. 4 vols. Berlin: Mittler.

Diehl, Peter 1989 *Ad abolendam* (X 5.7.9) and Imperial Legislation against Heresy. *Bulletin of Medieval Canon Law* 19: 1–11.

1991 The Papacy and the Suppression of Heresy in Italy, 1150–1254. PhD diss. University of California, Los Angeles.

Döllinger, Ignaz von 1890 *Beiträge zur Sektengeschichte des Mittelalters*. 2 vols. Munich: Beck.

Dondaine, Antoine 1947 Le Manuel de l'inquisiteur 1230–1330. *Archivum fratrum praedicatorum* 17: 85–194.

Fraher, Richard M. 1984 The Theoretical Justification for the New Criminal Law of the Middle Ages: "Rei publicae interest, ne crimina remaneant impunita." *University of Illinois Law Review* 577–95.

Frugoni, Arsenio 1954 *Arnaldo da Brescia nelle fonti del secolo XII*. Istituto storico italiano per il medio evo, studi storici, nos. 8–9. Rome: Istituto storico italiano per il medio evo.

Grundmann, Herbert 1961 *Religiöse Bewegungen im Mittelalter. Untersuchungen über die geschichtlichen Zusammenhänge zwischen der Ketzerei, den Bettleorden und der religiöse Frauenbewegungen im 12. und 13. Jahrhundert und über die geschichtlichen Grundlagen der deutschen Mystik*, 2nd edn. Hildesheim: G. Olms.

Guiraud, Jean 1935–8 *Histoire de l'Inquisition au moyen âge*. 2 vols. Paris: A. Picard.

Hageneder, Othmar 1963 Studien zur Dekretale *Vergentis* (X 5.7.10). *Zeitschrift der Savigny-Stiftung für Rechtsgeschichte, Kanonistische Abteilung* 49: 138–73.

Havet, Julien 1880 L'Hérésie et le bras séculier au Moyen Age jusqu'au treizième siècle. *Bibliothèque de l'Ecole des Chartes* 41: 488–517, 570–607.

Heers, Jacques 1977 *Parties and Political Life in the Medieval West*. Europe in the Middle Ages, Selected Studies 7. Amsterdam: North Holland.

Hinnebusch, William A. 1966–73 *The History of the Dominican Order: Origins and Growth to 1500*. 2 vols. Staten Island: Alba House.

Kuttner, Stephan 1952 Papst Honorius und das Studium des Zivilrechts. In Ernst von Caemmerer *et al.*, eds., *Festschrift für Martin Wolff: Beiträge zum Zivilrecht und internationalen Recht*, 79–101. Tübingen.

Little, Lester K. 1978 *Religious Poverty and the Profit Economy in Medieval Europe*. Ithaca: Cornell University Press.

Maisonneuve, Henri 1960 *Etudes sur les origines de l'Inquisition*, 2nd edn. L'Eglise et l'Etat 7. Paris: J. Vrin.

1965 Le Droit romain et la doctrine inquisitoriale. In *Etudes d'histoire du droit dédiées à Gabriel Le Bras*, II.931–54. 2 vols. Paris: Sirey.

Manselli, Raoul 1971 De la *persuasio* à la *coercitio*. In *Le Crédo, la morale et l'Inquisition*, 175–97. Cahiers de Fanjeaux 6. Toulouse: Edouard Privat.

1983 Aspetti e significato dell'intoleranza popolare nei secoli XI–XIII. In *Il secolo XII: Religione popolare ed eresia*, 27–46. Rome: Jouvence.

Mariano d'Alatri 1979 I francescani e l'eresia. In *Espansione del francescanesimo tra Occidente e Oriente nel secolo XIII. Atti del VI convegno internazionale, Assisi, 12–14 ottobre 1978*, 241–70. Assisi: Società internazionale degli studi francescani.

Meersseman, Gilles 1951 Etudes sur les anciennes confréries dominicaines. II. Les confréries de Saint-Pierre Martyr. *Archivum fratrum praedicatorum* 21: 51–196.

Merlo, Grado 1984 Pietro da Verona – S. Pietro Martire: Difficoltà e proposte per lo studio di un inquisitore beatificato. In Sofia Boesch Gajano and Lucia Sebastiani, eds., *Culto dei santi, istituzioni e classi sociali in età preindustriale*, 473–88. Collana di studi storici 1. L'Aquila: L. U. Japadre.

Milano, Ilarino da 1942–5 Il *Liber supra stella* del piacentino Salvo Burci contro i catari e altre correnti ereticali. *Aevum* 16 (1942): 272–319; 17 (1943): 90–146; 19 (1945), 281–341.

Moore, R. I. 1977 *The Origins of European Dissent*. London: Allen Lane.

1984 Popular Violence and Popular Heresy in Western Europe, c. 1000–1179. In W. J. Shiels, ed., *Persecution and Toleration*, 43–50. Studies in Church History 21. Oxford: Basil Blackwell.

1987 *The Formation of a Persecuting Society: Power and Deviance in Western Europe, 950–1250*. Oxford: Basil Blackwell.

Moorman, John 1968 *A History of the Franciscan Order from its Origins to the Year 1517*. Oxford: Oxford University Press.

1983 *Medieval Franciscan Houses*. St. Bonaventure, N.Y.: Franciscan Institute.

Pennington, Kenneth 1978 "Pro peccatis patrum puniri": A Moral and Legal Problem of the Inquisition. *Church History* 47: 137–54.

Racine, Pierre 1979. *Plaisance du Xème à la fin du XIIIème siècle: essai d'histoire urbaine*. 3 vols. Paris: H. Champion.

Robinson, I. S. 1990 *The Papacy 1073–1198: Tradition and Innovation*. Cambridge Medieval Textbooks. Cambridge: Cambridge University Press.

Somerville, Robert 1977 *Pope Alexander III and the Council of Tours (1163): A Study of Ecclesiastical Politics and Institutions in the Twelfth Century*. Publications of the Center for Medieval and Renaissance Studies, UCLA, 12. Berkeley: University of California Press.

Sutter, Carl 1891 *Johann von Vicenza und die italienische Friedensbewegung im Jahre 1233*. Freiburg: J. C. B. Mohr.

Theloe, Herrmann 1913 *Die Ketzerverfolgungen im 11. und 12. Jahrhundert*. Berlin: Dr. Walther Rothschild.

Thompson, Augustine Craig 1988 The Year of the Alleluia: Preachers and Preaching during the Great Devotion of 1233. PhD diss. University of California, Berkeley.

Ullmann, Walter 1965 The Significance of Innocent III's Decretal *Vergentis*. in *Etudes d'histoire du droit dédiées à Gabriel Le Bras*, I.729–41. 2 vols. Paris: Sirey.

Vauchez, André 1966 Une campagne de pacification en Lombardie autour de 1233: L'action politique des ordres mendiants d'après la réforme des statuts communaux et les accords de paix. *Mélanges d'archéologie et d'histoire de l'Ecole française de Rome* 78: 519–49.

Vitale, Vito 1951 *Il comune del podestà a Genova*. Milan: Ricciardi.

Waley, Daniel 1961 *The Papal State in the Thirteenth Century*. London: Macmillan.

Webb, Diana M. 1984 The Possibility of Toleration: Marsiglio and the City-States of Italy. In W. J. Shiels, ed., *Persecution and Toleration*, 99–113. Studies in Church History 21. Oxford: Basil Blackwell.

3   Social stress, social strain and the inquisitors of medieval Languedoc

James Given

Introduction

This is an essay on the political sociology of thirteenth- and fourteenth-century Europe. In particular it describes some aspects of medieval Languedocian social organization that facilitated the repressive work of the inquisitors of heretical pravity. The central Middle Ages were an era of major political developments. These included a great expansion in the size of political units and an intensification of rulership. To be sure, these subjects have often been discussed, but the conceptual tools employed by medievalists to understand these developments have not always been completely satisfactory.

In general, there seem to be two models commonly employed by medievalists to explain the phenomenon of political development in the central Middle Ages. On the one hand, there is a species of explanation, much favored by administrative historians, that can perhaps best be termed neo-Weberian. This sees political development as primarily a matter of growing rationality. For these scholars, the key development within the field of medieval politics is the gradual move away from traditional forms of authority, personal and charismatic in nature, toward more institutionalized and organized forms of government and political authority. This development is seen most clearly in the fashioning of ever more elaborate, specialized, professionalized, and coordinated organs of government. The ability of these organs to carry out their duties in a progressively more efficient and effective manner not only gave the politicians who commanded the services of these mechanisms a competitive advantage in the arena of politics; they also provided better forms of justice and better means of mutual defense. Hence, they ultimately promoted the creation of a civic order that was perceived by its subjects as better serving the interests of all members of the community.[1]

On the other hand, there is a model that can be described as neo-Marxist. Scholars of this persuasion believe the driving force behind the development of

---

[1] See, for example, Strayer 1970: 10. For a critique (perhaps a little too vehement in its rhetoric) of this type of explanation, see Given 1990: 254–69.

the state to be the need of the ruling class (that is, the landed aristocracy) to create a political organization capable of defending its interests against the subordinate classes of medieval society.[2] Although this line of reasoning has an undeniable attractiveness to it, as yet it does not seem that the neo-Marxists have adequately worked out the details of the way in which medieval state mechanisms were actually built up.

Scholars of both groups, however, have seldom addressed themselves to the question of precisely how the new governing institutions of the central Middle Ages interacted with the peoples whose affairs they sought to control. How the rulers of medieval Europe sought concretely to make their claims to leadership real, what factors facilitated their work, what factors retarded it, and how their subjects reacted to these efforts are issues that have often not received as much attention as they should. This is due largely to the fact that the nature of medieval administrative documents does not let us explore these questions in any detail.

Fortunately, the material left behind by the inquisitors of heretical pravity in medieval Languedoc allows us to address these matters with an unusual wealth of detail. Elsewhere I have discussed how the inquisitors took existing techniques of rule, emphasized some, developed others, and knit them together into an apparatus that gave them an impressive ability to manipulate the individuals to whom they directed their inquiries.[3] In that essay I stressed what might be called matters of agency and contingency.

In this essay, however, I shall discuss, not what the inquisitors did, but some preexisting social factors that facilitated their work. We will thus be entering into a discussion of the unacknowledged, and often unrecognized (at least by the people of the late thirteenth and early fourteenth centuries), factors that helped control and shape the work of the inquisitors.

My argument is a simple one. One of the techniques employed by the inquisitors was the systematic social isolation of those they investigated, a goal pursued through such things as the systematic use of imprisonment and the permanent insertion of individuals into the readily recognizable and stigmatized category of penitent heretic.[4] In short, the inquisitors sought to extract the people they prosecuted from the social networks in which they were embedded. In pursuing this goal they were assisted by the fact that certain important Languedocian social organizations were marked by characteristic cleavages and conflicts. To borrow some terminology from the anthropologists, we can say that these social organizations displayed characteristic

---

[2] For an example of this line of reasoning, see Brenner 1985. See also Anderson 1974: 151–3.

[3] Given 1989.

[4] *Ibid.*, 343–7, 352–6.

strain systems.[5] To these strain systems the inquisitors applied, in the form of their investigations, a novel and threatening outside stress. Under the right conditions this external stress could so exacerbate an already existing strain system as to lead to conflict and breakdown within a network of social solidarities, thus facilitating the work of the inquisitors.

Lordship

Lordship is probably the social bond that first springs to the minds of medievalists when they think about social solidarities. Accordingly I will begin with a consideration of the strains that afflicted this particular bond in Languedoc.

The thirteenth century was a great age of lordship in the south of France. Everywhere after the end of the Albigensian crusades lords, whether the Capetian kings, newly implanted aristocrats from the north, or native Languedocians, perfected their means of governance and consolidated their lordships. This process has been best studied in ecclesiastical lordships, especially in the diocese of Albi.[6] In Albi the bishops took advantage of the upheaval caused by the Albigensian crusades and the imposition of Capetian overlordship to develop significantly their secular authority within the diocese. The seigneurial rights of the Trencavel family, viscounts of Carcassonne and Albi, were destroyed. Throughout the first half of the thirteenth century the bishops conducted a long, and relatively successful, struggle against the pretensions of royal agents. In this effort to consolidate their authority, the bishops at first had as their allies the inhabitants of the city of Albi. To reward this support the bishops in the first half of the thirteenth century granted various privileges to the townsmen. Although we cannot say that the bishops took a benevolent attitude toward heresy, their alliance with the townspeople may have something to do with the fact that the inquisitors, after their early, occasionally unpleasant experiences with trying to ferret out heretics in Albi, left the city largely alone until the 1270s.[7]

In the second half of the thirteenth century, however, relations between the bishops and their subjects became strained. The growth of episcopal lordship, which ultimately included an intensive campaign against lay possessors

---

[5] My concept of strain and strain system is derived from that of Alan R. Beals and Bernard J. Siegel, who argue that "strain has to do with those areas of life in which culturally induced expectations tend to be frustrated most frequently" (1966: 68–9). It should be noted that my understanding of "strain system" has less to do with notions of culturally induced expectations, the factor stressed by Beals and Siegel, than with the existence in any social organization of certain fundamental contradictions of interests.

[6] See the essays of Jean-Louis Biget (1971, 1972) and of Auguste Molinier (1872–1904).

[7] Biget 1971: 274–8.

of tithes and attacks on the judicial and political prerogatives of the townsmen, came increasingly to seem a threat to the bourgeoisie of Albi. Many of
the town's leading elements decided that a way out of their dilemma was to
attempt to foster the growth of royal authority at the expense of that of the
bishop.

One result of this growing tension within the city, aside from rioting,
assassinations, and a general atmosphere of violence,[8] was a dramatic increase
in inquisitorial activity. Bernard de Castanet, who became bishop of Albi in
1276, quickly realized that a judicious use of heresy prosecution could assist
him in his difficulties with the people of his diocese. Tithes were prised out of
the hands of recalcitrant lay possessors by the expedient of threatening them
with prosecution for heresy.[9] In the 1290s Castanet tried to break opposition
within the city by arresting several of the town's leading citizens on the
suspicion that they had had dealings with the remaining Cathar heretics in the
region, trying them quickly in cooperation with Nicholas d'Abbeville, the
inquisitor of Carcassonne, and sentencing them to imprisonment in the dreaded
mur, or inquisitorial prison, in Carcassonne.[10]

It was not only in the diocese of Albi that the growing tensions between
aggressive lords and recalcitrant subjects facilitated the work of the inquisitors.
The same factor seems to have been at work in the diocese of Pamiers, which
embraced much of the county of Foix. One of the factors that caused Jacques
Fournier, bishop of Pamiers from 1317 to 1326, to press heresy investigations
in his diocese was the determined resistance of the inhabitants of the region
known as the Sabarthès to the bishop's efforts to increase his tithe revenue.[11]
Indeed, failure to pay tithes figured in six of the ninety-eight heresy investigations known to have been conducted by Fournier.[12]

So the strains involved in the consolidation of lordship often functioned in
such a way as to facilitate the work of the inquisitors. Not only were some lords
unwilling to protect their subjects from the attentions of the inquisitors, some
ecclesiastical lords were even willing to mount their own inquisitorial investigations. Although a bishop like the zealous Jacques Fournier was probably
genuinely concerned with heresy in his diocese, one is tempted to believe, as
did many of his contemporaries, that Bernard de Castanet made a cynical use

---

[8] An atmosphere vividly described in testimony delivered to papal commissioners investigating
Castanet in the early fourteenth century and recorded in Archivio Segreto Vaticano,
Collectorie 404.

[9] *Ibid.*, fol. 104r.

[10] The records of this investigation are printed in Davis 1948.

[11] Tithes had been a matter of dispute in the diocese of Pamiers since at least the 1250s. For
information on the protracted disputes over tithes in this diocese, see de Llobet n.d.: 30–1,
49–54. See also Duvernoy 1965: III.337–41.

[12] Le Roy Ladurie 1975: 15, 49.

of inquisitorial techniques to crush men whose fault was not heresy, but opposition to his will.[13]

Kinship

I shall now shift my attention from the vertical bonds of lordship and clientage to the horizontal bonds that united Languedocians. In particular we shall focus on two very important types of horizontal tie, first, those that united kinsmen, and second, those that united the inhabitants of the same residential community. Here once again we will see that these bonds were characterized by particular strain systems that much facilitated the work of the inquisitors.

In discussing the strains that afflicted kinship ties, we will focus on the diocese of Pamiers and the county of Foix. Thanks to the unusual detail in the inquisitorial register of Jacques Fournier and the researches of Le Roy Ladurie, we are relatively well informed about the nature of kinship ties in this part of Languedoc. At first glance, one might think that kinship ties would present a real problem for the inquisitors. In many ways, the family was the basic unit of medieval society, the center not only of biological reproduction, but of economic, cultural, and, to an extent, political reproduction as well. As Le Roy Ladurie has made clear, among the very well documented peasants of the Ariège, the kinship unit, incarnated in the household (conceived of both as a domiciliary unit and a network of relatives) was not only central to their social life, but was the object of considerable emotional investment.[14] And, as students of heresy have noticed, in Languedoc Catharism tended to propagate itself along family lines.[15] So one might believe that the inquisitors would find the family a very tough nut to crack.

These kinship groups, however, were afflicted with certain strains that ultimately facilitated the work of the inquisitors. For one thing, the rules for determining membership or leadership in the kinship group seem to have been

---

[13] The reader should note the existence of a problem with the discussion in the preceding paragraphs. It is clear that several different phenomena lurk under the loose heading of "lordship." By the thirteenth century lordship could take several different forms. On the one hand, there were the highly institutionalized forms of lordship, such as that exercised by the bishops of Albi. By the central Middle Ages many of these seigneuries were far down a path that seems to end in the construction of small-scale "statelike" organizations. On the other hand, there was a more informal, less institutionalized form of lordship, that uniting a single patron with a number of personal clients. It is much easier to observe how lordships of the more institutionalized form responded to inquisitorial stress. Therefore, in the preceding paragraphs I have found myself forced, for lack of available evidence, to focus on these institutionalized forms of lordship. For one of the rare glimpses of how the strains that afflicted the more informal, personal types of lordship could be exacerbated by the stress of inquisitorial investigations, see the discussion of Planissoles on pp. 78–9.

[14] Le Roy Ladurie 1975: 51–107.

[15] See Roquebert 1985.

fluid and unclear. The kinship groups that found their physical manifestations in the *ostal* appear to have had some of the characteristics associated with cognatic, or bilateral, kindreds.[16] The evidence concerning peasant family organization, largely derived from Fournier's inquisitorial register, is not always as clear about the nature of the kinship system of the Sabarthès as one would like. However, we know a fair amount about peasant family organization elsewhere in southern France, in the central Pyrenees, and the Basque country. And it is perhaps worthwhile to employ this information to illuminate the material we do have about the county of Foix.

Throughout the Pyrenees the primary focus of kinship groups appears to have been the household, the *domus* of Fournier's register, the *ostau* of the central Pyrenees, and the *etxe-ondo* of the Basques. The continued existence of the *ostal* was the primary concern of the kinship system. To guarantee its continuance, in the western Pyrenees the eldest child, whether male or female, inherited the entire household. In some places, it was held improper for a female heir and a male heir to marry, since this would extinguish one of the households. Thus, only younger children, whether male or female, could marry an inheritor. Among the Basques, when a male younger son of one *etxe-ondo* married the female heir of another *etxe-ondo*, he had to provide a dowry. Once the marriage had been consummated, he moved into his wife's household and assumed her name, which would be borne by their children.[17]

Something like this situation seems to have prevailed in the county of Foix in the early fourteenth century, although the peasants of Foix tended to emphasize the principle of patrilineal descent. But the matrilineal principle was not totally obliterated. The chief goal of the family remained the preservation of the *ostal*, and it could be passed through both males and females.[18] The adoption by children of their mother's family name rather than their father's seems to have been not uncommon. It was also not unheard of for a man to adopt his wife's family's name if he took up residence in her *ostal*.[19]

Cognatic descent groups of the sort that appear to have existed in the county of Foix can be divided into those with an ancestor-focus and those with an ego-focus.[20] In descent systems with an ancestor-focus people reckon kinship by tracing a line of descent from a common ancestor, say a paternal great-grandfather. In descent systems with an ego-focus individuals reckon their kin by working outward from themselves, first counting ascendants among both

16 For this terminology, see Fox 1967: 146–74; also Goody 1983: 222–39.
17 Poumarède 1974: 25–6; see also the following articles from the *Proceedings of the Fourth Annual Meeting of the Western Society for French History*: Goyheneche 1977: 6; Frank and Lowenberg 1977: 15; and Frank, Laxalt, and Vosburg 1977: 22–4.
18 For Le Roy Ladurie's views on inheritance and descent, see 1975: 64–6.
19 Duvernoy 1965: II.129; Le Roy Ladurie 1975: 64.
20 Fox 1967: 164.

their maternal and paternal kin and then working downward from these ascendants to determine their collateral kin. In such a system kindreds are essentially personal, each individual, with the exception of full siblings, having a different kin group.

The kin groups of the county of Foix seem to a certain extent to have combined the two principles. They had an ancestor-focus, in that what mattered most to members of the family in reckoning their kinship ties was the *ostal* to which they belonged. But these kinship groups seem also to have had something of an ego-focus. At least there always seems to have been a certain amount of ambiguity surrounding the reckoning of kinship ties. Indeed, individuals often appear to have had a degree of freedom in choosing the *ostal* and the kinship group to which they wished to affiliate themselves.[21] The upshot of all this is that the strength of the moral bonds that attached one member of a kinship group to another were often fairly loose.

Not only did the kinship system of the county of Foix not provide firm rules for determining the membership of a kin group, it also did not provide clear-cut rules for allocating leadership roles within kindreds. Age seniority alone was not a decisive criterion for determining leadership.[22] Particularly among members of the same generation there was often conflict over who would exercise effective leadership. Within the *ostal* one brother did not necessarily exercise complete control over his other siblings. Bishop Jacques Fournier's inquisitorial register, for example, reveals brothers from the Clergue *ostal* in Montaillou seemingly working at cross purposes. While Bernard Clergue, the count's *bayle* in Montaillou and a supporter of the Cathar heretics, was trying to persuade one Bernard Benet to go to Carcassonne to give testimony to the inquisitors against the Faure and Guilhabert families, his brother, Raimond Clergue, approached Martin Guilhabert with a scheme for keeping Benet's mouth shut by means of a bribe.[23] If age was not a clear-cut criterion for the establishment of leadership within the kin group, neither, surprisingly enough for one acquainted with the more patriarchal peasant societies of northern Europe, was sex.[24]

It is thus clear that there were several sources of potential strain within the kinship structures of the Fuxéen peasant family. The pressures that the

---

[21] Arnaud Sicre, Jacques Fournier's spy, preferred to attach his fortunes to his mother's kindred and *ostal* in Ax-les-Thermes rather than to that of his father's kindred in Tarascon.

[22] For example, Bernard Rives of Montaillou found himself forced to cede effective leadership of his *ostal* to one of his sons. When his daughter Guillemette, who had married and moved out of the household, tried one day to borrow a pack animal from her father, he told her that he neither could nor dared to give her an animal without his son's approval; Duvernoy 1965: I.340. See also Le Roy Ladurie 1975: 65.

[23] Duvernoy 1965: I.431.

[24] Sibille den Baille of Ax-les-Thermes, a Cathar adherent ultimately burned at the stake, clearly assumed leadership in her own household. See n. 28.

inquisitors exerted on local society as they pursued their investigations exacerbated these strains. In effect, there was added to the preexisting strain systems characteristic of the peasant family a new stress, that is, a novel, externally applied pressure, that could not be dealt with through the routine or traditional devices offered by local society.[25] This new stress so aggravated the preexisting strains within some kinship groups that it produced unregulated, divisive, and disruptive conflict among kin members.[26]

Jacques Fournier's register contains several examples of how the new stress constituted by inquisitorial activity could cause family groups to shatter along just such lines as our analysis of family structure would indicate. In a kinship system such as that in the Sabarthès, where age by itself did not constitute a clear-cut title to positions of leadership in the kin group, we would not be surprised to find that inquisitorial pressure generated conflicts between parents and children. We can find several examples of such conflicts in Fournier's register. One particularly vivid instance is found in the deposition of Bernard Marty. Bernard's father, Pierre, was a blacksmith in the town of Junac. Arnaud, one of his sons, was an ardent believer in the Cathar heretics. He was frequently away from home guiding the Cathar *Bonshommes* around the countryside. One day when he returned from a night journey to Quié, his father queried him about his activities. Arnaud refused to explain. That night at dinner Pierre upbraided his son, "Arnaud, your ways do not please me, because you go out by night and you come back by night." Arnaud replied, "Be quiet, father, else bad fortune will come to you." To which his father replied, "You speak to me like this?" In his anger he threw a container of salt at Arnaud. Arnaud seized it and lunged at his father, but was restrained by one of his friends, Pierre Talha, who was also sitting at the table. Arnaud told his father that bad luck would come to him. Pierre, reacting to what was evidently a veiled threat on the part of his son, picked up the bench on which he was sitting and threw it at his son. He also proclaimed that Arnaud was no son of his and that he would see to it that he came to a bad end, which was evidently a threat to inform on him to the inquisitors. Arnaud thereupon stormed out of the house. Thereafter, according to Bernard Marty, there was for a long time bad blood between Arnaud and his father.[27]

Inquisitorial activity could also turn spouses against one another. Sibille den Baille of Ax-les-Thermes was a dedicated Cathar adherent. Indeed, she ultimately died at the stake. Her husband, Arnaud Sicre, however, was hostile to the heretics. Therefore she threw him out of her house and he was forced to

[25] Beals and Siegel 1966: 91.

[26] I follow Beals and Siegel in their classification of types of conflicts (1966: 22).

[27] Duvernoy 1965: III.261–2. For another example of inquisitorial-induced stress between generations of the same household, see *ibid.*, II.186–7.

move back to the town of Tarascon. Subsequently, Arnaud became one of the agents of Jacques Fournier, searching out fugitive heretics in the diocese, and participating in the mass arrest of the inhabitants of the village of Montaillou on the suspicion of abetting heresy.[28] And in the next generation, Arnaud and Sibille's son, also named Arnaud, became a spy for Jacques Fournier in the hopes of recovering his mother's inheritance.[29]

The way in which inquisitorial pressure could exacerbate the strains inherent in Fuxéen peasant families is nicely illustrated by the internal quarrels that afflicted the exile community that took shape in the early fourteenth century in the kingdom of Aragon. One member of this group was Emersende Marty who, to escape from the inquisition, had fled with her daughter Jeanne from Montaillou to Beceite in Catalonia. Jeanne married one Bernard Befayt, also a devotee of Catharism. In Montaillou Jeanne had been a good Cathar; but in Catalonia she became, if not a good Catholic, at least a good hater of Cathars. She constantly harassed her mother, and later her husband. She amused herself by calling her mother "a little old heretic" and threatening to have her burned at the stake. On occasion she even came to blows with her mother. The pair's bickering eventually became a public spectacle. One day Emersende and Jeanne argued during dinner, and Jeanne began beating her mother. Her husband Bernard was summoned to administer husbandly correction, which he did with great zest, tossing his wife out of the house. The commotion brought all of the neighbors to watch.[30]

Eventually Emersende and the other Cathar exiles attached to the circle of the *Bonhomme* Guillaume Belibaste began to fear that Jeanne would betray them to the inquisitors. To deal with this threat, they discussed a whole series of possible actions. The idea of taking her to a distant town and abandoning her was broached. Not surprisingly, this was thought to be a rather inadequate measure, as was that of returning her to Montaillou, since there would be nothing to prevent her from going to the inquisitors once she had been abandoned. Finally, it was decided that the best solution was murder.

Lengthy discussions then followed as to the best person and method to carry out the deed. A large variety of possible homicidal techniques was evaluated. The methods considered included throwing Jeanne off various cliffs and bridges, stabbing her with an assortment of lances and swords, and poisoning her. After much discussion the plotters settled on poison as the best method. However, the apothecary from whom an effort was made to purchase some poison (under the guise of treating some diseased animals) refused to sell it,

[28] *Ibid.*, II.9, 20, 28, 170–1, and n. 299.
[29] Arnaud's deposition is printed *ibid.*, II.20–81.
[30] *Ibid.*, III.178.

suspecting the purpose for which it might be used, and Jeanne escaped with her life.[31]

This circle of exiles also hatched another murderous plot which set one kinsman against another. This time they planned to kill Jean Maury of Montaillou, Emersende Marty's nephew. Jean Maury had fallen very ill, and was expected to die. His fellow Cathar sympathizers therefore approached him about receiving the *consolamentum*, the Cathar baptism that washed away the effects of sin and enabled one to attain salvation. Since any sins, which included the eating of flesh or cheese, that were committed after the reception of the *consolamentum* cancelled out its effects, steps were taken to keep the dying from eating any unclean foods. To guarantee that the sufferers would die in a sanctified state, they were placed in a state the inquisitors called the *endura*, in which they were deprived of all food except water. Of course, the *endura* helped guarantee not only a good death and ultimate salvation but also a sharply reduced chance of recovery. Maury, unwilling to commit what in effect would be suicide, refused to have anything to do with the *consolamentum*. Moreover, he threatened to have those who had suggested the matter to him arrested by the inquisitors. When he recovered from his illness, the exiles, fearing that he would disclose them, contemplated poisoning him. To his credit, Jean's brother Pierre refused to have anything to do with the plot and told Jean what was afoot. Subsequently, Jean's enemies repented of their schemes and asked him to forgive them for wanting to poison him. Jean did so, but prudent man that he was, he henceforth tested his food by giving some of it to a dog.[32]

There is a difficulty with the argument that I have been making up to this point. Although we can say without too much hesitation or ambiguity that Languedocian family life was marked by certain strains and that inquisitorial pressure helped to exacerbate these, it is hard to point to concrete instances where such strains played directly into the hands of the inquisitors. Of the material that I have amassed it seems that the only unambiguous instance where we can see family strains push people into the arms of the inquisitors is the case of Sibille den Baille's family. The frictions generated by the adherence of this devout Cathar believer to heresy not only led to the break-up of her marriage but seem ultimately to have turned her husband and her son into agents of the Inquisition. But such dramatic evidence is hard to come by. At this stage, about all I can do is suggest that surely, out of the thousands of people who passed through the hands of the inquisitors, strains within the Languedocian family played a role in delivering some of them into the hands of their persecutors.

[31] *Ibid.*, II.55–7, III.172–8, 247.   [32] *Ibid.*, II.484–5, III.114–15.

Neighborhood

If we turn to another important horizontal bond in Languedocian society, that of co-residence in a local community, we can also detect a pattern in which preexisting strains were exacerbated by the added stress of inquisitorial activity. The twelfth and thirteenth centuries saw much development of horizontal ties among the people of Languedoc. This phenomenon is best known for the major cities and towns of the region, which gained often large degrees of political autonomy from their masters, created their own legal systems, formed organs of self-administration, the most important of which were boards of elected consuls, and, in the case of the city of Toulouse, came for a time fairly close to fashioning something like an independent city-state.

Less well known is the fact that similar organization around ties of co-residence was going on among the peasantry as well. In the eleventh and twelfth centuries there was a major reorganization of settlement patterns in parts of Languedoc. This phenomenon has been best studied by Monique Bourin-Derruau in the region around the city of Béziers. In the earlier Middle Ages, settlement in this region had been relatively scattered. In the eleventh and twelfth centuries, however, the inhabitants of the Biterrois began to group themselves into compact, densely inhabited fortified settlements known as *castra*. In the late twelfth century the people of many of these *castra* began to organize themselves politically. During the thirteenth century many *castra* equipped themselves with self-governing consulates modeled on those of the larger towns of the region.[33]

These self-conscious, organized communities, whether towns or villages, could present serious difficulties for the inquisitors. Indeed, it is probably safe to say that the inquisitors experienced their greatest challenges and some of their worst defeats in trying to deal with outraged communities. In the 1230s inquisitors were expelled from Toulouse by the city consuls and confronted with rioting and organized opposition in Albi and Narbonne.[34] At the end of the thirteenth century the people of Albi and Carcassonne succeeded in creating an interurban alliance against the inquisitors of Carcassonne and their ally, the bishop of Albi, that embraced not only these towns but a number of others in the region as well, and which, supported by public subventions, managed to win a sympathetic hearing, for a time, from the French king, Philip the Fair.[35]

Yet, there were strains in these communities that created situations that

[33] Bourin-Derruau 1987: II.145–80.
[34] Dossat 1959: 131–5; Bibliothèque Nationale, Collection Doat, vol. 31, fols. 29r–32v; "The Chronicle of William Pelhisson," translated by Walter L. Wakefield (1974: 218–22, 226–8). (I have been unable to consult the Latin original in Douais 1881: 81–118.) See also Emery 1941.
[35] Discussions of these events can be found in de Dmitrewski 1924–5 and Hauréau 1877.

played into the hands of the inquisitors. Some of these strains stemmed from the economic growth that Languedoc experienced in the thirteenth century, growth that in many towns led to a widening gulf between rich and poor. The development of institutions of self-government created political rivalry between groups of ins, who attempted to monopolize control of these institutions, and outs, who wanted to force their way into the charmed circle of governmental power. Many of these issues were exacerbated by taxation, which became especially heavy at the end of the thirteenth century, when Philip the Fair found himself involved in wars with the Flemish and the English.[36]

On the one hand, the local nobility, which had often been deeply involved in the communal life of the towns, began to insist on its legal separateness from the townsmen in the hopes of escaping the burden of war taxation.[37] On the other, strife grew over how taxation was to be apportioned. The rich, who tended to dominate town governments, favored regressive forms of taxation, while the poor just as adamantly wanted progressive taxation.[38]

I shall illustrate how this tension between ins and outs, rich and poor, could facilitate the work of the inquisitors with two examples, one relating to the small affairs of a ruffian named Aycred Boret from the Fuxéen town of Caussou, the other to the rather larger business of the *bourg* of Carcassonne's experiment with treason.

Boret was a thug, one of the specialists in personal violence who tended to gravitate around the households of the Fuxéen aristocracy. And, in what seems to have been an interesting phenomenon that was rather widespread in Foix, and which I unfortunately do not have space to discuss here,[39] he had developed the habit of disposing of his enemies by informing on them to the inquisitors.[40] When *tailles* were levied in Caussou, Boret found himself offended by the behavior of some of his fellow townsmen. As he told one man, the members of two particular households had taken "the part of the devils and thus cast down us poor people." As a result he seems to have conceived the plan of delivering some members of these households into the prisons of Jacques Fournier.[41]

In connection with my earlier discussion of the way in which the stresses in vertical relationships facilitated the work of the inquisitors, it is interesting to note that the issue of the levying of *tailles* also turned Boret against the

---

[36] On the development of social tensions in Languedocian cities, see Wolff 1978a.

[37] Dognon 1895: 156–60. See also Given 1990: 196.

[38] Wolff 1978a: 81–3; Pélissier 1914–16; Wolff 1974: 169–70; and *idem* 1978b: 341.

[39] But see Given 1988.

[40] At least he claimed to have had one Raimond Becque imprisoned by the bishop of Pamiers; Duvernoy 1965: III.348.

[41] *Ibid.*, III.348, 350.

Planissoles, an aristocratic family which had long had Cathar leanings and which had patronized Boret. As Boret told the inquisitors, his ties with the Planissoles family had been, to say the least, intimate; Boret had once helped Raimond de Planissoles murder and secretly bury one Pierre Plani.[42] But Boret was so infuriated by the role that the lord of Caussou, Guillaume de Planissoles, had played in the levying of the *tailles* that he openly referred to him as a devil, and was willing to denounce him to the inquisitors.[43]

An even better illustration of the way in which social tensions within co-residential communities facilitated the work of the inquisitors is the series of events which took place in the city of Carcassonne in the late thirteenth and early fourteenth centuries. Carcassonne, in addition to being the seat of a royal *sénéchaussée* and a bishopric, was the headquarters for one of the permanent Dominican inquisitorial tribunals. In the last half of the thirteenth century this organization gave many of the inhabitants of the *bourg* of Carcassonne a difficult time.[44] The extent to which the Carcassonnais were involved in heresy is not clear. Over the years, however, the inquisitors developed evidence that in their eyes implicated many of the townsmen. In response the Carcassonnais in the 1280s began organizing against the inquisitors. Proclaiming their innocence and the inquisitors' malevolence, they appealed variously to king and pope for protection.[45]

In the 1290s the resistance began to turn violent. In 1295 the inquisitor Nicholas d'Abbeville was driven from the pulpit and stoned through the streets when he tried to preach. Other Dominicans were assaulted, and the entire order was boycotted.[46] In 1296 an attempt by the inquisitors to arrest several suspects who had taken refuge in the local Franciscan convent set off a riot.[47] For a time King Philip IV showed himself willing to temper the authority of the inquisition, but his support proved short-lived.[48] Pope Boniface VIII was also deaf to the entreaties of the Carcassonnais.[49]

With neither king nor pope willing to protect the Carcassonnais, the inquisitors were able to grind them down. By 1299 Nicholas d'Abbeville had brought his enemies to the point of surrender. In October the *bourg*'s consuls

[42] *Ibid.*, III.347.
[43] *Ibid.*, III.353–4.
[44] Carcassonne, like many Languedocian cities, was divided into a *cité* around the local cathedral, usually older and more ecclesiastically oriented, and a *bourg*, usually newer and more commercially oriented.
[45] Guiraud 1935–8: II.295–302; Mahul 1857–85: V.635–6, 638–43; Bibliothèque Nationale, Collection Doat, vol. 26, fols. 153v–4v, 215v–16v, 245r–57v, 261v–4r, 266r–7r; vol. 27, fols. 235v–7r; vol. 28, fols. 166v–70r; Devic and Vaissète 1872–1904: IX.334–7; Vidal 1903: 39–43. See also Lebois 1970.
[46] Lea 1922: II.68–9; Gui 1961: 102.
[47] Bibliothèque Nationale, MS Lat. 4270, fols. 231r–2v, 238r–v.
[48] Lea 1922: II.65–7; Devic and Vaissète 1872–1904: X (*Preuves*), cc. 273–81.
[49] Bibliothèque Nationale, MS Lat. 4270, fols. 119v–20r.

and the inquisitors negotiated a settlement.[50] The exact terms of this agreement were, however, kept secret. In a few years they were to become the subject of considerable controversy and not a little fear.

As d'Abbeville negotiated with the people of Carcassonne, events were transpiring in Albi that were to give the Carcassonnais new allies in their struggle. The bishop of Albi, Bernard de Castanet, was at loggerheads with the subjects of his diocese.[51] His difficulties with the people of Albi may have prompted his decision to begin a heresy investigation late in 1299. Setting up his own inquisitorial tribunal with assistance from the Dominicans of Carcassonne, he arrested over forty suspects, seventeen of whom had been town consuls between 1280 and 1298. With the help of Nicholas d'Abbeville, Castanet tried and condemned twenty-four Albigeois. These men were removed from Albi and lodged in the inquisitorial prison in Carcassonne.

It was widely believed in Albi that the condemned were innocent and had been forced to confess through the vigorous application of torture. The Albigeois found a spokesman in the Franciscan Bernard Délicieux, a long-time critic of the inquisitors. In the next few years Délicieux took on himself the task of organizing opposition to the inquisitors. Under his leadership the Albigeois and the Carcassonnais set about trying to form an anti-inquisitorial league. Appeals were made to Pope Boniface VIII and King Philip IV for intervention against the inquisitors. Although Boniface was deaf to these entreaties, Philip was, for a time at least, willing to take steps against the bishop of Albi and to trim the powers of the inquisitors.[52]

But the king was never willing to do all that Délicieux and his comrades wished. By the end of 1303 the Carcassonnais had decided that they could hope for no real assistance from the king. This realization spurred a number of them to launch themselves down the path of treason. A number of the *bourg's* consuls invited the king of Majorca's son, Prince Ferrand, to seize the lordship of Carcassonne and drive out the French. In the conditions of the early 1300s, this was not a serious plan. Indeed, the king of Majorca put an end to it during an interview with Ferrand in which he was so carried away with rage that he ripped clumps of hair out of his son's scalp. All that this plot did was deliver a number of the *bourg's* consuls to the gallows as traitors.[53]

The difficulties that Bernard Délicieux and the Carcassonnais experienced in

---

[50] Bibliothèque Nationale, Collection Doat, vol. 32, fols. 283r–8r, 299r–308r.

[51] My description of Castanet's inquisitorial work is based on Biget 1971.

[52] Compayré 1841: 239–40; Lea 1922: II.79–80; de Dmitrewski 1924–5: 208; Devic and Vaissète 1872–1904: X (*Preuves*), cc. 379–84.

[53] Bibliothèque Nationale, MS Lat. 4270, fols. 76r–8r, 113r–14r, 195r–9r, 204r–7v, 219r–v, 284r, 294r–6r. Finke 1908–22: III.131–4. Mahul 1857–85: VI.1.10–11; Devic and Vaissète 1872–1904: IX.277–80, X (*Preuves*), cc. 461–3; Hauréau 1877: 126–8; Gui 1961: 105. As for Délicieux, he was arrested by the king but eventually set free. In 1319, however, he fell victim to his old enemies, the inquisitors, and was condemned for heresy. Ultimately he died in prison.

trying to recruit allies illustrate nicely how social and political rivalry could facilitate the work of the inquisitors. Bernard was successful in enlisting the bulk of the population of the *bourg* of Carcassonne against the inquisitors. But to do so he had to exacerbate tension in the town. In the summer of 1303 Délicieux managed to secure a copy of the secret 1299 agreement between the *bourg*'s consuls and the inquisitor Nicholas d'Abbeville. The interpretation that the friar gave this document was a very dark one. By its terms, so he claimed, the consuls had admitted that they and all the people of the *bourg* had aided and abetted heresy. This meant that if the inquisitors thereafter proceeded against any of the *bourg*'s inhabitants, they could treat them as relapsed heretics and consign them to the flames.

Bernard communicated his view to the Carcassonnais in an inflammatory sermon. An attempt by the incumbent inquisitor, Geoffroy d'Ablis, to provide a more palatable exegesis of the terms of the 1299 agreement only succeeded in touching off a riot, in which the houses of several of the consuls of 1299 were destroyed.[54] Délicieux had succeeded in mobilizing the bulk of the town against the inquisitors, but at the cost of setting one part of the population against the other. Some of the former consuls whose houses were destroyed in the riot were driven into exile and, seemingly, into the arms of the inquisitors.[55]

The chronic conflicts that pitted urban rich against urban poor also hampered the anti-inquisitorial party's search for allies. In those towns where the consuls favored the idea of joining the alliance, the poor were often hostile. This hostility stemmed not so much from Catholic bigotry as from resentment against the taxes levied to defray the expenses of the campaign against the inquisitors. For example, Délicieux's efforts to raise money in Cordes and Rabastens aroused opposition. Certain factions insisted that any money raised should be used only for the good of the towns themselves. Even at Albi the consuls' attempt to fund their exertions on behalf of their imprisoned citizens met with resistance; compulsion had to be employed to make the recalcitrant pay up. At Limoux, on the other hand, it seems that the poor favored Délicieux while the rich opposed him. When the town consuls proved unwilling to take any action against either the king or the inquisitors, the friar's response was to liken them to ignorant pigs and to appeal over their heads to the town's poor. These, he claimed, lacking the connections and influence of the rich, would not be able to protect themselves from the inquisitors. The poor of Limoux apparently took Bernard's words to heart; his visit was followed by rioting.[56]

---

[54] Bibliothèque Nationale, MS Lat. 4270, fols. 160r–1r, 194r–v, 199r–v, 206v, 211r–13r, 224v, 287r–v.

[55] *Ibid.*, fols. 199r–v, 212r, 223v–4v, 281v, 286v–7r.

[56] *Ibid.*, fols. 212r–v, 243r–v, 265v–6r, 301r–2r.

Conclusion

In concluding this essay, I think that a few words of caution are in order. I have argued, first, that various forms of Languedocian social organization were marked by certain characteristic forms of social strain, and, second, that these patterns of strain helped the inquisitors to prise apart social organizations that might have been expected to offer more effective resistance to their investigations.

The reader should be aware that this argument is a very hypothetical one. There is much that we would like to know, both about Languedocian social organization and about the operations of the medieval inquisitors that, given the vagaries of record survival, will forever be beyond our grasp. It is therefore very difficult to establish unambiguously the sort of connections for which I have argued here. At most I can claim that the evidence I have assembled is consonant with my argument, although I would be the first to recognize that it in no way constitutes irrefutable proof of that argument. This may seem an embarrassing position in which to find oneself, but it is a familiar one to anyone who wishes to make any but the simplest generalizations about medieval social and political organization.

Although my conclusions should be regarded as little more than working hypotheses, they are not without value. The central Middle Ages were a great age in the development of European governing institutions. But how those institutions, usually decentralized, fragmented, and uncoordinated, functioned in the context of a society composed of social classes and organizations that were themselves often poorly unified and organized is a difficult puzzle. Medievalists, seduced by the impressive achievements of generations of administrative historians, have tended to see medieval political development primarily from a top-down perspective, as a matter of the progressive rationalization of governing organizations. Such a perspective is perforce a partial one. Those interested in medieval politics need to return to the task, Marxisant though it may seem, of understanding the social conditions of political behavior. We need to do so not merely to understand the dynamics of the social forces that generated conflict and dissent and made repression necessary; we need to understand how the social organizations of Europe functioned as political action groups, how they organized opposition to the wishes of their ostensible masters, and how their internal contradictions offered hooks and cleavages which the directors of medieval repressive institutions could exploit. In exploring these questions we will undoubtedly never arrive at certainty. But I hope that this essay may suggest to others that there are valuable things to be learned through the effort to find answers to them.

REFERENCES

Anderson, Perry 1974 *Passages from Antiquity to Feudalism*. London: NLB.

Beals, Alan R., and Siegel, Bernard J. 1966 *Divisiveness and Social Conflict: An Anthropological Approach*. Stanford, Calif.: Stanford University Press.

Biget, Jean-Louis 1971 Un procès d'inquisition à Albi en 1300. In *Le Crédo, la morale, et l'Inquisition*, 273–341. Cahiers de Fanjeaux 6. Toulouse: Edouard Privat.

1972 La Restitution des dîmes par les laïcs dans le diocèse d'Albi à la fin du XIIIe siècle: contribution à l'étude des revenus de l'évêche et du chapitre de la cathédrale. In *Les Evêques, les clercs et le roi (1250–1300)*, 211–83. Cahiers de Fanjeaux 7. Toulouse: Edouard Privat.

Bourin-Derruau, Monique 1987 *Villages médiévaux en Bas-Languedoc: Genèse d'une sociabilité (Xe–XIVe siècle)*. 2 vols. Paris: Editions L'Harmattan.

Brenner, Robert 1985 The Agrarian Roots of European Capitalism. In T. H. Aston and C. H. E. Philpin, eds., *The Brenner Debate: Agrarian Class Structure and Economic Development in Pre-Industrial Europe*, 213–327. Cambridge and New York: Cambridge University Press.

Compayré, Clément 1841 *Etudes historiques et documents inédits sur l'Albigeois, le Castrais et l'ancien diocèse de Lavaur*. Albi: Imprimerie de M. Papilhiau.

Davis, George W., ed. 1948 *The Inquisition at Albi, 1299–1300: Text of Register and Analysis*. New York: Columbia University Press.

Devic, Claude, and Vaissète, Joseph, eds. 1872–1904 *Histoire générale de Languedoc*, ed. A. Moliner. 16 vols. Toulouse: Edouard Privat.

Dmitrewski, Michel de 1924–5 Fr. Bernard Délicieux, O.F.M., sa lutte contre l'Inquisition de Carcassonne et d'Albi, son procès, 1297–1319. *Archivum Franciscanum Historicum* 17: 183–218, 313–37, 457–88; 18: 3–32.

Dognon, Paul 1895 *Les Institutions politiques et administratives du pays de Languedoc du XIIIe siècle aux guerres de religion*. Toulouse: Edouard Privat.

Dossat, Yves 1959 *Les Crises de l'inquisition toulousaine au XIIIe siècle (1233–1273)*. Bordeaux: Imprimerie Bière.

Douais, Célestin, ed. 1881 *Les Sources de l'histoire de l'Inquisition au moyen âge*. Paris: V. Palmé.

Duvernoy, Jean 1965 *Le Registre d'inquisition de Jacques Fournier, évêque de Pamiers (1318–1325)*. 3 vols. Toulouse: Edouard Privat.

Emery, Richard Wilder 1941 *Heresy and Inquisition in Narbonne*. New York: Columbia University Press.

Finke, Heinrich, ed. 1908–22 *Acta aragonensia: quellen zur deutschen, italienischen, französischen, spanischen, zur Kirchen- und Kulturgeschichte aus der diplomatischen Korrespondenz Jaymes II. (1291–1327)*. 3 vols. Berlin and Leipzig: W. Rothschild (reprint 1966).

Fox, Robin 1967 *Kinship and Marriage: An Anthropological Perspective*. Harmondsworth: Penguin.

Frank, Rosalyn M., Laxalt, Monique, and Vosburg, Nancy 1977 Inheritance, Marriage, and Dowry Rights in the Navarrese and French Basque Law Codes. In Joyce Duncan Falk, ed., *Proceedings of the Fourth Annual Meeting of the Western Society for French History, 11-13 November 1976, Reno, Nevada*, 22–31. Santa Barbara, Calif.: Western Society for French History.

Frank, Rosalyn M., and Lowenberg, Shelley 1977 The Role of the Basque Woman as *Etxeko-Andrea*, the Mistress of the House. In Joyce Duncan Falk, ed., *Proceedings of the Fourth Annual Meeting of the Western Society for French History, 11–13 November 1976, Reno, Nevada*, 14–21. Santa Barbara, Calif.: Western Society for French History.

Given, James 1988 Factional Politics in a Medieval Society: A Case Study from Fourteenth-Century Foix. *Journal of Medieval History* 14: 233–50.

1989 The Inquisitors of Languedoc and the Medieval Technology of Power. *American Historical Review* 94: 336–59.

1990 *State and Society in Medieval Europe: Gwynedd and Languedoc under Outside Rule.* Ithaca, N.Y.: Cornell University Press.

Goody, Jack 1983 *The Development of the Family and Marriage in Europe.* Cambridge and New York: Cambridge University Press.

Goyheneche, Eugene 1977 Medieval French Basque Economic and Political Institutions. In Joyce Duncan Falk, ed., *Proceedings of the Fourth Annual Meeting of the Western Society for French History, 11–13 November 1976, Reno, Nevada*, 1–13. Santa Barbara, Calif.: Western Society for French History.

Gui, Bernard 1961 *De fundatione et prioribus conventuum provinciarum Tolosanae et Provinciae Ordinis Praedicatorum*, ed. P. A. Amargier. Monumenta Ordinis Fratrum Praedicatorum Historica 24. Rome: Institutum Historicum Fratrum Praedicatorum.

Guiraud, Jean 1935–8 *Histoire de l'Inquisition au moyen âge.* 2 vols. Paris: A. Picard.

Hauréau, B. 1877 *Bernard Délicieux et l'Inquisition albigeoise (1300–1320).* Paris: Hachette.

Lea, Henry Charles 1922 *A History of the Inquisition of the Middle Ages.* 3 vols. New York: Macmillan (orig. 1887).

Lebois, Michèle 1970 Le Complot des Carcassonnais contre l'Inquisition (1283–85). In *Carcassonne et sa région, Actes des XLIe et XXIVe Congrès d'études régionales tenus par la Fédération Historique des Sociétés Académiques et Savantes de Languedoc-Pyrénées-Gascogne, 17–19 mai 1968*, 159–63. Montpellier: Fédération Historique du Languedoc et du Roussillon.

Le Roy Ladurie, Emmanuel 1975 *Montaillou: village occitan de 1294 à 1324.* Paris: Gallimard.

Llobet, Gabriel de n.d. *Foix médiéval: recherches d'histoire urbaine.* Foix: Société Ariégeoise des Sciences, Lettres et Arts.

Mahul, M., ed. 1857–85 *Cartulaire et archives des communs de l'ancien diocèse et de l'arrondissement administratif de Carcassonne.* 7 vols. in 8. Paris: Didron.

Molinier, Auguste 1872–1904 Etudes sur les démêlés entre l'évêque d'Albi et la cour de France au treizième siècle. In Devic and Vaissète 1872–1904: VII.284–95.

Pélissier, E. 1914–16 La Lutte des classes à Foix au XIVe siècle. *Bulletin Périodique de la Société Ariégeoise des Sciences, Lettres et Arts et de la Société des Etudes de Cousserans* 14: 96–103.

Poumarède, J. 1974 Les Coutumes successorales dans les Pyrénées au moyen âge. *Revue de Pau et de Béarn* 2: 23–34.

Roquebert, Michel 1985 La Catharisme comme tradition dans la "Familia" languedocienne. In *Effacement du Catharisme? (XIIIe–XIVe s.)*, 221–42. Cahiers de Fanjeaux 20. Toulouse: Edouard Privat.

Strayer, Joseph R. 1970 *On the Medieval Origins of the Modern State*. Princeton, N.J.: Princeton University Press.

Vidal, J.-M. 1903 *Un inquisiteur jugé par ses "victimes": Jean Galand et les Carcassonnais (1285–1286)*. Paris: A. Picard.

Wakefield, Walter L. 1974 *Heresy, Crusade and Inquisition in Southern France, 1100–1250*. Berkeley: University of California Press; London: G. Allen & Unwin.

Wolff, Philippe, ed. 1974 *Histoire de Toulouse*. Toulouse: Edouard Privat (orig. 1967).

1978a Les Luttes sociales dans les villes du Midi français du XIIIe au XVe siècle. In his *Regards sur le Midi médiéval*, 77–89. Toulouse: Edouard Privat (orig. 1947).

1978b. Réflexions sur l'histoire médiévale de Montauban. In his *Regards sur le Midi médiéval*, 333–45. Toulouse: Edouard Privat (orig. 1956).

4   The schools and the Waldensians: a new work by Durand of Huesca

Mary A. Rouse and Richard H. Rouse

At the end of the twelfth century and the early years of the thirteenth, Christendom spawned a number of heterodox movements that one can justifiably consider pre-Mendicant. In general, their beliefs were properly orthodox. But among their practices, two that were modeled upon their perception of first-century Christians – a renunciation of all material wealth and an insistence upon the unlimited right to preach – rendered them suspect in the eyes of the Church. We are often ignorant of the factors that determined whether such communities as these, groups like the Waldensians, the *Humiliati*, the many varieties of "Poor Men," would eventually cross the boundary into heresy and excommunication, or would instead accommodate themselves, and be accommodated, within the greater family of the Church – or indeed, as sometimes happened, would take first one route and then the other.

It is difficult to know these groups well – their learning or lack of it, their intellectual formation, the distance of their mental horizons, the development of their philosophy. Whatever of self-revelation might have appeared in their writings has, along with those writings, been deliberately destroyed; and we are left to rely upon the unsympathetic and usually uninformed comments of the orthodox who suspected or despised them. Thus, the discovery of a new work written by the leader of such a group admits a thin ray of sunlight into this stubbornly benighted area of medieval intellectual history.

An early thirteenth-century manuscript at Yale University, Beinecke Library MS Marston 266, contains a hitherto unknown work by Durand of Huesca, a collection of biblical *distinctiones*. The collection is a revision of Peter of Capua's *Alphabetum in artem sermocinandi* which appears to antedate the surviving manuscripts of Peter's original. Durand reveals his responsibility for

We are grateful to Louis Bataillon OP, Robert L. Benson, Nicole Bériou, and Peter Diehl, who read this article in draft and graciously shared with us their knowledge of heretics, preachers, and canonists in twelfth- and thirteenth-century Italy and Provence. We thank Barbara Shailor, who is currently cataloging the Beinecke's medieval manuscripts, for her discussion of Marston 266's place of origin in Appendix 1 below.

this new version in a verse prologue to the work (lines 37–44);[1] and he dedicates it – or "submits it for correction," an ecclesiastical equivalent – to Bernard of Pavia (lines 53–60), for reasons and under circumstances that are not explained.

Durand of Huesca in Aragon[2] (*c.* 1160–1224?), a well-known follower of Waldes, led the body of Waldensians who in 1207 left the heretical group, to be legitimized by Innocent III in 1208 as the *Pauperes catholici.* The pope laid upon the Poor Catholics, with Durand as their prior, the special charge to preach against the Catharist heresy. The charge suited them well, since combating Catharist dualism had from the start been a major goal of the Waldensians; the anonymous Waldensian polemic against the Cathars entitled *Antiheresis,* written *c.* 1191–2, has been attributed to Durand. In about 1222–3, as orthodox prior of the Poor Catholics, he composed a second anti-heretical tract, the *Liber contra Manicheos.*[3]

Peter of Capua (d. 1214) taught theology at Paris, and founded in his native Amalfi a house of canons that was subsequently, with his consent, transformed into a Cistercian abbey. As cardinal deacon of S. Maria in Via lata (from 1193) and cardinal priest of S. Marcello (1200–14), he served as papal legate in France and elsewhere, and in 1202–4 as legate with the Fourth Crusade. Peter's known writings consist of a theological *summa* thought to have been written at Paris in the late 1180s, and a lengthy alphabetized collection of biblical *distinctiones* meant particularly for the use of preachers, the *Alphabetum,* which he began as classroom lectures at Paris, and finished at Rome as cardinal.[4]

Bernard of Pavia (d. 1213), an important canonist and teacher at the University of Bologna in the late twelfth century, compiled at Bologna between 1188 and 1191/2 the *Breviarium extravagantium* that came to be known as

---

[1] Line references correspond to the verse prologue edited and translated in Appendix 2 below.

[2] This, the conventional interpretation of the Latin *Durandus de Osca,* was questioned by Dossat 1969. His suggestion has not won general support.

[3] For a brief recent summary of the known biographical facts, see Sarasa Sánchez 1981; Sarasa, on unspecified grounds, names 1224 as the year of Durand's death. The most detailed recent discussion of Durand's life and writings remains Thouzellier 1969 and the bibliography cited there, above all the earlier works of Thouzellier herself and the articles of A. Dondaine. Concerning the early Waldensian community and Durand's role in it, see Selge 1967b. See also the chapters pertinent to many aspects of Waldensian and Poor Catholic history and development in *Vaudois languedociens et Pauvres catholiques,* especially Vicaire 1967a and 1967b, as well as Selge 1967a: 227–31.

[4] Peter's prologue and rubric to the *Alphabetum* provide the biographical data about its composition. Concerning Peter see Maleczek 1988. Among other services, Maleczek's work sorts out Peter's complex family ties and distinguishes this Peter of Capua (d. 1214), who became cardinal in 1193, from his nephew Peter of Capua (d. 1237), who became cardinal in 1219; previously, scholars had confounded uncle and nephew with regularity. For example, it has been mistakenly supposed that the younger Peter compiled the *Alphabetum*; see Rouse and Rouse 1979: 8 and *idem* 1982a: esp. 218–19 and n. 52.

the *Compilatio prima*; this was perhaps the earliest, and certainly the most influential, systematic collection of decretals of the era between Gratian's *Decretum* and Innocent III's accession. From 1191 or 1192 until 1198 Bernard was bishop of Faenza, and from 1198 until the end of his life bishop of his native Pavia.[5]

There are obvious but superficial parallels here. These three men were contemporaries, all ecclesiastics, all native to the Mediterranean world; and each today enjoys a modest celebrity in his own specific corner of late twelfth- and early thirteenth-century history. But until now there has been nothing to suggest any relationship among them; to the contrary, it has been our experience that a study which treats any one of these figures will make no mention of either of the others.

Durand, clearly, is the odd man out. A prominent Waldensian, he was thus by definition a proponent of the right and obligation of all Christians, including – some said, comprising almost exclusively – the untutored, to preach the faith, guided by the Holy Spirit and without concern for ecclesiastical permissions and prohibitions, in response to Christ's unequivocal command, "Go ye into all the world, and preach the gospel to every creature" (Mark16.15). Coming from this position, which was opposed to the accepted teachings of the Christian Church, Durand moved what seems a great distance in a short time, not only submitting to the authority and tutelage of the Church but actively seeking contact with powerful men and with ideas from the rapidly growing schools of Paris and Bologna, bastions of orthodoxy.

The work that brings these three names together is a collection of *distinctiones*. A biblical distinction lists or "'distinguishes'" the figurative meanings of a word from scripture, supported by pertinent examples.[6] This device, part serious exegesis and part rhetorical conceit, is a product of the Paris schools. The appearance of distinctions, toward the end of the twelfth century, accompanied the emergence of the so-called thematic or scholastic sermon, the dominant form of Latin sermon in the later Middle Ages – a sermon built upon a single verse or phrase of scripture as its "theme" (e.g., "In the beginning God created"); after stating the theme, the preacher then announces its divisions ("Now, there are three sorts of beginnings created by God") which, suitably expanded and subdivided, result in a three-part sermon. The elements of the thematic sermon were firmly in place by the 1230s, but one can see the nascent form growing and developing in Parisian sermons through the second half of the twelfth century, sermons that explored the layers of meaning in the words of a single scriptural passage. Furthermore, during the

---

[5] For recent though brief biographies of Bernard of Pavia, see Liotta 1967 and Chodorow 1984: IV.123–4. For a longer consideration of Bernard's importance as a canonist, see LeBras 1937.

[6] A complete *distinctio* is too lengthy to cite here; for a representative sampling, see the *distinctiones* quoted *in extenso* below.

same period when this sermon-form was evolving, the Church began to expect, and then to require, much more frequent sermons from its preachers. Collections of biblical distinctions – offering ready-made thematic divisions and subdivisions – therefore became the basic, near-indispensable, reference works for busy preachers writing thematic sermons.[7]

In this essay we explore the possible nature of the connections between Durand of Huesca and the two prelates Bernard of Pavia and Peter of Capua, indicated by the text in Marston 266. We consider the date and character of Durand's revision, and we document his use of these distinctions in his best-known work, the *Liber contra Manicheos*. Finally, we look at wider implications of Marston 266. An appendix presents an edition and translation of Durand's verse prologue.

Yale University, Beinecke Library Marston MS 266

The text in Marston 266 comprises an alphabetical collection of *distinctiones*, containing a section analogous to a "book" for each letter of the alphabet; the "book" is divided in turn into a series of articles, each devoted to a keyword beginning with the appropriate letter, and these articles or "chapters" distinguish the various figurative and allegorical meanings of the keywords. The manuscript was written in northern Spain, or at least by north Spanish hands; a date in the first quarter of the thirteenth century is suggested by the primitive nature of the decoration, such as the use of acanthus leaf without pen flourishing, and by the fact that the text is written on, not under, the top line of the ruling. Two representative folios are reproduced (see Ills. 1–2).

Parchment, fols. ii + 284; 250 × 177 (162 × 125) mm. Quires of ten, with catchwords; at least one quire missing between fols. 128 and 129. Two columns of thirty-one lines, ruled in lead or crayon. Written in early gothic bookhand by several scribes; there are distinctive Spanish features in script and decoration, although *qui* is consistently abbreviated in the northern form q^i (see Appendix 1 below). Large (three-line to seven-line) and mid-sized (two-line) initials, blue with red flourishing or the reverse; chapter numbers in red; majuscules in the text stroked with yellow. Bound in fifteenth-century Spanish tooled morocco. Purchased from L. C. Witten in 1959;[8] it is one of the Spanish manuscripts that Witten acquired, beginning in 1957, through the Italian entrepreneur Enzo Ferrajoli de Ry.[9]

---

[7] See Rouse and Rouse 1982a: esp. 214–18.
[8] For a full description see Shailor 1992. See her discussion of the manuscript's place of origin in Appendix 1 below.
[9] For an account of acquisitions from this source see Witten 1989. It has been said that Ferrajoli was involved in the sale of about 100 manuscripts and about 180 incunables from the chapter library of the cathedral of Saragossa, and that in the course of the sale the ex-libris marks were altered. For example, see Shooner 1985: 33–4, who describes the alterations of the ex libris in Marston MSS 231 and 232 made by "quidam mercator," now known to have been Ferrajoli.

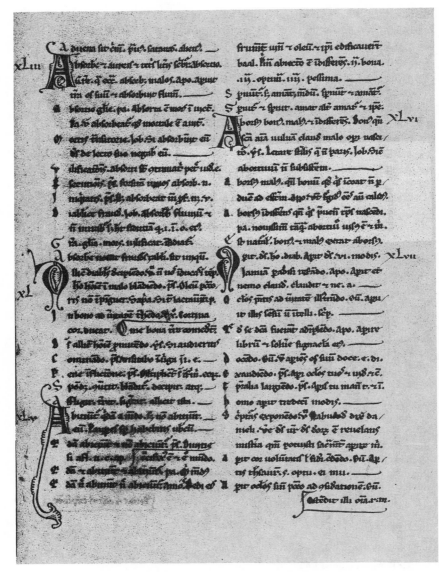

Ill. 1 Yale University, Beinecke Library MS Marston 266, fol. 9

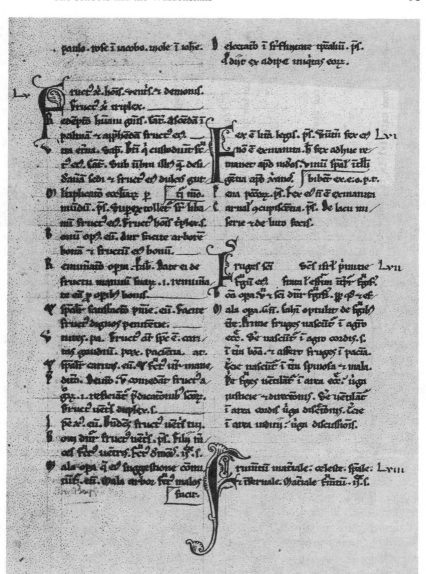

Ill. 2 Yale University, Beinecke Library MS Marston 266, fol. 71

The state of this manuscript is something of a puzzle. It is not an author's rough draft; although the presentation is modest, several elements – the addition of color, the hierarchy of initials, the formal bookhand – indicate that the manuscript is finished, up to a point. It is curious, however, that the list of chapter headings that precedes each letter of the alphabet seldom matches precisely the actual number and titles of the chapters, though naturally enough the correspondence is close. To take the most glaring example, the list of chapter titles beginning with C runs to 120 items (fol. 24), but the last actual chapter, *Confessio* (fol. 41), is chapter 85. Not only are chapters 86–120 unwritten, but in addition there is no title in the list that corresponds with actual chapter 85 *Confessio* itself – nor with the preceding chapters, 84 *Compedes* and 83 *Casus*; *Cete* (chapter 82) is numbered 80 on the list; two successive chapters are numbered 81 (*Canales, Cisterna*); chapters 78 *Calculus* and 79 *Cristallus* again do not correspond with the titles on the list; and so on. The first eighty titles on the list correspond with Peter of Capua's C-list, but – aside from the anomalies just specified – the actual chapters are not quite identical in rubric and sequence with Peter's. There are similar discrepancies elsewhere. The chapter list for the letter D contains the names of twelve chapters that are not actually present – and all twelve are titles added by Durand to Peter's original list; this is quite apart from the fact that the rubricator has mis-numbered (by five) the chapters in the margins. There are three more actual chapters under the letter I than there are names on the chapter list. Even so short an entry as Q, with only sixteen chapters listed, does not correspond; there are no chapters to correspond to the last five titles on the list.

An equally striking suggestion of an unfinished state is the blank space that has been left between the end of one "book" or letter and the beginning of the next. With few exceptions, there is seldom less than a full column blank,[10] and commonly a full page or more[11] has been deliberately left vacant, between letters. There is, for example, more than sufficient blank space in most cases to have accommodated the "missing" chapters mentioned above. Save for two occasions that seem merely accidental,[12] the letter-ends and subsequent blank spaces do not coincide with quire divisions in the manuscript. Although there might be other explanations for the blanks, the most likely is that the spaces left in this manuscript faithfully reproduce spaces in its exemplar, which was probably Durand's own draft. It is our assumption that Marston 266, given its early date, is a fair copy made at Durand's behest, and was in either his possession or that of one of his companions.

---

[10] Exceptions: roughly a half-column is blank at the end of letters A, B, and L; and at the end of M, only four lines.

[11] At the end of letter C, slightly more than three pages are blank; and at the end of D, slightly more than four.

[12] The end of G and I, with sections H and K (respectively) beginning new quires.

Date and place of Durand's composition

The content of Marston 266 raises several other questions not easily answered: where and when did Durand of Huesca discover Peter of Capua's *Alphabetum*? Where and when did Durand revise Peter's work? Why did Durand dedicate the revision to Bernard of Pavia?

Peter of Capua explains in his own prologue that he had begun collecting *distinctiones* as a classroom exercise, but that he completed the work at Rome after he had become cardinal – so, at some date between 1193 and his death in 1214. However, the earliest surviving manuscript of Peter's *Alphabetum*, Vatican Library MS Vat. lat. 4304,[13] can only be dated, on paleographic grounds, to the "first half of the thirteenth century." In other words, the survivors offer no hint of the sort of immediate and widespread circulation that would easily have reached Durand when he was still a Waldensian preacher in the south of France, before his conversion. Moreover, it is unlikely that as a Waldensian he would have dedicated his work to the orthodox bishop of Pavia. The best date one can offer for the completion of Durand's revision of Peter's work, therefore, is circumscribed by Durand's formal conversion to orthodoxy and Bernard of Pavia's death: between 1208 and 1213.

Durand's visits to Rome are the likely means of transmission. Christine Thouzellier[14] identifies three such visits, all dating after Durand's conversion and all related to his need for papal support for the Poor Catholics: the first lasting from September 1207 to the end of 1208, the second from July 1209 to May 1210, and the third during the spring of 1212. Probably one of these was the occasion of his encounter with a manuscript of the *Alphabetum* of Peter of Capua; given that Bernard of Pavia, Durand's dedicatee, died in 1213, the third visit in 1212 is probably too late to have occasioned Durand's introduction to Peter's text.

Although Durand's prologue praises Peter warmly (lines 29–37), it does not include any facts about the cardinal that Durand could not have extrapolated from Peter's prologue; thus, it is not requisite that Durand have met Peter. The fact remains, however, that Durand's revision is the earliest evidence of the existence of Peter of Capua's *Alphabetum*. At this early date (1208–13), Durand almost certainly acquired his exemplar of the *Alphabetum* either from Peter directly or from someone who knew Peter. Durand's group of converted heretics was in due course supported by quite a number of cardinals, several of

---

[13] This is treated as the earliest by Maleczek 1988: 231–45. To Maleczek's list of *Alphabetum* manuscripts add Durham, N.C., Duke University MS 104 (s. XIII[1], Italy); we are grateful to Paul Meyvaert for this reference.

[14] Durand de Huesca 1964: 36, hereafter cited as *Contra Manicheos*.

whom Durand thanks by name in the prologue of his *Contra Manicheos*;[15] and one of these men may have introduced Durand either to Peter of Capua or to Peter's *Alphabetum*.[16]

The most attractive candidate as intermediary between Peter and Durand is Leo Brancaleoni, member of an important Roman family who was cardinal deacon of S. Lucia in Septasolio (1200) and cardinal priest of S. Croce in Gerusalemme (1202–*c.* 1224). On the one hand, Durand addresses the *Contra Manicheos* "to the very reverend pillar of the church of Christ" Leo Brancaleoni, and submits the work to his correction, calling Leo the special protector of the Poor Catholics.[17] Probably Cardinal Leo had given Durand's followers his support from the time of their first appearance in Rome.[18] On the other hand, there is evidence of a connection between Leo and Peter of Capua. Their signatures appear together on literally dozens of papal documents in the years between 1200 (Leo's creation) and 1214 (Peter's death).[19] The case of Andreas the chaplain suggests an even closer association: when Peter of Capua established, in 1212, S. Pietro della Canonica as a house of regular canons in his native Amalfi, this Andreas was singled out from among the canons of the Lateran to be the first prior of the new house; but when the conversion of S. Pietro to a Cistercian abbey in 1214 left Andreas without a position, he immediately returned to Rome as a chaplain in the household of Leo Brancaleoni.[20] Surely, either Leo must first have recommended Andreas to Peter, or Peter must later have recommended Andreas to Leo.

---

[15] Of the two extant manuscripts, Prague Metr. Kap. 527 merely commends itself in general to the "cardinals of the holy Roman church"; but the other, Paris, Bibliothèque Nationale lat. 689, names "Pelagius, Nicholas [of Clermont], Stephen [of Fossanova], Guala [Bicchieri], John of Colonna, and others"; both versions name Leo Brancaleoni. See *Contra Manicheos* 84 and n., and Thouzellier 1969: 299. Concerning the careers of these prelates, see two recent prosopographical studies – Kamp 1973–82: I and especially Maleczek 1984.

[16] It is worth noting that Peter of Capua on at least one occasion preached against contemporary heresies. Paris, Bibliothèque Nationale MS nouv. acq. lat. 999 (s. XIII; the abbey of Silos) contains on fols. 243v–4v a sermon entitled "Sermo magistri Petri de Capuis in die assumptionis BMV," beginning *"Luna signum diei festi* [Sir. 43.7]. Sicut dicit glosa super illud locum Psalmi, *Ut sagitent in obscuro rectos corde* [Ps. 10.3]," which explicitly addresses heretical views on the conception of the Virgin and on the Incarnation; another sermon attributed to Master Peter of Capua begins on fol. 266v of this manuscript. We are grateful to Nicole Bériou for this information. At present, it is not clear which Peter of Capua, uncle or nephew, composed these sermons; see n. 4 above.

[17] "Reverentissime columpne ecclesie Christi domino Leoni tituli sancte Crucis in Iherusalem presbytero cardinali, pauperes katholici gratiam in presenti et gloriam in futuro . . . Yperaspistem nostrum dominum Leonem tituli sancte Crucis in Iherusalem presbiterum cardinalem, cui hoc opus proposuimus destinandum et reverentissimos fratres eius sancte romane ecclesie cardinales, in assercionibus nostris eligimus correctores": *Contre Manicheos* 66, 82–4.

[18] This is the assumption of Thouzellier 1969: 298 and of Maleczek 1984: 139.

[19] See the tables "Die Unterschriften der Kardinäle 1191–1216" in Maleczek 1984: 380–90.

[20] Maleczek 1988: 223 and n. 70; *idem* 1984: 123, 139.

In sum, although Durand's prologue does not state that he knew Peter of Capua, it is not difficult to imagine how Durand might have acquired a manuscript of the *Alphabetum*, either directly or indirectly, from its compiler.

Durand's prologue (lines 53–64) clearly indicates, on the contrary, that he had met Bernard of Pavia, that he had received or hoped to receive Bernard's favor, and that he completed his revision – or at any rate completed the verse prologue – in the city of Pavia. Unfortunately, the prologue does not go even further, to hint at the nature of Durand's connection with Bernard and Bernard's city. We know that Innocent III in commissioning the Poor Catholics to preach against heresy had, nevertheless, placed them under the customary discipline of obtaining permission from the bishop of any diocese in which they proposed to preach. Innocent at the same time enjoined the bishops to welcome the help of the Poor Catholics, and to grant them license to preach in public. Many bishops, however, were unenthusiastic, suspicious, or overtly hostile to this group composed of and led by men that had themselves so recently been condemned as heretical. In southern France, for example, where heresy was endemic, episcopal opposition to the preaching of the Poor Catholics out-weighed episcopal approval.[21] Any bishop who gave them a welcome would have been doubly appreciated by Durand's order.[22]

Between his first and second trips to Rome – that is, between December 1208 and July 1209 – we know that Durand spent at least a part of the time preaching and converting heretics in northern Italy. In January or February 1209 he stopped for a while in Milan, known as a center of heterodoxy, where he was courteously received by the cardinal-archbishop, Uberto de Pirovano (d. *c.* 1211), and where he participated with Uberto in the conversion and reconciliation of a body of Milanese Waldensians.[23] Perhaps it was at this same time that Durand went to Pavia, a short journey (less than twenty miles) from Milan; 1209, in fact, is one of the rare times when Milan and Pavia were not warring with one another. The basis for Durand's gratitude to Bernard, bishop of Pavia, may well have been that Bernard, like Uberto, offered welcome and encouragement for the Poor Catholics and their prior. Durand's prologue fancifully depicts his distinction collection as setting out to sea *urbe Pavia* (lines 63–4), from the city of Pavia, which suggests that he had settled there long enough to revise, or to finish revising, Peter of Capua's *Alphabetum*.

---

[21] Concerning specific instances of opposition to the Poor Catholics, see Selge 1967a: 238–9 and the sources cited there.

[22] As M.-H. Vicaire observed (1967b: 178), the Poor Catholics were not really an order; however, as he goes on to demonstrate ("Chr. Thouzellier emploie à leur sujet des expressions variées ... *institut* ... *fondation* ... *nouvel ordre* ... *ordre séculier* ... *organisation sérieuse* ... *grands corps de communauté*"), it is awkward to discuss the Poor Catholics without giving this group of religious some sort of designation. For the sake of simplicity, therefore, we occasionally use the term "order," despite its imprecision.

[23] Thouzellier 1969: 225.

The nature of Durand's revision

As a preliminary to characterizing Durand's revision, we might first consider the nature of the *Alphabetum* that Durand had to hand: are the elements of the text in Marston 266 that seem shorter than or different from the *Alphabetum* as we know it evidence of changes by Durand? Or do they, coupled with the earliness of the date of Marston 266, imply that Durand's exemplar was an unfinished state of Peter of Capua's text? There can be no definitive answer, but it seems likely that the text Durand saw was the same *Alphabetum* that survives. One of the clearest indications is this: Peter of Capua wrote two prologues to his work, evidently meant to follow one upon the other and almost certainly not composed until the distinction collection was finished; and Durand's verse prologue quotes from both of them.[24]

Durand's prologue implies (lines 37–52) that he has made major alterations in Peter of Capua's collection of *distinctiones*, abridging it but also inserting material and, a novel idea, converting Peter's prose into verse. To judge from test passages that we suppose to be representative, it seems that Durand abbreviated a lot, by eliminating many of the biblical quotations and a good deal besides, and that he added material, often at length; but the versification is a different matter. To be sure, Durand replaced Peter of Capua's lengthy prose prologue with sixty-eight lines of verse. The wording of Durand's prologue implies more to come. As far as we can see, however, Durand has not converted any of the distinction collection itself into verse. Nevertheless, the force of Durand's excisions often emphasizes the metric or even rhymed elements of Peter of Capua's distinctions. A comparison of the two versions of the first article (Peter's on the left, Durand's on the right)[25] will show the effect of a combination of excision and addition:

Est ALPHA sive principium creature.	ALPHA deus est. Unde in Apocalipsim
Unde Apocalipsim "Ego sum alpha	"Ego sum alpha et omega etc."
et omega etc." Alpha scripture, unde	Alpha est prima littera alphabeti
ab illa prima littera usitata	que latine dicitur .a. Primum est
appellatione alphabetum appellamus.	supra nos, secundum extra nos.
Primum est supra nos, secundum	Primum nos produxit, secundum
extra nos. Primum nos produxit,	instruxit. Primum scribitur in
unde in Genesi [2.7] "Formavit igitur	tabulis carnalibus, secundum in
deus hominem de limo terre."	tabula lapideis. [All that follows
Secundum nos instruxit primo.	is Durand's addition:] Et quia

---

24 Lines 21–6 quote from Peter of Capua's first prologue, lines 65–6 from the second.

25 In the absence of an edition, the text of Peter of Capua's *Alphabetum* cited here is based on Vatican Library Vat. lat. 4304 (s. XIII[1]), emended against two later thirteenth-century Vatican manuscripts of the *Alphabetum*, Vat. lat. 1157 and 1158.

Concupiscentiam nesciebam esse peccatum nisi lex dicet vel scriptura, "Non concupisces" [Deut. 5.21 (cf. Exod. 20.17)]. Primum est eternale, secundum temporale. Primum scribit, unde in Job [13.26], "Scribes enim contra me amaritudines," et in evangelio [Io. 8.6], "Jhesus inclinans se deorsum digito scribebat in terra," et in Exodo [34.1] domini ad Moysem, "Precide tibi duas tabulas ad instar priorum et scribam in eis verba que abuerunt tabule quas fregisti"; idem, "dedit Moyse duas tabulas scriptas digito Dei" [Deut. 9.10, Exod. 31.18]. Secundum scribitur. Unde in Exodo [17.14], "Scribe hoc in libro ob monimentum" et ibidem "Scripsit Moyses in lamina aurea nomen domini tetra grammaton." Primum scribit in tabulis cordis carnalibus. Secundum scribitur in tabulis lapideis pro duris iudeorum cordibus. Primum est principium et finis omnium, quia nichil ante ipsum nichil erit post ipsum. Unde in Apocalipsim dicit primis et novissimis et in Isaia "Ante me non est formatum Deus et post me non erit." Secundum tamen principium elementorum. Unde aliud elementum quam alpha habitur in fine greci Alphabeti. [end of Peter of Capua's chapter]

alpha idem est quod .a. de eius significationibus uideamus:

A nomen est indeclinabile, quandoque tenetur materiabiliter. ratione ipsius nominis, unde Priscianus [1.6], accidunt littere .iii. Nomen, Figura, Potestas. Nomen unde .a.b.[26]

Quandoque ponitur pro figura. unde hic, a est littera triangularis.

Quandoque ponitur in designatione littere[?], unde Priscianus hic nomen littere[?] finitur unde[?] a.

Quandoque ponitur pro figura et elementa. Unde Priscianus: Ago mutat principalem litteram scilicet .a. in e. hec enim figura e. ponitur pro hac figura .a. et hoc elementum .e. pro hoc elemento .a.[27]

Quandoque est prepositio, et secundum hac quandoque notat auctoritatem. unde "a domino factum est istud."

Quandoque processionem, unde hic. "Spiritus qui a patre procedit" [Io. 15.26].

Quandoque notat inspirationem. unde "responsum accepit Symeon a Spiritus sancto" [cf. Luc. 2.26] id est, per inspirationem Spiritus sancti.

Quandoque notat principium. unde "incipiens a Moyse" [Luc. 24.27].

Quandoque notat causam. unde

---

[26] Priscian book 1.6/7, ed. Hertz 1855–9: I.7 lines 26–7, cited hereafter by book and paragraph of Priscian, with the volume, page, and line numbers from Hertz's edition in parentheses.

[27] Cf. Priscian 1.28 (Hertz 1855–9: I.22 lines 1–7), 8.84 (*ibid.*, I.437 lines 7–8).

hic. "**a** tonitrui tui formidabunt" [Ps. 103.7], id est, tonitrus erunt causa formidinis.

Locum notat tripliciter. cum motu, unde hic, "iste exivit **a** domo."

Locum notat cum extensione. unde "**a** solis ortu cardin'."

Locum notat cum permanentia. unde "sede **a** dextris meis" [Ps. 109.1 etc.].

Quandoque notat tempus. unde "**a** seculo et usque in seculum tu es Deus" [Ps. 89.2].

Quandoque notat ortum vel generationem. unde "exivi **a** Patre et veni" [Io. 16.28].

Quandoque notat vim concludendi, unde hic. "<*illeg.*> locus a simili."

Quandoque ponitur privative. unde cum dicitur "Iste est **a**mens," id est, sine mente.

Quandoque notat dispositionem. unde hic. "Joseph secundus **a** rege" [cf. Gen. 41.40 etc.].

Quandoque notat separationem. unde "aufertur **ab** illo mnam etc." [Luc. 19.24].

Quandoque ponitur instantive. unde "iste percutitur **a** isto." unde versus:

Dicitur alpha deus .**a**. sit sermone latino
Nomen signat. trahitur. profertur. utrumque
Colligit. auctorat. inspirat. progrediturque
Concludit. privat. disponit. separat. infert.
Principium. causam. loca. tempora. signat et ortum.

The changes made to this chapter suggest that the intent of Durand's revision was more simplification than versification – his lengthy addition of a grammatical consideration of **a**, for example. In a sense, the emphasis on verse is itself a method of simplification, as in the sacrifice of Peter's wise play on words (the first alpha produced us, the second taught us the first; I should not have known desire to be a sin, if writing had not said, "Do not covet") in favor of the baldly mnemonic *Primum nos produxit, secundum instruxit*; again, Durand shifts Peter's observation – the first alpha writes, the second is written – to emphasize the medium written upon (*primum scribitur in tabulis carnalibus, secundum in tabulis lapideis*), in the process casually relegating God to the same passive role as the letter **A**.

As an example of extreme abridgment, compare the beginning, roughly one third, of Peter's chapter on the allegorical meaning of the hawk, *Accipiter*:

Accipiter sancti. Iob [39.26]: "Numquid per sapientiam tuam plumescit accipiter," pennis virtutum scilicet; et diabolus: Leviticus [11.13–16], "Hec sunt que comedere non debetis, larum et accipitrem iuxta genus suum." Primus rapit regnum celorum: Evang. [= Matth. 11.12], "Regnum celorum vim patitur et violenti rapiunt illud." Secundus rapit sanctos: Ps. [9:30], "Insidiatur ut rapiat pauperem." Primus instruxit, secundus destruxit. Primus aliquando capitur a secundo: Ps. [34.25], "Nec dicant devoravimus eum"; Evang. [= Matth. 6.13], "Ne nos inducas in temptationem"; Ps. [7.3], "Ne forte rapiat ut leo animam." Secundus quandoque a primo: Gen. [3.15], "Ipsa conteret caput tuum et tu insidiaberis calcaneo eius"; Ps. [17.38], "Persequar inimicos meos," etc.[28]

with Durand's edition of this same section:

Accipiter sancti: Iob, "Numquid per sapientiam tuam plumescit accipiter," plumis virtutum. Diabolus: Leviticus, "Hec sunt que comedere non debetis, larum et accipitrem." Primus rapit regnum celorum. Secundus rapit sanctos. Primus instruit. Secundus destruit. Primus aliquando capitur a secundo, et secundus quandoque a primo.[29]

In omitting all but two biblical quotations, Durand's version is shorter, more memorable, and now and then metrical. What it gains in punch it seems to us that it loses in intelligibility, but perhaps it did not seem so to a Poor Catholic preacher of the early thirteenth century. Durand's abridgment of this particular chapter went so far as to replace all of the remaining two-thirds of Peter's chapter on *accipiter* – entirely devoted to examples of the hawk as a symbol of Satan – with a single hexameter, "Accipiter sancti, satanas est accipiterque."

---

[28] Again, this text is an emended version of the three Vatican manuscripts.
[29] Marston 266, fol. 5.

Durand's use of distinctions

Three quatrains of Durand's prologue are given over to lavish praise of the *distinctio* as a rhetorical device (lines 5–16). His express delight in the utility and grace of this figure matches the frequently cited reaction of Peter of Cornwall, who a few years earlier had recorded his enthusiasm upon first hearing a sermon that incorporated *distinctiones*.[30] It should come as no surprise, therefore, to see Durand subsequently making extensive use of distinctions in his writings.

Christine Thouzellier devoted a section of her study of heresy in Languedoc to an examination of the distinctions in Durand's works.[31] Durand had not employed *distinctiones* in the *Antiheresis*, written *c.* 1191–2 before his conversion to orthodoxy. In contrast, his second anti-heretical tract, the *Liber contra Manicheos*, composed about 1222–3, incorporates a number of lengthy *distinctiones*. Thouzellier discussed and tabulated more than a dozen of these, comparing Durand's explanations in the *Contra Manicheos* with those of a number of sources known to her, including Peter the Chanter's *Summa Abel* and the *distinctiones* of Alan of Lille. No single source or combination of sources tallies with the text of *Contra Manicheos*, however. She goes on to ponder the extent to which the distinction material may have been created by Durand for inclusion in this tract.

Thouzellier was unacquainted with Peter of Capua's *Alphabetum*, and of course did not know of Thomas Marston's uncataloged manuscript at Yale. If she had, her puzzle would have been solved. Peter of Capua, as reworked by Durand of Huesca in Marston 266, is the storehouse of distinctions that supplied Durand when, some ten or fifteen years after revising the *Alphabetum*, he composed the *Liber contra Manicheos*. Although it is long, we should like to quote *in extenso* the distinction on the word *tabernaculum* from Durand's *Contra Manicheos*, one for which Thouzellier found only partial sources and near-matches in a combination of five earlier collections:[32]

Beata virgo dicitur tabernaculum; unde in libro Sapientie: "Qui creavit me requievit in tabernaculo meo." Caro Christi; unde in Psalmo: "In sole posuit tabernaculum suum." Corpus humanum; unde apostolus Petrus: "Certus sum quod velox est depositio tabernaculi mei, secundum quod Dominus Ihesus Christus significavit michi." Mens humana; unde Iob: "Deus erat in tabernaculo meo." Et sacra Scriptura dicitur tabernaculum et protectio divina; ecclesia presentis temporis; unde beatus Iohannes in

---

30 Concerning the twelfth-century origin of distinction collections, see Rouse and Rouse 1982a: 210–18. For the passage from Peter of Cornwall, see Hunt 1936: 33–4, 40–1. Peter of Cornwall is further cited, through Hunt, by Smalley 1952: 248; Mackinnon 1969: 38 n. 16; and Rouse and Rouse 1982a: 214 n. 34.

31 Thouzellier, "Les *distinctiones* de Durand de Huesca," 1969: 322–45.

32 See Thouzellier's discussion, 1969: 324–5, 327, and the table of sources on 326.

apocalipsi: "Ecce tabernaculum Dei cum hominibus, et habitabit cum eis." Celum, id est requies sempiterna; unde in Psalmo: "Domine, quis habitabit in tabernaculo tuo aut quis requiescet in monte sancto?" Et hoc est tabernaculum de quo dixit Apostolus non manu factum, quod intravit Ihesus quadragesimo die resurrectionis sue, sicut discipuli manifestant. Et pro omnibus istis tabernaculis dicit Psalmographus ad amorem celestium nos hostando: "Quam dilecta tabernacula tua, Domine virtutum, etc."[33]

The first interpretation, that the Virgin is a tabernacle, is a commonplace; it appears, for example, in the venerable collections of Pseudo Melliton and Pseudo Rabanus.[34] All the remaining interpretations – including the specific turns of phrase and, uncharacteristically, the biblical citations – appear at the beginning of the article *tabernaculum*, on folios 214v–15v of Beinecke Library MS Marston 266.[35]

Conclusion

Marston 266 is an extraordinarily early witness to the transmission of sermon material from the northern university community to the context of popular preaching in the south. Occasional use of biblical distinctions in sermons can be seen in northern France by the third quarter of the twelfth century, and Peter of Cornwall reports, as a novelty, hearing a sermon filled with distinctions preached in London by Gilbert Foliot, probably in the 1170s.[36] The practice of distinguishing the figurative meanings of biblical terms grew out of the theology classrooms at Paris, with simultaneous adoption by preachers for use in sermons. By the end of the twelfth century, a number of Paris masters had begun to gather large numbers of distinctions into collections, organized according to various principles, for use primarily by school-trained preachers. The earliest known collections were the distinctions restricted to the words of the Psalter, by the Parisian masters Peter of Poitiers (*c*. 1190) and Prepositinus (1196–8); the terse, almost telegraphic collection, the *Summa Abel*, of Master Peter the Chanter (*c*. 1190); and the more general collections, the *Summa quot modis* of Master Alan of Lille (before 1195) and, of course, the *Alphabetum* of Master Peter of Capua (1193–*c*. 1209/13).[37]

In date, Durand – and this manuscript – stand with the generation that

---

[33] *Contra Manicheos* 200 line 26–201 line 10.
[34] For printed references, see Thouzellier 1969: 326.
[35] Other *distinctiones* from Durand's *Contra Manicheos* tabulated by Thouzellier likewise come from Marston 266 – distinctions on the words *celum* (see table: Thouzellier 1969: 228), *terra* (*ibid.*, 229), *mundus* (*ibid.*, 231), *regnum* (*ibid.*, 334), *oves* (*ibid.*, 336), *seculum* (*ibid.*, 338). We selected the distinction on the word *tabernaculum* as an example because its difference from the other available sources makes the correspondence with the text of Marston 266 all the more significant.
[36] See n. 30 above.
[37] See Rouse and Rouse 1982a: 211 and *idem* 1974.

created the first collections of biblical distinctions. It would seem that Peter of Capua, in the act of leaving the teaching of theology for the life of a prelate, personally transported the genre from the Paris schools to the curia, where he completed the *Alphabetum* for the benefit of the clergy of Rome,[38] sometime after 1193; and between 1208 and 1213 Durand of Huesca came across Peter's collection and completed a revision of it. Since there is little unbiased information about the sermons of the *Pauperes catholici*, either before or after their conversion to orthodoxy, it is instructive to learn that their prior Durand in the earliest months of the order's existence eagerly seized upon a university device such as the *Alphabetum* and devoted time and effort to adapting it for his followers to use in preaching against heresy.

Students of scholasticism often ponder the influence of the schools on the larger world outside, considering (for example) how and whether schoolroom theories were transmitted to the frontline of pastoral care. A part of the story is already known. Just as Durand did for the Poor Catholics, so Franciscan and Dominican scholars were to do later in the thirteenth century, compiling and adapting collections of distinctions for the use of the preachers in their orders – men such as Maurice of Provins OFM in *c.* 1248, and Nicholas Gorran OP and Nicholas Biard (OP or OM) probably in the 1270s.[39] The Mendicant collections – composed at the University of Paris, reproduced by the university stationers, and destined for university-trained preachers – were disseminated by Mendicants as they traveled about western Europe in the second half of the thirteenth century and on into the fourteenth. This is a well-known route for the transmission of intellectual artefacts.

The distinction collection in Marston 266, in contrast, adds depth and shading to our sketchy image of the pre-Mendicant dissemination of the sermon materials and preacher's handbooks emanating from Paris in the early thirteenth century. Durand's collection shows how simply and directly the influence of the northern schools could reach the south, through the career of a prelate such as Peter of Capua, and how readily the curia might serve the exchange of ideas. Marston 266 fits together pieces that one had not even

---

[38] There is no one quotation that states all this. But see, for example, the passage from the beginning of Peter's first prologue (quoted below in the note to lines 29–36) addressed to "venerando clero romano et viris scholasticis' (the reverend clergy of Rome and the men of the schools); the "dedication," toward the end of the first prologue: "Suscipiat itaque caritas vestra benigne et munusculum presens in quo et venerandus clerus exercitetur facilius ad loquendam et sollicitudo scolastica presto et ad manum pleniorem habet copiam ad scrutandum" (Therefore, may your charity kindly receive this small present, in which both the worthy clergy may be easily trained to speak and scholarly solicitude may have quickly to hand a fuller abundance to examine); and Peter's second prologue or "response," which begins thus: "Responsio magistri Petri facta scolaribus in ipsis scolis insistentibus per presenti opere inchoando" (The response of Master Peter made to the students in the schools who urged the undertaking of the present work).

[39] See Rouse and Rouse 1974: 33–5.

recognized as parts of the same puzzle: Durand of Huesca, former heretic and leader of a group of popular preachers of questionable orthodoxy; the Paris-trained theologian Cardinal Peter of Capua; a powerful Roman politician and curialist Cardinal Leo Brancaleoni; and the eminent canon lawyer and former Bolognese master, Bishop Bernard of Pavia.

In short, Durand inhabited a world with broader intellectual horizons than one had formerly assumed. He made early, vivid, and important use of a work for the training of preachers, adapting it and trying to popularize it further; and just as he was innovative in adopting the new distinction form, product of the northern schoolroom, so was he also in making contact with a leader of the new and rapidly maturing discipline of canon law, in the person of Bernard to whom he dedicated his work. That the man who did these things began his public life beyond the boundaries of established belief reminds us of the remarkable vicissitudes in clerical and religious careers around the year 1200.

Appendix 1
Spanish features of MS Marston 266

Barbara Shailor

Several features of the script and decoration of Marston 266 suggest that the manuscript was copied in Spain (see Ills. 1 and 2). The script, written in very dark ink throughout, is characterized by a spiky appearance due to the lateral compression of vertical strokes in words containing the letters *l*, *m*, *n*, cursive *s*, *h*, *i*, and *j*. The abbreviations for the conjunction *et* are especially distinctive. The ampersand is tall, angular, and vertically rather than horizontally oriented; the tironian *et* has a very long horizontal bar. The abbreviation for *qui* is represented by the letter *q* with a suprascript *i*. The majuscule letter *Q* resembles the arabic numeral 2, with a small upper loop on the left and a flat horizontal base.

The decoration consists of finely executed red and blue initials, whose unusual shapes and designs are often reminiscent of those found in Visigothic manuscripts. These distinctive designs are apparent both in the tables that precede the entries for each letter of the alphabet and within the text itself, where several styles of initials may be juxtaposed on the same folio. One can note, for example, the various forms of *A* on fol. 9 (see Ill. 1) and of *F* on fol. 71 (see Ill. 2). Comparable penwork initials are illustrated in M. Gullick, *Working Alphabet of Initial Letters from Twelfth Century Spain* (The Red Gull Press, 1987), a facsimile of Philadelphia, Free Library MS Lewis 22, fols. 181v–2.

104

Appendix 2
Text and translation

Durand of Huesca's rhymed prologue[40] to his revision of Peter of Capua's collection of *distinctiones*, the *Alphabetum*, in Yale University, Beinecke Library MS Marston 266, fol. 1r–v, is written with only one ending for four verses (indicated here by the equals sign), this common ending enclosed in a red box. Verses 1 and 3 begin at the left margin, while 2 and 4 are in the middle of the same lines respectively as 1 and 3, with the whole joined by a web of horizontal lines (see Ill. 3). Each quatrain is laid out like this:

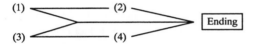

For the most part, the "voice" that speaks here is an abstraction, perhaps *Rhetorica*, rather than Durand himself, although there is a shift in narrator for verses 53–6.

[A]lta supern=orum	I, sprung from that high race
de stirpe creata de=orum	created by the most high gods,
Alloquor ista ch=orum	deliver as fitting chorus about this
sermonis supra arte dec=orum	art of the sermon,
5 Lux. dux. serm=onis	That leading light of the sermon,
distinctio fons rati=onis	the *distinctio*, wellspring of
Artibus et d=onis	reason, in devices and gifts as
locuples sceptrum Salom=onis	opulent as Solomon's scepter.
Qui non dist=ingit	Whoever does not "distinguish" does
10 non mira poema<t>a f=ingit	not fashion wondrous verse, [but]
Verba decus c=ingit	elegance encircles the words that the
pia que distinctio p=ingit	pious *distinctio* adorns.

[40] The prose translation offered here has benefited from the suggestions of a number of generous scholars, to whom we are most grateful: Louis J. Bataillon OP, Nicole Bériou, Alain Boureau, Leonard E. Boyle OP, Valerie I. J. Flint, Anthony Forte SJ, Margaret T. Gibson, Carol D. Lanham, and Barbara Shailor. The stylistic infelicities are our own contribution.

Unde juvat fl=ores
decerpere⁴¹ nunc meli=ores
15 Quos distinct=ores
sparsim posuere pri=ores

Whence it is gratifying now to gather
the better of the "flowers" which
earlier *distinctio*-makers placed here
and there.

Alfa .b. dum seq=itur [*sic*]⁴²
series levius reper=itur
Carmen fin=itur
20 dum littera .z. repet=itur

When B follows A, it is easier to
learn the sequence. The song is
finished when the letter Z is reached.

Queque deo d=antur
hec prima fronte loc=antur
Troni subd=antur
polus. aera. virque sequ=antur

All matters devoted to God are
placed first. The order of angels
comes next; the heavens, the air, and
man should follow.

25 Hinc animal sequ=itur
humus. equor'. abissus ad=itur
Regula perfic=itur
hec carmina cuncta met=itur

Then comes the brute beast, the
earth, the waters, and the abyss. The
pattern is complete; these songs treat
of all these things.

[interlin. over following line: "Sistole hic est"; beside it and down the
margin in reduced script is a passage not entirely decipherable: "Sistole est
quidam < . . . > scil. quando sillaba < . . . > brevis. producitur licentia

---

⁴¹ The combination of words *juvat flores decerpere* comes ultimately from Lucretius (book 1
line 928 = book 4 line 3), *iuvatque novos decerpere flores*; we are grateful to Carol D. Lanham
for this reference. There is no indication, however, that anyone was acquainted with the text of
Lucretius between the early ninth century and its rediscovery in the early fifteenth. This four-
word passage from Lucretius is quoted by the grammarian Nonius Marcellus, 252.9. But the
text of Nonius, though not as rare as Lucretius, was itself quite uncommon in the Middle Ages.
See Reynolds 1983: 218–22 (Lucretius) and 248–52 (Nonius). Durand might have come across
this phrase in a *florilegium*, although we cannot suggest a particular one; the language in the
prologue of the *Liber deflorationum* ("Florilegium Duacense"), *flores decerpere ceu de pratis*,
is insufficient, but it demonstrates how such a phrase might have been employed. See Rouse
and Rouse 1982b: esp. p. 169. Perhaps instead the phrase was transmitted by the Latin grammarians; again, we do not have one to suggest.

⁴² Verses 17–28 abridge, to the point of incomprehensibility, the explanation in Peter of Capua's
own prose prologue of the two-tiered organization of his topics, namely, alphabetical and
(within each letter's topics) hierarchical, beginning with the highest and ending with the
lowest: "Ordinem duplicem in eo [= opere] curavimus adhibere. Primo enim ponuntur
dictiones qui incipiunt ab .A., secundo qui a .B., tertio qui a .C., et sic per totum ordinem
alphabeti. Ad maiorem etiam operis distinctionem et ut quod queritur facilius inveniatur, in
singulis litteris ordo alius autem notatur. Nam inter illas que incipiunt ab .A., primo pronuntur
dictiones ille que proprie conveniunt Deo, vel his que circa Deum attenduntur. Secundo que
angelis, vel circa angelos. Tertio, que firmamento vel circa firmamentum. Quarto que aeri, vel
circa aerem. Quinto, que homini vel circa hominem. Sexto, que brutis vel circa bruta. Septimo,
que terre vel circa terram. Octavo, que aquis que sunt sub terra vel circa aquas. Nono et
ultimo, pronuntur que conveniunt abysso vel his qui attenduntur circa abyssum" (Vat. lat. 1157,
1158).

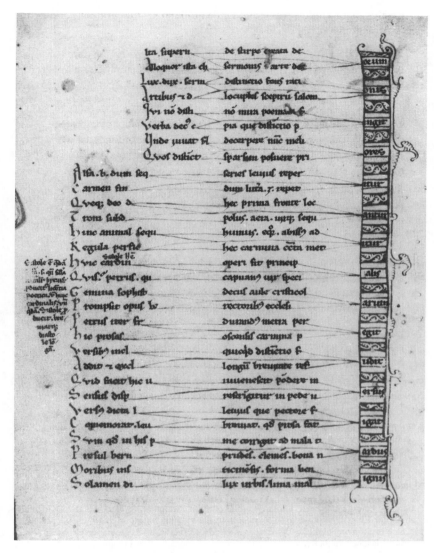

Ill. 3 Yale University, Beinecke Library MS Marston 266, fol. 1

poetica. unde 'huic cardinalis.' Unde quidam. sistole producit. breviatque diastole longam."][43]

	Huic cardin=alis	Let the cardinal be the chief of this
30	operi sit princip=alis	work. Who? Peter. Which one? of
	Quis? Petrus. Qu=alis?	Capua, a special man.
	Capuanus vir speci=alis[44]	

	Gemma sophist=arum	Jewel of philosophers, glory of
	decus aule cristicol=arum	Christians, he produced a work dear
35	Prompsit opus k=arum	to the rectors of churches.
	rectoribus ecclesi=arum	

	Petrus iter fr=egit	Peter broke the trail; Durand
	Durandus metra per=egit	composed the verses. The former[45]
	Hic prosas =egit	produced the prose; the man from
40	Oscensis carmina p=egit	Huesca composed the poetry.

	Versibus incl=udit	He [= Durand] puts into verse
	quicquid distinctio f=udit	whatever the *distinctio* poured forth.
	Addit et excl=udit	He adds and removes; he checked
	longum brevitate ref=udit[46]	long-windedness with brevity.

45	Quid facit hic v=ersus	What does this verse do? All that
	juvenescit pondere m=ersus	was weighed down recovers its
	Sensus disp=ersus	vigor; loose meaning becomes taut
	retringitur in pede v=ersus	in a foot of verse.

---

[43] We have not identified the source of this aside. Definitions and uses of *systole* and *diastole* occur in several of the grammarians edited by Keil (1855–80); but not in these words, and never as opposites. See Charisius (Keil 1955–80: I.279 line 1); Diomedes (*ibid.*, I.435 lines 10ff., 442 line 5); Probus (*ibid.*, IV.263 line 19); Donatus (*ibid.*, IV.372 line 5, 396 line 16); Sergius (*ibid.*, IV.482 line 11, 484 line 14); Pompeius (*ibid.*, V.132 line 12, 297 line 14); Consentius (*ibid.*, V.389 line 7, 400 line 22); Victorinus (*ibid.*, VI.194 line 3); Marius Plotius Sacerdos (*ibid.*, VI.452 line 15).

[44] Cardinal Peter of Capua (d. 1214), compiler of the collection of *distinctiones* that Durand has abridged. Lines 29–36 are extrapolated from the opening words of Peter's own prologue: "Dilectis plurimum et diligendis semper in visceribus Ihesu Christi venerando clero romano, et viris scolasticis prophetarum filiis epulantibus in domo calvi Elisei pulmentum ex vase fictili, Petrus divina permissione sancte romane ecclesie cardinalis indignus sic ex vase littere gustare pulmentum scripture ut per nostrum Elyseum apposita farine spiritualis intelligentie pulmentum ipsum gustantium dulcescat in ore quantinus sicut olim discipulis ita et ipsis sensum aperiat et intelligendas scripturas."

[45] *Contra* the more frequent meaning of *hic* = the latter.

[46] The claim (lines 37–44) means less than at first appears. Durand did indeed compose the poetry of this prologue, replacing Peter of Capua's prose; but Durand did not versify, nor apparently did he add verse to, Peter's text. See the discussion of this point above. The tenses in lines 41–4 seem dictated more by the rhyme scheme than by sense.

Versus dicta l=igat
50 levius que pectore f=igat
Comemorat. lev=igat
breviat. quod prosa fat=igat

Verse binds together *dicta*, that it may more easily implant them in the understanding; it reminds; it lightens and shortens that which prose makes wearisome.

Sum quod in his p=ardus
me corrigat ad mala t=ardus
55 Presul Bern=ardus[48]
prudens. clemens. bona n=ardus[49]

Because I am but a sinner[47] in these matters, I ask correction from Bishop Bernard, who is slow to evil, prudent, compassionate, a good balm.

Moribus ins=ignis
Ticinensis. forma ben=ignis
Solamen di=ignis [*sic*]
60 lux urbis. lima mal=ignis[50]

The Pavian, outstanding in conduct, a model for the good, solace for the deserving, light of the city, a corrector for the wicked.

Vsia[51] summa p=ia
comitetur et alma Mar=ia
Alta petit mar=ia
remus urbe Pap=ia[52]

May the benevolent Supreme Being and holy Mary be in attendance. My oar seeks the high seas, from the city of Pavia.

---

[47] *Pardus* means "sinner," in the standard medieval exegesis of the statement that "the leopard cannot change his spots" (Jeremiah 13.23: "Si mutare potest Aethiops pellem suam aut pardus varietates suas, et vos peteritis benefacere cum didiceritis malum"); and such an interpretation would fit well here with the sense of the following line. To cite an example from among Durand's contemporaries, *peccator* is a figurative meaning for *pardus* in the distinction collection of Alan of Lille; ironically, given Durand's personal history, Alan also interprets *pardus* as *hereticus* (for both meanings, cf. the *Novum Glossarium Mediae Latinitatis* ad verb.).

[48] Bishop Bernard of Pavia (d. 1213).

[49] A pun on the name Bernardus; this is not Durand's invention, of course.

[50] Horace (*Ars* 291) uses *lima*, "file," figuratively when he speaks of polishing his composition. Peter of Blois uses the phrase *castigatoris lima* in referring to a friend who is correcting his work.

[51] Greek *'Ousia*; in his *Contra Manicheos* Durand uses such Greco-Latinity as calling Christ God's "homousion Filium" (consubstantial Son) and saying that Jesus was "ex theothoco natum" (born of the mother of God); cf. prologue, 68 lines 17–18. As the reader will have recognized, Durand's vocabulary is eccentric. See Thouzellier's three lists from *Contra Manicheos* of "mots formés sur le grec," of "locutions latines généralement peu usitées," and of "vocables personnels," 1969: 311.

[52] Describing one's composition as a boat putting out to sea is a well-established metaphor. For example, St. Jerome, epistle 1, uses this figure to dramatize his expression of the conventional reluctance to write about matters beyond an author's abilities: "Super onerariam nauem rudis uector inponor et homo, qui necdum scalmum in lacu rexi, Euxini maris credor fragori" ("A novice in ship-craft, I am put on board a vessel heavily laden; a poor fellow who has never steered a skiff upon a lake, I am entrusted to the roar of the Euxine Sea"); see Jerome 1910 and 1933: 3. We thank Carol D. Lanham for this reference.

65   Alfa[53] sit in pr=imis   May that "Alpha" take first place
     summis qui regnat et =imis   Who reigns in the highest places and
     Cum sit subl=imis   the lowest; since He is sublime may
     donis me ditet op=imis   He enrich me with abundant gifts.

REFERENCES

Chodorow, Stanley 1984 Decretals. *Dictionary of the Middle Ages*, IV.122–4. New York: Scribners.

Dossat, Yves 1969 A propos du prieur des Pauvres catholiques: Durand de Huesca ou de Losque en Rouergue? *Bulletin philologique et historique (jusqu'à 1610), année 1967*: 673–85. Reprinted in his *Eglise et hérésie en France au XIIIe siècle*, ch. 5. London: Variorum Reprints, 1982.

Durand de Huesca 1964 *Une Somme anti-Cathare: Le "Liber contra Manicheos" de Durand de Huesca*, ed. Christine Thouzellier. Spicilegium sacrum Lovaniense, Etudes et documents 32. Louvain: Spicilegium sacrum Lovaniense Administration.

Hertz, Martin 1855–9 *Institutionum grammaticarum libri XVIII*. 2 vols. (= vols. II–III of Keil 1855–80). Leipzig: B. G. Teubner.

Hunt, Richard W. 1936 English Learning in the Late Twelfth Century. *Transactions of the Royal Historical Society* 4th ser. 19: 19–42.

Jerome, St. 1910 *S. Eusebii Hieronymi Epistulae* I. *Corpus scriptorum ecclesiasticorum latinorum* 54.1–2, ed. I. Hilberg. Vienna: F. Tempsky; Leipzig: G. Freytag.
    1933 *Select Letters of St. Jerome*. Trans. F. A. Wright. Loeb Classical Library. London: W. Heinemann; New York: G. P. Putnam's Sons.

Kamp, Norbert 1973–82 *Kirche und Monarchie im staufischen Königreich Sizilien*, I: *Prosopographische Grundlegung*. 4 vols. Münstersche Mittelalter-Schriften 10.1. Munich: W. Fink.

Keil, Heinrich 1855–80 *Grammatici latini*. 6 vols. + supplement, ed. H. Hagen. Leipzig: B. G. Teubner.

LeBras, Gabriel 1937 Bernard de Pavie. *Dictionnaire de droit canonique*, II.782–9. Paris: Librairie Letouzey et Ané.

Liotta, Filippo 1967 Bernardo da Pavia. *Dizionario biografico degli italiani* IX.279–84. Rome: Istituto della Enciclopedia Italiana.

Mackinnon, Hugh 1969 William de Montibus: A Medieval Teacher. In T. A. Sandquist and M. R. Powicke, eds., *Essays in Medieval History Presented to Bertie Wilkinson*, 32–45. Toronto: University of Toronto Press.

Maleczek, Werner 1984 *Papst und Kardinalskolleg von 1191 bis 1216*. Publikationen des Historischen Instituts beim Österreichischen Kulturinstitut in Rom, 1st sect. 6. Vienna: Verlag des Österreichischen Akademie der Wissenschaften.

---

[53] Lines 65–6: it is not uncommon to justify the starting point of a medieval alphabetical reference work with an allusion to God as alpha and omega; but in this case, Durand's language at the end of his prologue specifically echoes the last sentence of Peter of Capua's prologue: "Et ut nostrum principium ad eum referatur qui est principium quod loquebatur nobis, ad alpha incipiemus propter eum qui est alpha et omega."

1988 *Petrus Capuanus: Kardinal, Legat am Vierten Kreuzzug, Theolog.* Publikationen des Historischen Instituts beim Österreichischen Kulturinstitut in Rom, 1st sect. 8. Vienna: Verlag des Österreichischen Akademie der Wissenschaften.

Reynolds, Leighton D., ed. 1983 *Texts and Transmission: A Survey of the Latin Classics.* Oxford: Clarendon Press.

Rouse, Richard H., and Rouse, Mary A. 1974 Biblical Distinctions in the Thirteenth Century. *Archives d'histoire doctrinale et littéraire du moyen âge* 41: 27–37.

1979 *Preachers, Florilegia and Sermons: Studies on the Manipulus florum of Thomas of Ireland.* Toronto: Pontifical Institute of Mediaeval Studies.

1982a. *Statim invenire*: Schools, Preachers, and New Attitudes to the Page. In R. L. Benson and G. Constable, eds., with C. D. Lanham, *Renaissance and Renewal in the Twelfth Century*, 201–25. Cambridge, Mass.: Harvard University Press.

1982b. *Florilegia* of Patristic Texts. In *Les Genres littéraires dans les sources théologiques et philosophiques médiévales*, 165–80. Louvain-la-Neuve: Institut d'Etudes Médiévales de l'Université Catholique de Louvain.

Sarasa Sánchez, Estéban 1981 Durán de Huesca, un heterodoxo aragonés en la Edad Media. In *Miscelánea de estudios en honor de D. Antonio Durán Gudiol*, 225–38. Sabiñánigo: Amigos de Serrablo.

Selge, Kurt Victor 1967a L'Aile droite du mouvement vaudois et naissance des Pauvres catholiques et des Pauvres réconciliés. In *Vaudois languedociens et Pauvres catholiques*, 227–43. Cahiers de Fanjeaux 2. Fanjeaux: Edouard Privat.

1967b *Die ersten Waldenser, mit Edition des Liber antiheresis des Durandus von Osca.* Arbeiten zur Kirchengeschichte 37. 2 vols. Berlin: de Gruyter.

Shailor, Barbara 1992 *Catalogue of Medieval and Renaissance Manuscripts in the Beinecke Rare Book and Manuscript Library, Yale University*, vol. III: *Marston Manuscripts.* Binghamton, N.Y.: Medieval & Renaissance Texts & Studies.

Shooner, H. V. 1985 *Codices manuscripti operum Thomae de Aquino*, vol. III. Montreal: Les Presses de l'Université de Montréal; Paris: J. Vrin.

Smalley, Beryl 1952 *The Study of the Bible in the Middle Ages.* 2nd edn. Oxford: Blackwell.

Thouzellier, Christine 1969 *Catharisme et valdéisme en Languedoc à la fin du XIIe et au début du XIIIe siècle.* 2nd edn. Louvain: Editions Nauwelaerts; repr. Marseilles: Laffitte, 1982 (orig. 1966).

Vicaire, Marie-Humbert 1967a Ecrits anti-cathares de Durand et de ses compagnons vaudois. In *Vaudois languedociens et Pauvres catholiques*, 251–7. Cahiers de Fanjeaux 2. Fanjeaux: Edouard Privat.

1967b Rencontre à Pamiers des courants vaudois et dominicain (1207). In *Vaudois languedociens et Pauvres catholiques*, 163–94. Cahiers de Fanjeaux 2. Fanjeaux: Edouard Privat.

Witten, Laurence C., II 1989 Vinland's Saga Recalled. *The Yale University Library Gazette* 64 (October): 10–37.

5 The reception of Arnau de Vilanova's religious ideas

Clifford R. Backman

Prominent among the conflicts of the late Middle Ages was the dispute over knowledge – its nature, origin, and control. The enormity of the debate's implications accounts for the length and aggressiveness with which it was pursued, for the rise of literacy, and the concomitant widening and deepening of knowledge, challenged the primacy of the west's traditional authorities.[1] Advances in learning in almost any field could be, and often were, perceived as veiled or indirect threats to the established order, thus prompting earnest inquiries into the purpose as well as the content of the new learning. The study of the physical laws of impetus, for example, seems an unlikely venue for revolutionary connivance, but a theory of motion that made no needful mention of a Mover proved threatening, in such an atmosphere, to the Mover's earthly vicars and stewards – hence the attention paid by the Church to Peter John Olivi's scientific efforts.[2] "He who increases knowledge increases sorrow" warned scripture; but the masters of Paris were more prescriptive still, decreeing that any scholar who propagated any new ideas "which seem to undermine the faith," regardless of their viability or the evidence for them, had to refute them publicly or risk heavy punishment.[3] Perhaps only in the eighteenth century, with the works of Hume, Berkeley, and Kant, did the very idea of knowledge – its processes and potentialities – undergo such close and repeated scrutiny as in the late medieval world. This conflict marked a revolution of sorts, for the sources of new learning and the receptivity to new ideas won in this debate altered not only the intellectual terrain of western Christendom but also its political and social ordering.

Arnau de Vilanova's clamorous career, which ranged from medical practice to international diplomacy by way of alchemy and apocalyptic prophecy, offers a compelling perspective on this conflict around the year 1300. A true polymath, few of his contemporaries could equal him in the diversity of his interests or

---

[1] Good introductions to this topic are McLaughlin 1977; Moore 1987; and Stock 1983.
[2] Maier 1955.
[3] Thorndike 1944: 85–8.

the alert and restless energy he brought to them. He wrote scores of treatises – occasionally, he tells us, an entire work at a single sitting – and is credited with dozens of others. He translated Greek and Arabic texts into Latin and a variety of his own Latin works into Catalan and Greek, even while continuing to practice medicine and to propagate his unorthodox spiritual message of reform and apocalyptic expectation. But although his disciples and admirers were many, it has proved difficult to fix Arnau's place in the medieval intellectual tradition, for his varying activities have appeared erratic if not contradictory, the works of a capacious but divided mind. Consequently, the individual aspects of his career have been examined only in isolation to one another as discrete, though not discreet, phenomena. His scientific writings are the best known. Drawing simultaneously on Greek and Arabic scholarship and his own clinical experience, Arnau made important advances in anatomical science, pharmaceutical theory, nutrition, and the treatment of epilepsy. These accomplishments won him a professorial chair in medicine at the University of Montpellier and appointments as physician to a variety of kings and popes. His non-scientific work, by contrast, has received until recently far less attention. His ambiguous yet influential role as mentor to groups like the Beguins and the Franciscan Spirituals has inspired interest in his religious ideas; but this attention has focused chiefly on the details of his Joachimite eschatology, leaving other areas of his religious thought unexplored. Likewise, Arnau's most unscientific endeavors, in astrology, alchemy, and popular magic, remain largely unexamined. As his many writings were presumably the work of a single mind, it is necessary, if we are to understand his role in the intellectual development of the late medieval world, to reconfigure his intellectual activity, to see his ideas in a broader yet more clearly defined context, and to reconcile the scientist and the vision-haunted prophet.[4]

Arnau's ideas reached a wide audience and were enthusiastically received. Support for him personally and interest in his works remained strong throughout his life among the urban professional classes of the Mediterranean lands. Moreover, consciously exploiting his position as a court figure, he remonstrated and lectured wherever he went – Barcelona, Paris, Avignon, Naples, and Messina, among other capital cities – and secured an influential following among the ruling elites. To reach ever larger audiences he often personally directed the distribution of his writings in manuscript as well as their translation into the vernacular. Thus works like the *Regimen sanitatis*, written for the Aragonese King James II, found an eager readership in the prominent

---

[4] The best introductions are Paniagua (Arellano) 1951, for general biography; *idem* 1969; Diepgen 1909a; Verrier 1947–9; Manselli 1951; and Lee, Reeves, and Silano 1989: 27–46. See also Batllori 1954, supplemented by Santi 1983. Two important studies are Diepgen 1911 and 1937. Five valuable collections of documents have appeared: see Martí de Barcelona 1935a, 1935b; Alós Moner 1909–12; McVaugh 1982; and Lizondo 1981.

French and Italian courts and the English universities; later, a translation into Hebrew brought it to the attention of Jewish scholars. Copies of Arnau's treatise on wine, the *Liber de vinis* written (according to one tradition) as he was evangelizing in Tunis, rapidly appeared throughout Europe and was translated into Hebrew and Dutch.[5] In 1308 at Marseilles his unexpected contact with Hesychast monks from Mount Athos resulted in his preparation of Greek translations of five eschatological works (*Dialogus de elementis catholice fidei*; *Responsio ad cavillationes*; *Philosophia catholica et divina*; *Eulogium de notitia verorum*; *Allocutio super significatione nominis Tetragrammaton*), which he later supplemented with an additional four texts – one of which comprises our only surviving version of an otherwise lost work.[6] The following year Arnau boasted in his *Interpretatio de visionibus in somniis* that Catalan versions of five of his exegetical and moral writings had been requested by James in Barcelona for the education of his wife and children. The interest in his ideas expressed by so many influential figures – an interest clearly cultivated by Arnau himself – was as much a strategy as a symptom of his success; and the way in which his ideas were received by others may be a reflection of the manner in which Arnau himself received them and propagated them.

Nevertheless, while the wide currency of his ideas, both religious and scientific, clearly indicates his intellectual notoriety, a detractor existed for every disciple; and worse, the enthusiasm with which his works were received in some circles – whether or not their ideas were put into effect – was matched by the bemused boredom they met with in others. Frederick III of Sicily, we are told, received Arnau at court in 1304 "like Plato resurrected"; devoting himself eagerly to Arnau's apocalyptic message, he issued shortly thereafter a curious flurry of new laws that enacted Arnau's demanded reforms of slave-practice and evangelical efforts towards Muslims and Greeks.[7] James of Catalonia continually sought Arnau's advice, both medical and spiritual, despite diplomatic embarrassments like his violently passionate outburst before the College of Cardinals in 1305 (the result of the examination of his ideas by inquisitors at Bordeaux); and both Robert of Naples and Philip IV of France, who assigned

---

[5] For the Hebrew versions of the *Liber de vinis* and the *Regimen sanitatis ad regem Aragonum*, see Paris, Bibliothèque Nationale, Hebr. 1128 and 1176, respectively. For the Dutch text, see Braekman 1974.

[6] St. Petersburg, Publichnaja Biblioteka CXIII, in 222 folios, contains these texts, none of which has ever been edited. For description of the manuscript, see Carreras i Artau 1932. Batllori 1964 offers a Catalan translation of the Greek version of *De humilitate et patientia Jesu Christi*, in an attempt to approximate Arnau's lost Catalan original.

[7] Cánovas and Piñero 1976: 32. The laws referred to are the *Capitula alia*, one of six main legislative efforts by Frederick's government. They appear in Testa 1741–3: I.65–88 (where they are misdated to 1296); fragments can be found in the more easily available Finke 1908–22: II.695–9. Cf. Barcelona, Arxiu de la Corona d'Aragó, Cartas Jaume II, no. 3792.

him to several ambassadorial errands, dutifully adhered to his health regimens while yawning through his sermons. His following was not limited to the ruling caste, however. Eager evangelists and would-be mystics, especially from his native Catalonia, sent him a steady stream of requests for prayers, elucidations of puzzling dreams, and remedies for physical ailments. On occasion he even received manuscript writings from anxious new authors seeking his advice on the value of their spiritual insights. Beguin and Franciscan Spiritual groups too, of course, turned to him regularly for aid and inspiration in the hope that his prominence at Rome, and later at Avignon, might win them a respite from ecclesiastical ire.

Yet despite that very prominence and the avowedly radical stance of his religious prescriptions, Arnau was surprisingly successful in avoiding papal censure. On at least one occasion, at Perugia in 1304, he barely escaped with his life; but the fact that he avoided punishment even then – when his accusers had him in prison, with no papal or royal protector on the scene – suggests a broader receptivity to his ideas, or at least an inability to marshal a definitive case against them, than has previously been thought. No less than three consecutive popes, all of whom employed him as physician, tolerated his visionary warnings as well as his condemnations of Church corruption and malfeasance, although they did so with widely varying degrees of calm.[8] In 1301, for example, Arnau treated Boniface VIII for a painful attack of kidney stones and followed the treatment by composing a health regimen for him. According to an eyewitness to the events, these services (apparently successful in the short term) prompted an elated Boniface to declare to his court: "I did not until now realize it, but now I proclaim it aloud – this man is the greatest cleric in the world!" His gratitude was understandable, but it left both doctor and patient exposed to the anger of a number of churchmen who had hoped to see Arnau's book on the Antichrist condemned and Boniface's aged body laid to rest. According to the same eyewitness one of the conspiring clerics was over-heard to say: "If only Arnau had not come! For the truth is that the pope would be dead by now, if not for him."[9] Arnau's newly reedited treatise on the Antichrist was the occasion of his being present at court. Arnau had presented his *Tractatus de tempore adventus Antichristi*, originally composed a decade earlier, to the theology masters at the University of Paris in 1299. The subsequent controversy over the book had made Arnau a *cause célèbre* by the time his appeal reached Rome. His case went before the 1301 consistory

---

[8] Manselli 1959. Arnau's relationship with Boniface VIII has received the most attention; see especially Lerner 1988–9 and 1992.

[9] The witness was Guerau d'Albalat, Catalan envoy to the papal court; see Alós Moner 1909–12: doc. 20, "Iste homo maior clericus mundi est, et hoc fatemur, et adhuc per nos cognoscitur," followed by "et dixerunt isti cardinales: 'Magister Arnaldus, utinam non venisset. Fama enim est hic; et est verum, quod iam papa fuisset sepultus nisi magister.'"

court at roughly the same time that the errant kidney stones came so rudely to Boniface's attention. After long arguments and a confusing series of renunciations of the text followed by renunciations of the renunciations, Boniface ultimately albeit unenthusiastically allowed Arnau's apocalyptic warnings (after they were reexpressed a few months later in the treatise *De mysterio cymbalorum ecclesie*) to stand despite the Dominican masters' passionate opposition. Sitting no doubt somewhat uncomfortably on the papal throne, he voiced strong disapproval of Arnau's ideas, but, as Arnau himself emphasized later in the *Protestatio facta Perusii*, he specifically refused to anathematize them and asserted that Arnau had erred only in not presenting the work first to the Holy See.[10] Boniface's refusal to suppress these warnings entirely convinced Arnau that his ideas had Rome's tacit approval and inspired him to write still another work that his critics found equally offensive – the *Philosophia catholica et divina* – but which likewise received no censure. This implied endorsement not only vindicated Arnau in his own eyes but also in the eyes of others, for Guerau d'Albalat later tells us that from early 1302 on Arnau's apocalyptic warnings began to gain followers "even among the leaders [of the Church] . . . they say that his predictions have already begun to come true, and they fear that all his warnings will come to pass."[11]

The next pope, Benedict XI, was determined to put an end to these fears. As a Dominican he was perhaps predisposed against Arnau (who, in addition to his other sins, had quarreled publicly with several influential members of that order in Catalonia) and had little patience with popular prophets of any sort. Compounding Arnau's difficulties was the fact that since 1302 he had turned gradually away from millennial prophecy and towards radical reform propaganda, in the process allying himself, however indirectly, with the heterodox Franciscan Spiritual faction.[12] Benedict, understandably offended by Arnau's newly proclaimed "evangelical detestation of the corrupt practices within the Catholic orders" and particularly among the "dragons and serpents" of the Dominican order, was almost certain to provide the long desired condemnation.[13] Arnau arrived before the new pontiff at Perugia in early 1304 in an apparent, though ill-considered, attempt to win a new papal defender. Clear evidence of the ensuing events is wanting, but Arnau certainly failed to

[10] See the fragment of the *Protestatio* in Finke 1902: cxcii–cxciii.
[11] Alós Moner 1909–12: doc. 22, "Sciat Regio Celsitudo, quod magnus rumor est in curia de verbis magistri Arnaldi de Villanova, etiam apud maiores. Dicunt enim, quod ipsius prenuntiationes iam incipiunt verificari, et timent, quod verba ipsius veniant ad effectum." See also Carreras i Artau 1950: 15 and 19; and *idem* 1988–9, a useful text, but not a critical edition. No edition, critical or otherwise, exists for the *Philosophia catholica*.
[12] See Backman 1990.
[13] *Protestatio facta Perusii*, see Finke 1902: cxcvi, "ad detestationem evangelicam viciorum in catholicis statibus." Cf. Rubió i Lluch 1908–21: I, doc. 28, for the full text of the *Protestatio*; and *ibid.*, I, doc. 25 ("drachones et colubri").

convince Benedict of the correctness of any of his eschatological views. Whatever Benedict thought of Arnau's religious ideas, however, he placed high value on his medical skills. Suddenly stricken with grievous illness, the pope placed himself under Arnau's care, but died shortly after. Prior to Benedict's death, Arnau was no doubt under some form of detention or surveillance so that his inquisitors might have sufficient time to investigate the charges against him thoroughly. The pope's sudden demise had not only removed from the scene the only figure with the potential influence to protect Arnau against his foes, as Boniface had done, but in fact presented those enemies with an additional charge to mount against him, namely murder. Rumors of Arnau's supposed poisoning of the pope spread quickly, and the doctor found himself imprisoned. Had Benedict lived there is little doubt that Arnau would have been convicted of heresy; now, with no pope or king present to come to his defense, nothing stood in the way to stop his condemnation. Yet the College of Cardinals must have voted, after no doubt highly contentious debate, to release him, for he was inexplicably set free sometime in late August or September.[14] We know from Guerau d'Albalat's testimony that Arnau had won many converts among the curial leaders; and the support given by cardinals such as Napoleone Orsini to controversial figures like Fra Liberato (leader of a Franciscan Spiritual faction then prominent in the area around Perugia) is also well known.[15] Hence it seems likely – in the absence of any other satisfactory explanation for Arnau's release – that his religious ideas were sufficiently acceptable to a sufficiently large portion of the College at Perugia to win his freedom once the panic-inspired poisoning rumors were dispelled. None of his writings was condemned, none of his pronouncements withdrawn or recanted, and no strictures were placed on his further writing or preaching. Granted this reprieve, though evidently shaken, Arnau ventured to Sicily and the worshipful attention of Frederick III, before allegedly moving on to Tunis.

The third pope to confront the problem of Arnau treated it with a sense of detachment, almost of dismissal. Despite continuing pressure from various quarters, Clement V – who, when still archbishop of Bordeaux, had expressed sympathy for Arnau's treatment at the hands of the Dominicans and had thus unwillingly earned his relentless devotion – supported him in yet another

---

[14] Barcelona, Arxiu de la Corona d'Aragó, Canc. Reg. 335, fol. 312, top and middle. These are two letters from James II (dated 23 August 1304) – one addressed to the imprisoned Arnau, promising to exert all necessary force to have the false charges dismissed, and one to Cardinal Matteo Rosso, seeking his assistance in winning Arnau's release. Their language is vague, but they imply that Arnau's imprisonment was on account of the suspected poisoning rather than the accusation of heresy. The ever-cautious James would not have intervened, nor would his appeal have been heeded, had Arnau been jailed for heresy.

[15] Lerner 1988: 616–17.

inquiry at Bordeaux. Arnau's Sicilian wanderings had kept him away from the papal court throughout the interregnum; but the election of his supposed friend Clement had quickly brought him in search once again of a papal champion.[16] Few details survive about this meeting. It certainly lacked the drama of Perugia, for Arnau's support from the royal house of Aragon had been reaffirmed during the interim, while overtures had been made as well to influential Carthusians (for whom he wrote his *Tractatus de esu carnium pro substentatione ordinis Carthusiensis contra Jacobitas*) and to several bishops (such as Bishop Guillem of Majorca, dedicatee of the *Antidotum contra venenum . . . adversus denunciationes finalium temporum*). Clement gave no endorsement to Arnau's work, yet refused to condemn it, and then dismissed him. This was the last major attempt by Arnau's opponents to have his work condemned during his lifetime. Given his advanced age, it is likely that they simply decided to wait for him to pass away. The strategy, if such it was, may have paid off, for Arnau seldom again commanded so much attention and his influence seems to have declined somewhat in his last years. Nevertheless, Clement was held captive to a reading of the *Interpretatio de visionibus c. 1310*. Despite that work's alarming (and, as it turned out, false) claims – namely, that James of Catalonia had given himself over wholly to Arnau's apocalypticism – Clement daydreamed through the entire episode: "While Arnau was reading I did not bother to apply my mind to what he said, and rather sat thinking about other, more important, matters. I did not then or later understand what his book said; nor have I ever placed any faith or credence in his ideas."[17]

This relative absence of papal concern throughout his prophetic career (with the exception of Benedict) contrasts strikingly with the angry opposition offered by his foes, who were chary that Arnau's prominence as a court figure and a man of science might lend an undeserved air of authority to his apocalyptic warnings. There was good reason for this chariness. His teachings, after all, posited not only the advent of Antichrist (calculated, on the basis of Daniel 9 and 12, to occur between 1366 and 1376), but also the spent spiritual authority of the clergy, the supremacy of scripture to *magisterium*, the validity of ecstatic visions as sources of evangelical truth, the necessity of radical *paupertas*, and the demand for the immediate and sweeping reform of Christendom under the guidance of an angelic pope, a God-elected king,

---

16 See the *Presentatio Burdegalie*, in Finke 1902: cci–ccxi at cciii–cciiii, repeating that such support had been sought from Benedict until his death had unfortunately intervened.

17 Cited in Menéndez y Pelayo 1946–8: VII.315, "Verumtamen sciat Regalis Sinceritas, quod ad scripturam illam . . . nos, dum legebatur, cogitantes circa alia negotia graviora, que nostris tunc cogitationibus imminebant, mentem nostram non curavimus apponendam, nec ad illa, que prelibata continebat scriptura, tunc vel postea direximus intellectum, neque illis fidem vel credulitatem aliquam diximus adhibendam."

and the company of divinely appointed *precones incorrupti* or *speculatores ordinarii*. None of these ideas, in broad outline, originated with Arnau, most of them having been presented in varying forms by earlier or other contemporary writers. But he brought to their service a prominent and respected voice; a powerful, energetic prose style; and above all a gift for synthesis and simplification. Agilely shifting discursive modes, he united the ecstasy of prophetic visions with the analytic method, indeed the very language, of science, to produce a body of thought that was at once passionately felt and coolly (or at least, consistently) reasoned. Arnau's religious vision, so persuasive to so many, was convincing above all because of its forceful simplicity. And that very simplicity comprised its chief threat, in the opinion of writers like Augustinus Triumphus, whereas other religious scholars viewed Arnau's work as an important contribution, false in its conclusions perhaps but valuable for its insights and methods.

For example, in the *Tractatus contra divinatores et sompniatores* Augustinus bitterly attacked what he thought to be the sophomoric scholarship of unlettered divines like Arnau, who, he maintained, deluded their listeners with an ignorant flashiness that passed for brilliance.[18] But John of Paris, by contrast, took a rather more moderate stance and sought to mediate between Arnau and his Dominican opponents. While rejecting Arnau's specific calculation of 1376 as the year of Antichrist's arrival he accepted, and indeed promoted, the idea that Armageddon was imminent. Arnau's emphasis on the visionary experience which had inspired his understanding of scripture, John wrote, was valid but had to be tempered with and modified by the sure knowledge discovered by scholastic natural philosophy. Divine illumination was a necessary though not sufficient source of religious truth for so grave an issue, particularly when that illumination was experienced by a layman.[19]

Arnau's conflict with his opponents was personal as well as theological or epistemological. He had received his early education from Dominican masters, and the experience seems to have left him disaffected.[20] Although he referred to St. Dominic as the "very image of a celestial angel," a second Jeremiah to whom God had entrusted the mission of exposing and correcting the *ignorantia* which blocked the faithful from recognizing the truth of God's message,[21] the

[18] See Scholz 1911–14: I.190–7 and II.481–90. Scholz maintains that the *Tractatus contra divinatores et sompniatores* was directed chiefly against Ramon Llull, but cf. Hitzfeld 1930: 17–37. Hitzfeld's conclusions are affirmed by Manselli 1951: 19–20. Augustinus castigated Arnau, Llull, and Olivi for propagating their ecstatic imaginings: "visiones factas talibus non esse divinas revelationes sed Diaboli illusiones." See Hillgarth 1971: 56; Crisciani 1978: 246.
[19] Lerner 1983: 63–6; Pelster 1951: 36–41.   [20] Batllori 1951.
[21] See his *Epistola fratribus ordinis predicatorum qui sunt Parisiis*, Vatican City, Vat. Borgh. 205, fols. 63–5; Vat. Lat. 3824, fols. 98–100v. Cf. the opening passage of the *Tractatus de tempore adventus Antichristi*, in Finke 1902: cxxix, "quod carere studet, ne ipsum per ignorantiam ruina preoccupet."

Dominicans' scholastic methods stood at odds with the inductive nature of much of Arnau's own thinking. Working within established models – whether Galenic for medicine or Joachimite for eschatology – Arnau readily revised or adapted those models when necessary in order to accommodate individual facts and *exempla* drawn from other credible sources. For example, a major medical treatise traditionally ascribed to him, the *Breviarium practice*, dismissed the Parisian scholars who "strive exceedingly to gain knowledge of a universal principle while caring nothing for specific facts and *experimenta*. I recall having seen [there] a certain *maximus* in the [medical] arts – an *optimus* in natural philosophy, logic and theory – who did not know how to administer a simple clyster or any other specific remedy."[22] All knowledge, to Arnau, had an immediate and practical value since all knowledge derived ultimately from God and was to be employed to the glory of the Creator. Echoing Amos, he held that the Lord does nothing in this world without revealing His secrets to His servants the prophets.[23] The aim of the scholar, he argued, should be not only to learn but to put to use the knowledge or understanding he has gained; for only thus can the Creator be fully glorified and the truths which He had implanted in creation for us to see be perceived.[24]

Still, this divergence in intellectual approach might very well have come to nothing, but for two facts. First, Arnau was a layman. As such his religious teaching, with its implicit claims to unique prophetic gifts, could only be considered presumptuous and dangerous meddling. He admitted on several occasions – at times with true pride, at others with false humility – to having had only six months of formal theological study in his lifetime. His letter to the College of Cardinals in 1302 described himself as a *parvulus* of low birth, vulgar profession, and shadowy origin; while his angry essay *De morte Bonifacii VIII* declared: "I am the most contemptible of men – contemptible in origin, rank, office, daily life, and endeavor – for I have always labored in the secular sciences (from my very infancy and childhood, it seems), and apart

---

[22] An excellent new series of Arnau's medical works, the *Opera medica omnia*, is now appearing under the general editorship of Michael McVaugh, Juan Antonio Paniagua Arellano, and Luis García Ballester (Arnau 1975–). Until this project is complete, recourse will have to be made to the much older, and variously reliable, sixteenth-century editions; here see Arnau 1585: 1392, "et propter hoc Parisiense et Ultramontani medici plurimum student, ut habeant scientiam de universali, non curantes habere particulares cognitiones et experimenta. Memini enim vidisse quendam maximum in artibus – naturalem, logicum et theoricum optimum – in medicina tamen unum clystere seu aliquam particularem curationem non novit ordinare." On the old editions, see McVaugh, García Ballester, Sánchez Salor, and Trias 1985. On the debated authenticity of the *Breviarum practice*, see Diepgen 1909b; Batllori 1934; and Paniagua (Arellano) 1969: 53–5.

[23] Amos 3.3–8. This is an important text for Arnau who, despite his obvious reliance on Daniel for the Antichrist prophecy, turned regularly to the minor prophets of the scriptures. Echoes of this passage can be found, among other places, in the *Allocutio christiani*.

[24] *De diversis intentionibus medicorum*, in Arnau 1585: 645.

from six months of study, or thereabouts, I have never attended the classrooms of the theologians."[25] This lack of professional credentials accounts, in part, for the ten-year delay between the original composition of the Antichrist treatise and its presentation to the Parisian faculty, just as it accounts, in part, for the persistent attack upon his teachings by the schoolmen. For the Dominicans, of course, this sort of lay study of scripture, even though sanctioned by St. Augustine and other authorities, too easily exposed the unlettered faithful to the dangers of heresy. Since Arnau was a respected figure in intellectual circles, entrusted by popes and kings with their very lives, the potential harm of his forays into religious matters was deemed too great to be tolerated.

Secondly, the bits of knowledge that Arnau gathered and manipulated to form his religious ideas were not, in themselves, self-evident phenomena but the products of a unique and private ecstatic vision, or rather a continuing series of visions. Ideas received in this fashion, when they seemed not only contrary to the general current of Church belief but also suspiciously political in intent, were bound to confront resistance. Arnau's visions were impressively vivid and oddly all of a piece. They seem in general to have occurred at times of emotional stress or intense mental concentration, and they commonly took the form of an angelic voice unexpectedly heard, or of a miraculous text suddenly seen. Through whichever avenue the message was received, its import was usually the same and always urgent. His letter to Boniface accompanying the *Philosophia catholica et divina*, for example, tells how he came to compose the work: "While pacing alone in a certain chapel, turning over in my mind ways in which I might be of aid to you . . . suddenly a miraculous scripture appeared before my eyes, which said 'Sit down, quickly and write!' "[26] Doing so, Arnau found himself "starting to write with incredible speed."[27] The same verse from Luke prompted him to action in another episode described in the *De morte Bonifacii VIII*. Being "a poor son of the Church, repudiated in my spiritual mission," Arnau took up solitary residence at S. Niccolò di Sculcola in order to reflect upon the numerous criticisms his works had received ever since he began presenting them publicly. At this point, in 1301, he seems to

---

[25] See Finke 1902: clxiii, "procul dubio parvulus in catholicorum collegio, qui statu est infimus et officio fetidus et origine tenebrosus," and cxc–cxci, "cum sim despectissimus hominum, quia despectus origine et statu et officio et vita et studio, quia semper in scientiis secularibus ab infantia quasi vel pueritia studui, et nunquam scolas theologorum nisi sex mensibus aut circiter frequentavi."

[26] Luke 16.6.

[27] Finke 1902: clx–clxi, "Ego servus tuus in quandam capella solus deambulans et pre desiderio assistendi tibi mecum revolvens in animo, qualiter ad te possem securus accedere quidve tibi gratum et utile in obsequium exhiberem, dum aliquantulum stetissem immobilis, ecce repente coram oculis meis apparuit scriptura mirabilis, in qua sub formatissima litera michi videbatur, quod legerem: 'Sede cito et scribe!' . . . incredibili celeritate concipiens atque scribens composui."

have doubted for the first time the authenticity of his mystical experiences and the knowledge he had derived from them. Praying alone at the altar each day he implored Christ to speak to him: his entreaties were evidently successful, for after only a few days he could not enter the chapel without hearing a heavenly voice cry out "Write quickly!". Still doubtful, he approached the chapel's copy of the Bible, and, Augustine-like, opened it at random: Luke 16.6 stood out in huge capital letters. Arnau closed the book, reopened it to the same place, and saw the verse written in the same lower-case script as the rest of the text. Exulting in this confirmation of his earlier illuminations, he began once again to write "with miraculous speed" and completed an entire treatise before looking up from his desk to find a querulous papal official staring at him.[28] Given the intense nature of these experiences – one of which he later described in terms of a painful lance-blow to his chest and a ball of fire consuming his head – and their great number, it is hardly surprising to encounter references, among uninvolved witnesses, to Arnau suffering terrible, indeed debilitating, headaches.[29]

The problem with mystical visions is that they are not only viewed with suspicion by those who have not experienced them, but that they are frequently viewed in contrast to or in competition with those who have. Without other evidence to enhance or corroborate them, one man's visions are as good as another's. An important element, however, distinguished Arnau's epiphanies from those of many other mystics of the thirteenth and fourteenth centuries – namely, his success at harmonizing his ecstatic experiences with his critical science. And in this harmony we see one of the keys to the unique appeal of Arnau's religious ideas for his avid followers, and to the unique threat those ideas represented to his ecclesiastical opponents.

This harmony went beyond a simplistic discovery of joy in science and *scientia* in ecstasy, although it included that. He clearly derived a profound satisfaction from his scientific work – which he continued to labor at until the end of his life, even while preparing for the end of the world – for it not only provided his livelihood and made him a celebrated figure, but the knowledge generated by it had a glorious, even salvific, utility: "All the sciences share in a common usefulness, namely the acquisition of perfection in the human soul, preparing it, in effect, for all future happiness."[30] Despite the sternness with which he enjoined his listeners to embrace the spiritual virtues of humility and

---

[28] *Ibid.*, clxxix–clxxx.

[29] Alós Moner 1909–12: doc. 20, "alia die duxi Berengarium de Monte Alacri ad locum ubi magister Arnaldus de Villanova patitur dolorem magnum in capite propter solem, qui mense Julii caput et eius cerebrum perforavit ac etiam penetravit."

[30] *Commentum super canonem "Vita brevis,"* in Arnau 1585: 1693, "quod omnes scientie communicant in una utilitate, que est acquisitio perfectionis humane anime in effectum preparantis eam ad futuram felicitatem."

modesty (virtues which he emulated in his repeated references to his lowly state of birth and vulgar profession) he always referred to himself by his title of *magister* or *doctor*, to highlight his status as a learned man. He praised Robert of Naples for the number of scholars in all fields to be found in his court and for the honors paid to them; and he regularly singled out medicine as *scientiarum nobilissima, preciosior scientiis cunctis*, and as the *apicem nobilitatis*.[31] As a faculty of certain knowledge, he wrote, medical science is hampered by the constantly changing nature of the human organism; the signs (*signa*) which a physician must read in order to diagnose and treat effectively are themselves always in flux. But sure knowledge, and its consequent joy, are yet available through divine providence, which desires our physical health just as it desires our spiritual salvation, and which makes clear to the chosen physician the proper understanding of the body, its functions, and its maladies.[32] But such understanding is not for everyone, he argued. The mind acquires knowledge (*scientia*) through any number of channels – traditional authority, deductive models, or simple observation – but true understanding (*intellectus*) can be acquired only when the beneficent Lord allows one, by means of a divine illumination or vision, to comprehend the majestic whole.

While a belief in a providential ordering and intent in Creation permeated Arnau's approach to both scientific and scriptural study, his persistent devotion to both endeavors in the stormy last decade of his life – when one might expect him to have relinquished the former activity – reflects their interrelation, indeed their unity, in his intellectual outlook. He appropriated the image from *Revelation* of the book sealed with seven seals to describe the heavenly mysteries of natural and evangelical truth: the words are unalterably and eternally there, divinely authored and intended to be known, although the book can be read only by those few whom God allows to view the miraculous text.[33] To Arnau, the astronomer's ability to anticipate solar and lunar eclipses proves, on the one hand, that the ability to prophesy events is directly based upon the existence of a divine ordering of nature perceivable to a select few, while it

---

[31] *De conservanda juventute ac retardanda senectute* (another work of debated authenticity), dedicated to Robert, in Arnau 1585: 813, 838; but cf. *Antidotarium, ibid.*, 385; and *Tractatus contra calculum, ibid.*, 1565. I owe these references to Crisciani 1978: 258–9. On the authenticity of *De conservanda*, see Paniagua (Arellano) 1969: 50-1.

[32] *Liber de vinis*, in Arnau 1585: 588, "Ideo bene definit quidam dicens: 'Medicina scientia est, que nescitur . . . Deus autem Benedictus faciat nos scire et intelligere, et secundum Suum beneplacitum operari'"; *Tractatus contra calculum, ibid.*, 1565, "Reor quod medicina est scientia, quam Divina statuit Providentia fore auxiliatricem hominique contra incommoda, necessitatem, quam genus humanum ob prevaricationem primi parentis incurrerit delictuose, persuadens remedium medicinale adhibere forte inter creata, increata divina virtute excepta, apicem nobilitatis." Other examples, also in Arnau 1585, include *De diversis intentionibus medicorum*, 639; *Medicationis parabole secundum instinctum veritatis eterne*, 913; and *De epilepsia*, 1624. For the larger tradition of all science being a divine gift, see Post *et al.* 1955.

[33] Manselli 1951: 15.

vindicates, on the other hand, the contention that laymen may be the possessors of such knowledge and power.[34] "God and Nature do nothing in vain" – *Deus et natura nichil faciant frustra* – he asserted,[35] adding that their common desire to profit and redeem mankind is revealed in every aspect of God's holy, yet interpretable, creation.[36] Finally, he not only correlated true understanding (*intellectus*) with divine revelation, but he boldly posited, in his more radical moments, the special and perhaps unique enjoyment of such revelation by the various sciences' humblest practitioners.[37] This trend in his religious thought emerged explicitly after 1302, since prior to his reception of papal approval for his speculations (an approval that perhaps existed only in his own mind) he felt compelled, as a layman, to avoid the dangerous claim of possessing prophetic gifts.[38]

Having argued for an evangelical purpose in all science, he inevitably equated bad science with spiritual error – and hence the criticisms of the

[34] *Tractatus de tempore adventus Antichristi*, in Finke 1902: cxxxiv, argues that, because "Suam potentiam et sapientiam Deus non alligavit naturalibus causis," God has the power to alter the laws governing the movement of the planets, should be desire to do so. But this passage – an apparent response to certain criticisms he received – is intended rather to justify Arnau's substitution of years for days in Daniel 12.12 than to admit of any arbitrariness in natural laws.

[35] *Ibid.*, cxxxvii.

[36] See the remarkable opening to the *Allocutio christiani*, in Perarnau i Espelt 1992: 75–8 "Volens Deus propter immensitatem Sue bonitatis communicare Suam beatitudinem rationali creature insignivit eam illis potentiis, quibus posset acquirere qualitatem, per suam disponeretur ad consequendum eam. Qualitas autem, per quam rationalis creatura disponitur ad hoc, ut elevetur ad divinam beatitudinem consequendam, est summa justitia, quoniam gloriam Summi Regis non potest consequi creatura ex parte sui nisi per actum summe justitie, sicut est ei possibilis. Summa vero justitia est suum factorem seu creatorem pre cunctis rebus amare atque laudare. Ideo vero dictum est ex parte sui, quia Deus ex Sua mera liberalitate potest eam conferre cui voluerit absque aliquo merito recipientis, quemadmodum dat infantibus, qui obeunt post baptismum, sed adultis, qui habent usum rationis, non dat, nisi mediante aliquo justitie merito. Dedit igitur Deus homini rationem et intellectum: scilicet intellectum dedit, ut per ipsum cognoscat Deum in se, quoniam Deus, cum sit spiritus et res solum intellectualis, solo intellectu apprehenditur in se ipso; rationem vero dedit ei, ut a sensibilibus ad intelligibilia ratiocinando sciat Dei excellentias sive dignitates animadvertere per ea, que in sensibilibus experitur, ut sit per cognitionem ipsius in se quantum possibile est in presenti vita, et per cognitionem Suarum dignitatum incalescat eius animus ad amandum eum et amando sollicitetur ad laudandum eundem. Cognoscit autem homo Deum in presenti vita primo per creaturas, in quibus consideratis secundum originem et multitudinem et magnitudinem et pulchritudinem et ordinem et operationem relucent ista – scilicet, potentia immensurabilis, sapientia inexplicabilis, bonitas interminabilis Creatoris; secundo per Scripturas divinas, in quibus ipse Deus, qui Se ipsum tantummodo plene cognoscit, voluit propter exuberantiam Sue bonitatis notificare Suas dignitates hominibus, ultra noticiam quam de Se ipso dabat in creaturis, ut per radios Scripturarum illustraret caliginem Sue cognitionis in illis." I am preparing a critical edition of this work. Cf. the *Introductionum medicinalium speculum* in Arnau 1585: 57–8, 63–4, 214–19.

[37] Crisciani 1978: 270–1.

[38] See Arnau's letter of 12 October 1300, in Denifle and Chatelain 1889–97: II.87–90.

medical faculty at Paris attributed to him.[39] Hence, too, his insistence that all Jews be banned from the practice of medicine; for despite the noted expertise of Jewish physicians, Arnau's certainty of Antichrist's imminent arrival demanded the immediate enactment of the spiritual reforms he prescribed for Christendom. Since the health of the body was so closely linked with the health of the soul, the unequivocal segregation of the Jews was required.[40] For good measure, he enumerated among the religious failings of the Dominicans their continued recourse to Jewish doctors.[41]

Inversely, Arnau brought the language of science to the description and defense of his visionary experiences, and in so doing produced an argument that was both rhetorically powerful and uniquely challenging to his adversaries. This was, to a degree, inevitable; and we should not be wholly surprised to find a prolific writer of scientific tracts utilizing a scientific vocabulary when he turns his mind to other matters. For example, he frequently described his visions clinically, with reference to physical symptoms. Thus he tells us, in one case, that he initially misinterpreted the onset of a mystical experience as an attack of the spleen, while at another time the text *Homines pestilentes dissipant civitatem* appeared miraculously before his eyes.[42] Arnau repeatedly justified his visionary work with reference to St. Luke, the physician-evangelist: Christ Himself did not exclude physicians from understanding the divine mysteries, he argued, nor did any of the other apostles tell Luke, as Boniface had once enjoined Arnau, to "Immerse yourself in medicine, not theology."[43] Moreover, Arnau saw a symbolic, and obvious, purpose in God's choice of a medical practitioner to receive the new revelation, for the corruption of the church and the sinfulness of the world were nothing less than diseases to be cured prior to Judgment; hence the title, and rhetorical style, of works such as the *Antidotum contra venenum*. After he had written the *Philosophia catholica et divina* he saw in another epiphany that the papal office was gravely endangered by the corruption existing in the religious orders. Too frightened to present the news to Benedict XI, who appeared to have been struck with a rigid morbidity, Arnau waited "until another vision comforted me, in which [Benedict] was shown to me to be looking miserable (which he could not explain), when [suddenly] a voice said to me: 'Touch him!' And when I touched him, the vision ended."[44] In one of his medical writings he

---

[39] See n. 22 above.
[40] Manselli 1951: 21; cf. the *Capitula alia* (see n. 7 above), no. 70. For a discussion of Arnau's general relation to Judaism, see Carreras i Artau 1947 and 1954–6.
[41] *D morte Bonifacii VIII*, in Finke 1902: clxxxiv.
[42] Prov. 29.8.
[43] *Presentatio Burdegalie*, in Finke 1902: ccvi.
[44] *De morte Bonifacii VIII*, *ibid.*, clxxxii (for rhetorical reasons, Arnau here speaks of himself in the third person), "Set unum hic exprimo, quod cum *Philosophia* scripsisset *catholicam*, in qua demonstratur catholice Jhesum Nazarenum fuisse Messiam verum, et in qua subversiones

explicitly juxtaposed the frustration he felt toward those who refused to recognize the truth of his medical researches and his impatience with the haughty skeptics who refused to admit the validity of his religious vision.[45] Summing up these arguments, he complained: "I tell you, that if anyone rejects my religious writings simply because they were written by a physician, then he does not walk in the path of Christ, since Christ Himself did not exclude physicians from understanding the sacred teachings."[46]

Arnau's impatience and frustration – which are evident on nearly every page of his religious writings – stemmed from his certainty that God in fact wanted His divine secrets to be known to man, and that He had therefore established the numerous signs and portents visible in scripture and in human history just as He had created the bodily symptoms, physical laws, and natural properties necessary to the successful practice of medicine. For Arnau, the revealed truth of scripture, with its message of approaching Armageddon and the subsequent call for complete spiritual and moral reform, was quite literally the best medicine for mankind: in several texts he identified Christ, most strikingly, not as the Savior of mankind but as the *medicus supremus* of this world and the next.[47] The failure of the established ecclesiastical authorities to recognize or comprehend the truths hidden in the scriptures inspired God, in His wisdom, to grant a unique illumination to the *speculatores ordinarii*. God's selection of these *ordinarii* or *simplices*, Arnau wrote, coincided with the scriptural tradition of elevating the lowly; but it also indicated the providential role of these "simple laymen" as living *exempla* of the evangelical perfection that was required. After all, if God had chosen to elevate "the most contemptible of men . . . in origin, rank, office, daily life, and endeavor" to the status of

catholicorum statuum declarantur et omnes Antichristi versucie suorumque membrorum animadverti et evitari docentur, cum videret, quod status pontificis percuteretur rigidius, quodam quasi terrore compressus non concipiebat audaciam presentandi opus illud per se vel per alium eidem pontifici, donec quedam visio confortaret eum, in qua pontifex fuit ostensus ei sub tam miserabili specia, quod nullomodo explicare, fuitque dictum eidem: 'Tange ipsum!' Et cum tetigisset, disparuit visio."

[45] Crisciani 1978: 270–1.

[46] *Presentatio Burdegalie*, in Finke 1902: ccvi, "Protestor etiam et confiteor me dixisse, quod, si quis predictas scripturas orreret quia sunt edite per ministerium medici corporalis, non ambularet in spiritu Jhesu Christi, quoniam Ipse medicos non exclusit ab intelligentia sacrorum eloquiorum."

[47] *De epilepsia*, in Arnau 1585: 1624, "Medicum supremum Jhesum Christum obsecro, compatiens toti generi humano ab hoc languore infelici obsesso et potissime populo Christiano . . . ut valeam doctrinam componere, per quam hec species lugubra morbi lunatici curetur faciliter"; and 1629, "Repellantur . . . ignominiosi incantatores, conjuratores, spirituum invocatores, divinatores et augures in ministerio medicinali . . . ministri iam facti Diaboli, de Deo diffidentes, et summum medicum Jhesum Christum regnantem in coelis occidentes"; *Contra catarrhum, ibid.*, 1590, "Obsecro dominum nostrum Jhesum Christum, qui est summus medicus corporis mystici ecclesie Dei, ut per Suam misericordiam donare dignetur in me sensum, fidem et motum charitatis infundere, ut omnem defectum meum suppleat."

Christendom's preeminent professor of medicine and physician to the Holy Pontiff himself, how can one doubt that He would also select the obscure and low-born to receive the gift of divine revelation and *intellectus*?[48]

Arnau hoped, and insisted, that the *simplices* to whom that understanding had been granted would be allowed to use their gifts to reform a corrupted Christendom. He never intended, however, for his *illuminati* to take the place of the traditional clergy. Indeed, he strongly championed the absolute authority of the ecclesiastical hierarchy to guard over man's spiritual life. "Obey all ecclesiastical commands," he wrote to the Provençal Beguins in 1305;[49] the *custodia* of religious truth rests solely upon the Church's prelates.[50] But those outside of the traditional hierarchy and who would yet presume to sit in judgment of matters which they are fundamentally and intellectually incapable of understanding; those *pseudoreligiosi* who "walk in the spirit of haughty pride and pompous teaching";[51] those *pseudotheologi* whose chief concern is to increase the number of their colleges;[52] that is to say, the Dominican schoolmen, have no authority to judge the ideas of men like Arnau or the actions of groups like the Beguins or Franciscan Spirituals.

To offer, then, some preliminary conclusions. The success of Arnau's religious message depended upon an exceptionally wide variety of factors. Among these are, of course, his prominence as a court figure and respected intellectual, which gave his pronouncements an air of authority, in some circles, that other mystics' assertions might not have enjoyed. But we cannot credit solely to his medical skills the toleration with which he was treated by the papacy. Boniface's bowels, no matter how painful their condition, will not suffice to explain the papal refusal to censure; they certainly played no part in the adherence of other *curiales* to Arnau's prophecies. Perhaps Arnau's consistent, and generally unrecognized, championing of the Church hierarchy as the sole possessor of authority to judge religious debates provides an answer. It is clear that Boniface, Benedict, and Clement profoundly disagreed with Arnau's apocalyptic convictions – and that they considered him to be, respectively, brattish, brutish, and boring – but the court's reluctance to prosecute might be attributed to a belief that his ideas, while wrong, were not theologically false or harmful. (Benedict is a possible exception here.) Until the dispute could be decided – as, of course, it could not be until 1376 – Boniface and Clement, at least, were content to follow his health regimens,

---

[48] Manselli 1951: 64, 74–5, 90.
[49] *Informatio beguinorum*, in Finke 1902: ccii.
[50] *Presentatio Burdegalie, ibid.*, ccviii–ccix.
[51] *Ibid.*, ccviii: "qui ambulant in spiritu superbie et magistralis inflationis."
[52] *De morte Bonifacii VIII, ibid.*, clxxxv: "cum illorum studium sit multiplicare collegia numerum personarum."

wince at his more embarrassing pronouncements, and smile at his assertions of papal authority.

Arnau's forceful juxtaposition of critical science and joyous vision must have been a key factor for those who did accept his teachings. Evocative, powerful language was commonplace in mystical writing and preaching, but Arnau's approach seems likely to have convinced many of his followers. It must be remembered that unlike other mystics, many of Arnau's followers were to be found in the most prominent social, political, and ecclesiastical circles. This was a natural consequence of his professional life; and it does not seem unreasonable to suggest that such audiences as Arnau was likely to have had in Barcelona, Naples, Paris, Palermo, or Avignon (whether in the courts or among the urban professional classes) might require an intellectually satisfying, somewhat scientific, mysticism. Whatever their requirements, Arnau certainly took advantage of his high connections in order to broadcast his views and to win new disciples. It is clear, despite his encomiums to poverty, modesty, and low birth, that he chose to pass at least the last two decades of his life, from 1288 to 1311, in the most prominent society.

Lastly, concerning the Dominicans. This group offered, consistently and aggressively, the greatest challenge to Arnau's religious work. Their reaction may be attributed in part to a fundamental divergence in philosophical (in fact, epistemological) outlook. But other possibilities are suggested. Arnau's writings, especially after his trial in 1302, comprise a formidable attack upon scholasticism in general, but a particular – and particularly effective – attack on the Dominican order (and consequently of course the Inquisition). He ridiculed their deductive methods and the inability of their physicians to carry out the simplest of medical cures; he castigated their hypocritical relations with the Jews; and he consistently argued against their right – either a canonical or a philosophical right – to participate in the judgment of new developments in Christian spiritual life. His attack upon the Order of Preachers is, in fact, reminiscent of the powerful criticisms leveled, in an earlier time, against an earlier foe, by another prophet whom he quoted often – Malachi, the contemnor of failed clerics.

REFERENCES

Alós Moner, Ramon d' 1909–12 Collecció de documents relatius a l'Arnau de Vilanova. *Estudis universitaris catalans* 3: 47–53, 140–8, 331–2, 447–9, 531–4; 4: 110–19, 496–8; 6: 98–103.
Arnau de Vilanova 1585 *Opera omnia cum Nicolai Taurelli medici et philosophi in quosdam libros annotationibus.* Basel: Conrad Waldkirch.
    1975– *Opera medica omnia.* Ed. Michael McVaugh, Juan Antonio Paniagua Arellano, and Luis García Ballester. 5 vols. to date. Barcelona: Seminarium

Historiae Medicae Cantabricense; and Granada: Seminarium Historiae Medicae Granatensis.

Backman, Clifford R. 1990 Arnau de Vilanova and the Franciscan Spirituals in Sicily. *Franciscan Studies* ser. 2, 50: 3–29.

Batllori, Miquel 1934 Un carteig erudit sobre l'autenticitat del Breviarium. *Analecta sacra tarraconensia* 10: 25–43.

    1951 Arnau de Vilanova antiscolastique d'après les textes catalans et italiens. In *Scholastica ratione historico-critica instauranda. Acta Congressus Scholastici Internationalis Romae anno sancto MCML celebrati*, 567–81. Bibliotheca pontificii athenaei antoniani 7. Rome: Pontificum Athenaeum Antonianum.

    1954 Orientaciones bibliográficas para el estudio de Arnau de Vilanova. *Pensamiento* 10: 311–23.

    1964 Opusculum Arnaldi de Villanova nondum editum. In Isidorus a Villapadierna, OFM Cap., ed., *Miscellanea Melchor de Pobladura*, I.215–23. 2 vols. Bibliotheca seraphico-capuccina, sect. historica 23–4. Rome: Institutum Bistorium OFM Cap.

Braekman, W. L. 1974 Het *Liber de vinis* van Arnaldus de Villanova in het Middel-nederlands. *Verslagen en mededelingen van de Koninklijke Academie voor Nederlandse Tall- en Letterkunde* 3: 275–318.

Cánovas, Elena, and Piñero, Félix, eds. and trans. 1976 *Arnaldo de Vilanova: Escritos condenados por la Inquisición*. Madrid: Editora Nacional.

Carreras i Artau, Joaquim 1932 Una versió grega de nou escrits d'Arnau de Vilanova. *Analecta sacra tarraconensia* 8: 127–34.

    1947 Arnaldo de Vilanova, apologista antijudaico. *Sefarad* 7: 49–61.

    1950 *L'Epistolari d'Arnau de Vilanova*. Institut d'Estudis Catalans, Memòries de secció històrico-arqueològica 10. Barcelona: Institut d'Estudis Catalans.

    1954–6 Arnau de Vilanova y las culturas orientales. In *Homenaje a Millás-Vallicrosa*, I.309–22. 2 vols. Barcelona: Consejo Superior de Investigaciones Científicas.

    1988–9 El text primitiu del *De mysterio cymbalorum ecclesiae* d'Arnau de Vilanova. *Arxiu de textos catalans antics* 7–8: 7–169.

Crisciani, Chiara 1978 Exemplum Christi e sapere: sull'epistemologia di Arnaldo da Villanova. *Archives internationales d'histoire des sciences* 28: 245–92.

Denifle, Heinrich, and Chatelain, Emile, eds. 1889–97 *Chartularium universitatis Parisiensis*. 4 vols. Paris: ex typis fratrum Delalain.

Diepgen, Paul 1909a *Arnald de Villanova als Politiker und Laientheologe*. Abhandlungen zur mittleren und neueren Geschichte 9. Berlin and Leipzig: W. Rothschild.

    1909b Zur Echtheitsfrage des Breviarium. *Archiv für Geschichte der Medezin* 3: 188–96.

    1911 Arnalds Stellung zur Magie, Astrologie und Oneiromantie. *Archiv für Geschichte der Medezin* 5: 88–115.

    1937 Die Weltanschauung Arnalds von Vilanova und seine Medezin. *Scientia* 61: 38–47.

Finke, Heinrich 1902 *Aus den Tagen Bonifaz VIII: Funde und Forschungen*. Vorreformationsgeschichtliche Forschungen 2. Münster im Westfalen: Aschendroffsche Buchhandlung. Repr. Rome: Bardi Editore, 1964.

1908–22 *Acta aragonensia: Quellen zur deutschen, italienischen, französischen, spanischen, zur Kirchen- und Kulturgeschichte aus der diplomatischen Korrespondenz Jaymes II. (1291–1327).* 3 vols. Berlin and Leipzig: W. Rothschild (repr. 1966).

Hillgarth, J. N. 1971 *Ramon Lull and Lullism in Fourteenth-Century France.* Oxford: Clarendon Press.

Hitzfeld, Karl Leopold 1930 *Studien zu den religiösen und politischen Anschauungen Friedrichs III von Sizilien.* Berlin: E. Ebering. Repr. Berlin: Vaduz, Kraus Reprint, 1965.

Lee, Harold, Reeves, Marjorie, and Silano, Giulio 1989 *Western Mediterranean Prophecy: The School of Joachim of Fiore and the Fourteenth-Century Breviloquium.* Pontifical Institute of Mediaeval Studies, Studies and Texts 88. Toronto: Pontifical Institute of Mediaeval Studies.

Lerner, Robert E. 1983 *The Powers of Prophecy: The Cedar of Lebanon Vision from the Mongol Onslaught to the Dawn of the Enlightenment.* Berkeley, Los Angeles, and Oxford: University of California Press.

1988 On the Origins of the Earliest Latin Pope Prophecies: A Reconsideration. In *Fälschungen im Mittelalter: Internationaler Kongress der Monumenta Germaniae historica, München, 16.–19. September 1986,* 611–35. MGH Schriften XXXIII.5.

1988–9 The Pope and the Doctor. *Yale Review* 78: 62–79.

1992 Ecstatic Dissent. *Speculum* 67: 33–57. Originally presented at conference on "Christendom and its Discontents," Los Angeles, January.1991.

Lizondo, Mateu Rodrigo 1981 La protesta de Valencia de 1318 y otros documentos inéditos referentes a Arnau de Vilanova. *Dynamis* 1: 241–73.

McLaughlin, Mary Martin 1977 *Intellectual Freedom and its Limitations in the University of Paris in the Thirteenth and Fourteenth Centuries.* New York: Arno Press (© orig. 1955).

McVaugh, Michael M. 1982 Further Documents for the Biography of Arnau de Vilanova. *Dynamis* 2: 363–72.

McVaugh, Michael M., García Ballester, Luis, Sánchez Salor, Eustaquio, and Trias, Ana, 1985 Les ediciones renacentistas de Arnau de Vilanova: su valor para la edición crítica de sus obras medicas. *Asclepio* 27: 39–66.

Maier, Anneliese 1955 Die naturphilosophische Bedeutung der scholastischen Impetustheorie. *Scholastik* 30: 321–43. Repr. in her *Ausgehendes Mittelalter: Gesammelte Aufsätze zur Geistesgeschichte des 14. Jahrhunderts,* I.353–79. 3 vols. Storia e letteratura 97, 105, and 138. Rome: Edizioni di storia e letteratura, 1964–77.

Manselli, Raoul 1951 La religiosità d'Arnaldo da Villanova. *Bollettino dell'Istituto Storico Italiano per il Medio Evo e Archivio muratoriano* 63: 1–100.

1959 Arnaldo da Villanova e i papi del suo tempo: tra religione e politica. *Studi romani* 7: 146–61.

Martí de Barcelona, P., OFM Cap. 1935a Nous documents per a la biografia d'Arnau de Vilanova. *Analecta sacra tarraconensia* 11: 85–127.

1935b Regesta de documents arnaldians coneguts. *Estudis franciscans* 47: 261–300.

Menéndez y Pelayo, Miquel 1946–8 *Historia de los heterodoxos españoles.* Ed. Enrique Sánchez Reyes. 8 vols. Santander: Aldus, S. A. de Artes Gráficas (orig. 1880–1).

Moore, R. I. 1987 *The Formation of a Persecuting Society: Power and Deviance in Western Europe, 950–1250*. Oxford: Basil Blackwell.

Paniagua (Arellano), Juan Antonio 1951 Vida de Arnaldo de Vilanova. *Archivo iberoamericano de historia de la medicino y antropología médica* 3: 3–83.

1969 *El maestro Arnau de Vilanova, médico*. Valencia: Cátedra e Instituto de Historia de la Medicina.

Pelster, Franz 1951 Die Quaestio Heinrichs von Harclay über die zweite Ankunft Christi und die Erwartung des baldigen Weltendes zu Anfang des XIV Jahrhunderts. *Archivio italiano per la storia della pietà* 1: 25–82.

Perarnau i Espelt, Josep 1992 L'Allocutio christini d'Arnau de Vilanova: Edició i estudi del text. *Arxiu de textos catalans antics* 11: 7–135.

Post, Gaines *et al.* 1955 The Medieval Heritage of a Humanist Ideal: "Scientia donum Dei est unde vendi non potest." *Traditio* 11: 195–234.

Rubió i Lluch, Antoni, ed. 1908–21 *Documents per l'història de la cultura catalana mig-eval*. 2 vols. Barcelona: Institut d' Estudis Catalans.

Santi, Francesco 1983 Orientamenti bibliografici per lo studio di Arnau de Vilanova, spirituale: studi recenti (1968–1982). *Arxiu de textos catalans antics* 2: 371–95.

Scholz, Richard 1911–14 *Unbekannte kirchenpolitische Streitschriften aus der Zeit Ludwigs des Bayern (1327–1354)*. 2 vols. Rome: Loescher.

Stock, Brian 1983 *The Implications of Literacy: Written Language and Models of Interpretation in the Eleventh and Twelfth Centuries*. Princeton, N.J.: Princeton University Press.

Testa, Francesco, ed. 1741–3 *Capitula regni Siciliae, quae ad hodiernum diem lata sunt*. 2 vols. Palermo: A. Felicella.

Thorndike, Lynn, ed. 1944 *University Records and Life in the Middle Ages*. New York: Columbia University Press.

Verrier, René 1947–9 *Etudes sur Arnaud de Villeneuve v. 1240–1311*. 2 vols. Leiden: Brill.

6 "Springing cockel in our clene corn": Lollard preaching in England around 1400

Anne Hudson

As late as 1511 the London heretic Joan Baker claimed that "she cold here a better sermond at home in hur howse than any doctor or prist colde make at Poulis crosse or any other place."[1] The claim was doubtless largely evaluative, but its terms are perhaps more illuminating than Joan Baker realized or intended: the contrast between home and *Poulis crosse* overtly directs attention to the location of Lollard preaching by the beginning of the sixteenth century, and less overtly to its restriction to a group of familiars, to a conventicle if not to an underground cell; implicit in the comment is also the contrast between the standing of the preacher, a *doctor* or *prist* to the orthodox, and the Lollard teacher who was apparently not either and was presumably lay. That she was a qualified critic of the excellence of sermons evidently was an unquestioned assumption by Joan, and in her praise for the discourses of her own sect and her dismissal of the worth of orthodox preachers she followed a long line of Wyclifite sermon-tasters.[2]

Joan Baker's comment is late, and, as I shall argue, some of its implications are misleading for earlier Lollardy. But it raises in stark form some of the questions that I wish to address in this essay. Most simply, what was it like to attend a Lollard sermon? Where and when were they preached? What was the nature of the sermon delivered? Who was the preacher? What was expected of the congregation? In all of these aspects what differences were to be observed between Lollard preaching and contemporary orthodox preaching? For late

---

[1] London reg. FitzJames fol. 27v; for the date see Ussher's transcript, Dublin Trinity College MS 775, fol. 112v; Baker was dead by 1514 when she was defended by Richard Hunne (Wunderli 1982: 209–24 and earlier bibliography there).

[2] An interesting example is Thomas Boughton of Hungerford, who in 1499 commented that "sith the tyme of my first acqueyntaunce with the said heretikes I haue had a great mynde to here sermouns and prechynges of doctours and lerned men of the church. And, as long as they spack the veray woordys of the gospels and the epistles such as I had herd afore in oure Englissh bookys, I herkned wele vnto them and had great delight to here them. But as sone as they began to declare scripture after their doctouris, and brought in other maters, and spack of tythes and offrynges, I was sone wery to here them and had no savour in their woordys, thykyng that it was of their owen makyng for their profight and avauntage" (Salisbury reg. Blythe fol. 74v).

sixteenth- and seventeenth-century puritan sermons and lectures much evidence has been preserved, in the form of diaries, parish ledgers, and memoirs.[3] No such easy source of information is available for the first 150 years of English Protestantism; the material has to be pieced together from odd references in documentary sources and polemical writings, most of them being outspokenly hostile to the activities they note, and from the surviving Lollard sermons.[4] These latter are, fortunately, very numerous; but, whilst they provide ample evidence of the content and style of Lollard instruction, they are unfortunately more reticent about the circumstances of their delivery, intended or actual.[5] But from them, either directly or indirectly by means of scrutiny of the manuscripts in which they occur, the most important material derives.

Before looking at this detail, it is important to notice the centrality of preaching to Wyclifism. This was perhaps apprehended by the first opponents of the movement more quickly than by its initiators: to the latter the written word remained for some time an equal or even a superior mode of communication, whilst as early as spring 1382 the realization by bishops such as Wykeham of Winchester or Buckingham of Lincoln that the spoken word could reach far more widely than the written is shown by their edicts against the new preachers.[6] From then on almost every episcopal and later royal proclamation against the new sect specifically prohibited the preaching of its doctrines and the hearing of its preachers; the early investigations of its adherents concentrated, logically enough, upon the teachers; the counter-measures were directed towards making the activities of these preachers more difficult to pursue.[7] In particular, the rather vague requirements concerning authority to preach at the end of the fourteenth century were gradually clarified and more closely specified. Archbishop Arundel in his *Constitutions*, devised in 1407 and promulgated in 1409, effectively prevented the preaching of anyone other than the benefice holder in his own parish, unless a licence had been individually given by the diocesan bishop; a belated realization that this

---

[3] For material on these see especially Collinson 1975: 181–213; a particularly interesting picture of the parish life, the place of preaching in it, and its interaction with secular activity, is Spufford 1974.

[4] Details about these sources, and their problems, may be found in Hudson 1988: 32–58.

[5] The main examples that I shall use in the essay are, apart from Wyclif's own sermons (ed. 1887–90; abbreviated as Wyclif *Sermones* I–IV), the cycle of 294 English sermons, *English Wycliffite Sermons* (appreviated as *EWS*), a shorter and incomplete collection of English sermons edited Cigman, *Lollard Sermons* (abbreviated as *LS*), and a number of unpublished sermons, English and Latin, details of which will be given as they are quoted.

[6] Kirby 1896–9: II.337–8 concerning a preaching expedition in and near Odiham (Hants.) by Nicholas Hereford, John Aston, Robert Alyngton, Laurence Bedeman and others, preaching errors about the Eucharist and other sacraments; Lincoln reg. Buckingham fols. 236v–44 on the heterodox preaching of William Swinderby in and around Leicester.

[7] For a survey of the material in the early period see Richardson 1936: 1–28; some of the early episcopal activity is summarized in Hudson 1988: 73–81.

precluded the activities of the friars was rectified by a subsequent proclamation – but the very fact that the friars had been overlooked highlights the anxiety that the authorities felt about illicit preaching.[8] In retrospect Arundel's legislation may seem to mark a watershed in Lollard fortunes, but, as will be seen, its effect may actually have confirmed old tendencies rather than initiating a complete change of operation.

Turning to the questions that were raised earlier, my first example may seem to contradict that claim. Joan Baker contrasted the sermons she approved *at home in hur howse* with those she could hear at St. Paul's Cross in London, in the late medieval and early modern periods perhaps the most renowned of preaching sites.[9] But on Sunday 21 November 1406 the Oxford Lollard William Taylor had delivered a sermon there, a sermon which evidently found favor with many in the congregation even if it annoyed the orthodox clerk Richard Alkerton. Alkerton the following day preached at the same place, refuting the arguments that Taylor had put forward. Taylor's sermon survives, though not, unfortunately, Alkerton's reply; the reasons for orthodox outrage are easy enough to perceive.[10] But from the evidence available, although that evidence was provided by a source hostile to Lollardy, it was Alkerton's sermon that provoked the congregation's anger, not Taylor's: Alkerton was seriously insulted by Sir Robert Waterton, the close friend of Henry IV.[11] As late as November 1406 Wyclifite sermons could be delivered publicly, in the heart of London and at its most prestigious pulpit; though the authorization and instigation of sermons there at this early period seems obscure, it seems clear that Taylor's sermon cannot have been private enterprise by the preacher. Other examples of early Lollard sermons from pulpits provided by the established church, even if in less prominent places than St. Paul's Cross, can be readily given: William Thorpe preached in London at St. Martin's Orgar on Corpus Christi day and at St. Benet's on the Sunday after Trinity, some time between 1382 and 1386; John Coryngham used his pulpit in the village of Diddington near Huntingdon to disseminate heresy before his prosecution in March 1384; John Aswardby, vicar of St. Mary's Oxford, argued heretical views in several sermons against the Carmelite Richard Maidstone *in lingua*

---

[8] For Arundel's legislation see Wilkins 1737: III.314–19 and, concerning the exemption of the friars, 324; a detailed analysis of the regulations before this is provided in Spencer 1993: 163–88.

[9] For the later period see MacLure 1958.

[10] Taylor's sermon in Bodleian MS Douce 53 is edited in Hudson 1993, where the background to its preaching and more information about its author's career is also provided. A sermon by Alkerton survives in Oxford, Trinity College MS 42, fols. 56–9, and in English partially in London, British Library MS Additional 37677, fols. 57–61, but this dates from Easter week 1406 and was preached at St. Mary Spitel; see O'Mara 1994: 21–80.

[11] The story is told in Thomas Walsingham's *St. Alban's Chronicle 1406–1420* ed. 1937: 1–2.

materna some time between 1384 and 1392.[12] That the early English sermon cycle was designed for use in a public place, for formal reading, even if that public place cannot be proved to be a church, is suggested by the format and layout of most of the numerous early manuscripts in which it occurs.[13] The use of texts meticulously following the Sarum liturgy could be interpreted as mere uninventive imitation; but no such easy explanation is available for the displaying of the text in a script by the end of the fourteenth century rather old-fashioned in its formality, for its laborious marking of the translation of the lection on its first appearance, interrupted as that often is by exegesis, but no other biblical quotations, and for the sheer size of the books. These features, and others, make the manuscripts suitable for lectern use.[14]

Unorthodox preaching in consecrated places was certainly not stopped by Arundel's legislation. William Taylor himself continued the practice, albeit in less significant places, in the years before his investigations by Bishop Morgan of Worcester and Archbishop Chichele between 1417 and 1423; most notably, he had taken advantage of his friend Thomas Drayton's tenure of the living of Holy Trinity, Bristol, to disseminate heresy from its pulpit and from a preaching cross in the cemetery of St. Augustine's monastery in the town.[15] Robert Hoke, Lollard rector of Braybrooke (Northants.) from 1401 to 1425, certainly used his pulpit to full advantage; Drayton himself moved from Bristol to livings at Staines and then Snave, near Tenterden, in Kent, before being brought for trial.[16]

But it is clear that teaching, if not formal preaching – and the distinction is a hard one to maintain – in private places had begun long before Arundel's legislation restricted the venues for assembly. Wykeham's edict claims that the "Oxford apostles" had made *conventicula*, the first mention of a word that became, along with *scholae*, a particular mark of Lollard practice.[17] To some extent, of course, privacy was imposed by opposition, and the tighter the bishops' net was drawn to catch heretics, the greater the need for secrecy. But

---

12 For the first see *John Lydford's Book* ed. 1974: 109, though the editor's dating needs correction; the second is described by McHardy 1972: 131–3, 143; the third appears in Edden 1987: 113–34.

13 For these, and for details about the presentation of the text, see *EWS* I.124–51, supplemented by II.xxxi–xlvi, lxxi–lxxxii and III.xxvii–xxxvi, lix–lxiii.

14 The contrast with manuscripts of, for instance, John Mirk's *Festial* (see the list in Wakelin 1967: 93–118, supplemented by Fletcher 1980: 514–22) is striking.

15 For this part of the charges against Taylor see Worcester reg. Morgan pp. 33–8; later parts of the process that eventually led to Taylor's burning in 1423 are found in *Chichele Register* (ed. Jacob 1938–47, III.67–9, 160–73; abbreviated as *Chichele reg.*); the difficulties in the detailed chronology of Taylor's career are examined in the introduction to my edition of his sermon.

16 See *Chichele reg.* III.105–12; Drayton's moves appear in Worcester reg. Morgan p. 91 and *Chichele reg.* I.207 and his later trial in the latter III.107–9 – whether he continued in the same way after being given the cure of Herne following the trial (I.227), a living in the gift of the archbishop, is not known.

17 For Wykeham's edict see above n. 6; the meaning of the terms; and the novel use of the latter in regard to heretical groups, is discussed more fully in Hudson 1988: 174–80.

houses had certain positive advantages as compared with churches for the effective preaching of heresy: in particular, whilst audible congregational response to a preacher seems in the medieval church to have been commoner than is the case in mainstream present-day churches, Catholic or Protestant, it was easier in a setting outside the institutional building and outside the liturgical framework to engage a congregation in active involvement with the speaker's utterance. Evidence for what sort of active involvement was desired comes from a curious postscript added to a long sermon found in four manuscripts: this notes that the speaker has no time to make a recapitulation of his headings, but that he will leave a copy of it with his congregation for them to study; they may ask him questions next time he returns, and he asks them to note any arguments used against him by any opponent and to note specially the biblical texts which are used in that refutation.[18] Here, it might be said, we are closer to the study group than to the active preacher and receptive congregation; but the sermon starts with a text, to which it recurs, and continues with occasional reference in traditional form to a listening audience.[19] Though the sermon does not state where it was delivered, the questions and reports that are requested would seem more appropriately taken outside a church.

This particular sermon also highlights the questions of the length of Lollard sermons and the times at which they might be delivered, questions which are not unrelated. The example runs to about 3,000 lines in modern typescript; assuming a measured delivery from its at times rhetorical style, I would estimate that it would take approximately five and a half hours to read out. As such, the Egerton sermon could hardly have been delivered at the customary time during the service of mass, after the reading of the gospel; the postscript also seems to indicate that the discourse was free-standing, at least in regard to the liturgy. The Egerton sermon is unusual in its length; the nearest approximations to it are the "Sermon of Dead Men," intended, as its modern title suggests, for funerals, and the text known as *Of Mynystris in e Chirche*, if that is indeed a sermon and not a commentary.[20] But the typical Lollard sermon, at

18 British Library MS Egerton 2820, fols. 116r–v; I am preparing an edition of this sermon.
19 The text is "Omnis plantacio quam non plantauit Pater meus celestis eradicabitur," Matthew 15.13; this occurs in the Sarum rite within the gospel for the Wednesday in the third week of Lent, but it would seem from the content of the sermon itself that it was not necessarily preached then – if the fact that three of the surviving manuscripts are pocket books, two written by the same scribe, is put together with the speaker's intention to leave the sermon behind him, it seems more likely that this was a discourse that he gave several times to different groups and consequently on different days.
20 For the first see *LS* no. [17], with 1,164 lines in the modern edition, its purpose plain in lines 80ff "to preie deuoutli for e soule of oure deed frende . . . whiche is late passid fro vs"; for the second *EWS* II.328–65, with 1,029 lines (the relation to the main cycle is discussed *EWS* I.49–50). The uncertain boundary between sermons and commentaries is accentuated in Wyclifite cases by the fact that the typical mode of discourse in the former is exegetical, proceeding sentence by sentence, or even phrase by phrase through the lection.

least as that is preserved, was much briefer: the less amply preserved group that is here described as *Lollard Sermons* varies between 206 and 714 lines (though one has an optional extension to the main sermon that would increase the length to 926 lines); the average length of the widely circulated *English Wycliffite Sermons* is probably between 100 and 120 lines.[21] Sermons of this length could readily have been used in a liturgical context, and, from the care with which the appropriate occasion is noted in manuscripts of the latter group, it would certainly be logical to conclude that they were intended for this purpose – even if the liturgy were not within the Church itself.

The issue is, however, clouded by the indications in some Wyclifite sermons that the surviving texts were regarded as model sermons, and that the individual preacher was intended to extend the written text on his own initiative to suit his congregation's aptitude and needs. Wyclif's own sermons include such indications, and they are found in both the vernacular groups just mentioned.[22] The problem is whether the encouragement to improvisation was intended for the single sermon in which it occurs, or whether the directive should be regarded as covering all items within the group. The wording of a Sunday gospel sermon is typically ambiguous: "And mater of is net and brekyng erof ʒyuen men gret mater to speke Godis word, for vertuwes and vices and trew es of e gospel ben mater inow to preche to e peple."[23] The first part of the sentence refers back to the previous exegesis of the story of Peter's fishing expedition (Luke 5.1–11), whilst the second might look to a larger program of pastoral instruction. Such a larger program is found, for instance, in Wyclif's analyses of the ten commandments in ten sermons, interestingly, "ut mandatus sum a quodam devoto layco," or in the very elaborate sequence found in a number of manuscripts where the English long cycle gospel sermons are used as prothemes.[24]

A further complication is the sheer number of sermons provided by Wyclif's own collections and by the main English sermon cycle. It has been argued in regard to the dating of Wyclif's own sermons that no cleric could be expected to preach more than once on a Sunday; but the three groups of sermons usually thought to have been put together after his retirement to Lutterworth provide a

[21] *LS* nos. 7, 2, and 11 and 11a respectively; in *EWS* the sermons for the ferials (III, nos. 123–239) are, with the exception of those in the Lenten season and most notably that for Good Friday (no. 179, 391 lines), very brief, those for the Commune Sanctorum (II, nos. 55–85) on average relatively long, and those in the other three sets (I, nos. 1–54 and E1–55, II, nos. 86–122) between these two.

[22] For instance, Wyclif *Sermones* I.130/30 "Et dilatanda est materia sermonis secundum quod expedit populo audienti"; *LS* 1/377, 3/230, 5/454, 6/309 etc.; *EWS* I nos. 1/67, 2/102, 3/83 etc.

[23] *EWS* I no. 5/68.

[24] Wyclif *Sermones* I nos. 13–22, described at p. 89/22; for the derivative group see briefly *EWS* I.115–23 and much more adequately Spencer 1986: 352–96.

regular two, one on the gospel and one on the epistle, for each Sunday.[25] The vernacular material is even more ample: two sermons for each Sunday, one on the epistle and one on the gospel, plus a set of over a hundred on specified weekday occasions;[26] that these were envisaged as being sequential at least by some is indicated by arrangements of the sermons which intercalate epistle before gospel sermon on each Sunday, or add to this the appropriate weekday sermons after those for each Sunday.[27] A possible alternative interpretation of both Wyclif's and the vernacular's provision would obviously be that both aimed to furnish a corpus of preaching materials from which the individual *true priest* could select at will. I cannot see any means of proving or refuting this, but am not quite sure what evidence would provide final refutation. That the sermons were not to be chosen entirely at random is, however, shown not only by the expectation in both Latin and English that the example selected will correspond to the lection for a specific day; the existence of certain sequences, where an issue taken up in one sermon is pursued in ensuing examples, would also point at the very least to systematic selection.[28]

The evidence concerning time, and indeed place, of preaching is thus puzzling if not conflicting. Certainly, the importance of sermons emerges very clearly, but whether these were to be used in the traditional way, within the liturgical framework and within a church, or whether they were for weekly, and in the case of the vernacular cycle almost daily, reading in extra-ecclesial conventicles is less obvious. The possibility that they were intended for private use by individual sympathizers seems to me less likely, given the layout of the early manuscripts. But in the case of a sect that came under increasing persecution, of course, original intention is likely to have been overridden by practical necessity for concealment. To some of these problems I will return later.

Who preached Lollard sermons, a normally ordained priest or someone else?

---

[25] Mallard 1966: 86–105 at p. 89 etc.; the only failure of matching between Wyclif's Latin set 1, the sermons on the dominical gospels, and set 3, those on the dominical epistles, occurs in the Christmas season (confusingly alluded to in the preface to set 1).

[26] One for each day between Ash Wednesday and the end of Easter week and in the week between Whitsunday and Trinity Sunday, two per week from Advent to Lent and from the end of Easter week to Whitsunday, one per week in the Trinity season, plus one for each rogation day.

[27] See *EWS* I.9–35 for the details of this.

[28] The manuscript that formed Loserth's base text for Wyclif's *Sermones*, Cambridge, Trinity College B.16.2, does not specify the occasion for more than a small handful of sermons; but the close connection between sermon text and gospel or epistle for the day is often revealed in the opening words (e.g. *Sermones* I.43/7, 154/8, 215/4). Occasion is regularly indicated in all manuscripts of *EWS* whose rubrication has been completed (see *EWS* I.126–30). Reference has already been made to the sequence of sermons on the decalogue in Wyclif *Sermones* I nos. 13–22; see also the *De sex iugis* sequence in *Sermones* II nos. 27–8, 31–3. The sequence of English epistle sermons E11–15 deals with each of the "four sects" (pope and papal curia, monastic orders, canons, friars) and uses the provisions of 1 Cor. 13 to castigate all.

Amongst those investigated by the ecclesiastical authorities there are throughout Lollard history a fair number of clergy whose credentials seem not to have
been challenged: William Taylor, Thomas Drayton, Robert Hoke, Richard
Wyche, James Preston, William and Rafe Kent (uncle and nephew), John
Whitehorn, John Lydtister are just a few of those whose careers can to some
extent be traced.[29] Then there are those who claimed, perhaps justly, ordination
but whose claims were doubted by the investigating bishop or by the
subsequent recorder, men such as William Swinderby.[30] Once the alert had
gone out to the bishops to watch for heretical views, ordination might be
achieved by episcopal oversight or even by at least a mild duplicity on the part
of the candidate.[31] The ordination of a peripatetic Lollard such as William
Ramsbury as early as 1389 seems much more dubious; he claimed only to have
been tonsured and given the habit of a priest by a shadowy Thomas Fishburn
before he took up a life of preaching and reciting a curtailed version of the mass
around the villages and small towns of Wiltshire, Somerset, and Dorset.[32] It is
quite clear that in the later years of the movement their evangelists might be
laymen as often as priests: Thomas Man and his wife, who claimed to have
made between 600 and 700 converts in and around London before their
execution in 1518, or the ubiquitous John Hacker, at one point described
as "water-carrier", are typical examples.[33] But this indifference concerning
ordination was not one forced upon the sect by persecution. Wyclif
adumbrated, even if he did not fully develop, the idea of the priesthood of all
believers, an idea that his followers rapidly developed.[34] More importantly for
the present purpose, Wyclif emphasized and his followers loudly echoed the
view that all Christians had an overriding obligation to spread the gospel, and
hence to teach – and the distinction between teaching and preaching was one
consistently dismissed. Hence all need for sacerdotal license from a bishop to
preach was anathema; and the laity was encouraged, in default of proper
activity on the part of the priesthood, to take the initiative in sermonizing.[35]
Around 1400, however, it seems likely that most Lollard preaching, certainly
if done in the church or on consecrated ground, would be done by one who

---

[29] See the details in Hudson 1988; the first four and Whitehorn are more amply documented.

[30] Swinderby is described by Henry Knighton, *Chronicon*, ed. 1889–95, II.189 in 1382 as *quidam sacerdos*, but in Bishop Buckingham's register in the same year as *presbiter se dicens* (Lincoln reg. 12 fol. 236v).

[31] For the case of Peter Payne's ordination by Bishop Hallum of Salisbury in 1412, and the events leading to this, see Hudson 1988: 99–102.

[32] See Hudson 1972: 407–19.

[33] See Foxe ed. 1853–70: IV.208–13, 236, 239–40.

[34] Wyclif *Sermones* III.43/21, and see Hudson 1988: 325–7.

[35] For views on licenses see Wyclif *Sermones* III.75/20, 373/7, 374/12, Purvey's views in *Fasciculi Zizaniorum*, ed. 1858: 404, or those of William White, *ibid.*, pp. 428–9, and further discussion in Hudson 1988: 355–6.

claimed ordination. He might or might not be the holder of the benefice, or the holder's deputy; he might, like the preacher of the long Egerton sermon, be peripatetic. How peripatetic preachers gained access to pulpits or permission for churchyard preaching is often impossible to ascertain: as I have mentioned, William Taylor in 1420 took advantage of his friend Thomas Drayton's benefice in Bristol; William Swinderby allegedly around 1389–90 had used chapels that had fallen into disuse; but how William Thorpe had managed to preach *oruȝ leue grauntid to him* on 17 April 1407 in St. Chad's church in Shrewsbury we do not know.[36] But after the more rigorous provisions of Arundel's *Constitutions*, heterodox preaching in consecrated places was more difficult to arrange and more necessary to conceal.

What was the nature and composition of the congregation? To answer this question adequately would require a complete history of Lollardy, for which this is scarcely the suitable place. Only a few points can be mentioned. The first is that in the early period in some places the congregation was evidently large and illustrious: Swinderby in 1382 claimed to have preached before the mayor of Leicester, and certainly a number of important citizens of the town united to defend him; in Northampton ten years later an aggrieved citizen claimed that the mayor, trying to make the whole town Lollard, had "sent messengers to Oxford and to other places for to hire preachers of Lollardye, to be brought to Northampton to preach there euerie Sunday during Lent last past at the Cross in the churchyarde in the marketplace."[37] Once the need for secrecy became stronger, the majority of any congregation was doubtless already Lollard; extension of the sect continued, but proseletyzing seems to have occurred rather through private conversations, at work, over a meal or on a shared journey, as much as, if not more than, by direct preaching.[38] But the directing of sermons towards a group already converted seems perceptible from the earliest stages: in the long vernacular cycle many Lollard tenets are only tangentially described – there is little attempt to persuade the doubtful or recalcitrant, but rather a series of allusive references to doctrines shared between preacher and listener.[39] This may, of course, support the view that

---

[36] See above p. 135; for Swinderby see *Registrum Johannis Trefnant*, ed. 1916: 236, 249; for Thorpe the modernized version of the [1530] print in Pollard 1903: 121, see now my edition of the earlier manuscript, Oxford Bodleian Library Rawlinson C.208, 1993: 624–31. St. Chad's was a collegiate church. Thorpe was certainly a properly ordained priest, but he had been in trouble for heretical views in London in the 1390s.

[37] Quotation from a seventeenth-century copy of a badly damaged document (Public Record Office, Ancient Petitions SC.8/142/7099), printed by Powell and Trevelyan 1899: 45–50; for the whole episode see Hudson 1988: 78–81.

[38] For these situations see Hudson 1988: 131, 147, 153–7.

[39] For instance, *EWS* I nos. 8/25, 23/57, 32/14; that these and similar allusions *were* understood is shown by the omissions of the scribe of Bodleian MS Don.c.13, who regularly expurgated the sermons of many of their heresies (see Hudson 1971).

the sermons are in the nature of preaching materials rather than finished discourses. A greater difficulty concerns the similarly allusive references to questions of academic debate, most of them irrelevant to any question of orthodoxy or heterodoxy.[40] Here the vernacular sermons seem to be the inheritors of Wyclif's own predilections: though Wyclif describes his sermons in the preface to the Sunday gospel set as *rudes ad populum*, the discussion of matters such as the germination of seed, the properties of light or predication would seem to make them indigestible to any congregation outside the university world.[41]

An obvious question which I have hitherto not addressed is the puzzle in regard to language: a heresy that became typical of the *lay partie* might be expected to use English exclusively for its sermons.[42] Wyclif's use of Latin may be comparable to that of, for instance, Richard FitzRalph: Latin was the language of preservation, but English was the language of delivery.[43] But this divergence is not in the case of Wyclif made plain. More puzzling is the extensive set of sermons written by one of his followers, where again no indication that the preacher should translate them is given.[44] But these, along with other Wyclifite material in Latin (the *florilegia* known as the *Floretum* or in its abbreviated form *Rosarium*, the Apocalypse commentary *Opus Arduum*), presumably derive from a time when the supply of academic preachers was still assured.

This leads on to the question of the content and form of the sermons themselves. Here generalization is more difficult to provide, though a few points, some of which have been incidentally mentioned already, can be made. Almost every Wyclifite sermon is dominated by the text from which it starts, and in almost every case the whole lection for the occasion is used and not just a single verse.[45] The form of only one Lollard sermon is "modern," in the sense of using elaborate subdivisions.[46] Most would have to be classified as "ancient," though this is largely a negative description that covers a wide

---

[40] For example, *EWS* II nos. 59/12, 63 on the properties of seed, 61/29 on thunder, 62/19 on earthly and heavenly relations; none of these passages was expurgated by the scribe mentioned in the previous note.

[41] *Sermones* II.241/9, 380/17, and III.282/30 respectively. It is, of course, possible that the sermons, as they survive, represent revisions of sermons given originally in Oxford before Wyclif left in 1381; for the relation of the vernacular sermons in *EWS* to Wyclif's own see *EWS* III.xcix–cxlviii.

[42] The term is Reginald Pecock's; see Hudson 1988: 57.

[43] For the headings to FitzRalph's sermons which make this plain see Gwynn 1937: 1–57.

[44] For this set see von Nolcken 1986: 233–49.

[45] Even within the widely distributed *EWS* neither feature is invariable: nos. 206, 207, 221, 229, 237, 238 do not contain complete translation, but in every case the lection has been rendered in a sermon earlier in the provision; no. E5 uses only the first verse of the lection.

[46] This is the "Sermon of Dead Men", *LS* pp. 207–40 (on which see the editor's comments on pp. xlviii–li and the more detailed analysis in Spencer 1993: 264–5, 354–8).

variety of constructions. Wyclif's own sermons are often divisible into two parts: an opening exegesis of the lection, followed by an examination of doubts or questions – these may or may not arise from that lection; controversial material may be introduced into either part.[47] Some examples in the long English cycle follow a similar course; but more frequently exegesis of the lection is spread through the whole discourse, and polemical material is briefly interposed alongside this biblical commentary.[48] Commentary is the dominant impression, and it is the conventions of commentary that are followed in the layout of the text.[49] The apparently less popular sermons found in two manuscripts, edited under the title *Lollard Sermons*, are more unpredictable in form: some, like the previous cycle, work steadily through the matters in the lection that invite comment, but others diverge ingeniously after their opening on to more distant matters.[50] The sermon for the second Sunday in Lent uses the story of the woman from the coasts of Tyre and Sidon (Matt. 15.21–8) only in its second half, the whole of the first half being taken up with the implications of the alleged meaning of the name "Tyre" as "hunting"; this leads into an analysis of the activities of the devil as hunter and how these activities may be countered.[51] Neither this sermon, nor the majority of the others in this collection, contains a straightforward translation of the lection.

One of the most striking characteristics of all Wyclifite sermons that survive is the complete absence of stories beyond those in the lection, and occasionally an allusion to another biblical narrative. There are no *fablis, poesies or cronicles*, as Wyclifite preachers would derogatively describe them. The furthest extreme to which this is taken is in the few sermons for feasts of non-biblical saints, where the saint's life is not mentioned and indeed outside the heading the saint is not even named; even sermons for biblical saints restrict themselves rigidly to information from within scripture.[52] The Lollards

---

[47] For sermons that plainly divide in this way see, for instance, *Sermones* I nos. 1, 2, 3.

[48] An example of the first method would be *EWS* I nos. 10, 11, 16, of the second nos. 4, 6, 8.

[49] In particular in the underlining of the words of the lection on their first translation, but not of repeated words or of other biblical texts. The convention is followed in the Wyclifite *Glossed Gospels* and revisions of Rolle's Psalter commentary (for which see Hudson 1988: 247–64).

[50] For the first see, for instance, nos. 1, 3, 4. For some comments on the style of the sermons see Cigman 1988: 69–82 and 1989b: 479–96. Because of fluctuations between these sermons in length, verbal style, and exegetical technique (and even in one or two regards in ideological outlook), the possibility that the collection may not be the work of a single writer, or at least may reflect varying treatment of materials from divergent origins, should perhaps be considered.

[51] Lines 17–397; there is perhaps a distant allusion to the lection in 347, a clearer one in 358–9, but the story does not gain the preacher's main attention until 398 (the sermon ends at 540). Sections of these later 142 lines read like summaries to jog the user's invention, and this is implicit in the last sentence "And us, in is place, a man may touche of ese vertuis more or lasse at God 3yue hym grace, and after at he see e auditorie is disposid."

[52] For instance, *EWS* II nos. 108 for the translation of St. Martin and 110 for the feast of the Seven Brothers; see the sermons nos. 99, 102, 113–14, 116 for various feasts of the Virgin Mary.

associated *fablis, poesies and cronicles* particularly with the sermons of the friars, but the use of extra-scriptural material is, of course, typical of most later medieval vernacular preaching.[53] This distaste for sources other than the Bible is, of course, in accordance with Wyclifite theology. Less readily explicable is the general avoidance of exemplary tales, and of the sort of readily memorable concrete detail that makes handbooks such as the derivatives of the French *Miroir du monde* or *Somme le roi* so much more attractive than their function as confession handbooks might lead the modern reader to expect. The Additional/Rawlinson collection is in this, as in various other respects, atypical: here the analysis of, for instance, the sins is enlivened by details such as "a proude man mai wel be lickned to a tree   at is callid yuy, for iuy ha

is kynde: as long as it ha   hous, wal, or tree, or any   ynge to holde hit bi, it stie   euermore hiere and hiere, til it come to   e hiest place."[54] Wyclif's own sermons, and those of the main vernacular cycle, are unrelievedly plain – indeed, whilst one can understand the theological reasons for this, one might think the plainness evangelistically defeating. What enlivens the writing is rather polemic, a polemic that, at least in the form in which it is preserved and without the preacher's own embellishment, tends towards the shrill and repetitive. But, of course, the contemporary abuses to which that polemic is directed are not to the modern reader the cause of intense concern that they were to the original listeners.

To Wyclif and his followers the purpose of sermons was the instruction of the laity in scriptural history and doctrine, without the glosses of later canon law or of sophisticated interpreters, and without the facile adornment of ear-catching tricks. To their opponents, of course, the purpose and the reality were different: Bishop Trefnant of Hereford in 1391 fulminated against "predicatores . . . verius prevaricatores execrabilis nove secte, Lollardos vulgariter nuncupatos" who, under the guise of sanctity, were running around his diocese, assailing the unity and safety of the ship of Peter by teaching, and worse preaching publicly, matters repugnant to "sacris canonibus et decretis sanctorum patrum"; he described their method

exponendo videlicet sacram scripturam populo ad litteram more moderno aliter quam spiritus sanctus flagitat, ubi vocabula a propriis significacionibus peregrinantur et novas divinari videntur, ubi non sunt iudicanda verba ex sensu quem faciunt sed ex sensu ex quo fiunt, ubi construccio non subjacet legibus Donati, ubi fides remota a racionis

---

[53] For Wyclif's disapproval of this type of preaching see *Sermones* II.57/17, 448/7; III.39/1; for that of his followers, for instance, Arnold ed. 1869–71, III.147/27, 180/4, 274/30, 299/31, 376/14. Extra-scriptural stories are common in Myrc's sermons, and in the collections known as *Jacob's Well*, ed. 1900, the *Northern Homily Cycle*, ed. 1972–84, or the sermons of Robert of Greatham (English version unprinted).

[54] *LS* no. 11A/366ff.; cf. also much of sermons 12 and 13.

argumento sed suis principiis, doctrinis, et dogmatibus publicis et occultis virus scismatum inter clerum et populum ebullire.[55]

Alongside the necessary and largely formulaic expression of episcopal outrage against those who refused to observe normal ecclesiastical proprieties, a few more interesting and particularizing details emerge: that these preachers taught scripture *ad litteram*, that their interpretation was *more moderno* and that they forced words *a propriis significacionibus*. The first of these echoes Wyclif's own concern with the "literal sense" of scripture. But it is important to recognize that by that term Wyclif and his followers meant something rather different from the obvious modern apprehension. Certainly there was stress, a stress that indeed, as Trefnant recognized, was innovatory, on historical and textual context; thus Wyclif, echoed by the English sermons, mocks the opposing fraternal claims of Franciscans and Dominicans to find justification for their own rules concerning footwear in the Gospels – such a claim was manifestly anachronistic in historical terms, and also seized upon an unimportant detail or a plain figure of speech to the exclusion of the intended sense of the passage in which they occurred.[56] But it was acknowledged that some parts of the Bible were figurative: Old Testament writers, even if they used the present or even the past tense, might wittingly or unwittingly be prophesying events to come; the gospel parables declaredly had a didactic moral purpose, and this purpose might be discerned legitimately also in events such as Christ's miracles. Hence Wyclifite sermons include interpretations that we should describe as "allegorical" rather than as "literal": as has been mentioned, biblical place names are interpreted for moralization, the loaves and fishes of the stories of the feeding of the multitudes are understood as food for spiritual hunger and hence as the various parts of the Bible, the parables are explored beyond the interpretation provided in the Gospels for current lessons.[57] All of this is obviously traditional. Where Trefnant would part company with the writers of these sermons is where the Wyclifites hold up the mirror of scripture to the contemporary ecclesiastical world, and demand where in scripture is to be found the *grounding* for institutions of the papacy, the monks, friars or for the temporalities with which all these are maintained, or for practices such as oral confession, honor of images, pilgrimages, obligatory tithes, and so forth. Basically, the issue was one of authority: was scripture the sole legitimating law, and, even if so, who was a proper interpreter of it?

[55] *Trefnant reg.* ed. 1916: 232; the chronology at this part of the register is not entirely clear, but the sidenote dating of 1389 probably needs modification.
[56] Wyclif *Sermones* I.24/4, 53/17; *EWS* I no. 29/74. The influence of Wyclif in forcing his opponents into a more historical approach to doctrine, reflected in the work of Netter in contrast to the ahistoricism of Woodford, has still to be fully appreciated.
[57] For instances of these see *EWS* I nos. 12/30ff., 7/66ff., 38/69ff.

So sermons were at the heart of Wyclifism and of the orthodox opposition to that sect. Not only because it was by means of sermons that the sect gained many if not most of its adherents, but because the nature of the sect's preaching, scriptural, literal, exegetical, forced its claims concerning authority, explicitly and implicitly, to the fore. Arundel's *Constitutions* were directed at two targets, the university world and the world of the ordinary parishes; in regard to the latter he singled out two objects for control: biblical translation into the vernacular and preaching. Modern summary has concentrated on the former, but Arundel himself would probably have regarded the second as the more crucial. The Wyclifite Bible was, apart from a few glosses in a very few manuscripts, uncontroversial in its renderings; it was dangerous for the same reason as preaching, as a route towards unauthorized interpretation. Control of interpretation was at the heart of the stringent licensing of preaching. And interpretation was not just that of the preacher: it rested with the individual listener. Arundel could foresee the situation described by the captive Jesuit William Weston in 1588, when he saw a puritan assembly: "Each of them had his own bible, and sedulously turned the pages and looked up the texts cited by the preachers, discussing the passages among themselves to see whether they had quoted them to the point, and accurately, and in harmony with their tenets."[58]

REFERENCES

Arnold, Thomas, ed. 1869–71 *Select English Works of Wyclif*. 3 vols. Oxford: Clarendon Press

Brandeis, Arthur, ed. 1900 *Jacob's Well*. Early English Text Society, O.S. 115. London.

Capes, William W., ed. 1916 *Registrum Johannis Trefnant, episcopi Herefordensis*. London: Canterbury and York Society.

Cigman, Gloria 1988 The Preacher as Performer: Lollard Sermons as Imaginative Discourse. *Journal of Literature and Theology* 2: 69–82.

    1989a *Lollard Sermons*. Early English Text Society, O.S 294. London.

    1989b *Luceat Lux Vestra*: The Lollard Preacher as Truth and Light. *Review of English Studies* n.s. 40: 479–96.

Collinson, Patrick 1975 Lectures by Combination: Structures and Characteristics of Church Life in 17th-Century England. *Bulletin of the Institute of Historical Research* 48: 182–213.

Edden, Valerie 1987 The Debate between Richard Maidstone and the Lollard Ashwardby (ca. 1390). *Carmelus* 34: 113–34.

Fletcher, Alan J. 1980 Unnoticed Manuscripts from John Mirk's *Festial*. *Speculum* 55: 514–22.

---

[58] Quoted Spufford 1974: 263.

Foxe, John 1853–70 *The Acts and Monuments*. Ed. Stephen R. Cattley and Josiah Pratt. 8 vols. in 16. London: Seeley and Burnside.

Gwynn, Aubrey 1937 The Sermon Diary of Richard FitzRalph, Archbishop of Armagh. *Proceedings of the Royal Irish Academy* 44C: 1–57.

Hudson, Anne 1971 The Expurgation of a Lollard Sermon-Cycle. *Journal of Theological Studies* n.s. 22: 435–42. Repr. in her *Lollards and their Books*, 201–15. London: Hambledon Press, 1985.

1972 A Lollard Mass. *Journal of Theological Studies* n.s. 23: 407–19. Repr. in her *Lollards and their Books*, 111–23. London: Hambledon Press, 1985.

1988 *The Premature Reformation: Wycliffite Texts and Lollard History*. Oxford: Clarendon Press; New York: Oxford University Press.

1993 *Two Wycliffite Texts*. Early English Text Society, O.S. London.

Hudson, Anne, and Gradon, Pamela, eds. 1983– *English Wycliffite Sermons*. 3 vols. to date. Oxford: Clarendon Press.

Jacob, Ernest F., ed. 1938–47 *The Register of Henry Chichele, Archbishop of Canterbury, 1414–1443*. 4 vols. Oxford: Clarendon Press.

Kirby, Thomas F., ed. 1896–9 *Wykeham's Register*. 2 vols. Hampshire Record Society. London: Simpkin & Co.

Knighton, Henry *Chronicon*. Ed. Joseph Rawson Lumby, 1889–95. 2 vols. Rolls Series. London: HM Stationery Office.

Lydford, John *John Lydford's Book*. Ed. Dorothy M. Owen, 1974. Devon and Cornwall Record Society 20. London: HM Stationery Office.

McHardy, A. K. 1972 Bishop Buckingham and the Lollards of Lincoln Diocese. In D. Baker, ed., *Schism, Heresy and Religious Protest*, 131–45. Studies in Church History 9. Cambridge: Cambridge University Press.

MacLure, Millar 1958 *The Paul's Cross Sermons 1534–1642*. Toronto: University of Toronto Press.

Mallard, William 1966 Dating the *Sermones Quadraginta* of John Wyclif. *Medievalia et humanistica* 17: 86–105.

Nevanlinna, Saara, ed. 1972–84 *The Northern Homily Cycle*. 3 vols. Mémoires de la Société Néophilologique de Helsinki 38, 41, 43. Helsinki: Société Néophilologique.

Nolcken, Christina von 1986 An Unremarked Group of Wycliffite Sermons in Latin. *Modern Philology* 83: 233–49.

O'Mara, Veronica 1994 *A Study and Edition of Selected Middle English Sermons*. Leeds Texts and Monographs n.s. 13. Leeds.

Pollard, Alfred W. 1903 *Fifteenth Century Prose and Verse*. Westminster: A. Constable.

Powell, Edgar and Trevelyan, George M. 1899 *The Peasants' Rising and the Lollards*. London and New York: Longmans, Green.

Richardson, H. G. 1936 Heresy and the Lay Power Under Richard II. *English Historical Review* 51: 1–28.

Shirley, Walter W., ed. 1858 *Fasciculi Zizaniorum magistri Johannis Wyclif*. Rolls Series. London: Longman, Brown, Green, Longmans, & Roberts.

Spencer, Helen L. 1986 The Fortunes of a Lollard Sermon-Cycle in the Later Fifteenth Century. *Mediaeval Studies* 48: 352–96.

1993 *English Preaching in the Late Middle Ages*. Oxford: Clarendon Press.

Spufford, Margaret 1974 *Contrasting Communities: English Villagers in the Sixteenth and Seventeenth Centuries*. London and New York: Cambridge University Press.

Wakelin, Martyn R. 1967 The Manuscripts of John Mirk's *Festial*. *Leeds Studies in English* n.s. 1: 93–118.

Walsingham, Thomas *St. Alban's Chronicle 1406–1420*. Ed. Vivian H. Galbraith, 1937. Oxford: Clarendon Press.

Wilkins, David, ed. 1737 *Concilia Magnae Britanniae et Hiberniae*. 4 vols. London: R. Gosling.

Wyclif, John *Iohannis Wyclif Sermones*. Ed. Johann Loserth, 1887–90. 4 vols. Wyclif Society. London: Trübner.

Wunderli, Richard 1982 Pre-Reformation London Summoners and the Murder of Richard Hunne. *Journal of Ecclesiastical History* 33: 209–24.

Note: the paper here was completed in 1991, and is printed here with only minor modifications; a full account of material published since that date has not been possible.

Part II

Women's religious aspirations

7 Repression or collaboration? The case of Elisabeth and Ekbert of Schönau

Anne L. Clark

Misogyny may be seen as one of the more subtle ideologies of otherness that undergird institutional repression or exclusion in medieval culture. After all, there are no treatises *Contra Mulieres* (that I know of), as there are *Contra Hereticos* or *Contra Judaeos*, although certainly much monastic and clerical vituperation against marriage, later medical writings about female anatomy, and much secular love literature are marked by perspectives in which women are treated as an undifferentiated category of creatures who are naturally inferior to men.[1] Instead of a demonization of the female sex (comparable to the demonization of the Jews in late medieval culture), women were often denigrated as the lower rank of any number of significant hierarchies.[2] But hierarchy implies a continuum of value, rather than complete otherness and disjunction. And although hierarchy is crucial to the way most medieval Christians articulated their views of reality, it also lends itself to another favorite Christian theme for meditation, that of paradox and reversal. The treasured beliefs that God scatters the proud and exalts the lowly (Luke 1.51–2), uses the humble to put down the mighty, the fool to receive revelation (2 Cor. 11), or social outcasts and children to recognize the truth that their learned religious leaders ignore (Matt. 21.14–17), allow for the possibility of a certain disruption of the ordered ranks of hierarchy.[3]

The fact that one finds images of disrupted gender hierarchy does not mean, however, that misogyny was not real, and that women did not live in

In addition to acknowledging the comments offered by the conference participants, I would also like to thank Alfred Andrea, Luther Martin, Mary Martin McLaughlin, Robert Somerville, and Kevin Trainor, who read earlier versions of this paper.

[1] See, e.g., the remarks of a fourteenth-century commentator on the pseudo-Albertus *De Secretis Mulierum*, quoted in Thorndike 1955: 430. For the prevalence of misogyny in medieval religious and secular literature, see Bloch 1987: 1–24.

[2] For the development of a Christian view of Jews as "mysterious and incomprehensible, alienated and demonized," see Funkenstein 1971: 373–82, esp. 380. Cf. Cohen 1982: 19–32 for a challenge to Funkenstein's dating of this development.

[3] There are many striking examples in late medieval spiritual writings that evoke a subversion of gender hierarchy. For Hildegard of Bingen, see Newman 1985: 174; for Elisabeth and Ekbert of Schönau, see below n. 47; for Catherine of Siena and Raymond of Capua, see Scott 1992: 45.

circumstances constrained by the limited social, economic, and religious roles deemed appropriate for them.[4] Rather, my point is to address the complexity of the relationships between men and women, and, specifically, the effect of misogyny on the inclination of women to express in writing their religious experience. To conclude simply from an observation of medieval culture that "women were repressed" fails to acknowledge that women strove to shape their own lives and make them meaningful. In seeing women only as *objects* of repression rather than also as acting *subjects*, we also limit our understanding of the dynamics of exclusion by not acknowledging the extent to which culture is created in the interaction between groups and between individuals. Thus an attempt to understand repression must involve an examination of how the "repressed" group actually related to the dominant group; for example, in the case of women, how particular women absorbed, resisted, ignored, or transmuted the dominant ideology and how this very behavior on the part of women was itself part of medieval culture.[5] As Joan Scott has observed, power is not consolidated in a unified, coherent, and centralized force; rather, it is dispersed in the dynamics of individual, unequal relationships.[6] With this view in mind, I will focus on the relationship between Elisabeth and Ekbert of Schönau, a sister and brother, whose interactions can be traced in the texts of visionary experiences ascribed to Elisabeth.

Elisabeth and Ekbert came from a well-established family in the Rhineland, apparently with connections to the family of Count Rupert of Laurenburg.[7] Rupert's father had founded the cloister of Schönau in 1114 as a Benedictine priory dependent on the abbey of Schaffhausen in Swabia.[8] Its foundation in connection with Schaffhausen established Schönau as part of the Hirsau movement, a movement of monastic reform that dominated German Benedictine life from about 1080 to 1150. Two aspects of the Hirsau network are particularly important here: the frequent establishment of nuns' cloisters in conjunction with those for monks and the ties maintained between these monasteries and local bishops and lay nobles.[9] Elisabeth, who came to Schönau at the age of twelve,

---

4 For example, see in Coakley 1991b: 458–9 and Coakley 1991a: 236–40 the important reflections on how role reversal in gendered relationships may not ultimately alter the established, institutionalized power of men.

5 A similar concern can be seen in Katherine Gill's essay in this volume, in which legislation for women's communities (that is, the prescriptions often coming from male authorities) is explored within the context of how women actually responded to, incorporated, or rejected these prescriptions.

6 Scott 1988: 42.

7 Köster 1965: 18–20.

8 Rupert himself converted the priory into an independent monastery in 1125 or 1126, and soon thereafter the nuns' cloister was added. See Becker 1965: 80–1 and Wilhelm Günther, *Codex Diplomaticus Rheno-Mosellanus*, I (Coblenz: B. Heriot, 1822), 231 n. 2.

9 Küsters 1985: 142–55, 73–5. Küsters also traces other patterns of women's affiliation with the Hirsau monasteries.

was nourished in an environment that had a self-conscious commitment to spiritual renewal and to women's monastic life as part of that reform. Elisabeth's own concerns for religious renewal, in which wider issues of ecclesiastical morality came to the fore, can be seen, for example, in her letters to Archbishop Hillin of Trier.[10] Her letters of admonition and advice, even on negotiating the deeply troubling developments of the papal schism of 1159, not only show that Elisabeth considered Hillin's episcopal office a mouthpiece for her own pronouncements about the state of the Church, but they also suggest that the alignment between monasteries and local bishops and lay patrons characteristic of the Hirsau movement may have encouraged her sense of connection to the larger political controversies of her day.

Elisabeth's religious concerns were articulated in her descriptions of her visionary experiences, which began in 1152 when she was twenty-three years old.[11] Three years later, her brother Ekbert entered the community at Schönau, despite his well-placed connections (for example, his relationship with Rainald of Dassel) and ostensible preparation for a life of ecclesiastical promotion.[12] From this point on, he became Elisabeth's secretary: she dictated to him the contents of her visions and he "investigated" her claims, recorded her messages, and led her to consider subjects she might never have turned to herself. The result of this "collaboration" was the production of three chronologically arranged diaries of visionary experience, a work of moral exhortation entitled *Liber viarum Dei*, a collection of revelations about the martyrdom of St. Ursula and her 11,000 virgin companions, a brief series of visions about the bodily assumption of Mary, and about a dozen extant letters. The texts circulated in England, France, and Germany, and by the end of the fifteenth century, some had been translated into Anglo-Norman, Provençal, German, and Icelandic. There are 145 known manuscripts transmitting these works, 45 of which contain collections of these texts, while the remainder transmit individual works or fragments.[13]

---

[10] The letters to Hillin are found in *Die Visionen der hl. Elisabeth und die Schriften der Aebte Ekbert und Emecho von Schönau*, ed. F. W. E. Roth (Brünn: Verlag der Studien aus dem Benedictiner- und Cistercienser Orden, 1884) (hereafter cited as *Visionen*), 122, 140–1.

[11] *Visionen* 1.

[12] For Ekbert's relationship with Rainald, see his letters to Rainald in *PL* CXCV.12–14, and *Visionen* 311–17. For the Parisian education of German canons in preparation for ecclesiastical promotion, see Barrow 1989: 126–8. For the surprise of Ekbert's colleagues at his monastic conversion, see Emecho of Schönau, *Vita Eckeberti*, ed. S. Widmann, *Neues Archiv* 11 (1886): 450.

[13] The manuscripts are catalogued in Köster 1951: 243–315, and Köster 1952: 114–19. To this list should be added Cologne, Stadtarchiv MS GB 8° 60; Cologne, Stadtarchiv MS W133; and Troyes, Bibliothèque Municipale MS 946; +Trier, St. Eucharius-Matthias Abbey MS 148 (D56); and +Trier, St. Eucharius-Matthias Abbey MS 524 (I66). From this list should be deleted Trier, Stadtbibliothek 646/869 8°, a manuscript in which letters of Hildegard of Bingen are ascribed to Elisabeth.

Throughout her adult life, Elisabeth sought an outlet for her spiritual tension by confiding her thoughts to her fellow nuns and her brother. She and Ekbert shared a sense of the importance of her visions, but decided not to publish them during her lifetime.[14] When Elisabeth began to understand her experiences as having a pedagogical significance for the entire Christian world, she moved beyond this circle of confidants to allow her abbot Hildelin access to her visions. Hildelin initially saw himself as the primary medium for publishing the content of Elisabeth's revelations; he preached her most provocative vision despite her objections, but then lost exclusive control of the material when someone else sent out letters announcing the same message.[15] With Ekbert's move to Schönau, Hildelin institutionalized the relationship between Elisabeth and Ekbert by ordering their mutual cooperation in creating the literary records of Elisabeth's visions. Ekbert then became a filter through which all of Elisabeth's discourse passed and he became a shaper of that discourse by his investigations. Elisabeth seems to have been fairly confident in her brother's intentions and judgments, yet she still strove to retain some control over the public version of her inner experience.[16]

The bare fact of this literary relationship is a phenomenon comparable to the circumstances of many medieval women religious writers. Hildegard of Bingen, Angela of Foligno, and Margery Kempe are examples of women who – to varying degrees – engaged the services of men in their efforts to produce texts recording their religious experiences.[17] These collaborative relationships were always marked by questions of authority which were inextricably linked to the fact that women were not associated with writing.[18] The institutional correlate of this negative association was that the educational opportunities for women were much more restricted than those for men, particularly with the development of universities and the movement of higher education out of the cloister. The ideological correlate is the general view of women as inferior to men by nature. As an appropriate punishment for Eve's transgressions, women were viewed as properly subordinated to men. Women were associated with body or the animal, irrational part of the soul, and this suggested women's

[14] *Visionen* 38.
[15] Elisabeth recounts this event and its repercussions in a letter to Hildegard of Bingen, *Visionen* 70–4.
[16] For example, despite the arrangement that Elisabeth was to tell Ekbert everything that she has learned, she explicitly asserts that she has not announced all her visions. *Visionen* 22, 26–7.
[17] There are also examples of literary collaboration between women: Umtilà of Faenza dictated her sermons to a female disciple and some of the texts issuing from the convent of Helfta in the thirteenth century were collaborative compositions. For an examination of some collaborative works and the possibility of uncovering a substratum of female mystical experience beneath the hagiographical overlays, see Peters 1988.
[18] See Johnson 1991: 820–38.

intellectual inferiority to men, greater sexual appetite, and greater vulnerability to demonic suggestion.[19]

The general aspects of the cultural subordination of women to men can be seen in the concrete details of the lives of Elisabeth and Ekbert. Ekbert's piety reveals his absorption of the association of femaleness with sensuality. Commenting on Ecclesiasticus 42.14 ("Better indeed is the iniquity of a man than a woman who does good"), Ekbert offers an allegorical interpretation that links male with spirit, and female with flesh:

Wisdom is called that sense by which [the soul] is lifted up to contemplate celestial things, to ponder eternal life, the angels, and that creator of all things. That sense is called "spirit" and "man" of the soul. Prudence is that sense by which we think about those things which are necessary to the flesh – food, drink, and clothing. This is called "sensuality" and "woman." It is, moreover, called "woman" according to that analogy in which woman is given for the assistance of man, and with the result that she is ruled by him.[20]

Furthermore, Elisabeth lived in a women's community that was governed both administratively and liturgically by a man, the abbot Hildelin, to whom she also confessed her personal sins. Her education was limited to her reading knowledge of Latin gained in order to participate in the monastic divine office, whereas Ekbert had traveled abroad to study philosophy at one of the most exciting university cities of the day. Ekbert was ordained and could celebrate the Eucharistic mysteries that were central to Elisabeth's piety.

The dynamics of misogyny are also revealed in Elisabeth's relationships to Ekbert, to Hildelin, to ecclesiastical authorities, and to the public at large. She feared that the world would receive her words as *muliebria figmenta*.[21] Some unnamed churchmen suggested that she was deluded by the devil.[22] Her abbot insisted on publishing what she wished to keep private. Ekbert, as "the more learned one," sought to channel her inner life towards issues that were of particular interest to him. And yet the existence of the corpus of visionary writings itself suggests that the religious expression of this woman was not totally repressed. Elisabeth was manipulated by some and dismissed by others, but she nevertheless articulated her experience and her meditations upon it, and the wide dissemination of manuscripts suggests that the literary versions of

---

[19] For the development of these views within exegetical and moral treatises of early and medieval Christian authors, see d'Alverny 1977, and Bloch 1991: 37–46.
[20] "Sapientia dicitur ille sensus quo elevatur ad contemplanda celestia, de eterna vita cogitanda, de angelis, de ipso creatore omnium. Iste sensus dicitur spiritus et vir anime. Prudentia est ille sensus quo cogitamus ea que carni necessaria sunt, in cibo et potu et vestitu. Hic dicitur sensualitas et mulier. Dicitur autem mulier secundum hanc similitudinem quod mulier data est in adiutorium viro, et ut ab ipso regatur" (*Sermones per annum*, Trier, Stadtbibliothek MS 229/1397 8°, fol. 111r).
[21] *Visionen* 2.
[22] *Visionen* 72.

these expressions were widely read.[23] The question remains then about the potential discrepancy between Elisabeth's oral expression of her religious vision and the literary documents that purport to record it.

Although Ekbert and the nuns of Schönau recorded Elisabeth's pronouncements almost from the beginning of her visionary episodes, it was not until sometime after 1159, at least seven years after she began discussing these experiences, that the first collection of her visions was published.[24] Intervening between the beginning of Elisabeth's announcements and the publication of texts recording them is an event of extreme importance in her life: the entry of Ekbert into the community at Schönau in 1155. It was Ekbert who compiled the material recorded by himself and the Schönau nuns into the texts as they have been preserved. Ekbert described his role in an expanded introduction to the first visionary diary:

> Since therefore all the things which took place concerning her appeared to pertain to the glory of God and the edification of the faithful, they were for the most part transcribed in writing in the present little book according to her narration in which she expounded each thing to one of her brothers from the order of clerics whom she knew better than the others. Although she had hidden many things from questioners because she was very timid and most humble in spirit, she was forced by the order of the abbot and for the sake of love and kinship to explain intimately in detail all things to that one who was diligently investigating everything and desirous of handing it all down to posterity.[25]

In the final version of the collection, which was completed at least a year after Elisabeth's death, Ekbert further expanded this introduction to include his explicit identification of himself as the investigating cleric. He also acknowledged that sometimes Elisabeth dictated her revelations in German, which he translated into Latin, "adding nothing from my own presumption, seeking nothing of human favor nor earthly advantage, with God as my witness to whom all things are exposed and open" (cf. Heb. 4.13).[26]

Ekbert's description of his activity bears further scrutiny. First, his insistence that he wrote everything according to Elisabeth's narration should not be taken

---

[23] For other evidence of the popularity of Elisabeth's works, see Clark 1992: 25, 34, 37, 48–9.

[24] The last event recorded in the earliest collection of texts took place on 25 March 1159. The first outside evidence for the existence of a collection is Ekbert's letter (1164/5, before Elisabeth's death) to Reinhard of Reinhausen (*Visionen* 319).

[25] "Quoniam igitur omnia, que circa ipsam gesta sunt, ad gloriam dei et ad edificationem fidelium pertinere visa sunt, in presenti libello ex magna parte conscripta sunt iuxta narrationem ipsius, qua uni ex fratribus suis de ordine clericorum, quem pre ceteris familiarem habebat singula exposuit. Cum enim ab inquirentibus multa occultaret, eo quod esset timorata valde et humillima spiritu, huic diligenter omnia investiganti et memorie ea tradere cupienti germanitatis et dilectionis gratia, et abbatis iussione cuncta familiariter enarrare coacta" (*Visionen* 2). Roth's edition does not distinguish between the various redactions of the texts, so the three versions of this introduction are represented only by the latest, longest version.

[26] " . . . prout expressius potui, nihil mea presumptione adiungens, nihil favoris humani, nihil terreni commodi querens, testis mihi deus, cui nuda et aperta sunt omnia" (*Visionen* 1).

for granted. There was authoritative precedent for admitting that one was deliberately not transcribing a story as it was originally narrated, as seen, for example, in the introduction to his *Dialogi de miraculis*, where Gregory the Great distinguishes between the stories in which he gives *sensum solummodo* and those in which he gives *verba cum sensu*.[27] Ekbert chose to emphasize that Elisabeth's narration had been preserved, even when he mediated the language of her narration through translation.[28] His concluding oath of innocence suggests that he was responding to the suspicion that he had had a more active role in creating these records.[29]

Ekbert also acknowledged that Elisabeth's narrations had "for the most part" (*ex magna parte*) been captured in writing for posterity. This may be a some-what muted reference to what he describes elsewhere as his failure to record everything related to Elisabeth's visionary life. In a letter to Reinhard of Reinhausen, Ekbert gives three reasons for the incomplete records: his other obligations, the scarcity of parchment, and the negative reactions of some people who have heard about Elisabeth.[30] Ekbert's biographer goes even further and praises Ekbert's deliberate suppression of certain parts of Elisabeth's experience: "Diligently investigating all the marvels which our Lord worked with her, he put into writing those things that he saw to be appropriate for the use of the faithful, but those things that he knew would not profit the readers, he totally concealed."[31] Thus the visionary texts as they survive include only the material that Ekbert thought was fit for public consumption.

By comparing the various redactions of the visionary collections, one can get some sense of Ekbert's suppression of questionable texts. Elisabeth's unfulfilled prophecy of apocalyptic punishment upon an erring Christendom, an impolitic vision criticizing the tepid veneration of a coveted relic at the Premonstratensian cloister of Ilbenstadt, and a brief warning to future scribes copying the *Liber viarum Dei*, appear in early versions of the collection and are later suppressed.[32] But these are texts that Ekbert had initially included and then rejected. It is unclear what kinds of material and how much of it he may have never allowed into his collection. In addition to these suppressions, minor editorial revisions can also be seen in his refinement of the later versions of the

---

[27] Grégoire le Grand, *Dialogues: Texte critique, notes, et traduction*, ed. Adalbert de Vogüé, trans. Paul Antin, Sources Chrétiennes, no. 260 (Paris: Les Editions du Cerf, 1980), 16, 18.

[28] No original German records are extant.

[29] Cf. a similar assertion by Burchard of Worms in his preface to his *Decretum*, *PL* CXL.540, which did not keep him from extensive tampering with his sources.

[30] *Visionen* 318.

[31] "Qui universa magnalia, que dominus noster cum ipsa operatus est, diligenter perscrutans, ea que fidelium utilitati congruere videbat, conscripsit, ea vero, que legentibus non prodesse sciebat, omnino reticuit" (Emecho, *Vita Eckeberti*, 448–9).

[32] Köster 1952: 95–7.

collection. And yet, despite his total control over the publication of Elisabeth's visions after her death, remarkably little suppression and revision can be traced from the earliest to the latest version.[33]

This suppression of "inappropriate" material can be seen as a clear case of the repression of a woman's religious expression by a man whose authority over her was made possible by an ideology of female inferiority and by social structures that supported male dominance. But their relationship was even more complex than this, and correspondingly, the composition of the visionary texts was not as simple as a straightforward dictation that was censored in parts. There are three problems within the corpus of visionary texts that I believe reveal further dynamics of this collaborative relationship. These are: the shift in subject and genre after Ekbert's move to Schönau; the publication of potentially misunderstood texts; and what I would call the "negotiation of misunderstanding."

The shift in subject and genre

The corpus of Elisabeth's visionary work can be clearly divided between the texts that record her experience before August 1155, and those that record later material. This is the point at which Ekbert established his permanent residence at Schönau and undertook the role of investigating and recording for posterity the marvelous acts of God manifested in the life of his sister. The first visionary diary and the first version of the second diary contain earlier material.[34] The continuation of the second diary, the third diary, *Liber viarum Dei*, the revelations about the martyrdom of Ursula, and the revelations about the bodily assumption of Mary all record Elisabeth's announcements from the period after Ekbert's arrival.

While all the visionary texts share the same basic focus – the recording of Elisabeth's descriptions of what she saw and heard in her ecstatic trances – the style, content, and genre of text change after Ekbert's arrival. The earliest material focuses primarily on the person of Elisabeth and her inner experience. She describes the physical and emotional qualities of her various experiences, the content of the visions and auditions, and her reactions to them. The content of her visions is closely related to the annual liturgical calendar as well as the daily schedule of worship. It is clear that Elisabeth's participation in the regular liturgical life of her community provided the basis for her meditation on questions of her relationship to God, the saints, and the world

---

[33] Clark 1992: 46–8.

[34] The original version of the second visionary diary corresponds to *Liber visionum secundus*, chapters 1–18 (*Visionen* 40–8), although the chapters often do not follow the sequence found in this edition.

beyond her own, and this meditation is reflected in her descriptions of her visions.

In contrast, the actual quality of Elisabeth's experiences receives less attention in the later records. Her physical and mental states and the nature of her ecstatic experience are no longer recorded in much detail. Instead, the content of what she sees and hears predominates. Furthermore, Elisabeth is guided by Ekbert to explore specific questions once she has established contact with her celestial interlocutors. Thus her attention is directed to subjects other than those that naturally preoccupied her and found their way into her visionary announcements. The later works include questions such as how Dionysius the Areopagite could be correct in identifying the Seraphim, Cherabim, and Thrones with beings who did not know of Christ's work of human redemption. These and other questions proposed in these visions seem to have originated in the world of scholarly study and the examination of contradictory texts, not in the world of the daily round of the divine office and the veneration of saints that is so evident in the records of the earlier period.

In its most extreme form, this "investigatory" role of Ekbert led to the production of a different type of text. After Ekbert joined the monastery, most of the visions were recorded in thematic collections that were often, at least in part, inspired by the posing of particular questions to Elisabeth. For example, *Visio de resurrectione beate virginis Marie* begins with Elisabeth's description of how these visions were initiated:

Then, just as I had been forewarned by one of our elders, I asked her [i.e., Mary], saying: My lady, may it be pleasing to your kindness to deign to settle this for us, whether you were assumed into heaven in spirit only or also in body. I was mentioning this because, as they say, writing on this in the books of the Fathers is still met with doubt.[35]

The text that follows records a series of pronouncements by Elisabeth over the course of two and a half years in which she finally affirms that she has learned from Mary and her angelic guide that the Virgin was in fact corporeally raised into heaven forty days after her death. Ekbert had led Elisabeth squarely into the midst of this theological controversy, and had attempted to use her to answer a question about which scripture was silent and patristic writers disagreed.[36] This perception of the inadequacy of patristic tradition and the need

---

[35] "Tunc, sicut ab uno ex senioribus nostris premonita fueram, rogavi illam dicens: Domina mea placeat benignitati tue, ut de hoc certificare nos digneris, utrum solo spiritu assumpta sis in celum, an etiam carne. Hoc autem idcirco dicebam, quia ut aiunt, de hoc dubie in libris patrum scriptum invenitur" (*Visionen* 53).

[36] Peter Abelard had suggested that what was unknown to the early Fathers about this issue could be revealed to later generations: "potuit contingere, ut quod tempore Hieronymi latuit incertum, postmodum relevante Spiritu fieret manifestum" (Peter Abelard, *Sermo in assumptione beate Mariae, PL* CLXXVIII.543). For a discussion of Abelard's views on the Assumption, see Graef 1963: 233–4.

to supplement it fits well into what Edward Peters has described as the commonplace twelfth-century concern about deviating from the Fathers.[37]

The fact that Ekbert provided the impetus for the production of the text about Mary's corporeal resurrection does not mean that Elisabeth's role was simply one of passive submission. Her immediate response to his request is that Mary will reveal nothing to her for at least one year. She appears to hesitate when she senses that she is being used to resolve such a controversial problem. She creates a temporal space for herself, resisting pressure to make an immediate announcement. Having given herself time for further meditation on this issue, she later reaches the point where she literally *sees* the bodily assumption of Mary as a divinely revealed truth. Moreover, in this process, Elisabeth never seems to have become totally reliant upon the promptings of Ekbert. In the course of her visionary pronouncements, she revealed that the Church was incorrect in its present celebration of the feast of the Assumption: the correct date for the observance was 23 September, not the traditional date of 15 August. This news – not solicited by any recorded question from Ekbert and unprecedented in earlier discussions of Mary's assumption – seems unlikely to have been part of any preparation Elisabeth would have received from Ekbert regarding doubts found in patristic writing.

A somewhat more complex case of Ekbert's potential influence can be seen in Elisabeth's interest in the Cathars. She probably learned about the activities of Cathars in the Rhineland at least in part from Ekbert – he had been interested in the spread of this group before he came to Schönau.[38] But despite her contact with his views on the Cathars, her pronouncements about this group remain decidedly different from his. For example, they both addressed the alleged Cathar restriction of marriage to people who are virgins at the time of the nuptials. In his *Sermones contra Catharos*, Ekbert methodically argues from scripture about the remarriage of widows, and cites testimony from Augustine and Jerome against the Cathar prooftext of John Chrysostom.[39] In contrast, in the *Liber viarum Dei*, Elisabeth ignores the question of remarriage of widows, which was not the main issue of debate in any case. Instead, she announces the straightforward remarks of her angelic informant: "When such a marriage is possible, it is pleasing to the Lord." This response is qualified by a wry observation: "But it is very rare for such a thing to happen." And a final

---

[37] See Edward Peters, this volume. Cf. Elisabeth's reference to Origen as an example of someone whose excessive fervor in exploring the profundities of scripture got him into trouble, *Visionen* 62–3. Cf. also Lerner 1992. Both Peters and Lerner discuss the perceived limitations of the traditional body of exegetical knowledge and strategies for negotiating these limitations. Elisabeth's works, as well as the works of numerous other women visionaries of the twelfth to fifteenth centuries, offer rich sources for expanding these discussions beyond the question of scriptural exegesis *per se* to the larger issue of theological innovation in general.

[38] Ekbert, *Sermones contra Catharos*, PL CXCV.13–14; Emecho, *Vita Eckeberti* 452–3.

[39] Ekbert, *Sermones contra Catharos*, PL CXCV.34–5.

pragmatic point succinctly concludes the argument: "Besides, the number of the people with God would be excessively diminished."[40]

Basic differences in style and message are apparent in the two discussions of the same question, even though Elisabeth's *Liber viarum Dei* is a thematic collection of texts postdating Ekbert's arrival at Schönau, and even though Elisabeth's concern about the Cathars may have been fueled by Ekbert's own zeal. Thus even his direction of Elisabeth's attention to particular issues and his continuing presence at Schönau did not efface Elisabeth's own style and religious expression.

It is difficult to assess Elisabeth's overall reaction to her brother's increased influence in shaping the visionary texts through his posing of specific questions. I can trace no consistent dynamic of either resistance or unquestioned compliance. Instead, Elisabeth's reaction seems always to depend on the specific nature of the requests being made of her. Her responses to Ekbert's attempts to manipulate her visionary experience range from her refusal to offer any answer to his questions, sometimes including a divine warning against this type of intrusion, to her genuine interest in the questions when they correspond to concerns that are already meaningful to her. For example, her conclusion that Mary was bodily assumed into heaven accords well with the spirituality in the earlier records of her visions of a regal, powerful Mary in heaven.

In the case of her revelations about Ursula, Elisabeth recognized the high stakes in the production of this text – she was being asked to provide a celestial guarantee that would turn bones from a newly discovered graveyard into precious relics of early martyrs. The financial implications of her actions were well known to her, as were what she considered to be the spiritual implications. Her discomfort with this situation is palpable – in order to validate the bones as genuine relics of the 11,000 female virgins believed to have been martyred outside Cologne, she had to reinvent the legend through her visionary conversations with the martyred virgins. This text stands as one of the most striking examples of the attempt of "certain men of good repute" (Ekbert was not alone in this effort) to exploit Elisabeth's claim to celestial contact. It also stands as Elisabeth's most imaginative creation, one in which she could give full expression to a very profound aspect of her spiritual life, her devotion to the saints.

The publication of potentially misunderstood texts

I have already noted that Ekbert exercised control over Elisabeth's religious expression by suppressing records that he felt would be "misunderstood" or not

---

[40] "Ubi tale coniugium esse potest, gratum est domino. Sed rarum est valde, ut ita contingat . . . Alioquin nimis contraheretur numerus populi dei" (*Visionen* 104).

edifying to the general public. But his editorial prerogative also included the opposite possibility: the publication of texts whether or not Elisabeth wanted them made public. There is one place in the collection where it is possible to discern such a strain between brother and sister. In the revelations about the assumption of Mary, Elisabeth is acutely aware that her pronouncements bring her into tension with tradition: "I hesitated to publish a written form of this revelation, fearing that perhaps I would be judged as an inventor of novelties."[41] Elisabeth's concern takes the form of a dialogue with Mary, who reassures her that the revelations were not given merely to pass into oblivion. However, she cautions, because of the evil of the times, the visions should only be shared with those who are Mary's special devotees. Despite Elisabeth's assertion that these revelations were to be shared only with a small circle of Mary's devotees, this text is present in all the major versions of the visionary collections.

I think we can discern here a discrepancy between Elisabeth's preferences and the publication strategy undertaken by Ekbert. Given Ekbert's general caution not to scandalize or bring disrepute upon his sister and his monastery, he must have decided that Elisabeth's revelations would not too greatly shock the public, that in fact the time might be ripe for such a new declaration. The popularity of this text, witnessed by its extensive transmission both in the collections of her works and on its own, vindicates Ekbert's judgment about its timeliness. Yet it also seems to be the case that Ekbert's theological agenda led him first to direct Elisabeth to this subject and then to ignore her judgment and her desire to protect herself from potential criticism.

The "negotiation of misunderstanding"

The foregoing discussion of publication and suppression hinges on the question of potential misunderstanding. For both Elisabeth and Ekbert, this meant misunderstanding by those outside the cloister. However, there also occurred moments of misunderstanding or confusion between Elisabeth and Ekbert. An example of this misunderstanding is one of the most famous incidents recorded in the visionary collection. In one of the late diary entries, Elisabeth describes a vision which occurred during mass on Christmas Eve. In this vision, she sees a beautiful virgin sitting in the middle of the sun. The virgin weeps at the repeated approach of a dark cloud that causes the earth to be covered in shadows. Elisabeth then announces the allegorical meaning of this vision: the virgin represents "the sacred humanity of Lord Jesus" (*domini*

---

[41] "Post hec cum dubitarem publicare scriptum revelationis huius, metuens ne forte iudicarer quasi inventrix novitatum" (*Visionen* 54).

Jesu sacra humanitas), the sun represents the divinity of Christ, and the cloud is sin reigning in the world.

Elisabeth's meditation on the salvific nature of Christ is unexpected and elicits a question from her secretary. She is asked why the humanity of Christ is represented in this female image rather than in a male form. Elisabeth responds by describing another visionary exchange with the angel in which she is supplied with the answer: the virgin also represents the blessed mother of Christ. Elisabeth's further reflection on this image, coaxed by Ekbert, produced the more conventional interpretation.

In addition to observing here the dynamic of interaction between visionary and investigator, there are two important things to note about this incident. First, the unexpected announcement of a female image for the humanity of Christ appears to have made Ekbert uncomfortable, but, nonetheless, he did not suppress the passage describing it. Second, in elaborating her vision to include another meaning of the troubling image, Elisabeth was not simply conceding to more conventional theology under Ekbert's pressure. The second interpretation was not meant to correct or replace the earlier association of the female image with the humanity of Christ. Rather she reports that "it [the female image] could the more easily be adapted to *also* signify his blessed mother" (emphasis added).[42] Thus for Elisabeth, the symbol of the virgin is multivalent – it represents both the "sacred humanity of the Lord Jesus" and Mary the mother of Jesus. The richness of this symbol is facilitated by the intimate connection between Christ's humanity and his birth from Mary, which itself was the focus of the liturgical context of this particular visionary experience.

Ekbert's confusion at Elisabeth's original interpretation of the female symbol led her to meditate further upon it. Elisabeth complies with his request for clarification – she does cede to him the authority to "investigate" what she says. But she does not withdraw her surprising interpretation, nor does Ekbert decide to record only what is most comprehensible to his own sensibilities. In fact, the dialectic of their relationship here served to become the occasion for Elisabeth's further exploration and didactic exposition of her vision.

Conclusion: repression or collaboration?

I have considered throughout this essay the question of medieval misogyny and its impact on the religious expression of Elisabeth of Schönau. Before drawing out my conclusions from this analysis, one further question deserves notice,

---

[42] " . . . ut tanto congruentius etiam ad significandam beatam matrem eius visio posset aptari" (*Visionen* 62).

that of modern misogyny and its influence on the interpretation of Elisabeth's work. In his edition of Elisabeth's visions (1884), F. W. E. Roth asserted that the *Liber viarum Dei* reflects much more the thought of Ekbert than that of Elisabeth. He saw in it the work of a farsighted man of the world who had first-hand experience of the various ways of life described in the book, not of a woman who had spent most of her life within the walls of a cloistered convent.[43] This has been a very influential opinion.[44] And yet, there is very little "worldliness" in this text that cannot be paralleled in other traditional moral, exhortatory works. Roth's judgment about the authorship of the visionary texts can in general be traced along gender lines. The early diary accounts of emotional and physical experience, in which he saw evidence of spiritual immaturity and even psychosis, he attributed to Elisabeth and her unhealthy convent life. The more focused, ethical preaching of the *Liber viarum Dei*, to which he accorded a higher value, he attributed to Ekbert.

Looking at Elisabeth a century after Roth's investigation, we can draw upon some of the basic insights of feminist analysis to draw a different picture of her life. Our awareness of misogyny and the structures of male dominance gives us a different perspective on the religious lives of medieval women. We have become suspicious of the tendency to diagnose women as hysterical and are more likely to highlight the social roles that institutionalize and reinforce the perceived inferiority of women.

Nevertheless, I would also like to suggest that the case of Elisabeth and Ekbert of Schönau allows us to see the limitations of the category of misogyny as well. Even within the context of an ostensibly stable, even "monotonous" tradition of misogyny within medieval culture,[45] we cannot assume that particular articulations of gender were not problematic at any given moment. Assertions about the nature of men and women and prescriptions that organized gender hierarchy, even when we can find no extant literary challenges to them, were attempts to create and consolidate particular social realities, not witnesses to a fixed order.[46] Thus the tensions of social reality at any one time are masked by the consistency of an ideology, in this case, the consistent iteration of the divinely ordained subordination of women to male authority. What I have tried to suggest in my analysis is the inadequacy of projecting this ideology as a blueprint for the behavior of individuals. Knowing the contours of a cultural ideology and its corresponding social structures does not exhaust the content of the lives of specific individuals. Thus, in the context of the institutionalized and theologically supported subordination of women, Elisabeth and Ekbert had a complex relationship that

---

[43] Roth, *Visionen*, CIX–XC.   [44] See, e.g., Köster 1965: 28.
[45] On the "monotony" of medieval misogyny, see Bloch 1991: 47.
[46] Scott 1988: 5–7, 42–3.

resulted in the creation of texts that echo Elisabeth's voice, even if that voice is muffled at times.

Ekbert had his own way of understanding – or rationalizing – why the words of a woman were compelling and worthy of publication. He condemns those who would be scandalized at God's choice of a member of "the weak sex." Why, he asks, don't they remember "that it happened like this in the days of our fathers, when, while men were given over to negligence, holy women were filled with the spirit of God so that they prophesied, vigorously governed the people of God, and even triumphed gloriously over the enemies of Israel, women such as Huldah, Deborah, Judith, Jael and others of this kind?"[47] He offers biblical precedent for the current circumstance that seemed to defy the prescription of female silence. Of course, he offers no biblical precedent for his own activities of questioning and censoring. These were activities that needed no rationalization. As we have seen, his biographer took it for granted that these activities redounded to his credit.

Ekbert was clearly drawn to Elisabeth's visionary piety. In an early collection of Elisabeth's revelations, Ekbert included a vision that he himself had had.[48] In his description of Elisabeth's last days, he portrays his own request to his dying sister that he might inherit her prophetic spirit.[49] In addition to his attraction to Elisabeth's visionary spirituality, he also shared her zeal for addressing the decaying morals of Christendom. In coming to Schönau, he worked with Elisabeth and used her visions for ends that they shared as well as for his own interests, and he suppressed her voice when he felt that he should. Elisabeth accepted his authority to question, and seems to have been relieved, at least at points, to have his collaboration. She recognized manipulation when she saw it, and sometimes resisted when she disapproved. The dynamics of power were certainly in Ekbert's favor. Yet it is clear that his authority to investigate Elisabeth's pronouncements had another side to it. Ekbert's "use" of Elisabeth must not obscure Elisabeth's "use" of Ekbert. *His* authority to investigate became *her* opportunity to teach, to expound, to clarify her visions for the edification of the faithful, which is what she understood her divinely appointed commission to be.

---

[47] "Sed cur in mentem non venit, quoniam simile factum est in diebus patrum nostrorum, quando viris socordie deditis, spiritu dei replete sunt mulieres sancte, ut prophetarent, populum dei strennue gubernarent, sive etiam de hostibus Israel gloriose triumpharent, quemadmodum Olda, Debora, Judith, Jahel, et huiusmodi?" (*Visionen* 40).

[48] F. W. E. Roth, "Aus einer Handschrift der Schriften der heil. Elisabeth von Schönau," *Neues Archiv der Gesellschaft für ältere deutsche Geschichtskunde* 36 (1911): 222–3.

[49] *Visionen* 271. Cf. 4 Kings 2.9, in which the prophet Elijah, about to die, is asked by his successor Elisha for a share in his spirit, a passage which Ekbert is clearly echoing in this text.

REFERENCES

PRIMARY SOURCES

Abelard, Peter. *Sermo in assumptione beate Mariae. Patrologia Latina* 178, 539–47.
Burchard of Worms. *Decretum. Patrologia Latina* 140, 537–1058.
Ekbert of Schönau. *Sermones contra Catharos. Patrologia Latina* 195, 12–98.
   Sermones per annum. Trier, Stadtbibliothek MS 229/1397 8°, fols. 78v–131r.
Emecho of Schönau. *Vita Eckeberti.* Ed. S. Widmann. *Neues Archiv der Gesellschaft für ältere deutsche Geschichtskunde* 11 (1886): 447–54.
Grégoire le Grand. *Dialogues: Texte critique, notes, et traduction.* Ed. Adalbert de Vogüé. Trans. Paul Antin. Sources Chrétiennes, nos. 251, 260, 265. Paris: Les Editions du Cerf, 1980.
Günther, Wilhelm. *Codex Diplomaticus Rheno-Mosellanus,* I. Coblenz: B. Heriot, 1822.
Roth, F. W. E. Aus einer Handschrift der Schriften der heil. Elisabeth von Schönau. *Neues Archiv der Gesellschaft für ältere deutsche Geschichtskunde* 36 (1911): 219–25.
Die Visionen der hl. Elisabeth und die Schriften der Aebte Ekbert und Ermecho von Schönau. Ed. F. W. E. Roth. Brünn: Verlag der Studien aus dem Benedictiner- und Cistercienser Orden, 1884.

SECONDARY REFERENCES

Barrow, Julia 1989 Education and the Recruitment of Cathedral Canons in England and Germany 1100–1225. *Viator* 20: 117-38.
Becker, Hans 1965 Das Kloster Schönau (Übersicht). In *Schönauer Elisabeth Jubiläum 1965: Festschrift anlässlich des achthundert jährigen Todestages des heiligen Elisabeth von Schönau,* 80–1. Limburg: Pallottiner Druckerei.
Bloch, R. Howard 1987 Medieval Misogyny. *Representations* 20: 1–24.
   1991 *Medieval Misogyny and the Invention of Western Romantic Love.* Chicago: University of Chicago Press.
Bullough, Vern L. 1973 Medieval Medical and Scientific Views of Women. *Viator* 4: 485–501.
Bynum, Caroline Walker 1987 *Holy Feast and Holy Fast: The Religious Significance of Food to Medieval Women.* Berkeley: University of California Press.
Clark, Anne L. 1992 *Elisabeth of Schönau, a Twelfth-Century Visionary.* Philadelphia: University of Pennsylvania Press.
Coakley, John 1991a Friars as Confidants of Holy Women in Medieval Dominican Hagiography. In Renate Blumenfeld-Kosinski and Timea Szell, eds., *Images of Sainthood in Medieval Europe,* 222–46. Ithaca: Cornell University Press.
   1991b Gender and the Authority of Friars: The Significance of Holy Women for Thirteenth-Century Franciscans and Dominicans. *Church History* 60: 445–60.
Cohen, Jeremy 1982 *The Friars and the Jews: The Evolution of Medieval Anti-Judaism.* Ithaca: Cornell University Press.
d'Alverny, Marie-Thérèse 1977 Comment les théologiens et les philosophes voient la femme. *Cahiers de civilisation médiévale X–XIIe siècles* 20: 105–29.

Funkenstein, Amos 1971 Basic Types of Christian Anti-Jewish Polemics in the Later Middle Ages. *Viator* 2: 373–82.

Graef, Hilda 1963 *Mary: A History of Doctrine and Devotion*. London: Sheed and Ward.

Johnson, Lynn Staley 1991 The Trope of the Scribe and the Question of Literary Authority in the Works of Julian of Norwich and Margery Kempe. *Speculum* 66: 820–38.

Köster, Kurt 1951 Elisabeth von Schönau: Werk und Wirkung im Spiegel der mittelalterlichen handschriftlichen Überlieferung. *Archiv für Mittelrheinische Kirchengeschichte* 3: 243–315.

—— 1952 Das Visionäre Werk Elisabeths von Schönau. *Archiv für Mittelrheinische Kirchengeschichte* 4: 79–119.

—— 1965 Elisabeth von Schönau: Leben, Persönlichkeit und visionäres Werk. In *Schönauer Elisabeth Jubiläum 1965: Festschrift anlässlich des achthundert jährigen Todestages des heiligen Elisabeth von Schönau*, 17–46. Limburg: Pallottiner Druckerei.

Küsters, Urban 1985 *Der verschlossene Garten: Volkssprachliche Hohelied-Auslegung und monatische Lebensform im 12. Jahrhundert*. Studia humaniora: Düsseldorfer Studien zu Mittelalter und Renaissance, Band 2. Düsseldorf: Droste Verlag.

Lerner, Robert 1992 Ecstatic Dissent. *Speculum* 67: 33–57.

Newman, Barbara 1985 Hildegard of Bingen: Visions and Validation. *Church History* 54 (1985): 163–75.

Peters, Ursula 1988 *Religiöse Erfahrung als literarisches Faktum: Zur Vorgeschichte und Genese frauenmystischer Texte des 13. und 14. Jahrhunderts*. Hermaea Germanistische Forschungen, Neue Folge Bd. 56. Tübingen: Max Niemeyer.

Scott, Joan Wallach 1988 *Gender and the Politics of History*. New York: Columbia University Press.

Scott, Karen 1992 St. Catherine of Siena, "Apostola." *Church History* 61: 38–46.

Thorndike, Lynn 1955 Further Considerations of the *Experimenta, Speculum Astronomiae*, and *De Secretis Mulierum* Ascribed to Albertus Magnus. *Speculum* 30: 413–43.

Wood, Charles T. 1981 The Doctors' Dilemma: Sin, Salvation and the Menstrual Cycle in Medieval Thought. *Speculum* 56: 710–27.

8   Prophetic patronage as repression:
Lucia Brocadelli da Narni and Ercole d'Este

E. Ann Matter

As the scholarship of Caroline Walker Bynum has shown, the concept of "holy woman" was well developed in late medieval and Renaissance Christian society; my own recent work has begun to delineate the ways in which this concept functioned through to the last quarter of the seventeenth century.[1] In this essay I will focus on the life and legend of the official "holy woman" of the sixteenth-century court of the Este family of Ferrara, Lucia Brocadelli da Narni, in order to explore the connections between women's sanctity and political power.

Lucia Brocadelli was born in Narni (Umbria) on 13 December 1476. From childhood, her hagiographers tell us, the girl was filled with a desire to live a life like that of Catherine of Siena.[2] This orientation to Dominican spirituality was encouraged by her confessor. After the death of her father in 1490, the girl (now fourteen) was given in marriage to Count Pietro di Alessio of Milan. The marriage was, on her insistence, a chaste one: the hagiographers relate that every evening Lucia would sprinkle the bedroom with holy water, place a crucifix in bed between herself and her husband, and spend the night in fervent prayer. Familial life with Lucia was also marked by fasts, corporal discipline, frequent communion, and other activities *in imitatione Christi*.

Throughout this period, in spite of the increasing and understandable ire of her husband, Lucia moved resolutely towards religious life. On 8 May 1494, she was dressed by her confessor in the habit of a Dominican tertiary. Early in 1495, she was accepted into the house of Dominican tertiaries in Rome, where Catherine of Siena herself had once lived.

Lucia's position in this house seems to have been one of some authority, for a year later, on the order of the General of the Dominicans, she was sent to

A version of this paper was presented at the Sixteenth Century Studies Conference, St. Louis, October 1990. I would like to thank Anne Schutte for her advice and encouragement in pursuing this subject.

[1] Bynum 1987; Matter 1989–90; Matter 1993.

[2] The earliest life of Lucia Brocadelli was written by Serafino Razzi (1577: 151–7). A very similar account is in Marcianese 1663. For a modern summary of her life, see Prosperi 1972.

Viterbo to take charge of and reform the house of Dominican tertiaries of that city. Shortly after her arrival, on 25 February 1496, while praying at Matins between the prioress, Suor Diambra, and Suora Leonarda, Lucia received the stigmata. At first the wounds were invisible, but during Passion Week of 1496, they began to bleed profusely. Her mother and her former confessor were summoned to her bedside, and the entire community expected her to die. Instead of dying, however, Lucia became a celebrity, one of the most revered persons of Viterbo. As one modern historian has described it: "Her life at Viterbo seemed to become a perpetual mystery. Before the Crucifix and at mass she had wonderful ecstasies, in which she cried 'Fuoco, fuoco, amore, amore!' . . . She talked with Christ and suffered His Passion, and revealed hidden things of celestial mysteries, such that the nuns could find no words in which to record them."[3] When the local inquisitor showed up to examine these wonders, Lucia simply told him: "St. Catherine of Siena by her prayers has obtained from our Lord Jesus Christ that the Stigmata should be visible and palpable in me, as a pledge and testimony of the Stigmata of St. Catherine herself."[4]

This story is one which was repeated in the lives of scores, perhaps hundreds, of religious women of her century.[5] This proliferation of visions of Christ and reception of the stigmata does not in any way devalue the experience; in fact, it is evidence of how important these marks of holiness were to late medieval and Renaissance Italian society. Only from such a perspective can we understand the attention that Lucia's visions and stigmata received from one of the most powerful, and most pious, men of her day, Ercole d'Este, duke of Ferrara. As Werner Gundersheimer has eloquently pointed out, a large part of Ercole's *magnificentia* was lavished upon the Church: rebuilding and redecorating existing institutions, and financing religious congregations, sometimes from scratch.[6] Ercole's devotional life included a searching correspondence with the Dominican friar and prophet of the doom of the worldly Church, Girolamo Savonarola.[7] Many things about the spirituality of Lucia Brocadelli fascinated the duke of Ferrara; in a treatise dated 4 March 1500, the year after Lucia finally, after many difficulties, arrived at his court at Ferrara, Ercole wrote about her stigmata: "These things are shown by the Supreme Craftsman in the bodies of His servants to conform and

---

[3] Gardner 1968: 368.
[4] *Ibid.*
[5] See Bell 1985, especially the chart, pp. 215–37. Bell's study, it should be remembered, is limited to women who were actually beatified or canonized; Lucia appears on p. 228. See also Pozzi and Leonardi 1988 for summaries of many lives of Italian holy women.
[6] Gundersheimer 1973, especially ch. 6, "Hercules Dux Ferrariae," pp. 173–228. Ercole was preceded by his brothers Leonello and Borso.
[7] The correspondence between Savonarola and Ercole is printed in Cappelli 1869.

strengthen our Faith, and to remove the incredulity of impious men and hard of heart."[8]

Given the religious context of late fifteenth-century Italy, it is not so surprising that the duke of Ferrara would wish to have a holy woman at his court. What does seem unusual, however, is the length to which Ercole was persuaded to go to assure Lucia's presence at Ferrara. In the summer of 1497, Ercole wrote to Lucia in Viterbo, inviting her to move to Ferrara, and promising the construction of a convent of Dominican tertiaries over which she would have control. Lucia accepted at once, with gratitude, a sentiment echoed by her mother, who also wrote directly to Ercole.[9] But the people of Viterbo, beginning with the nuns of her own community, absolutely refused to let her leave. Ercole sent Alessandro da Fiorano and his son Ippolito, the nineteen-year-old cardinal-archbishop of Milano, to Rome to plead his case in the papal court of Pope Alexander VI. Lucia in the meantime grew very unhappy with the furor over where she should practice her spiritual gifts. In letters to Ercole, she complained that she had no peace, and could no longer dedicate herself to a spiritual life. Throughout the year 1498, as the tug-of-war between the duke and the city over the visionary continued, she wrote of her state as a spiritual hell. Such a description would perhaps be appropriate for the Italian Church in general, for this was, of course, also the year in which the increasingly dramatic story of Girolamo Savonarola reached its climax. When Savonarola and his two companions, Fra Domenico and Fra Silvestro, were hanged and burned in the Piazza della Signoria of Florence on 23 May 1498, a chronicle of Ferrara reported that a nun of Viterbo saw in a vision the three Dominicans called up into Paradise by singing angels. Since this was precisely the time in which the retinue of the duke of Ferrara was engaged in trying to bring one particular nun of Viterbo to be a prophet in their midst, it is not unlikely that this nun was Lucia Brocadelli, the apocalypticism of her vision a reflection of her own struggle to find a safe haven for her continuing reception of spiritual gifts.[10]

Finally, Ercole resorted to bribery, buying off no less a figure than the *podestà* of Viterbo, who was promised a better position in Ferrara for his treachery. On 14 April 1499, Lucia was smuggled out of Viterbo in a basket of linen, on the back of a mule. She was taken to her mother's house in Narni, where Alessandro da Fiorano was waiting to escort her through the states of

---

[8] Letter of 4 March 1500, printed as the *Spiritualium personarum feminei sextus facta admiratione digna*, a tract of twelve unpaginated leaves (six in Latin, six in German), in Nuremberg in 1501.

[9] The letters of Lucia to Ercole are preserved in Modena, Archivio di Stato, Giurisdizione sovrana, Santi e beati 430A.

[10] Muratori 1723–51: XXIV.353. The tentative identification of this nun with Lucia is made by Gardner 1968: 368 n. 1.

the duke of Urbino to Ferrara. She and her entourage (including her mother) arrived at Ferrara on 7 May. Ercole came out to meet her and escort her into the city, as seems only proper, considering the lengths to which he had gone to hasten the day of her coming. The duke, in fact, did all that he could to make his prize visionary comfortable in Ferrara: he sent for her confessor (perhaps partly to protect the priests of Ferrara from such a demanding penitent), he gathered a group of Ferrarese girls to become her novices in the community of Dominican tertiaries he had promised, and, less than a month after her arrival, he began work on the monastery he had promised her.

For the next two years, while the new convent was being built, Lucia lived in a temporary house with a small group of young girls of Ferrara, whom she hoped to make the nucleus of the new community. Lucia firmly believed herself to be the earthly representative of Catherine of Siena, indeed, she had a waking vision of the saint, who led her around the building, singing *Ave maris stella*, blessing every room, leaving her with a rod as a token of her authority. Other visions, all duly related to Duke Ercole, had Catherine calling Lucia to walk with her on a path paved with thorns, and the Madonna and angels taking up residence in the convent.

Ercole, feeling his unorthodox methods of bringing a holy woman to Ferrara fully justified by these visions, developed a theory of the efficacy of holy women. In the text of 1500, Ercole describes (besides Lucia) Suor Colomba da Rieti in Perugia, Stefana Quinzani in Crema, and Osanna Andreasi of Mantova, the latter of whom he also tried to tempt to Ferrara, at least for a visit.[11] This text, published in Nürnberg (1501) in German and Latin as a small pamphlet of letters relating to Lucia, may well have been a declaration of orthodoxy in the wake of the trauma of the demise of Ercole's old friend Savonarola. Ercole here grounds Lucia's authority on her reception of the stigmata.[12]

It may also be possible that this text was meant to attract the attention of Pope Alexander VI. Indeed, Ercole was aware of the fact that he needed papal permission to open the house of Dominican tertiaries he was building for Lucia. Ercole asked that the nuns be allowed, along with the privileges of cloistered nuns of St. Dominic, freedom to come and go from the monastery necessary truly to imitate Catherine. Alexander VI, who had not taken any particular interest in the movement of holy women of his Church, saw the importance of allowing Lucia to live out her special relationship with Catherine. On 29 May 1501, he promulgated the privileges of the new house, including freedom of movement, and the final authority of "our beloved

---

[11] For this document, see above, note 8. For discussion of and selections from the lives of Stefana and Osanna, see Pozzi and Leonardi 1988: 287–91, 295–300. See also Gardner 1968: 365–6, 375–7, and appendix 22 for a letter of Ercole's daughter Isabella of Mantua about the proposed visit of Osanna to Lucia from the Archivio di Modena, Cancelleria Ducale.

[12] A point emphasized by Prosperi 1972: 382.

daughter in Christ, Lucia da Narni, sister of the said third Order, who (as it is asserted) devotes herself so far as she can to following the footsteps of the Blessed Catherine."[13] It is doubtless significant that Alexander VI made this concession exactly at the time in which he was negotiating with the duke of Ferrara about the marriage of his daughter, Lucrezia Borgia, to Ercole's son Don Alfonso.

On 5 August 1501, Lucia Brocadelli entered her long-awaited new convent, named, of course, for Catherine of Siena. The occasion was solemn and marked by ecclesiastical privilege and great signs of favor: Ercole gave the house an Italian Bible from his own library and many relics of Dominican saints. Ironically, though, after all of the drama involved in settling Lucia Brocadelli in the promised community in Ferrara, one thing was missing: a community. The nuns recruited from among Ferrarese girls had stayed only briefly in the community, not finding the visionary at the head of the house nearly as inspirational as did the duke of Ferrara.

At Lucia's request, Ercole sent out messengers to a number of Dominican tertiary houses in Umbria and Lazio, inviting Lucia's old companions to join her in the new community. Lucia was especially anxious to be joined by her mother, and by seven of her former community at Viterbo, including Diambra and Leonarda, who had been next to her when she had received the stigmata. The duke's messenger soon found, however, that only Lucia's mother would come willingly; in Narni, the fathers of two young cousins greeted the request with *male parole*. And in Viterbo, even though members of Lucia's former community spoke movingly of the wonders Lucia had wrought during her stay there, none of the women requested to join the new community in Ferrara would agree to come. This time, Ercole went right to the top, enlisting the help of Lucrezia Borgia. There was soon a papal decree that all of the nuns listed by Lucia and Ercole had been summarily reassigned to Ferrara, and no excuse – lameness, dropsy, old age – was considered a valid reason for failing to comply. Lucrezia herself spoke to several of the women, assuring them the protection of her men on the trip to Ferrara (a trip she would take some months later) and threatening to find every woman on the list if she did not voluntarily come to Rome to prepare for the journey.[14] In this way, Lucia Brocadelli da Narni was finally installed as the official visionary of Duke Ercole d'Este of Ferrara.

For the next four years, until Ercole's death in 1505, Lucia lived a life marked by vast privilege and official respect. When her stigmata were

---

[13] Gardner 1968: 379, quoted from Ponsi, pp. 227–8. The documents are preserved in the Archivio della Curia Vescovile of Ferrara: *Annali di S. Cattarina di Siena MDII al MDCCLIII*; see pp. 11–12, letter of 1501.

[14] Gardner 1968: 380–1, 401–3, quoting from Gandini.

bleeding most profusely (on Wednesdays, Fridays, and during Holy Week), the duke would come to Santa Caterina for deep mystical talks; the cloths used to staunch Lucia's wounds became precious relics, one was said to have cured Don Alfonso, Ercole's heir and husband of Lucrezia Borgia, from a serious illness.[15] An emissary from Alexander VI examined these stigmata in 1502, and declared them real. Besides the stigmata, Lucia was famed in Ferrara for her clairvoyant powers, for guessing thoughts and foretelling the future.

Upon Ercole's death, however, Lucia's position in Ferrara changed dramatically. Never having developed any real following in the city, even in her own house, except that enforced by the duke, Lucia was left defenseless by his demise. The nuns of Santa Caterina turned against her (one was even said to have tried to stab her), and she was stripped of the authority and of the privileges granted by Alexander VI, who had died the year before. Worst of all, the signs of the stigmata disappeared, and Lucia was even accused of having fabricated them all along. She was not yet twenty-nine years old. For nearly another four decades, until her death at sixty-eight, on 15 November 1544, Lucia Brocadelli da Narni was kept under close supervision, a virtual prisoner in the house that had been built as a testimony to her spiritual gifts. In these years, she continued to have visions of Catherine of Siena, the Virgin Mary, and Christ, and wrote an account of these visions, one of a very few texts known to come directly from her hand, in the year of her death.[16]

Perhaps partly because of this book, her community changed their minds about Lucia after her death. Certainly, she had achieved some fame in her own lifetime, serving as a model of the holy life for Dominican tertiaries such as María de Santo Domingo, a Spanish *beata* who died in 1525.[17] Her life was first collected from oral tradition in 1577, the more popular hagiographical account dates to 1663.[18] The nuns of Santa Caterina of Ferrara successfully sponsored her cause before the Holy See; in 1710, Lucia Brocadelli was beatified (an honor denied to many other holy women of early modern Italy) and her body was placed as a sacred relic in the cathedral of Ferrara, where it remained until the mid-twentieth century.[19]

The comedy of errors by which Lucia was finally able to accept the duke's invitation to take up residence in Ferrara has its strongest parallel in the brisk

---

[15] *Ibid.*, 380, quoting Marcianese.

[16] Pavia, Biblioteca Civica "Bonetta," MS 11.112, an autograph.

[17] See Bilinkoff 1989: 55–66 for the religious career of this *beata*. The connection between Maria de Santo Domingo and Lucia Brocadelli da Narni was discussed in Bilinkoff 1987.

[18] For these printed sources, see above, n. 1, and Zarri 1980: 388–9. Documents regarding the canonization of Lucia Brocadelli are collected in cartella 25 of the Biblioteca della Curia Archivescovile of Ferrara: *Beata Lucia 3: Processus de vita, de mortibus et fama sanctitatis Ven: Sor: Lucia de narni fabricatus Anno 1644.*

[19] Lucia Brocadelli's tomb in the cathedral was replaced by the tomb of a bishop of Ferrara in the 1950s.

competition for *dead* saints which Patrick Geary has described for the central Middle Ages.[20] Gabriella Zarri, in fact, has pointed to the early *Cinquecento* as a time of special importance for the typology of what she calls *le sante vive*: live women saints.[21] Lucia Brocadelli, as Zarri points out, certainly fits this typology, especially as manifested by Duke Ercole's desperate efforts to have the "saint" in Ferrara, interceding on his behalf. As a live human being, Lucia might have been able to explain much better than the bones of dead holy people her desire to share her grace with a particular community; nevertheless, just as the dead saints Geary discusses, she managed best to make her desires known by miracles and apparitions. And, although she was a live human being, Viterbo and Ferrara fought over her as though she were a bone. Unfortunately, in building her community in Ferrara, Lucia treated her former colleagues in the same way, changing the discourse of *furta sacra* from "the saint wants to go to Ferrara" to "the saint wants *you* in Ferrara."

I find the role of the duke of Ferrara one of the most intriguing aspects of this story. The somewhat fickle (or perhaps simply prudent) supporter of Savonarola was deeply and loyally attached to the nun from Narni. Why was Suor Lucia Brocadelli so important to him? The answer is to be found in the power of the paradigm embodied by Lucia. He wanted her near him, so that he could turn to her for inspiration, particularly when the blood was flowing from her stigmata. He wanted to stay close to the signs of her passion *in imitatione Christi*, literally collecting her bloody bandages as trophies. And, most of all, he wanted her to pray for God's blessing on the duke of Ferrara. Ercole apparently believed deeply in Lucia's access to special grace, for he abandoned altogether the prudence with which he dealt with Savonarola, pressing soldiers, municipal officials, the general of the Dominicans, his own family, and even the pope into assistance in bringing about his plan for Lucia. Imprudence is probably an excellent word for the way Ercole proceeded, for he left his beloved visionary with no support besides his own, not even from her fellow sisters. Lucia Brocadelli's most extensive written work, the series of five visions dating from the last year of her life and preserved in her own hand, suggests that the visionary activity did not stop simply because its patronage ended. But these final visions are sad testimony to Lucia's abandonment: with sweeping apocalyptic imagery, they portray in graphic detail the crowns and thrones awaiting her in heaven.

As Michel de Certeau has pointed out, an important aspect of mystical discourse of the early modern period is its dialogical nature.[22] This is mysticism that was conceived in response to another. This accounts in some part for what I have pointed out as the formulaic or paradigmatic nature of Lucia

---

[20] Geary 1978.
[21] Zarri 1980: 371–445, especially 374–5.   [22] De Certeau 1982: I.216–21.

Brocadelli's story. In their studies of women mystics of the late Middle Ages, John Coakley and Karen Scott have especially investigated the answering voice of the male confessor.[23] With this essay, I hope to open discussion on the ways in which the political system of sixteenth-century Italy answered the woman mystic. A preliminary conclusion, drawn from the case of Lucia Brocadelli, is that holy women were sometimes exploited by the system of political patronage; that fleeting fame and political favor could be swiftly followed by repression, and justified by the same system of religious symbols.

REFERENCES

Bell, Rudolph M. 1985 *Holy Anorexia*. Chicago: University of Chicago Press.

Bilinkoff, Jodi 1987 A Spanish Prophetess and her Patrons: The Case of María de Santo Domingo. Paper presented at the meeting of the American Historical Association, San Francisco, Calif., December.

    1989 Charisma and Controversy: The Case of María de Santo Domingo. *Archivio Dominicano* 10: 55–66.

Bynum, Caroline Walker 1987 *Holy Feast and Holy Fast: The Religious Significance of Food to Medieval Women*. Berkeley: University of California Press.

Cappelli, Antonio 1869 *Fra Girolamo Savonarola e notizie intorno il suo tempo*. Modena: Coi tipi di C. Vincenzi.

Certeau, Michel de 1982 *La Fable mystique*, I: *XVIe–XVIIe siècle*. Paris: Gallimard.

Coakley, John 1991 Gender and the Authority of Friars: The Significance of Holy Women for Thirteenth-Century Franciscans and Dominicans. *Church History* 60: 445–60.

Gardner, Edmund G. 1968 *Dukes and Poets in Ferrara: A Study in the Poetry, Religion and Politics of the Fifteenth and Early Sixteenth Centuries*. New York: Haskell House (repr. of 1904 edn.).

Geary, Patrick 1978 *Furta sacra: Thefts of Relics in the Central Middle Ages*. Princeton, N.J.: Princeton University Press.

Gundersheimer, Werner L. 1973 *Ferrara: The Style of a Renaissance Despotism*. Princeton, N.J.: Princeton University Press.

Marcianese, P. F. G. 1663 *Vita della b. Lucia da Narni* . . . Viterbo.

Matter, E. Ann 1989–90 Discourses of Desire: Sexuality and Medieval Women's Visionary Narratives. *The Journal of Homosexuality* 18: 119–31.

    1993 Interior Maps of an Eternal External: The Spiritual Rhetoric of Maria Domitilla Galluzzi d'Acqui. In U. Wiethaus, ed., *Maps of Flesh and Light: Aspects of the Religious Experience of Medieval Women Mystics*, 60–73. Syracuse, N.Y.: Syracuse University Press.

Muratori, L. A., ed. 1723–51 *Diario Ferrarese, 1409–1502*. In L. A. Muratori, ed., *Rerum italicarum scriptores*, 24. 25 vols. in 28. Milan: Ex Typographia Societatis Palatinae.

Pozzi, Giovanni, and Leonardi, Claudio, 1988 *Scrittrici mistiche italiane*. Genoa: Marietti.

---

[23] Coakley 1991; Scott 1992.

Prosperi, A. 1972 Brocadelli (Broccadelli), Lucia. *Dizionario biografico degli italiani* XIV.381–3. Rome: Istituto della Enciclopedia Italiana.

Razzi, Serafino 1577 *Vite dei santi e beati, così huomini come donne del sacro Ordine de' frati predicatori*. Florence.

Scott, Karen 1992 St. Catherine of Siena, *Apostola. Church History* 61: 34–46.

Zarri, Gabriella 1980 Le sante vive: Per una tipologia della santità femminile nel primo Cinquecento. *Annali dell'Istituto storico italo-germanico in Trento* 6: 388–9. Repr. in *Le sante vive: cultura e religiosità femminile nella prima età moderna*, 87–163. Sacro/Santo 2. Turin: Rosenberg & Sellier, 1990.

Scandala: controversies concerning *clausura*
       and women's religious communities in late
       medieval Italy

Katherine Gill

If we look closely at religious women in the fourteenth and fifteenth centuries, images of community life emerge which do not conform to ecclesiastical legislation and religious rules. This is especially true with respect to enclosure. We see that strict claustration was not normative for many, perhaps most, women's religious communities during the last centuries of the Middle Ages. Contrary to what is often claimed or assumed, Boniface VIII's constitution *Pericoloso* did not represent either a dramatic turning point or a culmination in the history of women's religious institutions. It neither reflected nor achieved a general acceptance of strict enclosure as a necessary and validating feature of women's religious life. Routine processes (and a few extraordinary inventions) in the chanceries of Boniface's successors took the bite out of *Pericoloso*, as they did with other of the imperious pope's decisions. Likewise, both the quotidian and extraordinary actions of religious women defied the constitution.[1]

---

[1] Scholars writing about enclosure, particularly those looking forward to *Pericoloso* from the perspective of the early Middle Ages, often give a positivist presentation in which ideas and practice regarding *clausura* move continually toward greater institutional uniformity and increasingly universal application. In one of the more respected treatments of the subject, James R. Cain sums up the history of *clausura* through the thirteenth century: "We have seen the evolution of the cloister grow from scattered beginnings until it became nearly a universal custom. It became the master solution to most of the problems arising in communities of nuns." On *Perocoloso* Cain writes, "[Boniface VIII] imposed strict cloister upon all nuns, obliging them to accept it regardless of their past customs. His was the first papal legislation on the matter . . . and [it] had *a tremendous impact* on feminine religious life for centuries to come" (emphasis mine; see Cain 1968–9: 27.2.266). Yet the magnitude of impact claimed here is undermined in subsequent pages of Cain's study by statements such as "[Many] paid no heed . . . and abuses continued" (27.2.268), "By the time the Council of Trent had convened, [*Pericoloso*] had fallen into disuse in many localities" (27.2.269), and "the practice [of enclosure] varied from province to province and even from house to house" (27.2.269).
   Schulenberg 1984 is a very useful study for the early and central Middle Ages. Because the author accepts what others have erroneously claimed for the period after the twelfth century, however, she projects a momentum of increasing uniformity in women's religious institutions and places the high point of "flexible monastic structures" for women in the Merovingian period (p. 78). For Schulenberg *clausura* primarily emanates from "clerical reformers' fear of female sexuality" (p. 79). Schulenberg's notes provide a very good bibliography.
   More specific studies of women's communities or movements have tended to make

The fact that practice did not conform to precept is neither surprising nor, in itself, especially interesting. Why and how individual communities transgressed can be both. But to appreciate fully what we see, we must abandon the position of earlier scholars who, by presuming norms that never existed, were quick to frame evidence of nonconformity in terms of decadence and abuse in women's communities. The images of loose nuns and uncloistered religious women crafted by the authors of *fabliaux, novelle,* and by zealous male reformers have perhaps made too deep an impression on the historical imagination. Titillated by tales of sexual escapades or content with conventional wisdom regarding the "fragilis sexus," historians have generally missed the political, social, economic, and religious dimensions of non-compliance.[2] As an ecclesiastical and civic issue in the later Middle Ages, controversies about *clausura* were not so much about promiscuity and bad behavior as about incompatible political, social, and institutional visions. Conflict turned on the issue of woman and her political stature at least as much as woman and her sexual nature.

In the following pages I will present two cases in which controversies over *clausura* were clearly *not* about the circumscription of sexual activity or the preservation of honor, but rather about the control of political activity in the forms of self-governance, collective organization, and social influence. An anachronistic understanding of the term *scandalum* has often yielded conclusions that trivialize the roles of religious women in medieval societies and what is actually at stake in their frequent conflicts. To move toward a

---

Boniface a landmark and to adjust their presentations accordingly: see, e.g., Novelli 1975: especially 201; and Occhipinti 1978. In contrast to the preceding, Mario Sensi considers that, in Umbria, *Pericoloso* actually stimulated movement toward para-institutional or *bizzochale* communities (see Sensi 1985a). But Sensi tends to see a *bizzocaggio* (Italian version of a beguinage) in every non-*clausura*-abiding group. In this way he, like the rest, assumed a norm of crushed or compliant regular communities, which stand in contrast to uncloistered beguine-like groups. In reality, the contrast between convents and houses of *bizzoche* was not so stark. Many observers from the thirteenth through twentieth centuries have considered Sensi's *bizzoccagi* to be convents.

Raymond Creytens is more or less alone in asserting the atypicalness of *clausura* for the fifteenth and early sixteenth centuries; see especially his discussion of "monasteri aperti" (1965: 47–8). This article and Creytens 1964 are the best general presentations I know of for the legal and institutional situation of women's religious communities in the Tridentine period. Zarri 1986 complements Creytens with a panoramic and carefully documented treatment of social and political contexts.

2 The economic dimension of strict enclosure has been the most easily recognized by those who have cared to go beyond sex and sin explanations. John Freed has put it most succinctly, "only the wealthy could afford the poverty of the cloister" (1973: 324). Most recently, Penelope D. Johnson has confirmed this hypothesis statistically for thirteenth-century France and concludes, "Indeed, those houses that had few qualms about violating claustration were the most prosperous. [And] . . . poverty rather than wealth correlates with evidence of monastic decadence" (1991: 158). For work of other scholars who link loose cloister to prosperity and stability, see Johnson 1991: 160 n. 181.

picture which includes a greater awareness of women's interests and initiatives, I will then give a number of examples demonstrating why women's communities wanted latitude in the ordering of their lives. For this I will use the evidence of papal responses to requests from women's communities for exemption from the restrictions of enclosure. Paradoxically, the principal authority legislating constraints for female religious, the papacy, also provides in its most routine records some of the best evidence for the nature of women's religious life operating outside the bounds of legislation.[3]

The Perugian controversy

On a spring day in 1483, two of the several local communities of religious laywomen in the Umbrian hilltown of Perugia, Sant' Agnese and San Antonio da Padova, decided to make their position on *clausura* perfectly clear. The Sant' Agnese and San Antonio communities happened to consider themselves members of the "order of penitents of St. Francis," which indicates more a devotion to the saint than to his order, as we shall see. In the presence of recording public notaries, forty-four sisters from Sant' Agnese and thirty-nine sisters from San Antonio staged separate but procedurally identical demonstrations in the form of *public* chapter meetings. Each notarial record reports the events with the same words. The *ministra*, or leader, of each group initiated the business, stating:

Since the sisters . . . are being harassed by the Observant Franciscan friars concerning the implementation of *clausura* and the modification of [sisters'] rules or their manner of life, [the *ministra*] desiring that the intention of the sisters on the aforesaid matters be called forth and carried out, proposes [that the current meeting proceed in the following manner]: if any sister wants to practice *clausura* or to modify her rules or *modus vivendi*, she should now stand; but anyone who wants to live according to the rule and *modus vivendi* which she has followed up to now should stay sitting down.

After deliberation and consultation . . . , all remained sitting and not one [woman] rose up; in fact, each said in unison [with the rest] that she desired to live and remain [as before] . . . , that she in no way wanted to observe strict enclosure and neither did she want anything appended to her rule. Thus was the consensus among them.[4]

---

[3] My information comes primarily from four major series of the Archivio Segrego Vaticano (ASV): Registra Vaticana (RV), Registra Avenionensia (RA), Registra Lateranensia (RL), and Brevia Lateranensia (Brev. Lat.). The last two proved particularly useful in the degree of detail they provided. The early volumes (pontificate of Alexander VI) of the Brev. Lat. series (originally registered by papal domestic secretaries) contain an unusually high number of responses to petitions from women and women's communities. This is especially true of Brev. Lat. 2, where briefs concerning women are both numerous and registered in their entirety rather than in the more typical abbreviated versions.

[4] The public chapter of the community of San Antonio was recorded as follows: "Convocato et cohadunato publico et generale capitulo seu congregatione ministre et sororum . . . loci Sancti Antonii de Padua; quibus sic congregatis et cohadunatis prefata ministra [soror Maria d. Iacobi

180   *Katherine Gill*

The tertiaries' public action and its record suggest a judicious show-down. We are, in fact, witnessing the Perugian laywomen's attempt to force to conclusion a conflict which other sources indicate had been raging inter- mittently at least since 1461. In that year, with a bull beginning *Ut tolletur discursus* ("In order to settle the debate"), Pope Pius II had ruled that the women of San Antonio were not obliged to observe *clausura*.[5] Despite this decision, in 1469 the friars of the Observant branch of the Franciscan order in Perugia denied spiritual direction to the penitent women of San Antonio because they had refused to accept the innovation of strict enclosure. At that juncture, the commune of Perugia had risen to the defense of their pious laywomen, sending to the friars' regional assembly a lawyer who argued that the women should be allowed to keep their "original and accustomed rule."[6] In his oration to the Observant Franciscans, the lawyer decried their efforts to control the sisters, declaring that the imperious brothers had brought shock and scandal to the city (*tota civitas in admiratione ducta est cessitque in scandalum civium omnium non modicum*), and portraying the community of San Antonio as one of the finest institutions (*optimatibus*) in the city and close to the hearts of its citizens (*valde carus*). Finally, Perugia's representative maintained that San Antonio's spiritual value to the city was intimately related to its accessibility

de Perusio] dixit et proposuit, cum a fratribus sancti Francisci de Observantia sint dicte sorores molestate de faciendo clausuram vel aliquid addendo earum regule vel modo vivendi, volens suscitari voluntatem dictarum sororum in predictis circa predicta, ideo proposuit quod si aliqua ipsarum esset voluntatis facere clausuram vel quod aliquid addaretur dicte earum regule seu modo vivendi, debeat surgere; que vero vellet vivere in ea regula et modo vivendi in quibus hactenus vissit [*sic*], deberet sedere. Et habito inter eas ratiocinio et parlamento et misso partito de levando ad sedendum, omnes steterunt ad sedendum nec aliqua earum subrexit, immo qualibet [*sic*] predictarum una prout hattenus steterunt et nullatenus velle facere clausuram nec etiam velle quod aliquid dicte earum regule addatur; et sic inter eas predictum fuit obtemptum." This notarial record, which ended up in the archive of the friars of the monastery of Monteripido (Perugia), is partially published by Giovanna Casagrande (1984: 460). A record of the public chapter enacted by the second group of tertiaries, those of the house of Sant' Agnese, is in the protocol of notary Matteo di Nardo, Archivio di Stato Perugia (ASP), *Protocolli* 328 fol. 33; see Casagrande 1979: 157. Both notarial records describe the voting procedures with the same words. The fullest reproduction of either record appears in Casagrande 1984.

The starting point of the following discussion of Sant' Agnese, San Antonio, and their troubles with the Franciscan friars is information taken from the two articles cited above, together with a third article by Casagrande (1980).

5 For Pius II's *Ut tolletur discursus* (1461) see Hüntemann and Pou y Martí 1929–49: II, no. 971, cited in Casagrande 1980: 384 n. 56 and 1984: 491. The effects of this letter made their way to the Perugian tertiaries via a letter of Cardinal Alessandro Oliva, dated 22 June 1461 (Rome), in which Cardinal Oliva officially released the tertiaries from the obligation of *clausura*. Copies can be found in ASP, Corporazioni Religiose Soppresse, S. Antonio da Padova, *Pergamene* 9; and ASP, Corporazioni Religiose Soppresse, S. Francesco al Prato (a monastery of Observant friars), *cassetto* 5.

6 For the mission and the speech of the Perugian orator Mansueto dei Mansueti, see ASP, Consigli e Riformanze 105 fols. 53v–4r. It has been published in part by Casagrande (1984: appendix II n. 3 [p. 487]).

(*liber . . . accessum mulierum*).[7] This speech and the commune's support seem to have achieved about a decade of calm before the conflict between the tertiaries and the friars flared up again.

Apparently unaware of the suasions of 1469 or of Pius II's earlier decision in 1461, Sixtus IV, in September 1482, granted permission to the Observant Minors of Umbria to relinquish their responsibilities to tertiaries who refused *clausura*.[8] The women of San Antonio and Sant' Agnese, banding together with other penitent communities in Umbria, quickly and successfully addressed a petition in their own defense to Sixtus, who, in a swift volte-face, revoked his September decision.[9]

As is often the case in papal briefs responding to supplications, Sixtus's affirmation of the religious women's position incorporates part of the text of their appeal. Their argument, as recapitulated by a now more informed curial official, reveals how the Perugian tertiaries expressed in words what they would openly dramatize less than a year later. Enclosure, they claimed, was neither compatible with the vision of religious life they had embraced, nor with the nature, traditions, and functions of their houses:

for [women] who want to live under *clausura* certain monasteries have been designated, which these *ministrae* and sisters would have entered, if they had wanted to. And, they can enter [them now], if they want to live under this sort of *clausura*; furthermore, given their great number, [religious laywomen] could not easily survive from the unreliable income of alms if constrained by this kind of strict enclosure. Few women would be found in the future, who would want to enter these houses under the obligation of this kind of enclosure, and many [women currently living in these communities], granting their kin wanted it, would rather return to their family homes, than to stay in the afore-mentioned sort of houses under perpetual *clausura*, living from the uncertain income of alms, like the nuns of the order of S. Clare and her first institution.[10]

---

[7] *Ibid.* According to Mansueto, the esteem in which the townspeople held the women of San Antonio was due to "ob earum optimam et regularem vitam et tota civitas de ipso loco magnam habet consolationem et presertim spiritualem *ex quo ad eum liber est accessum mulierum*" (emphasis added).

[8] Hüntemann and Pou y Martí 1929–49: III, no. 1641; see Casagrande 1979: 158 n. 152.

[9] Hüntemann and Pou y Martí 1929–49: III, no. 1677 (December 1482); see Casagrande 1979: 158–9 and 1984: 461.

[10] *Ibid.*: "pro volentibus vivere sub clausura sunt certa monasteria deputata, quae ipsae ministrae et sorores proprium intrassent, si voluissent, et intrare possunt, si volunt sub huiusmodi clausura vivere; quodque, attento magno earum numero, difficulter vivere possent ex incerta mendicitate sub clausura [huiusmodi], et paucae in posterum reperirentur, quae vellent domos ipsas intrare cum huiusmodi clausura obligatione, et quamplurime ex eis, etiam consanguineis earum id volentibus, potius redirent ad paternas domos, quam non starent in predictis sub clausura perpetua, vitam ducentes ex incerta mendicitate, ad instar monialium ordinis S. Clarae et primariae instituionis illius." Both the enduring strength and the embattled character of the Umbrian tertiaries' position are suggested by the fact that the points of their 1482 argument find echoes in late sixteenth-century defenses of noncloistered convents. A speech of Alvaro Cabredo, a defender of "open" monasteries, delivered before the Sacred Congregation del Consilio in the mid-1560s is a case in point. Arguing for a more nuanced application of

The Perugian tertiaries' firm sense of corporate identity and its confident expression in script and public gesture emerge from the context of a century of well-organized self-government. Since 1392, Perugian laywomen living in communities or in private homes had maintained a city-wide network by means of a central committee composed of a *ministra* (in this case, a head of associated houses) and two representatives selected from the five regions of the town. The representative procedures of their federation (*congregatio*), similar to those of communal government in medieval hilltowns, gave the Umbrian tertiaries a corporate identity and public voice which would have been recognized locally as reasoned and politically potent.[11] These administrative practices, coupled with a sustained public presence, placed the Perugian penitents in an unusually strong position. It enabled them, when necessary, to coordinate efforts with groups living in other towns and villages, as the above quoted papal brief demonstrates. With such structures in place it is not surprising that the religious women of Sant' Agnese and San Antonio managed to make themselves credibly heard. Not only had Pius II and Sixtus IV accepted the tertiaries' arguments against enclosure, but the city officials of Perugia consistently lent their support.[12] Even the Franciscan vicar general, fra Pietro da Napoli, who had been deputized by Sixtus IV to investigate the issue, criticized the "immoderate zeal" of the Umbrian friars. Pietro contrasted the friars' aggressive behavior with his vision of the order as a cooperating family, and refused to support compulsory *clausura*.[13]

Tridentine decrees regarding religious women, Alvaro Cabredo asserted that the non-observance of *clausura* was a defining characteristic of tertiary communities and that, if they had to accept *clausura*, many tertiaries would not have entered religious life. Furthermore, without civic interrelations they would die of hunger. For this defense see Creytens 1965: 55, citing Biblioteca Apostolica Vaticana, Borgiani Latini 61 fols. 88–95.

The Perugian tertiaries' final statement that they emphatically did not want their institutions to be like those of St. Clare is a striking one for Umbrian Franciscan tertiaries to make. It suggests that they remained keenly aware of how institutionalization and subjection to the Franciscan order had operated to betray Clare's ideals. For an impassioned and powerful presentation of this process see Gennaro 1980; also de Fontette 1967 and Lainati 1973.

[11] The practice of forming ten-member representative committees was characteristic of town government in Perugia. Both *ad hoc* and standing commissions typically included two members from each of the five neighborhoods associated with each of the five city gates. See Casagrande 1979: 157–8.

[12] In addition to the above-mentioned commissioning an orator in 1468, in June 1482, when the Observant Franciscans again threatened to withhold spiritual services from the tertiaries, the city priors elected a committee of six, which included well-known legal experts, to help find a resolution to the standoff (ASP, Consigli e Riformanze 117 fol. 96r). The priors would do the same shortly after the public meetings, selecting on 22 April 1483 ten citizens, two for each city gate (or neighborhood), to deal with the issue. The committee members included persons from the most prominent families of Perugia (ASP, Consigli e Riformanze 118 fol. 25v). See Casagrande 1979: 157–8.

[13] For Pietro da Napoli's involvement in the controversy see Casagrande 1979: 158–60 and 1984: 459. One might wonder why, faced with such opposition, the Observant Franciscans persisted in their demand for strict enclosure. Relative newcomers to the ecclesiastical scene during the

Evidently unwilling to rest their hopes on the power of Pietro's familial metaphors, the Perugian penitents executed one final maneuver. Soon after the public chapter meetings Sant' Agnese and San Antonio arranged for local Amadeti friars, a group of male religious with no connection to the Observant Franciscans, to assume their spiritual care. Having slipped the noose of Observant *cura*, these communities did not adopt *clausura* until 1572. This was six years after Pius V issued *Circa pastoralis*, a constitution intended to add emphasis and force to the decisions of the Council of Trent by requiring strict enclosure for all women's communities, regardless of their rules, customs, or traditions.

I have chosen to begin with the Perugian tertiaries because the evidence of their resistance to strict enclosure is both extensive and exceptionally expressive of the women's point of view. The issues and arguments so clearly voiced here are paradigmatic of what one finds, albeit expressed either more indirectly or framed by adversaries of the women's position, in the records of many controversies involving both so-called regular monastic communities and quasi-regular tertiary or beguine-like communities in the late Middle Ages. First, it is significant that the uncloistered Perugian women did not regard their way of life as a degenerated or lax version of a truer form of religious life for women. Their *modus vivendi* was not hapless; they were aware of other options, but had not chosen them. Their status commanded local support and they were able to enlist the assistance of friends, neighbors, notaries, jurists, and civic councils. Tenacious and resourceful, they repeatedly received papal corroboration.

In the controversy, the Perugian women emphasize that enclosure was an economic issue: their collective survival depended on contact with the world outside their houses. Enclosure also emerges as a political issue: *clausura* would have made them subject and dependent. These women's communities

---

fifteenth century, the reformed branch of the Franciscan order was in the process of consolidating its own institutional power. In 1447 Eugenius IV had offered the Observants a new arena of leadership when, with an ambiguously worded bull, he had entrusted to them the *cura* of religious women associated with the Franciscan order. The friars were to extend spiritual services to sisters "of the first and the second and the third and any other order of St. Clare and the blessed Francis" ("moniales et sorores sive primi sive secundi sive tertii aut alterius ordinis Sancte Clare et Beati Francisci presertim collegialiter et in communi viventes et earum monasteria et loca," Hüntemann and Pou y Martí 1929–49: I, no. 1045). Indicative of the diversity of customs current among women's communities, Eugenius's bizarre wording encouraged ambitious efforts on the part of the Observants to exact obedience from all women's communities over which they thought they could assert a claim. Although the bull contained no mention of it, *clausura* became the goal and instrument of control. In the course of the fifteenth century, many women's communities sought papal exemptions to protect themselves from Observant dominance. For the history of the Observants in Italy see Sensi 1985b. Chapters 8 and 9 are the most relevant to the present discussion. For Roman examples of resistance to the Observant Franciscans see below, n. 36.

wanted to maintain their capacity for self-direction. Moreover, despite a general identity with the Franciscan Third Order, these tertiaries did not feel a strong obligation to or an abiding identification with the Franciscan order as an administrative entity. They did not want to see their organizational structures and highly valued local labors coopted and compromised by the ecclesio-political program of the expanding Observant wing of the Franciscan order. Although rebels against dominance by the Observant branch of the Franciscans, the Perugian communities were in no way heretics: they wanted regular access to the sacramental practices of the Church. The friars designated to provide these offices demanded administrative subjugation, epitomized and insured by *clausura*, in exchange for sacramental services, or *cura*. Their reference to San Damiano, "Clare and her first institution," in their supplication to Sixtus IV is extremely interesting in its rejection of the female religious model promoted by the Franciscans. This dissent indicates a keen historical awareness of how poorly early Poor Clares had been served by their alliance with the Franciscan order.[14] Finally, the duplicate public chapter meeting and, even more, the petitions to the pope indicate a capacity for coordinated "extra-mural" efforts. The tertiaries, like numerous women's communities in the later Middle Ages, existed in close connection with other similar communities, networks, which were sometimes administratively refined to the status of congregations. As we will see again, enclosure is incompatible with networks. Enclosure limits effective solidarity with (or even awareness of) groups sharing similar goals and problems, it hampers systems of clientage and patronage, and it assures that the resources and horizons of women's communities will remain predominately local.

Scandal, decadence, and abuse

It is not particularly useful when considering women's religious life of the fourteenth and fifteenth centuries, to draw a strong line between "regular" and "extra-regular" groups. The caveat of one historian of beguines applies, without extensive qualification, to women's religious life in general: "one cannot overemphasize the inherent diversity of their status, organization and function."[15] Many factors evacuate the meaningfulness of categorical distinctions between so-called regular monasteries and communities of beguines, *pinzochere*,[16] penitents, tertiaries. These include the diversity

---

[14] See nn. 9 and 12.
[15] Simons 1989: 63.
[16] *Pinzochera*, one of the vernacular Italian designations for uncloistered religious women, designates a female religious whose social status was similar to that of the northern European beguine. The Italian *pinzochere* are the subject of my doctoral dissertation (Gill 1994). See also Gill 1992.

of house customs, the accumulation of dispensations and exemptions, inadequate support services from designated ecclesiastical persons, and the powerful role of lay patronage. Furthermore, a proclivity for metamorphosis is characteristic of women's religious institutions. Some communities had pedigrees of affiliation and transformation which beg the services and branching schemata of a genealogist. Sant' Agnese in Perugia, for example, went from being a twelfth-century community of lay penitents, to a fourteenth-century monastery of Poor Clares, to a fifteenth-century tertiary house – with a few annexations and incorporations in between.[17] Today's hermitage might be tomorrow's monastery; today's convent, tomorrow's beguinage. Despite this historical recurrence of unstable boundaries around and between women's religious communities, scholars have persistently suspected foul play when viewing resistance to or disregard of strict enclosure. Moreover, they have privileged sexual activity or fear of sexual activity as a root cause of legislation and controversy. As we have seen, the Umbrian friars sought to impose *clausura* not to subdue sexual activity, but political activity and autonomy. Why then has the wayward nun, rather than the collectively self-conscious community, dominated explanations for turbulence with regard to enclosure?

Doubtless, the word *scandalum*, which so often emerges in the context of *clausura* controversies, is at least partially culpable for our association of sex with convent troubles. However, a careful survey of this term in late medieval documents shows that "public conflict," or "disruptive polarization of potent interest groups," or even "disturbance of the peace" would all be better translations than our tabloid tainted word "scandal." The Perugian orator accused the Observant friars, not the penitents, of causing "scandal among many." The term also frequently designated situations in which the authority of prominent persons, offices, or institutions was in some way jeopardized. Scandal acquired increasingly potent juridical usage in the later Middle Ages, heightening the criminal coloration of an already descriptively dramatic word. In both its descriptive and legal meanings, the word scandal insisted on the public ramifications of what might otherwise have been regarded as a private, domestic, or in-house affair.[18]

---

[17] Women's religious communities could be quite protean. It was not uncommon for communities to change locations, rules, functions, patrons, and ecclesiastical affiliations. Frequently one community absorbed another, thereby changing the character of both. Houses also exchanged lay for religious status and vice versa. For Sant' Agnese's metamorphoses from a lay to a religious and back to a lay status, see Casagrande 1979: 137–8 and 1980: 374–5. Casagrande's articles include other examples as well. I treat this aspect of women's religious life extensively in Gill 1994.

[18] While not all scandals were sexual in character, sexual misconduct could often only be prosecuted in the Middle Ages on the basis of scandalousness or notoriety. A reason for the term *scandalum* being increasingly invoked in connection with sexual misconduct, and thereby associated with it, is suggested by the work of Richard M. Frayer, in particular 1984 and 1989.

Socially and politically, scandal represented a public evil. For example, when papal soldiers bivouacked near St. Peter's after the return of the pope from Avignon, dramatically altering the urban environment around the convent of Santa Maria *prope Portium santi Petri*, the nuns asked permission to move in order to avoid "scandal." These women, living at the gateway of St. Peter's basilica, most of whom came from aristocratic Roman families, were not thinking primarily of sexual scandal. They wanted to avoid the public violence which would ensue between their kinsmen and the papal soldiers if one of them should suffer insult or assault. Doubtless, they also wanted to reduce the possibility that any of their relatives might have reason to be in the vicinity. At this moment in Rome, amid the havoc of schism, anti-papal feeling was running high. Especially restive were Rome's politically tethered magnates, some of whose anxious sisters and daughters lived at St. Peter's Gate. In the event of an incident, feminine honor would not have been the only issue in the hopper.[19] Similarly, when an unexpected pregnancy precipitated the shotgun marriage of a couple in the diocese of Cambrai, and this misadventure was followed first by the discovery of consanguinity and then by adultery on the part of the husband, the unhappy couple petitioned Eugenius IV for a divorce dispensation. The motive they gave for requesting divorce and the legitimization of their children was "to prevent scandals among our friends," friends who evidently were of hotly different minds as to what should be done in such a situation.[20] Even in this situation, scandal was only superficially connected with sexual misconduct; so too, I would argue, was sexual

From the twelfth century (but especially from the late thirteenth) jurists "expanded the sphere of public interest in criminal prosecutions" to include actions that had previously resided outside the reach of prosecution in what had been deemed the private sphere, particularly if the action was notorious (Frayer 1984: 583). In this context, scandal – together with terms such as ill-fame (*fama*) – assumed new legal import. Now "public scandal" could serve as grounds for prosecuting private acts. These included sex crimes, which, because they tended to be elusively private in nature, had previously been difficult to prove according to early medieval criteria for due process (Frayer 1989: 224–5). The valence of most forms of sexual misconduct was such that it easily combined with scandal – with conflict and uproar – because consequences frequently brought to loggerheads ecclesiastical, civil, and familial authorities (1989: 217 and 233). I am grateful to Edward Peters for pointing out Frayer's work to me and to Alan Bernstein for also highlighting the developing connotations of *scandalum* in canon law.

19 For the convent of Santa Maria *prope Portium santi Petri*, see the nun's petition in ASV, RL 156 fol. 95r–v (14 June 1411).

20 For the couple whose vexed marriage stirred up scandal in the diocese of Cambrai, see ASV, RL 398 fol. 304r–v (23 August 1443). In the preceding two examples I have given instances in which a "scandal" was only superficially about sexual behavior. Documents also frequently deploy the term to characterize situations in which sexual misconduct plays absolutely no part, for example, to describe the result of clerical misappropriation of funds pertaining to a benefice (ASV, RL 17 fols. 173v–5v). In like manner, the possible disagreement or resentment that might arise if the bishop of Poitiers intervenes to enable a certain widow to enter a convent is designated *scandalum* (ASV, RL 267 fol. 135r–v [22 July 1427]). The work of James Given, particularly his contribution to this volume, informed my thinking about group conflict.

misconduct only superficially connected, if at all, with the scandals of breaking *clausura*. The term signals if anything the public relevance not the private lives of religious women.

Together with "scandal," attributions of "abuse," "decadence," and "disobedience" are also commonly associated with the non-observance of *clausura* and other deviations from the purest versions of approved rules. Women's communities had no reason to believe that they should apply to themselves the ideas of every bishop, ordinary, or monastic superior who set himself up in their diocese. And neither should we. Nor should we embrace with so little scrutiny the perspective of complaining male authorities.[21] By failing to look carefully at factors producing such variance and variety in women's monastic and semi-monastic arrangements, we have missed evidence of the purposefulness, the social roles, and identity-giving traditions of many women's communities.

Santuccia Carabotti: leadership constrained

"It is not expedient for that sex to enjoy the freedom of having its own governance."[22] So wrote the twelfth-century German school teacher, Idung of Prüfening, whose rather unexemplary personal pilgrimage brought him eventually into the fold of the Cistercian order and into the fray of that century's debates about the purpose of monastic life. In one of his polemical works, entitled *An Argument on Four Questions*, Idung takes up the question of whether the Benedictine Rule should apply equally to men and women in matters of enclosure. His stance is clearly an emphatic no. Benedict never intended his Rule for women's religious communities. Interestingly, this is a judgment he shares with another contemporary exegete of the Rule, Heloise, who takes this position, rhetorically in a radically different direction.[23] The rise

---

21 "Toutes les réformes de monastères de femmes jusqu'au XVIIIe siècle ont toujours commencée par la remise en vigueur d'une stricte clôture"; see Jombart and Viller 1953: 999. Statements like this, which ignore changes in customs initiated by women, are fairly characteristic of the literature on *clausura*. The small complaints and the big decrees of ecclesiastical officials, whose routinely recorded statements were in practice almost as routinely overridden by quieter amendments, have been used to construct a misleading picture. For one example of a reform led by a woman see the discussion of Santuccia Carabotti, below.

22 The context of this quotation is Idung's third question, where he marshals authorities to support a case for female claustration and attempts to justify why monastic women should accept this restriction but not men; cited in Schulenberg 1984: 63 n. 82. Schulenberg offers an interesting discussion of Idung and his argument on pp. 61–3.

23 See Georgiana 1987, which beautifully positions Heloise's third letter to Alebard "in context of contemporary controversies concerning the monastic life and other forms of spirituality" (224). Georgiana demonstrates how Heloise casts doubt on the value of any outward regulation of religious life by directing attention toward the centrality of unruly passions and by transforming feminine weakness into a metaphor for human frailty.

of the mendicant orders in the early thirteenth century did not, apparently, quell all interest in possible meanings and adaptations of the Benedictine Rule. The late thirteenth-century reformer to whom we now turn, Santuccia Carabotti of Gubbio, engaged the traditional Rule experimentally together with another Umbrian religious leader named Sperandio. Like Heloise she established a confederacy of women's communities, united under a single, abbess-led, central administration and a single rule.[24] Like Heloise she was a married woman. We do not know what her opinion was on the ultimate value of religious rules; but her actions clearly indicate that she believed that in matters of governance women's communities should be no more constrained by enclosure than men's. Santuccia, whom Pope Clement V would dub *planatrix ordinis santucciarum*, founder of the order of the Sanctuccias, led what was probably one of the most radical and well-articulated of any of late medieval efforts to establish a women's religious order run by and for women.[25]

Santuccia's religious career began in the mid-thirteenth century when she and her husband embraced a religious form of life which enjoyed a marked popularity then and during the next 100 years: the chaste marriage.[26] The continent couple first affiliated themselves as oblates to the Benedictine monastery of San Pietro at Gubbio, a religious house recently revived under the leadership of fra Sperandio, who was yet another continent spouse.[27] Soon Santuccia and her husband took another step, this time separately. While her husband entered Sperandio's monastery as a monk, Santuccia established a women's convent based on the revised version of the Benedictine Rule developed by Sperandio for his monastery, San Pietro.

Santuccia's success in this project produced both popular support and numerous requests from central Italian bishops that she establish or reform existing monasteries in their dioceses. In 1262, Santuccia accepted an oratory and hermitage offered by a female recluse. Located on the edge of nearby

---

[24] Some of the more famous women's congregations include the Brigittines, the Observant communities associated with Sainte Colette in France or Blessed Angelina of Montegiove in central Italy, and later the Ursulines. Convents like Heloise's Paraclete functioned as mother houses for a number of smaller houses. There are many less famous examples; see, e.g., Casagrande 1984: 438–45 and 1980: 371–5 for the Perugian penitent house of Santa Maria de Valfabbrica and its extensive network of dependent houses in Assisi, Città di Castello, Borgo San Sepolcro, and Florence.

[25] The fundamental sources for the life and projects of Santuccia have been published and discussed by Leandro Novelli (1975). New documents concerning various monasteries, particularly three in Rome belonging to the "congregatio" or "ordo Santucciarum," inform my treatment of Santuccia's legacy in Gill 1994. For Santuccia, see also the work of Cardinal Giuseppe Garampi (1775).

[26] For continent couples pursuing religious vocations see Vauchez 1987: especially 83–92, 203–10, and 211–24.

[27] These two celibate couples, together with Speradio's sister, a recluse, comprised what we can still trace of a spiritual circle, or *cenacolo*, with a monastic and administrative reforming bent.

Perugia, at one of the city gates, this hermitage became the site and first affiliate of a nascent congregation which would include over twenty communities throughout central Italy before Santuccia's death in 1305.[28]

Santuccia's reform activities soon landed her in the first of a series of controversies involving the issue of enclosure. Her former spiritual guide and supporter, Sperandio, had died in 1260 and the new abbot of San Pietro in Perugia, reckoning Santuccia under his jurisdiction by virtue of her earlier act of oblation to his monastery, required that she tailor the rules of her new foundation and the scope of her own activities so that both conformed to expectations associated with *clausura*. Santuccia responded by asserting that she was no longer an oblate of San Pietro, but rather the abbess of an independent monastery. The abbot promptly excommunicated her, but the papal penitentiary, to whom Santuccia then appealed, upheld Santuccia's claim and formally released her from obedience to the abbot on 1 June 1265.

From this point on Santuccia's intentions for her congregation emerge more clearly. In her view women's convents would always fall victim to the debilitating designs of local families and bishops if they did not have recourse to a centralized, non-local, political structure whose female leadership would be primarily concerned with the spiritual and material well-being of nuns.[29] "Because the feminine sex is weak," Idung had written, "it needs greater protection and stricter enclosure."[30] In Santuccia's view feminine *fragilitas* was constructed rather than protected by the current institutional practices. Women's monasteries would always be vulnerable without the continuous leadership of truly interested parties, insiders who understood first hand the genesis of problems and would have to live intimately with the consequences of any solution adopted.[31]

---

[28] Novelli, in discussing the rapid diffusion of Santuccia's influence and its coagulation into a congregation of women's houses, adds, 'Si ha l'impressione che se la Congregazione non avesse trovato ostacoli da parte di alcuni vescovi e superiori religiosi a causa soprattutto della clausura e di altre novità di costititzione, avrebbe potuto avere una diffusione anche maggiore" (1975: 192).

[29] For kin and convent life, see Zarri 1986: especially 365–72. Sometimes family interference could be quite extreme; e.g., ASV, Archivum Arcis, *Armaria* I–XVII, vol. 6493 fol. 28r, contains an angry supplication from a father who insists that the pope should order his daughter into a convent because his wife and brother-in-law have connived a matrimonial match requiring a dowry the enormity of which, he claims, will undo him.

[30] Schulenburg 1984: 62 and 83 n. 77.

[31] Abundant evidence supports Santuccia's conviction that neither the traditional nor the new male orders could be consistently counted on for good leadership of women's convents. The interests and priorities of male ecclesiastical bodies would always contribute to, if not guarantee, patterns of neglect and overweening intervention in their dealings with women's communities. For instance, de Fontette documents well the poor record of male groups in the *regimen* and *cura* of women's communities; see especially her chapter on Franciscans (1967: 129–51). The inconsistent and usually disadvantageous administration endured by women's groups associated with the Franciscans could not have escaped Santuccia in Gubbio. See also

While Idung had declared that St. Benedict had never intended the licenses of his rule to apply to nuns, stating that it was obvious to everyone that business travel and commercial dealings were "unfitting . . . for any reason for the spouse of an earthly king, much less for the bride of the King of heaven,"[32] Santuccia took a different position. Mobility and autonomy were essential for the leaders and representatives of women's communities.[33] The houses of her order were subject to the rule of an "abbess general," whose role included regular visits for the purpose of assessing their condition. To maintain collective and individual equilibrium the abbess general could transfer nuns from one house to another, a practice which further increased movement in and out of her communities. She intended that collective issues be handled, as they were in male orders, in general chapters at which abbesses and representatives from the various houses would come together. For all its apparent novelty, Santuccia's principal innovation consisted in adopting for her congregation the Benedictine Rule, as it was practiced by men.[34]

While bishops of ordinaries were happy to be relieved of the burden of maintaining the well-being of their convents, they were not always enthusiastic about losing control of them. According to Santuccia's plan even a bishop's wishes regarding one of her communities were subject to the approval of the abbess general. As one might imagine, having to do business with a surveillant, politic, and juridically independent abbess cramped the style of some bishops, accustomed to regarding the women's communities in their diocese as ecclesiastical colonies and ready resources for their gracious exercise of regional power. (After all, a bishop never knew when he or a well-placed friend might have an illegitimate daughter needing to be conveniently placed some-where.) The inconsistent pattern of support and opposition in the attitude of

---

Creytens 1949: he cites, among others, an instance in which, in 1370, nuns of the diocese of Basel confront the College of Cardinals with their grievances deriving from the *malo regimine* of friars (p. 39 n. 109); he also charts the withdrawal of women's groups from the Dominican order in the fourteenth century (pp. 36–42).

32 Schulenburg 1984: 62.

33 Johnson's excellent study of nuns in thirteenth-century France bears out Santuccia's assertion that freedom from strict enclosure was necessary to the continued maintenance of a community's economic and political strength (1991: especially 153–5).

34 The issues of a nun's freedom to govern, to travel, and to participate in policy making together with the male members of her order had come up before. Santuccia was more successful than some of her predecessors. In a letter directed to the abbess and the nuns of Santa Maria di Bourbourg in 1166, Alexander III addressed the problem of egress from monasteries by abbesses – a habit the abbesses justified with the example of some Cistercian nuns who went to the general chapters convened by the abbots of their order. Alexander took a hard line: "nulli episcopo, in cuius episcopatu ecclesias possideant, liceat abbatissam ad synodum ex debito vel ex distractione vocare, nisi fuerit diocesanus episcopus vel metropolitanus," in Jaffé 1888: 200 n. 11297, cited in Occhipinti 1978: 205, where other examples of the same sort of conflict are included.

various local authorities required that Santuccia secure the rights of her congregation to their administrative practices through papal approval.

After Santuccia's death in March 1305, the central house at S. Maria in Julia at Rome continued to request confirmation of the right to follow the *regula sanctucciarum* and to receive the *subsidio defensionis* of a cardinal protector against any "prelates, rectors, clerics and other priests who, contrary to the privileges granted by the Holy See, without grounds, might harass and impede" the congregation.[35] All the confirmations contain the phrase "not withstanding the decisions of our predecessor Boniface VIII." Many other women's communities would in the course of the fourteenth and fifteenth centuries seek privileges and exemptions which would require and receive this same "non obstantibus" clause, *Pericoloso*'s legal solvent.[36]

The receipt of papal exemptions by no means meant that "the order of Santuccia" or other similarly licensed communities were home free. The women of such institutions would incessantly battle to reclaim the same territory: collecting contingent liberties and angling for equilibrium amid the political and ideological contradictions of their culture. We will now look at the ways in which some groups of women, who for various reasons lived in nonconformity with rules created by leaders of male orders for religious women, strengthened their positions through appeal to the papacy.

Labile liberties

"You already know how rights depend on one's petition being granted."[37] This statement from the autobiography of a Castilian noblewoman could serve as a political maxim for medieval women in general. It seems to hold, however, a special truth with regard to women's religious institutions. The papal registers of the fourteenth and, especially, the fifteenth centuries contain many papal responses to petitions from (or on behalf of) women seeking juridical backbone for their particular religious *modus vivendi*. Typically they sought exemptions from obedience to those who would normally exercise jurisdiction over them (a bishop or an ordinary), exemptions from practices prescribed by their rules or status, or the reconfirmation of exemptions granted at an earlier

---

[35] "Regula sanctucciarum" is Clement V's term. See Novelli 1975: 204 n. 11, where he excerpts from a 5 January 1306 bull cited as "Dal Regesto n. 52 di Clemente V, edito dai benedettini di S. Callisto 1885, vol. I, fol. 116." The specific reference to protection against clerical harassment comes from ASV, RA 6 vols. 656v–7r (31 May, John XXII, year I, thus 31 May 1317).

[36] Two fifteenth-century Roman examples: Paleotia's community in Rome (Trastevere), and that of Caterina of Orte, who headed a Roman group of tertiaries "de penitentia beati Francisci." Caterina, whose community was vernacularly dubbed "le perugine," sought help from Nicholas V in the face of harassment by the Observants. There may well have been a bond between this Roman house and the Perugian tertiaries discussed above.

[37] Lacey 1986: 331.

time.[38] The papacy, for its part, demonstrated its prerogative to loose, as well as bind, nowhere more consistently than in its dealings with religious women. The registers abound with letters which free communities from local control, from fasting and from limits on the personal control of property. Some letters, like those addressed to tertiaries who have renovated and occupied the uninhabited palace of a cardinal in Rome, authorize even more eccentric arrangements.[39] Frequently, some sort of conflict, an intervention from outside the community (usually referred to as *molestia* [harassment]), "discordia" within the community, or both concomitantly, precipitated recourse to the papacy. *Clausura* is often explicitly at issue in the controversy.

Unlike the male religious orders, we have few records of general or particular chapter meetings which reveal the way policy took shape and decisions evolved. Petitions to the Holy See, which often retain the wording of the request as received, are therefore even more valuable for what they tell of the conditions and choices of women's religious life. Too long viewed by post-Tridentine ecclesiastical historians as signs of conniving evasion or moral hebetude, exemptions and their confirmations allow us to observe the institution-building efforts of women in a world in which their rights did "depend on [their] petition being granted."

Probably the most frequent restrictions waived by papal largesse were those concerning the flow of people in and out of cloistered areas. Isabelle, daughter of Philip the Fair, received permission in 1320 for unlimited visits to a monastery of Poor Clares near Paris, together with an entourage of soldiers and women.[40] In early March 1493, a papal secretary registered the following message to John, "electoral prince of the Holy Roman Empire" and his brothers, Frederick and Sigismund, dukes of Brandenburg:

You have written that you have a sister [named] Dorothea in the monastery of St. Clare at Bamberg, whom you have always loved more than all your other sisters with a

---

[38] For exemptions see Creytens 1965 *passim.* Creytens makes the point that webs of exemptions conflicted with enforcement of a rigorist position on *clausura.* The pattern one typically sees in letters requesting approval of "irregularities" is that, having first established a community along certain lines, the women in it then ask permission to continue in the same way. I have never found a request for practices merely contemplated. Doubtless numerous para-institutional groups went about their business for decades without ever feeling the need for or seeking papal corroboration. Sensi offers a diplomatic description of privileges and exemptions to nuns, outlining the form and content of a typical document (1985b: 90–4).

[39] ASV, RV 403 fol. 13r–v. This letter from Nicholas V (21 April 1451) reiterates the right bestowed by Eugenius IV (21 September 1441) on the Dominican tertiaries *de penitentia,* allowing them to continue to reside in the palace of the cardinal of Santa Cecilia, which they had occupied and restored. Nicholas's reconfirmation describes a multi-purpose collection of buildings ("domus [residential structures] singulasque suas officinas"), which the tertiaries may continue to have "pro habitatione et aliis usibus vestris." This Roman parish hosted other groups with histories of innovation, including Humiliati and Brigittine canons.

[40] ASV, RA 14 fol. 342r (13 December 1320). Isabelle's sister Blanche receives the same license.

special fraternal love, and that you would like your current wives and Anna your mother, and your other sisters to be able to visit and converse with Dorothea for their consolation.[41]

Less regal petitioners regularly received the same sorts of permissions. The daughters, granddaughters, and all the female members of the household of the Venetian, Marinus Yenerius, could visit four times a year the recluses of Santa Maria Magdalena in Padua, in order to seek "spiritual renewal," as long as they did not stay overnight.[42] And Lucia de Crivellis of Milan received an affirmative reply to her petition to enter and "(se) spiritualiter recreare" four times a year whatever monasteries of nuns she elected, including communities of Poor Clares. Two or three other women of her choosing might go with her, but, again, they were not to spend the night inside the convent.[43] By virtue of an indult issued by Boniface IX in 1400, the parents of the canonesses of Venice could visit them when they were ill. (A privilege confirmed by Alexander VI, 5 July 1493.)[44] The fact that the responses to three out of four of the above petitions occur in a single register and within two weeks of each other gives some idea of their routine nature in the fifteenth century.

Friendship, family affection, and spiritual renewal are just one set of reasons why *clausura* prohibitions against outsiders might be abrogated. Ingress often meant income: an exchange of services, spiritual and otherwise.[45] In the case of six fifteenth-century Benedictine nuns in Yugoslavia, access to their convent allowed them a necessary labor force. They presented their predicament to Alexander VI in the following manner: their endowed income was so slight that

---

[41] Brev. Lat. 2 fol. 14r–v.

[42] Brev. Lat. 2 fols. 69v–70r (16 March 1493).

[43] Brev. Lat. 2 fol. 40v (1 March 1493). The frequent specification "even convents of St. Clare," which regularly appears in grants of this sort toward the end of the fifteenth century, may very well be a pointed "hands-off" message to the Observant friars.

[44] For Alexander's bull see Jombart and Viller 1953: 999. Parental affection and piety often merged, e.g., the duchesses of Brandenburg mentioned above and ASV, Archivum Arcis, *Armaria* I–XVIII 5029, fol. 39r (Alexander VI, *Minutae brevium*). The latter yields a letter to Julia de Quistelle, described simply as *mulieri Mirandulen(si)*, who receives permission to visit triennially, in the company of three *honestis matronis per te eligendis* a reformed (Observant) Franciscan monastery in her diocese dedicated to St. Louis in which she has a daughter. The matrons may also remain to eat and drink with the sisters. The letter is dated 8 May 1502.

[45] According to Jean Leclercq, the chief effect of enclosure was to reduce the possibility of work (1980: 86). This problem was generally recognized, if often managed differently, by both male and female religious. Poverty was an eloquently persuasive argument against observation of *clausura* from the first years after Boniface's constitution, and it continued to be so through the first years after the Council of Trent. Among the post-*Pericoloso* salvoes is the successful protest of the nuns of the Cistercian monastery of Santa Maria di Brione in the Piedmont, resisting the abbot of Lucedio's attempt to enforce strict enclosure, "quod cum ipse tanta essent pauperate [*sic*] gravate quod non haberent unde possent huiusmodi clausuram facere nec etiam congruam sustentacionem habere nisi interdum fidelium elemosinis iuvarentur" (Sella 1913: document 96; cf. Boyd 1943: 109 n. 17). See below for Trent.

they had to depend on manual labor for most of their food; for this reason they also had lay persons working in the monastery. Furthermore, they allowed women into their church and within the cloistered part of the monastery where they talked together about the needs of the monastery. Recently, however, they had heard a report that a former papal nuncio (now, a bishop) had once declared that if any nuns of any monastery should break *clausura* they would *ipso facto* incur excommunication. Troubled, the impoverished Yugoslavian nuns wondered if the nuncio's pronouncement held true for them. No, Alexander VI informed them, it did not.[46]

Neither did it seem unreasonable to Pius III and Julius II for Elizabeth, the duchess of Norfolk, a widow, to adopt a monastery of Poor Clares as her executive cockpit. The brief responding to the second supplication of this *dame d'affaires*, who resided permanently within the convent, runs as follows:

> Some time ago she made representation to Pope Pius III that following the death of her husband she wished, in order to live more quietly and to win salvation, to dwell with two or three upright women in the monastery of nuns outside Algate, London, of the order of St. Clare, though without taking the habit or making regular profession. At her supplication, Pius granted her license and faculty to dwell for life in the said monastery, including its inner cloisters, with two or three upright women, and in time of her infirmity or other necessities, with five or six such [women] without taking the habit or making regular profession, and [she would like] occasionally . . . to leave the monastery to pursue her affairs and then to return, and to have a suitable confessor, secular or regular, to absolve her and enjoin a penance . . . and to assist her in her infirmities . . . Her recent petition stated that she, now infirm and worn out with age, dwells in the said monastery in an honorable place and separated from the abbess and nuns, . . . that from time to time she requires the counsel of prudent persons for her arduous business and affairs, and a servant especially at table and for writing her business, and also other women.[47]

Duchess Elizabeth's letter also obtained for her the attendance of four priests and permission to enlarge the monastery's garden and ambulatory.

Not all long-term guests were so cumbersome or well-provisioned as the duchess; Elizabeth represents just one end of the spectrum of those "others residing in the monastery," who may be mentioned in passing documents.[48]

---

[46] Brev. Lat. 2 vols. 8v–9v (2 March 1493).

[47] ASV, RL 1184 fol. 318r–v (8 August 1506), published and translated in Haren 1989: 483–4.

[48] The imported staff of the duchess was most likely matched by an internal staff serving similar functions for the nuns. Two documents concerning the monasteries of the Santuccia congregation indicate that in addition to the sisters, the populations of the congregation's houses included "chaplains, confessors, and household staff (*familiares*)" as well as unspecified "others," ASV, RA fol. 657r–v (31 May 1317). See also Creytens 1949: 36–42, where the fourteenth- and fifteenth-century process whereby Dominican nuns gained more control over the friars and conversi who lived in their monasteries is discussed. Creytens also asserts that service to convents became increasingly attractive to Dominican friars and lay brothers after the Black Death, from which female institutions rebounded more readily than male ones.

Moreover, complex business concerns like those which involved the duchess of Norfolk were not always imported into convents by outsiders. With or without dispensation, nuns, particularly of aristocratic monasteries, frequently managed the responsibilities of private property. In 1399, Mascia de Haniballis sought permission for her two daughters, nuns of the Franciscan convent of S. Silvestro in Rome, to receive extensive properties and to be able to control them.[49]

In addition to the "passive" rupture of *clausura* effected by visitors, the active puncture of *clausura* by departing nuns was also the subject of numerous petitions. The poverty, elective or otherwise, of many communities required that sisters traverse their cities and towns soliciting alms. Even a relatively stable community like San Antonio in Perugia needed an advance on its annual allotment of civic grain when a cold spell kept them from their usual rounds of alms seeking.[50] With reference to religious women in the late medieval city, our concept of begging (*mendicare* and *elimosinare*) should probably be expanded to include fund raising as well as many sorts of social and personal services. Many of a city's mendicant tertiaries and nuns might function as a kind of respectable, flexible work force. Other uncloistered women regularly applied specific skills, among which medical arts and midwifery were prominent.[51] Extra-mural social contact was essential to the survival of many groups, as desperate petitions to the Holy See in the wake of Trent dramatically illustrate. For instance, in a petition of the later sixteenth century, the deputies of the *convertite* convent in Rome wrote that, having been denied the possibility of "begging," the 108 women of the house were "without wine, oil, wood, grain and other things necessary to eating." To emphasize their point, the deputies described the living conditions within the monastery as so poor "that if the Lord God himself were to convert some sinner who then

---

[49] Both Mascia and her husband, Jordanus Agapiti de Columpna (described as *domicellus Romanus* to the pope), were of most prestigious baronial families of Rome: ASV, RL 69 fols. 88r–9r (27 March 1399). The work of Etienne Huber on the financial records of San Silvestro has revealed its nuns to be real-estate moguls of major stature in thirteenth-, fourteenth-, and, to a lessening degree, fifteenth-century Rome (1988: especially 101–3). The nuns' preference for long-term leases eventually caused them to fall behind the enterprising canons of St. Peter's and those of St. John Lateran, who dealt in the more lucrative and adjustable short-term contract. It is likely that the impediments of enclosure regulations influenced the nuns' choice of a more passive and less lucrative policy of property management. Sensi offers an example of consistently aggressive property acquisition and management by female religious (1985b: 86–7).

[50] ASP, Consigli e Riformanze 105 fol. 114r–v, cited in Casagrande 1984: 458.

[51] Numerous wills leaving bequests to Italian *pinzochere* declare gratitude for unspecified *servitia* given and hoped for. See also Creytens 1949 for "open" monasteries and for examples of hardship caused for poorer nuns when public presence is denied them. Charting the occupations of female household heads in fifteenth-century Florence, David Herlihy determined that, after servants, *pinzochere* made up the second largest group of working women (1990: 159; see also Gill 1994).

desired to become a nun, [the *convertite*] would be forced, with great sorrow, to turn her away."[52]

Infirmity, her own or that of a relative, frequently impelled a nun to leave the cloister. In March 1493, Catherine Boudemanis "ordinis minorissarum," who described herself as "hunchback and scrofulous" and unable to remain in the monastery where she has professed "because of the feebleness (*imbecilitas*) of her body and frequent illness," received permission to live out her days, devoutly, in a house which her brother had given her.[53] Then there were also cases like Piera of Todi, whose mother had arranged for her to enter the Benedictine Annunciata when she was eleven, just after the death of her father. After years during which she comported herself with impeccable piety ("altissimo famulatum exhibendo"), Piera fell sick and moved out to stay with relatives. For her health's sake Piera now wanted to move to the Benedictine monastery of Santa Caterina, also in Todi, where the air was reputedly better; but her paternal inheritance had been used up during her stay at the Annunciata. Furthermore she was loathe to renege on her original agreement with the Annuciata, which stipulated that after she died the sisters there would receive the twelve ducats she had as annual income. The Holy See found all this reasonable. Neither is there any hint that Piera's convalescence in the home of relatives was perceived by her local bishop or by the papacy as anything extraordinary.[54]

A nun's simple act of leaving a monastery, particularly if it was to go into a private home or another convent, did not usually draw much concern or attention. She, after all, unlike Santuccia or the Perugian tertiaries, was not asking to take a place in the public sphere. Thus, when Elvira of a monastery in the diocese of Toledo, a house which she designated as "of the order of St. Augustine, under the care of the preachers," declared that for certain reasons she could no longer remain where she was with a tranquil soul, she received

---

[52] ASV, Archivum Arcis, *Armaria* I–XXII, 6493 fol. 5r. This letter is one of thirteen petitions from or concerning women's communities that have been bound together in a single volume entitled *Monialium diversa*. The letters seem to have been collected in the early sixteenth century to serve as case studies for the reflection of one or more members of one of the new papal commissions (*congregationes*) in charge of enforcing the new regulations regarding women's religious communities. Each one seems chosen to illustrate a different woe. This letter collection is more fully discussed and illustrated in Gill 1994.

[53] Brev. Lat. 2 fol. 3r.

[54] For Piera of Todi, see Brev. Lat. 2 fols. 66r–7r (12 March 1493). Anthony Molho, in his study of the Florentine dowry bank (*Mons dotalis*) and women who entered convents despite accrued savings for marriage dowries, presents cases of women who entered, rather than exited, monasteries because of illness. He makes the interesting suggestion that frequent accounts of miraculous healings in convents are due to the fact that so many nuns were sickly (1989: 22–6).

papal permission to leave. Furthermore, having explained that she was forty-five years old and the illegitimate daughter of a noble bachelor and a married woman, Elvira received an additional dispensation enabling her to serve as abbess, if ever elected, in whatever new institution she chose.[55] Two weeks later, Gratia de Gutzman petitioned to leave the same Toledan monastery and to move to "a monastery or *locus* of St. Clare," where she might experience "a greater feeling of devotion, since she has no hope of remaining in [her current monastery of] San Domenico with a tranquil soul and clear conscience."[56] Clearly, as Santuccia had long before recognized, both personal and institutional equilibrium could require the transfer of nuns in and out of monasteries. A community needed to be able to make these kinds of adjustments, without having the roof come down on their heads. This was the unfortunate case for a Dominican community in southern Italy who petitioned for papal protection against local secular and ecclesiastical authorities who were responding punitively to what they judged to be a violation of *clausura* in their house. The sisters also requested and received papal support for their desire that a certain nun formerly of their monastery not be forced to return by means of ecclesiastical censures and secular judicial procedures.[57]

Multiple goings and comings not only worked to make women's communities "irregular" but even "multi-regular." Papal permissions for transfers frequently allowed dislocated nuns to retain their original habit and rule if they chose a monastery with different customs.[58] Incorporation and annexations of one community with another sometimes led to situations in which women who professed different rules would find themselves living together. In 1402, the dean of the cathedral of Strasbourg wrote Boniface IX, describing a convent of the Holy Cross in his diocese, which "is said to be of the order of St. Augustine." However, disagreement had arisen among the twelve sisters as to what form of life the group should follow. The abbess and six followers claimed that they were bound by no rule and that this arrangement had been instituted by former ordinaries. Others wanted the Augustinian habit and rule as designated by the original institutes. A single nun preferred a rule "of regular observance" and strict enclosure. Differing positions on rules and habits, like the one above, often emerge in a context of *scandalum*, or public disagreement and factionalism. This was because adherence to a particular rule often promised the material or spiritual support of a certain lay or ecclesiastical

---

55 Brev. Lat. 2 fol. 4r (2 March 1493).
56 *Ibid.* fol. 109r; license conceded on 25 March 1493.
57 *Ibid.* fol. 2v (2 March 1493).
58 For example, a concession similar to the two above granted license to transfer to Maria de Molina, a nun who could no longer remain "cum animi . . . quiete et sana conscientia" at Santa Clara in Venice. Maria could go to any monastery, regardless of the strictness or laxness of the rule, and retain her clarisse habit (*ibid.* fol. 62r–v [2 March 1493]).

patron. Two or three proposed rules doubtless indicate as many vying outside interest groups.[59]

In general, a high degree of tolerance for variations among women's religious communities prevailed in the fourteenth and fifteenth centuries. The papacy's gracious practice of releasing groups and individuals, on a case by case basis, from obligation to strict adherence to monastic rules assisted and protected discrete solutions. Invention, whether mothered by necessity or creative vision, might find some latitude. At the same time, custom, tradition, and long-standing local recognition were powerful levers, as we have seen in Perugia, which women's communities could operate to secure their unique *modus operandi.* But, while the papacy's gracious exercise of power and respect for local custom fostered diversity, there was no consistent, benevolent, papal policy regarding women's communities. Popes who professed interest in the reform and improvement of women's religious institutions, for example Innocent III and Eugenius IV, seem to have been quite enamoured of uniformity and quite ruthless in the face of the small and the idiosyncratic.[60]

Certainly, the involvement of the Roman curia in the affairs of a house did not always work to the advantage of religious women. If the Holy See was called in to settle a conflict the community entered a sphere of heightened vulnerability. Official inquiries often led to accusations of irregularity and loss of autonomy. One papal *inquisitio* into the troubles of a convent outside Florence records:

Bartolomea and Picarda are quarreling with an intense hatred and competing for control of the convent. The bishop of Fiesole and . . . a notary have investigated and discovered that many if not all the nuns are not obeying the Benedictine Rule they professed. [Furthermore] they are living in such a way that jeopardizes even jettisons their souls.[61]

As a result of this report, a Florentine abbot was empowered to punish the monastery, transferring or even banishing nuns if expedient. The risk involved in inviting outside intervention to settle a community dispute was probably what led the Perugian federation of tertiaries to include in their 1392 consti-

---

[59] For the nuns of the Holy Cross, whose discord led to loss of liberties and autonomy, see ASV, RL 100 fol. 3r–v. An excellently presented and analyzed example of such a "scandal," involving multiple rules connected with multiple interest groups, appears in McLaughlin 1989. For other fifteenth-century examples of mixed communities see ASV, RL 474 fols. 121v–2v (1451), Augustinian and Dominican lay sisters living as a single community; and ASV, group of Franciscan tertiaries in Rome gaining a Dominican "sister of penitence" as prioress.

[60] Maccarrone 1972 and Bolton 1990: 107–15. Interestingly, in the related context of imposing uniformity on the Humiliati, Innocent III links diversity of religious practice with increased possibility for "scandal" (for this see Potthast 1874–7: I. 1192 and Bolton 1990: 108).

[61] ASV, RV 366 fol. 23r (28 September 1434).

tutions a statement that in the case of a dispute no individual or house would seek outside arbitration.[62]

Carefully managed, however, appeals to the gracious functions of larger political bureaucracies, and the Roman curia in particular, allowed women's communities to create a wider margin of maneuvering than local authorities could be counted on to provide. This channel enabled religious women to collect rights and privileges which could gloss the asperity of their rules. As the evidence of the papal registers makes clear, women's communities used petitions as a way of mitigating strictures so that they could grow, adapt, keep true to a founding ideal, or simply survive. These petitions reveal the diversity, the protean mutability, and the particularity of membership and function which characterized the institutions women created and struggled to maintain.

Conclusion

There was no steady progression toward stricter enclosure of religious women in the fourteenth and fifteenth centuries. Even the decisions of the Council of Trent regarding *clausura* were as cautious as those ventured by the fifteenth-century vicar Pietro da Napoli, who had hesitated to oppose the desire either of the Perugian tertiaries or the Observants. After just enough discussion to remind themselves of the well-established varieties among women's religious communities, the participants of Trent's Session 25 hurriedly decided to fight complexity with ambiguous generalities and hope for the best. Pope Pius V's later constitution, *Circa pastoralis* (29 May 1566), not the Council, was the real herald and agent of change.[63]

Historians have not been surprised enough that, unlike *Pericoloso*, *Circa pastoralis* did have far-reaching and lasting effects. A satisfactory explanation for its sticking power does not reside in a vision of women's religious history which attempts to connect legislative dots in such a way as to render a picture of accumulating consensus powering a steady progression toward a strict enclosure. This was an ideal which required the ambitions and the instruments of the Catholic Reformation bureaucracy for its full realization. *Circa pastoralis* and its fallout were stunning; many bishops, nuns, and tertiaries were caught completely off guard.[64] Close scrutiny of the various

---

[62] See McLaughlin 1989 for the anguish reflected in the writings of Catherine Vegri as a result of dissent within her community and outside intervention. See also Casagrande 1979: 143 for the constitutions of Perugian tertiaries that forbade recourse to outside arbitration for disputes among tertiaries.

[63] For *Circa pastoralis*, Pius V, and the subsequent legislation of Gregory XIII aimed at closing loopholes, see Creytens 1964 and 1965 as well as Cain 1968–9: 27.2.272–80.

[64] Perhaps the most obvious example of a group surprised by the unbending imposition of *clausura* in the sixteenth century consists of Angela Merici's Brescia communities; see

contemporary religious cultures (curial, communal, etc.), but particularly women's religious culture, and its traditions in late medieval Italy does not yield a rich crop of compelling reasons why the possibilities for autonomy, self-direction, and public contact would be so drastically curtailed by the end of the sixteenth century. Rather, I suspect one would have more luck finding reasons in the values and practices of aristocratic households, in courtesy books, in the domestic and professional backgrounds of ecclesiastical leaders, in emergent political ideologies, and especially in ideals of marriage.[65] In other words, places where one might be able to trace changed expectations for and structurings of the most basic kind of (political) relations between men and women.

The post-Tridentine erasure of all forms of women's religious life except a single model has contributed to a misreading of the variety which characterizes women's religious communities in the later Middle Ages. The consequent depreciation of female accomplishments is something George Eliot ponders in her Prelude to *Middlemarch*. Reviewing the role of women in history, Eliot asks: what has happened to the ambitions of the "heroic female spirit," to the ideals of women like St. Theresa, who "found her epos in the reform of a religious order? . . . [To] common eyes, their struggles seem mere inconsistency and formlessness." This, she continues, is because no social or political forms have received and given enduring shape to women's effort. Moreover, the resulting "indefiniteness" of their hampered lives has then been ascribed to woman's nature. In this way the particularity of women, the range of "variation" among them goes unrecognized. Judged according to models of male institution building, a woman like "St. Theresa remains a 'foundress of nothing' whose energies 'are dispersed among hindrances, instead of centering in some long-recognizable deed.' "[66]

Cozzano 1968. For another new Cinquecento foundation that did not expect to be bound by strict enclosure see the superbly documented study by Gabriella Zarri (1976: especially 62–3).

[65] Courtesy and devotional books are used to explore the way in which changing social values, particularly those of the upper urban classes, reflect and foster an increasingly narrow role for women in Gill 1994. There I suggest that we hear reformers and administrators speaking not so much as clerics educated in the Fathers or experienced in spiritual care, but as the aristocratic brothers and uncles of female relations and dependants, toward whom they might feel alternately protective or suspicious. In regions where Protestant ideas had a strong following, many other factors worked, of course, to undermine credibility of women living in religious communities: their association with liturgical prayer, alms soliciting, monks, a rejected economy of salvation, etc. For the concept of religious cultures see Davis 1982.

[66] Eliot 1872–3: II.8, "Some have felt that these blundering lives are due to the inconvenient indefiniteness with which the Supreme Power has fashioned the natures of women . . . Meanwhile the indefiniteness remains, and the limits of variation are really much wider than any one would imagine from the sameness of a woman's coiffure and the favorite love-stories in prose and verse . . . Here and there is born a S. Theresa, foundress of nothing, whose loving heart-beats and sobs after an unattainable goodness tremble off and are dispersed among hindrances, instead of centering in some long-recognizable deed."

I hope that this essay has begun to bring some definition to what religious women intended and achieved. If so, the shifts and disclaimers recorded in responses to their petitions will no longer be adduced as so much evidence of "inconsistency," but rather efforts to protect the particularity of their institutions. Instances of avoidance of committed affiliations with male orders and their rules may indicate a policy of survival, rather than contrariness. Finally, I would hope that institutional indefiniteness, that very quality which has made women's communities historiographically volatile and elusive, once admitted as both a condition and style of *politique*, might produce a new and more inclusive kind of institutional history.

REFERENCES

Bolton, Brenda 1990 Daughters of Rome: All One in Christ Jesus. In W. J. Sheils and Diana Wood, eds., *Women in the Church*, 101–15. Papers Read at the 1989 Summer Meeting and the 1990 Winter Meeting of the Ecclesiastical History Society (*Studies in Church History* 27). Oxford: Basil Blackwell.

Boyd, Catherine E. 1943 *A Cistercian Nunnery in Mediaeval Italy: The Story of Rifreddo in Saluzzo, 1220–1300*. Cambridge, Mass.: Harvard University Press.

Cain, James R. 1968–9 Cloister and the Apostolate of Religious Women. *Review for Religious* 27.2: 243–80, 27.4: 652–71, 27.5: 916–37, and 28.1: 101–21.

Casagrande, Giovanna 1979 Il monastero di S. Agnese in Perugia nei secoli XIV e XV. *Studi franciscani* 76: 137–69.

1980 Aspetti del Terz'Ordine francescano a Perugia nella seconda metà del secolo XIV e nel XV. In Mariano D'Alatri, ed., *Il movimento francescano della Penitenza nella società medioevale*, 371–95. Rome: Istituto Storico dei Cappuccini.

1984 Terziarie Francescane Regolari in Perugia nei secoli XIV e XV. In R. Pazzelli and M. Sensi, eds., *La Beata Angelina da Montegiove e il movimento del Terz'Ordine Regolare Francescano femminile: Atti del Convegno di studi francescani Foligno, 22–24 settembre 1983*, 437–91. Roma: Analecta TOR.

Cozzano, G. 1968 Risposta contra quelli persuadono la clausura alle Vergini di Sant'Orsola. In Teresa Ledóchowska, ed., *Angèle Merici et la compagnie de Ste-Ursule à la lumière des documents*, II.332–59. Milan and Rome: Ancora.

Creytens, Raymond 1949 Les Convers des moniales dominicaines au moyen âge. *Archivum Fratrum Praedicatorum* 19: 5–48.

1964 La giurisprudenza della Sacra Congregazione nella questione della clausura della monache (1564–1576). In *La Sacra Congregazione del Consilio: Quarto centenario della fondazione (1564–1964), studi e ricerche*, 563–97. Vatican City: Sacra Congregazione del Consilio.

1965 La riforma dei monasteri femminili. In *Il Concilio di Trento e la riforma tridentina: Atti del Convegno storico internazionale, Trento 2–6 settembre 1963*, I.45–83. Rome: Herder.

Davis, Natalie Zemon 1982 From "Popular Religion" to Religious Cultures. In Steven Ozment, ed., *Reformation Europe: A Guide to Research*, 321–41. St. Louis: Center for Information Research.

Eliot, George (Mary Ann Evans) 1872–3 *Middlemarch*. 2 vols. New York: Harper Brothers (orig. 4 vols., Edinburgh: Blackwood, 1871–2).

Fontette, M. de 1967 *Les Religieuses à l'âge classique du droit canon*. Paris: J. Vrin.

Frayer, Richard M. 1984 The Theoretical Justification for the New Criminal Law of the High Middle Ages: "Rei publicae interest, ne crimina remaneant impunita." *University of Illinois Law Review* 3: 577–95.

1989 Preventing Crime in the High Middle Ages: The Medieval Lawyers' Search for Deterrence. In James Ross Sweeney and Stanley Chodorow, eds., *Popes, Teachers, and Canon Law in the Middle Ages: Essays in Honor of Brian Tierney*, 212–33. Ithaca, N.Y.: Cornell University Press.

Freed, John B. 1973 Urban Development and the *Cura Monialium* in Thirteenth-Century Germany. *Viator* 3: 311–27.

Garampi, Giuseppe (Cardinal) 1775 *Memorie ecclesiastiche appartenenti all'istoria e al culto della B. Chiara di Rimini*. Rome: Pagliarini.

Gennaro, Clara 1980 Chiara, Agnese e le prime consorelle: dalle "Pauperes dominae" di S. Damiano alle Clarisse. In *Movimento religioso femminile e francescanesimo nel secolo XIII: atti del VII Convegno internazionale, Assisi, 11–13 ottobre 1979*, 167–91. Assisi: Società Internazionale di Studi Francescani.

Georgiana, Linda 1987 Any Corner of Heaven: Heloise's Critique of Monasticism. *Medieval Studies* 49: 221–53.

Gill, Katherine 1992 Open Monasteries in Late Medieval Italy. In Craig Monson, ed., *The Crannied Wall: Women, Religion and the Arts in Early Modern Europe*, 15–47. Ann Arbor: University of Michigan Press.

1994. Penitents, Pinzochere and Pious Laywomen: Varieties of Women's Religious Communities in Central Italy c. 1300–1520. PhD diss., Princeton University.

Haren, Michael J., ed. 1989 *Calendar of Entries in the Papal Registers: Registers relating to Great Britain and Ireland. Papal Letters, XVIII: Pius III and Julius II: Vatican Registers (1503–1513), Lateran Registers (1503–1508)*. Dublin: Dublin Stationery Office for the Irish Manuscripts Commission.

Herlihy, David 1990 *Opera muliebria: Women and Work in Medieval Europe*. New York: McGraw-Hill.

Huber, Etienne 1988 Un censier des biens romains du monastère S. Silvestro in Capite (1333–1334). *Archivio della Società Romana di Storia Patria* 111: 93–160.

Hüntemann, Ulrich, and Pou y Martí, José M., eds. 1929–49 *Bullarium Franciscanum*, 2nd ser. 3 vols. Quaracchi: ex Typographia Collegii S. Bonaventurae.

Jaffé, Philipp 1888 *Regesta pontificum romanorum ab condita ecclesia ad annum post christum natum MCXVIII*, 2nd edn. Vol. II. Leipzig: Veit.

Johnson, Penelope D. 1991 *Equal in Monastic Profession: Religious Women in Medieval France*. Chicago and London: University of Chicago Press.

Jombart, Emile and Viller, Marcel 1953 Clôture. In *Dictionnaire de spiritualité, ascétique et mystique, doctrine et histoire*, II.979–1007. Paris: G. Beauchesne et ses fils.

Lacey, Kathleen, trans. 1986 The Memories of Doña Lenor López de Córdoba (c. 1362–c. 1412). In Elizabeth Alvilda Petroff, ed., *Medieval Women's Visionary Literature*, 329–34. Oxford: Oxford University Press.

Lainati, C. A. 1973 La Clôture de sainte Claire et des premières clarisses dans la legislation canonique et dans la pratique. *Laurentianum* 14: 223–50.

Leclercq, Jean 1980 Il monachesimo femminile nei secoli XII e XIII. In *Movimento religioso femminile e francescanesimo nel secolo XIII: atti del VI Convegno internazionale, Assisi, 11–13 ottobre 1979*, 61–99. Assisi: Società Internazionale di Studi Francescani.

Maccarrone, Michele 1972 Il progetto di un *universale cenobium* per le monache di Roma. In his *Studi su Innocenzo III*, 272–8. Padua: Antenore.

McLaughlin, Mary M. 1989 Creating and Recreating Communities of Women: The Case of Corpus Domini, Ferrara, 1406–1452. *Signs: Journal of Women in Culture and Society* 14.2: 293–320.

Molho, Anthony 1989 Tamquam vere mortua: Le professioni religiose femminili nella Firenze del tardo medioevo. *Società e storia* 43: 1–44.

Novelli, Leandro 1975 Due documenti inediti relativi alle monache benedettine dette "Santuccie." *Benedictina* 22: 189–253.

Occhipinti, Elisa 1978 Clausura a Milano alla fine del XIII secolo: il caso del monastero di S. Margherita. In *Felix Olim Lombardia: Studi di storia padana dedicati dagli allievi a Giuseppe Martini*, 197–212. Milan.

Potthast, August, ed. 1874–7 *Regesta pontificum romanorum inde ab a. post Christum natum MCXCVIII ad a. MCCCIV*. 2 vols. Berlin: Rudolf de Decker; repr. Graz: Akademische Druk- und Verlaganstalt, 1957.

Schulenburg, Jane Tibbets 1984 Strict Active Enclosure and its Effects on the Female Monastic Experience (500–1100). In John A. Nichols and Lillian Thomas Shank, eds., *Distant Echoes: Medieval Religious Women*, I.51–86. Cistercian Studies Series 71. Kalamazoo, Mich.: Cistercian Publications.

Sella, Giacomo, ed. 1913 *Cartario del monastero di Santa Maria di Brione fino all'anno 1300*. Biblioteca della Società Storica Subalpina 67. Pinerolo: Municipio de Vercelli.

Sensi, Mario 1985a La Monacazione delle recluse nella valle Spoletina. In Claudio Leonardi and Enrico Menestò, eds., *S. Chiara de Montefalco e il suo tempo: atti del quarto Convegno di studi storici ecclesiastici organizzato dall'Archidiocesi di Spoleto (Spoleto 28–30 dicembre 1981)*, 71–121. Perugia: Regione dell'Umbria, and Florence: La Nuova Italia Editrice.

1985b *L'Osservanze francescane nell'Italia centrale (secoli XIV–XV)*. Rome: Istituto Storico dei Cappuccini.

Simons, Walter 1989 The Beguine Movement in the Southern Low Countries: A Reassessment. *Bulletin de l'Institut Historique Belge de Rome/Bulletin van het Belgisch Historisch Instituut te Rome* 59: 63–105.

Vauchez, André 1987 *Les Laïcs au moyen âge: pratiques ex expériences religieuses*. Paris: Cerf.

Zarri, Gabriella 1976 *Il carteggio tra don Leone Bartolini e un gruppo di gentildonne bolognesi negli anni del Concilio Trengo (1545–1563): Alla ricerca di una via spirituale* (= *Archivio italiano per la storia della pietà* 7). Rome: Storia e Letteratura (repr. 1986).

1986 Monasteri femminili e città (secoli XV–XVIII). *Storia d'Italia: Annali* 9 (Turin: Einaudi): 359–429.

Part III

Non-Christian minorities within medieval Christendom

10   The conversion of Minorcan Jews (417–418): an experiment in history of historiography

Carlo Ginzburg

1. This is an experiment *in corpore nobilissimo*. Peter Brown's *The Cult of the Saints* (1981) is a splendid book, full of learning, imagination, and grace. Even the perplexities I am going to express will show how deep is my intellectual debt towards Peter Brown's work.

At the end of chapter 5 (*"Praesentia"*) Brown illustrates the "ideal 'clean' power associated with the relics of the saints" with an episode which followed the arrival of St. Stephen's relics in Minorca in 417. The peaceful coexistence of Jews and Christians in the town of Mahon came brusquely to an end. Tensions emerged; the Jews locked themselves into the synagogue, collecting stones and clubs. After some clashes in the streets, the Christians razed the synagogue to the ground. Then they urged the Jews to convert. Their efforts were largely successful, although Theodore, the *defensor civitatis*, who was the most prominent representative of the Jewish community, for some time stubbornly resisted the joint pressures exerted on him by Christians and converted Jews. In a public debate on religious matters Theodore nearly defeated the bishop himself. Finally he gave up. Then the last Jewish resistance (which included some women) collapsed. "Through becoming Christians" Brown writes "[the Jews] maintained their full social status within their own community, though now subject to the higher *patrocinium* of Saint Stephen, and seated beside the Christian bishop as Christian *patroni*. Thus, far from being eradicated, the 'unclean' power of the established Jewish families has been 'washed clean' by being integrated into the Christian community under Saint Stephen."[1]

Brown does not deny that "violence and fear of yet greater violence played a decisive role" in these events. But his final comments emphasize the integration of Jews and Christians in a single community, not the human costs paid for it. This conclusion is prepared by the use of negative analogies like "it was something marginally more decent than a mere *pogrom*," or "his [i.e.,

I am very grateful to Peter Brown, Sofia Boesch Gajano, Augusto Campana, and Richard Landes for their help.
[1] Cf. Brown 1981: 103–5.

Stephen's] arrival on the island was not seen as an occasion to purge the island of Jews."[2] Deliberate anachronisms like *pogrom* or "purge" do not seem particularly illuminating in a case like this, which is among the earliest occurrences of Jewish–Christian tensions. Even more perplexing is the opposition between "clean" and "unclean" power, which plays a crucial role in Brown's presentation of the Minorcan events. "The reader must bear with me" Brown says "if, in describing a thoroughly dirty business . . . I limit myself to the perspective of bishop Severus, our only source, and speak of the *patrocinium* of Saint Stephen as 'clean' power." The problem raised here (to see other religions through Christian eyes) is at the very heart of this volume. But this slightly ambiguous passage could be wrongly interpreted by some readers as if it meant that categories like "clean" and "unclean" derive from the evidence itself. On the contrary, they are "etic," not "emic" categories, implicitly inspired by Mary Douglas's *Purity and Danger*, not by Severus's long letter on the Minorcan events.[3] A perfectly legitimate choice, of course, although somebody could object to the idea of lumping together pagans and Jews under the category of "unclean" power, in the light of the much later hostile association between Jews and dirt.[4]

But these remarks on Brown's historical approach to the Minorcan episode are bound to remain inconclusive, if they would not be supplemented by an analysis of the primary evidence on which Brown relies: the letter written by Severus, bishop of Minorca, in 418. This statement is not as obvious as it should be. "History of historiography without historiography," as Arnaldo Momigliano ironically defined it, has become in the last two decades more and more fashionable.[5] A radical disjunction between historical narratives and the spade-work on which they rely had been already suggested by Benedetto Croce in 1895.[6] One century later, in a largely different intellectual climate, this approach to historiography has become widespread, for reasons I will not try to explain.

---

[2] *Ibid.*, 104.

[3] On "emic" and "etic" cf. Pike 1967: 37ff; Gellner 1985: 144–5. For Brown's praise of another work by Mary Douglas (*Natural Symbols*) cf. 1981: 177 n. 102; "Douglas's seminal *Purity and Danger*" is mentioned in Brown 1983: 11, in a context suggesting the author's growing distance from "a strand of post-Durkheimian and of British functionalist anthropology."

[4] Cf. for instance Kriegel 1976: 26–30.

[5] Cf. Momigliano 1990: 198 (this final sentence was Momigliano's last-minute addition: see the editor's note, p. 11). For a similar rejection of "history of historiography as history of historical thought (*pensiero storico*)" see Cantimori 1971: especially 407–9. Momigliano's implicit target was history *à la* Hayden White; Cantimori's explicit target, some unnamed followers of Croce as well as, to a certain extent, Croce himself. I tried to explore the reasons of this convergence in Ginzburg 1992.

[6] Cf. Croce 1927: 36ff (the importance of this early essay has been stressed by White 1975: 381ff).

Its limitations (not to say dangers) are obvious, as the case I am dealing with, which is based on a single piece of evidence, immediately shows.[7] Doubts about the authenticity of Severus's letter had been raised in the past, as Gabriel Seguí Vidal has shown in the critical edition he prepared in 1937.[8] More recently, an authoritative evaluation of the letter as a seventh-century fake has been expressed on several occasions by Bernhard Blumenkranz (even if a detailed demonstration has been so far postponed).[9] Neither Seguí Vidal's edition nor Blumenkranz's criticism is mentioned by Peter Brown, who quotes Severus's letter from one of the two nearly identical texts reproduced in Migne's *Patrologia Latina*; both of them are based (except for some minor correction) on the *editio princeps* provided by Baronio in his *Annales ecclesiastici* (1588). In order to evaluate Brown's approach to the Minorcan events, a discussion of Severus's letter seems unavoidable.[10]

Let me immediately say that Brown was absolutely right in his tacit acceptance of its authenticity: some recently discovered evidence has proved it beyond any reasonable doubt. But a quick recapitulation of the discussions concerning the letter's authenticity will shed, I hope, some additional light on the events mentioned in it.

2. In his edition of Severus's letter Seguí Vidal observed that the style of the document was perfectly compatible with an early fifth-century date.[11] Nearly twenty years later, in an essay written with J. N. Hillgarth, Seguí introduced two additional arguments: (a) the identification of a pseudo-Augustinian treatise, *Altercatio Ecclesiae contra Synagogam*, with the *commonitorium* mentioned by Severus in his letter; (b) some archeological excavations suggesting the existence of a large paleo-Christian basilica in Minorca.[12] The irrelevance of the latter argument in a discussion concerning the date of Severus's letter – which in any case is probably earlier than the basilica – has been rightly emphasized by J. Vives (who, on the other hand, accepted the identification of the *commonitorium* with the *Altercatio*).[13] The former argument has been effectively rejected by Blumenkranz, who demonstrated that the *Altercatio* is a later (probably tenth-century) text.[14] Moreover, he claimed that the letter ascribed to Severus (or Pseudo-Severus, as he says)

---

[7] See Ginzburg 1992.
[8] Cf. Seguí Vidal 1937: 1ff. Castilian translations: Dameto 1632: 150ff; de la Puerta Vizcaino 1951 (originally 1857). The Latin text has recently been republished, followed by a Castilian and a Catalan translation: Severus 1981.
[9] Cf. Blumenkranz 1954: 46; *idem* 1960: 282–4; *idem* 1963: 106–10; *idem* 1977: 419–20.
[10] As far as I know, the issue has not been mentioned by the numerous reviewers of Brown 1981.
[11] Cf. Seguí Vidal 1937: 130ff.   [12] Cf. Segui Vidal and Hillgarth 1955.
[13] Cf. Vives 1956.   [14] Cf. Blumenkranz 1954.

reflects the preoccupations of a later period: the episode of Bishop Severus being nearly defeated by Theodore, for instance, would suggest the risks involved in public religious confrontations with the Jews. Blumenkranz added to this a (rather vague) linguistic argument: the words "Theodorus in Christum credidit", shouted by the Christians and misunderstood by the Jews as "Theodore crede in Christum", seems to imply a homophony between the Spanish "cree" (imperative) and "cree" (indicative) which would be incompatible with an early fifth-century date.[15]

Fifth or seventh century? L. Cracco Ruggini rightly rejected Blumenkranz's last date, but she gave a disproportionate importance to a more than doubtful argument – the archaeological evidence mentioned by Seguí and Hillgarth.[16] On the other hand, Díaz y Díaz's unfounded skepticism about an early date was supported by some valuable suggestions.[17] He noted that all five manuscripts used by Seguí Vidal for his critical edition include, besides the letter by Severus, the so-called *Liber de miraculis sancti Stephani Protomartyris*, which describes the miracles performed by St. Stephen's relics in an African town, Uzalis.[18] Both texts begin with the same biblical quotation (Tobit 2.7); the latter mentions the former, saying that the saint's relics were brought to Uzalis with a letter, written by Bishop Severus of Minorca, which was read aloud from the pulpit: it announced the extraordinary feats already performed by the same relics in converting the Jews of Minorca.[19] Díaz y Díaz suggests two alternative possibilities: (a) the allusion to Severus's letter in the *Liber de miraculis*, which is the only external proof of the former's early date, has been interpolated; (b) the letter itself is a late fake built up on the basis of the *Liber*'s allusion.[20]

These clever conjectures have been disproved by the discovery made by J. Divjak of a group of letters to and by Augustine. They include two letters written from the Baleares by Consentius (known already on an independent basis as a correspondent of Augustine).[21] One of them (12*) mentions Severus's letter on the conversion of the Jews, even claiming a certain responsibility in

---

[15] Cf. Blumenkranz 1963: 108 n. 14. On Severus's letter from a linguistic point of view cf. Paucker 1881 (not mentioned by Blumenkranz). Strangely enough, no commentator has ever discussed the word *abgistinum*, mentioned by Severus as a vernacular Minorcan word meaning "small hail" (1900: 742, "grando minutissima, quam incolae insulae illius gentili sermone Abgistinum vocant"). As far as I know, *abgistinum* is a hapax legomenon.

[16] Cf. Cracco Ruggini 1964: above all 936–8.

[17] Cf. Díaz y Díaz 1956.

[18] Severus 1900.

[19] *Liber de miraculis sancti Stephani Protomartyris, PL* XLI.835.

[20] Cf. Díaz y Díaz 1956: 12 n. 30.

[21] Some unconvincing doubts about this identification have been raised by R. Van Dam (1986).

the wording of it.[22] It has been remarked, however, that Severus's plain and straightforward style is very different from Consentius's.[23]

3. The discussion about the date and authenticity of Severus's letter has come to a conclusion. All residual doubts concerning these two issues stem from a hypercritical attitude.[24] Other problems are far from settled. Two recent essays insist in analyzing the letter as a self-standing document, related to a more or less isolated event.[25] This approach is far from useless. Here I will try to suggest the potentialities of another approach, based on a larger series of documents, related to a longer series of events; an approach implying the construction (and reconstruction) of a different historical object.

The connections between Severus's letter and the *Liber de miraculis sancti Stephani* have been already pointed by Díaz y Díaz. Both texts are related to the same person: Paulus Orosius, the author of *Historiarum Adversus Paganos libri VII*, the first universal history written in a Christian perspective. The circumstances of Orosius's biography explain this double involvement. Having left his birthplace, Braga (a formerly Spanish, now Portuguese town) Orosius had come to Africa in order to meet Augustine and become his pupil. Augustine trusted him so much as to send him to Jerusalem (415) in order to fight against Pelagius and his ideas.[26] Orosius took part in the Council of Diospolis, which turned out to be a success for Pelagius. During the synod the relics of St. Stephen, Gamaliel, and Nicodemus were found at Caphar-Gamala, not far from Jerusalem. A priest named Lucianus, who had been led there by a series of nocturnal visions, was asked by Avitus, a priest from Braga, to dictate to him the circumstances of the extraordinary discovery he had made. Lucianus spoke Greek, a language Avitus was familiar with. Having prepared a Latin translation of Lucianus's report (known to us as *De revelatione corporis sancti Stephani*) Avitus entrusted it, with some relics of St. Stephen, to his fellow

---

[22] Cf. St. Augustine 1936– : 46B.184ff. For the relevant passage (12*, 13) see pp. 248–50: "Eodem tempore accidit, ut quaedam apud nos ex praecepto domini mirabilia gererentur. Quae cum mihi beatus antistes, frater paternitatis tuae Severus episcopus cum ceteris qui affuerant retulisset, irrupit propositum meum summis viribus caritatis et, ut epistolam quae rei gestae ordinem contineret ipse conscriberet, sola a me verba mutuatus est." Consentius mentions also an anti-Jewish treatise of his, which he insisted be kept anonymous. Apparently it did not survive. The relevance of Consentius's letter, as well as some articles on it, have been kindly pointed out to me by Peter Brown.

[23] Cf. J. Wankenne, in St. Augustine 1936– : 46B.492.

[24] Cf. Moreau 1983: 215–23.

[25] Cf. Hunt 1982b; Wankenne and Hambenne 1987. Both articles take for granted the early date as well as the authenticity of Severus's letter; only the latter (which is more circumscribed in its scope) takes into account the letter by Consentius (12*). For an early discussion of it cf. Amengual i Batle 1980.

[26] Not in order to "acquire relics of St. Stephen" (they had not been discovered yet) as stated by W. H. C. Frend (1988: 164).

citizen Orosius, who was supposed to bring them to Palchonius, bishop of Braga.[27] In 416 Orosius left Jerusalem with his precious baggage, and after a halt in Africa went to Minorca in order to reach Spain. This never happened. In his letter, written at the beginning of 418,[28] Severus speaks of a priest coming from Jerusalem who, unable to go to Spain, after a while changed his mind and went back to Africa, having left in Minorca, "by divine inspiration," some fragments of St. Stephen's body. For a long time this anonymous priest has been identified as Orosius. What convinced him to give up his original project – whether winter storms, Vandal ships or both – we do not know. In any case, I think we can trust the passage from the *Liber de miraculis sancti Stephani* mentioning Severus's letter. The unnamed individual who brought it to Uzalis, with some more fragments from that apparently inexhaustible treasure – St. Stephen's relics – can be safely identified with Orosius. His *Historiae Adversus Paganos* were probably published in the same year (418).[29]

4. Orosius could be mistakenly regarded as the main hero in this story. In fact he played only the role of an (admittedly important) intermediary. The real hero is Stephen. The arrival of his relics to Africa triggered a series of miracles, duly recorded some years later in the *Liber de miraculis sancti Stephani protomartyris*, written under the impulse of Evodius, bishop of Uzalis. Evodius had been since his youth one of Augustine's closest pupils.[30] In the past Augustine had expressed an open skepticism towards miracles. The discovery of the relics of two unknown martyrs, Gervasius and Protasius, made in Milan in 386, and immediately exploited by Ambrosius as a symbolic weapon in his struggle against the Arians, had left Augustine unmoved.[31] In his treatise *De vera religione* (389–91) he explained that, after the diffusion of the Christian faith, miracles had become impossible: otherwise people would have craved only for visible things.[32] The title of chapter VIII of the last book (XXII) of the *City of God*, written in 425, sounds like a recantation of the aforementioned passage, as well as like a turning point in the history of the cult of the saints:

---

[27] Lucianus 1900: 805–16.

[28] On its date, corresponding to 2 February 418, see Saxer 1980: 246.

[29] I am very grateful to Richard Landes for having pointed this out to me: see in general his essay 1988: especially 156–60, on the discussion, which took place either in 418 or 419 (i.e., at approximately the time of Severus's epistle) between Augustine and Hesychius, a bishop from Dalmatia, concerning the end of the world. On the date of Orosius's work cf. Lippold 1976: I.xxii.

[30] Cf. Brown 1967 *passim*; Monceaux 1923: VII.42–5.

[31] Cf. Cracco Ruggini 1974; Simonetti 1976; Lenox-Conyngham 1982; Nauroy 1988.

[32] *De vera religione* 25.47, "Cum enim Ecclesia catholica per totum orbem diffusa atque fundata sit, nec miracula illa in nostra tempora durare permissa sunt, ne animus semper visibilia quaereret, ut eorum consuetudine frigesceret genus humanum" (quoted by G. Bardy in a note on miracles included in his edition of *The City of God*: St. Augustine 1936– : 37.825–31). Cf. Courcelle 1968: 139ff.

"De miraculis, quae ut mundus in Christum crederet facta sunt et fieri mundo credente non desinunt" ("On miracles, which have been performed in order to convince the world to believe in Christ, and are still performed even if the world believes in Him"). The cult of the martyrs' relics was widespread in Africa: the Council of Carthago (398) had tried to exert some control on it, ordering the destruction of all superstitious, or illegitimate, altars.[33] But the change in the attitude of Augustine was specifically related, as Victor Saxer has shown, to the wave of miracles connected to St. Stephen's cult-place (*memoria*) in Uzalis.[34] Why was St. Stephen so important? He had been, of course, the proto-martyr; his passion had echoed the passion of Christ. Other elements will become immediately evident by focusing on the momentous discovery of his relics. We started from 418 (the date of Severus's letter); then we went forward. Let us go back to 415.

5. The discovery of St. Stephen's relics took place at the right time and in the right place – a remark made by an eminent scholar like Saxer, whom nobody will suspect of militant anti-clericalism.[35] The event enhanced the prestige of a man who had clearly played a major role in it: John II, bishop of Jerusalem. In a recent essay Michael van Esbroeck has argued that some cults actively supported by John II – St. Stephen's being the most prominent of them – implied a coherent religious policy, consciously addressed towards Jewish–Christian groups.[36] This is a valuable suggestion: but the polemical, even aggressive implications of the event have been disregarded by van Esbroeck. The discovery of Nicodemus's and Gamaliel's tombs, suggesting a continuity between the Old and New Testaments, was more than counterbalanced by the discovery of the relics of St. Stephen, the proto-martyr, the first man who "fought for the Lord against the Jews" (*primum adversus Judaeos dominica bella bellavit*).[37] These words, included in both versions of the *De revelatione corporis Sancti Stephani*, are eloquent enough.[38] Religious closeness implied religious competition. As Marcel Simon has shown in his great book, the Christians' claim of being "the true Israel" had ambivalent, potentially tragic overtones.[39]

These tensions lurk behind the discovery of St. Stephen's relics. Even scholars who have emphasized the perfect timing of this event have, as far as I

---

[33] Cf. Cecchelli 1939: 131–2.
[34] Cf. Saxer 1980: 245ff. See also Lambot 1947: especially 105–6; *idem* 1969: 84; Verbraken 1976: serms. 314–20.
[35] Cf. Saxer 1980: 293–4.
[36] Cf. van Esbroeck 1984.
[37] Lucianus 1900: 813, 815–16.
[38] On the two versions cf. P[eeters] 1908: 364–7; Martin 1958. On the event cf. Hunt 1982a: 212–20.
[39] Cf. Simon 1964.

know, disregarded the element I am going to mention. On 20 October 415 the emperor deprived Gamaliel II, patriarch of Jerusalem, of his traditional title of *praefectus honorarius*. The reason mentioned for the title's suppression was, significantly, Jewish proselytism, exemplified by the construction of new synagogues and the circumcision of Christians and Gentiles.[40] The patriarch was the highest spiritual and political authority for the Jews of Palestine and the Diaspora; Origen regarded him as a kind of monarch of the Jews.

The suppression of the *praefectura honoraria* led, a few years later, to the disappearance of the Patriarchate.[41] The weakened position of the Jews under the Christian emperors was made evident, less than two months later, by another symbolic blow: the sudden reemergence of the relics of St. Stephen, announced by Lucianus's visions at the beginning of December 415.

6. Retrospectively, it seems obvious that they were bound to reemerge, sooner or later. In order to justify this statement, we need to make another step back – to the well-known sermons against Judaizing Christians pronounced by St. John Chrysostom in Antioch in 385–6.[42] The complex religious reality they reveal has been analyzed by Marcel Simon in a magisterial essay.[43] Both Jews and Christians, for instance, paid a fervent cult to the relics of the seven Maccabees and their mother, which were preserved (so people believed) in a synagogue in Antioch. Around 380 the synagogue was taken by force and transformed into a Christian church. This gesture (which was far from exceptional)[44] embodies the ambivalent implications of a formula like *verus Israel*. The desire to emphasize the continuity between the Old and the New Testaments inspired the inclusion of the Maccabees in the Antioch religious calendar, as well as the violent seizure of the holy place in which their relics were preserved.[45]

The cult of the Maccabee brothers and their mother was not circumscribed to Antioch. In 388, as we learn from a letter of St. Ambrose, at Callinicon, on the Euphrates's left bank, some heretics attacked a group of monks who, "following an ancient tradition," were singing psalms on the road to a sanctuary of the Maccabees. For some obscure reason, even in this case the local synagogue was destroyed by the same monks, inspired by the bishop

[40] Cf. Mommsen and Meyer 1962: 892–3.
[41] Cf. Juster 1914: 391ff; Rabello 1980: 713–16 (but in 415 Patriarch Gamaliel was not "deposed," as stated on p. 714 n. 212); Bachrach 1985: 412–15; Stemberger 1987: 208–13.
[42] Cf. St. John Chrysostom 1979. See also Wilken 1983; Meeks and Wilken 1979.
[43] Simon 1962a.
[44] Cf. Rampolla [del Tindaro] 1899: especially 388ff.
[45] E. J. Bikerman (1951: 74–5) remarks that synagogues were regarded as holy places in the Roman law, not in the Jewish ritual; but the attitude of the Christians (including those who seized the Antioch synagogue) was presumably closer to the former.

(*auctore episcopo*).[46] A cult so widespread, shared by Jews and Christians, had undoubtedly deep roots. The model of 2 Macc. 7 has been detected behind the description of Blandina, the Christian martyr put to death at Lyon in AD 177.[47] It has been suggested that the very notion of *martyrium* ultimately derives from the story of the seven Jewish brothers and their mother, tortured and killed for their refusal to eat pork.[48]

Some attempts to Christianize the cult of those Jewish proto-martyrs have been already mentioned. The new balance of power, which had emerged between the end of the fourth and the beginning of the fifth centuries, led to the discovery of the relics of the Christian proto-martyr, who according to the tradition had been killed by the Jews. Stephen was thus raised up against the Maccabees.[49] In Minorca (Severus wrote in his letter) the tensions generated by the arrival of St. Stephen's relics turned into a real fight: "the Jews encouraged each other by recalling the examples of the age of the Maccabees, willing to die in order to defend their Law."[50]

7. So far I have dealt with a hagiographic stereotype, attached to a name ("Stephen"). It would be possible to go beyond it, trying to disentangle, on the basis of Acts 6–8, the historical Stephen and his attitude towards the Jewish tradition.[51] Obviously I have no competence to do that. But the evidence I have assembled shows, I think, that the extremely ambivalent attitude towards the Jews played a crucial role in the emergence of the cult of the Christian saints. The religious violences which took place in Minorca are just an episode in a much longer story in which St. Stephen, or at least his relics, inevitably played an anti-Jewish role.[52]

This role is so obvious that Peter Brown, in the pages I started from, did not even mention it. Such a silence becomes relevant in so far as it can be related to a wider propensity to underplay tensions, divisions, oppositions (of all kind: social, cultural, religious). In a fragment of intellectual autobiography he remarked (with a touch of self-criticism) that British functionalist anthropology had a "tendency to isolate the holy man . . . from the world of shared values in which he operated as an exemplar."[53] Brown's tendency to focus on elements shared by the whole community has become more and more evident.

---

[46] Cf. Ambrosius, epistle 40.16, quoted by Cracco Ruggini (1959: 198–9).
[47] Cf. Frend 1978: especially 173.
[48] Cf. Frend 1958; this connection has been sharply denied by H. Delehaye (see Frend 1958: 151 n. 7).
[49] Cf. Simon 1962b: especially 157 (Gregory of Nazianzus 1885: 627).
[50] Severus 1981: 734, "Judaei igitur exemplis se Machabaei temporis exhortantes, mortem quoque pro defendendis legitimis suis desiderabant."
[51] A challenging attempt in this direction has been made by M. Simon (1958).
[52] The relevance of this topic has been emphasized by Blumenkranz (1963: 108 n. 14).
[53] Cf. Brown 1983: 12.

I strongly sympathize with the criticism, addressed in the first chapter of *The Cult of the Saints*, to all kinds of paternalist attitudes concerning the religious history of illiterate groups. I find much more debatable Brown's silent shift from this criticism to a rejection of what he labels "two-tier model" – an approach focused on cultural religious dichotomies.[54]

The Cult of the Saints is an irreplaceable book. But the way in which it dealt (or did not deal) with the Jewish–Christian dichotomy seems to me difficult to accept.

REFERENCES

Amengual i Batle, J. 1980 Noves fonts par a la història de les Balears dins el Baix Imperi. *Bolletí de la Societat Arqueológica Lulliana* segona època 96 vol. 37: 99–111.

Augustine, St. 1936– *Oeuvres*. Bibliothèque Augustinienne. Paris: Desclée, De Brouwer.

Bachrach, Bernard S. 1985 The Jewish Community of the Later Roman Empire as Seen in the *Codex Theodosianus*. In Jacob Neusner and Ernest S. Frerichs, eds., *"To see ourselves as others see us": Christians, Jews, "Others" in Late Antiquity*, 399–421. Chico, Calif.: Scholars Press.

Bikerman, Elias J. 1951 Les Maccabées de Malalas. *Byzantion* 21: 63–83.

Blumenkranz, Bernhard 1954 Altercatio Ecclesie contra Synagogam: texte inédit du Xe siècle. *Revue du moyen âge latin* 10.1–2: 5–159.

  1960 *Juifs et Chrétiens dans le monde occidental (430–1096)*. Paris and The Hague: Mouton.

  1963 *Les Auteurs chrétiens latins du moyen âge sur les Juifs et le judaïsme*. Paris and The Hague: Mouton.

  1977 Juden und Jüdische in christlicher Wundererzählung. In his *Juifs et Chrétiens: Patristique et moyen âge*, article IX. London: Variorum Reprints.

Brown, Peter R. L. 1967 *Augustine of Hippo: A Biography*. Berkeley and Los Angeles: University of California Press.

  1981 *The Cult of the Saints: Its Rise and Function in Latin Christianity*. Chicago: University of Chicago Press.

  1982 *Society and the Holy in Late Antiquity*. Berkeley and Los Angeles: California University Press.

  1983 The Saint as Exemplar in Late Antiquity. *Representations* 1.2: 1–25.

Cantimori, Delio 1971 Storia e storiografia in Benedetto Croce. In his *Storici e storia*, 397–409. Turin: G. Einaudi (orig. 1966).

Cecchelli, Carlo 1939 Note sopra il culto delle reliquie nell'Africa romana. *Rendiconti della Pontificia Accademia Romana di Archeologia* 15: 125–34.

Courcelle, Pierre 1968 *Recherches sur les "Confessions" de saint Augustin*. New edn. Paris: E. de Boccard.

---

[54] On the implications of this rejection see, for instance, Brown's presentation of the medieval cult of Sainte Foy (1982: 302–32, especially 318, 321, 330) to be compared with Stock 1983: 64–72.

Cracco Ruggini, Lellia 1959 Ebrei e Orientali nell'Italia settentrionale fra il IV e il VI sec. d. Cr. *Studia et monumenta historiae et iuris* 25.

1964 Note sugli ebrei in Italia dal IV al XVI secolo (a proposito di un libro e di altri contributi recenti). *Rivista storica italiana* 76: 926–56.

1974 Ambrogio e le opposizioni anticattoliche fra il 383 e il 390. *Augustinianum* 14: 409–49.

Croce, Benedetto 1927 La Storia ridotta sotto il concetto generale dell'arte. In his *Primi saggi*, 36ff. 2nd edn. Bari: G. Laterza (orig. 1895).

Dameto, Juan Bautista 1632 *La Historia general del reyno balearico.* Majorca: en casa de Gabriel Guasp.

Díaz y Díaz, Manuel C. 1956 De patristica española. *Revista española de teologia* 17: 3–12.

Esbroeck, Michel van 1984 Jean II de Jérusalem et les cultes de S. Etienne, de la Sainte-Sion et de la Croix. *Analecta Bollandiana* 102: 99–134.

Frend, William H. C. 1958 The Persecutions: Some Links Between Judaism and the Early Church. *Journal of Ecclesiastical History* 9: 141–58.

1978 Blandina et Perpetua: Two Early Christian Heroines. In Jean Rouge and Robert Turran, eds., *Les Martyrs de Lyon (177)*, 167–77. Colloques Internationaux du CNRS. Paris: Editions du CNRS.

1988 The North African Cult of Martyrs. In his *Archaeology and History in the Study of Christianity*, article XI. London: Variorum Reprints.

Gellner, Ernest 1985 *Relativism and the Social Sciences.* Cambridge and New York: Cambridge University Press.

Ginzburg, Carlo 1992 Just one Witness. In Saul Friedlander, ed., *Probing the Limits of Representation: Nazism and the "Final Solution,"* 82–96. Cambridge, Mass.: Harvard University Press.

Gregory of Nazianzus 1885 *Hom 3 in Mach.* In *PG* XXXV.627.

Hunt, E. D. 1982a *Holy Land Pilgrimage in the Later Roman Empire, AD 312–460.* Oxford: Clarendon Press; New York: Oxford University Press.

1982b St. Stephen in Minorca: An Episode in Jewish–Christian Relations in the Early 5th Century A.D. *Journal of Theological Studies* 2nd ser. 33.1: 106–23.

John Chrysostom, St. 1979 *Discourses against Judaizing Christians.* Trans. P. W. Harkins. Washington, DC: Catholic University of America Press.

Juster, Jean 1914 *Les Juifs dans l'empire romain: leur condition juridique, économique et sociale*, I. Paris: P. Geuthner.

Kriegel, Maurice 1976 Un trait de psychologie sociale. *Annales: Economies, Sociétés Civilisations* 31: 26–30.

Lambot, Cyrille 1947 Collection antique de sermons de saint Augustin. *Revue bénédictine* 57: 89–108.

1969 Les Sermons de saint Augustin pour les fêtes de martyrs. *Revue bénédictine* 79: 82–97.

Landes, Richard 1988 Lest the Millennium Be Fulfilled: Apocalyptic Expectations and the Pattern of Western Chronography 100–800 CE. In W. Verbeke, D. Verhelst, and A. Welkenhuysen, eds., *The Use and Abuse of Eschatology in the Middle Ages*, 137–211. Leuven: Leuven University Press.

Lenox-Conyngham, A. 1982 The Topography of the Basilica Conflict of A.D. 385/6 in Milan. *Historia: Zeitschrift für alte Geschichte* (Wiesbaden) 31: 353–63.

Lippold, Adolf 1976 Introduction. In *Le storie contro i pagani Orosio*. Trans. A. Bartalucci. 2 vols. Milan: Fondazione L. Valla.

Lucianus 1900 *De revelatione corporis Stephani martyris*. In *PL* XLI.807–16.

Martin, J. 1958 Die Revelatio S. Stephani und Verwandtes. *Historisches Jahrbuch* 77: 419–33.

Meeks, Wayne A. and Wilken, Robert L. 1979 *Jews and Christians in Antioch in the First Four Centuries of the Common Era*. Sources for Biblical Study 13. Missoula, Mont.: Scholars Press.

Momigliano, Arnaldo 1990 In R. Di Donato, ed., *La Contraddizione felice? Ernesto De Martino e gli altri*, 197–8. Pisa: ETS.

Mommsen, Theodor and Meyer, Paul M. 1962 *Codex Theodosianus*. 2 vols. in 3. 3rd edn. Berlin: Weidmann.

Monceaux, Paul 1923 *Histoire littéraire de l'Afrique chrétienne depuis les origines jusqu'à l'invasion arabe*, VII. Paris: E. Leroux.

Moreau, Madeleine 1983 Lecture de la Lettre 11* de Consentius à Augustin. In *Les Lettres de saint Augustin découvertes par Johannes Divjak, communications présentées au colloque de 20 et 21 septembre 1982*, 215–33. Paris: Etudes augustiniennes.

Nauroy, Gérard 1988 Le Fouet et le miel: le combat d'Ambroise en 386 contre l'arianisme milanais. *Recherches Augustiniennes* 23: 3–86.

Paucker, C. 1881 De latinitate scriptorum quorundam saeculi quarti et ineuntis quinti p. C. minorum observationes. *Zeitschrift für die oesterreichischen Gymnasien* 32: 481–99.

P[eeters], P. 1908 Le Sanctuaire de la lapidation de S. Etienne. *Analecta Bollandiana* 27: 359–68.

Pike, Kenneth L. 1967 *Language in Relation to a Unified Theory of Structure of Human Behaviour*. 2nd edn. The Hague and Paris: Mouton.

Puerta Vizcaino, Juan de la 1951 *La Sinagoga Balear; ó Historia de los Judíos de Mallorca*. Palma de Majorca: Editorial Clumba (reprint of 1857 edn.).

Rabella, Alfredo M. 1980 The Legal Condition of the Jews in the Roman Empire. In H. Temporini, ed., *Aufstieg und Niedergang der römischen Welt*, II.13: 662–762. Berlin and New York: De Gruyter.

Rampollo [del Tindaro], Cardinal [M.] 1899 Martyre et sépulture des Macchabées. *Revue de l'art chrétien* 42 (4th ser. 10): 290–305, 377–92, and 457–65.

Saxer, Victor 1980 *Mort, martyrs, réliques en Afrique chrétienne aux premiers siècles*. Paris: Beauchesne.

Seguí, Vidal, G. 1937 *La carta-encíclica del obispo Severo* . . . Palma de Majorca: Seminario de los Misioneros de los Sagrados Corazones de Jesús y María.

Seguí, Vidal G., and Hillgarth, J. N. 1955 *La "Altercatio" y la basilica paleocristiana de Son Bou de Menorca*. Palma de Majorca: Sociedad Arqueológica Lulliana.

Severus *Epistola de judaeis*. In *PL* XX.731–46.

    1900 *Liber de miraculis sancti Stephani protomartyris*. In *PL* XLI.833–54.

    1981 *Epistola Severi episcopi – Carta del Obispo Severo – Carta del Bisbe Sever*. Ed. E. Lafuente Hernandez. Minorca.

Simon, Marcel 1958 *St. Stephen and the Hellenists in the Primitive Church*. London and New York: Longmans, Green.

1962a La Polémique antijuive de saint Jean Chrysostome et le mouvement judaïsant d'Antioche. In his *Recherches d'histoire Judéo-Chrétienne*, 140–53. Paris and The Hague: Mouton.

1962b Les Saints d'Israel dans la dévotion de l'église ancienne. In his *Recherches d'histoire Judéo-Chrétienne*, 154–80. Paris and The Hague: Mouton.

1964 *Verus Israel: Etude sur les relations entre Chrétiens et Juifs dans l'empire romain (135–425)*. 2nd edn. Paris: E. de Boccard (orig. 1948).

Simonetti, Manlio 1976 La politica antiariana di Ambrogio. In Giuseppe Lazzati, ed., *Ambrosius Episcopus: Atti . . .* , I.266–85. 2 vols. Milan: Vita e pensiero.

Stemberger, Günther 1987 *Juden und Christen im Heiligen Land*. Munich: C. H. Beck.

Stock, Brian 1983 *The Implications of Literacy: Written Language and Models of Interpretation in the Eleventh and Twelfth Centuries*. Princeton: Princeton University Press

Van Dam, Raymond 1986 "Sheep in Wolves' Clothing": The Letters of Consentius to Augustine. *Journal of Ecclesiastical History* 37: 515–35.

Verbraken, Pierre-Patrick 1976 *Etudes critiques sur les sermons authentiques de Saint Augustin*. The Hague and Steenbergen: In abbatia S. Petri.

Vives, José 1956 Review of G. Seguí [Vidal] and J. N. Hillgarth, *La "Altercatio" y la basilica paleocristiana de Son Bou de Menorca* (1955). *Hispania sacra* 9: 227–9.

Wankenne, Ludovic-Jules, and Hambenne, Baudouin 1987 La Lettre-encyclique de Severus évêque de Minorque au début du Ve siècle. *Revue bénédictine* 97: 13–27.

White, Hayden V. 1975 *Metahistory: The Historical Imagination in Nineteenth-Century Europe*. Baltimore: The Johns Hopkins University Press.

Wilken, Robert L. 1983 *John Chrysostom and the Jews: Rhetoric and Reality in the Late 4th Century*. Berkeley: University of California Press.

11   The deteriorating image of the Jews –
twelfth and thirteenth centuries

Robert Chazan

Toward the end of the tenth century, the vitalization of northern Europe resulted, *inter alia*, in the attraction of southern European Jewish immigrants into an area that had previously lain outside the orbit of Jewish settlement. This immigration was, in many instances, fostered by perceptive rulers, who saw in these Jewish settlers potential contributors to the economic development of their principalities and useful allies in the expansion of their own power. The support of these rulers was, for the Jewish newcomers, indispensable, since the area into which they had chosen to immigrate was generally insecure and they in particular were broadly unpopular. These Jews were viewed negatively by their neighbors for a number of reasons: they were newcomers; they dissented from the Christian religious vision that bound all the rest of society; they were business people in a generally agrarian environment; they were the sworn allies of rulers sometimes popular and sometimes not; above all, they brought with them a series of negative images that often typified the Christian sense of Jews and Judaism. Despite considerable impediments to successful Jewish settlement, small but important Jewish communities rooted themselves all across northern Europe, as a result of the genuine needs of this developing area, the valuable contribution that the immigrant Jews were able to provide, and the mutually useful alliance between the Jews and their overlords.[1]

From the late tenth through the middle of the twelfth century, Jewish settlement proceeded effectively, although not without incident. By the mid-twelfth century, Jewish communities could be found from England in the west to Poland in the east. The Jews, who had come largely as business people, had, particularly in the economically better developed areas of the west – England and northern France – turned to moneylending, a specialty that seems to have contributed to general economic development, that was supported strongly by

---

[1] This essay is excerpted from an early draft of *Medieval Stereotypes and Modern Antisemitism*, to be published in mid-1996 by the University of California Press.

the Jews' baronial and royal protectors, that seems to have provided for the Jews considerable profit, and that further strained their relationship to their neighbors. As a result of this new economic specialization, the links that bound the Jews to their baronial and royal protectors were intensified. The Jews now turned to these rulers for physical security and for business assistance without which their flourishing money trade would have collapsed. Thus, two of the popular anti-Jewish perceptions prevalent in northern Europe from the onset of Jewish settlement – resentment of Jewish business activity and of the political alliance between the Jews and the authorities – were much sharpened by the middle of the twelfth century.[2]

More striking than the imagery of the Jewish moneylender and the Jewish protégé of the authorities was the mid-twelfth-century broadening and deepening of the historic sense of the Jews as hostile, as the unyielding enemies of the Christian world. Firmly rooted in New Testament imagery, this perception of the Jews took diverse forms and exhibited varying levels of intensity over the ages. In northern Europe, the sense of the Jews as enemies of the Christian faith was fairly strong from the outset. This stereotype of the Jews was at the root of the anti-Jewish riots that developed in the Rhineland during the spring months of 1096, in the wake of the popular preaching of the First Crusade.[3] By the middle of the twelfth century, the sense of the Jews as historic enemies of the Christian world had elided into a perception of real-life Jews as murderously hostile to their immediate neighbors, so venomous in fact as to take every opportunity to commit murder on unsuspecting and defenseless Christians, particularly Christian youngsters.[4] This sense became so widespread that the Jews of Paris considered themselves signally successful when they elicited from the sympathetic King Louis VII the following public announcement, in the wake of the execution of more than thirty Jews in the town of Blois on the charge of murdering and drowning a Christian child:

Now then, you Jews of my land, you have no cause for alarm over what that persecutor [Count Theobald of Blois] has done in his domain. For people have levelled the same accusation against the Jews of Pontoise and Janville, but, when the charges were brought before me, they were found false . . . Therefore, be assured, all you Jews in my land, that I harbor no such suspicions. Even if a body be discovered in the city or in the

[2] Chapter 2 of *Medieval Stereotypes* treats some of the twelfth-century transformations in Jewish economic affairs.
[3] For a full analysis of these matters, see Chazan 1987.
[4] While Gavin I. Langmuir sees the ritual-murder allegation that surfaces in the middle of the twelfth century as the key index of the deteriorating popular image of the Jews, I have come to the conclusion that the key index of this deterioration is reflected in the broader sense of the Jews as murderers. For my full argument on this matter, see chapters 3 and 4 of *Medieval Stereotypes*.

countryside, I shall say nothing to the Jews in that regard. Therefore, be not frightened over this issue.[5]

That such formal royal repudiation of the murder accusation should be required speaks volumes about the deteriorating image of the Jews at this critical and creative juncture in the history of northern European civilization.

The enhanced perception of the Jews as ranged in unceasing animosity against Christianity and Christians gave rise, with the passage of time, to a series of imaginative embellishments. The first of these was the allegation that the murderous Jews carried out their heinous acts in a ritualized manner, that they did more than simply murder, that they in effect repeated their historic sin of deicide by crucifying Christians. This allegation, innovated by Thomas of Monmouth in support of his argumentation for the sainthood of William of Norwich, recurs throughout the second half of the twelfth and into the thirteenth century. During the middle decades of the thirteenth century, a second and more tenaciously maintained embellishment of the murder motif made its appearance: the charge that Jews killed Christians in order to utilize their blood as part of the Passover ritual. For reasons that are not altogether clear, this embellishment became far more popular than the allegation of ritual murder, maintaining its potency down into our own century.[6] The middle decades of the twelfth century thus saw marked intensification of anti-Jewish imagery, an intensification that proceeded apace into the following century as well.

The focus of this brief essay is to identify those factors that gave rise to this deteriorating image of the Jews. The first direction that might be essayed is to examine the conditions of Jewish life. Were there factors in Jewish life itself which might have played some discernible role in the enhanced sense of the Jews as enemies of Christian society? A number of facets of Jewish life may indeed have contributed to the deepening sense of the Jews as malign forces. The most obvious of these factors is surely the twelfth-century Jewish specialization in moneylending, with all the traditionally negative imagery associated with the figure of the moneylender. Likewise significant was the intensified alliance between the Jews and the baronial and royal lords. This enhanced alliance – in fact interwoven with the moneylending specialization – surely served to convince many of the pernicious impact of Jews on life in northern European society. To be sure, not everyone would see this Jewish

---

[5] This text can be found in Neubauer and Stern 1892: 34; and Habermann 1945: 145. A full English translation can be found in Chazan 1979: 115–16. I have treated this incident at length in Chazan 1968.

[6] The account of Thomas of Monmouth has been brilliantly analyzed by Gavin I. Langmuir (1974). In chapter 4 of *Medieval Stereotypes*, I discuss the development of these and other stereotypes.

political role as harmful; however, all I am suggesting is that this role would be perceived by some as deleterious.

Jewish moneylending and the role of the Jews in augmentation of central authority both stem from the sphere of economic and political realities. Were there developments in the spiritual realm as well that might have served to buttress the sense of the Jews as implacably opposed to Christianity and Christians? Two related suggestions have occasionally been made, one having to do with enhanced commitment of the Jews of northern Europe to their historic talmudic tradition and growing Christian awareness of both the tradition and the commitment and the other to the related phenomenon of rejection of Christianity as reflected, for example, in the reactions to the crusader assaults of 1096 and to the new missionizing campaign of the mid-thirteenth century. There is some truth to both of these suggestions. It does seem likely that the enhanced commitment of the young Ashkenazic Jewish communities to their own rabbinic tradition may have deepened the perception of the Jews as different and perhaps therefore as dangerously different.[7] By the middle of the thirteenth century, as the leadership of the Church became increasingly aware of the Talmud and its teachings (in particular through the agency of former Jews), there was a heavy emphasis on talmudic tradition as hostile to Christian teachings and to Christian society.[8] While this arcane material was surely not known by broad segments of European society, it may well be that perceptions based on this information filtered into a variety of strata of European society or – more important – that broad suspicions of anti-Christian hostility, which predated the evidential base provided by the thirteenth-century converts from Judaism, were at least buttressed by the new information available on rabbinic Judaism.

I have argued elsewhere that, in the Christian world, the anti-Jewish riots of 1096 were not at all well known. Likewise, the conversionist efforts of the mid-thirteenth century were hardly the equivalent of front-page news. Again, however, it might plausibly be suggested that some awareness of solid Jewish intransigence in the face of both illegitimate and legitimate conversionist pressures filtered into Christian consciousness. Even Christian observers who were hostile to the popular crusading bands that assaulted the Rhineland Jews in 1096 were appalled by the violent Jewish responses. In particular, slaughter of youngsters by zealous Jewish parents evoked highly emotional condemnation by such Christian observers.[9] Similarly, I have suggested in my study of

---

[7] This is a point emphasized by Gavin I. Langmuir in his comments on the papers of Jeremy Cohen and David Berger in the *American Historical Review* (Langmuir 1986).

[8] See the discussion of the condemnation of the Talmud in Cohen 1982: 51–76, and in Chazan 1988.

[9] See my analysis of these matters in Chazan 1987.

the new missionizing of the mid-thirteenth century that, like all serious missionizing efforts, it was bound to bring harm to the targeted minority community. Either significant segments of the targeted minority would in fact succumb to the pressures, or, alternatively, failure to succumb to what was regularly perceived in the majority camp as unassailable truth could only be understood as some kind of intellectual or moral failure on the part of the minority group.[10] Thus, it does seem fair to suggest that Jewish behaviors in the religious realm may have contributed in some minimal way to the enhanced perceptions of Jewish enmity, as did developments in the economic and political spheres.

At the same time, it is surely clear that the search for developments in Jewish life that would aid substantially in comprehending the deterioration of the Jewish image – whether in terms of Jewish economic activity, political alliances, or religious behaviors – is ultimately of limited value. To focus on the minority and its behaviors is to accept at face value the judgments of the majority society that rejected the Jews and a number of other groupings as well. R. I. Moore, in *The Formation of a Persecuting Society*, expressed incredulity at the possibility that a number of different groups posed much the same threat to western Christendom at precisely the same time. For Moore, the coincidence of such parallel perceptions and programs means that, in fact, no one of these groupings posed the kind of threat that was projected. This then suggests to Moore that the explanation for the parallel perceptions and programs must lie within majority society itself.[11]

I would add to Moore's case another set of considerations drawn from my fuller analysis of deteriorating perceptions of the Jews. I would urge that the fundamental irrationality of this deteriorating perception again leads us in the direction of majority society, its thinking, tensions, and fears. When all due allowance for the realities of Jewish economic, political, and religious behavior has been made, we emerge with the sense that the threat of Jewish hostility and the danger flowing therefrom is rather obviously overblown. I am suggesting that the level of concern over what was after all a tiny and relatively weak minority group far exceeds all bounds and justifies the appellation irrational. The irrationality of the perceptions of the Jewish threat leads in the same direction proposed by Moore, and by others such as Gavin I. Langmuir and John Boswell as well: comprehension of the perceptions of minorities – Jewish and otherwise – spun out in majority northern European

---

[10] See my study of this innovative program in Chazan 1989.

[11] Moore 1987. While I share Moore's sense of the need to focus on majority society and its circumstances, I do not agree with all of Moore's positions. I disagree, for example, with his suggestion of the interchangeability of persecuted outgroups and with his view that anti-outgroup imagery was created by the societal elites in order to further their power aspirations.

society of the late twelfth and thirteenth centuries requires, above all, understanding of the majority, its spiritual and psychic state.[12]

Procedurally, it seems best to begin this discussion of the majority spiritual
and psychic state with some observations on changes in patterns of thinking
and then proceed – with all due caution and tentativeness – to the realm of the
irrational. The period under discussion has long been recognized as a period of
more than economic and political progress across northern Europe. It has been
acknowledged also as a period of major cultural advance, a period which was
sufficiently exciting in intellectual and spiritual terms to warrant utilization of
the term "renaissance." It does not seem exaggerated to suggest that many
facets of the intellectual progress that propelled northern European society to
the fore of western civilization owe their origins to this period and that many
important features of western thinking made their appearance or reappearance
at this juncture.[13] For our purposes, a number of these positive developments
had important and sometimes negative concomitants.

The first such development that we might note is the growing commitment
to rational philosophizing that looms so large in the history of western
speculation. The emphasis on reason, its powers, and the extent to which it
might undergird both the life of society and the dictates of traditional religion
represent important steps in the direction of much modern sensibility. Yet, as
noted in a penetrating observation by Amos Funkenstein, this stress on
rationality, which might have meant a new kind of openness and tolerance,
actually became a factor in a growing intolerance for non-Christians.[14] Given
the twelfth-century sense that reason would buttress the teachings of
Christianity, a sense that was substantially augmented by some of the rational
speculation of the thirteenth century, the conviction that non-Christians were
ultimately non-rational was, for many, inescapable. To the extent that
comprehending the truth of Christianity was either a divinely dispensed grace
or, at least, the fortuitous result of being born into the Christian fold, non-
believers were in many ways the subject of condescending pity; to the extent
that Christian truth was deemed obvious to anyone pursuing rational understanding with a measure of desire and objectivity, then non-believers were
subject to a problematic question – why could they not discern what reason so

---

[12] Langmuir 1990; Boswell 1980. I have consciously chosen to utilize a definition of "irrational"
different from that used by Langmuir in his important work. Langmuir draws a distinction
between non-rational and irrational: for him, irrationality involves assertions of truth for
"expressions of belief that could be demonstrated at the time to be empirically false (e.g., Jews
have horns)." This definition seems to me unduly limited, and I have chosen to treat the
irrational somewhat more loosely, including perceptions of danger posed by Jews that, while
not demonstrably false empirically, are wildly overblown.

[13] The legacy of this period is emphasized by R. W. Southern in his introduction to *The Making
of the Middle Ages* (Southern 1953).

[14] Funkenstein 1968.

clearly taught? In a real sense, the problem was compounded with respect to the Jews. While one might wonder about other groups and their failure to heed the dictates of reason, with the Jews the problem was doubled. They after all were the people who shared – and misunderstood – the message of divine revelation, which they obstinately refused to acknowledge; in parallel fashion, they resisted the obvious lessons of reason, which should likewise have led them to embrace Christian truth. The end result was not a pretty picture of the Jews. I acknowledge that many modern readers may find this line of thinking a rationalization for majority doubts, rather than an assertion of majority rationality. I do not rule out such a possibility, which we shall address shortly. For the moment, I am suggesting that the rationality of the period – surely a positive development from the modern perspective – had the potential for generating curious and harmful implications.

Yet another positive development widely noted was the growing awareness of human experience in all its complexity and at its deepest levels. There was heightened sensitivity to the range of human experience and human emotion.[15] This new sensitivity certainly enhanced and vivified the artistic creativity of the period. It had significant impact on the religious life of the period as well. Numerous observers have noted the growing humanization of the deity in Christianity, particularly the humanization of Jesus, in literary sources as well as in artistic representation. Once again, however, positive developments – at least from the modern western perspective – had the potential for negative implications with respect to the image of the Jews. At the core of Christian–Jewish tension lay a problematic dyadic relationship, viewed in traditional Christian thinking as the Jesus-victim and the Jews-aggressors. As the effort to deepen understanding of human experience proceeded, it bore in its wake a twofold negative implication with respect to the Jews, one flowing from enhanced humanization of the victim figure in the traditional Christian–Jewish dyad and the other resulting from the effort to understand in more profoundly human terms the aggressor.

Let us begin with the first. As sensitivity to the humanity of Jesus increased, one of the key elements of his humanity that came most strikingly to the fore was his suffering. Thus, just as the call to the crusade, with its emphasis on the Holy Sepulcher, had as an inevitable concomitant the stirring up of animosity against those who had allegedly been responsible for the laying of Jesus in his grave, so too did the enhanced concern with Jesus's humanity and his suffering accentuate the guilt of those who had purportedly caused this suffering. We can see this dynamic at work in Thomas of Monmouth's

---

[15] This new sensitivity is emphasized in numerous studies. For particularly compelling presentations of this theme, see a number of the essays collected in Chenu 1968 and in Benson and Constable 1982.

depiction of the suffering of the young William of Norwich.[16] Thomas identifies the saintly William with Jesus. The tale of the suffering of William-Jesus is as explicit as one could conceive. The depiction of the torture and crucifixion of William of Norwich is excruciatingly detailed. The primary goal of this detailed portrait of Jewish cruelty may not have been vilification of the Jews. It is arguable that what Thomas of Monmouth was most concerned to convey was the gruesome suffering of his hero, with the purpose of high-lighting William's martyrdom, in particular through an identification with the suffering Jesus.[17] Accepting for a moment that the goal of the lavishly depicted suffering was the emphasis on the nobility and heroism of William of Norwich, it was unfortunately the case that this emphasis could not be achieved except through a concomitant highlighting of the bestiality of his Jewish tormenters. Thus, again, a positive development of the period turns out to have damaging implications for the Jews.

The deepening of sensitivity to human experience had yet a second negative implication for the Jews. While the suffering of the Jesus-victim and associated martyr figures produced one kind of negative result, the alleged behavior of the Jews-aggressors produced yet another, flowing from enhanced focus on the intentionality of human actions. As is well known, there was an intense new concern, from the mid-twelfth century on, with the intentions of human behavior. This represents, again from a modern perspective, a considerable advance over the more behaviorist attitudes of the prior centuries. No longer was the action alone the only dimension to human experience and the sole basis for judgment of human behavior. In this more sensitive age, there was a growing awareness of and concern for the intentions that lay behind action and behavior. Once more, this positive development boded ill for the Jews. In a brilliant study of the motif of the Jews as killers of Christ, Jeremy Cohen has delineated a marked deterioration in the image of the Jew as Christ-killer.[18] Cohen associates this deterioration with his case for a new ecclesiastical perception of the Jews. I would suggest an alternative approach to the phenomenon to which he has drawn our attention. It is the concern with human intentionality that resulted in this new deepening of the sense of Jewish culpability. Since thinkers were now more attuned to the depths of human feeling and to human intentions, the question that this enhanced concern raised

---

[16] The full text of Thomas's treatise was published by Augustus Jessopp and Montague Rhodes James (Thomas of Monmouth 1896). Note again Langmuir 1984.

[17] Without arguing the point in full detail, let me indicate that sainthood for the young William was claimed by Thomas on three grounds: the pure childhood of the lad, his martyrlike death at the hands of the enemies of Christendom, and the miracles produced at his graves. While the first and third of these claims were important, the case for sainthood ultimately rested on the middle contention, and, in order for William's death to be considered martyrdom, the Jews had to be depicted as the implacable enemies of Christianity and Christians.

[18] Cohen 1983.

had to do with the feelings, intentions, and nature of the Jews who had been responsible for the death of Jesus. While the purported act of deicide had always been judged reprehensible, the more that Christians focused on this act as a reflection of thinking and feeling persons, the more they would be ineluctably drawn to questioning the nature of such persons and, almost inevitably, to judging those persons with greater severity. Thus, once again, an advance in spirituality had, as a concomitant, the deepening – rather than the lessening – of hostility toward the Jews.

Thus far, our look at majority society has focused on beneficial changes – or at least changes that have been by and large deemed beneficial by subsequent observers. The time has come now to raise the issue of tensions that might have eventuated in irrational fears and perceptions of the Jews, and other minority groupings as well. The argument is a simple one: as so often happens, a society discomfited and anxious is led to exaggerate the dangers lurking about it, to identify an alleged series of threats, and to exaggerate the significance of these threats to the point that one can no longer speak of reasonable responses to real forces. The question with which we are left is the identification of factors that might have led northern European society of the second half of the twelfth century to the point of high anxiety and considerable irrationality.[19]

Let us begin our search for factors contributing to societal anxiety and disequilibrium in the realm of the realistic. At least two major factors can be discerned in late twelfth-century northern Europe that in realistic terms disturbed the equilibrium of individuals and groups. The first and less obvious of the factors is the accelerating rate of change. It is of course impossible to be as specific as social scientists would be with regard to contemporary societal situations. Nonetheless, there is broad agreement among medievalists that the rate of change in societal life in northern Europe accelerated markedly during the middle decades of the twelfth century. To be sure, most of the direction of this change was positive, as we have noted repeatedly. What has not been sufficiently emphasized, however, is the tendency for even positive change to be disruptive. While a majority of members of a society may benefit from change, there is always a minority group adversely affected by the same changes. In fact, one need not think simply of positive and negative change. The status quo, however problematic it might be, has nonetheless the virtue of familiarity; new circumstances, however beneficial they might be, are uncomfortable in their very newness. It hardly seems amiss to suggest that the fact of rapid change itself meant some loss of societal equilibrium, a measure of enhanced anxiety, and therefore augmented concern with dangers real and fancied.

---

[19] Again, recall my divergence from Langmuir in utilization of the term "irrational" – see above, n. 12.

A more obvious factor in augmenting societal anxiety is the reality of challenges and dangers, both external and internal. Let us begin with the former. For approximately 150 years, a fairly lengthy stretch of time from the perspective of individual life span, northern European civilization had been maturing and expanding significantly at the expense of its neighbors. Particularly stunning were the remarkable successes associated with the First Crusade. While modern historiography has tended toward skepticism as to the overall significance of the successes of 1095–9, the emotional importance of the symbolic city of Jerusalem was enormous and the crusading victories were perceived as the hand of God at work in favor of a powerful and divinely favored society. The impact of the reverses of the mid- and late twelfth century was considerable. There was confusion, consternation, and anxiety in the wake of the fall of Edessa and – more important – the failure of the grand army organized by St. Bernard. Something was clearly wrong on both a terrestrial and heavenly level.[20] Indeed, as a result of the achievements of the eleventh and early twelfth centuries, this awareness of difficulty was absorbed within a new framework. There was now far greater appreciation of the vastness of the Muslim world and considerable fear of its massive resources. The older and naive optimism began to give way to a more realistic appraisal of the forces ranged against Christendom. This new awareness of external threat surely played a role in the anxieties that beset European society. It might well be objected that the Christian world was, in fact, stronger in relation to the Muslim world than it had been heretofore. This hardheaded appraisal is, for our purposes, beside the point. What counts for us is twelfth-century understanding of circumstances. An unreasonably self-confident western Christendom now found itself beset with serious concerns and misgivings. In such a state of disequilibrium, societies often turn against perceived threats existing within their midst. The tendency to magnify the danger flowing from minor threats that can be fairly readily contained is a constant of both individual and societal response to feelings of insufficiency and lack of control. So it seems to have been in mid-twelfth-century northern Christendom. The new awareness of external threat galvanized a concern with a variety of alleged internal dangers, which had the virtue of being far more readily controllable than the powerful Muslim world lurking beyond the borders of Christendom.

There was yet a second danger that threatened mid-twelfth-century western Christendom, and that was the internal danger of dissension and dissidence. While from a modern perspective – and this was appreciated to some extent even by medievals – new ideas and ideals have the capacity to vitalize

---

[20] Much has been written on the changing mood of the twelfth century. See, in particular, the broad depiction of Giles Constable (1953).

and revitalize a society, in traditional societies such new notions are often perceived as threatening the core of authoritative belief by which society – in particular a religious society – orients itself. Despite Moore's lumping together heretics, Jews, and lepers, I would argue that in fact heretics constituted a realistic challenge to the stability of at least the established church.[21] To be sure, one may well contend that the definition of heresy may have been unduly strict or that the means of repression of perceived heresy were ultimately counter-productive. Nonetheless, a realistic threat did exist, one that – in tandem with the external danger of which we have just now spoken – upset the equilibrium of society. I am not suggesting that there was necessarily a simple identification of heretics and Jews, although such an identification did on occasion manifest itself. What I am proposing, rather, is that the perception of internal threat contributed to a sense of insecurity that focused attention on and concern over a number of minority groupings, among them the Jews. Thus, perceived external and internal dangers raised the anxiety level in mid-twelfth-century northern Europe, making broad segments of the populace uncomfortable and fearful, predisposing them to a level of anti-outgroup hostility that would not have been present under stabler circumstances.

Both of the factors discussed thus far – the reality of rapid social change and the perception of external and internal threat – constitute developments that took place in the outer world of twelfth-century men and women and predisposed them to unrealistic perceptions of Jews and others, in particular of the dangers posed by these Jews and others. In addition, the inner spiritual developments of which we have spoken reinforced this uneasiness and anxiety. The enhanced sensitivity to the complexities of the human psyche worked in subtler ways to discomfit northern European society at this juncture. I have already suggested that growing awareness of the complexities of human behavior had directly deleterious consequences for stereotypes of the Jews, focusing attention on the suffering of Jesus and associated saint-figures, enhancing the sense of malevolence of those who persecuted him and them, and raising distressing questions about the nature of people who could behave in this manner. Beyond this immediate impact, awareness of the complications of the human psyche aroused distress at yet another set of dangers – less tangible perhaps than the dangers posed by external enemies and internal dissidents, but real nonetheless. Members of mid-twelfth-century northern European society found themselves frightened by more than real developments; they were also discomfited by the dangers increasingly perceived as lurking within the complex human psyche. While the issues involved were murky, the implications were significant. The complications of human thinking meant a fresh look at the potential for both beneficent and malevolent

---

[21] Note my earlier mention of disagreement on this matter – see above, n. 11.

behavior. The kind of portrait of Jewish cruelty notable in Thomas of Monmouth is in part an offshoot of this troubling new sense of human capacities for both good and evil. One of the striking manifestations of this intensified awareness of human capacity for evil is the proliferating sense of the ubiquity of the devil and his emissaries. In his major recent investigation of witchcraft, Jeffrey Burton Russell has the following to say, in a chapter significantly enough entitled "Demonology, Catharism, and Witchcraft, 1140–1230," reflecting much the same time frame with which I have been working.

The result [of a series of economic and social changes such as have here been discussed] was a great transformation in man's view of the supernatural. The saints, the Virgin, and God himself were progressively humanized. The stiff, composed, majestic Christ of the Romanesque crucifixes yielded to the suffering, compassionate Christ of Gothic art. Christ the awesome and remote Creator was replaced by the brother and lover of men, and his new gentleness was supplemented by the tenderness and warmth of the cult of the Virgin. The very same impetus humanized Satan. Christ, the Virgin, Satan – all three were no longer remote principles but immediately present, every moment, in the bustle of the day and in the stillness of the night. The eternal Principle of Evil walked in solid, if invisible, substance at one's side and crouched when one was quiet in the dark recesses of room and mind.[22]

Again, while there is much that is generally appealing in the transformation depicted by Russell, this shift held appalling implications for the image of European Jewry. To the extent that satanic forces became real and the agents of the devil were sought throughout society, the Jews (and others as well) were marked with a new intensity as potentially dangerous forces operating within an ever more threatened Christian society. The heretofore stereotypic Jewish enemy, whose ancestors had brought about the crucifixion, was transformed, like the deity and the devil, into something more real and ubiquitous, a group of neighbors consumed by hatred, involved in endless designs against their Christian hosts, and devoted to murderous violence.

Thus, while there were some aspects of Jewish behavior that contributed to the deterioration of the Jewish image in late twelfth and early thirteenth-century northern Europe, ultimately the critical shift took place within the collective psyche of the Christian majority in this rapidly maturing area. New patterns of thinking, by and large positive in their central thrusts, had damaging implications for the image of the Jews, and of other outgroups as well. More important, dangers real and imaginary heightened the anxieties of the majority and spurred a search for enemies immediate and potential. Given the earlier legacy of Christian thinking about the Jews and the prior realities of Jewish life in this area, it was almost inevitable that the heightened anxieties

[22] Russell 1972: 102.

and the resultant effort to identify sources of threat would fasten intensely, although not exclusively, upon the Jews.

The deteriorating image of the Jews, whose wellsprings I have attempted to identify, played a considerable role in the broad decline of Jewish life in northern Europe that began to manifest itself during the second half of the twelfth century.[23] This negative imagery had direct impact upon many of the leaders in both ecclesiastical and secular society. In addition, leaders in both establishments had much to gain from exploiting these negative perceptions of the Jews, winning accolades from the populace by acting as protectors of Christian interests in the face of the Jewish threat.[24] Indeed, the deteriorating image of the Jews, whose dynamics I have tried to sketch, left a lasting legacy. Given the centrality of these areas of northern Europe in the subsequent development of western civilization, it is hardly surprising – although highly lamentable – that much of the imagery created under the particular circumstances just now delineated has come to pervade western perceptions of the Jews down into the late twentieth century. The special circumstances of the late twelfth and thirteenth centuries created an enduring legacy that has plagued Jewish life and sullied western history from then till now.[25]

REFERENCES

Benson, Robert L. and Constable, Giles, with Lanham, Carol D., eds. 1982 *Renaissance and Renewal in the Twelfth Century*. Cambridge, Mass.: Harvard University Press.

Boswell, John 1980 *Christianity, Social Tolerance, and Homosexuality: Gay People in Western Europe from the Beginning of the Christian Era to the Fourteenth Century*. Chicago: University of Chicago Press.

Chazan, Robert 1968 The Blois Incident of 1171: A Study in Jewish Intercommunal Organization. *Proceedings of the American Academy for Jewish Research* 36: 13–31.

1979 *Church, State, and Jew in the Middle Ages*. New York: Behrman House.

1987 *European Jewry and the First Crusade*. Berkeley, Los Angeles, and London: University of California Press.

1988 The Condemnation of the Talmud Reconsidered (1239–1248). *Proceedings of the American Academy for Jewish Research* 45: 11–30.

---

[23] Chapters 6 and 7 of *Medieval Stereotypes* are devoted to sketching the dimensions of this broad decline and the factors that occasioned it.

[24] Let me clarify a bit further the disagreement with Moore indicated in n. 11. I believe that the negative popular imagery was exploited by the secular and religious elites; I do not believe that they created and disseminated the imagery.

[25] Langmuir's analysis and my own, while differing in certain details, agree on the onset of deterioration during the middle decades of the twelfth century. Both of us further agree on the enduring impact of the enhanced negative imagery on subsequent Jewish life in the western world.

1989 *Daggers of Faith: Thirteenth-Century Christian Missionizing and Jewish Response*. Berkeley, Los Angeles, and Oxford: University of California Press.

Chenu, Marie-Dominique 1968 *Nature, Man, and Society in the Twelfth Century: Essays on New Theological Perspectives in the Latin West*. Ed. and trans. Jerome Taylor and Lester K. Little. Chicago: University of Chicago Press.

Cohen, Jeremy 1982 *The Friars and the Jews: The Evolution of Medieval Anti-Judaism*. Ithaca, N.Y.: Cornell University Press.

1983 The Jews as the Killers of Christ in the Latin Tradition, from Augustine to the Friars. *Traditio* 39: 3–27.

Constable, Giles 1953 The Second Crusade as Seen by Contemporaries. *Traditio* 9: 213–81.

Funkenstein, Amos 1968 Changes in the Patterns of Christian Anti-Jewish Polemics in the Twelfth Century (Hebrew). *Zion* 33: 124–44.

Habermann, Abraham 1945 *Sefer Gezerot Ashkenaz ve-Zarfat*. Jerusalem: Sifre Tarshish.

Langmuir, Gavin I. 1984 Thomas of Monmouth: Detector of Ritual Murder. *Speculum* 59: 820–46. Repr. in his *Toward a Definition of Antisemitism*, 209–36. Berkeley, Los Angeles, and Oxford: University of California Press, 1990.

1986 Comment on David Berger, "Mission to the Jews and Jewish–Christian Contacts in the Polemical Literature of the High Middle Ages," and Jeremy Cohen, "Scholarship and Intolerance in the Medieval Academy." *American Historical Review* 91: 614–24.

1990 *History, Religion, and Antisemitism*. Berkeley, Los Angeles, and Oxford: University of California Press.

Moore, R. I. 1987 *The Formation of a Persecuting Society: Power and Deviance in Western Europe, 950–1250*. Oxford: Basil Blackwell.

Neubauer, Adolf, and Stern, Moritz, eds. 1892 *Hebräische Berichte über die Juden-verfolgungen während der Kreuzzüge*. Berlin: L. Simion.

Russell, Jeffrey Burton 1972 *Witchcraft in the Middle Ages*. Ithaca, N.Y.: Cornell University Press.

Southern, Richard W. 1953 *The Making of the Middle Ages*. New Haven, Conn.: Yale University Press.

Thomas of Monmouth 1896 *The Life and Miracles of St. William of Norwich*. Ed. and trans. Augustus Jessopp and Montague Rhodes James. Cambridge: Cambridge University Press.

12 Monarchs and minorities in the Christian western Mediterranean around 1300: Lucera and its analogues

David Abulafia

Writing from Anagni in August 1301, King Charles II of Naples expressed the fervent wish that "the Holy Mother Church be venerated and the Christian faith be cultivated in praise of God where once the profane rite of the Synagogue of the damnable Prince Muhammad" had been conducted, in Città Santa Maria, formerly known as Lucera.[1] The words were apparently not his, but those of his principal minister, the protonotary Bartolomeo da Capua, who was one of the most skilled Latinists of his day, and perhaps too much should not be made of the rhetorical reference to the mosque of Lucera as a synagogue. In fact, the equation of the biblical Sarah with the Christian Church and of Abraham's handmaid Hagar with the rejected Synagogue was current at this time, and coincided with an awareness among Christian authors that Islam traced its origin to Hagar and her son Ishmael.[2] When the terms *Synagoga* and *Muscheta* were used interchangeably, this was not necessarily the result of ignorance or of overblown rhetoric. It is one period in the coming together of attitudes to Jews and Saracens that this essay seeks to analyze, concentrating mainly on what might be termed "official" attitudes at certain royal courts, and concentrating on Jews and Muslims who found themselves under Christian rule.

The chronological limits of this essay are set by a series of events and non-events during a twenty-year period: the destruction of the Muslim enclave of Minorca, in 1287; the expulsion of the Jews from Anjou and Maine, in 1289; the mass conversions of Jews in southern Italy, from about 1290; the destruction of the Muslim colony at Lucera in southern Italy in 1300; the decision by the kings of Majorca and Naples not to expel the Jews from the Balearics, Roussillon, and Provence in 1306. The geographical limits of the essay are set within the western Mediterranean (with one obvious exception), a region

---

[1] *Codice Diplomatico dei Saraceni di Lucera*, ed. P. Egidi (Naples, 1917) (hereafter: *CDSL*) no. 611; the same words are used in *CDSL* no. 654 of 10 January 1302; here Nicola de Friczia, Bartolomeo da Capua's deputy, lifts large passages from his master's text in no. 611. See also Egidi 1915; this originally appeared in the *Archivio storico per le province napoletane* between 1911 and 1914: 36 (1911): 597–694; 37 (1912): 71–89, 664–96; 38 (1913): 115–44, 681–707; 39 (1914), 132–71, 697–766. References here are to this edition.

[2] Zacour 1990.

where Angevins of Naples and Aragonese of Aragon–Catalonia, Majorca, and Sicily competed but also at times collaborated, so that marriage alliances brought Spanish princesses to southern Italy and vice versa. The inclusion of one northern French territory, Anjou–Maine, in this conspectus is justified by the retention of the counties in the hands of the royal house of Naples until 1302, and by the close interest that the Angevins of Naples retained in their original patrimony. In any case, it is also clear that policy towards the Jews in Capetian France had great influence on their treatment in the lands of both Aragon and of Anjou.

I

The Muslim colony at Lucera was founded in the 1220s, at the same time as the kings of Aragon and Castile were beginning a victorious drive southwards. The deportation of the Muslim rebels who had held out in the mountains of Sicily against Frederick II began six years before James the Conqueror added Majorca to the lands of the house of Barcelona, and the last phase of deportations was probably completed in the 1240s, around the time that the Castilians seized Seville. What was original about Lucera was that it did not simply involve the expulsion of the Muslims out of the conquered lands, as happened in parts of Andalucia; the entire Muslim population of Sicily of 15,000–30,000 was supposedly uprooted and taken far into the northeast of the Sicilian kingdom, to a point whence access to the Islamic world would be exceptionally difficult. The Lucera Muslims were deliberately isolated. They had, while in Sicily, received succor from North Africa. Henceforth they would be all but forgotten by the Muslim world.[3] Thus this case falls half way between the mass expulsions often carried out by the Castilians and the policy of retention of the *mudéjar* population characteristic of Aragon.[4]

Even so, the apparent oddity of the Lucera colony must not be exaggerated. The south of Italy was dotted with small communities of Greeks, Bulgars, and others, whose origins in some cases lay in earlier deportations by the Byzantine rulers of Langobardia. The deportation of Lucera thus fits into an ancient local tradition of population transfers, irrespective of what it reveals about Frederick's attitude to Muslims. In the second place, a small Christian community continued to exist there, if only in the suburbs; and there were Dominican attempts to convert the Muslims which met with official imperial approval, and which may even have produced some results. It is possible

---

[3] This is still in a sense the case: there is no heading *Lucera* in the *Encyclopaedia of Islam*, second edition.

[4] For the variations in policy, see the surveys by J. O'Callaghan (for Castile and Portugal) and by R. I. Burns (for Aragon) in Powell 1990.

that Frederick saw the isolation of the Saracens at Lucera as a means of assimilating them into the Christian world; all alone *in media christianorum planitie* the Luceran Muslims would surely experience the same assimilation into the surrounding Latin society that so many Sicilian Muslims had experienced in the twelfth century. Many already understood Italian. In 1233 Gregory IX solicited Frederick's help in ensuring that the Dominicans be allowed to preach Christianity to the Lucerans.[5] Frederick insisted that he too was keen to convert all the Saracens in Lucera, and that many had already converted. It has been suggested that the pope was worried that the Lucerans spoke the same language as their Christian neighbors, and that they might therefore infect them with their misbeliefs.[6] This was a stock accusation against heretics and Jews; but more important was the feeling that this self-contained group of Muslims was an obvious first candidate for conversion, at a time when Gregory IX, Ramon de Penyafort, and others were beginning to plan still more ambitious preaching campaigns against Jews and Muslims, based on the close study of Arabic and Hebrew in special language academies set up for training missionaries.[7] The prospect of a quick strike against Islam in Apulia must have seemed too good to miss, especially since just now Frederick and the papacy were on reasonably good terms.

A second letter of Frederick II indicates that his concern for the Christianization of Lucera was still alive in 1236. Now we find him insisting that one third of the population has decided to turn Christian already, and rebutting accusations that he has been neglectful of the need to convert them. It has to be said that, even if as much as one third had really expressed an interest in Christianity, there is no evidence that the number of converts was anywhere nearly as high. Interestingly, though, Frederick claims credit not merely for deporting the Saracens from the Sicilian mountains to Apulia, which he obviously saw as a positive achievement for Christianity; he claims credit for Christianizing western Sicily by strengthening Christian settlement there, and by removing the Muslim menace from the island. Lucera has to be seen as a two-pronged policy, both arms of which are intended to benefit the Christians.[8] As Powell says, the letter of 1236, "which has been cited to show that Frederick had little interest in the conversion of the Luceran Muslims actually demonstrates the opposite."[9] But the great majority certainly

---

[5] J. L. Huillard-Bréholles, *Historia diplomatica Friderici Secundi*, 6 vols. in 12 parts (Paris, 1854–61; reprinted 1872–83), IV.452.

[6] James M. Powell, "The Papacy and the Muslim frontier," in Powell 1990: 195, where Powell assumes that *intelligunt* means "they speak," rather than the more probable "they understand."

[7] Cohen 1982: 107. In general, the interpretation of Chazan 1989 is preferable; on this point, see *ibid.* 29–30.

[8] Huillard-Bréholles, *Historia diplomatica*, IV.831.

[9] Powell 1990: 196.

remained Muslims until 1300, though how strong their commitment was is unknown.

The Lucera Muslims were given the task of cultivating a potentially fertile area whose wheat and barley became one of the prized assets of the Angevin kings of Naples. It is generally assumed that the Saracens all lived in Lucera City; however, some of the lands they cultivated were several miles from Lucera, and the presence of resident Saracens, officially or otherwise, in the surrounding countryside should not be discounted.[10] There were significant numbers of cattle and sheep, even a few pigs, on their land; skilled craftsmen in the town were given commissions by the Sicilian king, and some at least of the male Lucerans became soldiers, serving as far afield as northern Italy, Albania, and Tunis during the thirteenth century. The city was not a major cultural center, though the royal palace in Lucera was a favorite residence of Frederick II and his successors. In fact, many of the Saracen dancers and trumpeters in the emperor's service were probably Muslim slaves brought from overseas, not local Lucerans, though they may in time have added to the Luceran population.

Frederick's legislation of 1231 provides a valuable clue to the status of these Muslims. Frederick's laws speak of Jews and Saracens in the same breath, and insist that both groups must not be deprived of royal protection because their religion is hateful to Christians. Later documents reveal that the Saracens in the *Regno* are *servi camere nostre*. The phrase is adapted from the similar label attached to the Jews. Applied to Muslims, the label is apparently devoid of the complex theological background that was held to justify its use when applied to Jews. There simply did not exist a long history of Saracen subjection to Christian rulers, and the transfer of the term from Jews to Muslims was at least as much a practical political and fiscal convenience as it was a statement about the nature of Christian relations with Islam. Frederick had appropriated the community and had planted it on royal demesne lands; the Lucera Muslims were royal property, working on royal property. Their status thus differed markedly from that of those *mudejares* in Spain who had entered into a treaty, however unequal, with Christian conquerors. Like the Jews, they did not lack an internal political organization, under Muslim officials; this evolved into a Saracen *universitas* in all major respects similar to other south Italian *universitates*: a municipal government that was charged with the collection of local taxes and day-to-day affairs. A further feature of Luceran autonomy was the way the Sicilian administration countenanced the exclusion of the local Christians from all or most of their churches within Lucera; church lands were taken into the royal demesne to be handed on to the Muslims, but the churches that lost lands did receive other estates in compensation.

[10] The most recent study of Lucera concentrates on these aspects: Martin 1989: 797–810.

Lucera was rapidly cited by the papacy as evidence of Frederick's multi-faceted faithlessness. The emperor surrounded himself with Saracens and brought them on his campaigns in northern Italy. The existence of a Muslim community in southern Italy provided a central justification for the launching of a crusade against Manfred in 1258; the English nobles agreed that all vows to go to the Holy Land should be commuted in order to help Henry III conquer southern Italy on behalf of his son Edmund; "this can be done with honesty because of the town of Lucera in Apulia, which is inhabited by infidels."[11] When Charles of Anjou became papal champion, the existence of Lucera remained a prominent justification for his crusade against the Hohenstaufen. His failure to destroy the colony, despite its vigorous resistance to the Angevin usurpation, suggests a practical awareness of its value to the crown. The poll tax as well as taxes on local produce could not be ignored by a king who came to the throne already deeply in debt. Besides, the Muslim troops included effective archers and specialists in siege warfare, tent-making, and any number of other valuable skills. If he had to use further force against them, he would be faced with a costly struggle against a highly competent foe that had already held Frederick II at bay in Sicily for several decades. Charles did attempt to attract Provençal settlers to the Capitanata, near Lucera, and may have seen the resettlement of the region by an all-Christian population as a long-term objective.[12] Otherwise, Charles's anti-Muslim policy within his kingdom was probably limited to the expulsion, perhaps towards Lucera itself, of the last Muslims on Malta. In other respects, he took care to guarantee the rights of the Lucera *universitas*.

The integration of the Lucera Saracens into the administrative structure of the kingdom was also indicated by the apparently paradoxical policy of making *servi camere nostre* into knights. Salem Garuyno and Salem son of Ninabet were decorated *militari cingulo* by Charles II in 1291.[13] The knight Abraham was explicitly said to be liable *pro feudali servitio*.[14] Adelasisius or Abd-al-Aziz of Lucera, a member of what was clearly the wealthiest and most powerful family in Lucera, received a fief at Tortivoli near Lucera in 1296, and in fact his family was able to retain many of its possessions after the fall of Saracen Lucera since he and his relatives converted to Christianity.[15]

Although there are hints in the documents of unrest in Lucera during 1299 and early 1300, and although there was some tension between the Muslims and

---

[11] Huillard-Bréholles, *Historia diplomatica* V.680–1; Housley 1982: 65; Maier 1995.

[12] It is possible that the Franco-Provençal-speaking settlements in the hinterland behind Lucera represent the surviving residue of the colonization arranged by the early Angevin monarchs, but there are other explanations for their origin too. See most recently Kattenbusch 1982: 14–22; Castielli 1978: 7–21.

[13] *CDSL* no. 58.

[14] *Ibid.* no. 142.   [15] *Ibid.* nos. 206, 242, 323, etc.

their Christian neighbors, the destruction of the colony by order of Charles II
was sudden and unexpected. On 4 August Bartolomeo da Capua wrote to the
Lucerans advising them of the need to appoint new city officials. This was a
routine exercise, not by any means unique to Lucera; there was no hint that
strong action was in the king's mind. It is true that in June Bartolomeo da
Capua had written a strongly worded letter to the king's subjects condemning
the fact that the inhabitants of Lucera were Muslims and insisting that those
who became Christian would be exempt from all taxes for the rest of their
lives.[16] This letter may reflect a belief that the Lucerans should be given a
further chance to find the true faith before their expropriation; what is
important is that at no point does the letter suggest that the Saracens face
expropriation and sale as slaves.

The blow fell suddenly on 24 August 1300. Charles's men occupied the
town rapidly; the Muslims were all arrested; deportations began at once;
the town was renamed Città Santa Maria, a name which failed to stick. By
4 September 444 Saracens had already been taken in captivity to Naples.
Charles declared in the same breath that the Saracens were to be taken
away and that Christians were to be settled there: *iugiter in animo gessimus
depopulare et exhabitare terram ipsam Sarracenis eisdem, deinde christicolis
habitandum* (we arranged that the land be depopulated and evacuated by those
same Saracens, and then to be inhabited by Christians).[17] The policy was
carried out swiftly, efficiently and relentlessly, under the eye of Giovanni
Pipino, a trusted royal minister, who later gained virtual lordship over much of
the area. At least 10,000 Lucerans seem to have been deported, but the number
may be much higher; Frederick II appears to have brought about twice that
number to Lucera in the first place.

For Egidi there was a single explanation of the sudden abandonment of
royal tolerance towards the Saracens: "il movente primo ed essenziale della
distruzione della università dei Saraceni fu l'avida brama di confiscare i loro
beni e di far denaro delle loro persone" (the first and essential motive for the
destruction of the community of the Saracens was the avid desire to confiscate
their goods and to make money from their persons).[18] A more recent writer has
assumed that the fall of Lucera was "almost certainly a last desperate measure
to gain a financial respite."[19] It is certainly striking that very nearly the first
letters in the Angevin archives to deal with the Lucera Saracens after their
expulsion in late August address the problem of where the cattle of the
Lucerans have gone to.[20] Egidi's judgment has the force of finality since he

[16] *Ibid.* no. 294.
[17] *Ibid.* no. 318. The document was drawn up by Nicola de Friczia of Ravello, Bartolomeo da
Capua's deputy.
[18] Egidi 1914: 697.
[19] Housley 1982: 243.   [20] *CDSL* nos. 320–1.

based his conclusions on over 800 documents, nearly all from the State Archives in Naples which were destroyed in the Second World War. The Angevin registers consisted of administrative records to a high degree concerned with the state of royal finances and the rights of the crown over south Italian vassals. It is thus hardly surprising that the vast majority of the material examined by Egidi dealt with the disposal of the property of the Lucera Saracens after their dispersal in 1300, with the profits from the sale as slaves of Lucera Saracens, with the transfer of wheat and other supplies from Lucera to the royal army then fighting in eastern Sicily, with arrangements to resettle the land and to restore agricultural production, with the rights of ecclesiastical landlords in the Lucera region.[21]

Egidi argued that the destruction of Lucera resulted from a desperate financial emergency in 1300; the Angevins were making a vigorous, but horrendously expensive, attempt to recover the island of Sicily from Frederick of Aragon, at a moment when Frederick had been left politically isolated by deft papal diplomacy. It was a good moment to move against Sicily, yet Charles II had not received the substantial aid he had once naively expected from James II of Aragon, supposed ally of the Angevins after 1297. Charles thus sought a short-term objective: the realization of massive funds by the seizure of the persons and property of at least 10,000 Lucera Saracens. As has been seen, even the wheat and barley of Lucera was the subject of detailed orders, prompted by grain shortages during the summer of 1300 that left the Angevin armies poorly supplied. And, in defence of Egidi, it is noticeable that Charles II sought not to convert the Saracens and to keep them in place as Christians, but to take all that they had, including their bodies.

It is clear, nonetheless, that Muslim Lucera had been a valuable source of profit to the crown. Charles II recognized this in 1296 when he said of the Lucera Saracens: *hoc presertim tempore vexari nolimus et gravari, tum quia oportuni et utiles ad ipsius terre custodiam reputantur*.[22] Such remarks are reminiscent of the positive statements made by the Aragonese kings about the Muslims of Valencia, as late as the reign of Ferdinand the Catholic. Were the area to be resettled by Christians, the poll tax could not be levied on them. There are plenty of signs that the Lucera Saracens, like the Jews throughout Europe, suffered a significantly higher rate of taxation when asked to contribute to royal *collecta*. The sheer fact that Lucera lay in a fertile area of Apulia and that the Muslims had cultivated the restricted area of their settlement so intensively meant that these lands, and the population that worked

---

[21] There are ready comparisons to be made, for instance with the expropriation of the French Jews in and after 1306, notably the destruction of the princely house of Narbonne which (like Abd-al-Aziz's family) held lands and possessed a sort of noble status.

[22] *CDSL* no. 196.

them, were a major asset of the crown. To depopulate the area might produce short-term profit, but it was also certain to damage long-term revenues. New settlers would in addition need to be promised tax exemption and help with their travel expenses from other parts of Italy or Provence. Even the transformation of the mosques into churches was to cost the crown a handsome sum. Finally, the increasingly close links between the Florentine banks and the Angevin court resulted in a flow of credit into Charles II's treasury and proved an effective way to meet war costs and court expenses.[23] Indeed, the Florentines were much attracted by the wheat of Lucera, which was of high quality and which met some of the food needs of their expanding home city in Tuscany.[24]

It is worth asking what evidence exists for a less crudely materialistic explanation of what occurred. It has been seen that there was a last-minute attempt to encourage Saracens to convert to Christianity from their *profanato seu dapnate secte ac scismatis immo perfidie seu credulitatis errore.*[25] In fact there is evidence also for other recent attempts to win Saracens to Christianity. In 1294 (a year after Dominican preachers had been active among the south Italian Jews) Charles II gave the Dominicans approval in their attempts to search out Christians who had denied their faith and had fallen under the spell of the Muslims.[26] Most likely these "heretics" were relapsed Muslims who had been converted during previous preaching campaigns and had now abandoned their new religion. The Dominicans had also attempted a year and a half earlier to investigate new Jewish settlers in Lucera (the only evidence that Jews inhabited the town at this period).[27] Among the friars prominent in this program was Guglielmo di Tocco, already prominent in the anti-Jewish preaching taking place in southern Italy.[28] These Jews were described as protectors of heretics, which probably means that they were actively trying to wean back to Judaism some of the many recent converts won over by the Order of Preachers. These converts apparently assumed that Lucera was a safe place where the friars would be unable to touch them, though the Inquisition had for some time insisted that its rights extended over Jews who led Christians, including New Christians, astray.

Dominican attempts to penetrate Lucera can be traced back to Frederick II's correspondence with Gregory IX, cited earlier. But, as Kedar has remarked, there is virtually no evidence of sustained preaching campaigns in Saracen

[23] Abulafia 1981: 377–88.
[24] *CDSL* nos. 389a, 404, 434, 470a, 489, 517, 529, 534a, 559, 578, 581, 613a, 619, 640, 642, 644, 659.
[25] *Ibid.* no. 294.
[26] *Ibid.* no. 99.
[27] *Ibid.* no. 85.
[28] See the discussion *infra* of the persecution of the Jews in southern Italy around 1290.

Lucera.[29] It is hardly surprising that Lucera should have attracted the attention of so passionate a promoter of conversionist campaigns as Ramón Llull, as Angevin documents of February and May 1294 reveal.[30] They thus coincide with the Dominican initiative against relapsed Muslims in Lucera. Even so, it is uncertain whether Llull actually went to Lucera, which is not mentioned in his short semi-autobiographical *vita*. That he was in Naples during 1294 is clear, and that he encouraged Charles II to join in his schemes to send preachers to the infidel is also certain. The first royal letter concerning Llull dates from 1 February 1294 and is in the name of Charles, king of Hungary, that is, Charles II's eldest son, Charles Martel, claimant to the Hungarian throne. Addressed to the *capitaneus* or governor of Lucera, the Christian knight Enrico Girardi, the letter orders Girardi to provide all necessary help to Llull.[31] The letter was written in Naples and was clearly the result of Llull's own attempts to impress his aims on the royal family.

In the second letter, it is Charles II himself who writes, this time to the castellan of Castel dell'Ovo; the date is 12 May 1294, three and a half months after the first letter. Here the king is ordering facilities to be provided so that Llull may preach to the *Sarracenis in predicto castro morantibus*, that is, to Muslims detained for some reason in Naples.[32] The most likely candidates for the role of Saracen inmates in Castel dell'Ovo are leading Luceran Muslims arrested after outbreaks of arson and other trouble in the Lucera region the previous year.[33] Llull's interest in Lucera is, however, in accord with his attempts to organize preaching in synagogues and mosques in the lands of the king of Aragon. Here he was generally less energetic than the Dominicans, and the main target of his own campaigns was, as is well known, the Muslims of the Islamic world rather than non-Christians already under Christian rule. In 1293 he had been trying to persuade Pope Celestine V to encourage missions to the Muslims, Mongols, and other nations beyond the Latin frontiers.

The evidence for conversionist campaigns in Lucera is thus very patchy. On the other hand, the evidence that Charles II and his advisers saw the destruction of the colony as a worthy religious objective is fuller than Egidi allowed. Egidi made little reference in his monograph to the simple fact that the Lucerans were Muslims. He did not attempt to draw parallels with the treatment of Muslims in other western Mediterranean kingdoms, nor with the treatment of Jews in southern Italy. His assessment of Charles's aims no doubt reflects the pragmatic outlook of the new *Italia laica* of the 1910s in which he lived.

It is not surprising that royal letters concerned with administrative

---

[29] Kedar 1984: 145.
[30] *CDSL* nos. 98, 100.   [31] *Ibid.* no. 98.
[32] *Ibid.* no. 100.   [33] *Ibid.* nos. 90, 91, 92, 97.

arrangements in Lucera, such as the rounding up of the cattle of the Saracens, have little to say about Islam. The strength of royal feeling about the Muslims is expressed in the more general statements of policy contained in the orders to disband the colony and to erect a new, entirely Christian city on its site. Thus in his letter of 24 August 1300 to Giovanni Pipino, ordering the arrest of the Lucera Saracens, Charles II stresses that it is hardly surprising if one who has such devout ancestors as he does should aim to increase the Catholic faith. The presence of Saracens in his kingdom has long appeared to him to derogate from the Christian faith; it is to the honour of the King of Kings that he commits this act, and it is to the Virgin Mary that he dedicates the new, Christian city. While the letter avoids detail on the way in which these orders will be carried through, a single precise provision is made: the conversion of "that place known in Arabic as the *musquitum*, in which the said Saracens pray and are accustomed to come together for prayer" into the principal church of the city.[34]

In a letter of 8 September 1300 these themes are taken further. The Saracens had *proh pudor!* profaned and polluted the land; the king explicitly justifies his actions by saying that he considers it for the *bonum commune, salutem provincie et comoda subiectorum* (common good, safety of the province and advantage of the subjects) that the seed of Belial should be uprooted and wiped out in Capitanata.[35] This biblical language becomes the refrain of another major letter.[36] The presence of the Saracens endangered the whole kingdom and threatened to become a major scandal.[37] Their removal was necessary "because of many horrendous and detestable things inimical to the Christian name" that the Saracens regularly committed out of irreverence for God.[38] Islam was a contagion that threatened to become a plague in Apulia.[39] Charles's efforts were commended by Pope Boniface VIII, who wrote to Franciscan petitioners in 1301 to say that the obscene works of the Saracens had now been put to an end.[40] In the pope's eyes, Giovanni Pipino had achieved a great victory over perfidy.[41] Charles II was probably glad to have impressed a pope on whose support he must count if Aragonese power in the Mediterranean was to be restrained.

Charles's wish for an easy triumph over Islam is not difficult to explain. He was a very devout man, from a very devout family, nephew of St. Louis of

---

[34] *Ibid.* no. 318.

[35] *Ibid.* no. 323.

[36] *Ibid.* no. 325; *ibid.* nos. 611 and 654 also repeat the same phrases from one another, but are less obviously derived from biblical models.

[37] *Ibid.* no. 324.

[38] *Ibid.* no. 342; interestingly, one of their major crimes was the recent burning of the forests by Saracen rebels.

[39] *Ibid.* no. 655.

[40] *Ibid.* no. 470; Reg. Boniface VIII no. 4012.

[41] *CDSL* no. 478a; Reg. Boniface VIII no. 4070.

France and father of the future St. Louis of Toulouse, who renounced his claim to the throne in order to become a Franciscan. He was also nominal king of Jerusalem; the Angevins from 1277 entitled themselves *rex Jerusalem et Sicilie*, even when they owned neither, and they bore the arms of Jerusalem alongside those of cadet princes of France on their shield. The fall of Acre in 1291 is known to have deeply moved the Neapolitan court. Charles II was deeply conscious that he had failed to defend his most prestigious kingdom while distracted by the War of the Sicilian Vespers. His elaborate plans for the recovery of the Holy Land reveal an ambitious policy of linking the conquest of Sicily to a new crusade to the east; his projects have a good deal in common with those of Ramón Llull.[42]

The prospect of an easy victory against Islam within southern Italy was too good to miss; Lucera lay at the king's mercy. Moreover, the disbanding of Lucera involved the fulfilment of promises made thirty-five years earlier by Charles II's father Charles of Anjou when he entered southern Italy as a crusader against Manfred and his Saracen troops. There is thus some reason to accept Charles's insistence in his instructions to Giovanni Pipino during August 1300 that he had long been hoping to suppress the colony.[43] To insist on the importance of religious motives is not to deny that Charles was enthused by the prospect of making short-term profits from the sale of the inhabitants, their livestock and their crops, to help pay his war costs.

In January 1304 the king was at Foggia, near Lucera, and Bartolomeo da Capua wrote on his behalf to Giovanni Pipino to praise the overthrow of the *Sarracenici ritus et cultus fermentum vetus* (the old ferment of the Saracen rite and religion); the city now pullulated with new, Christian settlers (a claim that is contradicted by other evidence).[44] Yet an apparent contradiction in Charles's actions is the continued existence of Islam in southern Italy after 1300. The Lucerans were sold as slaves; they were not forcibly converted; forcible conversion was rarely regarded as permissible. The motive behind the suppression of the Lucera colony does not therefore seem to be the induction into Christianity of thousands of Muslims; the Christianization of Apulia would be engendered by the arrival of thousands of new Christian settlers from war-ravaged Calabria (where they were under threat from Aragonese armies) and from further afield. In fact, those Saracens who converted to Christianity after August 1300 could not be sure of their release from captivity. Some of the leading Saracens secured the return of their property, even a quantity of Saracen slaves, through baptism: Abd-al-Aziz and his family had been baptized within two years of the fall of Lucera.[45] Lucerans who had become

---

[42] Schein 1991: 108–10, where, however, a more skeptical view of Charles II's motives appears.
[43] *CDSL* no. 318.
[44] *Ibid.* no. 748.   [45] *Ibid.* no. 680.

Christian before the fall of the city were to be singled out and sent under safe guard to Naples; whether it was feared they might escape, or whether they were thought to be in danger from the king's subjects, who ruthlessly massacred fugitive Muslims, is unclear.[46] Most likely they were going to be interrogated to see if they were free of the taint of "heresy," that is, backsliding into Islam. But those Muslims who had rushed to the baptismal font between the destruction of the colony and their capture were in an even more difficult position. Asked what should be done with such people, Nicola de Friccia answered that "since the taking of baptism does not confer freedom on the slave (*servo*)" they should be treated like everyone else.[47] It is important to stress that this reply accords with practice elsewhere in the Mediterranean, notably at Genoa in the late thirteenth century. There were several categories of Christian slave in Christian lands, such as pagans who converted on being brought to western Europe and enslaved rebels against the Church.[48] Where canon law and secular rulers were tougher was in cases of Christian slaves owned by Jews or Muslims under Christian rule.

In a sense, the king had not enslaved the Saracens when Lucera fell. They were all already slaves. It has been seen that the Lucerans were *servi camere nostre*. The term was apparently understood by Bartolomeo da Capua and his colleagues to mean not just that they were serfs on the royal demesne; they were the property of the crown, and they and their goods could be disposed of by the crown. The interpretation of their status was closely modeled on what Roman law texts had to say about the lack of rights of a slave.[49] It is no coincidence that Naples was at this period a major center of study of the civil law. It will be necessary to return to this fundamental point later in this essay. The animals of the Lucerans were *curie nostre* too. As assets of the crown, many Lucerans were sold in the international slave markets for the profit of the *curia*: *in multo ex ipsorum Sarracenorum spoliis accrevit erarium* (the treasury grew greatly from the spoils of these Saracens).[50] But many became agricultural laborers, sold to new owners in southern Italy. In a sense, the Lucerans had been privatized. Once the slaves had been sold, the monarchy no longer insisted on its rights over them.

Despite an order in September 1300 not to permit groups of more than ten Saracens to remain together on estates in Capitanata, the crown later reversed

---

[46] *Ibid.* no. 460.
[47] *Ibid.* no. 498; cf. the slightly earlier no. 459 where a baptized Saracen and his mother are freed.
[48] Heers 1981.
[49] See Buckland 1908. In fact, the sections of Neapolitan legal treatises edited so far have little to say about slavery; see E. M. Meyers, *Iuris interpretes saeculi XIII curantibus scolaribus leidensibus* (Naples, 1924), where the passages by Bartolomeo di Capua dealing with *servi* such as pp. 203–4, nos. 49–50, clearly refer to serfs.
[50] *CDSL* no. 324.

its policy.[51] In an attempt to strengthen Egidi's argument that the fall of Lucera was motivated by financial motives alone, R. Bevere cited a document of June 1302 in which Charles II tolerated the establishment of a new Saracen settlement, consisting of 200 hearths, in Capitanata (quite near Lucera itself), and did not insist that these Muslims be converted to Christianity.[52] Thus, Bevere argued, Charles was not guided by religious motives when Lucera was disbanded. However, his belief that Charles II was explicitly tolerating the survival of Islam close to Lucera itself is given the lie by the wording of the king's instructions.[53] The Muslims were forbidden to have a mosque or to form a religious congregation; the call to prayer was forbidden too. Interesting is the reference to the fact that the Saracens might be either *liberi* or *servi*. Perhaps some Saracens had already managed to purchase their manumission, as Bevere hints.[54] The appearance of free Muslims poses problems: in Aragon it was assumed that even free Muslims were ultimately the property of the crown; this issue deserves further comparative study.[55] There remained Muslims in southern Italy under Charles II's son Robert the Wise (1309–43); in 1336 the king forbade their persecution so long as they did not themselves abuse the Christian faith; Robert even stated that he had heard that the Saracens played a useful role in the economy of Apulia.[56] There is little reason to doubt that most of these Saracens were free or unfree descendants of the Lucera community, though there were probably small groups of Muslim merchants present in several south Italian ports, comparable to the free Muslim merchants Elena Lourie has identified in thirteenth-century Majorca.[57]

II

It is now necessary to search for parallels to the treatment of the Lucera Saracens. There are two obvious directions in which to look: the treatment of other non-Christians (namely, the Jews) in southern Italy and the other lands of Charles II and his dynasty; and the treatment of Muslim enclaves elsewhere in the western Mediterranean. The major instance of the suppression of a Muslim territory contained within another western Mediterranean Christian kingdom is the conquest of Minorca in 1287 and the enslavement of its population. As Lourie has said, the Minorcans were denied the chance to become *mudéjares*.[58] There are some important analogies with Lucera: like Lucera, Minorca was a tolerated notch of Muslim-inhabited land within a Christian kingdom. It had submitted to James the Conqueror in 1231, in the wake of his conquest of

---

[51] *Ibid.* no. 327.   [52] Bevere 1935: 222–8.
[53] *Ibid.* 225.   [54] *Ibid.* 227.
[55] Burns 1973: 250.   [56] *CDSL* no. 818.
[57] Lourie 1970: 624–49.   [58] Lourie 1990a: 2–6.

Majorca, and was in Catalan eyes a fief held by its headman from the king of Aragon and/or Majorca.[59] Its inhabitants were originally permitted the free practice of Islam, and were even encouraged to come to Majorca, in the hope, it appears, that contact with Christians would be to their spiritual benefit. On the other hand, Minorca was not an artificial settlement like Lucera, but the rump of a disappeared Muslim state in the Balearics; it was not particularly fertile, but its pastoral products were valued in trade and as a major part of the annual tribute to the Aragonese kings.[60]

The dispersal of the Minorca Muslims once again is part of the side-history of the War of the Sicilian Vespers. The Aragonese had fought back against the French invasion of 1285 by attempting to dispossess James II of Majorca, brother of Peter of Aragon but apparent ally of Philip III and IV of France. Majorca and Ibiza were occupied in 1285 by the Infant Alfonso and there was fighting in the Majorcan-held lands in the Pyrenean foothills that separated Catalonia from Languedoc.[61] The Muslims of Minorca were suspected of plotting with the north African emirs against the Aragonese, notably during Peter's assault on Collo in north Africa which preceded his successful invasion of Sicily in 1282; besides, there was a danger that the French or Angevins might try to use the island, with its superbly endowed port at Maó (Mahón) as a base from which to attack Aragonese positions.[62] In 1287 Alfonso, now king of Aragon, invaded Minorca by way of Maó.[63]

The broad facts about the fate of the Minorcans are related in the chronicle of Ramón Muntaner, who was generally more interested in heroic deeds than in the niceties of Muslim–Christian relations. His insistence that Alfonso "se pensà que gran vergonya era de la casa d'Aragon que l'illa de Menorca tenguessen sarraïns, e així que era bo que els ne gitàs, e que la conqueris" (thought that it was a great shame for the house of Aragon that the island of Minorca contained Saracens, and thus that it was good that he should throw them out and conquer them) must be understood as part of his wider attempt to project a view of his masters as paragons of chivalry. He even papers over the deep gulf between Alfonso III and his uncle the king of Majorca by pretending

---

[59] Strictly, from James I of Aragon and Majorca till 1276; from James II of Majorca from 1276 to 1285; from Peter III of Aragon and his heir Alfonso III for the remaining couple of years.

[60] Jaume I, "Crònica o Llibre dels Feits," in Ferran Soldevila, ed., *Les Quatre Grans Croniques* (Barcelona, 1971), 59–61, caps. 117–23; Abulafia 1994: 65–8.

[61] For an outline of the make-up of the Majorcan kingdom, see Abulafia 1994: 34–55.

[62] Ramón Muntaner, "Crònica," in Ferran Soldevila, ed., *Les Quatre Grans Croniques* (Barcelona, 1971), 819, cap. 170.

[63] *Ibid.*, 820–2, cap. 172; Mata 1984: 9–62, especially 30–1 where stress is laid on the betrayal by the Muslim ruler of Minorca of Peter the Great's plan to attack Collo in 1282, and the conquest is explained as punishment for this betrayal; Rosselló Vaquer 1980, where details are given of links with Majorca before 1287. E. Lourie's studies in Lourie 1990a add much new documentation from the Arxiu de la Corona d'Aragó in Barcelona.

that a victory in Minorca would serve James II of Majorca's interests; the opposite was the case.[64] More revealing of Alfonso's outlook is what he did on his arrival in the island. Once he had reached the capital, Ciutadella, he "féu pendre totes les fembres e els infants de tota la illa, els hòmens qui romases eren vius, qui eren assats pocs, que en la batalla foren tots morts" (ordered to be taken all the women and children of the entire island and the men who remained alive, who were few in number, for all had died in the battle). Muntaner estimates the number of captives at 40,000, which may be a considerable exaggeration. The entire population was to be sold into slavery in Majorca, Sicily, and Catalonia.[65] Exceptions were made for those who could pay a ransom for themselves, who were nonetheless obliged to leave the island, which was to be repopulated "de bona gent de catalans" (good Catalan people). In fact, as Elena Lourie has discovered, some Muslims were retained on the island as agricultural laborers, but they were few and they were needed because of the great difficulty the kings of Aragon (and, after 1298, the restored kings of Majorca) had in attracting settlers to their wind-blown conquest.[66] These laborers were "ni esclaves ni libres" (neither slaves nor free), in Lourie's view.[67]

Recently, the mass enslavement of the Minorcan Muslims has been singled out by Henri Bresc as an important moment in the development of western attitudes to slavery. This was not just an expulsion, but an appropriation of human bodies and of their possessions, notably their lands, cattle, and sheep.[68] Even if earlier isolated examples of similar conduct can be found, the clearance of a whole territory in this manner cannot be paralleled, whether or not Muntaner greatly exaggerated his figure of 40,000 captives.[69] For Bresc, the assertion of royal rights over the Minorcans is an expression of the growing power of the state. The reappearance of slavery in the Christian Mediterranean world is thus seen as a symptom of the centralization of government during the late thirteenth and fourteenth centuries. Untidy exceptions such as enclaves of Muslims within Christian territories lay under threat from powerful unitary governments.

The occupation of Minorca was undoubtedly prompted by immediate political considerations. Alfonso III, like Charles II, had financial motives, and hoped to raise large sums from the sale of so many slaves.[70] The king seems to

[64] See the commentary by Soldevila (p. 975) on Muntaner, "Cronica," 819, cap. 170.
[65] Muntaner, "Cronica," 821, cap. 172.
[66] Lourie 1970: 622–3; *idem* 1983: 135–86; also repr. in *idem* 1990.
[67] Lourie 1983: 135.
[68] Bresc 1989–90: I.89–102.
[69] It is still unclear what happened to most Majorcan Muslims after 1229; the lack of a Muslim (as opposed to a Jewish) *aljama* in Majorca prompts the thought that a great many were unfree. See Abulafia 1994: 56–64.
[70] Lourie 1990b: 2–6.

have been of the opinion that he was free to dispose of the Minorcan Muslims since they were faithless on two counts: as Muslims, certainly, but also as people who had placed his father in jeopardy by alerting the north Africans to Peter's plans five years before. In a sense, then, they were war captives; captivity in war was an established justification for enslavement in Spain.

Whether the enslavement of the Minorcans influenced the enslavement of the Lucerans cannot be said. There is no sign of an argument that the Lucerans were war-captives, though this argument could have been pressed on historical grounds: they had, after all, been rounded up as rebels and dumped there by Frederick II. However, the basic idea of disposing of Muslims in this fashion may have been transmitted directly from the Aragonese lands to Naples. The royal house of Majorca built close ties to the Angevins of Naples, as the papacy tried to knit together the rival dynasties into a single clan that would be permanently at peace with its members. James II of Aragon married Blanche of Naples in 1295, while Robert of Anjou, the future king of Naples, married first Violante of Aragon in 1297, then Sancha of Majorca in 1304.[71] The personal and cultural links among the courts of Naples, Majorca, and Aragon were thus very close around 1300. The royal families shared an interest in the Spiritual Franciscans, while Queen Sancha of Naples displayed a hostility to the Jews that was moderated by the more benign outlook of King Robert, who continued the Angevin tradition of patronizing Jewish translators.

III

Patronage of Jewish translators did not automatically mean benevolence to the wider Jewish community. Court Jews were frequently exempted from legal requirements such as the wearing of a Jewish badge. If natives, they belonged generally to an elite group of families, who were recognizably the aristocracy of their people, and (like Abd-al-Aziz of Lucera) were recognized as such by monarchs who had a keen sense of nobility of birth.[72] The elite was also probably seen as a prime source of converts, whose baptism would act as an effective example to the wider population of Jews. In fact, many Jewish translators in southern Italy were not native-born, but originated in southern France or Spain.[73] Admittedly, some of Charles of Anjou's helpers were from Sicily (Faraj of Girgenti and Moses of Palermo), but Charles himself never took up residence on the island before he lost it, and Arabic-speaking Sicilian Jewry had a different cultural history from the communities of mainland

---

[71] Musto 1985: 182–5, where allusion is also made to the period when Robert was living as a hostage in Catalonia; his knowledge of Aragonese affairs must have been quite full.

[72] Suarez Fernández 1983: 113 describes how "d'authentiques aristocrates" developed at the Spanish courts, families such as de la Cavalleria, Benveniste, Abulafia, and ibn Shoshan.

[73] Abulafia 1988: 255.

southern Italy.[74] The status of the court Jews was thus quite different from that of the vast majority of south Italian Jews, who were a town-dwelling population of artisans, active in the textile and dyeing industry and similar pursuits. These Jews were mostly regarded as *servi camere regie*, as they had been in Frederick II's day, but several communities, such as that of dyers at Salerno, had been granted to the Church, whose *servi* they then became.[75]

The south Italian Jews were probably not the first Jewish subjects of Charles II to suffer from royal hostility. In December 1289 the Jews of Anjou and Maine were expelled.[76] Charles's action coincided with a wave of local expulsions in northern France, but had distinctive characteristics. Once again, the Sicilian Vespers affected the course of events. The settlement of the ransom demanded by his Aragonese captors was only possible with friendly help from Edward of England, who the previous year expelled the Jews from Gascony, and a few months later expelled the Jews from England. Charles II was thus in serious financial difficulty, and there is general agreement that the expulsion from Anjou was partly at least motivated by the need for money; the comparison with Lucera is obvious. What is striking is that much of this money was to be raised not from the Jews but from the Christians, who were to pay the count-king for the privilege of having their Jews removed.

Charles directed his decree of expulsion at the Jews, the Lombards, and the Cahorsins, but he singled out the Jews for especially lurid description: the document is quite plainly a denunciation of the Jews with an attack on the Italian and southern French usurers inserted as a bonus, perhaps at the prompting of the ecclesiastical and secular advisers who are said to have assented to the hearth and poll taxes (and who stood to suffer least from them). Alongside deep disapproval expressed for the usury practiced by all three groups, Charles condemns the Jews for the "subversion" of the Christians; they are "enemies of the life-giving Cross and of all Christianity," and they are the source of "crimes odious to God and abhorrent to the Christian faith." Charles recognizes that the Jews bring him financial benefit, but he says that he prefers "to provide for the peace of our subjects rather than to fill our coffers with the mammon of iniquity." While the goods of the Cahorsin and Lombard usurers are to be seized by local lords, whose help is solicited by the count, the goods of the Jews appear to fall to the count's officials, who will then presumably collect them for Charles. If this is the case, it reflects the special status of the Jews as the ruler's property. However, the principal source of profit to the

---

[74] Roth 5706: 93–5 for Faraj ibn Salim (Ferragut ben Solomon).

[75] Monti 1934: 174 made the error of assuming that *servus camere regie* was a title of honor applied (in this case) to Ribamelis, a Jew condemned by Bartolomeo dell'Aquila and another Dominican inquisitor.

[76] Chazan 1973: 184–6, with a partial translation of the decree of expulsion: Chazan 1979: 313–17, with a fuller translation; Jordan 1989: 181–2, 230.

count-king was to be a capitation tax of six *deniers* and a hearth tax of three *sous*, in return for which the debts to the Jews would apparently be cancelled.

As well as the corruption of usury, the Jews are held responsible for another form of pollution. "What is most horrible to consider, they evilly cohabit with many Christian maidens." The Jews have worked to impoverish the Christian population by "devious deceits" resulting in the loss of their goods and their reduction to the ranks of beggars. There is no doubt that, alongside the material gain that attracted Charles to the scheme, the decree exudes a contempt for the Jews that stands in the tradition firmly established at the court of Charles II's uncle Louis IX of France.[77] It is noticeable that Edward I also took the opportunity to claim a grant from his subjects when he expelled the Jews of England, and that he laid heavy stress on Jewish usury when explaining his action.[78] This curried favor with his subjects, and it is likely too that the expulsion from Anjou–Maine was greeted with some satisfaction by the count's subjects there.[79] Yet it would be a mistake to underestimate the sense that these rulers had that their expulsions were an act of piety.[80] Charles II was perhaps all the more inclined to acts of piety as a thank offering for his release from Aragonese captivity; the inception of his direct rule after his release must show that he aimed to reach a high moral standard in his methods of government. Usury was seen as a threat to the whole fabric of society, as well as being immoral because those who practiced it gained wealth without any input of labor.[81] The idea of usury as something destructive of the social and economic fabric is expressed with crystal clarity in Charles II's decree. While his levy of an expulsion tax on the Christians shows some originality, the attitudes underlying his action in 1289 closely reflect the hardline approach to the Jews that was gaining currency not merely in northern France and England at this time. To its impact in the crown of Aragon and in the southern lands of the house of Anjou it is now time to turn.

IV

On 9 November 1304 the Tuscan firebrand preacher Giordano da Rivalto described to his audience in the church of Santa Liperata in Florence how it had come to the attention of King Charles of Naples that the Jews were guilty of human sacrifice. They had supposedly put to death a boy in mockery of

---

[77] Jordan 1989: 181, stressing the importance of the image of the unnatural and beastly Jew at princely courts.

[78] *Ibid.* 182; Chazan 1979: 317–19.

[79] Chazan 1973: 186, speaks of the 'utilisation of anti-Jewish sentiment' by Charles II.

[80] Jordan 1989: 255–6, emphasizes the awareness of the French rulers that the Jews were a moral problem, as usurers and in other ways.

[81] Le Goff 1988 expounds the concept of the "Thief of Time."

Christ's Passion. The king had heard of this "perhaps fourteen or fifteen years ago, or a little more or a little less," that is, around 1290.[82] Thus the "re Carlo" to whom Giordano refers must be Charles II. Moreover, Giordano states that Charles heard of this accusation "per bontade d'un franco frate Bartolomeo, ch'era ministro"; Bartolomeo had reputedly found the Jews making "human sacrifices," and therefore claimed that there were ample grounds to kill or expel the Jews. It will be seen that there are good grounds for supposing this person to be Bartolomeo da Capua, who was first minister of Charles II in 1290, in 1304 when Giordano spoke, and under Charles's successor Robert.

The king accordingly arrested all Jews in "Puglia," that is, southern Italy, and gave them the option of converting to Christianity or of being exterminated. More than 8,000 Jews accepted baptism "dopo lungo consoglio"; those who had not been arrested fled the country, with the result that there were no longer any Jews in the kingdom. One of the converts had become a Dominican friar, like Giordano, and was a friend of his, but apparently lived in Naples.

Giordano's tale forms part of a wider attack on the Jews in this and other sermons. He insisted that the Jews constantly vilified and crucified Christ, blaspheming against Christ three times a day and cursing the Virgin as well. Giordano claimed to have studied their books and to have found evidence of their hostility to Christianity: not a new accusation by 1300. According to Giordano, they worship the wrong God, because they have lost the Bible which was once theirs; they circumcise Christian children, deface images of Jesus, desecrate the host and every year they are said to crucify a Christian child; he is glad to see them put to death for their crimes.[83] Jews are held to have no place in Christian society. Giordano's popular preaching is thus in certain respects reminiscent of themes present in Charles II's decree for the expulsion of the Jews from Anjou. Their corrupting influence on society is emphasized in both cases. But Giordano's medicine is far stronger, and his insistence on conversion or death is absent from the decree.

There is circumstantial evidence that Giordano's story of a mass conversion has a basis in fact.[84] The existence after the start of the fourteenth century

---

[82] Giordano da Rivalto, *Prediche* (Florence 1831), II.231; Delcorno 1975: 283–4, no. 62 [partial transcription].

[83] Giordano da Rivalto, *Prediche*, II.220–32; Cohen 1982: 238–41, identifying Bartolomeo dell'Aquila as the moving force in Naples (rather than Bartolomeo da Capua). It is to Cohen's credit that he has gone beyond the single passage that has attracted most attention among earlier writers, namely the description of the mass conversion in southern Italy, to look at the entire sermon.

[84] The basic study of this event is Umberto Cassuto 1912: 389–404; later studies by Cassuto add to and refine the original argument: U. Cassuto, 1931/2: 172–80; Moshe David Cassuto (his Hebrew name) 1950: M. D. Cassuto 1942: 139–52, which is an updated restatement of the original article of 1912. See also Ferrorelli 1915; Roth 5706: 100–1; Munkácsi 1940. There is valuable additional material in Starr 1946.

not merely of converts, *neofiti*, but of *universitates neofitorum*, and the transformation of synagogues into churches, notably in Trani, is well attested. Later
Hebrew sources knew that there had been an attempt at mass conversion but
were unsure when in the thirteenth century it had occurred. In the sixteenth
century a story was current that the son of Frederick II had been told by his
dying father to reward the Jews for their loyalty, and had been advised by
his counsellors that the best possible reward they could receive was the
salvation of their souls. The Jews tried to bargain with the king, and agreed to
be baptized only on condition that marriages would be arranged between themselves and the nobility of southern Italy. To their surprise, the king assented to
this and many were coerced into conversion. Others were massacred.[85] One of
the synagogues in Naples became the church of Santa Caterina (this part of the
tale seems to be true). The Hebrew chroniclers seem to date this event to 1250
or thereabouts, but in all likelihood this tale mirrors truer circumstances around
1290. The supposed intermarriage of the Jews and the nobility may reflect the
adoption at the font by *neofiti* of the family names of their noble patrons. This
was common practice in contemporary Spain.

On the other hand, the existence of converts to Christianity, not always
sincere, is attested from the time of Charles I of Anjou, when a more
enthusiastic convert named Manuforte urged the king to suppress Judaizing
neophytes.[86] In 1288 there was an attempt to disperse converts among the
population so that they would be more rapidly assimilated into the Christian
community.[87] Jews had become the victims of the inquisitors during
Charles II's reign. Partly as a result of Manuforte's reports to the king, and
partly as a result of similar measures taken by his brother the king of France
and by recent popes, Charles I ordered his own officials to go to the houses
of the Jews, in company with high-ranking ecclesiastical figures, and to
confiscate the Talmud and other books deemed harmful to Christianity.[88]

The spasmodic acts of hostility to the Jews in southern Italy were transformed into a concentrated campaign for mass conversion when Charles II
returned to Naples after his captivity in Aragonese hands. There is little
evidence for popular hostility to the Jews, whose communities in Apulia were
very ancient. All the signs are that this campaign was led from the front, by the
royal court and by the Dominicans, and that it dated to the period around 1290

[85] Solomon ibn Verga, *Shevet Yehudah*, ed. A. Shohat (Jerusalem, 1946), 66–7; Samuel Usque,
  Consolaçam ás tribulaçoens de Israel (Coimbra, 1906–8), pp. Xa–XIb and no. 11; Samuel
  Usque 1964: 178–80; Joseph ben Joshua ha-Cohen, *'Emeq ha-Bakha*, ed. M. Letteris
  (Jerusalem, 1967), 64–5; Joseph Hacohen and the Anonymous Corrector, *The Vale of Tears
  (Emek Habacha)*, trans. Harry S. May (The Hague, 1971), 40–1; Cassuto 1912: 396–400.
[86] Starr 1946: 203.
[87] Starr 1946: 203; Caggese 1922–30: I.299.
[88] Starr 1946: 204; Caggese 1922–30: I.298–9.

to 1294, when close investigation of dubious converts was frequently ordered; it will be recalled that in December 1292 the inquisitors were trying to trace Jews who had fled to Muslim Lucera.[89] Described as *hereticorum receptatores, fauctores et defensores*, these Jews were evidently being accused of trying to wean back to their old faith some of the recent converts to Christianity; in this capacity they fell under the remit of the inquisitors.[90]

Among the figures who planned this campaign can be identified two Bartolomeos: the Dominican inquisitor Bartolomeo dell'Aquila and the proto-notary Bartolomeo da Capua. Jeremy Cohen assumes that the former is the figure mentioned by Giordano da Rivalto, "un franco frate Bartolomeo, ch'era ministro" (a free brother, Bartolomeo, who was a minister). On the other hand, Delcorno, in his recent study of Giordano, provides several arguments to confirm the more common assumption that the "minister" intended by Giordano was Bartolomeo da Capua. Bartolomeo da Capua was a good friend of the Dominicans, even if he was never a member of the order; he was in fact married and a layman. He had been a pupil of Thomas of Aquinas and was later to give evidence in the process for the canonization of St. Thomas. Giordano perhaps never visited Naples, but he had close links with those who knew the Neapolitan court well.[91] In support of this argument it is possible to show that Bartolomeo da Capua was involved in royal policy towards the Jews; indeed, there were few aspects of royal policy in which he was not involved. An order of 1294 freeing the neophytes of Naples from the obligation to pay general subventions, *collecta*, and other taxes comes from his hand.[92] The motive was obviously to encourage conversion from Judaism. So too was Bartolomeo da Capua responsible for an act of February 1299 concerning a lapsed convert, Bonusmirus of Bari.[93] Thus Bartolomeo of Capua was active in the persecution of the Jewish communities, just as he was later to be active in the suppression of Lucera Saracenorum.[94]

Giordano's claim that Judaism had been suppressed in the *Regno* had lost whatever validity it had ever possessed by the time he delivered his fiery sermon in 1304. Inscriptions recovered from Jewish sites in Trani, a major Jewish center in medieval Apulia, indicate that Jews were still living and dying openly as Jews in 1293.[95] Although the *Universitas Judeorum* of Trani disappeared early in the fourteenth century, to be replaced by a *Universitas*

---

[89] *CDSL* no. 85.
[90] Cohen 1982: 48 rightly stresses the importance of accusations that Jews were aiding heretics, including Judaising ex-Jews.
[91] Delcorno 1975: 25, 234.
[92] Cassuto 1942: 152 doc. B.
[93] Monti 1934: 178–9.
[94] Bartolomeo dell'Aquila appears only in the margins of the events at Lucera: *CDSL* no. 142.
[95] Cassuto 1931/2: 172–8.

Neofitorum, Jewish settlements were still in existence elsewhere in the kingdom in the early years of the reign of Robert the Wise (1309–43). It is possible that as many as 8,000 Jews converted, as Giordano claimed, but Jews were still being taxed as such in Naples in 1294–5, and the king around this time permitted some fugitive Jews to return to the kingdom.[96] At most, there can only have been a period of a year or two in which it was impossible to live openly as a Jew in the *Regno*. Like his French counterparts, Charles II moderated his fury against the Jews; on the basis of French evidence, Jordan has argued persuasively that this "erraticism" in royal conduct damaged the social relations between Jews and Christians still further, since the king's subjects were unsure what was permitted of them, or the Jews.[97]

On the other hand, the conversionist campaigns continued throughout the 1290s, with a strong emphasis on the hunt for lapsed neophytes and on Jews who supposedly subverted the faith of new converts. Most likely the "mass conversion" was achieved more successfully in some areas of dense Jewish settlement, notably the major towns of Apulia (Giordano attributes the ritual murder to "Puglia" but the term was sometimes used for all the kingdom of Naples). Trani was certainly a center of the neophytes, and several synagogues, notably the *Scola Nova*, were seized from the Jews. The *Scola Nova*, built in 1247, still survives as the church of Santa Anna.[98] On the other hand, some old synagogues were not apparently expropriated, since at the end of his reign Robert of Naples guaranteed the right of Jews to keep the old ones but required the destruction of new ones.[99] He also expressed concern at mixing between neophytes and Jews, and it is clear that the neophytes long remained identifiable, and subject to suspicion, in the *Regno*: the parallels with fifteenth-century Castile are striking.[100]

It is now possible to suggest an explanation of the known events. Soon after his return to Naples from France, Charles II and the two Bartolomeos took advantage of renewed accusations of ritual murder to turn against the Jews of southern Italy. The emphasis of the campaign does not seem to have been on their involvement in usury, which was much less important an economic activity among the south Italian Jews than it was in Anjou and Maine; the legislation of Frederick II permitting Jewish moneylending in southern Italy under certain restraints should not lead to the conclusion that moneylending, rather than their industrial activities, was the main source of income to the Jews of the *Regno*. The driving force behind the campaign was a hatred for the

96 Starr 1946: 208, 210; Roth 5706: 259; Ferorelli 1915: 54.
97 Jordan 1989: 257–8.
98 Cassuto 1931/3: 178–80; Munkácsi 1940: 72–8. For a Neapolitan case, see Cassuto 1942: 161–2, doc. A.
99 Monti 1934: 179; Caggese 1922–30: I.309.
100 Vitale 1926: 233–46.

Jewish religion, accentuated by evidence that Jews were trying to draw back into their faith neophytes who had been converted in the wake of Manuforte's activities a few years earlier. The ritual murder accusation was apparently taken seriously, and past denunciations of it by Frederick II (though in Germany) and by the papacy were ignored. But ritual murder was seen as the most horrible and relatively rare manifestation of a daily cult of abuse of Christian beliefs. Judaism was believed to be impregnated with contempt for Christ; its character was thought to be that of a plot against Christ, a constant reaffirmation of the killing of Christ by the Jews. Thus the reasons given by Giordano da Rivalto for annihilating Judaism conform in striking measure with the passages in the decree of expulsion from Anjou–Maine where the count–king denounces the Jewish religion.

V

In view of his hostility to the Jews in Anjou and Naples, it is surprising that Charles II did not suppress the Jewish communities of Provence, a region that was in many ways his favorite possession. Indeed, Jews arrived in Provence during 1306, having just suffered the ignominy of expulsion from Capetian France. It has been suggested that it was the moderating influence of the royal heir Robert that prevented tougher action against the Provençal Jews than insistence that they should wear a badge, separate their markets from those of the Christians and not be approached for medical treatment by Christians; the ban on Jewish physicians treating Christians was, interestingly enough, also discussed by Bartolomeo da Capua in his commentary on the laws of Frederick II.[101] In fact, Charles spent 1306 and 1307 mainly occupied with Provençal affairs.[102] He seems simply to have lost his passion for the "Jewish problem." It was Robert who adopted a tough stance, and who ordered inventories to be made of Jewish property; Charles himself put an end to the scheme for their expulsion.[103] On becoming king, Robert merely confirmed his father's policy. Certainly, the Jews of Provence had close links to the former Occitan communities, and the count–king may have calculated that the Jews would generate wealth. More importantly, the towns of Provence had in several cases (notably Marseilles) granted special privileges to the Jews, with whom the Christian population generally lived in harmony.[104] On the other hand, the inquisitors were active in Provence against converted Jews, and on

---

[101] Jordan 1989: 230; Trifone 1921: cxcii, citing Bartolomeo da Capua on Constitutions of Melfi, book 3, cap. 46.

[102] Léonard 1967: 249.

[103] Kriegel 1978: 8.

[104] Shatzmiller 1990 shows that in 1317 Jews and Christians in the Marseilles business community had some esteem for one another.

one occasion the Provençal Jews persuaded Charles I of Anjou to restrain these investigators.[105] The Provençal communities thus survived by a hair's breadth, and were the beneficiaries of the "erraticism" in policy towards Jews observed by Jordan.

Similar plans for expulsion also nearly engulfed the Jewish communities of Roussillon and the Balearics, subjects of James II of Majorca, who was, as has been seen, deeply beholden to the French kings.[106] The Majorcan Jews continued to be subjected to royal fines, dispossession of their synagogues and other severe vexations, and were saved more by the greed of King Sancho, James's successor, than by adherence to any principles of *convivencia*.[107] As in Provence, the hope of financial benefit may have led the monarchy to tolerate the settlement in Roussillon of fugitive southern French Jews. The Majorcan Jews were expected to pay well for the right to live as a protected community. Equally, they were defended by the king himself against the sort of charges that had wrecked their security in southern Italy; in 1309 James II of Majorca instructed his officials to act against rumors of child murder, which were malicious nonsense.[108]

VI

There are some common threads in this evidence. The suppression of the Saracens of Lucera, like that of the Jewish communities in Anjou and southern Italy, has been attributed to the religious fervour of a king who sought divine support in his plans to recover Sicily, and ultimately the Holy Land. He was bitter in his denunciation of the supposedly corrupting influence of Jews and Muslims on the Christian inhabitants of his lands. In this policy he had the warm support, even the prompting, of the Dominicans, and also of his counsellors both in Anjou–Maine (as the expulsion decree makes plain) and in southern Italy. But he was not alone in adopting so aggressive an approach to his non-Christian subjects, as the case of Minorca indicates, and as the French and English precedents for his Jewish policy also suggest.

Just as the enslavement of the Minorcans, and by extension that of the Lucerans, has been associated by Henri Bresc with the growing power of the state, so too the expulsions of the Jews in the late thirteenth century and after have been seen by Maurice Kriegel as a stage in the definition of state authority. The ruler sought to win the approval of his subjects by persecuting an often unpopular minority; but rulers also sought a religious uniformity

---

[105] Kriegel 1977: 315–23.
[106] Kriegel 1978: 7–8.
[107] Abulafia 1992; Moore 1976; Pons 1957–60; the older work of Isaacs (1936) has a useful register of documents, though the text is very dated.
[108] Isaacs 1936: 241, doc. 87.

which would harmonize with their attempts at greater governmental central-ization. There was little room for minorities; Valencia may appear the obvious exception, but there it was the Christians who were numerically the minority in their own kingdom. The Jews in southern Italy were a scattered community and had few means of defence; the king, and some of the prelates to whom Jewish communities had been granted in the past, were *de jure* their defenders. If the king abandoned such a position, the Jews had little future in the *Regno* as Jews. Less implacable than the Ashkenazi Jews, who had preferred death to conversion, many Italian Jews went to the font, but not all those who did so abandoned their loyalty to the God of their fathers.[109]

The Muslims were in certain important respects in a similar position. Their status as royal *servi* was ruthlessly exploited by a government anxious to possess their goods. Islam was suppressed, in the sense that those who survived in southern Italy were denied the use of mosques; but forcible conversion seems not to have occurred. The crown sought the conversion of the Muslim leaders, and generally did not release from slavery those who converted after their capture. Yet it has been seen that in the case of Lucera religious motives of a different type cannot be discounted. Enslavement was a punishment for generations of obstinate commitment to Islam, just as expulsion and the threat of massacre was a punishment against Jews who for centuries had supposedly maligned Christ.

It is being suggested here that the royal court harnessed Roman law to argue that the state had the power and right to enslave its Muslim subjects. Indeed, they were already slaves before they were sent into slavery. The importance of the literal interpretation of the term *servus*, in *servus camere regie*, to mean "slave" in the sense understood by Roman law, cannot be under-estimated. In many ways, the use of Roman law to defend royal rights was what made possible that assertion of state control that Kriegel and Bresc have associated with the enslavement of Muslims and the expulsion of Jews. It is thus necessary to stress that at Charles II's elbow there stood one of the most eminent Roman lawyers in Italy, Bartolomeo da Capua. As royal proto-notary, from June 1290, he had a direct role in the enactment of decrees against Jews and Muslims. His influence and that of his circle deserve examination.

Bartolomeo was a product of a distinguished legal family. His services to the

---

[109] The different outlook of the Mediterranean Jews to the problem of forced conversion is perhaps expressed most clearly in the Letter on Persecution and Letter to Yemen of Moses Maimonides, written in the late twelfth century to deal with rare instances of forcible conversion by Muslim rulers; his pragmatic approach opened the door to insincere conversion which masked crypto-Judaism.

crown earned him lands and wealth.[110] It has been said of him that for forty years he was the fulcrum of all Angevin legislative initiatives; he was "la mente direttiva della loro azione politica."[111] He was at the core of a group of Roman lawyers who insisted on the fullness of royal authority; *rex in regno suo est imperator*: the idea was articulated in Naples, as in France, to fend off papal and (in the case of Naples) imperial assertions of authority over the *Regno*.[112] He prepared glosses on the laws of Frederick II and his successors, which were incorporated in the glosses of his colleague Andrea da Isernia, another vigorous protagonist of the autonomy of the *Regno*.

A fuller study of Bartolomeo's legal writings, many of which remain unedited, is needed, all the more so when legal historians insist so emphatically on his importance. Yet what is significant in the glosses on the Sicilian law codes is not his originality. The glosses prepared by Andrea da Isernia under his influence repeat with approval the position on the rights of Jews established in canon law: Jews are *peioris conditionis quam Christiani et debent esse*. Jews may not have authority over Christians.[113] They state too that *privilegia data Catholicis denegantur Iudaeis, et omnibus qui non sunt membrum Catholicae ecclesiae seu fidei*.[114] A law of Charles II of Naples states *quod Iudaeis, qui sunt vassalli ecclesiae nulla officia committantur, nec aliae oppressiones, vel gravamina inferantur*.[115] Andrea was clear that both Jews and Saracens lived *sub protectione principis, ne vindicta sua auctoritate quis recipiat*.[116] As has been seen, Bartolomeo was of the view that Jewish physicians are not to treat Christians; indeed, Christians are not even to receive food and drink from Jews.[117] As Roman lawyers, then, the close advisers of Charles II could add something to the odium for non-Christians that Bartolomeo apparently shared, if (as Giordano da Rivalto suggested) it was he who turned the king against the Jews in about 1290. When it came to the expropriation of Saracen property, or the condemnation of the Jews for insulting Christians and supposedly murdering children, the Jews and the Muslims faced the full force of Roman law. The slave condition of the king's non-Christian subjects placed them under his protection, as the glosses said, but also at his mercy.

---

[110] The best recent description of his career is by Walter and Piccialuti in the *Dizionario biografico italiano*, s.v. His family connections and administrative functions are explained in Minieri Riccio 1872: 135–48, and tables at end.

[111] Trifone 1921: xx.

[112] Monti 1941: II.13–54; Ullmann 1949: 1–33.

[113] Andraeas de Isernia *et al.*, *Constitutiones regni utriusque Siciliae, Glossis ordinariis, Commentariisque excellentiss. I.U.D. Domini Andraeae de Isernia, ac D. Bartholomaei Capuani, atque nonullorum veterum*, ed. Gabriele Sarayna (Lyons, 1568), 32.

[114] *Ibid.*

[115] Capitula Regis Caroli II, in *ibid.*, 316; Trifone 1921: 99, no. 59 (101).

[116] Andraeas de Isernia *et al.*, *Constitutiones*, 47.

[117] Trifone 1921: cxcii, citing Bartolomeo da Capua on Frederick II's Constitutions of Melfi, book 3, cap. 46.

The years around 1300 saw, therefore, the coming together at the court of Naples of the theme of the demonization of the Jew and the Saracen and the Roman law tradition that emphasized the subjection of *servi* and the rights of rulers over their property and persons. Roman law bolstered the authority of the state, but it also confirmed the lack of rights of non-Christian subjects, all the more so when they had for generations been called *servi camere regie*.[118]

REFERENCES

PRIMARY SOURCES

Andraeas de Isernia *et al. Constitutiones regni utriusque Siciliae, Glossis ordinariis, Commentariisque excellentiss. I.U.D. Domini Andraeae de Isernia, ac D. Bartholomaei Capuani, atque nonullorum veterum.* Ed. Gabriele Sarayna. Lyons, 1568.

Codice Diplomatico dei Saraceni di Lucera. Ed. P. Egidi. Naples: Pierro & Figlio, 1917.

Giordano da Rivalto. *Prediche.* 2 vols. Florence: Magheri, 1831.

Huillard-Bréholles, J. L. *Historia diplomatica Friderici Secundi.* 6 vols. in 12 parts. Paris: Henricus Pl., 1854–61. Reprinted 1872–83.

Jaume I. Crònica o Libre dels Feits. In Ferran Soldevila, ed., *Les Quatre Grans Cròniques.* Barcelona: Selecta, 1971.

Joseph ben Joshua ha-Cohen. *'Emeq ha-Bakha.* Ed. M. Letteris. Jerusalem, 1967.

Joseph Hacohen and the Anonymous Corrector. *The Vale of Tears (Emek Habacha).* Trans. Harry S. May. The Hague, Nijhoff, 1971.

Meyers, E. M. *Iuris interpretes saeculi XIII curantibus scolaribus leidensibus.* Naples: F. Perralla, 1924.

Muntaner, Ramón. Crònica. In Ferran Soldevila, ed., *Les Quatre Grans Cròniques.* Barcelona: Selecta, 1971.

Matthew Paris. *Chronica Majorca.* 7 vols. Rolls Series, 1872–83.

Samuel Usque. *Consolaçam ás tribulaçoens de Israel.* Coimbra: Franca Amado, 1906–8.

    Consolation for the Tribulations of Israel. Ed. and trans. Martin A. Cohen. Philadelphia: Jewish Publication Society of America, 1964.

Solomon ibn Verga. *Shevet Yehudah.* Ed. A. Shohat, Jerusalem: Mosad Bi'alik, 1946.

SECONDARY REFERENCES

Abulafia, David 1981 Southern Italy and the Florentine economy. *Economic History Review* ser. 2 33: 377–88. Repr. in David Abulafia, *Italy, Sicily and the Mediterranean, 1100–1400.* London: Variorum reprints, 1987: Essay VI.

---

[118] My understanding of these issues has been greatly enhanced by discussion with Anna Sapir Abulafia and with Norman Zacour, the latter of whom very kindly explored the resources of Trinity Hall Library, Cambridge, on my behalf, in pursuit of the almost non-existent civil law texts on Saracen slaves. Professor Zacour pointed out to me that Azo on Codex 1.11 states that when Justinian refers to pagans, Saracens are to be understood, *qui deos innumeros, deasque imo demones colunt et adorent.*

1988 *Frederick II. A Medieval Emperor.* London: Allen Lane.

1992 From Privilege to Persecution: Crown, Church and Synagogue in the City of Majorca, 1229–1343. In David Abulafia, Michael Franklin, and Miri Rubin, eds., *Church and City, 1000–1500. Studies in Honour of Christopher Brooke,* 111–26. Cambridge: Cambridge University Press.

1994 *A Mediterranean Emporium. The Catalan Kingdom of Majorca.* Cambridge: Cambridge University Press.

Bevere, R. 1935 Ancora sulla causa della distruzione della colonia saracena di Lucera. *Archivio storico per le provincie napoletane* 60 (n.s. 21): 222–8.

Bresc, Henri 1989–90 L'Esclavage dans le monde méditerranéen des XIVe et XVe siècles: problèmes politiques, réligieux et morales. In *XIII° Congrès d'història de la Corona d"Aragó,* I: 89–102, 4 vols. Palma de Mallorca: Institut d'Estudis Balearics.

Buckland, W. W. 1908 *The Roman Law of Slavery.* Cambridge: Cambridge University Press.

Burns, Robert I. 1973 *Islam under the Crusaders. Colonial Survival in the Thirteenth-Century Kingdom of Valencia.* Princeton: Princeton University Press.

Caggese, Romolo 1922–30 *Robert d'Angiò e i sui tempi.* 2 vols. Florence: R. Bemporad & Figlio.

Cassuto, Moshe David 1942 Hurban ha-Heshivot be-Italyah ha-deromit ba-Me'ah ha-13. In Simhah Assaf and Gerschom Gerhard Scholem, eds., *Studies in Memory of Asher Gulak and Samuel Klein* (Hebrew), 139–52. Jerusalem: Hebrew University.

1950 Od ketubot ivrit me'ir Trani. *Alexander Marx Jubilee Volume,* Hebrew section: Jewish Theological Seminary of America.

Cassuto, Umberto 1912 Un ignoto capitolo di storia giudaica. *Judaica. Festschrift zu Hermann Cohens 70. Geburtstag,* 389–404. Berlin: Verlag von Bruno Cassirer.

1931/2 Iscrizioni ebraiche a Trani. *Rivista di studi orientali* 13: 172–80.

Castielli, R. 1978 Saggio storico culturale. In M. Melilli, ed., *Storia e cultura dei Fran-coprovenzali di Colle e Faeto,* 7–21. Manfredonia.

Chazan, Robert 1973 *Medieval Jewry in Northern France. A Political and Social History.* Baltimore: Johns Hopkins University Press.

1979 *Church, State and Jew in the Middle Ages.* New York: Behrman House.

1989 *Daggers of Faith. Thirteenth-Century Christian Missionizing and Jewish Response.* Berkeley/Los Angeles: University of California Press.

Cohen, Jeremy 1982 *The Friars and the Jews. The Evolution of Medieval Anti-Judaism.* Ithaca, N.Y.: Cornell University Press.

Delcorno, Carlo 1975 *Giordano da Pisa e l'antica predicazione volgare.* Florence: L. S. Olschki.

Egidi, Pietro 1911–14 La colonia saracena di Lucera e la sua distruzione. *Archivio storico per le provincie napoletane* 36 (1911): 597–694; 37 (1912): 71–89, 664–96; 38 (1913): 115–44, 681–707; 39 (1914), 132–71, 697–766.

1915 *La colonia saracena di Lucera e la sua distruzione.* Naples: Pierro & Figlio.

Ferorelli, N. 1915 *Gli ebrei dell'Italia meridionale dall'età romana al sec. XVIII.* Turin: Il Vessillo Israelitico; new edn., Naples, 1990.

Heers, Jacques 1981 *Esclaves et domestiques au moyen-âge dans le monde méditerranéen*. Paris: Fayard.

Housley, Norman 1982 *The Italian Crusades. The Papal–Angevin Alliance and the Crusades against Christian Lay Powers, 1254–1343*. Oxford: Oxford University Press.

Isaacs, A. Lionel 1936 *The Jews of Majorca*. London: Methuen.

Jordan, William Chester 1989 *The French Monarchy and the Jews. From Philip Augustus to the Last Capetians*. Philadelphia: University of Pennsylvania Press.

Kattenbusch, D. 1982 *Das Franko-Provenzalische in Süditalien. Studien zur synchronischen und diachronischen Dialektologie*. Tübinger Beiträge zur Linguistik 176. Tübingen: G. Narr.

Kedar, Benjamin Z. 1984 *Crusade and Mission. European Approaches toward the Muslims*. Princeton, N.J.: Princeton University Press.

Kriegel, Maurice 1977 Prémarranisme et inquisition dans la Provence des XIIIᵉ et XIVᵉ siècles. *Provence Historique*, fasc. 109: 313–23.

1978 Mobilisation politique et modernisation organique. Les expulsions de Juifs au bas Moyen Age. *Archives de sciences sociales des religions* 46: 5–20.

Le Goff, Jacques 1988 *Your Money or your Life. Economy and Religion in the Middle Ages*. New York.

Léonard, Emile 1967 *Gli Angioini di Napoli*. Milan: dall'Oglio.

Lourie, Elena 1970 Free Moslems in the Balearics under Christian Rule in the Thirteenth Century. *Speculum* 45: 624–49. Repr. in Lourie 1990: Essay VI.

1983 La colonización cristiana de Menorca durante el reinado de Alfonso III "el Liberal", rey de Aragón. *Analecta Sacra Tarraconensia* 53/4: 135–86.

1990a. *Crusade and Colonisation. Muslims, Christians and Jews in Medieval Aragon*. Aldershot: Variorum.

1990b Anatomy of Ambivalence: Muslims under the Crown of Aragon in the Late Thirteenth Century. In Lourie 1990a: Essay VII.

Maier, C. 1995 Crusade and Rhetoric against the Muslim Colony of Lucera: Eudes of Châteauroux's *Sermones de rebellione sarracenorum Lucerie in Apulia*. *Journal of Medieval History* 21.

Martin, Jean-Marie 1989 La Colonie sarrasine de Lucera et son environnement. Quelques réflexions. *Mediterraneo medievale. Scritti in onore di Francesco Giunta*, II: 797–810. Soveria Mannelli: Rubbettino.

Mata, Micaela 1984 *Conquests and Reconquests of Menorca*. Barcelona.

Minieri, Riccio C. 1872 *De' grandi uffiziali del Regno di Sicilia dal 1265 al 1285*. Naples.

Monti, Gennaro M. 1934. Da Carlo I a Roberto d'Angiò: ricerche e documenti. *Archivio storico per le province napoletane* 59.

1941 La dottrina anti-imperiale degli Angioini di Napoli. I loro vicariati imperiali e Bartolomeo da Capua. In *Studi di storia di diritto in onore di A. Solmi*, II: 13–54. 2 vols. Milan: Giuffre.

Moore, Kenneth 1976 *Those of the Street. The Catholic Jews of Mallorca*. Notre Dame, Indiana: University of Notre Dame Press.

Munkácsi, E. 1940 *Der Jude von Neapel*. Zurich: Verlag "De Liga."

Pons, Antonio 1957–60 *Los Judíos de Mallorca durante los siglos XIII y XIV*. 2 vols. Palma de Mallorca: Miguel Font.

Powell, James M. 1990. *Muslims under Latin rule, 1100–1300*. Ed. James M. Powell. Princeton, N.J.: Princeton University Press.

Musto, Ronald G. 1985 Queen Sancia of Naples (1286–1345) and the Spiritual Franciscans. In J. Kirshner and S. F. Wemple, eds., *Women of the Medieval World*, 179–214. Oxford: Blackwell.

Rosselló Vaquer, Ramón 1980 *Aportació a la història medieval de Menorca. El segle XIII*. Ciutadella de Menorca.

Roth, Cecil 5706 [= 1946] *The History of the Jews of Italy*. Philadelphia: The Jewish Publication Society of America.

Schein, Sylvia 1991 *Fideles Crucis. The Papacy, the West and the Recovery of the Holy Land 1274–1314*. Oxford: Oxford University Press.

Shatzmiller, Joseph 1990 *Shylock Reconsidered. Jews, Moneylending, and Medieval Society*. Berkeley and Los Angeles: University of California Press.

Starr, Joshua 1946 The Mass Conversion of Jews in Southern Italy (1290–93). *Speculum* 21: 203–11.

Suarez Fernández, Luis 1983 *Les Juifs espagnols au moyen âge*. Paris: Gallimard.

Trifone, R. 1921 *La legislazione angioina*. Naples: L. Lubrano.

Ullmann, Walter 1949 The Development of the Medieval Idea of Sovereignty. *English Historical Review* 64: 1–33.

Vitale, Vito 1926 Un particolare ignorato di storia pugliese: neofiti e mercanti. *Studi in onore di Michelangelo Schipa*, 233–46. Naples.

Zacour, Norman 1990 *Jews and Saracens in the Consilia of Oldradus de Ponte*. Toronto: Pontifical Institute of Mediaeval Studies.

13 Muslim Spain and Mediterranean slavery: the medieval slave trade as an aspect of Muslim–Christian relations

Olivia Remie Constable

The medieval Iberian Peninsula has long been cited as a classic example of a land in which people of different religions lived side by side for centuries in a varying atmosphere of concord and conflict. Whether one subscribes to the alternate myths of harmonious *convivencia* or victorious *reconquista*, the so-called "land of three religions" provides an excellent setting for examining the changing relationship between Muslims and Christians from the eighth to the thirteenth centuries AD. Certain aspects of this relationship also had resonance in other regions of the western Mediterranean world.

This essay is concerned with the commercial side of interfaith relations in the western Mediterranean, and particularly with the Iberian slave trade as an aspect of Muslim–Christian interaction. The time frame spans the period from the rule of the Umayyad dynasty in al-Andalus (Muslim Spain) through the main Christian victories of the thirteenth century (Córdoba in 1236, Valencia in 1238, and Seville in 1248). This was a time of changing relations between Muslims and Christians, both in the Iberian Peninsula and elsewhere, and changes in the slave trade reflect one aspect of this interfaith dialogue. Slavery was a very real part of both Christian and Muslim life in the medieval Mediterranean world and it was primarily the result of economic demand, not of political events or interreligious friction. Nevertheless, changes in the slave trade appear linked to shifts in the balance of religious power in the Iberian Peninsula and wider Mediterranean, while its existence throws light on religious interaction and differences. Between the eighth and thirteenth centuries, the Iberian slave trade shifted from Muslim control, when Christian and pagan slaves were transported from Europe into the Islamic world by way of Andalusi markets, to a pattern whereby Spanish Muslims were enslaved in Christian Spain and sold throughout the northwestern Mediterranean.

The Iberian Peninsula functioned as a crossroads for trade in the medieval Mediterranean world, with goods from Christian Europe entering the Muslim world and commodities from Islamic lands coming northward through Iberian channels. These goods included raw fibers and woven textiles, spices, metals and metalwork, leather, furs, and slaves. For the purpose of this discussion, slaves are seen as one more category in the spectrum of Mediterranean commodities. Unlike the communities described by David Abulafia in his essay for this volume, collectively "owned" by a monarch, most of the slaves noted here were individuals, sold by and to other individuals for a price. Their unfree status was clear and unambiguous.

Slaves were unique, however, as being the only commodity in which religion played a crucial role. While most merchandise could be bought and sold without regard to religious considerations, faith was an extremely important – indeed crucial – issue in the slave trade.[1] The fact of slavery, and the right to hold, buy, or sell slaves, was usually justified by an appeal to religious differences. Medieval slaves and their masters were almost always of different religions. Christian, Muslim, and Jewish law codes all strictly forbade the enslavement of co-religionists, and while prohibitions on buying or keeping slaves of one's own religion may have been less strictly adhered to, violations appear rare. Usually slaves who were purchased by a co-religionist were manumitted immediately after purchase, as a pious and philanthropic gesture. Likewise, slaves who converted during their captivity were generally freed at the time of conversion or at the death of their master. Religious and secular legislation was quite clear on these points, and regulations often established a hierarchy of slave holding. Thus, Christian law codes stressed the inherently free status of Christians, although Muslims could be legally enslaved. Muslim legislation contained similar, though complementary, provisions. Not surprisingly, the most convenient slave was a pagan (i.e., not a Christian, Muslim, or Jew), whose servitude need never interfere with religious conscience.

The chronological changes in the Iberian slave trade from the eighth to the thirteenth centuries are striking, and follow in the wake of shifts in the political and religious balance of power. Christian military successes had a profound effect on the entire Iberian economy, altering patterns of production, import, and export in all areas of commerce, including the slave trade. Whereas Muslim and Jewish buyers of pagan and Christian slaves had predominated in the earlier Middle Ages, Christian buyers of Muslim slaves became increasingly common in the period following northern reconquest victories.

During the period of strong Islamic control in the south, from the eighth to the twelfth century, Andalusi cities had provided important markets for slaves, including slaves brought south from Slavic regions and northern Spain. These men and women would either remain with their new masters in Spain or be reexported to other parts of the Islamic world. It appears that most slaves in Muslim Spain at this time were either born into slavery or obtained through slaving expeditions across the Muslim–Christian frontier or farther

---

[1] Items of potential military use, including timber, arms, and food, were also restricted during periods of warfare between Muslim and Christian rulers.

afield.[2] In contrast to a later period, their enslavement was usually not directly connected with local political or military events.

By the eleventh century, the Iberian slave trade had grown more complex, and its commercial aspects became less clear-cut in the face of war. With the new military reality of the reconquest, an increasing number of Christian Spaniards were taken as prisoners of war by Muslims, destined either for ransom or for enslavement. At the same time, we find exactly parallel developments in the Christian slave trade, whereby large numbers of Muslim captives began to appear as slaves in Christian cities – perhaps even in the same reconquered city where they had once been free. Although there had been Saracen slaves in Christian Spain and other regions of southern Europe throughout the eleventh and twelfth centuries, the enslavement of Muslims in the thirteenth century can often be linked directly to Christian victories in Islamic lands.

Documentation for the Iberian slave trade tends to emphasize the changes taking place in the twelfth and thirteenth centuries, since materials on slavery in Muslim Spain during an earlier period are of a very different nature than later data. Evidence from Arabic sources provides a general picture of the Andalusi slave trade, through scattered references, and the same is true of contemporary Latin and Hebrew documentation. In contrast, later documentation tends to concentrate on particular periods or places. This is especially true of Italian and French notarial records, which contain contracts for the sale of Andalusi slaves. These contracts represent our earliest and most important external source demonstrating the dramatic changes taking place in Iberian economy and society in the wake of the thirteenth-century reconquest.

In accordance with this documentary dichotomy, the following discussion begins by looking at the Iberian slave trade during the early Middle Ages, providing a general description of the phenomenon in Muslim Spain. The second half deals with the period of the Christian reconquest, presenting a detailed examination of specific notarial materials on Muslim Spanish slaves sold in Genoese markets. By the thirteenth century, Muslim slaves were widely available in Christian Mediterranean cities, especially in Catalonia, Provence, and northern Italy. The Genoese data are of particular interest, because they represent some of the earliest and most abundant records of such sales. They also demonstrate the penetration of Spanish political events and commodities into other regions of the western Mediterranean.

During the Umayyad period (750–*c*. 1031), documentation from al-Andalus tends to provide a rather muddled picture of the slave trade, and it is often difficult to determine the identity, religion, and geographical origin of either

---

[2] There is not much Andalusi evidence of slavery as a punishment for crimes.

slavers or slaves. References may be further obscured by polemical overtones, particularly by writers outraged at the enslavement of co-religionists.

Reports from the ninth century indicate that Jewish and Muslim merchants brought slaves to al-Andalus from Europe and Christian Spain, then reexported them to other regions of the Islamic world.[3] Many of these slaves were pagan, taken in military or slaving raids along the northern and eastern frontiers of Europe, but others were Christian. The Arab geographer Ibn Khurrādadhbih remarked that one group of Jewish traders, the Rhadhanites, sold Andalusi slave girls, while his contemporary, Ibn al-Faqīh, listed slave girls among Andalusi exports to North Africa.[4] These women may well have been natives of northern Spain, as shown in another example, recorded by the ninth-century Muslim jurist Ibn Sacīd, in which Jewish merchants sold a number of Galician women in Merida.[5] Male slaves, like a certain Basque musician at the court of the emir cAbd al-Raḥmān II (822–52), were also imported from the north of Spain.[6]

Bishop Agobard of Lyons wrote in a famous passage (c. 826) of two young men abducted from Arles and Lyons by Jewish slavers. At least one of the pair was sent as a slave to Córdoba. Agobard went on to claim that instances of Jewish slaving were common, and that "it should not be permitted for Jews to sell Christians to Spain," particularly since the Jews sometimes "do things too horrible to write about."[7] The context of Agobard's complaint makes it difficult to judge the accuracy of his information. It is significant that this is the only source to object to the taking of Christian captives within Carolingian realms at this period. Other ninth-century sources show Jews operating as slave traders in France, but they do not suggest that these merchants enslaved local Christians.[8]

Information from the tenth century, however, may lend more credibility to Agobard's assertions. The Muslim geographer Ibn Ḥawqal (writing in the

---

[3] The number and variety of reports on Jewish slavers in the early Middle Ages (and the fact that these include rabbinic material) support their veracity. Only in a few instances, such as the remarks of Agobard of Lyons noted below, are there overtones of vilification in the mention of Jewish slave traders.

[4] Ibn Khurradādhbih 1967: 153–5; Ibn al-Faqīh 1967: 252.

[5] Ribera y Tarragó 1928: 24–5.

[6] Vernet 1950: 258; the *Annales regni Francorum* (Pertz 1895: 124) record an incident from 807 in which a group of monks from Pantellaria were captured by Muslims and sold in Spain.

[7] Agobard 1899: 183, 185.

[8] A charter of Louis the Pious (814–40) granted to a Spanish Jew, Abraham of Saragossa, permitted the latter to traffic in foreign slaves (*mancipia peregrina*) within Louis's kingdom. Another document concerning two Jews, David and Joseph of Lyons, and dated before about 825, granted similar rights to trade in foreign slaves. See Zeumer 1886: 325, no. 52, and 310, no. 31. About the same time, a rabbinic source cited the arrival of Jewish merchants bringing with them "slaves and young eunuchs" (Assaf 1928: 38–9).

970s) reported that "among the most famous exports [from al-Andalus to other Muslim lands] are comely slaves, both male and female, from Frankish (*Ifranja*) and Galician regions."[9] Ibn Ḥawqal went on to comment on another type of slave exported from Spain, the *ṣaqāliba* or Slavic slaves, remarking that "all Slavic eunuchs on earth come from Al-Andalus, because they are castrated in that region and the operation is performed by Jewish merchants." Al-Muqaddasî, another geographer writing at about the same time, provided similar information that Jews in "a town behind Pechina" (perhaps Luchena) produced Slavic eunuchs, who were later sent from al-Andalus to Egypt. However, not all Slavic slaves were handled by Jews, and a slightly later Muslim writer noted that both Jewish and Muslim slavers in the regions along the Andalusi frontier castrated slaves for export abroad.[10]

There is also evidence of eunuchs made and exported to the Iberian Peninsula from France. Liutprand of Cremona (*c.* 920–72) described traffic in eunuchs between Verdun and Muslim Spain, but cited neither Jews nor Slavs among the parties involved. This information may confirm Agobard's accusations in the previous century, although Liutprand did not refer to these Verdun slaves as either Christian or of local French origin.[11] No Arabic sources cite Verdun as a source of eunuchs coming to al-Andalus.

Continuing to concentrate on the Muslim south, we see that sources from the eleventh century begin to present a new picture of the Andalusi slave trade. The virtual disappearance of both Slavic slaves and Jewish slave traders in Muslim Spain during this period is particularly striking. Possibly the demise of the centralized Umayyad state, whose rulers had at one time employed

---

[9] Ibn Ḥawqal 1938–9: 110. In Arabic, Galician might apply to anyone from the northwestern peninsula – León, Galicia, Asturias, even Portugal.

[10] Ibn Ḥawqal 1938–9: 110, al-Muqaddasī 1950: 56, al-Maqqarī 1885–61: I.92 (al-Maqqarī attributed this information to Ibrāhīm b. al-Qāsim al-Qarawī, better known as al-Qayrawānī, who died in 1026; see Brockelmann 1937: 252). The *ṣaqāliba* were perhaps the best-known slave population in Al-Andalus. They rose from slavery, under the Umayyads, to form ruling dynasties in the eleventh-century Taifa period (which indicates that not all *ṣaqāliba* were eunuchs). Although chroniclers mention thousands of Slavic slaves at the court of the Umayyad caliph 'Abd al-Raḥmān III in the tenth century, they do not appear as slaves in later sources. The role of Spain in the transfer and production of these Slavic eunuchs is fairly clear, but the identity of the *ṣaqāliba* has been a matter for debate. Although many scholars have assumed that the term was generic, referring to any slave of northern origin, David Ayalon (1979) has argued convincingly that all of the *ṣaqāliba* were genuine ethnic Slavs, imported both to Spain and to the eastern Islamic world. The link between the name *ṣaqāliba* and Slav (as well as Romance derivatives, *esclave*, etc.) has been generally supported in modern scholarship; see Verlinden 1942; Kahane and Kahane 1962. Also on trade in Slavs during the tenth century, see Verlinden 1974 and 'Abbadī 1953. For a reconstructed map of traffic in Slavs, see Lombard 1975: 197.

[11] Liutprand 1915: 156. Scholars disagree on how slaves would have been brought to Spain from Verdun. Archibald Lewis opted for an entirely overland route, while Verlinden suggested a sea route departing from Arles (Lewis 1951: 180; Verlinden 1955–77: I.223–4). Also on the early slave trade and Verdun, see Verlinden 1983.

thousands of the *ṣaqāliba*, reduced the demand for a large and loyal corps of Slavic slaves. At the same time, Slavic slavery presumably declined in the eleventh and twelfth centuries with the eastward expansion of European kingdoms and the increasing Christianization of Slavic lands. Perhaps also, the arrival of the Almoravid and Almohad dynasties in al-Andalus created new markets and new channels of access to black slaves in Spain and North Africa.[12]

The apparent decline of Jewish slave trading in al-Andalus may be linked to these changes in the slave population. Black slaves do not seem to have been handled by Jewish slavers, possibly because their country of origin was outside the Jewish trading sphere. Nor did Jews have a large role in trading Christian slaves from northern Spain, which had become the main source of white slaves in al-Andalus by the year 1000. Documents from the Cairo Geniza indicate that Jews in al-Andalus and elsewhere continued to own slaves during the eleventh and twelfth centuries, but they do not record activity by Jewish slave traders.

Most evidence on Andalusi slavery during the eleventh, twelfth, and early thirteenth centuries comes from Arabic legal materials – judicial opinions (*fatwas*), manuals for market inspectors, and contractual handbooks. These sources do not provide information on exact numbers of slaves, nor is it wise to accept all their evidence at face value. The thirteenth-century jurist al-Saqaṭī, for example, was quoting a well-known list rather than empirical evidence when he described the merits and attributes of different female slaves: Berbers were voluptuous; Turks would bear valiant sons; Christians were careful with money and housekeeping; Africans made excellent wet-nurses, and so forth. Al-Saqaṭī continued his inventory for male slaves, but in every case – as with the women – the characteristic was a traditional attribute rather than an empirical observation. Nevertheless, his account indicates an expectation of considerable ethnic and religious diversity in the slave population.[13]

Other legal texts may provide a more accurate measure of different types of slaves available in Muslim Spain, particularly when their evidence is mutually corroborated. These sources suggest that the catchment area of the Andalusi slave trade had been reduced by the eleventh century, and the scale of international trade diminished. All the same, men and women of many varieties were still available. For example, a collection of contractual formulae by the jurist al-Fihrī (d. 1070) listed Galicians, Berbers, and "Africans" among the slaves an eleventh-century buyer might have encountered for purchase. Likewise, his contemporary, the Toledan legal scholar Ibn Mughīth (d. 1067),

---

[12] Brett 1969: 360.
[13] Al-Saqaṭī: 374–5. Other writers cited similar lists as, for example, in a passage from the eastern writer Ibn Buṭlān (died 1066), translated in Lewis 1974: II.243–51.

described formulae for sales of Galician slaves, most of whom were female.[14]

Another compendium of legal rulings, put together by the sixteenth-century jurist al-Wansharīsī, also contains *fatwas* relating to slaves in this period. One opinion, from the eleventh or twelfth century, dealt with the propriety of capturing Christians along the Andalusi frontier in order to sell them. Another case from about the same period arose when a group of Christian Spanish slaves held captive in the south commandeered a boat and escaped in it.[15]

Among legal opinions, the eleventh-century Cordoban judge Ibn Sahl's *fatwa* collection is particularly useful because it contains notations on prices for slaves and other commodities. These are isolated references, but Ibn Sahl cited them as normal rather than extraordinary examples. In one instance, a white female slave could be had for twenty-eight dinars (about the same price as a horse), while a black slave might fetch up to 160 dinars (for which one could obtain a small house in Córdoba).[16]

Female slaves in the Muslim world were usually employed in the household, and Islamic law also allowed their use as concubines. Male slaves were generally used for domestic or military service, and were rarely employed for agricultural or manual labor.[17] The predominance of female slaves, and their generally higher price, is striking both in al-Andalus at this period and later in the European slave trade.

Because so many different types of slaves could be had in Muslim Spanish markets, and because the Andalusi population itself was so ethnically mixed, all kinds of interesting legal conundrums might arise. For example, al-Saqaṭī told the story of how a buyer from out of town had purchased a Christian slave girl in Córdoba who, he was told, had been recently acquired from the frontier regions. This was demonstrated by the fact that she only spoke a northern language. Because she had been recently imported, he paid an exorbitant price, after which he bought beautiful clothes for her and prepared to take her home. However, at this point she revealed – in fluent Arabic – that she was actually a free Muslim woman, and threatened to take him before a judge unless he did as she instructed. She counseled that "if you fear [losing]

---

[14] Al-Fihrī n.d.: fol. 33r; Ibn Mughīth n.d.: fols. 17v, 46r–v, 47v, 48r–v, 49r.

[15] Al-Wansharīsī 1401–3: II.179; Idris 1974: 186.

[16] Cited by Lévi-Provençal (1953: 259). These figures cannot be accepted at face value, for we know nothing of the details of these sales, and little of the relative value of money in different periods. In the next century, however – c. 1138 – a Geniza letter (TS 12.285) mentioned a price of 20½ dinars for a young male slave, so perhaps Ibn Sahl's lower figure is more representative. See also Goitein 1967: 139 for a discussion of slave prices in the Geniza. Goitein considers 20 dinars to be an average and relatively stable price for slaves during the twelfth century. On the slave trade in eleventh-century Córdoba, with information drawn from Ibn Sahl, see Khallāf 1984: 110–16.

[17] Slave armies were never as common in the Muslim West as in the Near East.

your money, take me to Almeria, where you can increase what you originally paid [because] Almeria is a terminus for ships and a center for merchants and travelers." When the duped buyer tried to complain to the original seller, the latter claimed to have left the business. Therefore, the man heeded his slave's advice, allowed her to keep her new finery, took her to Almeria, and sold her at a profit – presumably handing over a certain amount of this to her. And so the deception continued.[18]

Aside from the interest of the scam itself, this tale demonstrates several points regarding the parameters of slavery. Most important was the fact that religion was crucial, although it was not always easy to tell a Christian from a Muslim in Andalusi society. Related to this, the fear of penalties for buying a free Muslim (even in error) which might be levied in either money or reputation, combined with the prospect of losing the purchase price, were sufficient to blackmail an innocent buyer into both continuing the fraud and making the journey to Almeria. If the deception continued, the woman either might have traveled abroad – probably reaping higher sums the further away she was sold – or, as seems more likely, she may have extricated herself from the Almerian sale, and returned to her partner (the seller in Córdoba) to repeat the cycle until a watchful market inspector put a stop to their business.

Thus far, this essay has looked at Christians and other non-Muslims sold as slaves in Andalusi markets. This traffic continued through the reconquest period, as long as economic demand in the Islamic world and the availability of suitable merchandise persisted. But the slave trade also went in the other direction, and Andalusi Muslims were sold in Christian lands, although this northward trade probably started somewhat later – at least in the Iberian Peninsula – than its southern counterpart. During the early Middle Ages, Muslims were only one among several varieties of slave available in Latin Europe, but they had become by far the predominant group by the later Middle Ages.[19]

To judge from the increase of documentation, trade in Andalusi slaves to Christian Spain, Italy, and southern France grew fairly rapidly in the twelfth century. Latin documents usually state that a particular slave was a Muslim, using either the term Saracen (*sarracenus/a*) or Moor (*maurus/a*), or else recently enslaved Muslims can be identified by characteristic names such as Fatima, Axia (ᶜAisha), Maomet (Muḥammad), or Alio (ᶜAlī). The unfree status of these men and women could be designated in several ways. They might be referred to as *sarracenus meus, servus, ancilla, sclavus,* or by other similar

---

[18] Al-Saqaṭī: 1931: 54–5. This reconstruction is an amalgam of two very similar stories. In this instance, al-Saqaṭī's account appears to be more solidly grounded in Spain than was his stereotypical description of slave types cited above (in n. 13).

[19] For a more general discussion of the medieval European slave trade, see Verlinden 1955–77 and other works by the same author.

terms. *Sclavus* appears with particular frequency in thirteenth-century documents.

Muslim slaves in Christian households were both outsiders and personal property. Although there are examples of conversion and manumission, whereby a former Muslim slave might be integrated into Christian society, this does not seem to have been the primary objective of Christian buyers in this period. Most Muslim slaves in Christian lands were employed in a domestic capacity, as house servants, maids, nurses, and the like.

The processes of enslavement are rarely clear. Before the middle of the twelfth century, Muslim slaves were probably procured in the same manner as other slaves – through capture in slaving expeditions, border raids, military conquests, or by birth. By the later twelfth and thirteenth centuries, however, slavery in the western Mediterranean was more directly linked with the Spanish reconquest, with Andalusi Muslims falling into Christian hands in the wake of military victories. Some men and women must have been prisoners of war, but others were enslaved after the conquest of their homelands, since Muslims living under Spanish Christian rule might legally lose their freedom as a punishment for certain crimes. Others were probably taken illegally, by slavers whose desire for profit outweighed their respect for royal decrees protecting conquered populations. Following the reconquest, Spanish Muslim slaves were increasingly regularized as legitimate commodities for sale in Christian markets, rather than military trophies.[20]

Not every prisoner of war was necessarily destined for slavery, since it was generally more profitable to hold captives for ransom than to enslave them immediately. Thus, there was often a delay between the time a person was captured, the time needed to seek a ransom, and (when the latter effort was unsuccessful) the time of sale. But redemption could be a complicated and expensive process, and the Christian community in Spain was better organized for the effort than their Muslim counterparts.[21] This may have been owing to a longer history of Christians held in Muslim lands. In general, there was no organized system for redeeming Muslims, and the unfortunate's family was largely responsible for the burden. When an entire Muslim city came into Christian hands, as in the case of Valencia in 1238, large-scale ransom of captured inhabitants would have been impossible.

Castilian, Catalan, and Portuguese town charters frequently listed tariffs levied on Muslim slaves sold in Christian markets during the twelfth and thirteenth centuries. The 1166 *Fuero* of Évora, for example, quoted a charge of one solidus levied on merchants for every "Moor whom they sell in the market," a phrase which was reiterated in other charters of the

---

[20] This point has also been made by Bensch (1991).
[21] See Brodman 1986.

period.[22] Muslim slaves became an important Catalan export during the reign of James I (1213–76), when their trade was subject to government license and regulation.[23] As with earlier tariff lists, charters granted to Aragonese and Catalan cities, including the 1238 *lezda* of Valencia, stated duties to be collected on Muslim slaves sold in the city.[24] Catalan notarial contracts also testify to slave trading, with one merchant sending a female slave for sale in Sicily in 1238, and another shipping six slaves to crusader Palestine in 1252.[25]

Outside of the internal Iberian market, the best evidence for trade in Andalusi Muslims is derived from records of slave sales by Catalan and Provençal merchants in southern French and Italian port cities. Tariff lists from these cities provide some data on trade in Andalusi slaves to southern France and Italy. When a 1128 tariff register from Genoa listed charges for "men who ... come from Barcelona to sell Saracens," it is reasonable to suppose that their wares were of Andalusi origin.[26] Sometimes, the evidence is more tenuous, as when tolls collected in Narbonne, in 1153, included Saracen slaves among the items liable for duties. Geography suggests that these Muslim men and women were most likely of Spanish origin, even though not specifically noted as such. The same is true for later tariff lists from other southern French cities which contained similar clauses.[27]

Genoese notarial records yield an important group of slave sales contracted in that city between the middle of the twelfth and the middle of the thirteenth century. These Latin registers from the Genoese Archivio di Stato date back to the 1150s, making them the earliest documents of their type to survive.[28] Notarial records of contracts for the sale of slaves are of unique value, for they demonstrate an unquestionable commercial transfer, together with data on price, seller, and a minimal description (sex, name, race, provenance) of the men or women sold. Not all of these sales relate to Andalusi slaves, and there is also evidence of men and women brought from Sardinia, North Africa,

---

[22] "De mauro quem vendiderint in mercato I solidum," Academia Real das Sciencias de Lisboa 1856–1936: I.393 (see also pp. 407, 412, 416, 419, 427, 431, 475, 488, 495, 496, 513). On Castilian and Catalan references, see Verlinden 1942: 116–17.

[23] Burns 1973: 111.

[24] Dualde Serrano 1950–67: 287.

[25] Madurell Marimón and García Sanz 1973: 151–4 (documents 2 and 5).

[26] "Homines qui veniunt ianuam pro mercato. si fuerit de barchinonia et vendiderit sarracenum debet dare" (Ricotti 1854: col. 32, no. 23).

[27] Mouynès 1871–9: 4. For other lists from the early thirteenth century, see Guillems de Montpellier 1884–6: 438 for Montpellier, and Guérard 1857: lxxvii for Marseilles.

[28] Most of the twelfth-century and a few of the early thirteenth-century Genoese notarial materials have been published, including the registers of Giovanni Scriba, Lanfranco, Salmon, Oberto Scriba, Giovanni di Guiberto, Bonvillano, and Guglielmo Cassinese (q.v. in bibliography). The majority of thirteenth-century registers are only available in manuscript.

Malta, and elsewhere.[29] The contracts relating to Andalusis are particularly interesting, however, in terms of the correlation between the progress of the Christian victories in the peninsula, most notably the Aragonese conquest of Valencia in 1238, and the dates of slave sales. This correlation demonstrates that repercussions of Iberian political and economic events were felt in other regions of the western Mediterranean.

Table 1 provides a rough chronological list of sales of Andalusi, or probably Andalusi, slaves in Genoa over the years 1160–1251.[30] Although this group of sales is not large enough to support much statistical analysis, we can see some interesting trends in the price of slaves, their race, their sex, their provenance, and the merchants who sold them. In contracts, the term "Saracen" was used to indicate religion, not race, and a slave was usually further designated as white (*blancus/a*), brown (*brunus/a*) or black (*nigrus/a*). This information is presented in Table 2.[31] Prices for women tend to be higher than those for men, and it is probable that the predominance of slaves in the domestic setting rendered females preferable.[32] However, the explanation of prices is particularly difficult, because we cannot know the multiple factors involved, such as the age, health, and appearance of the slave. Also, it is noteworthy that during a period when one would expect to see rising prices owing to inflation, prices for these slaves seem remarkably stable at roughly

---

[29] After Saracens, Sardinians were the most commonly noted type of slave sold in Genoa. Balbi (1966) has compared the frequency of sales of Sardinians, Saracens, and others. It is possible that slaves noted as "sardo/a" in Latin contracts were of Muslim origin, because Sardinia seems to have functioned as a distribution point for slaves in the twelfth century. This view is supported by an observation of the Muslim traveler Ibn Jubayr, who visited the island in the 1180s, that there was "a group of Muslim prisoners, about eighty men and women, being sold in the market. The enemy – may God destroy them – had just returned with them from the sea-coast of Muslim countries" (Ibn Jubayr 1952: 27).

[30] This table does not incorporate all notarial records of slave sales in Genoa, only those relating to Andalusis or probable Andalusis. There is a lacuna in the data between 1200 and 1237, and a similar gap is seen between these years for other Genoese contracts concerning Spain. In the table, published notaries are cited by name and document number; unpublished notaries are cited by Archivio di Stato di Genoa (ASG) cartulary number and folio. Several scholars have already studied the extensive subject of the Genoese slave trade, and this table incorporates their work as well as my own archival research. Sales marked with an asterisk (*) are also mentioned in Verlinden 1977, though he erroneously dates several contracts from August 1239 to August 1249 (p. 54). I have not seen the manuscript for the final sale, cited in Verlinden 1977: 54. Sales marked # are noted in Balard 1968: 635. The sale cited as "Tria" may be found in Tria 1947: 139.

[31] Head counts are taken of all individuals, though price information only includes those sales in which a price is stated. Average prices are expressed in decimal notation for *libra* only. The category "not stated" refers to race, not religion, and thus may include Saracens.

[32] Also, although the practice was less open than in the Muslim world, concubinage of female slaves was not unknown in Europe. For a discussion of this phenomenon, see Phillips 1985: 98–100. At least one Genoese notary, Giovanni di Guiberto (1930–40: 473, no. 1020), recorded the conversion of a female Muslim slave prior to her marriage to a Christian.

£4–£6.[33] The apparent stability of prices may stem from the fact that the advance of Christian victories in the peninsula created a glut in the western Mediterranean market for Andalusi slaves, with excess supply thus offsetting inflation. Later in the century, the price of slaves rose sharply, probably owing to reduced availability.[34]

These tables also suggest that price and availability varied according to race. White slaves appear to have predominated and fetched higher prices, whereas black and brown slaves, while less commonly found, sold for slightly less money. This is in contrast to the higher price cited by Ibn Sahl for a black slave in eleventh-century Córdoba.[35]

Unlike prices, which remained much the same through the early thirteenth century, the predominant sex of these slaves changed from male, in the period 1160–1200, to female, between 1237 and 1251. Perhaps this was because the men in earlier sales were true prisoners of war, while later sales of women represented captives taken after the surrender of cities. It is also possible that in a situation which required the ransoming of large numbers of people, such as the capture of a city, men would have been redeemed before women. Greater demand for female slaves, in preference for males, may have also affected the market.[36]

In terms of provenance, it is likely that most – if not all – of these slaves were Spanish. If they were not specifically documented as such, then a Catalan or Provençal seller supports this conclusion. Thus, we may conjecture that the thirteen Saracen slaves of unknown provenance, who were sold in Genoa by merchants from Narbonne, Nice, Marseille, Montpellier, and Cartagena between 1160 and 1200, were probably Andalusi. It is not clear why, in the 1230s, it became routine to note slaves' homelands in sale contracts, where notation of this sort had previously been rare. It is unlikely that this was done to distinguish Muslim Spaniards from Sardinians or other slaves, since these other varieties had become less common by the early thirteenth century. This

---

[33] By way of price comparison, other notarial contracts show two bolts of Valencian cloth selling for £9$^{1}/_{2}$ in 1253 (ASG 29, fol. 22r); 14 lb of Castilian alum costing £25 16s. in 1213 (ASG 5, fol. 60r), and a package of Cordoban leather priced at £11 15s. in 1248 (ASG 26/II, fol. 88r). For a comparison between slave prices and contemporary Genoese wages, see Epstein 1988: 134.

[34] Documents from the 1260s show sales of Muslim Spanish women at £12–£16; yet by the end of the century, £20 was common. See Balard 1968: 643–5, 661.

[35] It should be remembered, however, that Ibn Sahl's price represents an isolated figure.

[36] The predominance of female slaves persisted through the thirteenth century. Balard (1968: 650) has estimated that women comprised 62.9% of the slave population of Genoa in the period 1239–1300, while males made up 37.1%. This trend was also true in other contemporary Mediterranean slave markets. In his discussion of Muslim slavery in Barcelona, Bensch (1991) has proposed a link between the predominance of female slaves and the importance of patrician women as slaveholders.

Table 1. *Contracts for the sale of Andalusi slaves in Genoa*

ASG cartulary #		Date	Slave		Price	Seller
G. Scriba, # 788		11/25/1160	Ms		£3	P. V. de Narbonne
G. Scriba, # 837		6/10/1161	Ms		55s.	W. M. de Narbonne
Tria		10/18/1186	Fns		£6	V. P. de Marseille
O. Scriba, # 307		12/4/1186	Mns		£3 2s.	P. U. de Montpellier
O. Scriba, # 342		12/20/1186	Fns		manumission	A. de Narbonne
O. Scriba, # 121		2/11/1190	3Ms		£18	P. M. de Nice
O. Scriba, # 126		2/12/1190	Ms		£5	P. M. de Nice
O. Scriba, # 129		2/13/1190	Ms		£4 4¹/2s.	P. M. de Nice
O. Scriba, # 244		3/12/1190	Ms		50s.	R. de Nice
O. Scriba, # 582		8/2/1190	Fs		£9	G. Beneventer
G. Guiberto # 12		11/5/1200	F		£4	B. V. de Cartagena
20/II, 222v	*	8/6/1237	3M	[M]	–	–
21/I, 96r		8/17/1239	Mws	[Ma]	£5 5s.	T. S. de Tortosa
21/I, 96r–v		8/17/1239	Mws	[Ma]	£14	B. S. de Tortosa
			Fs	[J]	[¹/2 of above £14]	
21/I, 99r	*	8/18/1239	Mws [V]		£5	S. de Tortosa
21/I, 99v	*	8/1239	Mws	[V]	£4 12d.	T. S. de Tortosa
21/I, 104r	*	8/22/1239	Mws	[Mu]	£4	B. A. de Tortosa
21/I, 104r	*	8/22/1239	Mws	[J]	£5	B. A. de Tortosa
21/I, 106r	*	8/1239	Mws	[V]	£5 5s.	B. de Tortosa
21/I, 111r	*	8/31/1239	Mws	[V]	£4 16s.	B. de S. F. de Tortosa
24, 107v		9/24/1239	Fs	[V]	£4	A. A. de Narbonne
24, 114v		10/1239	Ms	[V]	£15	–
			Fs	[V]	[in above £15]	
			Fn	[V]	[in above £15]	
24, 114v	#	10/1239	Fs		£9	J. de M. de Tortosa
24, 115r	#	10/12/1239	Fbs	[V]	£7	J. de M. de Tortosa
24, 115v	#	10/13/1239	Fws	[V]	£5 15s.	B. de M. de Tortosa
24, 116r		10/13/1239	Fws	[V]	£5 12s.	R. M. de Tortosa
24, 120v		10/27/1239	Fws		35 sol.	B. de Tortosa
24, 120v	#	10/1239	Mws	[V]	–	J. de M. de Tortosa
24, 120v		10/1239	Fws		£6	–
26/I, 156r	*	6/10/1241	Fws	[G]	£5	P. de R. de Tortosa
26/I, 157v	*	6/12/1241	Fbs		£3 15s.	W. de G. de Tortosa
26/I, 158v		6/19/1241	Fbs		£6	P de Iacaro
26/I, 159r		6/20/1241	Fbs		£6	*to* P. de Iacaro
26/I, 159r		6/20/1241	Fbs		£6	P. de Iacaro
26/I, 168r	*	7/23/1241	Fbs	[A]	£4	P. O. de Tortosa
26/I, 168v	*	7/1241	Fns	[C]	£6 15s.	P. S. de Tortosa[a]
26/I, 226r	*	12/3/1241	Mws	[V]	£4 10s.	V. de Fontanella
143, 63v		5/14/1248	Ms	[Y]	£8 10s.	
			Fs	[Y]	[in above price]	
20/I, 122v	*	5/13/1248	F	[G]	£4 (?)	–
20/I, 125v	*	5/18/1248	M	[Y]	£6	M. C. de Tortosa
20/I, 126v	*	5/19/1248	Fb	[V]	£9 5s.	A. F. de Tortosa
20/I, 127r	*	5/19/1248	Fw	[V]	£8¹/2	M. C. de Tortosa

Table 1. (*cont.*)

ASG cartulary #		Date	Slave		Price	Seller
20/I, 127r	*	5/19/1248	Mw	[V]	£4 15s.	M. C. de Tortosa
20/I, 127r	*	5/19/1248	Fw	[V]	£8¹/₂	M. C. de Tortosa
20/I, 127v	*	5/19/1248	Fw	[V]	9¹/₂	P. de R. de Tortosa
143, 64v		5/19/1248	Fs	[Y]	£? 17s.	M. C. de Tortosa
20/I, 130r	*	5/21/1248	M	[V]	£5 7s.	M. C. de Tortosa
26/II, 88v	*	5/22/1248	Mbs	[V]	£5	M. C. de Tortosa
143, 129r		5/26/1248	Mws		£5 6s.	M. C. de Tortosa
143, 129v		5/26/1248	F	(illegible)		M. C. de Tortosa?
20/I, 135r	*	5/30/1248	Fb	[D]	£5¹/₂	P. de R. de Tortosa
21/I, 25r	*	8/22/1248	Fb	[D]	£5	–
21/I, 66v	*	10/20/1248	Mw	[S]	£3 10s.	–
Verlinden		1/6/1251	Fw	[Al]	–	–

*a*This slave was from Ceuta, but sold by a merchant from Tortosa, which shows that not all slaves handled by Tortosans were Andalusi.

Key:

identity codes: M = Male, F = Female, s = Saracen (i.e. Muslim), w = white, n = black, b = brown
Where a slave is not specified as from al-Andalus, no provenance is noted. Where specified:
[M] = Majorca, [V] = Valencia, [Y] = Yspania (usually used to designate the Levant region),
[D] = Denia, [G] = Granada, [Ma] = Malaga, [J] = Jativa, [Mu] Murcia, [A] = Algesiras,
[S] = Seville, [C] = Ceuta, [Al] = Almeria.

later period is also the time when Andalusi slaves are routinely referred to as *sclavus/a* rather than by other Latin terms signifying unfreedom.

The provenance of those slaves specifically noted as being Andalusi suggests that their enslavement was directly connected with the progress of the Christian Spanish reconquest. This is particularly true of slaves brought to Genoa from Valencia in 1239, almost exactly a year after the capture of the city by James I of Aragon.[37] The delay between the fall of the city and the sale of some of its inhabitants can be explained as the time-lag needed while waiting for ransom. It is also possible that these men and women were captured some time after the fall of the city. Although James I forbade the later enslavement of local Muslim populations in captured regions, some illegal sales almost certainly occurred.

There is no evidence of specific Aragonese legislation regarding the export of Muslim slaves to Italy. Nevertheless, Genoa had long-standing commercial

[37] Valencia fell in September 1238, and Valencians began to appear in Genoese sales in August and September of the following year. The two slaves brought from Denia in 1248 probably fit into a similar category, for their region was captured in the mid-1240s. The case is not so clear for slaves from Seville, sold on 20 October 1248, because the city was not taken until the following month (23 November 1248).

Table 2. *Price, race, sex and provenance of slaves*

			Race			
	Total	Saracen	White	Brown	Black	Not stated
I Slaves sold 1160–1200						
Men	9	9	–	–	1	8
Andalusi	–	–	–	–	–	–
Av. price	£4.3	£4.3	–	–	£3.1	£4.4
Women	4	3	–	–	2	2
Andalusi	–	–	–	–	–	–
Av. price	£6.3	£7.5	–	–	£6.0	£6.5
II Slaves sold 1237–51						
Men	19	13	11	2	–	6
Andalusi	18	12	11	1	–	6
Av. price	£4.9	£4.9	£4.8	£5.1	–	£5.0
Women	26	15	9	7	2	8
Andalusi	21	11	8	5	2	6
Av. price	£5.9	£5.3	£6.3	£5.8	£5.9	£5.5

relations with Aragon–Catalonia, dating back to the eleventh century. As recently as 1230, a treaty drawn up between James I and Genoa had permitted Aragonese and Catalan merchants (presumably including slave merchants) to trade in the Italian port.[38]

Data from the Genoese registers indicate that these merchants took advantage of their commercial privileges. The traders who sold Muslim slaves in Genoa deserve attention primarily because of the overwhelming majority of merchants from southern France and eastern Spain – particularly from the Catalan city of Tortosa.[39] During the 1230s and 1240s, at least a dozen Tortosan merchants were named in Genoese contracts for the sale of Andalusi slaves. In the 1240s, Tortosans were also active as buyers and sellers of Muslim slaves in Majorca, while in 1240 two Tortosans turn up as slave traders in notarial contracts from Marseille.[40] The number of men involved, and the reappearance of certain names, is illustrated in Table 3.

Most merchants' names appear only once, although one, Matthew Curtina,

---

[38] James I 1976: 240–7. On later Aragonese legislation on slavery, see Vincke 1970.

[39] The Tortosan majority is so striking that I have not included the names of merchants outside this category who were noted in Table 1. Tortosa's strategic location, and its long history as a commercial center, must have contributed to the prominence of Tortosans as slave traders during the main period of the Catalan–Aragonese reconquest.

[40] Contracts from Marseilles have been published in Blancard 1884–5: documents 97 and 148. I am most grateful to Larry Simon for references to Tortosan merchants working in Majorca during the 1240s.

Table 3. *Tortosan slave merchants*

Name of seller	Place and date		Source
Thomas de Sarabita de Tortosa	[G]	8/17/1239	21/I, 96r
Bernard de Sorgia de Tortosa	[G]	8/17/1239	21/I, 96r–v
Stephan (Seut?) de Tortosa	[G]	8/19/1239	21/I, 99r
Thomas Sarabita de Tortosa	[G]	8/19/1239	21/I, 99r
Bernard Alcan . . . de Tortosa	[G]	8/22/1239	21/I, 104r
Bernard Alcan . . . de Tortosa	[G]	8/22/1239	21/I, 104r
Barbaran de Tortosa	[G]	8/23–4/1239	21/I, 106r
Bernard de Sancto Felixio de Tortosa	[G]	8/31/1239	21/I, 111r
Johann de Mora de Tortosa	[G]	10/9–11/1239	24, 114v
Johann de Mora de Tortosa	[G]	12/12/1239	24, 115r
Bernard de Mora de Tortosa	[G]	10/13/1239	24, 115v
Raymond Marchilius (?) de Tortosa	[G]	10/13/1239	24, 116r
Berengar . . . de Tortosa	[G]	10/27/1239	24, 120v
Johann de Mora de Tortosa	[G]	10/1239	24, 120v
Guillem Vidal de Tortosa	[M]	1240	Reg. 342, 8v
Peter de Rivopullo de Tortosa	[G]	6/10/1241	26/I, 156r
William de Gironda de Tortosa	[G]	6/12/1241	26/I, 157v
Peter Obertus de Tortosa	[G]	7/23/1241	26/I, 168r
Peter Sartor de Tortosa	[G]	7/1241	26/I, 168v
Bernat de Mora de Tortosa	[M]	1242	Reg. 342, 91v
Ramon Cambrils de Tortosa	[M]	1247	Reg. 343, 200r
Johann de Mora de Tortosa	[G]	7/1243	Balard, p. 635
Nicholas Baronus de Tortosa	[Mr]	3/23/1248	Blancard, # 97
Peter de Hospitale de Tortosa	[Mr]	3/23/1248	Blancard, # 148
Matthew Curtina de Tortosa	[G]	5/18/1248	20/I, 125v
Astrugus Figueria de Tortosa	[G]	5/19/1248	20/I, 126v
Matthew Curtina de Tortosa	[G]	5/19/1248	20/I, 127r
Matthew Curtina de Tortosa	[G]	5/19/1248	20/I, 127r
Matthew Curtina de Tortosa	[G]	5/19/1248	20/I, 127r
Peter de Renes de Tortosa	[G]	5/19/1248	20/I, 127v
Matthew Curtina de Tortosa	[G]	5/19/1248	143, 64v
Matthew Curtina de Tortosa	[G]	5/21/1248	20/I, 130r
Matthew Curtina de Tortosa	[G]	5/22/1248	26/II, 88v
Matthew Curtina de Tortosa	[G]	5/26/1248	143, 129r
Matthew Curtina de Tortosa	[G]	5/26/1248	143, 129v[a]
Peter de Renes de Tortosa	[G]	5/30/1248	20/I, 135r

[a]This contract is very badly damaged, and the name of the seller cannot be read; however, it follows directly after a contract made by Matthew Curtina.
Place of sale indicated in square brackets: [G] = Genoa, [M] = Majorca, [Mr] = Marseilles. Genoese references are from the ASG (cited by cartulary and folio), unless noted as Balard (1968). References from Marseilles are from Blancard (1884–5). Majorcan references are from the Archivo del Reino de Mallorca, Real Patriminio, Escribania de Cartas Reales. I am indebted to Larry Simon for providing these Majorcan examples. Names have been anglicized, except for those provided by Prof. Simon which retain their Catalan forms.

contracted a number of sales recorded by different notaries. Another merchant, Bernard de Mora, made sales in both Genoa and Majorca, in 1239 and 1242 respectively, and may have been related to his Tortosan colleague Johann de Mora. The number of Tortosans, and the clustering of dates, suggests that these merchants worked and traveled in company. Together, they must have presented a significant force in the western Mediterranean slave trade until *c*. 1250. After this date, however, Tortosan preeminence seems to have faltered in the face of competition from other Catalan, Aragonese, and Provençal traders.

Although Jews continued to have some role as slave dealers during the twelfth century – a document dating to 1104 gives four Jews permission to import Muslim slaves to Catalonia[41] – most trade in Andalusi slaves shifted into the hands of Christian merchants. Jewish slaving activity appears to have remained low until the second half of the thirteenth century, after the main reconquest period, when records of Jewish merchants selling Muslim slaves reappear.[42]

The sale of Spanish slaves in Genoa and elsewhere did not cease after 1250, although it seems to have declined. In 1259, for example, several Muslim slaves from Majorca were sold in Perpignan.[43] Likewise, Genoese notaries recorded the sales of at least five Andalusi Muslims in 1266–7 – two from Murcia, which had fallen to James I in 1266 – by merchants from Valencia, Pisa, Bonifacio, and Palma.[44] Balard has estimated a total of ninety-four Spanish Saracen slaves sold in Genoa between 1239 and 1274, roughly 46% of the total number of Muslim slaves recorded.[45] This figure, which overlaps with the period covered in this essay (when Andalusi slaves predominated), indicates that imports from the Iberian Peninsula declined in the second half of the century. Certainly, as the pace of the Spanish Christian conquests slowed, Andalusis were increasingly replaced by slaves from the eastern Mediterranean and Black Sea.[46]

Genoese materials on the slave trade before 1250 provide an excellent example of the changing trading patterns in the western Mediterranean world following the increased militarization of relations between Christian and Muslim powers. These Italian records complement internal Iberian data to complete our picture of an economy in flux, as Christians and Muslims in the

[41] Verlinden 1937–8: 594.
[42] Recent work by Larry Simon demonstrates the role of Jewish slave traders during the later thirteenth and the fourteenth centuries.
[43] Heers 1981: 28.
[44] Ferretto 1901: 49, 91.
[45] Balard 1968: 643–5.
[46] On Genoese slaving in the eastern Mediterranean, see Ehrenkreutz 1981. Also on later slavery in Genoa, see Tria 1947; Gioffré 1969; and Vitale 1949.

thirteenth-century Iberian Peninsula struggled to redefine their political, social, and economic relationship.

Documentation from an earlier period provides a different view of the Iberian slave trade, and yet reflects a continuous phenomenon of interreligious friction. Slavery remained common in the Iberian Peninsula throughout the medieval period, but changes in slaves and slavers can be directly related to the changing religious and political balance over time. Whereas Christian slaves were traded southward, into al-Andalus (and from there to the rest of the Islamic world) in the early Middle Ages, by the thirteenth century we see Muslim slaves carried into Christian Europe. At the same time, there emerged a pattern whereby Muslims and Jews predominated as slave traders through the eleventh century, but were overtaken or rivaled by Christian slave merchants in the twelfth and thirteenth centuries.

Slavery represents only one aspect, albeit dramatic, of the shifting atmosphere of interreligious dialogue in medieval Iberia and the western Mediterranean. The enslavement of Christians by Muslims, and Muslims by Christians, was facilitated by the existence of the long-standing religious frontier between al-Andalus and the northern Spanish kingdoms. Human merchandise moved across this frontier both in times of war and peace, although the processes of enslavement, the buyers, the sellers, and the slaves themselves, would vary with time and political circumstance.

REFERENCES

PRIMARY SOURCES

Academia Real das Sciencias de Lisboa 1856–1936 *Portugaliae monumenta historica: leges et consuetudines*. Vol. I in 6 pts. Lisbon: Typis Academicis.

Agobard 1899 *Epistolae*. ed. Ernst Dümmler. *MGH Epistolae* V. Berlin: Weidmann.

Assaf, Simḥah, ed. 1928 *Gaonic Responsa from Geniza MSS* (Hebrew). Jerusalem: Darom.

Blancard, Louis, ed. 1884–5 *Documents inédits sur le commerce de Marseille au moyen-âge*. 2 vols. Marseilles: Barlatier-Feissat.

Bonvillano 1939 *Bonvillano (1198)*. Ed. J. E. Eierman, H. C. Krueger, and R. L. Reynolds. Genoa: R. Deputazione di Storia Patria per la Liguria.

Dualde Serrano, Manuel, ed. 1950–67 *Fori antiqui valentiae*. Madria and Valencia: Consejo Superior de Investigaciones científicas.

Ferretto, Arturo, ed. 1901 *Codice diplomatico della relazioni fra la Liguria, la Toscana, e la Lunigiana al tempi di Dante*. *Atti della Società ligure di storia patria* 31.

Al-Fihrī n.d. *Wathā'iq wa al-masā'il al-majmū'a min kutub al-fuqahā*. Miguel Asín Institute, Consejo Superior de Investigaciones científicas, Madrid, MS 11.

Giovanni di Guiberto 1939–40 *Giovanni di Guiberto (1200–1211)*. Ed. M. W. Hall-Cole, H. C. Krueger, and R. L. Reynolds. 2 vols. Genoa: R. Deputazione di Storia Patria per la Liguria.

Giovanni Scriba 1935 *Il cartolare di Giovanni Scriba*. Ed. Mari Chiaudano and Mattia Moresco. 2 vols. Turin: S. Lattes.

Guérard, Benjamin E. C., ed. 1857 *Cartulaire de l'abbaye de Saint-Victor de Marseille*. 2 vols. Paris: C. Lahure.

Guglielmo Cassinese 1938 *Guglielmo Cassinese (1190–1192)*. Ed. M. W. Hall, H. C. Krueger, and R. L. Reynolds. 2 vols. Genoa: R. Deputazione di Storia Patria per la Liguria.

Guillems de Montpellier 1884–8 *Liber instrumentorum memorialium; Cartulaire des Guillems de Montpellier*. Ed. Alexandre C. Germain. Montpellier: J. Martel aîné.

Ibn al-Faqīh 1967 *Kitāb al-buldān*. Ed. M. J. de Goeje. Bibliotheca geographorum arabicorum 5. 2nd edn. Leiden: E. J. Brill.

Ibn Ḥawqal 1938–9 *Kitāb ṣūrat al-arḍ*. Ed. J. H. Kramers. 2 vols. Leiden: E. J. Brill.

Ibn Jubayr 1952 *The Travels of Ibn Jubair*. Trans. R. J. C. Broadhurst. London: Jonathan Cape.

Ibn Khurradādhbih 1967 *Kitāb al-masālik wa al-mamālik*. Ed. M. J. de Goeje. Bibliotheca geographorum arabicorum 6. 2nd edn. Leiden: E. J. Brill.

Ibn Mughīth n.d. *al-Muqni' fī 'ilm al-shurūt*. Real Academia de la Historia, Madrid, MS 44.

James I 1976 *Documentos de Jaime I de Aragón*. Ed. Ambrosio Huici Miranda and María Desamparados Cabares Pecourt. Vol. I. Valencia: Anubar.

Lanfranco 1951 *Lanfranco (1202–1226)*. Ed. H. C. Krueger and R. L. Reynolds. 3 vols. in 2. Genoa: Società Ligure di Storia Patria.

Liutprand 1915 *Antapodosis*. Ed. J. Becker. *MGH SS rer. Germ.*

al-Maqqarī 1855–61 *Analectes sur l'histoire et la littérature des arabes d'Espagne*. Ed. Reinhart Dozy *et al.* 2 vols. Leiden: E. J. Brill.

Mouynès, German, ed. 1871–9 *Inventaire des archives communales antérieures à 1790: ville de Narbonne*. 6 vols. in 5. Narbonne: E. Caillard.

al-Muqaddasī 1950 *Description de l'Occident musulman au IVe–Xe siècle*. Ed. Charles Pellat. Alger: Editions Carbonel.

Oberto 1938 *Oberto, Scriba de Mercato (1190)*. Ed. Mario Chiaudano and Raimondo Morozzo della Rocca. Genoa: R. Deputazione di Storia Patria per la Liguria.

1940 *Oberto, Scriba de Mercato (1186)*. Ed. Mario Chiaudano. Genoa: R. Deputazione di Storia Patria per la Liguria.

Pertz, Georg H., ed. 1895 *Annales regni Francorum*. 2nd edn. F. Kurze. *MGH SS rer. Germ.*

Ricotti, Ercole, ed. 1854 *Liber iurium reipublicae genuensis*. Historiae patriae monumenta 7. Turin: ex Officina regia.

Salmon 1906 *Liber magistri Salmonis sacri palatii notarii (1222–1226)*. Ed. Arturo Ferretto. *Atti della Società ligure di storia patria* 36.

al-Saqaṭī 1931 *Kitāb al-faqīh al-ajall 'ālim al-'ārif al-awḥad (Un Manuel hispanique de ḥisba)*. Ed. Georges S. Colin and Evariste Lévi-Provençal. Paris: E. Leroux.

al-Wansharīsī 1401–3 (= 1981–3) *Mi'yār al-mu'rib wa al-jami' al-maghrib*, ed. Muḥammad Hajji. 12 vols. Rabat and Beirut: Wizarat al-Awqaf wa-al-Shu'un al-Islamiyah lil-Mamlakah al-Magribiyah.

Zeumer, C., ed. 1886 *Formulae merowingici et karolini aevi*. *MGH Leges* V (in quarto).

SECONDARY REFERENCES

'Abbadī, Ahmad M. 1953 *Los esclavos en España (al-Ṣaqāliba fī Isbāniyā)*. Trans F. de la Granja Santamaria. Madrid: Ministerio de Educación Nacional de Egypto.

Ayalon, David 1979 On the Eunuchs in Islam. *Jerusalem Studies in Arabic and Islam* 1: 67–124.

Balard, Michel 1968 Remarques sur les esclaves à Gênes dans la seconde moitié du XIIIe siècle. *Mélanges d'archéologie et d'histoire de l'Ecole Française de Rome* 80: 627–80.

Balbi, Giovanna 1966 La schiavitù a Genova tra i secoli XII e XIII. In Pierre Gallais and Yves-Jean Rion, eds., *Mélanges offerts à René Croset*, II.1025–9. 2 vols. Poitiers: Société d'Etudes Médiévales.

Bensch, S. 1991 From Prizes of War to Domestic Merchandise: Slaves in the Towns of Eastern Iberia. Unpublished paper delivered at the Medieval Academy's annual meeting, Princeton, N.J.

Brett, Michael 1969 Ifrīqiya as a Market for Saharan Trade from the Tenth to the Twelfth Century A.D. *Journal of African History* 10: 347–64.

Brockelmann, Carl 1937 *Geschichte der arabischen Literatur*. Supplemental vol. I. Leiden: E. J. Brill.

Brodman, James W. 1986 *Ransoming Captives in Crusader Spain*. Philadelphia: University of Pennsylvania Press.

Burns, Robert I., SJ 1973 *Islam under the Crusaders: Colonial Survival in the 13th-Century Kingdom of Valencia*. Princeton: Princeton University Press.

Ehrenkreutz, Andrew 1981 Strategic Implications of the Slave Trade between Genoa and Mamluk Egypt in the Second Half of the Thirteenth Century. In Avram L. Udovitch, ed., *The Islamic Middle East, 700–1900*, 335–45. Princeton: Darwin Press.

Epstein, S. A. 1988 Labour in Thirteenth-Century Genoa. In I. Malkin and R. L. Hohlfelder, eds., *Mediterranean Cities: Historical Perspectives*, 114–40. London: Cass.

Gioffré, D. 1969 Un studio sugli schiavi a Genova nel XIII secolo. *Atti della Società ligure di storia patria* n.s. 9: 321–5.

Goitein, Solomon D. 1962 Slaves and Slavegirls in the Cairo Geniza Records. *Arabica* 9: 1–20.

1967 *A Mediterranean Society*. Vol. I. Berkeley and Los Angeles: University of California Press.

Haverkamp, Alfred 1974 Zur Sklaverei in Genua während des 12. Jahrhunderts. In Friedrich Prinz, Franz-Joseph Schmale, and Ferdinand Sebit, eds., *Geschichte in der Gesellschaft: Festschrift für Karl Bosl*, 160–215. Stuttgart: A. Hiersemann.

Heers, Jacques 1981 *Esclaves et domestiques au moyen-âge dans le monde méditerranéen*. Paris: Fayard.

Idris, H. R. 1974 Les Tributaires en Occident musulman médiéval d'après le *Mi'yār* d'al-Wanšarīšī. In Pierre Salmon, ed., *Mélanges d'islamologie: volume dédié à la mémoire de Armand Abel*, I.172–96. 2 vols. Leiden: E. J. Brill.

Kahane, Renée and Kahane, Henry 1962 Notes on the Linguistic History of *Sclavus*. In *Studi in onore di Ettore Lo Gatto e Giovanni Maver*, 345–60. Florence: Sansoni.

Khallāf, M. A. 1984 *Qurṭuba al-islāmiyya*. Tunis.

Kleinclausz, Arthur J. 1934 *Charlemagne*. Paris: Hachette.

Lévi-Provençal, Evariste 1953 *Histoire de l'Espagne musulmane*. 2nd edn. Vol. III. Paris: G. P. Maisonneuve.

Lewis, Archibald R. 1951 *Naval Power and Trade in the Mediterranean, A.D. 500–1100*. Princeton: Princeton University Press.

Lewis, Bernard 1974 *Islam, from the Prophet Muhammad to the Capture of Constantinople*. 2 vols. New York: Harper & Row.

Lombard, Maurice 1975 *The Golden Age of Islam*. Trans. Joan Spencer. Amsterdam: North–Holland; New York: American Elsevier.

Madurell Marimón, José M. and García Sauz, Arcadio 1973 *Comandas comerciales barcelonesas de la baja edad media* (= *Anuario de estudios medievales, anejo* 4). Barcelona: Colegio Notarial de Barcelona.

Phillips, William D., Jr. 1985 *Slavery from Roman Times to the Early Transatlantic Trade*. Minneapolis: University of Minnesota Press.

Ribera y Tarragó, Julián 1928 *Disertaciones y opúsculos*. Vol. I. Madrid: E. Maestre.

Soto i Company, Ricard 1981 El primer tràfic esclavista a Mallorca. *L'Avenç* 35: 60–5.

Tria, L. 1947 La schiavitù in Liguria. *Atti della Società ligure di storia patria* 70: 139.

Verlinden, Charles 1937–8 La Place de la Catalogne dans l'histoire du monde méditerranéen médiévale (avant 1300). *Revue des cours et conférences* 39: 586–606.

1942 L'Origine de sclavus-esclave. *Bulletin du Cange: archivium latinitatis medii aevi* 17: 97–128.

1955–77 *L'Esclavage dans l'Europe médiévale*. 2 vols. Bruges: De Tempel.

1974 La Traité des esclaves: un Grand Commerce international au Xe siècle. In *Etudes de civilisation médiévale (IXe–XIIe siècles): mélanges offerts à Edmond-René Labande*, 721–30. Poitiers: CESM.

1977 Le Recrutement des esclaves à Gênes du milieu di XIIe siècle jusque vers 1275. In *Fatti e idee di storia economica nei secoli XII–XX: studi dedicati a Franco Borlandi*, 37–57. Bologna: Il Mulino.

1983 Les Radaniya e Verdun . . . in Maria del Carmen Carle, Hilda Grassotti, and German Orduna, eds., *Estudios en homenaje a don Claudio Sánchez Albornoz*, II.105–32. 2 vols. Buenos Aires: Instituto de Historia de España.

Vernet, Joan 1950 El Valle de Ebro como nexo entre orient y occidente. *Boletín de la Real Academia de Bellas Letras de Barcelona* 23: 249–86.

Vincke, Johannes 1970 Königtum und Sklaverei im aragonischen Staatenbund während des 14. Jahrhunderts. *Gesammelte Aufsätze zur Kulturgeschichte Spaniens* 25: 19–112.

Vitale, Vito 1949 La schiavitù in Liguria. *Bollettino ligustico per la storia de la cultura regionale* 1: 43–7.

Part IV

Christendom and its discontents:
rethinking the boundaries

14   The tortures of the body of Christ

Gavin I. Langmuir

The greatest persecution of any single group in the Middle Ages was the massacre of Jews during the Black Death between 1348 and 1350. But that persecution was not an expression of discontents inherent within Christendom; it was a reaction to a biological disaster. Confronted with a genuine disaster, Europeans reacted as have many other people in very different contexts; they looked for a scapegoat. Though old discontents within Christendom determined the choice of the scapegoat, Christian discontents did not initiate the urge to massacre. If we are looking for the greatest medieval persecution that was a direct expression of discontents and tensions inherent in Christendom, we must look a little earlier, to the massacres, also of Jews, between 1298 and 1338. Those massacres were not an irrational reaction to an external threat; they were a reaction to something that existed only in the minds of Christians – their beliefs and doubts about the physical presence of their god, *verus corpus Christi*.

"The Eucharist is the sacrament on which the devotion of moderns depends most of all," declared the Franciscan, John of Winterthur, in the chronicle he began no later than 1340. He also reported that in Constance, about 1332, a Christian servant fled from a house of Jews, crying out, "The body of Christ is being horribly tortured by the Jews," whereupon twelve Jews were burnt, six drowned, and ten cut down.[1] By the early fourteenth century, Jews were being accused of torturing the body of Christ and killed by the thousands. Though Jews thought that Jesus of Nazareth had been dead for thirteen centuries, they were massacred because of the symbolic significance for Christians of a piece of bread and the religious significance Christians attributed to suffering.

Suffering, both human and divine, has long been important in Christian faith. Unlike Jews or Muslims, Christians have believed that their god appeared bodily on earth, suffered flagellation and crucifixion under Pontius Pilate, and was resurrected, thereby saving those who believed in Him from death

---

[1] *Die Chronik Johanns von Winterthur*, ed. Friedrich Baethgen, 2nd edn. in *MGH SS rer. Germ.* n.s. III.64, 107. See Browe 1933: 22.

and damnation. Those fundamental beliefs about the incarnation of their god and the salvific effects of his passion have been a great comfort to Christians through the centuries. Yet starting around the year 1000, those beliefs also began to inspire profound anxieties that provoked dissent and lethal persecutions.

For the first thousand years, Christians in western Europe did not emphasize Christ's suffering; they celebrated his triumph over death. And though they believed that he was somehow still really present on earth when his sacrifice was offered back to him in the celebration of the Eucharist, they did not think much about how that was so. As the language they used suggests, they thought it a mystery. From early Christianity to the ninth century, the term *corpus Christi* was used by theologians and ordinary believers to denote two directly observable – and inextricably linked – realities they thought of as the body of Christ: the Catholic Church and the consecrated wafer of the mass. To distinguish between them, they used the term *corpus Christi* in slightly different ways. When they spoke of *corpus Christi* without an additional indication of what they meant, they were referring to the Church, but if they spoke of the mystical body of Christ, the *corpus mysticum*, they were referring to the consecrated wafer of the mass.[2] It was the mystery. The classic doctrine by which they explained how Christ's body could save them from the condemnation incurred by original sin was, however, remarkably concrete and legalistic. It depicted salvation as the outcome of a cosmic clash of legal rights over human beings between god and the devil; and in that drama, the human beings who were to be saved were more or less passive pawns, and Christ's humanity was a trick to deceive the devil.

Starting around the year 1000, however, thinking about Christ, the Catholic Church, and the consecrated wafer changed dramatically. Salvation became more personal and less a cosmic drama. More and more Christians began to read – or hear – the gospel stories about Jesus and to think ever more literally about his physical body as it had been historically, and as it was now present everywhere in their midst. For not only were there representations everywhere on crucifixes and in pictures and sculptures, there was also the true body of Christ, *verus corpus Christi*. Reflecting those new attitudes, theological language changed in a way that made Christ's body in the wafer seem more simply physical and factual, whereas the mystery was now the Catholic Church whose priests could make that reality present. The term *corpus Christi* without qualification now meant the consecrated wafer, whereas the term *corpus mysticum* was applied to the Church.[3] And that was accompanied by a dramatic change in soteriology.

However satisfying the classical explanation of how the incarnation had

---

[2] Lubac 1949: 34.   [3] *Ibid.* 276 and *passim*.

brought salvation may have been philosophically or legally, it was not very comforting psychologically for those suffering immediate evils here and now. But another and psychologically more comforting solution was potentially present in the Gospels. Undeveloped for a thousand years, it only became central after the first millennium, when the triumph of Christianity throughout Europe had made Christians more sensitive to the religious problem of their continued sufferings in this life. For the more people thought of their society as Christendom and believed that their world was ruled by Christ, the more striking and problematical became the continued presence of evil within it, and the greater became the need of Christians to find an explanation that provided psychological comfort for their sufferings.

The response was striking: suffering itself came to be valued as a contact, a mode of communion, with God. People began to emphasize that Christ too had endured torture; that because he had he could empathize with the sufferings of his worshipers, as they could with him; and that he would therefore comfort them. As early as the first half of the eleventh century, Romuald and Damian were preaching, not about the majesty of God, but about the vulnerability and sufferings of Jesus and the importance of compunction as a means of contact with him. And by the end of the century, Anselm had made Christ's suffering as a human being theologically central in the soteriological revolution he enunciated in *Cur Deus homo*. "In this way, also, by following the will received from the Father invariably, and of His own accord, the Son became obedient to him, even unto death; and learned obedience from the things which he suffered."[4]

Abelard went even further and held that people would be saved by the love of Christ that his suffering for them engendered. "And so our redemption is that great love awoken in us by the passion of Christ, which not only frees us from the slavery of sin, but acquires for us the true liberty of the sons of God, that we may fulfil all things more by love of him than by fear."[5]

Bernard of Clairvaux made Christ's suffering all the more real by emphasizing that it occurred in historical, in human, time.

For, as it is written of him, "He learned obedience by the things which he suffered," so may he have suffered that he might learn compassion. This, however, does not mean that he, whose compassion was eternal in its origin and duration, had not hitherto known pity, but that what he knew in an eternal sphere, he learned by experience in a temporal sphere.[6]

---

[4] *Cur Deus homo*, ch. 10. See also ch. 14: "God subjects himself to himself by torments, even against man's will, and thus shows he is the Lord of man, though man refuses to acknowledge it of his own accord."

[5] *PL* CLXXVIII.836.

[6] *De gradibus humilitatis et superbiae*, ch. 3.

From then on, the sufferings inflicted on the physical body of Jesus of Nazareth became important to Christians as never before and were reflected everywhere. In the following centuries, iconography, literature, and mystery plays would depict the agonies of Jesus ever more gruesomely and the sorrows of His mother ever more piteously. Inevitably, that new way of thinking about Christ's body gave new emotional significance to Christ's presence in the host. But it also raised new questions about that presence. However comforting psychologically for individuals the emphasis on shared suffering and divine empathy may have been, and however comforting the new sense of Christ's human presence, the new religiosity had a horrifying implication: if Christ's historical body was present here and now on earth, it could still suffer torture.

With the tortures of one of his earthly bodies, the Church, I shall not be concerned here.[7] I will concentrate on the other body, the consecrated wafer, *verus corpus Christi*. It was much more immediately vulnerable to attack than the Church because it was a concrete object that anyone could touch. Yet to describe the host simply as a concrete object is misleading, for it was the symbolization of that object by faith that made it Christ's body. And since both mind and material were necessary for the belief, that body could be assaulted both mentally and physically.

The attacks on the mental dimension of that belief are too well known to need much description. They were almost bound to occur as people began to think literally of Christ's body and compare it with bread they saw on the altar. Already in the middle of the ninth century, Ratramnus of Corbie had attacked Radbertus of Corbie's belief that the consecrated bread and wine were the historical body and blood of Christ. After the second wave of invasions had ended, challenges to the belief appeared at the popular level. In the first half of the eleventh century, several little movements appeared which denied that priests really made Christ physically present. And about 1040, the assault began in earnest when Berengar of Tours denied that the historical body of Christ became present when the bread and wine were consecrated. In horrified reaction, Cardinal Humbert reasserted the presence of Christ's body in a way that suggested its torture. Humbert forced Berengar to affirm that the bread and wine were "the true body of our Lord Jesus Christ . . . handled and broken by the hand of the priest and ground by the teeth of the faithful."[8] But that was only the beginning of the debate, for Berengar had made the issue of Christ's

---

[7] It may be noted, however, that the church was also suffering at the end of the thirteenth century. Anti-clericalism and heresy had risen sharply, the kingdom of Jerusalem had fallen by 1291, and by 1296 kings were successfully defying papal authority. Suffering from attacks by heretics, Muslims, kings, and regional loyalties, Christ's institutional body on earth, the *corpus mysticum*, seemed and was increasingly vulnerable by the end of the thirteenth century.

[8] Pelikan 1978: 198.

physical presence a central theological and ecclesiastical concern.[9] After 1050, awareness of doubts about the real presence was widespread both in educated and popular circles, and efforts to offset those doubts would preoccupy theologians throughout Europe for centuries to come.

The dissemination of doubts at the popular level is clear in the twelfth century. In the first half of the century, the Petrobrusians denied that any miraculous change occurred at the altar. In the second half of the century, the deviant Christian movement that spread most widely in medieval Europe, the Cathars, not only rejected that belief but also held that anything material came from evil. And in the thirteenth century, despite the dogmatic definition of transubstantiation in 1215, disbelief was by no means confined to open disbelievers; good Catholics were anxious too. There was now a nagging awareness that it was difficult to believe that something physical had changed in the host when no physical change could be seen. The enormity of the mental problem facing theologians and ordinary people would later be stated succinctly by Duns Scotus: "a philosopher, or anyone following natural reason, would see a greater contradiction in this negation of the bread than in all the articles of faith concerning the incarnation."[10]

So great was the problem and so important belief in the real presence for the authority of the Church,[11] that theologians from Lanfranc forward anxiously tried to demonstrate how a substantial change in the bread and wine could occur without its being physically evident. Even the Franciscans who later criticized the Thomistic arguments for transubstantiation did not go so far as to deny the real physical presence. Though Duns Scotus maintained that the substance of bread remained, he nonetheless developed his own remarkably subtle argument to demonstrate that Christ was physically present.[12]

Theological argument was not the only effort to protect the belief that Christ was physically present in the consecrated hosts; there was also ritual reinforcement. Not only were there additions to the liturgy and the interpretation of the mass, the most frequent ritual in Europe;[13] there was the creation of the new feast of Corpus Christi in the thirteenth century. The original impetus for the feast was the fervor of religious women, such as Marie of Oignies and Julianna of Mount Cornillon, who focused their emotions dramatically on the

---

[9] Even if he had few followers who adhered closely to his particular theses. See Macy 1990a and 1990b.

[10] Burr 1984 p. 88.

[11] Sacramentalism was fundamental for the authority of the Roman Catholic church, above all the monopoly its priests claimed of the power to operate the change of bread and wine into the real body and blood of Christ. See Troeltsch 1949: I.231–2.

[12] Burr 1984: 77–98.

[13] Jungmann 1951–5 I: 91–127.

consecrated bread and wine themselves.[14] It was Julianna of Cornillon who inspired John of Cornillon to create the first office of Corpus Christi between 1232 and 1246. With some modifications, the feast was celebrated for the first time by the Cistercians and Dominicans at Liège in 1247. There was considerable opposition then on the ground that the Eucharist was already venerated daily in the mass and that another office was therefore superfluous. But the spread of the feast was supported by a papal legate. Hugh of Saint-Cher had entered the Dominican order in Paris in 1225, and in 1244 he became the first Dominican to be made a cardinal. In 1251, he was appointed cardinal-legate to Germany, and in 1252 he gave his approval to the feast at Liège and authorized its use throughout Germany, where it first spread. The feast received further backing and spread more widely when Jacques of Pantaléone, formerly archdeacon of Liège, became pope as Urban IV and extended the feast to the whole Church in 1264 by the bull *Transiturus de hoc mundo*. But there was still opposition and the feast was not universally observed. Only after Clement V had confirmed *Transiturus* in the Council of Vienne in 1311/12 and after John XXII had inserted the bull in the Clementine collection of canon law in 1317 was the new feast observed throughout the Church.[15]

The centuries of theological concern, the dogma of transubstantiation in 1215, and the development of the feast of Corpus Christi were all symptoms of the mounting importance attributed to the host itself. But that increased attention had troubling side-effects. Although belief in Christ's physical presence was reinforced by doctrine, dogma, and ritual, the basic challenge to the belief was not any abstract philosophical or theological argument; it was the contrast, evident to anyone, between the officially prescribed belief and the lack of any visible change in the host. Perhaps most of the population believed unthinkingly that Christ somehow became present at the moment of consecration, even though they could see no change, but many educated and uneducated people were increasingly troubled and wanted evidence of a change in the host itself. Indeed, the desire was so ardent that some people satisfied it; they saw what they wanted to see.

There had, of course, been host miracles long before the eleventh century. The miracles usually confirmed faith, converted unbelievers, or confounded sinners. Thus, a guilty person might be unable to swallow a consecrated host, or a dove might fly up at the moment of consecration. Yet if miraculous events that legitimated belief in the real presence occurred in connection with the host, reports of physical changes in the host itself were almost completely unknown

---

[14] Bynum 1987 has described their religiosity in fascinating detail. This new kind of Eucharistic piety is first obvious about 1200 in Marie of Oignies (*ibid.*, 59, 119, 228).

[15] See Cottiaux 1963: 5–81, 405–59; and Forni 1984: 459–65. And see now Rubin 1991, a carefully detailed study of the rise of Eucharistic practice and devotion with an excellent bibliography.

before the eleventh century. Only after Berengar's challenge did reports of visions of changes in the host itself become frequent.[16]

As was recognized at the time, these miracle stories functioned to prove that Christ really was physically present in the consecrated host. After Berengar's challenge, supporters of the real presence such as Durand of Troarn, Lanfranc of Canterbury, Guitmond of Aversa, Alger of Liège, Gerhoch of Reichersberg, and others recounted various stories about miracles that they themselves or others had experienced. As Guitmond of Aversa explained, "the opponents of the eucharistic dogmas were refuted not only by authority but also by many clear miracles."[17] And since not only Berengar but many average Christians without theological pretensions had doubts, such miracles were valued as lessons for the laity.

In the chronicle he wrote between 1150 and 1186, Abbot Robert of Torigni of Mont-Saint-Michel recorded a number of host miracles in his entry for 1181/2.[18] A woman, who had not swallowed the host she had received at Easter, wrapped it in a cloth and placed it in her money box. When her sweetheart opened the box, he found it transformed into the likeness of flesh and blood. The same thing happened to a host held by a priest near Chartres, to a host a woman in Flanders put in a box, and to a host that a peasant in the diocese of Chartres put in the hood of his cape. More striking was a miracle at Anger. While a priest was singing mass, a small boy present saw the most beautiful small boy in the hand of the priest when he consecrated the wafer. The boy went out and cried to everyone to come and see the marvel of God, but when they came, they saw nothing but bread. The same thing happened to a priest at Fécamp. Robert concluded that "the Lord, out of pity, worked all these things to confirm our faith in his sacraments."

So valued were host miracles by the middle of the thirteenth century that Aquinas legitimated them by serious arguments first developed by Albert the Great.[19] Aquinas asserted that even when there were no real changes in the appearance of the host, God caused some people to have such visions "for the purpose of showing that Christ's body is truly under this sacrament." He even asserted that some people saw real changes in the host that God had caused in order to represent the truth that Christ's body and blood were truly in this sacrament. And although Aquinas held that what they saw was not the real body and blood but only an appearance, an apparent change in the accidents of the host, less sophisticated believers were unlikely to make that distinction.[20]

---

[16] Browe 1938: 95, 100, 179.

[17] *Ibid.*, 180–2.

[18] *Chronicles of the Reign of Stephen, Henry II, and Richard I*, ed. Richard Howlett (Rolls Series; London, 1884–9), IV.296–7; Gransden 1974–82: I.263.

[19] Macy 1991.

[20] *Summa theologica* III.76.8. See Browe 1938: 189–90.

But how was Christ seen? In his great pioneering book on the subject, Peter Browe showed that in some visions the host changed into the living Christ, sometimes as a child, sometimes as a martyred adult, sometimes as flesh and blood.[21] Many of the visions of the living Christ were visions of an infant which, though they may have emphasized Jesus's vulnerability, were not reminders of Christ's suffering.[22] Expressions of a particular type of religiosity, they emphasized love and nurture. In many visions, however, whether of Christ as a child, as the Lamb of God, or as an adult, Christ was seen as slaughtered, as crucified with blood flowing from His flesh, or even as being held by his feet by God the Father and being pressed into a mill. To these must be added the visions in which the host turned, briefly or lastingly, into flesh and blood,[23] obvious reminders of physical suffering. Thus, while some of these visions did not draw attention to Christ's physical suffering, others did. Indeed, one person could have both kinds of visions: Elisabeth of Schönau (d. 1164), who had a vision in which Christ appeared as a female virgin,[24] insisted that she had also seen true flesh in the pyx. I have not tried to count the number of reported visions of both types, but visions that focused on flesh and blood seem by far the more numerous. It is as if Christians needed to believe that their god was still suffering in order to believe that they themselves would be saved from their suffering.

When we look back over these developments, we can detect three major watersheds: around 1050, when Berengar denied that the consecrated wafer changed into Christ's historical body; around 1215, when the dogma of transubstantiation was promulgated; and around 1300, when the feast of Corpus Christi was widely celebrated, especially in Germany, and people were coming to focus obsessively on the host itself. Those dates were also, however, and by no means coincidentally, milestones in the development of beliefs about Jews. Indeed, when we examine the development of miracle stories about Jews and the host, we can only be struck by the extent to which they were a reverse or negative image of the changes in Christian religiosity I have just described.

Long before Berengar, there had been stories that connected Jews with the Eucharist, but they were rare. The most famous is the story which first appears in a Latin version in Gregory of Tours and was frequently repeated in the Middle Ages.[25] A Jewish boy went to mass with his Christian friends. When he told his father what he had done, his father threw him into a red hot oven. He

---

[21] Browe 1938: 93. See also Rubin 1991: 108–29.
[22] Browe 1938: 100–9; Rubin 1991: 135–9.
[23] See Browe 1938: 95–128.   [24] Bynum 1987: 264.
[25] Around 850, the pseudo-Bede attributed it to St. Boniface, and by the end of the Middle Ages, at least thirty-three different versions had appeared. See Parkes 1969: 296; Blumenkranz 1963: 68.

was rescued, miraculously unharmed, by his mother and neighbors, who threw the father in the oven, where he was thoroughly consumed. The boy and many other Jews then converted to Christianity.

Like the Christian doctrine about Jews that was established by the fourth century, the message the story conveys about Jews is ambivalent. The central theme is the conversion of Jews to Christianity by a miracle connected with a mass, although we should note that the story does not attribute any active role to the host itself. Yet if the function of miracle in the story is to convert Jews, not to incite hatred or punishment of them, the role of the father is a reminder that disbelieving Jews are evil and will be properly punished.

The same ambivalence characterized the story from the *Life* of St. Syrus, a third- or fourth-century bishop of Pavia which Radbertus of Corbie utilized in the ninth century in his famous treatise on the Eucharist, and which Geza of Tortona repeated in the late tenth century in his treatise on the Eucharist.[26] According to the story, a Jew attended a mass celebrated by Bishop Syrus to obtain a host, which he intended to throw in the privy. But he was unable to carry out his plans because the host stuck like fire to his mouth. Only after he had told the bishop and been aided by his prayer did the host come free, whereupon the Jew converted. This too is a story of miraculous conversion, but this time the host itself plays an active role, albeit its appearance does not change. And once again there is a reminder of Jewish evil, for the Jew's intention before conversion was to throw the host in a privy. Indeed, when Geza of Tortona retold the story, he was more worried about the danger of profanation than eager for miraculous conversions, for he recommended that Jews be kept away from masses since they always tried to profane the host.

Another story frequently repeated during the Middle Ages came from the fourth-century *Life of St. Basil*. A Jew who had attended a mass out of curiosity saw a slaughtered small child in Basil's hand and found that the consecrated host he received was real flesh and that there was real blood in the chalice. Needless to say, he converted.[27] Radbertus of Corbie used this story in the ninth century to support his argument that Christ's historical body was really present in the Eucharist. For, as Radbertus explained, such miraculous transformations of the host into visible flesh and blood occurred to convince those who doubted that Christ was really present. The same intent is obvious in another story used by Geza of Tortona in the tenth century. A Jew whose conversion had been peculiarly difficult was confirmed in his new faith when, at his first communion, he saw a butchered body on the altar and blood on the hands of the priests.[28]

[26] Browe 1938: 34; Blumenkranz 1963: 191–2.
[27] Parkes 1969: 296; Browe 1926: 167; Browe 1938: 93–4.
[28] Blumenkranz 1963: 233–5.

Yet if ecclesiastics welcomed conversions, they were well aware that conversions were rare and that most Jews disbelieved and mocked Christianity, and from an early date Christian authorities took measures to protect Christian beliefs from Jewish disbelief and mockery. Thus in 538, the Council of Orléans ordered that Jews should not mingle with Christians during the Easter weekend. The prohibition was included in Ivo of Chartres's *Decretum* and was repeated by the IV Lateran Council of 1215, with the explanation that Jews poked fun at Christian grief during those days of lamentation.[29] But only in the thirteenth century was that protective measure extended to the holy sacrament itself. In 1266, to protect the tender shoot of Christianity in Poland, the synod of Breslau ordered Jews to stay in their houses with their windows shut whenever a procession of the sacrament of the altar passed their houses.[30]

We can be sure that Jews did indeed mock Christian beliefs openly so long as it was safe, and it seems probable that Jews often treated the material symbols of Christianity that came into their hands with similar or greater disrespect. In any case, some Christians believed they did. From an early date, there were scattered stories that Jews showed their contempt for Christianity by attacking pictures and other images of Christ, which then bled copiously to manifest their holiness and reveal the Jewish crime.[31] To protect such things from maltreatment, Charlemagne forbade ecclesiastics to let Jews get their hands on the precious objects of churches.[32]

During the four hundred odd years from 600 to 1000, however, there was little serious animus against Jews in most of western Europe, and what little there was emphasized their disbelief and mistreatment of Christian objects but not their mistreatment of the host. But after 1000, the new attention to the sufferings of the historical Jesus made the Jews' objection that such a miserable body could not be God a much more serious challenge, as is evident from the sudden rash of anti-Judaic polemics, as well as Anselm's *Cur Deus homo*. Moreover, the new image of the humanity of Christ and the preaching of the First Crusade gave new and deadly significance to the old charge that the Jews were killers of Christ, as the first great massacres of 1096 demonstrate.

Jewish disbelief was by no means the only challenge to Christian beliefs. As early as the first half of the eleventh century, small Christian movements had been questioning many prescribed beliefs, including belief in the real presence, and larger movements of this kind appeared in the first half of the twelfth century. By the middle of the century, Peter the Venerable was so worried about the various challenges to his beliefs that he devoted much labor to

---

[29] Blumenkranz 1960: 316–17; Grayzel 1966–89: I.308, no. X.

[30] Grayzel 1966–89, II.245, no. VI.

[31] Parkes 1969: 292–3; Browe 1926: 169–71.

[32] Blumenkranz 1960: 318–19.

combating them.[33] And since anyone who was now worried by disbelief was bound to think of Jews, Peter wrote perhaps the most careful of the many polemics against Jews that appeared in the twelfth century. He also repeated the charge that Jews mistreated ecclesiastical objects, asserting that the Jews treated the chalices that came into their hands in ways too shameful to describe.[34] Not surprisingly in that worsening atmosphere, stories of Jewish mistreatment of Christian objects multiplied, and by the beginning of the thirteenth century, both ecclesiastical and secular authorities forbade churchmen to pawn Christian objects such as books, vestments, altar-covers, or chalices to Jews.[35]

A much deadlier and thoroughly irrational accusation had also been developing in the second half of the twelfth century, an accusation that depended on the image of Christ's historical body and focused directly on human suffering. Jews were accused of showing their contempt and hatred, not by assaulting the material symbols of Christian worship, but by ritually crucifying Christian children as substitutes for Christ. Such stories spread, and by 1205 even the pope was prepared to believe that Jews in France were secretly murdering Christians.[36]

The beginning of the thirteenth century was a second watershed in the development of beliefs about Jews. Up to 1200, Jews had rarely appeared as protagonists in stories of host miracles.[37] When they did, the stories were usually the old ones I have already described; and their example inspired few new ones. By 1200, however, liturgical developments had made the moment of consecration ever more impressive;[38] theologians had devoted a century and a half of disputation to producing a refined argument that Christ was substantially present in the consecrated water; Innocent III was about to proclaim the dogma of transubstantiation; and the host was beginning to be venerated in a way that would engender the feast of Corpus Christi. Great attention was now focused on the host in and of itself.

Just how concretely sophisticated people could think of the host is apparent from a letter of Innocent III to the archbishop of Sens and the bishop of Paris in 1205. Innocent reported that he had heard, possibly from the archbishop of Sens, that when Christian wet-nurses for Jews received the body and blood of Jesus Christ at Easter, the Jews forced them to empty their milk in the latrine for three days. The pope therefore prohibited Christians from serving Jews as wet-nurses or servants.[39] What is interesting here is the

---

[33] See Langmuir 1990: 197–208.

[34] *The Letters of Peter the Venerable*, ed. Giles Constable (Cambridge, Mass., 1967), I.328–30.

[35] *Recueil des actes de Philippe Auguste*, ed. H. F. Delaborde *et al.* (Paris, 1916–79), II, no. 955; Grayzel 1966–89: I.300, 319, 320.

[36] Grayzel 1966–89: I.108.   [37] Browe 1938: 128–9.

[38] See Rubin 1991: 129–55.   [39] Grayzel 1966–89: I.114–16.

implication that even Jews believed there was more to the host than mere bread.

Eight years later, Innocent gave credence to another story about Jews that focused directly on the miraculous powers of the host itself and contained many elements that would later be incorporated in the stories about Jewish torture of the host. According to Innocent's letter of 1213, again to the archbishop of Sens,[40] a Christian servant of Jews in the archdiocese had converted to Judaism and now thought that the host was only bread. Since she feared punishment if she denied faith in Christ publicly, she went to church at Easter and received the Eucharist. Instead of swallowing it, she hid it in her mouth and brought it to the father of the Jewish household, saying, "Here is my Savior, as Christians assert." Interrupted by someone at the door, the Jew hid the host in a box which contained seven coins. When he returned and opened the box, he found it full, not of coins, but of wafers. He summoned his friends, who were amazed and persuaded by the miracle to convert.

His son Isaac, who was present, entrusted his wife and sons to the royal marchal, asked him to have them baptized, and left himself for Rome. Once there, he told his story to the pope, was instructed in the Christian faith by the bishop of Tusculum, and was baptized. Innocent explained to the archbishop of Sens that he was recounting what he had been told about all this because it was lovely to recount the wonders of God. Then he got down to practical business. He ordered the archbishop to encourage this tender new plant by ensuring that he and his family would not suffer materially from their conversion and would not bother the pope further on that account. In conclusion, Innocent ordered the archbishop to discover the full truth about the miracle and send it to him.

I would dearly love to know more about the events behind this letter. Unfortunately, our only evidence is the papal letter, but it is interesting enough. Although the archbishop of Sens may have given Isaac a short letter to ensure his access to the pope, it is clear that Innocent had not received a letter describing the events from the archbishop but was relying solely on Isaac the convert's dubious assertions. Nonetheless, the papal letter is direct evidence of what Innocent III, aided by the bishop of Tusculum, was willing to believe on the basis of suspect testimony just two years before he promulgated the dogma of transubstantiation in 1215.

Curiously enough, no French chronicle reports such a miracle, which makes it unlikely that whatever happened in or around Sens had made much of a splash locally. Our knowledge of what actually happened is therefore limited. What does seem clear and surprising is that Isaac traveled all the way to Rome to be baptized, leaving his wife and sons behind, instead of getting baptized at Sens, and then returned with a papal letter whose practical import was that the

[40] *Ibid.* I.136–8.

archbishop of Sens was to ensure that he and his family did not suffer materially. Solomon Grayzel suggested that Isaac might have concocted the whole pretty story to ensure that he and his family would not lose materially from conversion,[41] but that seems highly unlikely. Had Isaac's story been a complete fiction, it would have been challenged as soon as he returned to Sens. It seems much more probable that someone had encouraged Isaac to make the long trip to Rome, and there is an obvious candidate.

Peter of Corbeil, the archbishop of Sens, was annoyed by the presence of Jews for other reasons.[42] Moreover, Peter had been the future Innocent III's admired teacher of theology at Paris, and in return, Innocent had actively supported his friend's career thereafter.[43] We might therefore suspect that Peter's teaching about the Eucharist had influenced Innocent's conception of transubstantiation, and that both Peter and Innocent were much concerned to reinforce beliefs about the sacrament. Be that as it may, we know that by 1213 perhaps the most powerful pope of the Middle Ages was willing to believe that a Jew had received a consecrated wafer from a Christian maidservant and treated it in a strange way that produced a miracle, doubtless because that highly suspect story supported his convictions about transubstantiation.

Fortunately for Jews, the story had no further immediate effect. Though hostility against Jews was rising rapidly in northern Europe in the thirteenth century, though stories about Jewish profanation of Christian objects were recorded more frequently, and though Jews in Germany were being accused increasingly frequently of ritual cannibalism after 1235, Jews were not accused of torturing the host. Caesarius of Heisterberg and Thomas of Cantimpré reported many host miracles and stories about Christians who mishandled the host, and Thomas hated Jews and believed they committed ritual murder, yet neither Caesarius nor Thomas accused Jews of trying to torture the host.[44] By the end of the thirteenth century, however, Jews were being accused, not of profaning the host, but of torturing the body of Christ.

The turning point came in 1290. The official story, literally, the story legitimated by the "official" of the episcopal court of Paris,[45] asserted that a Jew in Paris had bought a consecrated host from his Christian servant for £10. On Easter Sunday, the Jew put it on a table, summoned other Jews, and said to them, "Aren't the Christians who believe in this host stupid?" The Jews then tried without success to destroy it with knives and other instruments. Finally one of the Jews struck the host with a large knife; the host broke into three parts; and blood kept streaming from it. When they placed the host in boiling water to destroy it, the host, by divine grace, turned itself into flesh and blood.

---

[41] *Ibid.* I.17.   [42] *Ibid.* I.144–5.
[43] Baldwin 1970: I.46, 118, 343.   [44] Browe 1938: 129.
[45] *Chronicon Johannis de Thilrode* in *MGH SS* XXV.578; Browe 1938: 130.

The miracle persuaded many Jews to convert, including John, the bearer of the letter of the official of Paris, and all his family.

The brief notice of these events in the *Grandes Chroniques* of Saint-Denis agrees closely with the official's account but ascribes the tortures only to the Jew who acquired the host. It adds that the Jew was charged with the offense, that the charge was proved before Simon Matifas of Bucy, bishop of Paris (1290–1304), and that, with the counsel and consent of the regents in theology and canon law, the Jew was publicly burned and his twelve-year-old daughter was baptized by the bishop.[46] The story circulated widely and soon came to the ears of the pope. By 1295, when Renier the Fleming, a rich citizen of Paris active in Philip IV's administration,[47] sought papal permission to build a chapel on the spot, Boniface VIII had been told that a Jew had cut a host with a knife and plunged it into boiling water and that the host had bled. Boniface believed the story and authorized the famous Chapelle des Billettes,[48] which was enlarged in 1299 thanks to a grant of Philip IV.[49]

There are obvious similarities and dissimilarities between the 1290 story and the story of 1213. The most obvious similarity is that in both a Jew gets a consecrated host from his Christian servant girl at Easter, that a miracle occurs that corroborates transubstantiation, and that it leads to the conversion of some Jews. But whereas in the 1213 story the disbelieving servant brings the host to the Jew of her own volition, in the 1290 story the Jew pays the girl in order to obtain a host. And whereas in the 1213 story it is the servant who ridicules the belief, in the 1290 story it is the Jew who mocks the stupidity of the Christian belief. It would thus seem that the Jew is being made the scapegoat for Christian disbelief. But the treatment of the host and its reaction in the 1290 story contradicts such an explanation. Whereas in the 1213 story the Jew does not attack the host, the host shows no signs of suffering, and no Jews are killed, in the 1290 story the Jew tortures the host in various other ways, the host demonstrates signs of human suffering, and the cruel Jew nonetheless continues to assault the host even after it has demonstrated supernatural qualities. He does not doubt; he believes he is attacking Christ.

A great change has occurred. The Jew is not accused of mere profanation of a symbol of the faith he rejected and despised; he is accused of intentionally torturing the true body of Christ. The Jew's hatred and cruel torture of Christ are even more heavily emphasized in a later, fuller, but more fabulous and highly untrustworthy account of these alleged events. It was composed no earlier than 1299, and probably later, apparently to glorify the Chapelle des

---

[46] *Les Grandes Chroniques de France*, ed. Jules Viard (Société de l'histoire de France; Paris, 1920–53), VIII.144–5.
[47] Jordan 1989: 193.
[48] Grayzel 1966–89: II.197.
[49] Bouquet *et al.* 1738–1904: XXII.33.

Billettes. In this account, the Jew, who is explicitly described as cruel, gets a host by promising an impoverished woman that he will return without charge the clothes she has pawned with him. The Jew then tortures the host and the miraculous events occur. The Jew's wife and sons are astounded and ask the Jew to stop torturing the host. But the Jew shows no compunction, not even when the host exhibits itself in the species of the body of the crucified Lord. This account even asserts that the Jew's son told Christians who were hurrying to church to adore the mystery of the holy body of Christ that they would seek their god in vain in the church, for their god – whipped, insulted, and mistreated – had just been killed by his father. The host is then recovered unharmed; the Jew's wife, son, and daughter and many others are converted; and the Jew is burned unrepentant, despite his claim that a book he had (presumably the Talmud was meant) would save him from burning.[50]

Versions of what had happened at Paris in 1290 were spread rapidly by travelers and mendicant preachers, but their impact varied. No massacres occurred in England, where royal government was strong and the king was about to expel the Jews from the kingdom.[51] Nor were there massacres in France, which was under the strong government of Philip IV. Although he too would expel the Jews from his kingdom in 1306, he disapproved of unauthorized initiatives against them.[52] Conditions in Germany, however, were very different. Central government was weak since the mid-century, particularly during the competition for the crown between Albert of Austria and Adolf of Nassau, which broke out into civil war in 1298; and fantastic accusations

---

[50] *De miraculo hostiae* in Bouquet *et al.* 1738–1904: XXII.32–3. This account is highly untrustworthy. It was written after the Chapelle des Billettes was well established and after the massacres committed on the basis of the similar accusations by Rindfleisch and his followers in Germany in 1298. It is also unbelievably embellished, presumably to enhance the reputation of the chapel. I therefore disagree with Jordan's reliance on it: Jordan 1989: 193–4. As stories of events were handed down, they were often embellished with accusations that only emerged later and were absent from the earliest accounts. For example, at the Council of Oxford in 1222, a deacon who had converted to Judaism was degraded and burned for his apostasy. Later on, however, a chronicler added that the apostate deacon had taken part in the ritual crucifixion by Jews of a Christian boy. By the end of the thirteenth century, another chronicler even alleged that the deacon had thrown the Lord's body in a privy! See Maitland 1911: 385–406. The accusations that Jews attacked the host at Lauda in 1202, at Belitz about 1247, and at Cologne in 1250 were similarly later embellishments of earlier accounts. See Browe 1938: 129 n. 3; Lotter 1988a: 533–83.

[51] The Annals of Worcester reported the event at Paris, including the execution, and linked it with Edward I's expulsion of the Jews. See *Annales Monastici*, ed. H. R. Luard (Rolls Series; London, 1864–9), IV.503.

[52] In 1288, thirteen Jews were burned at Troyes after an ecclesiastical investigation, allegedly for killing a Christian, and probably on the basis of a ritual murder charge, since it alone would have justified the ecclesiastical intervention. When Philip heard what had happened, he immediately prohibited any prelates or members of any religious order from seizing and punishing Jews without royal approval. Presumably, Philip was thinking primarily of inquisitors, particularly the Dominicans. See Jordan 1989: 190–1.

against Jews had been spreading widely in the second half of the thirteenth century.

The first ritual murder accusation in Germany, the new accusation of ritual cannibalism at Fulda in 1235, had attracted attention throughout Europe, wider attention than any previous ritual murder accusation.[53] Other accusations followed in Germany, and in 1287 another ritual murder accusation attracted wide attention. The Jews at Oberwesel were accused of ritually crucifying – or killing and taking the blood of – a Christian named Werner, soon known as the "good Werner." He was then buried at Bacharach, where miracles promptly occurred. The accusation incited a major massacre of Jews in the surrounding region, which was stopped by Rudolf I. The emperor fined the inhabitants of Oberwesel and Boppard for their participation, and the archbishop of Mainz preached that the whole thing was a fraud.

Nonetheless, work was begun in 1288 to enlarge the chapel of St. Cunibert, where the body was placed; and in the following year, prelates of the Roman curia granted indulgences to aid the project. The new altar of the chapel was consecrated in 1293 by the auxiliary bishop of Cologne, acting for the archbishops of Cologne and Trier, and an indulgence of forty days was granted to pilgrims to Werner's tomb. By the first decade of the fourteenth century, a ballad in Flemish testified to the spread of Werner's fame, and by 1320, the archbishop of Mainz had changed his mind about the alleged martyr, for he granted new indulgences for the chapel.[54]

Given this atmosphere, it is not surprising that news of the new host miracle in Paris found a receptive audience in Germany. As early as 1294, Jews were killed at Laa, Austria, for mistreating a host.[55] Then, in 1298, just when the civil war broke out, the accusation that Jews were torturing the host incited the so-called Rintfleisch persecutions "whose scale in breadth, violence, and the number of the victims threw even the massacres of the First Crusade in the shade."[56] At least 3,441 Jews were massacred in some forty-four places in Germany by Rintfleisch's band and other groups and individuals.[57] A generation later, between 1335 and 1338, as many as 6,000 Jews were massacred over a wide area by the so-called Armleder movement.[58]

It would be easy to think of the massacres as but another stage in the mounting hostility to Jews and to consider the host accusation as but another

[53] See Langmuir 1990: 263–81.
[54] Vauchez 1984: 492–4.
[55] *Continuatio Zwetlensis Tertia* in *MGH SS* IX.658. The brief account only tells us that Jews had stolen a host and were caught burying it in a stable. But it reports that a chapel was built on the spot, and we may suspect that there was more to the story that justified the building of the chapel than the chronicler tells us.
[56] Lotter 1988b: 389.
[57] *Ibid.* 422 and *passim*.   [58] Lotter 1988a: 560–71.

justification for attacks on Jews inspired by many motives: the desire to kill and loot; xenophobic hatred of those who scorned Christianity; the debtor's hatred of creditors; anger at the authorities who protected Jews and their lending; and the hatred of people who were believed to kill innocent Christians for ritual purposes. Viewed in this light, and with the expulsions from England and France in mind, the accusations of 1298 may seem no more than a pretext to eliminate Jews from German society – especially since the great Armleder massacres in 1336–8 and the massacres in 1348–9 during the Black Death demonstrate just how broad and deep the desire to eliminate Jews from Germany and Austria was.

Yet to consider the massacres of 1298 as no more than an expression of mounting hatred inspired by social, economic, political, and old religious motives avoids the whole question of why hatred of Jews was expressed so intensely in that year. It neglects the fact that what catalyzed the massacres was a novel accusation. As we have seen, miracle stories about the consecrated host and Jews had been available for centuries, but they had not occasioned massacres, not even when Jews were accused of profaning the host by contemptuous treatment. In 1298, however, Jews were accused of torturing Christ himself, and that accusation provoked the worst massacres yet.

One reason the new accusation was much deadlier than the old accusations of profanation of Christian objects or ritual murder was material. With rare exceptions, the material prerequisite for an accusation of ritual murder was the body of some young Christian whose killers or cause of death were unknown. But such bodies did not turn up every day or in many places at about the same time. Even when there was a body, it would be found in a particular place. And despite the fantasy that the place was chosen by a conspiracy that involved all Jews, and even though the hate inspired by the story might threaten Jews in surrounding communities, only the Jews on the spot could have done the killing, and only they were likely to be killed in revenge. Hosts, however, were everywhere and could easily be planted in Jewish houses anywhere, as apparently happened at Plukau.[59] Moreover, Jews in any place could be accused of obtaining hosts by various means and distributing them to Jews in other places, so that Jews in any place, even where no host had been "found," could be accused of torturing Christ. The host accusation could therefore be used to justify massacres in many places and in many places at one time.

What made the accusation so deadly, however, was its great psychological appeal for anxious Christians. How troubled many Christians were is evident from the extreme irrationality of the fantasy they so eagerly embraced. If Christians had been told for over two centuries that Christ was physically present in the host, they had also been told for centuries that Jews did not

[59] See Browe 1938: 162–6.

believe in Christ and thought that the host was only bread. Up to 1290, all the host miracle stories about Jews had taken for granted that Jews did not believe that the host became God, and that, if a miracle persuaded them to believe that it did, they promptly converted to Christianity and ceased to be Jews. Yet those who believed the new fantasy in 1298 suppressed all that knowledge of Jewish disbelief. They neither accused Jews of disbelief nor punished them as scapegoats for their own doubts. Just the reverse. In order to accuse contemporary Jews of acquiring hosts in order to torture Christ, people had to believe – or badly want to believe – that although the Jews were so evil that they refused to worship Christ, even they believed that Christ was physically present in the consecrated wafer!

If the irrationality of the fantasy is obvious, there remains the question of who was responsible. The basis of the fantasy was, of course, the belief that ecclesiastics had instilled for centuries that priests could and did make Christ physically present in the host. That belief was the foundation of their prestige and authority, and clerics of all sorts – preachers, theologians, and popes – had sought to strengthen it by impressive ritual, theological argument, and stories about the host miracles experienced by Christians and Jews. Yet the responsibility of ecclesiastics for the new fantasy should not be exaggerated.

The host miracle stories that clerics supported before 1290 were not primarily directed against Jews. They were intended to convince Christians, including clerics, of the real presence, and they did not incite any persecution of Jews. Moreover, even after 1290, although some clerics were involved in the killing of Jews on the basis of such stories, the higher ecclesiastical authorities did not demand a general persecution of Jews for their alleged crime. From the point of view of the clerical interest, what was essential was that these stories about changes in the host be believed; and for that there had to be Jews. The continuing presence of Jews in a state of degradation was far more useful for clerics than their destruction – as the papal bulls of protection had long indicated.

Moreover, the clerics who welcomed host miracle stories were not all hypocrites, motivated only by socio-political considerations. Most of them were concerned with their own salvation and believed that the Eucharist was necessary for it – even though some may have doubted that the host changed physically into Christ's body. They therefore welcomed host miracle stories, not simply as a reinforcement of their authority but also as a confirmation of their faith and their hopes for salvation. Julianna of Mount Cornillon's devotion to the Eucharist was not inspired by any desire to strengthen the position of the clergy.

In any case, whatever the precise role of some clerics of various ranks in 1298, the massacres were not a systematic persecution directed by clerics; they were the uncontrolled reaction of a vastly larger number of lay people, who were concerned with salvation in their own way. Belief in Christ's presence was as important for them as it was for most clerics. Although anti-clericalism was rising by 1298, most lay Christians believed – or badly wanted to believe – that Christ's body was really present in the bread they used ritually. Some even ran from church to church, not to participate in the mass, but to see the elevation of the consecrated host. But there were doubts among the laity as well as the clergy by 1298, doubts to which they responded, not with theological or metaphysical arguments or by relying on priestly authority, but by their actions.

The lay people who believed the new fantasy were not defending the clergy. Indeed, a fascinating feature of the new accusations about Jews is that they relegated priests to the background. Although the new fantasies take for granted that priests had consecrated the tortured hosts, in striking contrast to most of the earlier host miracle stories, Christ does not appear physically in the hands of a priest when he pronounces the words of consecration. Christ materializes in the hands of the Jews, and the words that create his appearance are the insults of Jews – or rather the accusations of lay Christians.

The reason the massacres of 1298 were so sudden, widespread, and deadly was that the fantasy appealed widely to many lay people who acted on their own initiative to satisfy their own needs and overcome their own doubts. What the laity believed about the host may have been prescribed by clerics, but the laity had their own hunger to believe. For centuries, they had believed what they had been told, that their god could save them and that supernatural power emanated from material objects, especially the host. But they interpreted what their priests had told them in their own way, and their religiosity was affected by their limited horizons and immediate fears and desires. And by the end of the thirteenth century, lay people in Germany had many reasons to be fearful and to hunger for reassurance.[60]

Though many motives, including worldly ambitions, may have impelled different elements of the population to attack Jews in 1298, the Jews were not accused of harming Germans physically or economically. The catalyst for the massacres was purely religious: "The body of Christ is being horribly tortured by the Jews." What impelled so many Christians to believe so flagrantly false a fantasy should now be clear. For centuries, miracle stories about the host had functioned to offset doubts about the belief that the host really became Christ's body. By the end of the thirteenth century, after so much attention had been focused directly on the host itself, the need to repress doubts had apparently become so acute that many people were willing to accept a fantasy that contradicted what, for excellent reasons, Christians had long taken for granted about Jews. And not only did many Christians entertain the fantasy as an idea;

[60] See Delumeau 1978.

they tried to make it seem concrete and real by massacring Jews by the thousands.

Except for the persecutions in the thoroughly abnormal conditions of the Black Death, the persecutions of 1298 and 1335–8 were the deadliest of medieval persecutions. What made them so deadly was that more and more people were now of two minds. On the one hand, people had non-rational beliefs which they were told were necessary for their salvation; on the other hand, more and more people were thinking ever more rationally about what they could observe. That divided thinking made many doubtful about some of the beliefs they had internalized. Despite the efforts of the Inquisition to suppress the doubters, doubts had increased and would increase until they surfaced again dramatically in Wyclif, Hus, and Luther.

For those who felt themselves in this double-bind, doubt could be agonizing. It drove some to the extreme irrationality of 1298. Unfortunately, the chroniclers, who give differing accounts of the events of 1298,[61] were more concerned to record the events that followed the accusations than to describe in any detail the miracle stories that initiated them. It is therefore difficult to penetrate below the surface of the events to detect what was troubling Christians so deeply. Doubtless there was considerable variety. Yet whatever the variety, we know that thoughts about Jews attacking the consecrated host were their common denominator.

I cannot analyze all the stories about the massacres here, but I will examine one of the fuller stories because it is such a fascinating illustration of the tensions in Christian religiosity I have been discussing. It comes from the collection of marvelous stories about miracles, prophecies, Jews, the devil, and ghosts compiled between 1284 and 1303 by Rudolf, prior of the Dominicans at Schlettstadt in Alsace. The collection is particularly interesting for anyone concerned with Jewish history, for eighteen of Rudolf's fifty-six stories involve Jews. Of these, only two are versions of the ritual cannibalism or blood libel fantasy, while twelve are versions of the host fantasy, particularly the stories that sparked the widespread massacres in 1298.[62]

The first story describes the host miracle that allegedly incited Kraft I of Hohenlohe to burn the Jews in his lordship of Weikersheim in 1298. According to the story, the Jews of Weikersheim had bribed a church custodian

---

[61] For an excellent analysis of the accounts, see Lotter 1988a.

[62] Rudolf von Schlettstadt, *Historiae Memorabiles*, ed. Erich Kleinschmidt (Beiheft zum Archiv für Kulturgeschichte, vol. 10; Cologne, 1974), pp. 3, 9–11, 16–17. Rudolf was prior around 1300, and so far as his stories refer to events or people that can be dated, they describe events that allegedly occurred between 1284 and 1303. Since his purpose was presumably to provide *exempla* that Dominicans could use in sermons for clerical or lay audiences, the collection is valuable as an illustration of the kind of folktales that were current then and that the Dominicans were disseminating.

to leave the church open. Then, on the night of Easter Thursday, the Jews entered the church, threw the consecrated hosts on the altar, and stabbed them. The purest blood flowed from the wounds, covering the hands of the Jews and splattering the ground, and from the host came the voice of Christ hanging on the cross. "Hely, hely lamma sabacthani?" The sound was so great that although – miraculously – the Jews could not hear it, others did, and the Jews were caught red-handed and burned.[63]

We can be sure those events did not happen because the flowing blood and the cries of suffering are simply too unbelievable, as is the idea that Jews would engage in such dangerous conduct. We must therefore conclude that all those who genuinely believed the fantasy were reacting irrationally. Yet if what they imagined about Jews was totally false, what they told each other expressed something real that was going on in their own heads. What was it? The manifest message, of course, was that they believed that Jews then and there were torturing Christ and that Christ was suffering as intensely as he had on the cross. But what were the latent messages?

To decode the fantasy, we must keep firmly in mind that the despairing cry, "My God, my God, why hast thou forsaken me?" occurred only in the imagination of those Christians. And since they chose to focus on that striking expression of anxiety, one latent message is obvious. We know that host miracles had functioned for centuries to offset doubts about the real presence. Since the fantasy made the host cry out that God had forsaken it, people who believed the fantasy could use it to express – in a socially acceptable way – their fear that God was not in the host, while at the same time they suppressed the fear at the conscious level by attributing the cry to the host itself and killing Jews. The cry could also express another and much deeper anxiety, fear of the absence of God.[64] By using it, people could express their fear that their god had left them, a fear they then tried to overcome by fantasizing that Christ was really present, not only in their minds, but physically in the host, and that – like them – he was suffering intensely here and now.

We will never know all we would like to know about the anxieties of those who believed the fantasy in 1298, but one general conclusion seems warranted. Christians believed that the physical suffering of their god was necessary for their salvation, and they had been taught that he was physically present in the Eucharist. But what could be observed on the altar was bread, and consciously or subconsciously many Christians doubted Christ's presence. Those who were afraid to acknowledge their doubts even to themselves repressed them. To overcome their anxiety, they retreated into irrationality and accused

---

[63] *Ibid.*, pp. 41–3. It should be noted that Kraft was heavily indebted to Jews.
[64] For a very different kind of analysis of the importance of the sense of an absence, see Certeau 1982: 107–21 and *passim*.

contemporary Jews of torturing their god. And they gave their fantasy reality by inflicting undeniably real and horrible physical suffering on thousands of Jews. What a slaughter of Innocents! What torture for Christ!

REFERENCES

Baldwin, John W. 1970 *Masters, Princes, and Merchants.* 2 vols. Princeton: Princeton University Press.

Blumenkranz, Bernhard 1960 *Juifs et chrétiens dans le monde occidental, 430–1096.* Paris: Mouton.
     1963 *Les Auteurs chrétiens latins du moyen âge sur les juifs et le judaïsme.* Paris: Mouton.

Bouquet, M. *et al.* 1738–1904 *Recueil des historiens des Gaules et de la France.* 24 vols. Paris.

Browe, Peter 1926 Die Hostienschändungen der Juden im Mittelalter. *Römische Quartalschrift für christliche Altertumskunde und Kirchengeschichte* 34: 167–97.
     1933 *Die Verehrung der Eucharistie im Mittelalter.* Munich: M. Hueber.
     1938 *Die eucharistischen Wunder des Mittelalters.* Breslau: Verlag Müller & Seiffert.

Burr, David 1984 *Eucharistic Presence and Conversion in Late Thirteenth-Century Franciscan Thought.* Transactions of the American Philosophical Society 74.3. Philadelphia: American Philosophical Society.

Bynum, Caroline Walker 1987 *Holy Feast and Holy Fast.* Berkeley, Los Angeles, and Oxford: University of California Press.

Certeau, Michel de 1982 *La Fable mystique.* Paris: Gallimard.

Cottiaux, Jean 1963 L'Office liégois de la fête-Dieu: sa valeur et son destin. *Revue d'histoire ecclésiastique* 58: 405–59.

Delumeau, Jean 1978 *La Peur en Occident, XIVe–XVIIIe siècles.* Paris: Fayard.

Forni, Alberto 1984 Maestri predicatori, santi moderni e nuova aristocrazia del denaro tra Parigi e Oignies nella prima metà del sec. XIII. In Sofia Boesch Gajano and Lucia Sebastiani, eds., *Culto dei santi: istituzioni e classi sociali in età preindustriale,* 459–70. L'Aquila: L. U. Japadre Editore.

Gransden, Antonia 1974–82 *Historical Writing in England c. 550 to c. 1307.* 2 vols. London: Routledge and Kegan Paul; Ithaca, N.Y.: Cornell University Press.

Grayzel, Solomon 1966–89 *The Church and the Jews in the XIIIth Century.* Vol. I, 2nd edn., New York: Hermon Press. Vol. II, ed. Kenneth R. Stow, New York: Jewish Theological Seminary in America; Detroit: Wayne State University Press.

Jordan, William Chester 1989 *The French Monarchy and the Jews.* Philadelphia: University of Pennsylvania Press.

Jungmann, Josef A. 1951–5 *The Mass of the Roman Rite.* Trans. Francis A. Brunner. 2 vols. New York: Benziger.

Langmuir, Gavin I. 1990 *Toward a Definition of Antisemitism.* Berkeley, Los Angeles, and Oxford: University of California Press.

Lotter, Friedrich 1988a Hostienfrevelvorwurf und Blutwunderfälschung bei den Judenverfolgungen von 1298 ("Rintfleisch") und 1336–1338 ("Armleder"). In *Fälschungen im Mittelalter,* 533–83. *MGH Schriften* XXXIII.5.

1988b Die Judenverfolgung des "König Rintfleisch in Franken um 1298." *Zeitschrift für historische Forschung* 15: 385–422.

Lubac, Henri de 1949 *Corpus Mysticum: l'Eucharistie de l'Eglise au moyen âge.* 2nd edn. Paris: Aubier.

Macy, Gary 1990a Berengar's Legacy as a Heresiarch. In Peter Ganz, R. B. C. Huygens, and Friedrich Niewohner, eds., *Auctoritas und Ratio: Studien zu Berengar von Tours,* 47–67. Wiesbaden: Otto Harrassowitz.

1990b Reception of the Eucharist according to the Theologians: A Case of Theological Diversity in the Thirteenth and Fourteenth Centuries. In John Apczynski, ed., *Theology and the University,* 15–36. Lanham, Md.: University Press of America.

1991 The Sources of Thomas Aquinas' Theology of the Eucharist. Paper read at the annual meeting of the Medieval Academy of America, 13 April 1991.

Maitland, Frederic William 1911 The Deacon and the Jewess; or, Apostasy at Common Law. In H. A. L. Fisher, ed., *The Collected Papers of Frederic William Maitland,* I.385–406. Cambridge: Cambridge University Press.

Parkes, James William 1969 *The Conflict of the Church and the Synagogue.* New York: Atheneum.

Pelikan, Jaroslav 1978 *The Christian Tradition,* III: *The Growth of Medieval Theology (600–1300).* Chicago: University of Chicago Press.

Rubin, Miri 1991 *Corpus Christi: The Eucharist in Late Medieval Culture.* Cambridge and New York: Cambridge University Press.

Troeltsch, Ernst 1931 *The Social Teaching of the Christian Churches.* Trans. Olive Wyon. 2 vols. New York: Macmillan (repr. 1949).

Vauchez, André 1984 Antisemitismo e canonizzazione populare; san Werner o Vernier (d. 1287) bambino martire e patrono dei vignaioli. In Sofia Boesch Gajano and Lucia Sebastiani, eds., *Culto dei santi: Istituzioni e classi sociali in età preindustriale,* 491–508. L'Aquila: L. U. Japadre Editore.

15   The holy and the unholy: sainthood, witchcraft and magic in late medieval Europe

Richard Kieckhefer

Dorothea von Montau was by any standards an extraordinary woman – but was she a saint, or was she a witch? A moot distinction, concludes the narrator of Günter Grass's novel *The Flounder*, since she lived in that infamous fourteenth century, an age "when witches as often as not doubled as saints."[1] With perhaps equal plausibility, J. K. Huysmans has a character in his novel *Là-bas* conclude that in the following century Gilles de Rais combined Satanic practices with a genuinely mystical spirit: "Now from lofty Mysticism to base Satanism there is but one step. In the Beyond all things touch. [Gilles] carried his zeal for prayer into the territory of blasphemy." "Unresponsive to mediocre passions, he is carried away alternatively by good as well as evil, and he bounds from spiritual pole to spiritual pole."[2]

The relationship between the holy and the unholy has long been familiar not only in literary but in historical and anthropological circles. Sainthood and witchcraft are sometimes seen as mirror images of each other, alike in their patterns of behavior yet reversing each other's values. (Indeed, when he set forth new procedures for canonization in 1642 Urban VIII was keenly conscious of the danger of mistaking witchcraft for sanctity.)[3] Alternatively, they are seen as somehow fusing with each other in a coincidence of moral opposites. In a provocatively rich and useful essay Gábor Klaniczay has suggested that the "two poles of the popular magical universe – the beneficial and the harmful, or the positive and the negative – have in fact always developed in relation to each other. They have borrowed elements from each other, they have reflected changes occurring in the opposite domain." He cites the saintly and prophetic women of the later Middle Ages, such as Joan of Arc, who "produced such

[1] Grass 1978: 12–13, 122–68. I am grateful to Barbara Newman, Aviad Kleinberg, Gábor Klaniczay, and the participants in Robert Bartlett's medieval workshop at the University of Chicago for their comments on this essay.
[2] Huysmans 1972: 52, 206.
[3] Woodward 1990: 225. See Thomas Aquinas, *Summa theologiae* II–II, q. 63. See the case of St. Gemma Galgani, to whom the devil came disguised as Jesus, tempting them to disobey the priest who served as her confessor; she resisted the temptation. For the details of her life see Germanus of St. Stanislaus 1913, and Amedeo 1935. I am grateful to Laura J. May for information on this case.

anxiety in the male world that their saintly position became ambiguous," and whose status "contributed to a renewed diabolization of the female sex in the same period." Klaniczay proposes that *maleficia* are "nothing other than inverted miracles," that descriptions of the witches' Sabbath can be seen as parallel to accounts of holy visions, and that possession is a counterpart to mystical ecstasy.[4]

The notion that witchcraft is the inverse of sainthood may seem neatly and perhaps even self-evidently correct. Indeed, the demonologists in the age of the witch-hunt emphasized that witchcraft was a deliberate inversion and mockery of orthodox religion.[5] The conception of witches as the embodiment of evil and thus the antithesis of good is common in many cultures.[6] But if the witch is the consummate embodiment of evil, surely she must contrast most starkly with the supreme embodiment of virtue, the saint. The witch is the anti-saint, and contrariwise the saint is the anti-witch – or so it is argued.

Let us return to Günter Grass and J. K. Huysmans. In Grass's imaginative portrayal it is not the historical Dorothea von Montau who appears, nor even the Dorothea of hagiography, but rather Dorothea as fictionally reconstructed in words ascribed to her husband. She was, he insists, a religious fanatic committed to ascetic and devotional extremes, but not at all to him and to their family. To be sure, later generations would venerate her as a saint, but from his perspective she was less a saint than a witch, having destroyed him and their children with her neglect and fanaticism. Yet he wavers in his judgment: he insists that if she had been put on trial he could have testified about her witchcraft, yet when ecclesiastical authorities do investigate her and ask about witchcraft he can provide no evidence. "True, she stirred the ashes of burnt coffin wood into her Lenten soups, but this she did as a reminder of man's frailty before the Lord God." The authorities too are uncertain; they ponder sending her to Rome as a pilgrim, hoping she will die en route, and when they agree to have her immured as an anchoress they fear that "by Satan's help" she may live longer than they expect. Ultimately the husband-narrator acknowledges that she is neither a saint nor a witch, but a woman seeking liberation from the duties of hearth and bed, although her society could only see her eccentricities in terms of sanctity or witchery – virtually interchangeable categories in her era, we are to believe.

In Huysmans's novel the main character is himself a novelist named Durtal, who throughout the book is immersed in research on the life of Gilles de Rais. He learns much about Gilles's alleged Satanism, and he concludes that Gilles must have been the fifteenth century's great embodiment of evil, as his

---

[4] Klaniczay 1990: 220–48.

[5] On this point see now especially, Clark 1977: 174–6.

[6] Mair 1969: 38.

comrade in arms Joan of Arc was the era's supreme representative of goodness. A friend of Durtal agrees: "Since it is difficult to be a saint, there is nothing for it but to be a Satanist. One of the two extremes." Elsewhere, however, Durtal is more nuanced and ambivalent in his judgment. He sees Gilles as a "true mystic," whom Joan of Arc stimulated to desire for the divine, although Satanism combined in his soul with this mystical bent.[7]

It might seem at first that Grass and Huysmans are arguing the same point: the difficulty of distinguishing between religion and magic, sainthood and witchcraft, the holy and the unholy. To be sure, they do both address this issue, yet from essentially different perspectives. Huysmans is concerned with the psychological question of how a single individual can in fact combine opposite tendencies and hold them in tension, not so much creative as destructive. He takes it as established fact that Gilles de Rais was both a mystic and a Satanist (*simul sanctus et peccator*, as it were), and he is concerned with the ambiguity inherent in the historical character. Grass's more complex novel deals with the subtleties of how events and personalities are diversely perceived and interpreted by contemporaries and by succeeding generations. For him, Dorothea was neither a saint nor a witch but a liberated woman *avant la lettre*, for whom the culture of the day had only the two opposed categories of saint-hood and witchcraft. His preoccupation is not with ambiguity in the character, but with ambivalence in the society. With Huysmans's Gilles de Rais we have a combination of sainthood and witchcraft, but with Grass's Dorothea we have merely a confusion of the two.[8]

In one important respect, however, Grass and Huysmans are at one in their view of saintly witchcraft: they both see sainthood and witchcraft as funda-mentally distinct in principle. If the people of fourteenth-century Prussia (as portrayed by Grass) cannot decide whether Dorothea is a saint or a witch, this is not because sainthood and witchcraft represent closely related shades of gray; it is, rather, because they cannot decide whether she and others like her deserve to be painted in white or in black. If Gilles de Rais (as recreated by Huysmans's novelist) attempts to combine in himself the extremes of mysticism and Satanism, these extremes do not thereby neutralize each other; rather, they coexist in a state of conflict and rend his soul asunder. Could it

---

[7] Huysmans 1972: 52–4, 108.

[8] Furthermore, Huysmans's fictional novelist Durtal shares much of the ambiguity that he ascribes to Gilles de Rais, and because of the ambiguity in his own character he finds himself fascinated yet repulsed (and at any rate romantically involved) with a flesh-and-blood succuba who leads him to a Black Mass, thus replicating in his own person the subject matter of his attention. The male character invented by Grass, on the other hand, is a timeless male, a figure of the Eternal Masculine, who marries a series of wives over the centuries and thus interacts with a dizzying array of female types without ever identifying with any of them. Instead, he represents that patriarchal society in which he is rooted, which casts its ambivalent gaze at a woman such as Dorothea.

be otherwise? *Prima facie* one must say no: sainthood and witchcraft are by definition extreme types of virtue and vice respectively, so that ambiguity can only arise when an individual attempts (no doubt madly and in vain) to combine the extremes, while ambivalence can only be empirical indecision about which extreme lies at hand.

This glimpse of these works of modern literature may seem a stalling tactic, or a digression en route to the real subject of this essay: sainthood, magic, and witchcraft as these phenomena actually related to each other in late medieval Europe, not as modern novelists imagine them to have related. When we turn from Grass's Dorothea to the Dorothea of history, we find that she was never really suspected of witchcraft, although three years before her death there was loose talk of her being a heretic.[9] As for Gilles de Rais, he may well have kept company with necromancers, but his mystical leanings came from Huysmans's imagination, and he seems never to have been in imminent danger of canonization.[10] Nonetheless, the fictional works of Grass and Huysmans help to define what is at stake. The possibilities of ambiguity and ambivalence suggested in their writing are crucial for historical inquiry.

Within the strictly historical sphere, the problem more often addressed is the relationship between magic and religion. Keith Thomas, for example, is interested not only in the extreme case of witchcraft, and not at all in the opposite extreme of sainthood, but most fundamentally in the relationship between magic and the ordinary practice of religion. Particularly in his survey of "The Magic of the Medieval Church," he finds religious practices so interwoven with magic as to be virtually indistinguishable from it.[11] What we will be considering here, the more specific relatedness of witchcraft and sainthood, is an extreme version of this broader problem.

While the relationship between the holy and the unholy could be studied in virtually any historical context, it was in late medieval Europe that it became a particularly important issue, partly because society was increasingly complex: rising lay literacy gave wider access to spiritual literature and exercises, and the proliferation of religious orders, societies, and movements brought with it an unwieldy assortment of folk whose multiform pious activities were met with equally manifold distrust. Perhaps never before in the history of Christianity – at least never since the heyday of the Gnostics in late antiquity – were there so many people distrustful of each other's pieties. What could be more natural in such a culture than suspicions, first whispered and then shouted aloud, that the pretense of sanctity was a mask for the worst worm of impiety?

[9] Stachnik 1978: 108ff (cf. 473ff). It is interesting to note that two of Dorothea's posthumous miracles involved the relief of bewitchment: *ibid.* 44, 455ff.

[10] The dossier has been translated by Hyatte 1984. Butler (1949: 100–10) summarizes the evidence and proposes that Gilles's company was using a Solomonic text for its rituals.

[11] Thomas 1971: 25–50.

Sainthood and witchcraft: empirical confusion and conceptual conflation

There were indeed cases in which late medieval society found it difficult to determine whether a person was a witch or a saint. Apart from Joan of Arc, who was ultimately burned not as a witch but as a heretic,[12] other figures in late medieval Europe had reputations wavering between these extremes. Ursulina da Parma, for example, believed she had a divine mandate to reconcile the competing papacies during the Great Schism, but at one point she was accused of using *magica aut superstitiosa ars* and *maleficia diaboli*.[13] Magdalena Beutler "suffered great agony and illness for a long time; and in spite of the severe pain that she suffered, she spared her tender, virginal body not at all ... Her holy, blessed life was scoffed at and denied by many sinful people, and it was often taken as a sign that she was a sorceress." Colomba da Rieti too was accused of being not a saint but a *fattuchiera*, and her confessor an enchanter.[14]

Even in late antiquity, as Peter Brown has noted, confusion might arise at times between saints and magicians. There is evidence for this in Jerome's biography of St. Hilarion,[15] and Brown suggests that it may be more than coincidence that the sorcerers of popular Christian romance share their names with the great bishop-saints Cyprian and Athanasius. "The contrast between the saint is not that the saint commands the demons while the sorcerer is their agent: both can command; but the saint has an effective 'vested' power, whereas the sorcerer works with a technique that is unreliable and, above all, cumbersome."[16]

But we know more about the circumstances attending certain late medieval saints than about the immediate context for these particular figures of late antiquity. Suspicion of witchcraft might arise from inexplicable misfortune, as in the case of Eustochio da Padua, a fifteenth-century nun (1444–69). Eustochio's story is particularly instructive, and worth tracing in some detail.[17] She was the daughter of a nun, brought up from age four in her father's house and ill treated by her stepmother. Before long she became obsessed or

---

[12] On her trial see Jones 1980 and Kelly 1993. For the issues entailed in her proceedings see Christian 1981: 188–203.
[13] Simon de Zanaccis 1865: 727 (*Vita*, 1.25). Her response was "Maleficiis diaboli non utor, sed beneficiis Domini nostri Jesu Christi pro animarum salute fungor."
[14] Petroff 1986: 354; Bell 1985: 156.
[15] St. Jerome 1952: 258–60. The stories told here demonstrate the saint's power *against* magicians; for another such case see Paulinus 1952: 44–5 (*Life* ch. 6). See also Galatariotou 1984–5: 55–94.
[16] Brown 1970: 17–45.
[17] In this account I follow Thurston 1926: 134–48, who evaluates and summarizes the sources for the case. I have also consulted Cordara 1768. Dinzelbacher (1990: 42–4) deals briefly with the story.

possessed by the devil, who tormented her, whisked her through the air, and caused her to become intermittently ill tempered and refractory, although she was well behaved at other times. By age six she was returned to the convent where she had been born; there she spent nine years as a model of piety, even though her demonic obsession did not wholly cease. The convent in general, however, was known for its laxity. When Eustochio was sixteen the abbess died and the nuns intended to elect a successor who would permit them to continue in their accustomed ways, but the bishop insisted that the convent be reformed before a new abbess was elected. The nuns abandoned the house, and the bishop instated a new community with more observant nuns, with Eustochio as the only continuing resident. When she asked to be received into the religious life as a novice a year later, the newly established reformed nuns were reluctant to accept her, viewing her as a reminder of the convent's previous state, and fearing that her exposure to the earlier laxity might have corrupted her. The bishop, however, overruled the nuns and had her received into the community. Soon afterward the diabolical assaults resumed: her pious conduct was interrupted by intervals of unruly and disobedient behavior, and eventually she became straightforwardly possessed, howling and gnashing her teeth, contorting her face, writhing like a snake, bouncing about into the air, and rushing at the nuns with knife in hand. Exorcism did not provide a lasting cure, and when the nuns bound her for several days to a pillar she shrieked uncontrollably and felt the devil torture her, with attempts to draw out her intestines and to strangle her. Eventually, however, the condition abated and she resumed her normal functions in the convent.

The next stage in the case came when the abbess was struck with a strange disease that left the physicians baffled. The nuns discovered "certain super-stitious objects" in a corner of their house and concluded that Eustochio had poisoned or bewitched the abbess as revenge for her mistreatment during the possession. Soon the rumor spread outside the convent, and people crowded outside demanding that she be burned alive for sorcery. She was locked in a dark and tiny cell, with no possessions, with an intermittent supply of bread and water to sustain her, and with unsympathetic nuns to guard her. Her confessor protested this treatment, but when he visited with her she confessed that she was indeed guilty of using powerful magic against the abbess, having learned such diabolical arts from the earlier members of the convent. The confessor refused to believe this confession, and the next day she retracted it; she said she had many failings and deserved greater suffering than she had experienced, but disclaimed any thought of using magic. Nonetheless, the nuns refused to lighten her treatment until the abbess herself recovered and developed doubts about the convent's proceedings.

The abbess now proposed that Eustochio simply leave the convent, but she declined to do so, saying that she was not as miserable as she might seem, indeed when she entered religion she expected to suffer as Christ did. She stayed on as a peripheral member of the community, and her possession recurred: at one point the nuns heard her screaming in a locked room, and when they broke through the door they found her lying on the floor with marks suggesting the devil had tried to strangle her. When one of the nuns appeared (falsely, as it happened) to be suffering from the plague, Eustochio was assigned to care for her, and under these circumstances the two women became friends, although the other nuns still refused contact with Eustochio. The devil continued to torment her; he is reported to have scourged her with metal-studded cords and slashed her with a knife, dragged her to the door of the convent, lifted her into the air and let her fall, bound her with cords, placed a haircloth against her skin, crushed her head and immersed it in frigid water, attempted to destroy her health with tainted water and poisonous oil, caused her to vomit blood, made her feel intense heat, and given her the sensation of being chopped to pieces. (Although all this abuse is reported as the devil's work, comparison with young self-mutilating women in modern society is surely not irrelevant.)[18] We are told that when the devil raised her to a high roofbeam and threatened to cast her down if she did not consign her soul to him, she came safely down only when her confessor arrived and performed an exorcism. Seeing her subject to these assaults, and reassured by her virtuous behavior during calmer intervals, the nuns eventually became more sympathetic and allowed her to make solemn profession at age twenty-one.[19] Within two years, however, her seizures and lacerations brought her to a chronic bedridden state, in which she impressed those about her with her piety in illness and under continued diabolical affliction. By the time she died in 1469, she was recognized as a holy woman; the name of Jesus was discovered inscribed on her breast, and her demise was accompanied by miracles and apparitions.

Eustochio's story parallels interestingly that of Elizabeth Knapp in seventeenth-century Massachusetts: both vacillated between turbulent demonic possession and placidly submissive good conduct, both were suspected of being complicit with the devil and not merely victims, both seem ultimately to have been cleared of that suspicion, both wavered between confession and recantation, both had early childhood experience of being shamed by the misconduct of an adulterous father and abused in a dysfunctional household, and both were relegated to dubious havens into which they could not be fully incorporated as natural members. It is tempting to apply to Eustochio the diagnosis John Putnam Demos has suggested for Knapp: a

---

[18] McClory 1986: 29–38.

[19] Thurston adds, "though they probably all felt very jumpy and wished her a hundred miles away, they were at bottom really good women, even if they could not readily lay aside the prejudices of the times in which they lived and of the surroundings in which they had been brought up."

narcissistic personality, stemming from lack of nurture in early childhood, and manifesting itself in culturally conditioned exhibitionism, dependency, and anger.[20] Perhaps most basically, one could say that both these young women were demanding recognition as victims while at the same time fearing that they deserved their misfortune. Eustochio's case was in one important way more complicated than Knapp's: she was herself simultaneously the fruit both of her father's misconduct and of breakdown in the monastic system, and thus she was an embarrassment both to her original family and to the surrogate family to which she was entrusted. For our purposes, however, there are more important differences in the way her role became construed. The Puritan culture of New England knew well about the collective role of "the saints," but not about individual sainthood as a state that could be confused with either possession or witchcraft. This ambiguity was present in late medieval Europe, and it goes far toward explaining Eustochio's peculiar mixture of fortune and misfortune. Also of critical importance was the loyalty of Eustochio's confessor, who probably played a complex role for her as surrogate father, foil in the acting out of her crisis, and main interpreter of her state, like the parson in whose house Knapp resided. While Knapp's surrogate father eventually became alienated from her, Eustochio's confessor seems to have remained remarkably consistent in his sympathy and support for her.

While in Eustochio's case the renown for sanctity followed her earlier notoriety, the sequence of events was reversed in the life of Magdalena della Cruz, a Franciscan nun of sixteenth-century Spain (1487–1560). After decades of ecstasies, visions, prophecies, mortification, stigmata, levitation, miraculous cures, and inedia, Magdalena found herself accused of falsifying her experiences. Exorcised and interrogated by an inquisitor, she confessed that her holiness was not merely a fraud but a demonic ruse. When she was five years old a demon named Balban had come to her disguised as an angel and in other holy forms, deceiving her and enabling her to deceive others with feigned sanctity. At last he had revealed himself to her in his own bleak colors and demanded that she enter a pact with him as the condition for continuing to enjoy her renown. She had consented. Having confessed all this, she recanted, then confessed again and was condemned to life imprisonment.[21]

The cases of Eustochio and Magdalena demonstrate the role both of the community and of the accused in deciding the outcome of a contested case. It would be easy enough to posit some psychological origin for both of these cases. A psychoanalyst, for example, might take them as classic cases of those complementary mechanisms that have been seen to underlie other mystical

[20] Demos 1982: 97–131.
[21] Lea 1907: 82–3, drawing from Bibliothèque Nationale, fons espagnol, MS 354, fols. 248–69; Campan 1862–83; and other sources. See Dinzelbacher 1900: 44–5.

phenomena: female hysteria and male obsession. The behavior under interpretation is analyzed as hysterical in origin; the fear and suspicion regarding this behavior is said to be inspired by male obsession with fantasies about the ideal and the transgressive female.[22] However useful or problematic such analysis may be elsewhere, it has little explanatory value in the present cases, not only because it abstracts too much from the interpretive systems of the women's cultures, but also because both Eustochio and Magdalena were originally accused not by men but by other women within their convents. Eustochio was suspected by her fellow nuns of bewitching the abbess, and it was when an opponent of hers became abbess that Magdalena was first charged with feigning her sanctity. The men who entered into each of these cases did play crucial roles, but their stances cannot be categorized simplistically as obsessive, especially since Eustochio's confessor remained sympathetic toward her and did not share the nuns' suspicions. Both women confessed their guilt and later recanted, perhaps because their confessions had been extorted from them, but perhaps because they, like Birgitta of Sweden and other women of mystical proclivities, were themselves terrified at the possibility of demonic deception. But to say that the mystics could themselves be uncertain about their own experience is of course not to say (with Huysmans's Durtal) that they embraced both possibilities, demonic as well as divine. It is, rather, to admit that the ambivalence of the society might be internalized.

The model that works better in these cases, then, is that which Grass proposes. Eustochio and Magdalena were, like Dorothea, women whose aspirations to sanctity evoked a mixture of adulation and distrust. They were caught in a trap particularly dangerous for a holy nun: their life of apparent sanctity in the convent was at least an implicit reproach to those who took their vows and their devotions far less seriously. Essentially the same phenomenon might at times be observed outside the cloister as well. A woman such as Margery Kempe, for example, most often met disdain when she reacted with conspicuous devotion precisely in those places (such as a church, or on Golgotha itself) where bystanders might well consider themselves reproached for lack of spiritual fervor.[23] In Margery's case, as in Dorothea's, the danger was not being burned as a witch but being mistaken for a heretic.

In such cases there was no doubt a coalition of opponents, each of whom may have been motivated in part by some combination of conscious and unconscious ulterior motives; such motives, if they existed, no doubt differed from one member of the coalition to another. Yet none of these factors could lead to action without a legitimating appeal to theological principle which

---

[22] Freud 1959: 143, cited in Mitchell 1974: 90 and 112. I am grateful to Jennifer Ash for calling this material to my attention.

[23] See especially Kempe 1985: 105ff (*Book of Margery Kemp* 1.28).

could plausibly be made to fit the circumstances. The nuns who accused Eustochio of witchcraft did not convince others because the category of witchcraft did not fit the case: the abbess's recovery cast doubt on the allegation of sorcery, and while Eustochio's chronic possession might indeed link her to the devil it did not plausibly suggest that she was in league with him. The new abbess who accused Magdalena of false sanctity served as the channel for hostility within the monastic community; what the inquisitor did was to provide a theological rationale for reinterpreting Magdalena's behavior and for punishment. Neither element in this coalition – neither the hostile nuns nor the inquisitor who legitimated their hostility – would alone have sufficed for this reinterpretation.

The difficulty was compounded in cases of this sort because the communities that judged these women claimed to be judging objective qualities inherent in the women, while in fact what they were judging was their own relationship to the women. The judgment was essentially intersubjective but was treated as if it were objective. Pierre Deloz has reaffirmed the traditional notion that "one is never a saint except *for other people*,"[24] and the same is true of witches. To be sure, specific acts of heroic virtue and of *maleficium* are actually performed, but they are defined as such by the culture and recognized as such by the society, and the way they fit into a pattern of conduct – whether a person is sufficiently virtuous to qualify as a saint, or so fundamentally evil as to be branded for witchcraft – is a question the society must adjudicate. In ambiguous cases the community uses formal or informal tests to decide what will be taken as objective fact, but in the most difficult cases, where there is strong evidence for both verdicts, what these tests serve to establish is the way the community chooses to relate to the exceptional individual. The nuns of Padua decided, finally, that Eustochio was a holy woman; in Magdalena's case the ultimate judgment was less propitious, and the key factor was almost surely her lack of a strong clerical supporter.

When contemporaries of a potential saint were called upon to state their judgment, they clearly had categories other than sainthood and witchcraft from which to choose. Aviad M. Kleinberg, who more than any other historian has shown how such judgments were made in their microhistorical contexts,[25] has called attention to the interesting case of Marcolino da Forli. Marcolino was a simple Dominican, and when he died in 1397 it did not occur to his fellow Dominicans that he might have been a saint. At his burial, however, the church was crowded with people who protested, "You want to bury a saint in secret!" His devotees told how he had healed one man's hand, how a person had been stirred to repentance by a vision of Marcolino, how he had displayed great powers of prophecy by predicting hidden and future things. None of

[24] Delooz 1983: 194.   [25] Kleinberg 1992.

this testimony impressed the friars, who saw Marcolino as something of a simpleton with a tendency to doze off during mass and at meals. Besides, there were alternative explanations of his wonders: even during his life he had been said to predict the future not by prophecy but by divinatory art, and when he healed a man's hand he had employed some herb. The patient rejoined that the herb was of itself insignificant; humbly wishing to conceal the divine power at his command, Marcolino had simply plucked a herb at random and pretended that it was the healing agent. Eventually the friars had to allow veneration of their new *beatus*, although a compromise was reached: Marcolino was to be recognized as an exemplar of simple humility, not as a wonder-worker.[26]

In most instances the testimony that we have regarding prospective *beati* and saints comes from people already predisposed to recognize their extraordinary deeds as miraculous. To the extent that the *processus canonizationis* and *vitae* mask uncertainties, it was probably the case of Marcolino far more often than that of Eustochio da Parma that was replicated. Even Pope Celestine V, canonized under his lay name Pietro di Morone, was asked to recite healing charms on behalf of his devotees, to which he courteously replied that this was not his *métier* but that he would bless them instead.[27] The alternatives most likely to arise were not whether a person was a saint or a witch, but rather whether an alleged saint was in fact an ordinary Christian capable of using natural magic for healing and divination.

If the relationship between witchcraft and sainthood was sometimes difficult to disentangle on the plane of empirical fact, one might suppose that this was because of some underlying conceptual similarity between the two phenomena – not simply an accidental similarity, such as might lead to merely careless confusion, but a deeper and more systematic correspondence, a mirror-imaging between witchcraft and sainthood. Thomas Aquinas and the authors of the *Malleus maleficarum* shared the belief that the demonic hierarchy was a sinister inversion of the angelic prototype,[28] and it is possible to represent witchcraft as an exact phenomenological reversal of sainthood. How far this model can be applied within medieval European culture, however, is a question we must explore.

Citing cases such as those of Eustochio da Padua and Magdalena de la Cruz, Peter Dinzelbacher has recently compared witchcraft with the specifically mystical sanctity of the later Middle Ages.[29] He suggests a close parallel between the holy and the unholy, with one as indeed the mirror-image of the

---

[26] Kleinberg 1989: 183–95 and 1992: 31–6. Kleinberg draws upon the account by Giovanni Dominici.

[27] Vauchez (1981: 521) suggests that Pietro did not wish to be seen as a sorcerer. See the further discussion of Celestine in Kieckhefer 1994: 816 n. 14.

[28] *Summa theologiae* 1.109.1; Krämer and Sprenger 1928: 28–31 (*Malleus maleficarum* 1.4).

[29] Dinzelbacher 1990: 49–59.

other. His parallels can be divided into six general categories.[30] First of all, both saints and witches had privileged relationships with their deities (the devil being conceived here specifically as a sort of anti-God), who appeared to them in human form. In both cases the relationship could have a pronouncedly erotic element, and saints as well as witches were capable of supernatural pregnancy. Secondly, both made a quasi-juridical pact with their deity (Dinzelbacher reports seventy-seven medieval and modern cases of mystical betrothal to Christ, which he sees as corresponding to the witches' pact), and in both cases the pact might be sealed with a physical sign (the stigmata in one case, the devil's mark in the other). Thirdly, both were subject to supernaturally inflicted pains: mystics such as Dorothea von Montau experienced physical as well as inward agony, and witches found themselves beaten and tortured by their demons. Fourthly, saints as well as witches performed magic, sometimes in similar ways. For example, Blessed Sperandea da Gubbio urged a man to relinquish a woman he had abducted. When he refused, she cursed him with the words, "May the judgment of God come upon you, by the witness of Christ," and when he grew ill he recalled these words and complied with her command. The incident counted as evidence for her sanctity, but under slightly different circumstances might have marked her as a sorceress. Fifthly, both saints and witches encountered their deity at a feast – Dinzelbacher finds a parallel to the Sabbath in Francesca da Roma's vision of a verdant meadow on which people with bright clothes and garlands danced and sang in honor of the Lamb – and if witches could fly through the air en route to this feast, saints too could levitate. Finally, both saints and witches were keenly attentive to the Eucharist, whether for the mystical graces it imparts or for the magical powers ascribed to it. Noting that mystical sanctity and concern with witchcraft arose in European culture at roughly the same time (a proximity which he perhaps exaggerates),[31] Dinzelbacher suggests that they represent a common phenomenon: a sense of awe regarding unfamiliar spiritual powers.

Dinzelbacher has performed a great and useful service in laying out this schema, pressing the mirror-image theory as far as it can reasonably go. But while some elements in his schema are convincing, few of the paired categories are sufficiently interchangeable to have been the source of empirical confusion. The stigmata may have a certain functional similarity with the devil's mark, but there is no indication that one was ever mistaken for the other. The punitive miracles of the saints do at times resemble the curses of witches, and witches

---

[30] This is my own clustering of the categories, not Dinzelbacher's.

[31] Mystical sanctity had surely started to become a significant factor in European monasteries before the end of the twelfth century, and by the fourteenth it was already long established. If one discounts the forged evidence of Etienne-Léon de Lamothe-Langon, the kind of witch accusations that Dinzelbacher speaks of did not become a real concern in Europe until the fifteenth century.

may on rare occasions mimic the saints more closely: Dorothea Hindremstein, for example, was said to have used a magic ritual to multiply grain and feed ten people.[32] But whether Francesca da Roma's celestial vision resembles a Sabbath is less clear. The saints' avid craving for the Eucharist may arise out of the same sense of awe at the miraculous real presence that underlies magical use of the consecrated host, but that awe surely expresses itself in fundamentally different ways in the two contexts. The inner afflictions of the mystic might be confused with the torments of an energumen, but not with the literal pummelings of the devil at the Sabbath. Saints and witches might both fly, but the correspondence is at most a limited one; levitating saints did not usually fly to distant places, much less to assemblies nocturnal or otherwise.[33]

Even the delusions of pseudo-saints did not usually correspond very closely to the alleged experiences of witches. The apparitions that saints enjoyed might be construed as demonic illusions, but that does not in itself make them equivalent to the ways in which the devil appears to his witches: Satan may take on both the form of an angel of light and the form of an incubus, but these options did not lend themselves readily to confusion.

Furthermore, Dinzelbacher indiscriminately mingles phenomena that are central and routine with others that are peripheral and occasional. Thus, most saints perform miracles (though relatively few miracles *in vita* are punitive), and many female mystics experience a spiritual betrothal, but mystical pregnancy and visions of celestial dancing are less common. The Sabbath and flight through the air are basic to the mythology of witchcraft, but use of the Eucharist is incidental. The argument would work more effectively if the phenomena were weighted similarly on both sides of the chart, but they are not: the witches' pact and slight to the Sabbath, for example, are more fundamental to the mythology of witchcraft than spiritual betrothal and levitation are to mystical sanctity.

Nonetheless, Dinzelbacher has called attention to certain elements of both mythologies that are well worth noting. In particular, the areas of experience he highlights are areas that carry a strong emotional charge, positive or negative, often ambivalent, serving as fertile ground for fantasy: sexual intercourse and childbearing, exuberant festivity, release from the constraints of gravity, and (particularly a source of awe within later medieval culture) contact with God himself in the Eucharist. Even if sainthood and witchcraft are not so closely similar that they easily or normally lend themselves to confusion, it is nevertheless true that they both arise out of religious (or demonic) interpretation of those areas of life that are most deeply meaningful and call for imaginative

---

[32] Hoffmann-Krayer 1899: 33–9.   [33] Loomis 1948: 45–50.

symbolic representation. Dinzelbacher's typology of such representations is an important contribution toward an understanding of both phenomena.[34]

Much more might be said, to be sure, about parallels in the way saints and witches are perceived by their contemporaries. Gábor Klaniczay has shown important structural parallels in the way people tell stories about miracles and bewitchment.[35] In terms of social geography, too, there are interesting parallels: Robert Muchembled has written about women in early modern France who were perceived as sorceresses in their own villages but honored as healers by outsiders,[36] and holy men and women too are sometimes more easily recognized as saints by those outside their own milieu.[37] In both cases, however, what we have are mechanisms that apply to both sainthood and witchcraft – not factors challenging the distinction between these phenomena.

We would come closer to the heart of our inquiry by speculating about the psychological connections between cathexis and obsession, between the strong emotional bonding between devotee and saint on the one hand and the strong emotional repulsion that leads one person to accuse another of witchcraft. To be sure, a saint once established as such evokes routine and merely conventional devotion from many, but the onset of the cult (unless it is fundamentally political) presupposes the intense devotion of at least a small band of followers. The observer, as well as the saint and the witch, are emotionally charged figures in the relationship; if there is an appropriate analogy, it is not that of iron drawn to a magnet, but of two magnets acting on each other either to attract (in the case of the saint and the devotee) or to repel (in that of the witch and her victim or accuser).

To summarize, then, the argument made thus far: sainthood and witchcraft as defined in late medieval Europe might indeed be antithetical phenomena, but if they mirrored each other it was in non-systematic ways, and by virtue of their common focus on areas of life that are deeply charged with emotion and symbolic meaning; there was some possibility of mystical sainthood and diabolical deception being confused with each other, but the idea that sainthood and witchcraft could be combined is a literary fiction only; and even the confusion of these phenomena was dangerous to the prospective saint only

---

34 Gustav Henningsen (1990: 208–9) has formulated a similar set of inverse correspondences between the "white sabbath" or the "Italian fairy cult" and the "black sabbath" described by demonologists.

35 See especially Klaniczay 1992a. Klaniczay's unpublished and ongoing work will develop the analysis further, in important and interesting ways, and will discuss the ways late medieval society applied a dual classification system to women perceived as having extraordinary power; in some cases he cites, women were suspected not so much of witchcraft (with veneration of the devil and *maleficia*) but of demonic deception in simpler forms.

36 Muchembled 1979.

37 For two examples see Kieckhefer 1984: 31 and 42–3.

when she encountered a coalition of enemies who could add theological justification to communal hostility.

The transvaluation of the necromancers

The perspective alters radically, however, if we turn to another area of inquiry, the explicitly demonic magic of the necromancers (or "nigromancers," as the term often appears in late medieval texts). Demonic magic might be seen as essentially irreligious, but it is clearly not unreligious. It operates as a type of religious practice, calling upon spirits and paying them homage in return for favors. From the viewpoint of orthodoxy, demonic magic is of course a perversion of religion, but even to be that it must fall within the realm of religion. But does this mean that its practitioners thought of it as in any sense holy? Extravagant as it may seem, I wish to suggest that the necromancers of late medieval Europe who stood within magic circles invoking demons with the power of God's names and with other sacred ritual did indeed conceive their activity as holy, and that we have here the most real and most interesting fusion of the holy with the unholy.

Parallels can easily be found elsewhere in the history of magic. The magical papyri that have survived especially in Egypt, as well as the texts used in ancient Jewish magic, contain the same kind of interpenetration of the holy with the unholy, and it was not for nothing that early Christian writers had to ponder (in effect) what Jerusalem had to do with Alexandria. In medieval Europe there was similar precedent in the practical Kabbala, and in the Arabic astral magic upon which necromancy drew.[38] These parallels may themselves be difficult to account for, but their proliferation among the loosely defined and weakly disciplined elites of various traditions should at least temper our surprise at finding the phenomenon in late medieval Europe.

Here again fictional sources may serve as a useful starting point for inquiry – but this time medieval rather than modern fictions. What is most remarkable is that the invocation of demons could at times be presented as morally unproblematic even in sources otherwise deeply concerned with moral questions. The fifteenth-century story of Mary of Nijmegen, an extended exemplum ascribed to Anna Bijns, tells of "a holy priest called Sir Gilbert" whose niece is abducted by a suspicious stranger, all too veritably a devil. At one point she remarks to her companion: "Necromancy, that is a fine art. My uncle knows a lot about it, and sometimes he does marvels which he gets out of a book. I do not think that he has ever failed. They say he can make the devil crawl through a needle's eye, whether he likes it or not." But the devil refuses to teach her that art, and shortly

[38] See Betz 1986; Conybeare 1899; Morgan 1983; Ambelain 1951 and 1984; and Savage-Smith 1980.

explains to the audience the grounds of his reluctance: "If she had learned necromancy, the danger would be in case she were to call up all hell and put them in danger, and even to exercise her powers over me if she chose, or get me into some tight place. I teach her necromancy? Not likely!'[39] At no point is the uncle's holiness challenged on the grounds of his conjuring, nor are his motives impugned – or even explained.

Something similar occurs in the Cistercian *Quest of the Holy Grail*. A hermit is lamenting the fate of a companion, who, having "served Our Lord most faithfully over thirty years," has just died while wearing a soft white shirt in violation of his monastic rule. Fearing that the renegade has gone to hell, the hermit proceeds to conjure the devil in hopes of reassurance:

The good man went into his chapel then to fetch a book and a stole which he put round his neck, and on his return he set about conjuring the enemy. He had been reading the invocation for some while, when he looked up and saw the enemy before him in such hideous guise that the stoutest of hearts would have quailed at the sight of him.

The fiend, much like the shade of Samuel brought back by Saul (I Sam. 28: 15), grumbles that he is cruelly plagued, but does indeed reassure the hermit, telling him that his friend died innocently and has been saved.[40] At no point does either the hermit or the narrator feel obliged to explain why a holy man with profound scruples about fidelity to the habit has no scruples whatever about conjuring demons. How could these authors relate their tales without betraying the slightest *frisson* of disapproving horror? In part, at least, because real necromancers clearly and explicitly conceived their art as a holy one.

When people were accused of necromancy, the charges may well at times have been false, but the survival of necromantic materials suggests that someone was engaged in such practices, and the finger of suspicion points most clearly to members of what I have called a "clerical underworld," who possessed the requisite command of Latin and of ritual forms entailed in necromancy, and whose ordination itself (to orders including that of exorcist) gave them a putative authority in dealing with spirits.[41] That there were clerics of lax morality who conjured demons is surely not incredible; that there were men of dedicated if problematic piety who dabbled in necromancy is clearly harder to believe, and harder still to comprehend.

One must remember the intimate link between necromancy and exorcism. Mary of Nijmegen's uncle is spoken of as a necromancer, but the demons fear him as an exorcist, a bearer of extraordinary power that extends even to the

---

39 Colledge 1965; Petroff 1986: 355–72.
40 The story ends: "Having said this he departed suddenly, razing the trees in his path and whipping up such a violent storm that it seemed as though all the fiends of hell were tearing through the forest," Matarasso 1969: 136–40 (*The Quest of the Holy Grail* ch. 7).
41 Kieckhefer 1989: 153–6.

world of spirits. The disciples of Christ were seldom so animated as when they returned to their master and reported with breathless exhilaration that the very demons were subject to them (Luke 10.17), and the late medieval necromancer seems to have shared that feeling. This was the one realm in which mortals might claim powers of command over the spirit world – a disputed claim,[42] but a crucial one for the necromancers. Even more basically, the knowledge of how to conjure demons was itself a source of excitement.

One important clue to the mentality of the demonic magicians comes from *Picatrix*, the thirteenth-century translation of a classic Arabic compendium of astral magic. In the first chapter of the first book the compiler proclaims: "knowledge is an exalted and noble affair, and each day you should study in God . . . And this is the greatest gift that God himself has given to men, that they should study to have knowledge. For to study is to serve God."[43] The author explains that all things are created by God, which gives learning about all of creation a kind of divine character. Knowledge always accumulates and never diminishes, always raises up and never degrades, always appears and never hides itself (presumably once it has been gained). It leads a person to despise the things of this world, it cultivates good manners, and it directs itself only to what he (God?) wishes and loves. To grasp the full import of all this one must bear in mind that *Picatrix* proceeds to give folio upon folio replete with formulas for invoking stars and their attendant spirits, with breathtaking nonchalance about their angelic or demonic nature. Indeed, its "details . . . often much more curious than edifying" caused J. Wood Brown to hope "that it may never be translated into any modern language."[44] I do not wish to suggest that *Picatrix* or the manuals of astral and demonic magic that followed it are works of intellectual profundity. Far from it; such works tend to be conceptually simplistic, and perhaps the fullest and most explicit manual of late medieval necromancy that we have is marked by abominable Latinity.[45] Yet the writers and owners of such books clearly fancied that they possessed a wealth of occult learning that was in itself holy. The necromancer would essay to command the demons, but by virtue of power over them that he had gained from God in mock-humble supplication. Their purposes might be base: deception of their fellow mortals, adultery, and the like. But if their ends were unholy, their

---

[42] This is the central concern of Johann of Frankfurt, in his "Quaestio, utrum potestas cohercendi demones fieri possit per caracteres, figuras atque verborum prolationes," in Hanse 1901: 71–82.

[43] Pingree 1986: 4 "scire est res summa et nobilis, et quotidie studere debes in Deo . . . Et hoc est maximum donum quod ipse Deus hominibus dedit, ut studeant scire et cognoscere. Nam studere servire Deo est."

[44] Brown 1897: 183 and n. 1.

[45] I refer to materials in Munich, Bayerische Staatsbibliothek, MS Clm 849; I am preparing an edition of this material, with commentary.

means were of the holiest. Which, of course, was itself a form of blasphemy and therefore compounded their unholiness.

But to be more precise, one could say that for many of these necromancers this distinction between means and ends would be misleading. Doubtless there were cases in which the owners of necromantic books actually attempted the experiments contained therein. For others, and perhaps the majority, the greatest thrill came not in using but merely in possessing such lore. From the second century onward, the Alexandrian tradition regarding theology had in this respect prevailed within Christianity: Clement of Alexandria and Origen had taught the Christian Church that the attainment of knowledge was itself good and holy. Among the many permutations on this theme was the Dominican ideal, *contemplata aliis tradere*, the fruits of contemplation being taken here to include the riches of theological learning.[46] If for the Dominicans the goal was to share these riches, there was an esoteric strain in Christianity, again going back to the Alexandrians, which sought to maintain the elite character of the Christian intellectual precisely by hoarding such riches.[47] This was the tradition that the necromancer shared. No doubt he parodied it, debased it, transvalued its most cherished assumptions about the spiritual order – but even in so doing he shared its essential notion that the possession of knowledge is inherently holy, indeed so holy that it must be guarded as well as cherished. What we have here is, of course, the fountainhead of Faustian notions of magic: despite his fascination with power, what centrally concerns Faust is demolishing barriers to his quest for knowledge. Of all the forms of ambiguity and ambivalence that we have surveyed this is surely the most fascinating, precisely because the necromancer genuinely proposed a transvaluation of conventional values.

The conception of necromancy as a holy art is particularly clear in a *Liber consecrationum* that gives elaborate ritual for restoring the potency of necromantic experiments that have lost their force.[48] For this ritual to have its proper effect, the operator must have firm faith, for "one who does not believe firmly and faithfully cannot be saved." For one who does believe, a single word of these formulas is worth more than a pound of gold, for knowledge is superior to secular power, and this knowledge (which can give power to "corrupt" experiments) is of particular value. For nine days before the ritual, the operator must be free of pollution in mind and body, must abstain from food

---

[46] The *locus classicus* is Thomas Aquinas, *Summa theologiae* II–II, q. 188 a. 6, "maius est contemplata aliis tradere quam solum contemplari."

[47] To be sure, Alexandrian esotericism surely was not a goal in itself, but rather was ancillary to conceptions of how virtue could be inculcated through the mentorship of a theological instructor. For the context of this tradition see Wilken 1984: 15–30. Hall 1988: 2 is (perhaps ironically?) more of a popular account.

[48] Clm 849, fols. 52r–9v.

and drink and hateful or immoderate words. Each day he must attend mass and place the book of experiments on the altar, then take it home, sprinkle it with holy water, wrap a priestly cincture and stole around it in the form of a cross, kneel facing east and say various prayers (the Seven Penitential Psalms, the Litany of the Saints, and other prayers specifically for the occasion), then open the book with humble devotion, "so that Almighty God in his mercy and goodness may sanctify and bless and consecrate this book dedicated to his most holy names." In the prayers written for this ritual, the magician professes his own unworthiness and begs God's pardon for his sins. One of the prayers recites a long litany of divine names, and then proceeds:

By these most holy names, and by others which it is not lawful to name, I humbly beseech thee, that thou mayest bestow power and strength upon the prayers, consecrations, and invocations contained in this book, by thy divine power, for the consecration of all experiments and invocations of demons, so that wheresoever the malign spirits are summoned and exorcised by the power of thy names, they may come at once from every quarter and fulfill the will of the exorcist, without inflicting any harm or terror, but rather showing themselves obedient . . . Fiat, fiat, fiat. Amen.[49]

One might perhaps suspect that the labored protestations of purity and humility fall short of total sincerity, but in historical contexts even more than contemporary ones sincerity is a difficult quality to gauge. Few in their day would have questioned the efficacy of such rituals; the only question was whether they were legitimate. The necromancers clearly knew that they were violating orthodox norms, but evidently they had persuaded themselves that theirs was a deeper, if not higher, morality.

The same mentality can be seen in the *Liber iuratus* ascribed to one Honorius son of Euclid, probably a fourteenth-century text.[50] Like the author of the *Liber consecrationum*, the present author requires a regimen of penitence, ritual purity, fasting, prayer, and good works as preparation for invoking spirits. The bulk of the work consists of a series of prayers, many of which contain cryptic names for the divine. These are to be used in association with elaborately prepared magical seals and circles. The rituals herein prescribed may be used to gain a vision of God (indeed, this is the purpose highlighted by the author), for an increase of knowledge, or for other ends. They may also be used for an enormously broad array of further purposes, listed at the beginning and hinted at elsewhere: spirits may be constrained to bring precious metals, to destroy whatever the magician wishes destroyed, to teach him "the mixture of the elements," or to gain favor with others. The

[49] Clm 849, fol. 57r–v; see a similar prayer on fol. 58v.
[50] Driscoll 1983. The work is discussed briefly by Thorndike (1929: 283–9). The dating suggested by Cohn (1975: 178) is supported by the manuscript tradition. Robert Mathiesen is currently working on the text.

author speaks at several junctures about the kinds of spirits that can be conjured. The nine traditional choirs of angels are immune from such service, but the magician may call upon those planetary angels and elemental spirits which serve humans as well as God. The planetary angels are of various natures, some virtuous and others vicious; among the latter, some arouse sadness, anger, and hatred, while others arouse warfare, murder, death, and general destruction. The elemental spirits or demons are morally neutral, "capable of performing either good or evil according to the will of [him] who calls them"; these are the ones whom Solomon invoked and bound. Angels must be invoked cautiously, and must be adjured to come "without violence," "in an agreeable and pleasing form," desisting from their stubbornness and submitting to the magician's will.

The author repeatedly expresses his moral sensitivities, perverse by orthodox standards but not necessarily superficial or insincere. To take merely one example:

He who would work in magical art [must] beware that he not be in deadly sin, for if he be, he shall be mad ever after, for the soul, by its nature, desires to see God in whom it delights, but the impediment of sin frustrates its desire and it cannot see God. He who would work in magical art must be willing in his work and utterly cleansed from all filthiness, for the more he suffers the more he shall obtain. The sight of God will not be had without purity; God will not be constrained, but rather prayed to and entreated. Even so the sight of God is a difficult thing to obtain, for it is a thing above natural reason.[51]

The categories I have dealt with are to some extent gender-linked. Empirical confusion of sainthood and witchcraft arose, when it did at all, mainly in the case of women, for the obvious reason that women's spirituality was more often suspect, although not exclusively in the eyes of male critics. Combination of religious devotion with demonic magic was primarily an affair of that "clerical underworld" which by definition was populated only by men.

The Renaissance mages were often suspected of dabbling in such practices, and while they defended themselves vigorously against this charge they often left themselves open to it. They might perceive magic as itself a holy exercise, but the distinction between good and evil spirits was difficult for them to define as sharply as one might have liked. Thus, while Marsilio Ficino insisted that magic was a pious activity and merely made use of those powers bestowed from above – from God ultimately, but via the stars and planets – he also acknowledged that the heavenly bodies are ruled by evil as well as good

---

51 Driscoll 1983: 67–8. See also pp. 19 ("Take heed that you cannot receive the sacrament and intend evil, for that would be death to him who would try it, wherefore some men call this book a book of death, but it is only so for those who intend evil") and 98 ("Men who are good and faithful need fear no harm from magical art, for demons are conquerable and made subservient to the will of a good man by fortitude and courage").

spirits, and his critics were not quibbling when they suspected him of benefiting indiscriminately from spiritual ministrations.[52] Similar ambiguity arises with Cornelius Agrippa. Even in the first book of *De occulta philosophia*, Agrippa concedes that not only angels but "evil demons can be bound by evil and profane arts," while in the second book he tells of evil spirits being mastered by use of geometrical figures, and in the third book he again speaks of evil as well as good spirits invoked (for example) with demonic names to arouse storms. He tells of seeing a man inscribe the name and sign of a spirit on paper and giving it to a frog while murmuring an incantation, all to arouse storms. In his case it is difficult to distinguish between description and recommendation, especially in view of his explicit repudiation of all occult arts after writing (but before publishing) *De occulta philosophia*. Satan was notoriously able to disguise himself as an angel of light, and adepts who claimed to be working only with good or neutral spirits had no right to be surprised when contemporaries reacted skeptically to this claim. One cannot grasp the complexities of this situation, however, without realizing that there were manuals of necromancy in late medieval and Renaissance Europe, and there were surely eager users of these manuals who perceived *their* rituals as sharing in a kind of holiness. Only in this context does it become fully clear why mages such as Ficino and Agrippa (and one could add Johannes Trithemius, John Dee, and others to the list) had such difficulty persuading people of their orthodoxy.[53]

Is it possible, then, that necromancers were saints, or thought of themselves or were thought of in those terms? Were there those who effectively combined sanctity with witchcraft, or at least with demonic magic? Surely not. But neither were the necromancers merely functionaries who performed their rituals and expected them to take effect *ex opere operato*. While their purifications did not commit them to orthodox standards of moral behavior, they did claim for themselves a kind of numinous status. They claimed mastery in a spiritual realm beyond good and evil, a realm ruled ultimately perhaps by a sort of Jungian deity possessed of a dark or evil side,[54] yet a realm populated most importantly by demons. Commerce with these spirits required an amoral sort of "holiness": the sort which entails ritual purity, psychic concentration, and a fascination – perhaps even an obsession – with the dangers of transgressing the border between the natural and supernatural worlds. Those who flirted with that danger did so expecting a rush of numinous power to overwhelm them.[55] The holy was, for them, clearly a *mysterium tremendum et*

---

[52] Walker 1958: 45–53. The key text is Ficino 1989: especially III.1, III.23, III.26. See also Copenhaver 1984a and 1984b, and Tomlinson 1992.

[53] Nauert 1965: 242–51. See Arnold 1971; Brann 1981; and French 1972.

[54] Jaffé 1970: 98–100. For a recent critique see Sanford 1988: 109–30.

[55] See the experience related in Cellini 1946: 118-22.

fascinans,[56] at all levels, even if in different ways at the divine level and the demonic: the divine might be alluring as an inherently valuable and ultimate goal, but the demonic only as a means to particular ends; the majesty of God was absolute and illimitable, but the power of the demons could in principle be bridled, so that the necromancer adopted a supplicant pose before God in an effort to control the demons.

No one possessed of psychological insight could doubt that profound religious encounters can be spiritually disruptive even when they are perfectly orthodox in nature. After all, *ein jedere Engel ist schrecklich*.[57] Anthony Bloom warns of this possibility in his well-known book on prayer: "To meet God face to face in prayer is a critical moment in our lives, and thanks be to Him that He does not always present Himself to us when we wish to meet Him, because we might not be able to endure such a meeting."[58] Metropolitan Anthony speaks, of course, as one who believes firmly in God's existence. Those with equal faith in the existence of demons – which is to say virtually everyone in late medieval Europe – will fear encounters with them all the more because demons, unlike God, have no concern for the real interests of those who seek such encounter. The necromancers recognized this danger, and attempted to avert it by commanding the demons to come in non-threatening form and inflict no harm.[59] The danger of confronting the demons in their true form was surely never far from the necromancers' minds, and added to the excitement of their pursuit: these people were playing a spiritual equivalent of Russian roulette.

Yet the Nietzschean grandeur they might have claimed for their daring is often belied by the limited scope and even banality of their goals. They may at times have proclaimed grand or monstrous designs, but when they plunged into their conjuration they seem more often to have pursued petty illusions, love affairs, and knowledge of empirical particulars with little cosmic significance. Awestruck fascination could give way to playful fascination; a ludic element no doubt often lurked behind the dark seriousness of necromancy. In this respect they are again prototypes of Marlowe's Faustus, proudly declaiming their quest of surpassing knowledge and thus unsurpassable power, but within two or three acts preoccupied more with farcical pranks at the expense of prelates and carters.[60]

Necromancers were not easily mistaken for saints. One person we know of

---

56 Otto 1923: especially ch. 6 argues that the *mysterium tremendum* must also be *fascinans*.
57 Rilke 1955: 685 (first of the Duino elegies); cf. 689 (second elegy).
58 Bloom 1970: 27.
59 E.g., Clm 849, fols. 19r, 24r, 42r, 51r, 57v.
60 Marlowe 1969; the pranks in the papal court occur in Act 3, and others in Act 4. The farcical scenes occur already in the German source, the *Historia von D. Iohan Fausten*, chs. 22 and 29–40 (Barnet 1969: 236–44).

who had studied necromancy and then went on to become a *beatus*, Giovanni dalle Celle of Vallombrosa, repented between these stages of his career.[61] Joan of Arc was charged with conjuring spirits and other forms of divination – rather than with witchcraft in the fully developed sense emerging in her era – but these accusations were dropped by her judges because they could not be substantiated.[62] To be sure, those who burned her wanted her to be perceived as a dupe of demons if not an invoker of evil spirits,[63] but this charge had not been borne out in the trial. The saintly necromancer – the Gilles de Rais of *Là-bas* – is just as much a fiction as the saintly witch. The central difference is that witchcraft and sainthood are both in large measure ascribed roles, by which society finds its ideals and nightmares manifest in specific individuals, while in necromancy the holy and the unholy come together in a fusion that is real and complete, if only in the mind of the necromancer.

It is probably fair to speculate that the necromancer's typical attitude is one not of reverence but rather of fascination: not a submission of soul to a spiritual presence revealed in yet simultaneously concealed behind the appearances, a yielding of abyss to abyss, but an attraction primarily of the theoretical and practical intellect to the appearances themselves, to those spiritual beings who appear in the world and promise aid within the phenomenal order. The distinction is subtle but crucial. It is essentially that between reverence for the noumena behind the phenomena and fascination with noumenal beings made phenomenal. From a psychological viewpoint this distinction is perhaps as important as the theological divide between good and fallen spirits.

It may be heuristically useful to compare the necromancers with those other problem children of late medieval piety, the heretics of the Free Spirit.[64] Both the necromancers and the Free Spirits differed from orthodoxy, but in different ways (apart from the basic fact that the very existence of necromancers is

---

[61] Anonymous 1866: 49–50 (*Vita B. Catharinae Bononiensis* 2.16).

[62] Among the seventy articles brought forward in the trial begun on 27 March 1431, as given in Tisset 1960, thirteen dealt with divination and consultation of presumably malign spirits: she was charged with divination (art. 4, p. 196; art. 59, p. 271), consorting with demon-fairies (arts. 5–6, pp. 197–8), magical use of mandrake (art. 7, p. 199), invocation or conjuring of demons for divination (art. 2, pp. 194–5; art. 19, p. 216); invocation and consultation of demons (art. 23, p. 222; art. 50, p. 251); reliance on revelations ostensibly of saints but probably of demons (art. 32, p. 229; art. 51, pp. 254–5), veneration of these spirits (art. 49, p. 249), and reliance on the aid of demons (art. 56, p. 264). When the articles were reduced to twelve on 2 April 1431, only one preserved a trace of these earlier accusations: Joan was now reproached merely for placing absolute faith in the spirits that appeared to her, and being confident that they were not demonic, although she consulted no one regarding them (art. 11, pp. 295–6); the suggestion that those spirits probably were in fact demonic was now dropped.

[63] At her execution Jeanne wore a mitre inscribed with the words *heretique, relapse, apostate, ydolatre*, flande or held up by demons; see the reconstruction in Barrett 1931: facing 332.

[64] Lerner 1972.

better attested). In terms of inward disposition, orthodox Christianity insisted upon a state of reverence before the numinous order and a recognition of God as the proper object of that reverence; in the realm of outward conduct it prescribed certain ritual actions and moral behaviors. The heretics of the Free Spirit accepted the inward dispositions that orthodox Christianity enjoined, but they flouted its demands for proper outward conduct. The necromancers' stance was more nuanced: they accepted the subjective state of reverence, but in paying homage to demons they deviated from the strict monotheist orientation toward the divine; unlike the Free Spirits they relied on ritual actions largely derived from orthodox ceremonial, but they departed from orthodox conceptions of moral conduct. The antinomian element in the heresy of the Free Spirit transvalued the norms of orthodox Christianity, but as a radical version of Christian mysticism this heresy operated within a received conception of spiritual values. If some of the Free Spirits actually used antinomian principle as a justification for moral license, the tradition of radical mysticism in general leaned more toward indifference regarding the order of outward behavior. And the Free Spirits accepted an orthodox notion of the proper inward state – they shared with mystics generally the notion of inner detachment from the world – even if they challenged the traditional conception of how this related to outward conduct. The necromancers, on the other hand, accepted part of the traditional demands for inner disposition and followed part of the norms for outer conduct, but in both these spheres they turned Christian tradition against itself, holding God and the devil in a precarious balance and using ritual forms for radically non-traditional ends. Necromancy represented the more radical departure, the more thoroughgoing, subtler, and more complex transvaluation of traditional Christianity – the more serious flirtation with the perilous underside of spiritual experience.

Incidentally, at least two mystical writers of the late Middle Ages seem to have recognized the force of this inversion: Nicholas of Cusa referred to the demonic magician's bond with the devil as a parody of mystical relatedness to Christ, and *The Cloud of Unknowing* cited the necromancer as a negative analogue to the contemplative.[65] The *Cloud* author's point appears at first merely quaint: the necromancer who foolishly peers into the devil's single gaping nostril will go mad. The author is perhaps replicating a homelists' tale of caution against the hazards of necromancy,[66] but is more directly concerned with the deceptive nature of spiritual experience linked with bodily sensations and corporeal visions. Nicholas of Cusa comes closer to perceiving a genuine parallel between the magician's relationship with the devil and the mystic's with Christ; to dignify the former as even parodically similar to the latter is to

---

[65] Hopkins 1981: 152–3; Hodgson 1982: 57 (*The Cloud of Unknowing* ch. 55).
[66] Kieckhefer 1989: 174.

approach the necromancers' own apparent perception that they were engaged in an exercise of spiritual power, although the medieval necromancers seem to have commanded the demons without committing themselves to the Faustian relationship of a binding pact.

In short, sainthood and witchcraft were ascribed roles and could give occasion for competing ascription, with different observers thinking of a single person either as a saint or as a witch, but the necromancer's role was essentially self-defined, and in the necromancer's own mind the holy and the unholy, the sacred and the explicitly demonic, entered into a rare and fascinating alliance. Günter Grass provides a fitting model for society's ambivalence regarding the saint and the witch, but Huysmans comes closer to depicting the ambiguity found in the necromancer. Not surprisingly, both the ambivalence in the one case and the ambiguity in the other were disturbing: orthodox observers understandably felt threatened by such flirtation between heaven and hell.

REFERENCES

Ambelain, Robert 1951 *La Kabbale pratique*. Paris: Niclaus.
    1984 *La Géomancie arabe et ses miroirs divinatoires*. Paris: Laffont.
Amedeo, Father 1935 *Blessed Gemma Galgani*. Trans. Osmuand Thorpe. London: Burns, Oates & Washbourne.
Anonymous [Bollandists] 1866 *Vita B. Catharinae Bononiensis*. In *Acta sanctorum*, Mar., vol. II. Paris and Rome: Victor Palmé.
Arnold, Klaus 1971 *Johannes Trithemius (1462–1515)*. Würzburg: Schöningh.
Barrett, W. P., trans. 1931 *The Trial of Jeanne d'Arc*. London: Routledge.
Bell, Rudolf M. 1985 *Holy Anorexia*. Chicago: University of Chicago Press.
Betz, Hans Dieter, ed. 1986 *The Greek Magical Papyri in Translation, Including the Demotic Spells*, vol. I. Chicago: University of Chicago Press.
Bloom, Anthony 1970 *Beginning to Pray*. New York: Paulist Press.
Brann, Noel L. 1981 *The Abbot Trithemius (1462–1516): The Renaissance of Monastic Humanism*. Leiden: Brill.
Brown, J. Wood 1897 *An Enquiry into the Life and Legend of Michael Scot*. Edinburgh: Douglas.
Brown, Peter A. 1970 Sorcery, Demons and the Rise of Christianity: From Late Antiquity into the Middle Ages. In Mary Douglas, ed., *Witchcraft Confessions and Accusations*, 17–45. London: Tavistock. Reprinted in his *Religion and Society in the Age of St Augustine*, 119–46. London: Faber & Faber 1972.
Butler, E. M. 1949 *Ritual Magic*. Cambridge: Cambridge University Press.
Campan, Charles-Albert, ed. 1862–83 *Mémoires de Francisco de Enzinas: texte Latin inédit, avec la traduction française du XVIe siècle en regard, 1543–1545*. Brussels: Société de l'Histoire de Belgique.
Cellini, Benvenuto 1946 *The Autobiography of Benvenuto Cellini*. Trans. John Addington Symonds. Repr. Garden City, N.Y.: Doubleday.
Christian, William A. 1981 *Apparitions in Late Medieval and Renaissance Spain*. Princeton: Princeton University Press.

Clark, Stuart 1977 King James's *Daemonologie*: Witchcraft and Kingship. In Sydney Anglo, ed., *The Damned Art: Essays in the Literature of Witchcraft*, 156–81. London: Routledge & Kegan Paul.

Cohn, Norman 1975 *Europe's Inner Demons: An Enquiry Inspired by the Great Witch-Hunt*. New York: Basic Books.

Colledge, Eric, trans. 1965 *Medieval Netherlands Religious Literature*. New York: London House & Maxwell.

Conybeare, F. C. 1899 The Testament of Solomon. *Jewish Quarterly Review* 11: 1–45.

Copenhaver, Brian P. 1984a Astrology and Magic. *Renaissance Quarterly* 37: 274–85. 1984b Scholastic Philosophy and Renaissance Magic in the *De Vita* of Marsilio Ficino. *Renaissance Quarterly* 37: 523–54.

Cordara, Giulio 1768 *Vita, virtù e miracoli della B. Eustochio, vergine Padovana, monaca professa dell'Ordine Benedittino nel monastero di S. Prosdocimo di Padova*. Venice.

Delooz, Pierre 1983 Towards a Sociological Study of Canonized Sainthood in the Catholic Church. In Stephen Wilson, ed., *Saints and their Cults: Studies in Religious Sociology, Folklore and History*, 189–216. Cambridge: Cambridge University Press.

Demos, John Putnam 1982 *Entertaining Satan: Witchcraft and the Culture of Early New England*. New York: Oxford University Press.

Dinzelbacher, Peter 1990 Heilige oder Hexen? In Deiter Simon, ed., *Religiöse Devianz: Untersuchungen zu sozialen, rechtlichen und theologischen Reaktionen auf religiöse Abweichung im westlichen und östlichen Mittelalter*, 41–60. Frankfurt am Main: Vittorio Klostermann.

Driscoll, Daniel J. 1983 *The Sworn Book of Honourius the Magician*. Gillette, N.J.: Heptangle.

Ferzoco, George 1990 Historical and Hagiographical Aspects of the Religious World of Peter of Morrone. In Walter Capezali, ed., *Celestino V e i suoi tempi: Realtà Spirituale e Realtà Politica: atti del 40 Convegno Storico Internazionale l'Aquila, 26–27 agosto 1989*, 227–37. L'Aquila: Centrao Celestiniano.

Ficino, Marsilio 1989 *Three Books on Life: A Critical Edition and Translation with Introduction and Notes*, ed. and trans. Carol V. Kaske and John R. Clark. Binghamton, N.Y.: Medieval and Renaissance Texts and Studies in conjunction with the Renaissance Society of America.

French, Peter J. 1972 *John Dee: The World of an Elizabethan Magus*. London: Routledge & Kegan Paul.

Freud, Sigmund 1959 Inhibition, Symptoms and Anxiety. In James Strachey, ed. and trans., *The Standard Edition of the Complete Psychological Works*, XX.77–175. London: Hogarth Press.

Galatariotou, Catia 1984–5 Holy Women and Witches: Aspects of Byzantine Conceptions of Gender. *Byzantine and Modern Greek Studies* 9: 55–94.

Germanus of St. Stanislaud 1913. *The Life of the Servant of God, Gemma Galgani, and Italian Maiden of Lucca*, trans. A. M. O'Sullivan. London and Edinburgh: Sands; St. Louis: Herder.

Grass, Günter 1978 *The Flounder*. Trans. Ralph Manheim. New York: Harcourt Brace Jovanovich.

Hall, Manly P. 1988 *The Adepts in the Esoteric Classical Tradition,* II: *Mystics and Mysteries of Alexandria.* Reprinted Los Angeles: Philosophical Research Society.

Hansen, Joseph, ed. 1901 *Quellen und Untersuchungen zur Geschichte des Hexen-wahns und der Hexenverfolgung im Mittelalter.* Bonn: Georgi. Reprinted Hildesheim: Olms, 1963.

Henningsen, Gustav 1990 "The Ladies from Outside": An Archaic Pattern of the Witches' Sabbath. In Bengt Ankarloo and Gustav Henningsen, eds., *Early Modern European Witchcraft: Centres and Peripheries,* 191–215. Oxford: Clarendon Press.

Hodgson, Phyllis, ed. 1982 *The Cloud of Unknowing and Related Treatises.* Salzburg: Institut für Anglistik und Amerikanistik.

Hoffmann-Krayer, E. 1899 Luzerner Akten zum Hexen- und Zauberwesen. *Schweizerisches Archiv für Volkskunde* 3: 33–9.

Hopkins, Jaspar 1981 *Nicholas of Cusa on Learned Ignorance: A Translation and an Appraisal of "De Docta Ignorantia"* 23.11. Minneapolis: Arthur J. Banning.

Huysmans, J. K. 1972 *Là-bas (Down There).* Trans. Keene Wallace. New York: Dover (orig. Paris, 1928).

Hyatte, Reginald 1984 *Laughter for the Devil: The Trials of Gilles de Rais, Companion-in-Arms of Joan of Arc (1440).* Rutherford, Madison, and Teaneck, N.J.: Fairleigh Dickinson University Press.

Jaffé, Aniela 1970 *The Myth of Meaning in the Work of C. G. Jung.* Trans. R. F. C. Hull. London: Hodder & Stoughton.

Jerome, St. 1952 *Life of St. Hilarion.* In Roy J. Deferrari, ed., *Early Christian Biographies, The Fathers of the Church,* vol. XV, 245–86. Washington, DC: Catholic University of America Press.

Jones, A. E. 1980 *The Trial of Joan of Arc.* Chichester: Barry Rose.

Kelly, H. Ansgar 1993 The Right to Remain Silent: Before and After Joan of Arc. *Speculum* 68: 992–1026.

Kempe, Margery 1985 *The Book of Margery Kempe.* Trans. B. A. Windeatt, Harmondsworth: Penguin.

Kieckhefer, Richard 1984 *Unquiet Souls: Fourteenth-Century Saints and their Religious Milieu.* Chicago: University of Chicago Press.

    1980 *Magic in the Middle Ages.* Cambridge and New York: Cambridge University Press.

    1994 The Specific Rationality of Medieval Magic. *American Historical Review* 99: 813–36.

Klaniczay, Gábor 1990 Hungary: The Accusations and the Universe of Popular Magic. In Bengt Ankarloo and Gustav Henningsen, eds., *Early Modern European Witchcraft: Centres and Peripheries,* 219–55. Oxford: Clarendon Press.

    1990–1 *Miraculum* und *maleficium*: Einige Überlegungen zu den weiblichen Heiligen des Mittelalters in Mitteleuropa. *Wissenschaftskolleg – Jahrbuch*: 220–48.

    1992a Punitive Miracles and Evil Spells, Sainthood and Witchcraft: A Structural Comparison. Paper presented at the International Congress on Medieval Studies, Kalamazoo, Mich., May.

    1992b Witchcraft and Sainthood: Anthropological Problems and Structural

Comparison. Paper presented at a plenary session of the International Congress on Medieval Studies, Kalamazoo, Mich., May.

Kleinberg, Aviad M. 1989 Proving Sanctity: Selection and Authentication of Saints in the Later Middle Ages. *Viator* 20: 183–205.

1992 *Prophets in their Own Country: Living Saints and the Making of Sainthood in the Later Middle Ages.* Chicago: University of Chicago Press.

Krämer, Heinrich and Sprenger, Jakob 1928 *Malleus maleficarum.* Trans. Montague Summers. London: Rodker. Reprinted London: Pushkin, 1948.

Lea, Henry Charles 1907 *A History of the Inquisition of Spain,* vol. IV. New York: Macmillan.

Lerner, Robert E. 1972 *The Heresy of the Free Spirit in the Later Middle Ages.* Berkeley and Los Angeles: University of California Press.

Loomis, C. Grant 1948 *White Magic: An Introduction to the Folklore of Christian Legend.* Cambridge, Mass.: Medieval Academy of America.

McClory, Robert 1986 Cutters: Mutilation: The New Wave in Female Self-Abuse. *The Chicago Reader* 5 September: 29–38.

Mair, Lucy 1969 *Witchcraft.* New York: McGraw-Hill.

Marlowe, Christopher 1969 *Doctor Faustus.* Ed. Sylvan Barnet. New York: Signet.

Matarasso, P. M., trans. 1969 *The Quest of the Holy Grail.* Harmondsworth: Penguin.

Mitchell, Juliet 1974 *Psychoanalysis and Feminism.* New York: Pantheon.

Morgan, Michael A., trans. 1983 *Sepher-ha-Razim: The Book of Mysteries.* Atlanta: Scholars Press.

Stachnik, Richard, ed. 1978 *Die Akten des Kanonisationsprozesses Dorotheas von Montau von 1394 bis 1521.* Cologne and Vienna: Böhlau.

Thomas, Keith 1971 *Religion and the Decline of Magic.* New York: Scribners.

Thorndike, Lynn 1929 *History of Magic and Experimental Science,* vol. II. New York: Macmillan.

Thurston, Herbert 1926 A Cinderella of the Cloister. *The Month* 147: 134–48.

Tisset, Pierre, ed. 1960 *Procès de condamnation de Jeanne d'Arc,* vol. I. Paris: Klincksieck.

Tomlinson, Gary 1992 *Music in Renaissance Magic: Toward a Historiography of Others.* Chicago: University of Chicago Press.

Vauchez, André 1981 *La Sainteté en Occident aux derniers siècles du moyen âge d'après les procès de canonisation et les documents hagiographiques.* Rome: Ecole Française de Rome.

Walker, D. P. *Spiritual and Demonic Magic, from Ficino to Campanella.* London: Warburt Institute.

Wilkin, Robert L. 1984 Alexandria: A School for Training in Virtue. In Patrick Henry, ed., *Schools of Thought in the Christian Tradition,* 15–30. Philadelphia: Fortress Press.

Woodward, Kenneth L. 1990 *Making Saints: How the Catholic Church Determines Who Becomes a Saint, Who Doesn't, and Why.* New York: Simon & Schuster.

Edward M. Peters

Some discontents of Christendom

Fundamental to any conception of *Christianitas*, whether as polity or order (including intellectual order), was the distinction between orthodoxy and heterodoxy and the role of authority in establishing and maintaining that distinction. Heterodoxy represented one of the most dangerous manifestations of discontent, as Chenu once argued, because it attacked two vital structural principles of *Christianitas*: the proper bond between the individual Christian and God and the common fraternal bonds among believing individuals in the Christian community.[1] Both kinds of violation are iterated in the famous definition of heresy attributed by Matthew Paris to Robert Grosseteste and discussed by Chenu "Haeresis est sententia humano sensu electa, scripturae sacrae contraria, palam edocta, pertinaciter defensa."[2] The last two parts of Grosseteste's four-part definition address heresy as an offense against the community – the heretic's defiant public teaching of destructive error after formal, authoritative instruction and condemnation. The first two parts address the individual and his or her cognitive and moral fault – he has, by the exercise of his own powers of understanding (which were universally understood to be differentiated among humans according to differing proportions of faith and grace), reached an opinion concerning religious truth that is contrary to scripture, the only measure of religious truth.

From the Pauline and Pastoral Epistles to the Reformation it is in discussions of the misuse of scripture, measured according to juridical and magisterial tradition, that we often find characterizations of moral psychology and

I would like to thank Richard Newhauser, James J. O'Donnell, Karl F. Morrison, and the anonymous reader for the University of California Press for their generous readings of earlier drafts of this essay. Their advice saved it from much incoherence, if not from all remaining errors, which are entirely my own responsibility.

[1] Chenu (1963), repr. in Le Goff 1968: 9–14, most recently discussed in Vauchez 1990, in Mollat du Jourdin and Vauchez 1990: 320–51. For its use as early as Gregory the Great, see Straw 1988: 80.
[2] Le Goff 1968: 10; Matthew Paris 1880: 401, *ad an.* 1253. For other categorizations, particularly those of canonists, see Hageneder 1976, and in general, Grundmann 1963.

intellectual error that could apply to a wide variety of discontent. As Chenu shrewdly remarked of the first part of Grosseteste's definition,

> The [heretic's fervent] faith has released in his spirit – and, transcending his intellect itself, in his entire mental behavior – an avid curiosity to penetrate the mystery, to have of it, in the obscurity of its transcendence, certain knowledge, understanding, *intellectus fidei*. The intimacy of this demand is the moving grandeur of the heretic, even though it is sometimes effected by a certain psychological disequilibrium.[3]

Before the heterodox thinker was pertinacious, before he even took his convictions public, before he revealed himself as a *superbus*, he was first, therefore, a kind of *curiosus*.

Although *curiositas* never became one of the major vices that, with the virtues, stand at the root of Christian moral theology and palaeopsychology, it was frequently discussed by early Christian writers, sometimes attached to a major vice such as pride, avarice, or sloth, and built into the characterization of certain kinds of dissent, notably heresy and the practice of magic. From Tertullian on, it was regularly attributed to heterodoxy.[4] A particularly troublesome scriptural text in this regard was Matt. 7.7, *zetete kai euersete*, "seek and ye shall find," which, as Tertullian bitterly proclaimed, had been appropriated by every heresiarch in the first two centuries, particularly the Gnostics, out of a fatal spirit of *curiositas*. *Cedat curiositas fidei*, proclaimed Tertullian; after the epiphany of Christianity such seeking as Tertullian denounced was invariably a sign of *sacrilega curiositas*. The proneness of the human intellect, dominated by a Pauline "lower nature," abounding in curiosity and pride, and unaided by adequate faith or grace, to err in spiritual matters was a prominent concern of Pauline anthropology and one echoed by other early Christian writers besides Tertullian. Jerome and Augustine insisted that the intellect had to be supplemented by revelation itself, by the Spirit which was its author, by grace in proportion as God had given it, and by *auctoritas*, i.e., the interpretive construction given to revelation by those who were regarded as authoritative interpreters of its meaning and the rules of belief and practice they prescribed.

Concerning the general problem of human intellectual and spiritual capacity

---

[3] Le Goff 1968: 10. The intellectual passion of heterodox thinkers – as well as their apparent righteousness – led critics from Ambrose on to imply that their claims were based on *dissimulatio*, thus introducing the accusation, and assumption, of heterodox "hypocrisy" into patristic and later debates. Early writers did not neglect this "heroic" aspect of heterodox thinkers; cf. Grundmann 1963: 151 n. 55 on Augustine. For a full discussion of the *typus*, see Grundmann 1927 and Moore 1976.

[4] Newhauser 1982. There is growing literature on the varying concepts of *curiositas* in antique and medieval thought. See the studies of Newhauser, Oberman, Peters, and Blumenberg, cited below. For Tertullian, see especially Frédouille 1972: 427; Barnes 1971. Richard Newhauser and I are completing an extensive study of the term and its history.

in the face of the profound mysteries of revelation, as well as that of the limits that God had set to legitimate spiritual and intellectual inquiry, early Christian writers drew on a set of images from scripture and elsewhere and their elaboration in later exegesis. For example, the Pauline dicta, *noli altum sapere* (Rom. 11.20), *Non plus sapere quam opportet sapere* (Rom. 12.3), and *Scientia inflat* (1 Cor. 8.1), could be readily joined to such phrases from the wisdom literature as *Altiora te ne quaesieris* (Ecclus. 3.22) or to such tags from non-Christian morality as the alleged "Socratic dictum" of Lactantius: *Quae supra nos, nihil ad nos,* and other similar phrases.[5] In such imagery there is implied an "above" that is not a legitimate concern of humans. The precise nature of the "above and below" or "high and low" might be a matter of debate, but such imagery in any case governed the metaphorical nature and terms of any debate. In other related imagery, the *patres* were depicted as having provided all essential teaching in an exegetical aggregate from which it was forbidden to subtract and to which it was forbidden to add (Deut. 4.2, 13.1; Apoc. 22.18–19), or of having laid out a road from which deviation to the left or right was forbidden (Num. 21.21–2; 1 Sam. 6.12; Isa. 30.21). Images of high and low, unalterable aggregate of wisdom, and linear rectitude occur again and again in debates about the nature of theological/exegetical speculation, its proper and improper objects, the spirit in which it is undertaken, and the nature of the authority that must guide and judge it, not only in exegesis, but also in terms of dogma, liturgy, and canon law.

Such imagery did much to shape the mental perceptions of the problem of speculative exegesis and its limits, especially when raised in the context of other Pauline considerations such as those distinguishing *sapientia* from *scientia* (1 Cor. 12.8) or that calling the wisdom of this world "foolishness" in the eyes of God (1 Cor. 3.19).

The magisterial and juridical history of another image, that of "limits (or boundaries) set by the Fathers," *termini positi a patribus* (Prov. 22.28), offers a perspective from which a number of aspects of such debates may be considered. The exegetical fortunes of a particular biblical verse are not inherently compelling objects of study and do not always offer a coherent history, of course, but the case of this verse illustrates the intertwining of the juridical and magisterial dimensions of authority in Christendom that were so often brought to bear on troubling problems of exegesis and other disciplinary matters in which ancient and authoritative tradition needed to be invoked. Originally, this was cited in discussions of exegesis, in the formulation of dogma, and in matters of ecclesiastical tradition, largely in the texts of early canon law. By the middle of the twelfth century it came to be routinely and more narrowly cited in the case of exegesis and intellectual speculation. Thus,

---

[5] Some of these and their histories are discussed in Oberman 1973a and Ginsburg 1976.

the exegetical history of the verse offers materials for considering some characteristic discontents that the question of human intellectual capacity, its characterization in scriptural imagery, and its application to scripture generated. That is, the exegetical history illustrates equally the response to authority to heterodox devotional forms and to the misuse of the intellect that had generated them.

Prov. 22.28 and its analogous texts (Deut. 19.4, 27.17; Hos. 5.10; Job 24.2) originally described the sacrality of ancient boundary stones, a common concern of ancient Mediterranean societies. Similar texts are found in Egyptian literature, the laws of various Greek city states, in Plato's *Laws* (VIII 842e–843), and in Festus's citation of an ancient law of Numa.[6] The Romans even possessed a god named Terminus, of whom both Erasmus and Gibbon made good use.[7] In all of its citations, the injunction emphasized the sacrality of boundaries set in antiquity and the audacity of those who crossed or moved them.

In order to appreciate the importance of Prov. 22.28 between the ninth and the fourteenth centuries, it is necessary first to consider its exegetical history in the early Church, when ideas of authority and tradition were being shaped; that is, to consider the various early meanings of the term *patres* and the nature of the *termini* they were thought to have set.

Patres and *termini*

The term *patres* possessed a variety of meanings in the first few Christian centuries, from the general sense of "teachers" in Paul (1 Cor. 4.15) and others, to the more specific sense of the apostles and their successors as receivers of divine inspiration in the thought of a number of Greek Christian writers.[8] This characterization lay at the root of the concept of ancient tradition and its double role in the early Church; on the one hand, scripture, divinely inspired, was interpreted for the apostles by Jesus and for others by the apostles. Therefore, authentic exegesis had to derive from and coincide spiritually with this authentic tradition. On the other hand, the apostles were also taught how to live by Jesus, and their practices were also transmitted to their followers. The centrality to Christian identity of both interpretation and practice were strongly (and often equally) emphasized by second-century Christian writers, thus

---

6 Scott 1965: 135–8; Festus 1913: 505 (attested only by Paul the Deacon); for Chios, Humphreys 1988: 470–1.

7 Gilmore 1963: 141; Allen and Allen 1928: 430–2; Festus 1913: 505; Wind 1937–8: 66–9; den Boeft 1988: 19–23; for Gibbon, many editions, ch. 1.

8 General accounts in Quaesten 1966: 9–12; Amann 1933: 1192–215; de Ghellinck, 1948: 19–23. On the formation of tradition, see Van den Eynde 1933; Morrison 1969; Pelikan 1973; Brandmüller 1987.

establishing firmly the principles of antiquity and continuity that constituted an interpretive standard against which other interpretations and practices might be judged. Those found wanting by these standards could be dismissed and condemned as deriving from "one's own opinion," and therefore an illegitimate "novelty" (*chainautonomia*: 1 Tim. 6.20).

Both interpretations and practices are the *termini* set by the *patres* according to Papias, Polycarp, Origen, and Eusebius. The *patres* came to be understood as having possessed the authority – as heirs and interpreters of the apostolic tradition (*paradosis*) – to expound the rules of Christian life and the norms of the interpretation of scripture. But the opinions of individual *patres* were not considered sufficient in themselves to later writers. From Eusebius to Maximus the Confessor there emerged the idea of the consensus of the *patres* which regulated the proper investigation (*zetesis*) of scripture and determined which interpretations and practices were inconsistent with the patristic consensus and were therefore to be condemned as individual innovations, even when these might be the opinions of one or another individual *pater*. The first Christian writers who cited Prov. 22.28, Origen and Eusebius, understood the *patres* to have been the apostles and those of their successors who had been guided by the Holy Spirit, and the *termini* set by them to be the essentials of Christian belief.[9]

Augustine, whose own enthusiastic citations of Matt. 7.7 suggest how much more confident and hopeful Christian hermeneutics had become since the days of Tertullian, considered the *patres* primarily the figures of the Old and New Testaments – he referred to *patres temporis novi testamenti* and to *patres temporis veteris testamenti*, to *sancti antiqui patres* and *Hebraei patres*, and this understanding continued down to Isidore of Seville, whose *De ortu et obitu patrum* ended with the apostles and missionaries mentioned in the Pauline Epistles and Acts.[10]

The first Latin citation of Prov. 22.28, however, that of Siricius I in his *Ep. 6.1.2 Ad diversos episcopos*, added a new dimension to earlier, largely exegetical usage. Siricius cited the Proverbs text in conjunction with 2 Thes. 2.14, the Pauline command to hold fast to *traditiones*, a text that, with 1 Tim. 6.20, constituted another Pauline dimension of the discussion of ancient authority and boundaries.[11] Siricius was particularly disturbed at the variety of

---

[9] Pelikan 1973; Pelikan 1974: 52–3; Morrison 1969: 59–64, 71, 113–15; and especially Danielou 1975.

[10] Augustine, *De bono conjugali*, 18, 32; *Contra Faustum*, 22, 76.

[11] The earliest references to patristic citations of Prov. 22.28 are to those of Origen and Eusebius: Allenbach 1980a: 206; 1980b: 193. Virtually no scholarly research is cited in Sieben 1980 and 1983. It seems that the Prov. 22.28 text was first cited as a challenge to Jesus made by the scribes and Pharisees. Matt. 15.2, "quare discipuli tui transgrediuntur traditionem seniorum." Cf. Mark 7.1–23.

practices in the scattered churches of Christendom, and although he recognized much of the validity of local custom, he also warned against local presumption and observed that both local and universal traditions had to concur in belief and practice. The letter of Siricius added the dimension of orthopraxy to the earlier hermeneutic of Origen and Eusebius. Siricius's letter did not remain an isolated utterance; it was taken up in later canonical collections, notably those of Pseudo-Isidore and Regino of Prüm, and it gained particular currency in the divided world of Carolingian and post-Carolingian Europe.[12]

The themes worked out in early patristic literature and canon law, were taken up and transmitted to later ages by Vincent of Lerins, Cassiodorus, and Gregory the Great, which may be said to have completed the construction of the image of *patres* and *termini* in the early Church. Those who ventured to cross or remove these *termini*, whom Gregory identified as both heterodox dissenters and immoderate exegetes, shared the same trait: *plus quaerunt sentire quam capiunt*. In his *Moralia in Job* and elsewhere in his writings, Gregory explicitly identified those who transgressed the limits set by the *patres* with those who violated the *constitutiones patrum*. Gregory's focus upon the heretic's denial of faith and reason, his willfulness, and his meaningless isolation, reflects one of his central beliefs; as Carole Straw has characterized it, "For Gregory, self-sufficient autonomy is the true evil, the fatal mistake of seeking to stand in oneself (*stare in semetipso*)."[13] *Propria desideria, proprius sensus*, these are Gregory's characteristic explanations of the inappropriate address to exegesis.[14] This approach may explain why Gregory was more concerned with the heretic's willfulness, his *superbia*, than with his *curiositas*; that is, pride is the fundamental fault, *curiositas* being in this case a manifestation of underlying pride.

The various usages of Prov. 22.28 from Siricius to Gregory were put to active use between the late eighth and the early twelfth centuries. Carolingian scholars, eager to identify their own programs with authentic tradition, transformed the scattered dossiers of patristic texts into canon law, the regulation of monastic life, and the basis of a literary education. Having recovered a very wide range of patristic opinion, they brought the full weight of what they understood to be tradition – but which was just as often selective use of particular *patres* or local custom – to bear in their assertions of traditional

---

12 *PL* XIII.1187–8; there is a brief discussion in Morrison 1969: 80–1. For later citations see Hinschius 1963: 524, and below, p. 344.

13 Straw 1988: 79–80. Gregory's characterization of the misuse of scripture and the psychology of the misuser, with his descriptions of heterodox beliefs, were transmitted to Carolingian and later Europe by the *Moralia*, but also by his *Register* and by the *Dialogues*. For Vincent, see *PL* L.637–86; Madoz 1933; de Ghellinck 1935: 404 n. 5. For Cassiodorus, see Cassiodorus 1937: *Praef.*; Morrison 1969: 166; O'Donnell 1979. Cf. *Moralia in Job* 16. 4. 56; 20. 8. 18; de Lubac 1961: 99–128; Dagens 1977: 216–18, 340–2.

14 Gregory, *Moralia*, 30.1; de Lubac 1961: 301–17.

authority in the attack on Adoptionism and especially in their dispute with their Byzantine opposite numbers in the matter of iconoclasm, emphatically in the *praefatio* to the *Libri Carolini* and the canons of the Council of Frankfurt of 794, which confidently cited Prov. 22.28, and in the Pseudo-Isidorean decretals, which relied very heavily upon an alleged ecclesiastical tradition having the authority of antiquity to argue its ninth-century case.[15] In letters forged under the names of Victor, Alexander, and Calixtus, Prov. 22.28 is cited, and in letters attributed to Fabianus and Eusebius the analogous text of Deut. 27.17 conveys the identical sense. In addition, Pseudo-Isidore also includes the authentic letter of Siricius I with its own citation of Prov. 22.28.[16] The Pseudo-Isidorean forger knew perfectly well how effective appeals to such a notion of tradition and patristic authority might be in ninth-century Francia.

Carolingian authorities also cited Prov. 22.28 in their debates over the Eucharist and the doctrine of double predestination, over proper and improper exegesis, and over the allegorical interpretation of the liturgy provoked by the work of Amalarius of Metz. The prominence of Prov. 22.28, its analogous texts, and the Carolingian elevation of patristic authority generally help to explain the important citation of the text in the *De synodalibus causis* of Regino of Prüm.[17] In the letter to Hatto of Mainz that prefaces the *De synodalibus causis*, Regino states that although the faith is universal, joining all Christians in the *societas christiana*, it nevertheless lives according to different customs in different places. Just as diverse *nationes* of peoples differ from one another in kind, morals, languages, and laws – *genere, moribus, lingua, legibus* – so also different ecclesiastical provinces require suitable customs, addressing "modern" problems, but also consistent with the common *termini* set by the Fathers. Scripture warns that the *termini* – that is, the *leges et decreta* – that the Fathers have set, must in all cases be observed, and only with the most presumptuous *temeritas* may they be transgressed. Regino, following his predecessors, has laid out these and the modern *termini* in order. The judgment

---

[15] On Adoptionism, see Alcuin, *Ep.* 23; Bullough 1983; Riché 1981: 736–7. Cavadini 1993 is a major contribution to the subject. On the *Libri Carolini*, see Bastgen 1924: 3. For the Council of Frankfurt, Brandmüller 1987. For Pseudo-Isidore, see Hinschius 1963: 95, 128, 139, 162, 238, 524. On canon law in general, see Munier 1957. The text of the *Collectio canonum Hibernensis*, the first collection to use patristic material, is in Wasserschleben 1885. The best recent discussion is that of Reynolds 1983. On *florilegia* as dossiers against particular heresies, see Riché 1981: 726–9. Generally, see McKitterick 1977; Wallace-Hadrill 1983; Riché 1981; Contreni 1983; Bullough 1983.

[16] There is a brief discussion in Morrison 1969: 236–40. See Hinschius 1963: 95, 128, 139, 163, 238, 524.

[17] For the text of Amalarius, see Hanssens 1948–50. The case has often been misunderstood as an example of general ecclesiastical anti-intellectualism. Regino's text is in Wasserschleben 1840. On Regino's importance in early discussions of "national" identities, see the essays in Beumann 1978. On the frequency of references to *leges*, *statuta*, and *decreta patrum*, see de Lubac 1959: 282 n. 1.

of Hatto must decide which are to be chosen and approved for the province of Mainz. In Regino's thought fundamental and authoritative tradition remained crucial, but it also had to allow for regional variation in some practices and usages, a dilemma that characterized a number of thinkers in the tenth, eleventh, and twelfth centuries.

For Carolingian thinkers, such images as that of the *termini* set by the *patres* were not necessarily metaphors. The collections of individual patristic texts grew in number during the ninth century, as did those of dossiers and *florilegia*, collections of excerpts from the writings of the Fathers.[18] Before the eleventh century it really was possible to believe that one had the *termini* set by the *patres* in front of one as one read or wrote. As Chenu and others have pointed out, by the ninth century patristic *texts* themselves came to be understood as possessing an *auctoritas* that "no longer signifies the personal worth of a Gregory or an Augustine, but rather designates a *text* of Gregory or Augustine."[19]

The wide figurative uses of Prov. 22.28 in exegesis, authoritative custom, and the idea of tradition that were exercised in Carolingian and post-Carolingian Europe retained their versatility in the eleventh and early twelfth centuries, when boundaries and limits of many kinds were being sorely tested. Radulphus Glaber, for example, wrote of flying boundary stones in a territorial dispute between one family and its neighbors. Fulbert of Chartres and Berno of Reichenau cited the Proverbs text to justify, respectively, a procedure in a case of homicide and the insistence upon observing the rules of cult.[20] Still others – Abbo of Fleury, Cardinal Humbert, *The Collection in 74 Titles*, and Ivo of Chartres – cited Prov. 22.28 to emphasize the integrity of episcopal jurisdiction, sometimes literally in geographical and territorial terms.[21]

Between the fourth and the twelfth centuries, then, Prov. 22.28 had proven to be an extremely useful text in a number of different contexts: canon law, scriptural and liturgical exegesis, and the developing concept of authoritative tradition. The term *patres* itself had broadened to include not only apostolic Fathers, early councils and popes, and such figures as Ambrose, Augustine, Jerome, and Gregory, but later thinkers as well, beginning with Bede. The term proved versatile in matters of canonical authority, ecclesiastical practice and discipline, doctrinal disputes, and the cognitive limits of exegesis. In all cases

---

[18] See McKitterick 1977: 154–83.

[19] Chenu 1976: 355.

[20] For Glaber, see Fichtenau 1991: 101–9; for Fulbert, see Behrends 1976: 58–9; Peters 1990. For Berno, see de Lubac 1961: 36–41. The *glossa ordinaria* to the Bible allowed for both kinds of interpretation: *PL* CXIII.1106A, "Non transgrediaris terminos Catholicae fidei, quos ab initio statuere doctores."

[21] For Ivo, see *MGH LdL* II.642–55; Morrison 1969: 309–10. See also Robinson 1983; Mostert 1987: 115–19; Morris 1989: 219–26; for Abbo's (and generally monastic) versatility in justifying a status quo by appealing to patristic literature, see Fichtenau 1991: 286–9.

the temerity of the act of transgression and the audacity of the alleged transgressor remained a principal component of the image.

The very versatility of the verse, however, suggests the eagerness with which Carolingian and post-Carolingian thinkers seized upon patristic authority and tradition to control a diverse and rapidly changing world of thought and practice in the absence of any clear-cut contemporary central authority and in the actual existence of "the Church," outside of theoretical ecclesiology and polemic, as many local churches whose eleventh- and early twelfth-century disputes could only be settled by appeals to a universally recognized tradition and the authority it entailed. Beginning in the mid-eleventh century, however, just such an authority was formulated in the reform papacy of Leo IX and his successors. In matters of canon law and ecclesiastical discipline, although the papacy certainly acknowledged and claimed to incorporate tradition, the growing presence and enforceability of *auctoritas romana* came to determine definitions of those *termini* that had once and for a long time been left in the hands and diverse texts of the *patres*.[22] Perhaps the inherent lack of specificity in the phrase from Proverbs as well as the increasing academic awareness of the variety and apparent internal contradictions in the patristic corpus led to its disuse, particularly in those contexts in which efficient and comprehensive collections of authoritative texts were now available – the *glossa ordinaria* to scripture, Gratian's *Decretum*, Peter Lombard's *Liber senteniarum*, and the decretals and canons of twelfth-century popes and councils. But it survived in one earlier function, indeed came to be used more frequently – that of characterizing impious or erroneous exegesis, its old cognitive role, applied from the eleventh century on to the world of the new schools, first to the use of the liberal arts in interpreting scripture, and later to the interpretation of doctrine by techniques developed in natural philosophy.

Patres, *termini*, **and** *magistri*

One of the chief concerns in the cautionary citation of Prov. 22.28 in matters of exegesis had long been the ecclesiastical – chiefly, but certainly not exclusively monastic – distaste for the use of the *artes liberales* and the kinds of interpretive questions they raised in a hermeneutic enterprise that was thought to require spiritual, rather than primarily intellectual understanding. Although Augustine and Jerome had struck a widely accepted compromise between the two kinds of effort, subsequent thinkers, including Bede, had renewed the debate, and the question was only temporarily settled by

---

[22] Kuttner 1982; Morris 1989; Gratian, C. 24 q. 3 cc. 26–31.

Carolingian thinkers.[23] The Carolingian balance struck between the *artes* and contemplative reading of scripture was lost during the tenth and early eleventh centuries, and the debate was renewed in earnest in the eleventh and twelfth centuries. The *artes* survived in the external schools of some monasteries, in cathedral schools, and in some urban schools in northern Italy. Nor were the *artes* entirely unattractive to monastic scholars, although their reappearance during the early eleventh century certainly did not please all monks.

The new prominence of the propaedeutic studies – the *artes* – in monastic learning and exegesis shaped the legend of Gerbert and elicited the doubts and stinging protests of Otloh S. Emmeram, Peter Damian, and Manegold of Lautenbach, as well as the revival of the Augustinian sense of *curiositas* in the *De similitudinibus* long attributed to Anselm.[24] In the light of the instrumental use of grammar and dialectic in shaping the new academic forms of *quaestio* and *disputatio*, the monastic *lectio*, "oriented," as Jean Leclercq had said, "toward the *meditatio* and the *oratio*," stood in sharper and sharper contrast to the new methods and the new *theologia* that they purported to teach.[25] The monastic *lectio* fed memory and imagination, and when it inquired, its *quaerere* was a *studium* that came from the heart and sought God, not from the intellect seeking knowledge, nor, for that matter, teaching, preaching, and fighting heresy.

The Carolingian and later monastic deference to the *patres* here had to perform yet stronger service. In the late eleventh and twelfth centuries there was no longer a question of a few isolated debates concerning the correct interpretation of matters that had never been authoritatively settled, as there had been in the ninth century. Instead, the renovation of the curriculum of the *artes* brought them to bear consistently and in an original manner upon problems of exegesis and led ultimately to the discipline of theology. This new role of the *artes* was far removed even from the misgivings of Otloh and the outright hostility of Peter Damian. Although the reformed monastic tradition certainly did not entirely give way before it – indeed the greatest years of that tradition lay ahead during the twelfth century – it could, and did, reemphasize the *auctoritas patrum* as a means of control over what it considered the most extreme or superfluous manifestations of the new exegesis. Monastic critics took St. Paul's complaint about "novelties" straight to the new treatment of scripture, from the desacralization of the physical text to the new manner of disputing and expounding it.

---

23 Riché 1981; Contreni 1983; de Lubac 1961: 50–3, 381–93; D'Onofrio 1986; Gibson 1981, 1982; Wallace-Hadrill 1983; Sullivan 1989; d'Alverny 1946; Smalley 1983.
24 On Otloh, Evans 1980b: 60–2; Resnick 1987; on Peter Damian, Cantin 1975; Morrison 1983; on Manegold, Hartmann 1970; on Gerbert, Riché 1985. On the Anselmian *De similitudinibus* (*De Humanis moribus*), see Southern and Schmitt 1969.
25 Leclercq 1982: 72.

Central to both monastic consciousness and to the adaptation of the new learning to monastic standards, although often neglected in studies of monastic attitudes toward the new schools, was the form of the exposition of scripture. As John Van Engen has succinctly put it:

While a certain dialectic between reason and authority permeated this development, becoming especially prominent in public doctrinal controversies, the most fundamental change, overlooked in much of the older literature . . . was that which transformed Holy Scripture, the divine repository of sacred dogma, kissed, incensed, and invoked each day at mass, into a textbook routinely lectured upon in the schools and haggled over in public disputes.[26]

Central to monastic attitudes toward the new learning, and central to monastic self-awareness, was the *lectio divina* – the study and contemplation of scripture. Monastic discussions of the proper and improper approaches to scriptural exegesis formed the vocabulary applied by monastic critics and scholars to learning in general and to the new learning of the eleventh and twelfth centuries and to the problem of the *artes liberales*. From the tenth century on, monastic writers had readier access to patristic literature and regularly invoked it – and its heresiology – in a wide range of situations, not all of which appear to have borne on doctrine at all.

The *artes* in the eleventh and early twelfth centuries posed only one problem to the defenders of orthodoxy, as orthodoxy had come to be defined by 1100. A second, very old and potentially equally serious question, was the argument that scriptural exegesis could legitimately be extended beyond the comments of the *patres*, if it was inspired by the Holy Spirit. Origen had argued vigorously for an expanded exegesis, and even Augustine's and Jerome's tempering of Origen's enthusiasm allowed for an ongoing improved hermeneutic. Gregory the Great had anticipated an even clearer understanding of scripture in the future, and even Carolingian authorities allowed for a kind of *pia curiositas*, as long as it was accompanied by grace – as in Ambrosius Autpertus's remark that he had "added from my own resources, or rather from the gift of the grace of God, many things in which the *patres* seem to be deficient." Amalarius of Metz ran afoul of the irascible Florus of Lyons and the Council of Quierzy in 835 because he had omitted the qualifying "from the gift of the grace of God" when he explained that he had gotten many of his allegorical interpretations of the liturgy, "from inside myself" – Florus could then charge him with having displayed *ex proprii sensus temeraria praesumptio*. As Robert Lerner has pointed out, preserving the saving clause "with the aid of the Holy Spirit" led to the development of the "ecstatic

---

[26] Van Engen 1983: 97. See also Evans 1980b; Chenu 1968; Ferruolo 1985; Fichtenau 1992.

defense" of individual exegesis that might legitimately proceed *ultra patres*.[27]

This line of reasoning proved to be safest, however, in a monastic setting, more controversial in the schools, and most controversial when argued by individual dissenters, especially when these appeared to run afoul of monastic claims to intercessory functions or to challenge canonical authority of any kind. Within the monastic context the best – and one of the earliest – examples of this uneasiness is the reception of the work of Rupert of Deutz, his vast scriptural commentary produced in the first two decades of the twelfth century. Familiar with more of the exegetical tradition and literature than any writer before him, Rupert remained firmly within a distinctly monastic tradition of exegesis. Rupert's grand thematic focus on the Trinity and the Holy Spirit – as well as his involvement in disputes about specific doctrinal issues – made earlier commentaries less than useful for him, and his novel definition of monastic life as contemplation of scripture gave to the encounter between the individual monk and scripture a direct validity that ultimately reduced the role of the Fathers to a single stage of instruction; a monastic reader might very well find "more useful" meanings in his own encounters with the text of scripture than the Fathers themselves had produced.[28]

The scale and originality of Rupert's work drew from monastic critics the complaint that such a display of learning violated the warning of I Cor. 8.1, *scientia inflat*, as well as the charge from secular masters and their disciples that Rupert's ambitious commentary needlessly increased the literature in which the *patres* had said all that was sufficient. Rupert's Prologue to his commentary on the Apocalypse suggests strongly that he had been accused of going *ultra patres*, having produced superfluous exegetical material, offensive to the memory and judgment of the *patres*, a product of vainglory rather than piety.[29]

Rupert retorted, echoing Origen, that although the *patres* had opened one or two wells from which to draw the living water, he was opening new ones, as

27 Origen, *De principiis, Praefatio,* 3; Danielou 1975: 11. Augustine, *Confessions,* xiii, 18–24; Gregory, *Homil. in Ezech.* 2. 4. 10–12 (*PL* LXXXVI.979–81). On Ambrosius see Pelikan 1978: 9–23 at n. 10. For Amalarius and Florus, see Cabaniss 1954; McKitterick 1977: 149–53; Hanssens 1948–50: 19; de Lubac 1961: 40, 99–128. In addition, a number of exegetes pointed out that the heretics' misuse of scripture forced orthodox Christians to examine scripture more closely (Grundmann 1963), increasing the inherently and properly tantalizing invitation. See de Lubac 1961: 305 n. 3; Lerner 1992.

28 Van Engen 1983: 80.

29 Rupert, *Comm. in Apoc., Praef.* (*PL* CLXIX.825–8). See also Lerner 1992; Van Engen 1983: 71, 239–40, 343, 346. One of Rupert's critics, Alger of Liege, very carefully insisted that he did not interpret scripture "in my own sense," but in that of the Fathers. See Van Engen 1983: 171. Further on not proceeding *ultra patres*, Van Engen 1983: 184, 210, 219, 351; de Lubac 1959: 78–9, 84; de Lubac 1961: 219–38; Evans 1980: 57–79; de Ghellinck 1948: 250–77. On the image in Origen and Isidore see Gregoire 1965: 158.

had Isaac, when he opened new wells because the Philistines had closed the wells of Abraham.[30] For Rupert, such activity, because it lay at the heart of monastic life, could not repudiate the *patres*, but built upon and added to their work. His work expressed the matter better and more fully (*melius et compendiosius*). Rupert, "an ardent contemplative whose faith delighted in mystery," saw no conflict with the *patres* in what was, for him, a common enterprise.[31]

By the early twelfth century the concern over deviating from the *patres*, adding to or subtracting from their work in exegesis, had become a common-place; it is interesting to note that criticism of this kind came to Rupert from fellow monks as well as secular masters, among the latter no less than Anselm of Laon and William of Champeaux, who professed to build their own com-mentaries squarely upon the bases laid by the *patres*. But the prospects opened up with such obvious delight and devotion by Rupert of Deutz and other monastic exegetes were too bright to be dimmed by criticism that they consisted of a presumptuous rejection of the *patres*. Thus, Richard of St. Victor regarded such criticism as an excuse for laziness: "For our part, how-ever, let us take with all greediness what the *patres* have discussed; let us offer with all generosity the fruits of our research, that we may fulfill that which is written: Many shall pass over, and knowledge shall be manifold [Dan. 12.4]."[32] Elsewhere Richard repeated this idea – the *patres* had left many things unsaid; they were interested chiefly in allegorical problems; as in Origen, they had deliberately left things for later commentators to find: "Do you wish to honor and defend the authority of the *patres*? We cannot honor the lovers of truth more truly than by seeking, finding [Matt. 7.7], teaching, defending, and loving the truth. Do not ask whether what I say is new, but whether it is true."[33] Such sentiments as those of Rupert and Richard ring with the delight that the new exegesis had instilled in diligent mock-scholars, still secure in the monastic tradition, still confident that such seeking and finding would only redouble contemplative joy.

The defenses of Rupert and Richard appear to have succeeded, chiefly because of the popularity of their work in the world of monks and canons regular. But the practices of the masters in the schools soon passed well beyond the limited claims of Anselm of Laon and William of Champeaux, and many writers, notably St. Bernard, expressed great concern over the freedom with which the *mundanae artes* could be applied to the sacred pages. Here there

[30] Van Engen 1983: 71; Gregoire 1965: 158.
[31] Chenu 1968: 270–330; Chenu 1976: 351–65.
[32] Smalley 1983: 107–8; Chenu 1968: 310; de Lubac 1959: 109–10.
[33] Smalley 1983: 109. On defenses of *libertas inquirendi*, see McLaughlin 1977; Peters 1985. The forthcoming study of academic heresies by H. M. M. J. Thijssen properly criticizes the application to such conflicts of the modern term "academic freedom."

was less toleration for the ecstatic defense. The generation of Peter Abelard produced both praise of the new learning and bitter condemnations of it. In his own defense of his teaching at the Council of Reims in 1148, Gilbert of Poitiers claimed that he held the same faith as the Fathers, and that he knew their works not from *florilegiae* and excerpts, but from having read their entire books. It was the best defense that he could have offered.[34]

A related concern is that of spending too much time and energy on preliminary disciplines. The *Metalogicon* of John of Salisbury, with its criticism of students and masters who spend all of their lives on what ought to be a propaedeutic study, that of logic as one of the *artes*, is a well-known example. But excessively prolonged study of any one of the *artes* was only one kind of objection to the twelfth-century schools. The application of dialectic was not merely a tool for studying scripture and doctrine but also a principle of ordering the faith itself, a principle that insisted upon the debating of *quaestiones*, the puzzles of *sophismata*, the demystifying of the essential mystery of faith. There was little room here for the monastic *meditatio* or for the hieratic function of scripture. *Profanae novitates* appeared to critics to abound, not only in the schools, but in the character of heresies themselves. Thinkers during the second half of the twelfth century cited Prov. 22.28 again and again, not always from the same perspective, and not always with the same purposes, but from a general anxiety that old certainties were being discarded or ignored and that new approaches to scripture and its meaning were causing more discontent and anxiety than offering anything resembling new certainties. In many respects, the faith itself seemed to be becoming contingent, authority less fixed, and individual opinion, countered by other individual opinions, to be the chief medium of dialogue about matters essential to the salvation of mankind.

To others, however, far less secure in an intellectual and devotional tradition than Richard of St. Victor, the right to question, debate, and investigate was essential, even in matters of theology. In spite of the continuing assertion of patristic authority and tradition, some thinkers readily allowed for the importance of contemporary styles of thought and argument. From Abelard on, despite the occasional setbacks of condemnation and criticism, the new thinkers appropriated the title of *magistri*, and were acknowledged as such by their contemporaries.

Monastic culture could indeed contain the intellectual adventures of such figures as Rupert of Deutz and Richard of St. Victor, imbued as both were with its deepest spirit. In the case of monks going to the schools, however, and in the case of masters of the *artes* boldly undertaking the exposition of scripture with

---

[34] Offo of Freising 1974: I. 58 (59). For other defenses, see Peters 1985.

the tools of Aristotle, by the second half of the twelfth century many of the traditionalist advocates of the *patres* had turned against the *magistri*, and their opposition has been eloquently traced by Chenu and others, most recently by Stephen Ferruolo and Heinrich Fichtenau.[35]

Partly against the misuse of the *mundanae artes*, especially *disputatio*, in the exposition of scripture, St. Bernard launched his elaborate reconstruction of Augustinian *curiositas*, possibly through the medium of the Anselmian *De similitudinibus*. Gerhoch of Reichersberg cited Rupert of Deutz against the *magistri* and condemned *novitates* as violently as had any earlier exegete. Robert of Melun, Peter of Celle, Stephen of Tournai, and others took up the attack and its main themes. William of St. Thierry warned against ignoring "the limits of that faith that our *patres* established, nor to disregard them in any way."[36]

Within these contexts, the "novelties" condemned in 1 Tim. 6.20 and elsewhere in scripture and patristic literature figured prominently. Beryl Smalley traced the early medieval adventures of the idea and the term some years ago.[37] A term of opprobrium in 1100 (and for several decades after), "novelty" had become a largely honorific term by 1250. Smalley by no means insisted that *auctoritas antiqua* disappeared between 1100 and 1250, but that its privileged (and functional) place was modified in order to accommodate some concepts of a legitimate "novelty".

Throughout the twelfth century the debates concerning the limits of inquiry thus invoked Prov. 22.28 and the image of authority it conveyed more frequently and in more forms than had the juridical citations of the phrase and image between the fourth and the early twelfth centuries. The term was also apparently to be applied to intellectuals rather than to dissenters in general. It does seem to turn up in discussions of heterodoxy outside the schools. In spite of the many charges against heterodox thinkers outside the schools that they displayed considerable exegetical skills, even for rustics, the verse from Proverbs remained leveled primarily at early scholastic thinkers, not at dissenters with large "popular" followings. By the end of the twelfth century a contemporary and indisputable source of authority was in place – the papacy and its institution of judges-delegate. As in the case of Valdes, dissenters could be heard, their opinions assessed, and a confession of faith required – and given or not. If such assent were not forthcoming, the heretic could then be accused of pertinacity, increasingly the most important legal element in the charge of heresy. Heterodoxy then became the denial of legitimate contemporary

---

[35] Chenu 1976; Ferruolo 1985; Fichtenau 1992.

[36] Newhauser 1987; Leclercq 1982; Stock 1975; de Lubac 1961: 583–6.

[37] Smalley 1975. For an earlier manifestation of this spirit in episcopal circles see Fichtenau 1991: 286–7.

authority. There was no need to observe that Waldensians, Cathars, or others had transgressed the limits established by the Fathers. They had in any case transgressed the contemporary authority that mattered.

At the same time, scholars with opinions of the kind that had troubled William of St. Thierry, William of Champeaux, Bernard of Clairvaux, and others were not as readily controlable. The university was rapidly becoming, as Smalley observed, "a fact of life." The institution offered advantages to popes and rulers whose cultivation required considerable restraint on the part of authority, and permitted – sometimes grudgingly – considerable freedom within its relatively closed society. In the light of the new presence of the universities, once such charges as secret teaching and esoteric doctrines had been obliterated by public teaching and collegial familiarity, scholars were for the most part safe from the kind of exercise of authority that troubled dissenting groups outside the precincts of the universities.

On the other hand, the papacy of the twelfth and early thirteenth centuries took time to catch up with the thought of the scholars. Until it did, it could still resort to the last usage of the text from Proverbs. The limits set by the Fathers could still be invoked until the emergence of a concept of professional discipline in the thirteenth century. Withal, the form of earlier *auctoritas* itself was changed – into individual texts, propositions, and statements of doctrine excerpted in specialized, systematic, and increasingly authoritative collections of texts, usually according to the principles of one or another of the *artes*, chiefly logic. This was a far different use of *ratio* than the Carolingian exegetes had defended, or that even the best-intentioned early theological dialecticians would have allowed. It took time for the new theology to acquire respectability – and security – and to escape from the charges of introducing novelties and transgressing the limits set by the *patres*. The acknowledgment of ancient *auctoritas* survived into the textbooks and teaching of the later twelfth and thirteenth centuries, but it was an acknowledgment of a far different concept of *auctoritas* from that of the Carolingians, or even of Lanfranc. It did not refer to the compilation of patristic literature, but to patristic thought, which had to be arrayed side by side with the full apparatus of rational inquiry developed in the twelfth-century schools.

Peter Lombard concluded his prologue to the Books of Sentences with the insistence that his work echoes those of the Fathers, *non a paternibus discessit limitibus*. Although the contents of Peter's work most certainly did proceed well beyond the range of patristic exegesis, it is arguable that Peter's cautionary self-defense was not merely a *captatio benevolentiae*, but the expression of a genuine belief that his work was consistent with a constant tradition and that the phrase from Proverbs had by the mid-twelfth century lost some of its sharper overtones, at least in the schools.

Such a conclusion fits well with the first commentary on Peter's work, that of Peter Comestor.[38] In his commentary on the prologue, Peter Comestor interpreted the limits set by the Fathers not in terms of Proverbs 22.28 at all, but in terms of Exodus 19 and 24, the story of Moses placing boundaries around the mountain of the Lord. These images had long been a part of Jewish thought concerning tradition and the nature of authority. Exodus 19 and 24 provided the source for the expression "fences around the law" that is found in the Pirke Abot and echoed in Maimonides, where the phrase was understood to refer to the authority of sages to adapt the rules of Torah to particular circumstances.[39] It is possible that Peter Comestor knew something about this, since there had been increasing contact between Jewish and Christian scholars during the twelfth century, and the wisdom literature provided a ground more common to the two religions than many other parts of scripture. Whether he drew upon Jewish sources or not, Peter Comestor was certainly more concerned with the difficulties of intellectual motivation and effort than he was with any dangers that the hermeneutical *termini* might pose to ambitious students of theology. The mountain, Peter says, stands for the two testaments; the *limites* are the writings of the Fathers, who themselves could cross the *termini* because they were directly inspired by God. Others in the story are also allegorized in the spirit of the new learning; the elders who approach the *termini* and give up are those not sufficiently diligent in studying scripture. Others are lazy and do not even bother to begin the study of the Fathers. The work of the *patres* here seems to be rather an impenetrable forest than prohibitive boundaries, and Peter is far less concerned with transgressing hermeneutic limits than he is with the difficulties of understanding scripture and patristic literature concerning the exegesis of scripture. For Peter Comestor the purpose of Lombard's work was precisely the overcoming of this difficulty. Comestor is more concerned with lazy or insufficiently diligent scholars than with presumptuous ones.

The age of the new legitimacy of novelty, characterised by Comestor's distinctive reading of Peter Lombard's citation of Prov. 22.28, came to something of an end in the disputes between Mendicants at the University of Paris in the middle of the thirteenth century, in a revived Augustinian criticism of Aristotelian scholastic theology, in the condemnations of 1277, and in the new intellectual temper of the fourteenth century. Many of the themes and images considered already in this essay come together in the letter sent by Gregory IX on 17 July 1228, to the regent masters in theology at the University of Paris.[40] Old images usually applied to the study of secular literature – those of the spoils of the Egyptians (Exod. 3.21–2), the purified and shorn Egyptian

---

[38] Martin 1931.

[39] See Daly 1957 for a possible connection between Comestor and the Jews of his native Troyes. On the Jewish image see Neusner 1990.

[40] Denifle 1889: no. 59, 114–16; de Lubac 1959: 116. The forthcoming study by H. M. M. J. Thijssen on academic heresies will greatly illuminate a presently obscure subject.

handmaid (Deut. 21.11–13), and the children of Hagar (Gen. 17.20–7) – and other topoi from earlier Christian literature are all invoked to warn the masters that

It has reached our ears that some among you, distended like a skin by the spirit of vanity [1 Cor. 8.1], are working with profane *novitates* [1 Tim. 6.20] to pass beyond the *positi a patribus termini*, the understanding of the heavenly pages limited by the fixed *termini* of expositions in the study of the holy Fathers, *quos transgredi non solum est temerarium, sed prophanum*, inclining toward the philosophical doctrine of natural things.

They are doing this, not for their students' profit, but only for a show of knowledge, so that they might be thought to be God themselves. They should expound scripture according to the approved traditions of the saints, rather than by carnal means, but instead they reverse a natural hierarchy – they force the queen to be a servant to the handmaid. They confuse the realms of grace and nature, and thereby violate the strictures of 1 Tim. 6.20. Gregory commands them to teach theological purity, not adulterating the word of God with the figments of philosophers, but abiding by the *termini* established by the *patres*.

Gregory is here summing up a century of criticism of the misuse of the intellect and the confusion of disciplines that had characterized Latin theological studies from the days of Rupert of Deutz. It was illustrated not only in the quarrels between monks, but between monks and masters and between masters and masters, finally among popes, bishops, and masters. But Gregory's apparatus of scriptural references already sounds dated. Although the problem he addressed was a real one – and one that continued to be debated for the next half-century – its solution was not to be reached by the repetition of the familiar scriptural injunctions, but by the internal development of the schools themselves. By the end of the thirteenth century monks were no longer at the center of intellectual debates, and although the mendicant professors had appropriated some of the arguments of earlier monastic critics, they were themselves too involved in the intellectual life of their world to be as effective as the eleventh and early twelfth-century monastic critics had been. Moreover, the cognitive world of the late thirteenth and early fourteenth centuries had developed stability and internal rules of its own; it had become, as Miss Smalley suggested, a "fact of life." And it settled its cognitive and epistemological problems not by invoking either a set of undefined "limits" set by Fathers or the rhetoric of Gregory IX. Rather, it developed a line of argument that ran from Augustine to Aquinas and consisted of defining humility as being contained within one's own limits, and extending this definition to the idea of individual academic disciplines. The opening of the condemnation of the errors in the confusion of natural philosophy and theology at Paris in 1277 spoke of the arts faculty as having exceeded the proper limits of its discipline.[41]

From the limits of patristic authority to the limits of an academic discipline is a conceptual step that effectively characterizes the achievement of the twelfth- and thirteenth-century schools. Gregory IX cited Prov. 22.28 and other scriptural texts in a language and style characteristic of twelfth-century critics of the schools, but his citation was aimed at practitioners of a particular discipline, that of theology. Within the academic disciplines, of course, the sense of *terminus* itself resonated differently, since it too was a term of art – terminist logic had insisted that areas of thought, too, possessed *termini*, "limits" or "boundaries" that contained the rules, proper subject-matter, and specificity of each discipline. The Aristotelianism of Aquinas and other thirteenth-century thinkers was perfectly at home with such a notion, and remained at home with it until the debates of the later thirteenth and fourteenth centuries challenged the new theology in the name of a revived Augustinianism and a new anxiety about the limitations upon the omnipotence of God potentially posed by that theology.

But the later medieval debates about the integrity of theology did not void the sense of the limits of disciplines as characterizing the authority of those disciplines. Indeed, the safety of the schools proved remarkable in the face of ecclesiastical and temporal authority's assault on manifestations of religious discontent in the world outside the schools. Although individual masters ran the occasional risk of condemnation of their doctrines, not until the fourteenth century did any run the risk of the most severe punishments inflicted upon heretics convicted in spiritual or temporal courts, and then only rarely. Jan Hus was, after all, the first doctor convicted and executed for heresy. This remarkable – and quite practical – demonstration of academic freedom indicates one of the roles played by the schools of the twelfth and thirteenth centuries: what might be culpable *curiositas* and *superbia* in non-academics could be considered well within the limits of an academic discipline. As Heiko Oberman has pointed out, these notions of individual and professional limits ran down to the days of Jean Calvin:

To stay within one's personal limits – the medieval definition of humility and the alternative to proud curiosity – means now to stay within the limits of one's field of competence. The medieval differentiation between the university faculties – pragmatically transcended in the preceding stages of the Renaissance – is here recaptured by Calvin to defend and respect the different methods of illuminating the common object, the glory of God.[42]

---

[41] Denifle 1889: no. 473, 543.
[42] Oberman 1973b: 403. Oberman's study is a critique of the work on the subject by Blumenberg 1983.

Long before Calvin, St. Bonaventure had pointed out that even theologians may err when they assert opinions in areas where they have no disciplinary competence.[43]

In the fourteenth and fifteenth centuries, the notion of disciplinary competence attracted the attention of skeptics, critics of speculative theology, practical moralists like Jean Gerson, and humanist critics of scholastic thought generally. The images and scriptural armory of Cassiodorus and Gregory the Great had served a long and complex task, being invoked again and again in utterly different contexts in order to assert the existence, continuity, and authority of tradition, first in law and ecclesiastical politics, later in the study of theology, and finally in the restricted area of individual and professional capacities.

Oberman has suggested that nominalist thought, particularly the work of Nicole Oresme, in its restriction of the term *experientia*, either to recorded collective experience in the historical record or the use of inductive reasoning to produce general conclusions and the discovery of physical laws, constituted a revolution in the history of attitudes toward speculative thought. Lacking actual experience, we are permitted to use imagination until it is verified or refuted by actual experience: "In the field of theology, this would be vain curiosity; in the field of natural philosophy, this is research, *investigation*."[44] For expanding the concept of the universe to include natural philosophy, the heavens themselves became acceptable objects for human inquiry:

For Oresme as well as for those who stand in his tradition, the issue of the heavenly movements – of the orbits of the sun, the moon, the moving stars, and the earth – is no longer to be solved in terms of a deductive speculative cosmo*logy*, but in terms of an experimental inductive cosmo*nomy* – with the aid of imagination, but without claim on scientific accuracy until the mental experiments are confirmed by experience.[45]

For Oberman, such a transformation freed valid *curiositas* (the appropriate attitude for investigating the whole order of nature, now including both earth and heaven) from *vana curiositas*, the pointless attempt to penetrate the unknown and unknowable realm of God omnipotent. The *termini* set by the Fathers now applied to a *disciplina*, the discipline of theology, but the province of theology had been redefined and that of natural philosophy expanded. The uncertainties of the twelfth and thirteenth centuries were past, and the adventures of the modern world yet to come.

---

[43] Peters 1985: 94; Berubé 1976: 130–62.
[44] Oberman 1973b: 409; Oberman 1973a: 33–8.
[45] Oberman 1973b: 410–11.

REFERENCES

Allen, P. S. and Allen, H. M. 1928 *Opus Epistolarum Des. Erasmi Roterodami*, Tom. VII, 1527–8. Oxford: Clarendon Press.

Allenbach, J. 1980a *Biblia Patristica*, vol. III. Paris: Editions du Centre national de la recherche scientifique.

1980b *Biblia Patristica*, vol. IV. Paris: Editions du Centre national de la recherche scientifique.

d'Alverny, M.-T. 1946–9 La Sagesse et ses sept filles: recherches sur les allégories de la Philosophie et des arts liberaux du IXe au XIIe siècle. In *Mélanges dédiés à la mémoire de Félix Grat*, I: 245–78. 2 vols. Paris: Pecquer-Grat.

Amann, E. 1933 Pères de l'Eglise. *Dictionnaire de théologie catholique*, vol. XII.1: cols. 1192–215. Paris: Letouzet et Ane.

Barnes, Timothy David 1971 *Tertullian: A Historical and Literary Study*. Oxford: Oxford University Press.

Bastgen, Hubertus, ed. 1924 *Libri carolini, sive Caroli Magni Capitulare de imaginibus*. *MGH Leges* sec. 3, 2.

Behrends, Frederick 1976 *The Letters and Poems of Fulbert of Chartres*. Oxford: Clarendon Press.

Berubé, C. 1976 *De la philosophie à la sagesse chez Saint Bonaventure et Roger Bacon*. Rome.

Beumann, Helmut with Schröder, W. 1978 *Nationes. Historische und philosophische Untersuchungen zur Enstehung der europäischen Nationen im Mittelalter*. Sigmaringen.

Blumenberg, Hans 1983 *The Legitimacy of the Modern Age*. Trans. Robert Wallace. Cambridge, Mass.: MIT Press.

Blumenthal, Uta-Renate 1983 *Carolingian Essays: Andrew W. Mellon Lectures in Early Christian Studies*, Washington, DC: Catholic University of America Press.

Brandmüller, Walter 1987 *Traditio Scripturae Interpres*: The Teaching of the Councils on the Right Interpretation of Scripture Up to the Council of Trent. *Catholic Historical Review* 73: 523–40.

Bullough, Donald 1983 Alcuin and the Kingdom of Heaven: Liturgy, Theology and the Carolingian Age. In Blumenthal 1983: 1–69.

Cabaniss, Allen 1954 *Amalarius of Metz*. Amsterdam: North Holland Publishing Company.

Cantin, André 1975 *Les Sciences seculières et la foi: les deux voies de la science au jugement de S. Pierre Damien (1007–1072)*. Spoleto: Centro Italiano di Studi sull'alto Medioevo.

Cassiodorus 1937 *Cassiodori Senatoris Institutiones*. Ed. R. A. B. Mynors. Oxford: Clarendon Press.

Cavadini, John 1993 *The Last Christology of the West: Adoptionism in Spain and Gaul 785–820*. Philadelphia: University of Pennsylvania Press.

Chenu, Marie-Dominique 1968 *Nature, Man, and Society in the Twelfth Century: Essays on New Theological Perspectives in the Latin West*. Trans. Jerome Taylor and Lester K. Little. Chicago: University of Chicago Press.

1976 *La Théologie au douzième siècle*. Paris: J. Vrin.

Contreni, John J. 1983 Carolingian Biblical Studies. In Blumenthal 1983: 71–98.

Dagens, Claude 1983 *Saint Grégoire le Grand. Culture et experience chrétiennes.* Paris: Etudes Augustinienne.

Daly, Saralynn R. 1957 Peter Comestor: Master of the Histories. *Speculum* 31: 62–75.

Danielou, Jean 1975 Recherche et tradition chez les pères. *Studia Patristica* 12: 3–13.

den Boeft, J. 1988 *Illic aureum quoddam ire flumen:* Erasmus' Enthusiasm for the *Patres.* In J. S. Weiland and W. Th. M. Trijhoff, eds., *Erasmus of Rotterdam: The Man and the Scholar,* 172–81. Leiden and New York: E. J. Brill.

Denifle, H. 1889 *Chartularium Universitatis Parisiensis,* with A. Chatelain, vol. I. Paris: ex typis Fratrum Delalain.

D'Onofrio, Giulio 1986 Dialectic and Theology: Boethius' *Opuscula sacra* and their Early Medieval Readers. *Studi Medievali* 3rd ser. 27.1: 45–67.

Evans, G. R. 1980a *Old Arts and New Theology: The Beginnings of Theology as an Academic Discipline.* Oxford: Oxford University Press.

  1980b *Anselm and a New Generation.* Oxford: Oxford University Press.

Ferrulo, Stephen C. 1985 *The Origins of the University: The Schools of Paris and their Critics, 1100–1215.* Stanford: Stanford University Press.

Festus 1913 *Sexti Pompeii Festi De verborum significatu quae supersunt cum Pauli Epitome.* Ed. W. M. Lindsay. Leipzig: B. G. Teubueri.

Fichtenau, Heinrich 1991 Die Ketzer von Orléans. In Klaus Herbert, Hans Henning Kortüm, and Carlo Servatius, eds., *Ex ipsis rerum documentis. Beiträge zur Mediävistik. Festschrift für Harald Zimmermann zum 65. Geburtstag.* Sigmarigen: Thorbecke.

  1992 *Ketzer und Professoren. Häresie und Vernunftglaube im Hochmittelalter.* Munich: C. H. Beck.

Frédouille, Jean-Claude 1972 *Tertullien et la conversion de la culture antique.* Paris: Etudes Augustinienne.

de Ghellinck, Joseph 1935 Patristique et argument de tradition au bas moyen âge. In A. Lang, ed., *Aus der Geisteswelt des Mittelalters. Beiträge zur Geschichte der Philosophie und Theologie des Mittelalters,* 403–26. Texte und Untersuchungen, Supplementband III.1. Munster: Ock Aschendorff.

  1948 *Le Mouvement théologique du XIIe siècle.* Brussels and Paris: Editions "De Tempel."

Gibson, Margaret 1981 *Boethius: His Life, Thought and Influence.* Oxford: Blackwell.

  1982 Boethius in the Carolingian Schools. *Transactions of the Royal Historical Society* 5th ser. 32: 43–56.

Gilmore, Myron P. 1963 *Humanists and Jurists: Six Studies in the Renaissance.* Cambridge, Mass.: Harvard University Press.

Ginzburg, Carlo 1976 High and Low: The Theme of Forbidden Knowledge in the Sixteenth and Seventeenth Centuries. *Past & Present* 73: 28–31.

Gregoire, Reginald 1965 *Bruno de Segni exégète médiéval et théologien monastique.* Spoleto: Centro Italiano di Studi sull'alto Medioevo.

Grundmann, Herbert 1927 Der Typus des Ketzers in mittelalterlicher Anschauung. In *Kultur- und Universalgeschichte. Walter Goetz zu seinem 60. Geburtstag* (Leipzig) 91–107.

  1963 *Opporet et haereses esse.* Das Problem der Ketzerei im Spiegel der mittelalterlichen Bibelexegese. *Archiv fur Kulturgeschichte* 45: 129–64.

Hageneder, Othmar 1976 Der Häresisbegriff bei den Juristen des 12. und 13. Jahrhunderts. In Lourdaux and Verhelst 1976: 42–103.

Hanssens, J. M. 1948–50 *Amalarii Episcopi Opera Liturgica Omnia*. Studi e Testi 138–40. Vatican City: Biblioteca apostolica vaticana.

Hartmann, Wilfried 1970 Manegold von Lautenbach und die Anfänge der Frühscholastik. *Deutsches Archiv* 26: 47–149.

Hinschius, Paul 1963 *Decretales Pseudo-Isidorianae et Capitula Angilramni*. Repr. Aalen: Scientia Verlag.

Humphreys, S. C. 1988 The Discourse of Law in Archaic and Classical Greece. *Law and History Review* 6: 465–93.

Kuttner, Stephan 1982 On "Auctoritas" in the Writing of Medieval Canonists: The Vocabulary of Gratian. In G. Makdisi, Dominique Sourdel, Janine Sourdel-Thomine, eds., *La Notion d'autorité au Moyen Age. Islam, Byzance, Occident*, 69–81. Paris: Presses Universitaires de France.

Leclercq, Jean, O.S.B. 1982 *The Love of Learning and the Desire for God*. Repr. New York: Fordham University Press.

Le Goff, Jacques, ed. 1968 *Hérésies et sociétés dans l'Europe pré-industrielle 11e–18e siècles*. Paris and La Haye: Mouton.

Lerner, Robert 1992 Ecstatic Dissent. *Speculum* 67: 33–57.

Lourdaux, W., and Verhelst, D., eds. 1976 *The Concept of Heresy in the Middle Ages (11th–13th c): Proceedings of the International Conference Louvain May 13–16 1973*. Louvain: Louvain University Press.

de Lubac, Henri 1959 *Exégèse médiévale. Les quatre sens de l'écriture*. Première Partie, I. Paris: Aubier.

    1961 *Exégèse médiévale. Les quatre sens de l'écriture*. Seconde Partie, I. Paris: Aubier.

McKitterick, Rosamund 1977 *The Frankish Church and the Carolingian Reforms*. London: Royal Historical Society.

McLaughlin, Mary Martin 1977 *Intellectual Freedom and its Limitations in the University of Paris in the Thirteenth and Fourteenth Centuries*. New York: Arno Press.

Madoz, Jose 1933 *El Concepto de la Tradicion en S. Vincente de Lerins: Estudio Historico-Critico del "Commonitorio"*. Analecta Gregoriana, vol. V. Rome: Pontificiae Universitatis.

Martin, R.-M. 1931 Notes sur l'oeuvre littéraire de Pierre le Mangeur, *Recherches de théologie ancienne et médiévale* 3: 54–66.

Matthew Paris 1880 *Matthaei Parisiensis Chronica Majora*, ed. H. R. Luard, vol. V. London; repr., Wiesbaden, 1964.

Mollat du Jourdin, Michel, and Vauchez, André 1990 *Un temps d'épreuves*. Vol. VI of *Histoire du christianisme*. Paris: Fayard.

Moore, R. I. 1976 Heresy as Disease. In Lourdaux and Verhelst 1976: 1–11.

Morris, Colin 1989 *The Papal Monarchy: The Western Church from 1050 to 1250*. Oxford: Oxford University Press.

Morrison, Karl F. 1969 *Tradition and Authority in the Western Church, 300–1140*. Princeton: Princeton University Press.

    1983 Incentives for Studying the Liberal Arts. In David L. Wagner, ed., *The Seven Liberal Arts in the Middle Ages*, 32–57. Bloomington: Indiana University Press.

Mostert, Marco 1987 *The Political Theology of Abbo of Fleury*. Hilversum: Verloven.

Munier, Charles 1957 *Les Sources patristiques du droit de l'église du VIIIe au XIIIe siècle*. Mulhouse: Salvator.

Neusner, Jacob, ed. and transl. 1990 *Scriptures of the Oral Torah: Sanctification and Salvation in the Sacred Books of Judaism*. Atlanta: Scholars Press.

Newhauser, Richard 1982 Towards a History of Human Curiosity: A Prolegomenon to its Medieval Phase. *Deutsche Vierteljahrschrift* 56: 559–75.

  1987 The Sin of Curiosity and the Cistercians. In John R. Sommerfeldt, ed., *Erudition at God's Service*, 71–95. Cistercian Studies Series, 98. Kalamazoo.

Oberman, Heiko 1973a *Contra vanam curiositatem. Ein Kapitel der Theologie zwischen Seelenwinkel und Weltall*. Zurich: Theologischer Verlag.

  1973b Reformation and Revolution: Copernicus's Discovery in an Era of Change. In John B. Murdoch and Edith Dudley Sylla, eds., *The Cultural Context of Medieval Learning*, 397–435. Dordrecht and Boston: D. Reidel Publishing Company.

O'Donnell, James J. 1979 *Cassiodorus*. Berkeley and Los Angeles: University of California Press.

Otto of Freising 1974 *Gesta Frederici seu Rectius Chronica*. Ed. G. Waitz, B. Simpson, F.-J. Schmale, Ausgewahlte Quellen sur Geschichte des Mittelalters, Band XVIII. Darmstadt: Wissenschäftliche Buchgesellschaft.

Pelikan, Jaroslav 1973 Council or Father or Scripture? The Concept of Authority in the Theology of Maximus the Confessor. In David Neiman and Margaret Schatkin, eds., *The Heritage of the Early Church: Essays in Honor of the Very Reverend Georges Florovsky*, 277–88. Rome: Institutum Studiorum Orientalium.

  1974 *The Spirit of Eastern Christendom (600–1700)*. Chicago: University of Chicago Press.

  1978 *The Growth of Medieval Theology (600–1300)*. Chicago: University of Chicago Press.

Peters, Edward 1985 *Libertas Inquirendi* and the *Vitium curiositatis* in Medieval Thought. In G. Makdisi, J. Sourdel Thomine, D. Sourdel, eds., *La Notion de liberté au moyen âge*, 89–98. Paris: Société d'Editions les Belles Lettres.

  1990 The Death of the Subdean: Ecclesiastical Order and Disorder in Eleventh-Century Francia. In Bernard S. Bachrach and David Nicholas, eds., *Law, Custom, and the Social Fabric: Essays in Honor of Bryce Lyon*, 51–71. Kalamazoo: Medieval Institute Publications, Western Michigan University.

Quasten, Johannes 1966 *Patrology*, I: *The Beginnings of Christian Literature*. Utrecht and Antwerp: Spectrum.

Resnick, I. M. 1987 *Scientia liberalis*, Dialectics, and Otloh of St. Emmeram. *Revue bénédictine* 97: 241–52.

Reynolds, Roger E. 1983 Unity and Diversity in Carolingian Canon Law Collections: The Case of the *Collectio Hibernensis* and its Derivatives. In Blumenthal 1983: 99–135.

Riché, Pierre 1981 *Divina Pagina, Ratio et Auctoritas* dans la théologie carolingienne. In *Nascità dell'Europa ed Europa Carolingia: un'Equazione da Verificare*, II.719–63. Settimane di Studio del Centro Italiano di Studi sull'Alto Medioevo. Spoleto: Presso la Sede del Centro.

  1989 *Ecoles et enseignement dans le Haut Moyen Age. Fin du Ve siècle–milieu du XIe siècle*. 2nd edn. Paris: Picard.

Robinson, I. S. 1983 Political Allegory in the Biblical Exegesis of Bruno of Segni. *Recherches de théologie ancienne et médiévale* 50: 67–98.

Scott, R. B. Y. 1965 *The Anchor Bible. Proverbs and Ecclesiasticus.* Garden City, N.Y.: Doubleday.

Sieben, Hermann Josef 1980 *Voces. Eine Bibliographie zu Worten und Begriffen aus der Patristik (1918–1978).* Berlin and New York: W. de Gruyter.

1983 *Exegesis Patrum: Saggio bibliografico sull'esegesi biblica dei Padri della Chiesa.* Rome: Institute Patristico Augustinianum.

Smalley, Beryl 1975 Ecclesiastical Attitudes to Novelty, c. 1100–c. 1250. *Studies in Church History* 12: 113–31.

1983 *The Study of the Bible in the Middle Ages.* 3rd edn. Oxford: Blackwell.

Southern, R. W., and Schmitt, F. S. 1969 *Memorials of St. Anselm,* Auctores Britannici Medii Aevi, vol. I. London: published for the British Academy by Oxford University Press.

Stock, Brian 1975 Experience, Praxis, Work, and Planning in Bernard of Clairvaux: Observations on the *Sermones in Cantica.* In John Murdoch and Edith Dudley Sylla, eds., *The Cultural Context of Medieval Learning,* 219–68. Dordrecht and Boston: Reidel Publishing Company.

Straw, Carole Ellen 1988 *Gregory the Great: Perfection in Imperfection.* Berkeley, Los Angeles, and London: University of California Press.

Sullivan, Richard E. 1989 The Carolingian Age: Reflections on its Place in the History of the Middle Ages. *Speculum* 64: 267–306.

Van den Eynde, Damien 1933 *Les Normes de l'enseignement chrétien dans la litterature patristique des trois premiers siècles.* Gembloux and Paris: J. Duculot.

Van Engen, John 1983 *Rupert of Deutz.* Berkeley and Los Angeles: University of California Press.

Vauchez, André 1990 Contestations et hérésies dans l'église latine. In Mollat du Jourdin and Vauchez 1990: ch. 6.

Wallace-Hadrill, J. M. 1983 *The Frankish Church.* Oxford: Oxford University Press.

Wasserschleben, F. G. A. 1840 *Reginonis Abbatis Prumiensis Libri Duo de Synodalibus Causis et Disciplinis Ecclesiasticis.* Leipzig: Sumptibus G. Engleman.

Wasserschleben, Hermann 1885 *Die irische Kanonensammlungen.* Leipzig, Tauchnitz.

Wind, Edgar, 1937–8 *Aenigma Termini. Journal of the Warburg and Courtauld Institutes* 1: 66–9.

Zimmermann, Albrecht, ed. 1973 *Antiqui und Moderni. Traditionsbewusstsein und Fortschrittsbewusstsein im späten Mittelalter.* Miscellanea Medievalia, Band 9. Berlin and New York: de Gruyter.

Index

Abbo of Fleury, 345
Abd-al-Aziz, 238, 244, 249
cAbd al-Rahmān II, 267
Abelard, 289
Abraham, of the Bible, 350
Abraham, the Knight, 238
Abulafia, David, 10, 234, 264
acanthus leaf, 89
Accipter, 99
Acre, 244
Ad abolendam, 51
Ad diversos episcopos, 342
Adalbero of Laon, 33
Adelasisius, *see* Abd-al-Aziz
Additional/Rawlinson collection, 143
Ademar of Chabannes, 31–2, 34
Adolf of Nassau, 301
Adoptionism, 344
adultery, 186
Africa, 9, 210–13, 247, 249, 267; land shrines,
    38; north, 235, 269, 273
age, as factor in kin group, 72–3
Agobard of Lyon, Bishop, 267–8
Al-Muqaddasī, 267
al-Saqatī, 269–70
al-Wansharīsī, 270
Alan of Lille, 100–1
Albania, 237
Albert of Austria, 301
Albi, diocese of, 69–70, 77, 80–1
Albigensians, crusade, 23, 53, 69
Albigeois, 80
alchemy, 112–13
Alessandro da Fiorano, 170
Alexander, 344
Alexander III, Pope, 50
Alexander IV, Pope, 61–2, 193
Alexander VI, King, 170–3
Alexandria, 324
Alfonso, Don, 172-3
Alfonso, III, 247–8
Aldgate, London, 194

Alger of Liège, 293
Alio, 271
allegory, 88–9, 155, 162–3
Alleluia, 59-60, 62
Almeria, 271
Almohad dynasty, 269
Almoravid dynasty, 269
Alphabetum in artem sermocinandi, 86–7,
    93–6, 100–2, 105
Altercatio Ecclesiae contra Synagogam, 209
Amadeti friars, 183
Amalarius of Metz, 344, 348
Amalfi, 87, 94
Ambrosius, 212
Ambrosius Autpertus, 348
anathema, 28–30, 116, 139
anatomy, 113, 151
Andalusia, 264–71, 273–5, 277–8, 280
Anderson, Benedict, 6
Andrea da Isernia, 259
Andreas, the chaplain, 94
angels, 106, 119, 155, 163, 170–1, 317, 322,
    329–30
Angela of Foligno, 154
Anger (town), 293
Angevins, 235, 237–40, 242, 244, 247, 259
Anglo-Norman, 153
Anglo-Saxons, 2
Anjou, 39, 234–5, 250–2, 255–7
Anna Bijns, 324
Annales ecclesiastici, 209
Annibaldo, senator of Rome, 58
Annunciata, Benedictine, 196
Anselm, 289, 296, 350
Antichrist, 21, 31, 115, 118–19, 125
Antidorum contra venenum . . . , 118, 125
Antiherisis, 87
Antioch, 214
apocalyptic, 96, 112–14, 116, 118, 127, 157,
    170, 174, 349
apothecary, 75
Apulia, 236, 238, 240, 243–4, 246, 252, 254–5